GREAT BRITAIN
AND THE
AMERICAN CIVIL WAR

LORD JOHN RUSSELL
(*From Trevelyan's "Garibaldi and the Making of Italy"*)

EPHRAIM DOUGLASS ADAMS

GREAT BRITAIN AND THE AMERICAN CIVIL WAR

TWO VOLUMES BOUND AS ONE

S·A·R

New York
RUSSELL & RUSSELL

RUSSELL & RUSSELL INC.

LIBRARY OF CONGRESS CATALOG CARD NUMBER 58-5369

PRINTED IN THE U.S.A.

PREFACE

This work was begun many years ago. In 1908 I read in the British Museum many newspapers and journals for the years 1860-1865, and then planned a survey of English public opinion on the American Civil War. In the succeeding years as a teacher at Stanford University, California, the published diplomatic correspondence of Great Britain and of the United States were studied in connection with instruction given in the field of British-American relations. Several of my students prepared excellent theses on special topics and these have been acknowledged where used in this work. Many distractions and other writing prevented the completion of my original plan; and fortunately, for when in 1913 I had at last begun this work and had prepared three chapters, a letter was received from the late Charles Francis Adams inviting me to collaborate with him in preparing a "Life" of his father, the Charles Francis Adams who was American Minister to Great Britain during the Civil War. Mr. Adams had recently returned from England where he had given at Oxford University a series of lectures on the Civil War and had been so fortunate as to obtain copies, made under the scholarly supervision of Mr. Worthington C. Ford, of a great mass of correspondence from the Foreign Office files in the Public Record Office and from the private papers in the possession of various families.

The first half of the year 1914 was spent with Mr. Adams at Washington and at South Lincoln, in preparing the "Life." Two volumes were completed, the first by Mr.

Adams carrying the story to 1848, the second by myself for the period 1848 to 1860. For the third volume I analysed and organized the new materials obtained in England and we were about to begin actual collaboration on the most vital period of the "Life" when Mr. Adams died, and the work was indefinitely suspended, probably wisely, since any completion of the "Life" by me would have lacked that individual charm in historical writing so markedly characteristic of all that Mr. Adams did. The half-year spent with Mr. Adams was an inspiration and constitutes a precious memory.

The Great War interrupted my own historical work, but in 1920 I returned to the original plan of a work on "Great Britain and the American Civil War" in the hope that the English materials obtained by Mr. Adams might be made available to me. When copies were secured by Mr. Adams in 1913 a restriction had been imposed by the Foreign Office to the effect that while studied for information, citations and quotations were not permissible since the general diplomatic archives were not yet open to students beyond the year 1859. Through my friend Sir Charles Lucas, the whole matter was again presented to the Foreign Office, with an exact statement that the new request was in no way related to the proposed "Life" of Charles Francis Adams, but was for my own use of the materials. Lord Curzon, then Foreign Secretary, graciously approved the request but with the usual condition that my manuscript be submitted before publication to the Foreign Office. This has now been done, and no single citation censored. Before this work will have appeared the limitation hitherto imposed on diplomatic correspondence will have been removed, and the date for open research have been advanced beyond 1865, the end of the Civil War.

Similar explanations of my purpose and proposed work were made through my friend Mr. Francis W. Hirst to the owners of various private papers, and prompt approval given. In 1924 I came to England for further study of some of these private papers. The Russell Papers, transmitted to the Public Record Office in 1914 and there preserved, were used through the courtesy of the Executors of the late Hon. Rollo Russell, and with the hearty goodwill of Lady Agatha Russell, daughter of the late Earl Russell, the only living representative of her father, Mr. Rollo Russell, his son, having died in 1914. The Lyons Papers, preserved in the Muniment Room at Old Norfolk House, were used through the courtesy of the Duchess of Norfolk, who now represents her son who is a minor. The Gladstone Papers, preserved at Hawarden Castle, were used through the courtesy of the Gladstone Trustees. The few citations from the Palmerston Papers, preserved at Broadlands, were approved by Lieut.-Colonel Wilfred Ashley, M.P.

The opportunity to study these private papers has been invaluable for my work. Shortly after returning from England in 1913 Mr. Worthington Ford well said: "The inside history of diplomatic relations between the United States and Great Britain may be surmised from the official archives; the tinting and shading needed to complete the picture must be sought elsewhere." (Mass. Hist. Soc. *Proceedings*, XLVI, p. 478.) Mr. C. F. Adams declared (*ibid.*, XLVII, p. 54) that without these papers ". . . the character of English diplomacy at that time (1860-1865) cannot be understood. . . . It would appear that the commonly entertained impressions as to certain phases of international relations, and the proceedings and utterances of English public men during the progress of the War of Secession, must be to some extent revised."

In addition to the new English materials I have been fortunate in the generosity of my colleague at Stanford University, Professor Frank A. Golder, who has given to me transcripts, obtained at St. Petersburg in 1914, of all

Russian diplomatic correspondence on the Civil War. Many friends have aided, by suggestion or by permitting the use of notes and manuscripts, in the preparation of this work. I have sought to make due acknowledgment for such aid in my foot-notes. But in addition to those already named, I should here particularly note the courtesy of the late Mr. Gaillard Hunt for facilities given in the State Department at Washington, of Mr. Herbert Putnam, Librarian of Congress, for the transcript of the Correspondence of Mason and Slidell, Confederate Commissioners in Europe, and of Mr. Charles Moore, Chief of Manuscripts Division, Library of Congress, for the use of the Schurz Papers containing copies of the despatches of Schleiden, Minister of the Republic of Bremen at Washington during the Civil War. Especially thanks are due to my friend, Mr. Herbert Hoover, for his early interest in this work and for his generous aid in the making of transcripts which would otherwise have been beyond my means. And, finally, I owe much to the skill and care of my wife who made the entire typescript for the Press, and whose criticisms were invaluable.

It is no purpose of a Preface to indicate results, but it is my hope that with, I trust, a "calm comparison of the evidence," now for the first time available to the historian, a fairly true estimate may be made of what the American Civil War meant to Great Britain; how she regarded it and how she reacted to it. In brief, my work is primarily a study in British history in the belief that the American drama had a world significance, and peculiarly a British one.

EPHRAIM DOUGLASS ADAMS.

November 25, 1924

CONTENTS

OF

VOLUME ONE

LIST OF ILLUSTRATIONS

PART ONE

GREAT BRITAIN AND THE AMERICAN CIVIL WAR

CHAPTER I

BACKGROUNDS

IN 1862, less than a year after he had assumed his post in London, the American Minister, Charles Francis Adams, at a time of depression and bitterness wrote to Secretary of State Seward : " That Great Britain did, in the most terrible moment of our domestic trial in struggling with a monstrous social evil she had earnestly professed to abhor, coldly and at once assume our inability to master it, and then become the only foreign nation steadily contributing in every indirect way possible to verify its judgment, will probably be the verdict made against her by posterity, on calm comparison of the evidence."[1] Very different were the views of Englishmen. The historian, George Grote, could write : " The perfect neutrality [of Great Britain] in this destructive war appears to me almost a phenomenon in political history. No such forbearance has been shown during the political history of the last two centuries. It is the single case in which the English Government and public—generally so meddlesome—have displayed most prudent and commendable forbearance in spite of great temptations to the contrary."[2] And Sir William Harcourt, in September, 1863, declared : " Among all Lord Russell's many titles to fame and to public gratitude, the manner in which he has steered the vessel of State through the Scylla and Charybdis of the American War will, I think, always stand conspicuous."[3]

[1] State Department, Eng., Vol. LXXIX, No. 135, March 27, 1862.

[2] Walpole, *Russell*, Vol. II, p. 367. [3] *Life of Lady John Russell*, p. 197.

Minister Adams, in the later years of the Civil War, saw reason somewhat to modify his earlier judgment, but his indictment of Great Britain was long prevalent in America, as, indeed, it was also among the historians and writers of Continental Europe—notably those of France and Russia. To what extent was this dictum justified? Did Great Britain in spite of her long years of championship of personal freedom and of leadership in the cause of anti-slavery seize upon the opportunity offered in the disruption of the American Union, and forgetting humanitarian idealisms, react only to selfish motives of commercial advantage and national power? In brief, how is the American Civil War to be depicted by historians of Great Britain, recording her attitude and action in both foreign and domestic policy, and revealing the principles of her statesmen, or the inspirations of her people?

It was to answer this question that the present work was originally undertaken; but as investigation proceeded it became progressively more clear that the great crisis in America was almost equally a crisis in the domestic history of Great Britain itself and that unless this were fully appreciated no just estimate was possible of British policy toward America. Still more it became evident that the American Civil War, as seen through British spectacles, could not be understood if regarded as an isolated and unique situation, but that the conditions preceding that situation—some of them lying far back in the relations of the two nations—had a vital bearing on British policy and opinion when the crisis arose. No expanded examination of these preceding conditions is here possible, but it is to a summary analysis of them that this first chapter is devoted.

. . . . . .

On the American War for separation from the Mother Country it is unnecessary to dilate, though it should always be remembered that both during the war and afterwards there existed a minority in Great Britain strongly sympathetic with the political ideals proclaimed in America——regarding those ideals, indeed, as something to be striven for in Britain itself and the conflict with America as, in a measure, a conflict in home politics. But independence once acknowledged by the Treaty of Peace of 1783, the relations between the Mother Country and the newly-created United States of America rapidly tended to adjust themselves to lines of contact customary between Great Britain and any other Sovereign State. Such contacts, fixing national attitude and policy, ordinarily occur on three main lines: governmental, determined by officials in authority in either State whose duty it is to secure the greatest advantage in power and prosperity for the State; commercial, resulting, primarily, from the interchange of goods and the business opportunities of either nation in the other's territory, or from their rivalry in foreign trade; idealistic, the result of comparative development especially in those ideals of political structure which determine the nature of the State and the form of its government. The more obvious of these contacts is the governmental, since the attitude of a people is judged by the formal action of its Government, and, indeed, in all three lines of contact the government of a State is directly concerned and frequently active. But it may be of service to a clearer appreciation of British attitude and policy before 1860, if the intermingling of elements required by a strict chronological account of relations is here replaced by a separate review of each of the three main lines of contact.

Once independence had been yielded to the American Colonies, the interest of the British Government rapidly waned in affairs American. True, there still remained the valued establishments in the West Indies, and the less considered British possessions on the continent to the north of the United States. Meanwhile, there were occasional frictions with America arising from uncertain claims drawn from the former colonial privileges of the new state, or from boundary contentions not settled in the treaty of peace. Thus the use of the Newfoundland fisheries furnished ground for an acrimonious controversy lasting even into the twentieth century, and occasionally rising to the danger point. Boundary disputes dragged along through official argument, survey commissions, arbitration, to final settlement, as in the case of the northern limits of the State of Maine fixed at last by the Treaty of Washington of 1842, and then on lines fair to both sides at any time in the forty years of legal bickering. Very early, in 1817, an agreement creditable to the wisdom and pacific intentions of both countries, was reached establishing small and equal naval armaments on the Great Lakes. The British fear of an American attack on Canada proved groundless as time went on and was definitely set at rest by the strict curb placed by the American Government upon the restless activities of such of its citizens as sympathized with the followers of McKenzie and Papineau in the Canadian rebellion of 1837.[1]

None of these governmental contacts affected greatly the British policy toward America. But the "War of 1812," as it is termed in the United States, "Mr. Madison's War," as it was derisively named by Tory contemporaries in Great Britain, arose from serious policies in which the respective governments were in definite opposition. Briefly, this was a clash between belligerent and neutral interests. Britain, fighting at first for the preservation of Europe against the spread of French revolutionary influence, later against the Napoleonic plan of Empire, held the seas in her grasp and exercised with vigour all the accustomed rights of a naval

[1] There was a revival of this fear at the end of the American Civil War. This will be commented on later.

belligerent. Of necessity, from her point of view, and as always in the case of the dominant naval belligerent, she stretched principles of international law to their utmost interpretation to secure her victory in war. America, soon the only maritime neutral of importance, and profiting greatly by her neutrality, contested point by point the issue of exceeded belligerent right as established in international law. America did more; she advanced new rules and theories of belligerent and neutral right respectively, and demanded that the belligerents accede to them. Dispute arose over blockades, contraband, the British "rule of 1756" which would have forbidden American trade with French colonies in war time, since such trade was prohibited by France herself in time of peace. But first and foremost as touching the personal sensibilities and patriotism of both countries was the British exercise of a right of search and seizure to recover British sailors.

Moreover this asserted right brought into clear view definitely opposed theories as to citizenship. Great Britain claimed that a man once born a British subject could never cease to be a subject—could never "alienate his duty." It was her practice to fill up her navy, in part at least, by the "impressment" of her sailor folk, taking them whenever needed, and wherever found—in her own coast towns, or from the decks of her own mercantile marine. But many British sailors sought security from such impressment by desertion in American ports or were tempted to desert to American merchant ships by the high pay obtainable in the rapidly-expanding United States merchant marine. Many became by naturalization citizens of the United States, and it was the duty of America to defend them as such in their lives and business. America ultimately came to hold, in short, that expatriation was accomplished from Great Britain when American citizenship was conferred. On shore they were safe, foı Britain did not attempt to reclaim her subjects from the soil of another nation. But she denied that the American flag on merchant vessels at sea gave like security and she asserted a naval right to search such vessels in time of peace, professing her complete acquiescence in a like right to the American navy over British merchant vessels—a concession refused by America, and of no practical value since no American citizen sought service in the British merchant marine.

This " right of search " controversy involved then, two basic points of opposition between the two governments. First America contested the British theory of " once a citizen always a citizen " ;[1] second, America denied any right whatever to a foreign naval vessel in *time of peace* to stop and search a vessel lawfully flying the American flag. The *right of search in time of war*, that is, a belligerent right of search, America never denied, but there was both then and later much public confusion in both countries as to the question at issue since, once at war, Great Britain frequently exercised a legal belligerent right of search and followed it up by the seizure of sailors alleged to be British subjects. Nor were British naval captains especially careful to make sure that no American-born sailors were included in their impressment seizures, and as the accounts spread of victim after victim, the American irritation steadily increased. True, France was also an offender, but as the weaker naval power her offence was lost sight of in view of the, literally, thousands of *bona fide* Americans seized by Great Britain. Here, then, was a third cause of irritation connected with impressment, though not a point of governmental dispute as to right, for Great Britain professed her earnest desire to restore promptly any American-born sailors whom her naval officers had seized through error. In fact many such sailors were soon liberated, but a large number either continued to serve

[1] This was the position of President and Congress: yet the United States had not acknowledged the right of an American citizen to expatriate himself.

on British ships or to languish in British prisons until the end of the Napoleonic Wars.[1]

There were other, possibly greater, causes of the War of 1812, most of them arising out of the conflicting interests of the chief maritime neutral and the chief naval belligerent. The pacific presidential administration of Jefferson sought by trade restrictions, using embargo and non-intercourse acts, to bring pressure on both England and France, hoping to force a better treatment of neutrals. The United States, divided in sympathy between the belligerents, came near to disorder and disruption at home, over the question of foreign policy. But through all American factions there ran the feeling of growing animosity to Great Britain because of impressment. At last, war was declared by America in 1812 and though at the moment bitterly opposed by one section, New England, that war later came to be regarded as of great national value as one of the factors which welded the discordant states into a national unity. Naturally also, the war once ended, its commercial causes were quickly forgotten, whereas the individual, personal offence involved in impressment and right of search, with its insult to national pride, became a patriotic theme for politicians and for the press. To deny, in fact, a British "right of search" became a national point of honour, upon which no American statesman would have dared to yield to British overtures.

In American eyes the War of 1812 appears as a "second war of Independence" and also as of international importance in contesting an unjust use by Britain of her control of the seas. Also, it is to be remembered that no other war of importance was fought by America until the Mexican War of 1846, and militant patriotism was thus centred on the two wars fought against Great Britain.

[1] Between 1797 and 1801, of the sailors taken from American ships, 102 were retained, 1,042 were discharged, and 805 were held for further proof. (Updyke, *The Diplomacy of the War of* 1812, p. 21.)

The contemporary British view was that of a nation involved in a life and death struggle with a great European enemy, irritated by what seemed captious claims, developed to war, by a minor power.[1] To be sure there were a few obstinate Tories in Britain who saw in the war the opportunity of smashing at one blow Napoleon's dream of empire, and the American "democratic system." The London *Times* urged the government to "finish with Mr. Bonaparte and then deal with Mr. Madison and democracy," arguing that it should be England's object to subvert "the whole system of the Jeffersonian school." But this was not the purpose of the British Government, nor would such a purpose have been tolerated by the small but vigorous Whig minority in Parliament.

The peace of 1814, signed at Ghent, merely declared an end of the war, quietly ignoring all the alleged causes of the conflict. Impressment was not mentioned, but it was never again resorted to by Great Britain upon American ships. But the principle of right of search in time of peace, though for another object than impressment, was soon again asserted by Great Britain and for forty years was a cause of constant irritation and a source of danger in the relations of the two countries. Stirred by philanthropic emotion Great Britain entered upon a world crusade for the suppression of the African Slave Trade. All nations in principle repudiated that trade and Britain made treaties with various maritime powers giving mutual right of search to the naval vessels of each upon the others' merchant vessels. The African Slave Trade was in fact outlawed for the flags of all nations. But America, smarting under the memory of impressment injuries, and maintaining in any case the doctrine that in time of peace the national flag protected a vessel from inter-

[1] The people of the British North American Provinces regarded the war as an attempt made by America, taking advantage of the European wars, at forcible annexation. In result the fervour of the United Empire Loyalists was renewed, especially in Upper Canada. Thus the same two wars which fostered militant patriotism in America against England had the same result in Canadian sentiment against America.

ference or search by the naval vessels of any other power, refused to sign mutual right of search treaties and denied, absolutely, such a right for any cause whatever to Great Britain or to any other nation. Being refused a treaty, Britain merely renewed her assertion of the right and continued to exercise it.

Thus the right of search in time of peace controversy was not ended with the war of 1812 but remained a constant sore in national relations, for Britain alone used her navy with energy to suppress the slave trade, and the slave traders of all nations sought refuge, when approached by a British naval vessel, under the protection of the American flag. If Britain respected the flag, and sheered off from search, how could she stop the trade ? If she ignored the flag and on boarding found an innocent American vessel engaged in legal trade, there resulted claims for damages by detention of voyage, and demands by the American Government for apology and reparation. The real slave trader, seized under the American flag, never protested to the United States, nor claimed American citizenship, for his punishment in American law for engaging in the slave trade was death, while under the law of any other nation it did not exceed imprisonment, fine and loss of his vessel.

Summed up in terms of governmental attitude the British contention was that here was a great international humanitarian object frustrated by an absurd American sensitiveness on a point of honour about the flag. After fifteen years of dispute Great Britain offered to abandon any claim to a right of *search*, contenting herself with a right of *visit*, merely to verify a vessel's right to fly the American flag. America asserted this to be mere pretence, involving no renunciation of a practice whose legality she denied. In 1842, in the treaty settling the Maine boundary controversy, the eighth article sought a method of escape. Joint cruising squadrons were provided for the coast of

Africa, the British to search all suspected vessels except those flying the American flag, and these to be searched by the American squadron. At once President Tyler notified Congress that Great Britain had renounced the right of search. Immediately in Parliament a clamour was raised against the Government for the "sacrifice" of a British right at sea, and Lord Aberdeen promptly made official disclaimer of such surrender.

Thus, heritage of the War of 1812 right of search in time of peace was a steady irritant. America doubted somewhat the honesty of Great Britain, appreciating in part the humanitarian purpose, but suspicious of an ulterior "will to rule the seas." After 1830 no American political leader would have dared to yield the right of search. Great Britain for her part, viewing the expansion of domestic slavery in the United States, came gradually to attribute the American contention, not to patriotic pride, but to the selfish business interests of the slave-holding states. In the end, in 1858, with a waning British enthusiasm for the cause of slave trade suppression, and with recognition that America had become a great world power, Britain yielded her claim to right of search or visit, save when established by Treaty. Four years later, in 1862, it may well have seemed to British statesmen that American slavery had indeed been the basic cause of America's attitude, for in that year a treaty was signed by the two nations giving mutual right of search for the suppression of the African Slave Trade. In fact, however, this was but an effort by Seward, Secretary of State for the North, to influence British and European opinion against the seceding slave states of the South.

The right of search controversy was, in truth, ended when American power reached a point where the British Government must take it seriously into account as a factor in general world policy. That power had been steadily and rapidly advancing since 1814. From almost the first moment of established independence American statesmen visualized the separation of the interests of the western continent from those of Europe, and planned for American leadership in this new world. Washington, the first President, emphasized in his farewell address the danger of entangling alliances with Europe. For long the nations of Europe, immersed in Continental wars, put aside their rivalries in this new world. Britain, for a time, neglected colonial expansion westward, but in 1823, in an emergency of European origin when France, commissioned by the great powers of continental Europe, intervened in Spain to restore the deposed Bourbon monarchy and seemed about to intervene in Spanish America to restore to Spain her revolted colonies, there developed in Great Britain a policy, seemingly about to draw America and England into closer co-operation. Canning, for Britain, proposed to America a joint declaration against French intervention in the Americas. His argument was against the principle of intervention; his immediate motive was a fear of French colonial expansion; but his ultimate object was inheritance by Britain of Spain's dying influence and position in the new world.

Canning's overture was earnestly considered in America. The ex-Presidents, Jefferson and Madison, recommended its acceptance, but the Secretary of State, John Quincy Adams, opposed this, favouring rather a separate declaration by the United States, and of this opinion was also President Monroe. Thus arose the Monroe Doctrine announcing American opposition to the principle of "intervention," and declaring that the American continents were no longer to be regarded as open to further colonization by European nations. The British emergency situation with France, though already quieted, caused Monroe's Message to be greeted in England with high approval. But Canning did not so approve it for he saw clearly that the Monroe Doctrine was a challenge not merely to continental Europe, but to England as well and he set himself to thwart this threatening American policy. Had Canning's policy been followed by later British statesmen there would have resulted a serious clash with the United States.[1]

In fact the Monroe Doctrine, imposing on Europe a self-denying policy of non-colonial expansion toward the west, provided for the United States the medium, if she wished to use it, for her own expansion in territory and in influence. But for a time there was no need of additional territory for that already hers stretched from the Atlantic to the Rocky Mountains, two-thirds of the way from ocean to ocean. Her population was growing fast. But four millions at the time of the Revolution, there were thirteen millions in 1830, and of these nearly a third were already across the Appalachian range and were constantly pressing on towards new lands in the South and West. The Monroe Doctrine was the first definite notice given to Europe of America's preconceived "destiny," but the earlier realization of that destiny took place on lines of expansion within her own boundaries. To this there could be no governmental objection, whether by Great Britain or any other nation.

But when in the decade 1840 to 1850, the United States, to the view of British statesmen, suddenly startled the world by entering upon a policy of further territorial expansion, forsaking her peaceful progress and turning toward war, there was a quick determination on a line of British policy as regards the American advance. The first intimation of the new American policy came in relation to the State of Texas which had revolted from Mexico in 1836, and whose independence had been generally recognized by 1842. To this new state Britain sent diplomatic and consular agents and these reported two factions among the people—one

[1] Temperley, "Later American Policy of George Canning" in *Am. Hist. Rev.*, XI, 783. Also *Cambridge History of British Foreign Policy*, Vol. II, ch. 2.

seeking admission to the American Union, one desiring the maintenance of independence.

In 1841 Aberdeen had sent Lord Ashburton to America with instructions to secure, if possible, a settlement of all matters in dispute. Here was a genuine British effort to escape from national irritations. But before the Treaty of 1842 was signed, even while it was in the earlier stages of negotiation, the British Government saw, with alarm, quite new questions arising, preventing, to its view, that harmonious relation with the United States the desire for which had led to the Ashburton mission. This new development was the appearance of an American fever for territorial expansion, turning first toward Texas, but soon voiced as a " manifest destiny " which should carry American power and institutions to the Pacific and even into Central America. Among these institutions was that of slavery, detested by the public of Great Britain, yet a delicate matter for governmental consideration since the great cotton manufacturing interests drew the bulk of their supplies of raw cotton from the slave-holding states of America. If Texas, herself a cotton state, should join the United States, dependence upon slave-grown cotton would be intensified. Also, Texas, once acquired, what was there to prevent further American exploitation, followed by slave expansion, into Mexico, where for long British influence had been dominant?

On the fate of Texas, therefore, centred for a time the whole British policy toward America. Pakenham, the British minister to Mexico, urged a British pressure on Mexico to forgo her plans of reconquering Texas, and strong British efforts to encourage Texas in maintaining her independence. His theory foreshadowed a powerful buffer Anglo-Saxon state, prohibiting American advance to the south-west, releasing Britain from dependence on American cotton, and ultimately, he hoped, leading Texas to abolish slavery, not yet so rooted as to be ineradicable. This policy was approved by the British Government, Pakenham was sent to Washington to watch events, a *chargé*, Elliot, was despatched to Texas, and from London lines were cast to draw France into the plan and to force the acquiescence of Mexico.

In this brief account of main lines of governmental contacts, it is unnecessary to recite the details of the diplomatic conflict, for such it became, with sharp antagonisms manifested on both sides. The basic fact was that America was bent upon territorial expansion, and that Great Britain set herself to thwart this ambition. But not to the point of war. Aberdeen was so incautious at one moment as to propose to France and Mexico a triple guarantee of the independence of Texas, if that state would acquiesce, but when Pakenham notified him that in this case, Britain must clearly understand that war with America was not merely possible, but probable, Aberdeen hastened to withdraw the plan of guarantee, fortunately not yet approved by Mexico.[1]

The solution of this diplomatic contest thus rested with Texas. Did she wish annexation to the United States, or did she prefer independence ? Elliot, in Texas, hoped to the last moment that Texas would choose independence and British favour. But the people of the new state were largely emigrants from the United States, and a majority of them wished to re-enter the Union, a step finally accomplished in 1846, after ten years of separate existence as a Republic. The part played by the British Government in this whole episode was not a fortunate one. It is the duty of Governments to watch over the interests of their subjects, and to

[1] Much has recently been published on British policy in Texas. See my book, *British Interests and Activities in Texas*, 1838-1846, Johns Hopkins Press, Balt., 1910. Also Adams, Editor, *British Diplomatic Correspondence concerning the Republic of Texas*, The Texas State Historical Association, Austin, Texas, 1918.

guard the prestige and power of the state. Great Britain had a perfect *right* to take whatever steps she chose to take in regard to Texas, but the steps taken appeared to Americans to be based upon a policy antagonistic to the American expansion policy of the moment. The Government of Great Britain appeared, indeed, to have adopted a policy of preventing the development of the power of the United States. Then, fronted with war, she had meekly withdrawn. The basic British public feeling, fixing the limits of governmental policy, of never again being drawn into war with America, not because of fear, but because of important trade relations and also because of essential liking and admiration, in spite of surface antagonisms, was not appreciated in America. Lord Aberdeen indeed, and others in governmental circles, pleaded that the support of Texan independence was in reality perfectly in harmony with the best interests of the United States, since it would have tended toward the limitation of American slavery. And in the matter of national power, they consoled themselves with prophecies that the American Union, now so swollen in size, must inevitably split into two, perhaps three, rival empires, a slave-holding one in the South, free nations in North and West.

The fate of Texas sealed, Britain soon definitely abandoned all opposition to American expansion unless it were to be attempted northwards, though prophesying evil for the American madness. Mexico, relying on past favours, and because of a sharp controversy between the United States and Great Britain over the Oregon territory, expected British aid in her war of 1846 against America. But she was sharply warned that such aid would not be given, and the Oregon dispute was settled in the Anglo-Saxon fashion of vigorous legal argument, followed by a fair compromise. The Mexican war resulted in the acquisition of California by the United States. British agents in this province of

Mexico, and British admirals on the Pacific were cautioned to take no active steps in opposition.

Thus British policy, after Texan annexation, offered no barrier to American expansion, and much to British relief the fear of the extension of the American plans to Mexico and Central America was not realized. The United States was soon plunged, as British statesmen had prophesied, into internal conflict over the question whether the newly-acquired territories should be slave or free.

The acquisition of California brought up a new problem of quick transit between Atlantic and Pacific, and a canal was planned across Central America. Here Britain and America acted together, at first in amity, though the convention signed in 1850 later developed discord as to the British claim of a protectorate over the Atlantic end of the proposed canal at San Juan del Nicaragua. But Britain was again at war in Europe in the middle 'fifties, and America was deep in quarrel over slavery at home. On both sides in spite of much diplomatic intrigue and of manifestations of national pride there was governmental desire to avoid difficulties. At the end of the ten-year period Britain ceded to Nicaragua her protectorate in the canal zone, and all causes of friction, so reported President Buchanan to Congress in 1860, were happily removed. Britain definitely altered her policy of opposition to the growth of American power.

In 1860, then, the causes of governmental antagonisms were seemingly all at an end. Impressment was not used after 1814. The differing theories of the two Governments on British expatriation still remained, but Britain attempted no practical application of her view. The right of search in time of peace controversy, first eased by the plan of joint cruising, had been definitely settled by the British renunciation of 1858. Opposition to American territorial advance but briefly manifested by Britain, had ended with the annexation of Texas, and the fever of expansion had waned in America. Minor disputes in Central America, related to the proposed canal, were amicably adjusted.

But differences between nations, varying view-points of peoples, frequently have deeper currents than the more obvious frictions in governmental act or policy, nor can governments themselves fail to react to such less evident causes. It is necessary to review the commercial relations of the two nations—later to examine their political ideals.

In 1783 America won her independence in government from a colonial status. But commercially she remained a British colony—yet with a difference. She had formed a part of the British colonial system. All her normal trade was with the mother country or with other British colonies. Now her privileges in such trade were at an end, and she must seek as a favour that which had formerly been hers as a member of the British Empire. The direct trade between England and America was easily and quickly resumed, for the commercial classes of both nations desired it and profited by it. But the British colonial system prohibited trade between a foreign state and British colonies and there was one channel of trade, to and from the British West Indies, long very profitable to both sides, during colonial times, but now legally hampered by American independence. The New England States had lumber, fish, and farm products desired by the West Indian planters, and these in turn offered needed sugar, molasses, and rum. Both parties desired to restore the trade, and in spite of the legal restrictions of the colonial system, the trade was in fact resumed in part and either permitted or winked at by the British Government, but never to the advantageous exchange of former times.

The acute stage of controversy over West Indian trade was not reached until some thirty years after American Independence, but the uncertainty of such trade during a long period in which a portion of it consisted in unauthorized and unregulated exchange was a constant irritant to all parties concerned. Meanwhile there came the War of 1812 with its preliminary check upon direct trade to and from Great Britain, and its final total prohibition of intercourse during the war itself. In 1800 the bulk of American importation of manufactures still came from Great Britain. In the contest over neutral rights and theories, Jefferson attempted to bring pressure on the belligerents, and especially on England, by restriction of imports. First came a non-importation Act, 1806, followed by an embargo on exports, 1807, but these were so unpopular in the commercial states of New England that they were withdrawn in 1810, yet for a short time only, for Napoleon tricked the United States into believing that France had yielded to American contentions on neutral rights, and in 1811 non-intercourse was proclaimed again with England alone. On June 18, 1812, America finally declared war and trade stopped save in a few New England ports where rebellious citizens continued to sell provisions to a blockading British naval squadron.

For eight years after 1806, then, trade with Great Britain had steadily decreased, finally almost to extinction during the war. But America required certain articles customarily imported and necessity now forced her to develop her own manufactures. New England had been the centre of American foreign commerce, but now there began a trend toward manufacturing enterprise. Even in 1814, however, at the end of the war, it was still thought in the United States that under normal conditions manufactured goods would again be imported and the general cry of "protection for home industries" was as yet unvoiced. Nevertheless, a group of infant industries had in fact been started and clamoured for defence now that peace was restored. This situation was not unnoticed in Great Britain where merchants, piling up goods in anticipation of peace on the continent of Europe and a restored market, suddenly discovered that the poverty of Europe denied them that market. Looking with apprehension toward the new industries of America, British merchants, following the advice of Lord Brougham in a parliamentary speech, dumped great quantities of their surplus goods on the American market, selling them far below cost, or even on extravagant credit terms. One object was to smash the budding American manufactures.

This action of British merchants naturally stirred some angry patriotic emotions in the circles where American business suffered and a demand began to be heard for protection. But the Government of the United States was still representative of agriculture, in the main, and while a Tariff Bill was enacted in 1816 that Bill was regarded as a temporary measure required by the necessity of paying the costs of the recent war. Just at this juncture, however, British policy, now looking again toward a great colonial empire, sought advantages for the hitherto neglected maritime provinces of British North America, and thought that it had found them by encouragement of their trade with the British West Indies. The legal status of American trade with the West Indies was now enforced and for a time intercourse was practically suspended.

This British policy brought to the front the issue of protection in America. It not only worked against a return by New England from manufacturing to commerce, but it soon brought into the ranks of protectionists a northern and western agricultural element that had been accustomed to sell surplus products to West Indian planters seeking cheap food-stuffs for their slaves. This new protectionist element was as yet not crystallized into a clamour for "home markets" for agriculture, but the pressure of opinion was beginning to be felt, and by 1820 the question of West Indian trade became one of constant agitation and demanded political action. That action was taken on lines of retaliation. Congress in 1818 passed a law excluding from American ports any British vessel coming from a port access to which was denied to an American vessel, and placing under bond in American ports British vessels with prohibition of their proceeding to a British port to which American vessels could not go. This act affected not merely direct trade with the West Indies, but stopped the general custom of British ships of taking part cargoes to Jamaica while *en route* to and from the United States. The result was, first, compromise, later, under Huskisson's administration at the British Board of Trade, complete abandonment by Britain of the exclusive trade basis of her whole colonial system.

The "retaliatory system" which J. Q. Adams regarded as "a new declaration of independence," was, in fact, quickly taken up by other non-colonial nations, and these, with America, compelled Great Britain to take stock of her interests. Huskisson, rightly foreseeing British prosperity as dependent upon her manufactures and upon the carrying trade, stated in Parliament that American "retaliation" had forced the issue. Freedom of trade in British ports was offered in 1826 to all non-colonial nations that would open their ports within one year on terms of equality to British ships. J. Q. Adams, now President of the United States, delayed acceptance of this offer, preferring a treaty negotiation, and was rebuffed by Canning, so that actual resumption of West Indian trade did not take place until 1830, after the close of Adams' administration. That trade never recovered its former prosperity.

Meanwhile the long period of controversy, from 1806 to 1830, had resulted in a complete change in the American situation. It is not a sufficient explanation of the American belief in, and practice of, the theory of protection to attribute this alone to British checks placed upon free commercial rivalry. Nevertheless the progress of America toward an established system, reaching its highest mark for years in the Tariff Bill of 1828, is distinctly related to the events just narrated. After American independence, the partially illegal status of West Indian trade hampered commercial progress and slightly encouraged American manufactures by the mere seeking of capital for investment; the neutral troubles of 1806 and the American prohibitions on intercourse increased the transfer of interest; the war of 1812 gave a complete protection to infant industries; the dumping of British goods in 1815 stirred patriotic American feeling; British renewal of colonial system restrictions, and the twelve-year quarrel over "retaliation" gave time for the definite establishment of protectionist ideas in the United States. But Britain was soon proclaiming for herself and for the world the common advantage and the justice of a great theory of free trade. America was apparently now committed to an opposing economic theory, the first great nation definitely to establish it, and thus there resulted a clear-cut opposition of principle and a clash of interests. From 1846, when free trade ideas triumphed in England, the devoted British free trader regarded America as the chief obstacle to a world-wide acceptance of his theory.

The one bright spot in America, as regarded by the British free trader, was in the Southern States, where cotton interests, desiring no advantage from protection, since their market was in Europe, attacked American protection and sought to escape from it. Also slave supplies, without protection, could have been purchased more cheaply from England than from the manufacturing North. In 1833 indeed the South had forced a reaction against protection, but it proceeded slowly. In 1854 it was Southern opinion that carried through Congress the reciprocity treaty with the British American Provinces, partly brought about, no doubt, by a Southern fear that Canada, bitter over the loss of special advantages in British markets by the British free trade of 1846, might join the United States and thus swell the Northern and free states of the Union. Cotton interests and trade became the dominant British commercial tie with the United States, and the one great hope, to the British minds, of a break in the false American system of protection. Thus both in economic theory and in trade, spite of British dislike of slavery, the export trading interests of Great Britain became more and more directed toward the Southern States of America. Adding powerfully to this was the dependence of British cotton manufactures upon the American supply. The British trade attitude, arising largely outside of direct governmental contacts, was bound to have, nevertheless, a constant and important influence on governmental action.

Governmental policy, seeking national power, conflicting trade and industrial interests, are the favourite themes of those historians who regard nations as determined in their relations solely by economic causes—by what is called "enlightened self-interest." But governments, no matter how arbitrary, and still more if in a measure resting on representation, react both consciously and unconsciously to a public opinion not obviously based upon either national or commercial rivalry. Sometimes, indeed, governmental attitude runs absolutely counter to popular attitude in international affairs. In such a case, the historical estimate, if based solely on evidences of governmental action, is a false one and may do great injustice to the essential friendliness of a people.

How then, did the British people, of all classes, regard America before 1860, and in what manner did that regard affect the British Government? Here, it is necessary to seek British opinion on, and its reaction to, American institutions, ideals, and practices. Such public opinion can be found in quantity sufficient to base an estimate only in travellers' books, in reviews, and in newspapers of the period. When all these are brought together it is found that while there was an almost universal British criticism of American social customs and habits of life, due to that insularity of mental attitude characteristic of every nation, making it prefer its own customs and criticize those of its neighbours, summed up in the phrase "dislike of foreigners" —it is found that British opinion was centred upon two main threads; first America as a place for emigration and, second, American political ideals and institutions.[1]

British emigration to America, a governmentally favoured colonization process before the American revolution, lost that favour after 1783, though not at first definitely opposed. But emigration still continued and at no time, save during the war of 1812, was it absolutely stopped. Its exact amount is unascertainable, for neither Government kept adequate statistics before 1820. With the end of the Napoleonic wars there came great distress in England from which the man of energy sought escape. He turned naturally to America, being familiar, by hearsay at least, with stories of the ease of gaining a livelihood there, and influenced by the knowledge that in the United States he would find people of his own blood and speech. The bulk of this earlier emigration to America resulted from economic causes. When, in 1825, one energetic Member of Parliament, Wilmot Horton, induced the Government to appoint a committee to investigate the whole subject, the result was a mass of testimony, secured from returned emigrants or from their letters home, in which there constantly appeared one main argument influencing the labourer type of emigrant; he

[1] In my studies on British-American relations, I have read the leading British reviews and newspapers, and some four hundred volumes by British travellers. For a summary of the British travellers before 1860 see my article "The Point of View of the British Traveller in America," in the *Political Science Quarterly*, Vol. XXIX, No. 2, June, 1914.

got good wages, and he was supplied, as a farm hand, with good food. Repeatedly he testifies that he had "three meat meals a day," whereas in England he had ordinarily received but one such meal a week.

Mere good living was the chief inducement for the labourer type of emigrant, and the knowledge of such living created for this type remaining in England a sort of halo of industrial prosperity surrounding America. But there was a second testimony brought out by Horton's Committee, less general, yet to be picked up here and there as evidence of another argument for emigration to America. The labourer did not dilate upon political equality, nor boast of a share in government, indeed generally had no such share, but he did boast to his fellows at home of the social equality, though not thus expressing it, which was all about him. He was a common farm hand, yet he "sat down to meals" with his employer and family, and worked in the fields side by side with his "master." This, too, was an astounding difference to the mind of the British labourer. Probably for him it created a clearer, if not altogether universal and true picture of the meaning of American democracy than would have volumes of writing upon political institutions. Gradually there was established in the lower orders of British society a visualization of America as a haven of physical well-being and personal social happiness.

This British labouring class had for long, however, no medium of expression in print. Here existed, then, an unexpressed public opinion of America, of much latent influence, but for the moment largely negligible as affecting other classes or the Government. A more important emigrating class in its influence on opinion at home, though not a large class, was composed about equally of small farmers and small merchants facing ruin in the agricultural and trading crises that followed the end of the European war. The

British travellers' books from 1810 to 1820 are generally written by men of this class, or by agents sent out from co-operative groups planning emigration. Generally they were discontented with political conditions at home, commonly opposed to a petrified social order, and attracted to the United States by its lure of prosperity and content. The books are, in brief, a superior type of emigrant guide for a superior type of emigrant, examining and emphasizing industrial opportunity.

Almost universally, however, they sound the note of superior political institutions and conditions. One wrote "A republican finds here A Republic, and the only Republic on the face of the earth that ever deserved the name: where all are under the protection of equal laws; of laws made by Themselves."[1] Another, who established an English colony in the Western States of Illinois, wrote of England that he objected to "being ruled and taxed by people who had no more right to rule and tax us than consisted in the power to do it." And of his adopted country he concludes: "I love the Government; and thus a novel sensation is excited; it is like the development of a new faculty. I am become a patriot in my old age."[2] Still another detailed the points of his content, "I am here, lord and master of myself and of 100 acres of land—an improvable farm, little trouble to me, good society and a good market, and, I think, a fine climate, only a little too hot and dry in summer; the parson gets nothing from me; my state and road taxes and poor rates amount to $25.00 per annum. I can carry a gun if I choose; I leave my door unlocked at night; and I can get snuff for one cent an ounce or a little more."[3]

From the first days of the American colonial movement

[1] John Melish, *Travels*, Vol. I, p. 148.

[2] Morris Birkbeck, *Letters from Illinois*, London, 1818, p. 29.

[3] Letter in Edinburgh *Scotsman*, March, 1823. Cited by *Niles Register*, Vol. XXV, p. 39.

toward independence there had been, indeed, a British interest in American political principles. Many Whigs sympathized with these principles for reasons of home political controversy. Their sympathy continued after American independence and by its insistent expression brought out equally insistent opposition from Tory circles. The British home movement toward a more representative Government had been temporarily checked by the extremes into which French Liberalism plunged in 1791, causing reaction in England. By 1820 pressure was again being exerted by British Liberals of intelligence, and they found arguments in such reports as those just quoted. From that date onward, and especially just before the passing of the Reform Bill of 1832, yet always a factor, the example of a prosperous American democracy was an element in British home politics, lauded or derided as the man in England desired or not an expansion of the British franchise. In the earlier period, however, it is to be remembered that applause of American institutions did not mean acceptance of democracy to the extent of manhood franchise, for no such franchise at first existed in America itself. The debate in England was simply whether the step forward in American democracy, was an argument for a similar step in Great Britain.

Books, reviews and newspapers in Great Britain as the political quarrel there grew in force, depicted America favourably or otherwise according to political sympathies at home. Both before and after the Reform Bill of 1832 this type of effort to mould opinion, by citation of America, was widespread. Hence there is in such writing, not so much the expression of public opinion, as of propaganda to affect that opinion. Book upon book, review upon review, might be quoted to illustrate this, but a few notable examples will suffice.

The most widely read and reviewed book on the United

States before 1840, except the humorous and flippant characterization of America by Mrs. Trollope, was Captain Basil Hall's three-volume work, published in 1829.[1] Claiming an open mind, he expected for his adverse findings a readier credence. For adverse to American political institutions these findings are in all their larger applications. In every line Hall betrays himself as an old Tory of the 'twenties, fixed in his belief, and convinced of the perfection and unalterableness of the British Constitution. Captain Hamilton, who wrote in 1833, was more frank in avowal of a purpose.[2] He states in his preface:

> ". . . When I found the institutions and experiences of the United States deliberately quoted in the reformed parliament, as affording safe precedent for British legislation, and learned that the drivellers who uttered such nonsense, instead of encountering merited derision, were listened to with patience and approbation by men as ignorant as themselves, I certainly did feel that another work on America was yet wanted, and at once determined to undertake a task which inferior considerations would probably have induced me to decline."

Harriet Martineau, ardent advocate of political reform at home, found in the United States proofs for her faith in democracy.[3] Captain Marryat belittled Miss Martineau, but in his six volumes proved himself less a critic of America than an enemy of democracy. Answering a review of his earlier volumes, published separately, he wrote in his concluding volume: "I candidly acknowledge that the reviewer is right in his supposition; my great object has been to do serious injury to the cause of democracy."[4]

[1] *Travels in North America*, 1827-28, London, 1829.

[2] Captain Thomas Hamilton, *Men and Manners in America*, Edinburgh and London, 1833. 2 vols.

[3] *Society in America*, London, 1837. 3 vols. *Retrospect of Western Travel*, London, 1838. 2 vols.

[4] Captain Frederick Marryat, *A Diary in America, with Remarks on Its Institutions*, Vol. VI, p. 293.

The fact was that British governing and intellectual classes were suffering a recoil from the enthusiasms leading up to the step toward democracy in the Reform of 1832. The electoral franchise was still limited to a small minority of the population. Britain was still ruled by her "wise men" of wealth and position. Meanwhile, however, just at the moment when dominant Whig influence in England carried through that step forward toward democratic institutions which Whigs had long lauded in America, the latter country had progressed to manhood suffrage, or as nearly all leading Englishmen, whether Whig or Tory, regarded it, had plunged into the rule of the mob. The result was a rapid lessening in Whig ruling-class expression of admiration for America, even before long to the complete cessation of such admiration, and to assertions in Great Britain that the Reform of 1832 was "final," the last step toward democracy which Britain could safely take. It is not strange that the books and reviews of the period from 1830 to 1840, heavily stress the dangers and crudity of American democracy. They were written for what was now a nearly unanimous British reading public, fearful lest Radical pressure for still further electoral reform should preach the example of the United States.

Thus after 1832 the previous sympathy for America of one section of the British governing class disappears. More—it is replaced by a critical, if not openly hostile attitude. Soon, with the rapid development of the power and wealth of the United States, governing-class England, of all factions save the Radical, came to view America just as it would have viewed any other rising nation, that is, as a problem to be studied for its influence on British prosperity and power. Again, expressions in print reflect the changes of British view—nowhere more clearly than in travellers' books. After 1840, for nearly a decade, these are devoted, not to American political institutions, but to studies, many of them very careful ones, of American industry and governmental policy.

Buckingham, one-time member of Parliament, wrote nine volumes of such description. His work is a storehouse of fact, useful to this day to the American historical student.[1] George Combe, philosopher and phrenologist, studied especially social institutions.[2] Joseph Sturge, philanthropist and abolitionist, made a tour, under the guidance of the poet Whittier, through the Northern and Eastern States.[3] Featherstonaugh, a scientist and civil engineer, described the Southern slave states, in terms completely at variance with those of Sturge.[4] Kennedy, traveller in Texas, and later British consul at Galveston, and Warburton, a traveller who came to the United States by way of Canada, an unusual approach, were both frankly startled, the latter professedly alarmed, at the evidences of power in America.[5] Amazed at the energy, growth and prosperity of the country and alarmed at the anti-British feeling he found in New York City, Warburton wrote that "they [Americans] only wait for matured power to apply the incendiary torch of Republicanism to the nations of Europe."[6] Soon after this was written there began, in 1848, that great tide of Irish emigration to America which heavily reinforced the anti-British attitude of the City of New York, and largely changed its character.

Did books dilating upon the expanding power of America reflect British public opinion, or did they create it? It is

[1] James Silk Buckingham, *America, Historical, Statistic and Descriptive*, London, 1841-43. 9 vols.

[2] *Notes on the United States of North America during a phrenological visit*, 1838-9-40, Edinburgh, 1841. 3 vols.

[3] *A Visit to the United States in* 1841, London, 1842.

[4] George William Featherstonaugh, *Excursion through the Slave States*, London, 1844. 2 vols.

[5] William Kennedy, *Texas: The Rise, Progress and Prospects of the Republic of Texas*, London, 1841. 2 vols. George Warburton, *Hochelaga: or, England in the New World*, London, 1845. 2 vols.

[6] Warburton, *Hochelaga*, 5th Edition, Vol. II, pp. 363-4.

difficult to estimate such matters. Certainly it is not uninteresting that these books coincided in point of time with a British governmental attitude of opposition, though on peaceful lines, to the development of American power, and to the adoption to the point of faith, by British commercial classes, of free trade as opposed to the American protective system. But governing classes were not the British public, and to the great unenfranchised mass, finding voice through the writings of a few leaders, the prosperity of America made a powerful appeal. Radical democracy was again beginning to make its plea in Britain. In 1849 there was published a study of the United States, more careful and exact than any previous to Bryce's great work, and lauding American political institutions. This was Mackay's "Western World," and that there was a public eager for such estimate is evidenced by the fact that the book went through four British editions in 1850.[1] At the end of the decade, then, there appeared once more a vigorous champion of the cause of British democracy, comparing the results of "government by the wise" with alleged mob rule. Mackay wrote:

> "Society in America started from the point to which society in Europe is only yet adding. The equality of men is, to this moment, its corner-stone . . . that which develops itself as the sympathy of class, becomes in America the general sentiment of society. . . . We present an imposing front to the world; but let us tear the picture and look at the canvas. One out of every seven of us is a pauper. Every six Englishmen have, in addition to their other enormous burdens, to support a seventh between them, whose life is spent in consuming, but in adding nothing to the source of their common subsistence."

British governing classes then, forgoing after 1850 opposition to the advance of American power, found them-

[1] Alexander Mackay, *The Western World: or, Travels through the United States in* 1846-47, London, 1849.

selves involved again, as before 1832, in the problem of the possible influence of a prosperous American democracy upon an unenfranchised public opinion at home. Also, for all Englishmen, of whatever class, in spite of rivalry in power, of opposing theories of trade, of divergent political institutions, there existed a vague, though influential, pride in the advance of a people of similar race, sprung from British loins.[1] And there remained for all Englishmen also one puzzling and discreditable American institution, slavery —held up to scorn by the critics of the United States, difficult of excuse among her friends.

Agitation conducted by the great philanthropist, Wilberforce, had early committed British Government and people to a crusade against the African slave trade. This British policy was clearly announced to the world in the negotiations at Vienna in 1814-15. But Britain herself still supported the institution of slavery in her West Indian colonies and it was not until British humanitarian sentiment had forced emancipation upon the unwilling sugar planters, in 1833, that the nation was morally free to criticize American domestic slavery. Meanwhile great emancipation societies, with many branches, all virile and active, had grown up in England and in Scotland. These now turned to an attack on slavery the world over, and especially on American slavery. The great American abolitionist, Garrison, found more support in England than in his own country; his weekly paper, *The Liberator*, is full of messages of cheer from British friends and societies, and of quotations from a sympathetic, though generally provincial, British press.

From 1830 to 1850 British anti-slavery sentiment was at its height. It watched with anxiety the evidence of a developing struggle over slavery in the United States,

[1] This is clearly indicated in Parliament itself, in the debate on the dismissal by the United States in 1856 of Crampton, the British Minister at Washington, for enlistment activities during the Crimean War.—*Hansard*, 3rd. Ser., CXLIII, 14-109 and 120-203.

hopeful, as each crisis arose, that the free Northern States would impose their will upon the Southern Slave States. But as each crisis turned to compromise, seemingly enhancing the power of the South, and committing America to a retention of slavery, the hopes of British abolitionists waned. The North did indeed, to British opinion, become identified with opposition to the expansion of slavery, but after the "great compromise of 1850," where the elder American statesmen of both North and South proclaimed the "finality" of that measure, British sympathy for the North rapidly lessened. Moreover, after 1850, there was in Britain itself a decay of general humanitarian sentiment as regards slavery. The crusade had begun to seem hopeless and the earlier vigorous agitators were dead. The British Government still maintained its naval squadron for the suppression of the African slave trade, but the British official mind no longer keenly interested itself either in this effort or in the general question of slavery.

Nevertheless American slavery and slave conditions were still, after 1850, favourite matters for discussion, almost universally critical, by English writers. Each renewal of the conflict in America, even though local, not national in character, drew out a flood of comment. In the public press this blot upon American civilization was a steady subject for attack, and that attack was naturally directed against the South. The London *Times*, in particular, lost no opportunity of presenting the matter to its readers. In 1856, a Mr. Thomas Gladstone visited Kansas during the height of the border struggles there, and reported his observations in letters to the *Times*. The writer was wholly on the side of the Northern settlers in Kansas, though not hopeful that the Kansas struggle would expand to a national conflict. He constantly depicted the superior civilization, industry, and social excellence of the North as compared with the South.[1]

[1] Gladstone's letters were later published in book form, under the title *The Englishman in Kansas*, London, 1857.

Mrs. Stowe's *Uncle Tom's Cabin* excited greater interest in England than in America itself. The first London edition appeared in May, 1852, and by the end of the year over one million copies had been sold, as opposed to one hundred and fifty thousand in the United States. But if one distinguished writer is to be believed, this great British interest in the book was due more to English antipathy to America than to antipathy to slavery.[1] This writer was Nassau W. Senior, who, in 1857, published a reprint of his article on "American Slavery" in the 206th number of the *Edinburgh Review*, reintroducing in his book extreme language denunciatory of slavery that had been cut out by the editor of the *Review*.[2] Senior had been stirred to write by the brutal attack upon Charles Sumner in the United States Senate after his speech of May 19-20, 1856, evidence, again, that each incident of the slavery quarrel in America excited British attention.

Senior, like Thomas Gladstone, painted the North as all anti-slavery, the South as all pro-slavery. Similar impressions of British understanding (or misunderstanding) are received from the citations of the British provincial press, so favoured by Garrison in his *Liberator*.[3] Yet for intellectual Britain, at least—that Britain which was vocal and whose opinion can be ascertained in spite of this constant interest in American slavery, there was generally a fixed belief that slavery in the United States was so firmly

[1] "The evil passions which 'Uncle Tom' gratified in England were not hatred or vengeance [of slavery], but national jealousy and national vanity. We have long been smarting under the conceit of America—we are tired of hearing her boast that she is the freest and the most enlightened country that the world has ever seen. Our clergy hate her voluntary system—our Tories hate her democrats—our Whigs hate her parvenus—our Radicals hate her litigiousness, her insolence, and her ambition. All parties hailed Mrs. Stowe as a revolter from the enemy." Senior, *American Slavery*, p. 38.

[2] The reprint is without date, but the context shows the year to be 1857.

[3] For example the many British expressions quoted in reference to John Brown's raid, in *The Liberator* for February 10, 1860, and in succeeding issues.

established that it could not be overthrown. Of what use, then, the further expenditure of British sympathy or effort in a lost cause? Senior himself, at the conclusion of his fierce attack on the Southern States, expressed the pessimism of British abolitionists. He wrote, "We do not venture to hope that we, or our sons, or our grandsons, will see American slavery extirpated, or even materially mitigated." [1]

[1] Senior, *American Slavery*, p. 68.

CHAPTER II

FIRST KNOWLEDGE OF IMPENDING CONFLICT, 1860–61.

IT has been remarked by the American historian, Schouler, that immediately before the outbreak of the Civil War, diplomatic controversies between England and America had largely been settled, and that England, pressed from point to point, had " sullenly " yielded under American demands. This generalization, as applied to what were, after all, minor controversies, is in great measure true. In larger questions of policy, as regards spheres of influence or developing power, or principles of trade, there was difference, but no longer any essential opposition or declared rivalry.[1] In theories of government there was sharp divergence, clearly appreciated, however, only in governing-class Britain. This sense of divergence, even of a certain threat from America to British political institutions, united with an established opinion that slavery was permanently fixed in the United States to reinforce governmental indifference, sometimes even hostility, to America. The British public, also, was largely hopeless of any change in the institution of slavery, and its own active humanitarian interest was waning, though still dormant—not dead. Yet the two nations, to a degree not true of any other two world-powers, were of the same race, had similar basic laws, read the same books, and were held in close touch at many points by the steady flow of British emigration to the United States.

[1] Dr. Newton asserts that at the end of the 'fifties Great Britain made a sharp change of policy. (*Cambridge History of British Foreign Policy*, Vol. II, p. 283.)

When, after the election of Lincoln to the Presidency, in November, 1860, the storm-clouds of civil strife rapidly gathered, the situation took both British Government and people by surprise. There was not any clear understanding either of American political conditions, or of the intensity of feeling now aroused over the question of the extension of slave territory. The most recent descriptions of America had agreed in assertion that at some future time there would take place, in all probability, a dissolution of the Union, on lines of diverging economic interests, but also stated that there was nothing in the American situation to indicate immediate progress in this direction. Grattan, a long-time resident in America as British Consul at Boston, wrote:

> "The day must no doubt come when clashing objects will break the ties of common interest which now preserve the Union. But no man may foretell the period of dissolution. . . . The many restraining causes are out of sight of foreign observation. The Lilliputian threads binding the man mountain are invisible; and it seems wondrous that each limb does not act for itself independently of its fellows. A closer examination shows the nature of the network which keeps the members of this association so tightly bound. Any attempt to untangle the ties, more firmly fastens them. When any one State talks of separation, the others become spontaneously knotted together. When a section blusters about its particular rights, the rest feel each of theirs to be common to all. If a foreign nation hint at hostility, the whole Union becomes in reality united. And thus in every contingency from which there can be danger, there is also found the element of safety." Yet, he added, "All attempts to strengthen this federal government at the expense of the States' governments must be futile. . . . The federal government exists on sufferance only. Any State may at any time constitutionally withdraw from the Union, and thus virtually dissolve it."[1]

[1] Thomas Colley Grattan, *Civilized America*, 2 vols. 2nd ed., London, 1859, Vol. I, pp. 284-87. The first edition was printed in 1859 and a third in 1861. In some respects the work is historically untrustworthy since

Even more emphatically, though with less authority, wrote one Charles Mackay, styled by the American press as a "distinguished British poet," who made the usual rapid tour of the principal cities of America in 1857-58, and as rapidly penned his impressions :

> "Many persons in the United States talk of a dissolution of the Union, but few believe in it. . . . All this is mere bravado and empty talk. It means nothing. The Union is dear to all Americans, whatever they may say to the contrary. . . . There is no present danger to the Union, and the violent expressions to which over-ardent politicians of the North and South sometimes give vent have no real meaning. The 'Great West,' as it is fondly called, is in the position even now to arbitrate between North and South, should the quarrel stretch beyond words, or should anti-slavery or any other question succeed in throwing any difference between them which it would take revolvers and rifles rather than speeches and votes to put an end to."[2]

The slavery controversy in America had, in short, come to be regarded in England as a constant quarrel between North and South, but of no immediate danger to the Union.

internal evidence makes clear that the greater part of it was written before 1846, in which year Grattan retired from his post in Boston. In general he wrote scathingly of America, and as his son succeeded to the Boston consulship, Grattan probably thought it wiser to postpone publication. I have found no review of the work which treats it otherwise than as an up-to-date description of 1859. This fact and its wide sale in England in 1860-61, give the work importance as influencing British knowledge and opinions.

[2] Charles Mackay, *Life and Liberty in America : or, Sketches of a Tour in the United States and Canada in* 1857-8, one vol., New York, 1859, pp. 316-17. Mackay was at least of sufficient repute as a poet to be thought worthy of a dinner in Boston at which there were present, Longfellow, Holmes, Agassiz, Lowell, Prescott, Governor Banks, and others. He preached "hands across the seas" in his public lectures, occasionally reading his poem "John and Jonathan"—a sort of advance copy of Kipling's idea of the "White Man's Burden." Mackay's concluding verse, "John" speaking, was :

> "And I have strength for nobler work
> Than e'er my hand has done,
> And realms to rule and truths to plant
> Beyond the rising sun.
> Take you the West and I the East ;
> We'll spread ourselves abroad,
> With trade and spade and wholesome laws,
> And faith in man and God."

Each outbreak of violent American controversy produced a British comment sympathetic with the North. The turmoil preceding and following the election of Lincoln in 1860, on the platform of "no extension of slavery," was very generally noted by the British press and public, as a sign favourable to the cause of anti-slavery, but with no understanding that Southern threat would at last be realized in definite action. Herbert Spencer, in a letter of May 15, 1862, to his American friend, Yeomans, wrote, "As far as I had the means of judging, the feeling here was at first *very decidedly* on the side of the North . . ." [1] The British metropolitan press, in nearly every issue of which for at least two years after December, 1860, there appeared news items and editorial comment on the American crisis, was at first nearly unanimous in condemning the South.[2] The *Times*, with accustomed vigour, led the field. On November 21, 1860, it stated:

> "When we read the speech of Mr. Lincoln on the subject of Slavery and consider the extreme moderation of the sentiments it expresses, the allowance that is made for the situation, for the feelings, for the prejudices, of the South; when we see how entirely he narrows his opposition to the single point of the admission of Slavery into the Territories, we cannot help being forcibly struck by the absurdity of breaking up a vast and glorious confederacy like that of the United States from the dread and anger inspired by the election of such a man to the office of Chief Magistrate. . . . We rejoice, on higher and surer grounds, that it [the election] has ended in the return of Mr. Lincoln. We are glad to think that the march of Slavery, and the domineering tone which its advocates were beginning to assume over Freedom, has been at length arrested and silenced. We rejoice that a vast community of our own race has at

[1] Duncan, *Life and Letters of Herbert Spencer*, Vol. I, p. 140.

[2] R. C. Hamilton, Manuscript Chapters and Notes on "The English Press and the Civil War." Mr. Hamilton was at work on this subject, as a graduate student, but left Stanford University before completing his thesis. His notes have been of considerable value, both for suggested citations from the English Press, and for points of interpretation.

length given an authoritative expression to sentiments which are entertained by everyone in this country. We trust to see the American Government employed in tasks more worthy of a State founded on the doctrines of liberty and equality than the invention of shifts and devices to perpetuate servitude; and we hear in this great protest of American freedom the tardy echo of those humane doctrines to which England has so long become a convert."

Other leading journals, though with less of patronizing self-complacency, struck the same note as the *Times*. The *Economist* attributed Lincoln's election to a shift in the sympathies of the " lower orders " in the electorate who had now deserted their former leaders, the slave-owning aristocracy of the South, and allied themselves with the refined and wise leaders of the North. Lincoln, it argued, was not an extremist in any sense. His plan of action lay within the limits of statesmanlike moderation.[1] The *Saturday Review* was less sure that England should rejoice with the North. British self-esteem had suffered some hard blows at the hands of the Democratic party in America, but at least England knew where Democrats stood, and could count on no more discourtesy or injustice than that inflicted in the past. The Republican party, however, had no policy, except that of its leader, Seward, and from him might be expected extreme insolence.[2] This was a very early judgment of Seward, and one upon which the *Saturday Review* preened itself later, as wholly justified. The *Spectator*, the only one of the four journals thus far considered which ultimately remained constant in advocacy of the Northern cause, was at first lukewarm in comment, regarding the 1860 election, while fought on the slavery issue, as in reality a mere contest between parties for political power.[3]

[1] *Economist*, November 24, 1860. Six months later, however, the *Economist* pictured Lincoln as merely an unknown " sectionalist," with no evidence of statesmanship—*Economist*, June 1, 1861.

[2] *Saturday Review*, November 24, 1860.

[3] *Spectator*, November 24, 1860.

Such was the initial attitude of the English press. Each press issue for several weeks harped on the same chord, though sounding varying notes. If the South really means forcible resistance, said the *Times*, it is doomed to quick suppression. "A few hundred thousand slave-owners, trembling nightly with visions of murder and pillage, backed by a dissolute population of "poor whites," are no match for the hardy and resolute populations of the Free States," [1] and if the South hoped for foreign aid it should be undeceived promptly: "Can any sane man believe that England and France will consent, as is now suggested, to stultify the policy of half a century for the sake of an extended cotton trade, and to purchase the favours of Charleston and Milledgeville by recognizing what has been called 'the isothermal law, which impels African labour toward the tropics' on the other side of the Atlantic?" [2] Moreover all Americans ought to understand clearly that British respect for the United States "was not due to the attitude of the South with its ruffian demonstrations in Congress. . . . All that is noble and venerable in the United States is associated with its Federal Constitution." [3]

Did the British public hold these same opinions? There is no direct evidence available in sufficient quantity in autobiography or letters upon which to base a conclusion. Such works are silent on the struggle in America for the first few months and presumably public opinion, less informed even than the press, received its impressions from the journals customarily read. Both at this period and all through the war, also, it should be remembered, clearly, that most newspapers, all the reviews, in fact nearly all vehicles of British expression, were in the early 'sixties "in the hands of the educated classes, and these educated

[1] The *Times*, November 26, 1860.
[2] *Ibid.*, November 29, 1860.
[3] *Ibid.*

classes corresponded closely with the privileged classes." The more democratic element of British Society lacked any adequate press representation of its opinions. "This body could express itself by such comparatively crude methods as public meetings and demonstrations, but it was hampered in literary and political expression."[1] The opinion of the press was then, presumably, the opinion of the majority of the educated British public.

Thus British comment on America took the form, at first of moralizations, now severe toward the South, now indifferent, yet very generally asserting the essential justice of the Northern position. But it was early evident that the newspapers, one and all, were quite unprepared for the determined front soon put up by South Carolina and other Southern States. Surprised by the violence of Southern declarations, the only explanation found by the British press was that political control had been seized by the uneducated and lawless element. The *Times* characterized this element of the South as in a state of deplorable ignorance comparable with that of the Irish peasantry, a "poor, proud, lazy, excitable and violent class, ever ready with knife and revolver." [2] The fate of the Union, according to the *Saturday Review*, was in the hands of the "most ignorant, most unscrupulous, and most lawless [class] in the world—the poor or mean whites of the Slave States." [3] Like judgments were expressed by the *Economist* and, more mildly, by the *Spectator*.[4] Subsequently some of these journals found difficulty in this connection, in swinging round the circle to expressions of admiration for the wise and powerful aristocracy of the South; but all, especially

[1] R. L. Duffus, "Contemporary English Popular Opinion on the American Civil War," p. 2. A thesis presented in fulfilment of the requirements for the degree of Master of Arts, Stanford University, 1911. This thesis is in manuscript. It is a valuable study of the Reviews and of the writings of men of letters. Hereafter cited as Duffus "English Opinion."

[2] The *Times*, January 12, 1861.

[3] *Saturday Review*, January 12, 1861.

[4] *Economist*, December 8, 1860. *Spectator*, January 19, 1861.

the *Times*, were skilled by long practice in the journalistic art of facing about while claiming perfect consistency. In denial of a Southern right of secession, also, they were nearly a unit,[1] though the *Saturday Review* argued the case for the South, making a pointed parallel between the present situation and that of the American Colonies in seceding from England.[2]

The quotations thus far made exhibit for the leading papers an initial confusion and ignorance difficult to harmonize with the theory of an "enlightened press." The Reviews, by the conditions of publication, came into action more slowly and during 1860 there appeared but one article, in the *Edinburgh Review*, giving any adequate idea of what was really taking place in America.[3] The lesser British papers generally followed the tone of the leading journals, but without either great interest or much acumen. In truth the depth of British newspaper ignorance, considering their positiveness of utterance, appears utterly astonishing if regarded from the view-point of modern historical knowledge. But is this, after all, a matter for surprise? Was there not equal confusion at least, possibly equal ignorance, in America itself, certainly among the press and people of the Northern States? They also had come by experience to discount Southern threats, and were slow to understand that the great conflict of ideals and interests was at last begun.

The British press both influenced and reflected educated class opinion, and, in some degree, official opinion as well. Lord John Russell at the Foreign Office and Lord Lyons, British Minister at Washington, were exchanging anxious letters, and the latter was sending home reports remarkable for their clear analysis of the American controversy. Yet even he was slow to appreciate the inevitability of secession.

[1] *Spectator*, December 1, 1860. *Times*, January 29, 1861. *Economist*, May 25, 1861.
[2] *Saturday Review*, January 19, 1861.
[3] *Edinburgh Review*, Vol. 112, p. 545.

LORD LYONS

(From a photograph taken at Boston, U.S.A., in 1860)
(From Lord Newton's "Life of Lord Lyons," by kind permission)

Other officials, especially those in minor positions in the United States, showed a lack of grasp of the situation similar to that of the press. An amusing illustration of this, furnishing a far-fetched view of causes, is supplied in a letter of February 2, 1860, from Consul Bunch, at Charleston, S.C., to Lord Lyons, the British Minister at Washington.[1] Bunch wrote describing a dinner which had been given the evening before, by the Jockey Club of Charleston. Being called upon for a speech, he had alluded to the prizes of the Turf at home, and had referred especially to the Plates run for the various British colonies. Continuing, he said:

> " ' . . . I cannot help calling your attention to the great loss you yourselves have suffered by ceasing to be a Colonial Dependency of Great Britain, as I am sure that if you had continued to be so, the Queen would have had great pleasure in sending you some Plates too.'
>
> " Of course this was meant for the broadest sort of joke, calculated to raise a laugh after dinner, but to my amazement, the company chose to take me literally, and applauded for about ten minutes—in fact I could not go on for some time."

Bunch evidently hardly knew what to make of this demonstration. He could with difficulty believe that South Carolina wished to be re-annexed as a colony of Great Britain, and comments upon the episode in a somewhat humorous vein. Nevertheless in concluding his letter, he solemnly assures Lord Lyons that

> " . . . The Jockey Club is composed of the 'best people' of South Carolina—rich planters and the like. It represents, therefore, the 'gentlemanly interest' and not a bit of universal suffrage."

It would be idle to assume that either in South Carolina or in England there was, in February, 1860, any serious thought of a resumption of colonial relations, though

[1] Lyons Papers.

W. H. Russell, correspondent of the *Times*, reported in the spring, 1861, that he frequently heard the same sentiment in the South.[1] For general official England, as for the press, the truth is that up to the time of the secession of South Carolina no one really believed that a final rupture was about to take place between North and South. When, on December 20, 1860, that State in solemn convention declared the dissolution "of the Union now existing between South Carolina and the other States, under the name of the 'United States of America,'" and when it was understood that other Southern States would soon follow this example, British opinion believed and hoped that the rupture would be accomplished peaceably. Until it became clear that war

[1] Russell, *My Diary North and South*, Boston, 1863, p. 134. "Then cropped out again the expression of regret for the rebellion of 1776, and the desire that if it came to the worst, England would receive back her erring children, or give them a prince under whom they could secure a monarchical form of government. There is no doubt about the earnestness with which these things are said." Russell's *Diary* is largely a condensation of his letters to the *Times*. In the letter of April 30, 1861 (published May 28), he dilates to the extent of a column on the yearning of South Carolina for a restoration of colonial relations. But Consul Bunch on December 14, 1860, reported a Charleston sentiment very different from that of the Jockey Club in February. He wrote to Lyons:

> "The church bells are ringing like mad in celebration of a newly revived festival, called 'Evacuation Day,' being the *nefastus ille dies* in which the bloody Britishers left Charleston 78 years ago. It has fallen into utter disuse for about 50 years, but is now suddenly resuscitated apropos *de* nothing at all."

In this same letter Bunch described a Southern patriotic demonstration. Returning to his home one evening, he met a military company, which from curiosity he followed, and which

> "drew up in front of the residence of a young lawyer of my friends, after performing in whose honour, through the medium of a very brassy band, a Secession Schottische or Palmetto Polka, it clamorously demanded his presence. After a very brief interval he appeared, and altho' he is in private life an agreeable and moderately sensible young man, he succeeded, to my mind at any rate, in making most successfully, what Mr. Anthony Weller calls 'an Egyptian Mummy of his self.' The amount of balderdash and rubbish which he evacuated (*dia stomatos*) about mounting the deadly breach, falling back into the arms of his comrades and going off generally in a blaze of melodramatic fireworks, really made me so unhappy that I lost my night's rest. So soon as the speech was over the company was invited into the house to 'pour a libation to the holy cause'—in the vernacular, to take a drink and spit on the floor."

Evidently Southern eloquence was not tolerable to the ears of the British consul. Or was it the din of the church bells rather than the clamour of the orator, that offended him? (*Lyons Papers.*)

would ensue, the South was still damned by the press as seeking the preservation of an evil institution. Slavery was even more vigorously asserted as the ignoble and sole cause. In the number for April, 1861, the *Edinburgh Review* attributed the whole difficulty to slavery, asserted that British sympathy would be with the anti-slavery party, yet advanced the theory that the very dissolution of the Union would hasten the ultimate extinction of slavery since economic competition with a neighbouring free state, the North, would compel the South itself to abandon its beloved "domestic institution."[1]

Upon receipt of the news from South Carolina, the *Times*, in a long and carefully worded editorial, took up one by one the alleged causes of secession, dismissed them as inadequate, and concluded, ". . . we cannot disguise from ourselves that, apart from all political complications, there is a right and a wrong in this question, and that the right belongs, with all its advantages, to the States of the North."[2] Three days later it asserted, "The North is for freedom of discussion, the South represses freedom of discussion with the tar-brush and the pine-fagot." And again, on January 10, "The Southern States expected sympathy for their undertaking from the public opinion of this country. The tone of the press has already done much to undeceive them. . . ."

In general both the metropolitan and the provincial press expressed similar sentiments, though there were exceptions. The *Dublin News* published with approval a long communication addressed to Irishmen at home and abroad: ". . . there is no power on earth or in heaven which can keep in peace this unholy co-partnership. . . . I hope . . . that the North will quietly permit the South to retire from the confederacy and bear alone the odium of

[1] *Edinburgh Review*, Vol. 113, p. 555.
[2] The *Times*, January 4, 1861.

all mankind. . . ."[1] The *Saturday Review* thought that deeper than declared differences lay the ruling social structure of the South which now visioned a re-opening of the African Slave Trade, and the occupation by slavery of the whole southern portion of North America. "A more ignoble basis for a great Confederacy it is impossible to conceive, nor one in the long run more precarious. . . . Assuredly it will be the Northern Confederacy, based on principles of freedom, with a policy untainted by crime, with a free working-class of white men, that will be the one to go on and prosper and become the leader of the New World."[2] The *London Chronicle* was vigorous in denunciation. "No country on the globe produces a blackguardism, a cowardice or a treachery, so consummate as that of the negro-driving States of the new Southern Confederacy"—a bit of editorial blackguardism in itself.[3] The *London Review* more moderately stigmatized slavery as the cause, but was lukewarm in praise of Northern idealisms, regarding the whole matter as one of diverging economic systems and in any case as inevitably resulting in dissolution of the Union at some time. The inevitable might as well come now as later and would result in benefit to both sections as well as to the world fearing the monstrous empire of power that had grown up in America.[4]

The great bulk of early expressions by the British press was, in truth, definitely antagonistic to the South, and this was particularly true of the provincial press. Garrison's *Liberator*, advocating extreme abolition action, had long

[1] Letter to *Dublin News*, dated January 26, 1861. Cited in *The Liberator*, March 1, 1861. Garrison, editor of *The Liberator*, was then earnest in advocating "letting the South go in peace" as a good riddance.

[2] *Saturday Review*, March 2, 1861, p. 216.

[3] *London Chronicle*, March 14, 1861. Cited in *The Liberator*, April 12, 1861.

[4] *London Review*, April 20, 1861. Cited in Littel's *Living Age*, Vol. LXIX, p. 495. The editor of the *Review* was a Dr. Mackay, but I have been unable to identify him, as might seem natural from his opinions, as the Mackay previously quoted (p. 37) who was later New York correspondent of the *Times*.

made a practice of presenting excerpts from British newspapers, speeches and sermons in support of its cause. In 1860 there were thirty-nine such citations; in the first months of 1861 many more, all condemning slavery and the South. For the most part these citations represented a comparatively unknown and uninfluential section, both in politics and literature, of the British people. Matthew Arnold was among the first of men of letters to record his faith that secession was final and, as he hoped, an excellent thing for the North, looking to the purity of race and the opportunity for unhampered advance.[1] If English writers were in any way influenced by their correspondents in the United States they may, indeed, have well been in doubt as to the origin and prospects of the American quarrel. Hawthorne, but recently at home again after seven years' consulship in England, was writing that abolition was not a Northern object in the war just begun. Whittier wrote to *his* English friends that slavery, and slavery alone, was the basic issue.[2] But literary Britain was slow to express itself save in the Reviews. These, representing varying shades of British upper-class opinion and presenting articles presumably more profound than the newspaper editorials, frequently offered more recondite origins of the American crisis. The *Quarterly Review*, organ of extreme Conservatism, in its first article, dwelt upon the failure of democratic institutions, a topic not here treated at length since it will be dealt with in a separate chapter as deserving special study. The *Quarterly* is also the first to advance the argument that the protective tariff, advocated by the North, was a real cause for Southern secession;[3] an idea made much of later, by the elements unfriendly to the North,

[1] Matthew Arnold, *Letters*, Vol. I., p. 150. Letter to Mrs. Forster, January 28, 1861.

[2] Julian Hawthorne, *Nathaniel Hawthorne and his Wife*, Vol. II, pp. 271-78. *Life and Letters of John Greenleaf Whittier*, Vol. II, pp. 439 *seq.*

[3] *Quarterly Review*, Vol. 110, p. 282. July, 1861.

but not hitherto advanced. In these first issues of the Reviews for 1861, there was frequently put forth the "Southern gentlemen" theory.

> "At a distance of three thousand miles, the Southern planters did, indeed, bear a resemblance to the English country gentleman which led to a feeling of kinship and sympathy with him on the part of those in England who represented the old traditions of landed gentility. This 'Southern gentleman' theory, containing as it did an undeniable element of truth, is much harped upon by certain of the reviewers, and one can easily conceive of its popularity in the London Clubs. . . . The 'American,' so familiar to British readers, during the first half of the century, through the eyes of such travellers as Mrs. Trollope, now becomes the 'Yankee,' and is located north of Mason and Dixon's line."[1]

Such portrayal was not characteristic of all Reviews, rather of the Tory organs alone, and the Radical *Westminster* took pains to deny the truth of the picture, asserting again and again that the vital and sole cause of the conflict was slavery. Previous articles are summed up in that of October, 1863, as a profession of the *Westminster's* opinion throughout: ". . . the South are fighting for liberty to found a Slave Power. Should it prove successful, truer devil's work, if we may use the metaphor, will rarely have been done."[2]

Fortunate would it have been for the Northern cause, if British opinion generally sympathetic at first on anti-slavery grounds, had not soon found cause to doubt the just basis of its sympathy, from the trend of events in America. Lincoln had been elected on a platform opposing the further territorial expansion of slavery. On that point the North was fairly well united. But the great majority of those who voted for Lincoln would have indignantly

[1] Duffus, "English Opinion," p. 7.
[2] *Westminster*, Vol. LXXX, p. 587.

repudiated any purpose to take active steps toward the extinction of slavery where it already existed. Lincoln understood this perfectly, and whatever his opinion about the ultimate fate of slavery if prohibited expansion, he from the first took the ground that the terms of his election constituted a mandate limiting his action. As secession developed he rightly centred his thought and effort on the preservation of the Union, a duty imposed by his election to the Presidency.

Naturally, as the crisis developed, there were many efforts at still another great compromise. Among the friends of the outgoing President, Buchanan, whose term of office would not expire until March 4, 1861, there were still some Southern leaders, like Jefferson Davis, seeking either a complete surrender to Southern will, or advantages for Southern security in case secession was accomplished. Buchanan appealed hysterically to the old-time love of the Union and to the spirit of compromise. Great congressional committees of both Senate and House of Representatives were formed seeking a solution. Crittenden for the border states between North and South, where, more than anywhere else, there was division of opinion, proposed pledges to be given to the South. Seward, long-time champion of the anti-slavery North, was active in the Senate in suggestion and intrigue seemingly intended to conciliate by concessions. Charles Francis Adams, early a Free Soiler, in the House of Representatives Committee conducted his Republican colleagues along a path apparently leading to a guarantee of slavery as then established.[1] A constitutional amendment was drafted to this effect and received Lincoln's preliminary

[1] Adams' course was bitterly criticized by his former intimate friend, Charles Sumner, but the probable purpose of Adams was, foreseeing the certainty of secession, to exhibit so strongly the arrogance and intolerance of the South as to create greater unity of Northern sentiment. This was a purpose that could not be declared and both at home and abroad his action, and that of other former anti-slavery leaders, for the moment weakened faith that the North was in earnest on the general issue of slavery.

approval. Finally Lincoln, in his inaugural address, March 4, 1861, declared:

> "I have no purpose, directly or indirectly to interfere with the institution of slavery in the States where it exists. I believe I have no lawful right to do so, and I have no inclination to do so."

It should be no matter for surprise, therefore, that, as these efforts were observed in Great Britain, a note of uncertainty began to replace the earlier unanimity of opinion that the future of slavery was at stake in America. This offered an easy excuse for a switch-about of sympathy as British commercial and other interests began to be developed, and even dismayed the ardent friends of the anti-slavery North. Meanwhile the Government of Great Britain, from the very first appearance of the cloud of civil war, had focused its attention on the point of what the events in America portended to British interests and policy. This is the business of governments, and their agents would be condemned as inefficient did they neglect it. But did British governmental policy go beyond this entirely justifiable first thought for immediate British interests to the point of positive hope that England would find an advantage in the breaking up of the great American Republic? American opinion, both then and later, believed Great Britain guilty of this offence, but such criticism was tinged with the passions of the Civil War. Yet a more impartial critic, though possibly an unfriendly one because of his official position, made emphatic declaration to like effect. On January 1, 1861, Baron de Brunow, Russian Ambassador at London, reported to St. Petersburg that, "the English Government, at the bottom of its heart, desires the separation of North America into two republics, which will watch each other jealously and counterbalance one the other. Then England, on terms of peace and commerce with both, would have nothing to fear from either; for she would dominate them, restraining them by their rival ambitions." [1]

If, however, one turns from the surmises of foreign diplomats as to the springs of British policy, to the more authentic evidence of official and private diplomatic correspondence, there is found no proof for such accusations. Certainly neither Lord John Russell, Foreign Secretary, nor Lord Lyons, British Minister at Washington, reveal any animus against the United States. Considering his many personal ties with leaders of both factions Lyons, from the first, reported events with wonderful impartiality, and great clarity. On November 12, 1860, he sent to Russell a full description of the clamour raised in the South over the election of Lincoln, enumerated the resignation of Federal officials (calling these "ill-judged measures"), and expressed the opinion that Lincoln was no Radical. He hoped the storm would blow over without damage to the Union.[2] Russell, for his part, was prompt to instruct Lyons and the British consuls not "to seem to favour one party rather than the other," and not to express opinions or to give advice, unless asked for by the State Governments, in which case the advice should be against all violent action as tending toward civil war.[3]

This bare statement may indeed be interpreted as indicating an eager readiness on Russell's part to accept as final the dissolution of the Union, but such an interpretation is not borne out by a reading of his instructions. Rather he was perplexed, and anxious that British agents should not gain the ill-will of either American faction, an ill-will that would be alike detrimental in the future, whether the Union remained unbroken or was destroyed.

[1] *Services rendered by Russia to the American People during the War of the Rebellion*, Petersburg, 1904. p. 5.

[2] *Parliamentary Papers*, 1862, *Lords*, Vol. XXV, "Correspondence on Civil War in the United States," No. 1.

[3] *Ibid.*, No. 6. Russell to Lyons, December 26, 1860.

Strict instructions against offering advice are therefore repeated frequently.[1] Meanwhile the first concrete problem requiring British action came from the seizure by South Carolina of the Federal customs house at the port of Charleston, and the attempt of the State authorities to collect port dues customarily paid to Federal officials. British shipowners appealed to Consul Bunch for instructions, he to Lyons, and the latter to the American Secretary of State, Judge Black. This was on December 31, 1860, while Buchanan was still President, and Black's answer was evasive, though asserting that the United States must technically regard the events in South Carolina as acts of violent rebellion.[2] Black refused to state what action would be taken if Bunch advised British shipowners to pay, but a way out of the embarrassment was found by advising such payment to State authorities "under protest" as done "under compulsion." To one of his letters to Bunch on this topic, Lyons appended an expression indicative of his own early attitude. "The domestic slavery of the South is a bitter pill which it will be hard enough to get the English to swallow. But if the Slave Trade is to be added to the dose, the least squeamish British stomach will reject it."[3]

Nevertheless the vigorous action of South Carolina, soon followed by other Southern States, made a deep impression on Russell, especially when compared with the uncertainty and irresolution manifested in the attempted compromise measures of Northern statesmen. In a private letter to Lyons, January 10, 1861, he wrote "I do not see how the United States can be cobbled together again by any compromise. . . . I cannot see any mode of reconciling such

[1] *Ibid.* Russell to Lyons, No. 9, January 5, 1861, and No. 17, February 20, 1861.

[2] *Parliamentary Papers*, 1861, *Lords*, Vol. XVIII. Correspondence with U.S. Government respecting suspension of Federal Customs House at the Port of Charleston. Nos. 1 and 3.

[3] Lyons Papers. Lyons to Bunch, December 12, 1860.

parties as these. The best thing *now* would be that the right to secede should be acknowledged. . . . I hope sensible men will take this view. . . . But above all I hope no force will be used." [1] And again twelve days later, " I suppose the break-up of the Union is now inevitable." [2] To Russell, as to most foreign observers, it seemed that if the South with its great wealth, its enormous extent of territory, and its five and one-half millions of population, were determined to leave the Union, no force whatever could compel a return. History failed to record any revolution on so large a scale which had not succeeded. His desire, therefore, was that the North would yield to the inevitable, and would not plunge into a useless civil war disastrous alike to the prosperity of America and of foreign nations. Russell's first hope was that the South would forgo secession; his second, this accomplished, that there would be no war, and in this sense he instructed Lyons. The latter, less expectant of peaceful separation, and more aware of the latent power of the North, maintained throughout his entire service at Washington that there was at least a *chance* that the North could subdue the South by might of arms,[3] but he also, looking to British interests, saw his early duty, before war broke, in cautious suggestions against forcible Northern action. Thus from January to March,

[1] *Ibid*. The same day official instructions were sent permitting Bunch to remain at Charleston, but directing him, if asked to recognize South Carolina, to refer the matter to England. F.O., Am., Vol. 754, No. 6. Russell to Lyons, January 10, 1861.

[2] Lyons Papers. Russell to Lyons, January 22, 1861.

[3] This view was not shared by Lyons' colleagues at Washington. The Russian Minister, Stoeckl, early declared the Union permanently destroyed, and regretting the fact, yet hoped the North would soon accept the inevitable and seek close co-operation with the South in commerce and in foreign relations. This view was repeated by him many times and most emphatically as late as the first month of 1863. (Russian Archives, Stoeckl to F.O., January 29-February 10, 1863. No. 342.) It was not until September, 1863, that Stoeckl ventured to hope for a Northern re-conquest of the South. I am indebted to Dr. Frank A. Golder, of Stanford University, for the use of his notes and transcripts covering all of the Russian diplomatic correspondence with the United States, 1860-1865. In the occasional use made of this material the English translation is mine.

1861, British effort and indirect advice were based on the hope that British trade interests might escape the tribulations inevitable from a civil conflict in America. Beyond that point there was no grasp of the complications likely to arise in case of war, and no clear formulation of British policy.[1]

In fact up to the middle of March, 1861, both public and official British opinion discounted armed conflict, or at least any determined Northern effort to recover the South. Early British attitude was, therefore, based on a misconception. As this became clear, public opinion began to break from a united humanitarian pro-Northern sentiment and to show, in some quarters, quite another face. Even as early as January the *Economist* expressed wonder that the Northern States had not availed themselves gladly of the chance to "shake off such an incubus, and to purify themselves of such a stain,"[2] and a month later professed to believe that Great Britain would willingly permit the North to secure compensation for loss of territory by annexing Canada—provided the Canadians themselves desired it. This, it was argued, would directly benefit England herself by cutting down military expenditures.[3] The *London Press* indulged in similar speculation, though from the angle of a Canadian annexation of the Northern States, whose more sober citizens must by now be weary of the sham of American democracy, and disgusted with the rowdyism of political elections, which "combine the morals of a horse race, the manners of a dog fight, the passions of a tap-room, and the emotions of a gambling

[1] Stoeckl reported that at a dinner with Lyons, at which he, Mercier and Seward were the guests, Seward had asserted that if Civil War came all foreign commerce with the South would be interrupted. To this Lyons protested that England could not get along without cotton and that she would secure it in one way or another. Seward made no reply. (*Ibid.*, March 25-April 9, 1861, No. 810.)

[2] *Economist*, January 12, 1861.

[3] *Ibid.*, February 23, 1861.

house." [1] Probably such suggestions had little real purpose or meaning at the moment, but it is interesting that this idea of a "compensation" in Canada should have been voiced thus early. Even in the United States the same thought had occurred to a few political leaders. Charles Sumner held it, though too wise, politically, to advance it in the face of the growing Northern determination to preserve the Union. It lay at the bottom of his increasing bitterness toward his old friend Charles Francis Adams, now busy in schemes intended, apparently, to restore the Union by compromise, and it led Sumner to hope for appointment as Minister to England.[2]

The chief organ of British upper-class opinion, the *Times*, was one of the first to begin the process of "face about," as civil war in America seemed imminent.[3] Viewed from the later attitude of the *Times*, the earlier expressions of that paper, and in truth of many British journals, seem merely the customary platitudinous British holding up of horrified hands at American slavery. On January 19, 1861, a strong editorial still proclaimed the folly of South Carolina, as acting "without law, without justice," but displayed a real dismay at the possible consequences of war to British trade and commerce. On January 22, the *Times* reprinted an article from the *Economist*, on a probable cessation of cotton supply and editorially professed great alarm, even advocating an early recognition of the Southern confederacy if needed to maintain that supply. From this time on there

[1] *London Press*, March 23, 1861. Cited in Littell's *Living Age*, Vol. LXIX, p. 438.

[2] Before Adams' selection as Minister to England was decided upon, Sumner's Massachusetts friends were urging him for the place. Longfellow was active in this interest. *H. W. Longfellow*, by Samuel Longfellow, Vol. II, pp. 412-13.

[3] John Bright later declared "his conviction that the leading journal had not published one fair, honourable, or friendly article toward the States since Lincoln's accession to office." Dasent, *Life of Delane*, Vol. II, p. 38. The time is approximately correct, but the shift in policy began earlier, when it came to be feared that the North would not submit to peaceable secession.

is no further note in the *Times* of the righteousness of the Northern cause; but while it is still asserted that war would be folly, the strength of the South, its superiority as a military nation, are depicted.

A long break of nearly six weeks follows with little editorial comment. Soon the correspondence from New York, previously written by Bancroft Davis, and extremely favourable to the Northern cause, was discontinued. W. H. Russell, the famous war correspondent of the Crimea, was summoned to London and, according to his own story, upon being given papers, clippings, and correspondence (largely articles from the *New York Herald*) supporting the right of the South to secede, hastily took his departure for America to report upon the situation.[1] He sailed from Queenstown on March 3, and arrived in New York on March 16. At last on March 12, the *Times* took positive ground in favour of the justice of the Southern cause.

> "No treachery has been at work to produce the disruption, and the principles avowed are such as to command the sympathies of every free and enlightened people. Such are the widely different auspices under which the two rival Republics start into existence. But mankind will not ultimately judge these things by sympathies and antipathies; they will be greatly swayed by their own interest, and the two Republics must be weighed, not by their professions or their previous history, but by the conduct they pursue and the position they maintain among the Powers of the earth. Their internal institutions are their own affair; their financial and political arrangements are emphatically ours. Brazil is a slave-holding Empire, but by its good faith and good conduct it has contrived to establish for itself a place in the hierarchy of nations far superior to that of many Powers which are free from this domestic contamination. If the Northern Confederacy of America evinces a determination to act in a narrow, exclusive, and unsocial spirit, while its Southern com-

[1] Bigelow, *Retrospections*, Vol. I, pp. 344-45.

> petitor extends the hand of good fellowship to all mankind, with the exception of its own bondsmen, we must not be surprised to see the North, in spite of the goodness of its cause and the great negative merit of the absence of Slavery, sink into a secondary position, and lose the sympathy and regard of mankind."

This to Northern view, was a sad relapse from that high moral tone earlier addressed to the South notifying slave-holders that England would not "stultify the policy of half a century for the sake of an extended cotton trade." [1]

The *Economist*, with more consistency, still reported the violence and recklessness of the South, yet in logical argument proved to its own satisfaction the impossibility of Northern reconquest, and urged a peaceful separation.[2] The *Spectator*, even though pro-Northern, had at first small hope of reunion by force, and offered consolation in the thought that there would still remain a United States of America "strong, powerful and free; all the stronger for the loss of the Black South."[3] In short from all quarters the public press, whatever its sympathy, united in decrying war as a useless effort doomed to failure if undertaken in the hope of restoring the Union. Such public opinion, however, was not necessarily governmental opinion. The latter was indeed more slow to make up its mind and more considerate in expressing itself. When it became clear that in all probability the North would fight, there was still no conception, any more than in the United States itself, of the duration and intensity of the conflict. Indeed, Russell yet hoped, as late as the end of January, that no protracted war would occur. Nevertheless he was compelled to face the situation in its relation to British commerce.

On February 16, Russell addressed Lyons on that aspect of possible war which would at once call for a determination

[1] See *ante*, p. 40.
[2] *Economist*, March 2, 1861.
[3] *Spectator*, March 16, 1861.

of British policy. "Above all things," he wrote, "endeavour to prevent a blockade of the Southern coast. It would produce misery, discord, and enmity incalculable." [1] Within a week Forster, a thorough friend of the North throughout the whole war, was interrogating the Ministry in the House of Commons in regard to the situation at Charleston, and expressing the hope that England would not in any way attempt to interfere.[2] This was the first reference in Parliament, its sittings but just renewed after the long vacation, to the American conflict, but British commercial interests were being forced to a keener attention, and already men in many circles were asking themselves what should be the proper governmental attitude; how soon this new Southern Confederacy could justly claim European recognition; how far and how fast European governments ought to go in acknowledging such a claim; what ought to be the proper policy and position of a neutral power; whether, indeed, a declaration of neutrality ought to be issued.

With these questions rapidly coming to the front, it became important for British statesmen to know something about the leaders in this new Southern movement, the attitude of the people in general, and the purposes of the

[1] Lyons Papers.

[2] Hansard, 3rd. Ser., CLXI, p. 814. February 22, 1861. William E. Forster was of Quaker descent and had early taken part in public meetings called to express humanitarian sentiment. From 1850 on he was an acceptable public speaker in all matters Liberal, as free trade, social reform, and anti-slavery. Elected to Parliament in 1859 and again in 1861 from Bradford, where he was engaged in business as a woollen manufacturer, he sought, after the fashion of new Members, a cause to represent and found it in championship of the North. Having great native ability, as shown by his later distinguished career, it was the good fortune of the United States thus to enlist so eager a champion. Forster and John Bright were the two leading "friends of the North" in Parliament. The latter already had established reputation, but was more influential out of Parliament than in it. Forster, with a reputation to make, showed skill in debate, and soon achieved prestige for himself and his American cause. Henry Adams, son and private secretary of the American Minister to England, once told the writer that he regarded Forster's services as, on the whole, the most valuable rendered by any Englishman to the North.

new Government. Here, unfortunately, Lord Lyons could be no guide. The consuls in the South, however, were in a position to give their impressions. On February 28, 1861, Bunch wrote to Russell, describing the election of Davis and Stephens,[1] to the Presidency and Vice-Presidency of the Confederacy, and giving a personal characterization of many members of the Government. He was rather caustic. Davis, he said, was the only *able* man, and he, unfortunately, was a confirmed "manifest destiny" leader, so much so in fact that Bunch prophesied a renewal of filibustering when once the North had acquiesced in a Southern State and the fear of the North had passed. Bunch had no faith in any future greatness of the South, asserting that it would be a State despised among nations for its maintenance of slavery, and that it could not hope for any encouragement or sympathy from the humane nations of Europe; in fact, his entire characterization was wholly damning to the South. Yet it is to be noted that he never for a moment questioned that the South had already actually established its independence. This he seems to take for granted. Thus again, and from another quarter, there was presented the double difficulty of England in regard to the Civil War—the difficulty of reconciling sentiments of humanity long preached by Great Britain, with her commercial interests and her certainty that a new State was being born.

For men in the Northern Government Lyons was in a position to report, but up to the end of January he had not written in any great detail with regard to the new administration and its make-up, though on January 7, he had informed Russell that Seward would be the Secretary of State and had expressed the fear that with regard to Great Britain he would be "a dangerous Foreign Minister."[2] Lincoln was still in Illinois and the constituency of the

[1] F.O., Am., Vol. 780, No. 30.
[2] Newton, *Lord Lyons*, Vol. I, p. 30.

Cabinet was yet uncertain, but Seward's voice was sure to be a powerful one. Occasionally Lyons found some opportunity to talk with him. On February 4, 1861, in an official letter to Russell, Lyons reported at length an interview with Seward, in which the latter had expressed his extreme confidence that the trouble in America was but superficial and that union sentiment in the South would soon prevail.[1] In a private letter of the same date, however, Lyons asserted that Seward was indeed likely to be a very dangerous Secretary of State. He had told Lyons that if European governments interfered to protect their commerce, he could unite America by a foreign war in order to resist such interference.[2] Again, on February 12, while himself expressing hope that a solution might be found for the difficulties in America, Lyons warned Russell that there were those who would solve these difficulties by a foreign war, especially if foreign governments refused to acknowledge a United States declaration without formal blockade closing the Southern ports.[3] Writing privately, Lyons exhibited great anxiety in regard to Seward's attitude and suggested that the best safeguard would be close union by England and France, for if these two governments took exactly the same stand in regard to trade, Seward would hardly dare to carry out his threat.[4]

Lyons' letter of February 4 called out from Russell an instruction in which it was repeated that advice to either party should be withheld and a strictly neutral attitude maintained, and Russell concluded by an assertion that if the United States attempted a jingo policy toward England, the British Cabinet would be tolerant because of its feeling of strength but that "blustering demonstrations" must

[1] F.O., Am., Vol. 760, No. 40.
[2] Russell Papers. Lyons to Russell, February 4, 1861.
[3] F.O., Am., Vol. 760, No. 59.
[4] Russell Papers. Lyons to Russell, February 12, 1861.

not be carried too far.[1] Even as early as December, 1860, Russell had foreseen the possibility of what he considered a mere jingo policy for home effect in America. Now, however, upon the repeated expression of fears from Lyons that this might be more than mere "bunkum," Russell began to instruct Lyons not to permit English dignity to be infringed, while at the same time desiring him to be cautious against stirring American antagonism. Lyons' earlier disquietude seems, indeed, to have passed away for a time, and on February 26 he wrote that everyone was waiting to see what Lincoln would do when inaugurated, that there was still hope of compromise, and that in his own view this was still possible. In this letter the tone is more important than the matter, and so far as Lyons is concerned the tone is all distinctly hopeful, all favourable to a resumption of normal relations between the North and South. He at least had no hope of disruption, and no happiness in it.[2]

Before this communication could reach England Russell had thoroughly awakened to the seriousness of the American situation in relation to British foreign trade. On March 9, writing privately to Lyons, he stated, "I hope you are

[1] *Parliamentary Papers*, 1862, *Lords*, Vol. XXV. "Correspondence on Civil War in the United States," No. 17. Russell to Lyons, February 20, 1861.

[2] F.O., Am., Vol. 761, No. 78. Received March 11. It is curious that in the first period of the war Lyons made no extended characterization of Lincoln. Probably his contacts with the new President were insufficient to justify it. The first record of personal impressions was that made by W. H. Russell and later printed in his "Diary" but not reproduced in his letters to the *Times*. Russell was taken to the White House. "Soon afterwards there entered, with a shambling, loose, irregular, almost unsteady gait, a tall, lank, lean man, considerably over six feet in height, with stooping shoulders, long pendulous arms, terminating in hands of extraordinary dimensions, which, however, were far exceeded in proportion by his feet. . . . The impression produced by the size of his extremities, and by his flapping and wide-projecting ears, may be removed by the appearance of kindliness, sagacity, and awkward bonhomie of his face . . . eyes dark, full, and deeply set, are penetrating, but full of an expression which almost amounts to tenderness. . . . A person who met Mr. Lincoln in the street would not take him to be what—according to usages of European society—is called a 'gentleman' . . . but, at the same time, it would not be possible for the most indifferent observer to pass him in the street without notice."—*My Diary*, I, pp. 37-8.

getting on well with the new President. If he blockades the Southern ports we shall be in a difficulty. But according to all American doctrine it must be an actual blockade kept up by an efficient force." [1] Thus, before any act had really occurred in America, the matter of a blockade was occupying the attention of British statesmen. One difficulty at the time was that there was no one in England qualified to speak for the new administration at Washington. Dallas, the American Minister appointed under the Buchanan administration, while, unlike some other diplomatic representatives abroad, faithful to the cause of the United States, was nevertheless not wholly trusted by Lincoln or by Seward, and was thus handicapped in representing to Russell American conditions or intentions. Indeed he had very little communication with Russell. Adams' nomination to England was known to Lyons on March 20, for on that day he telegraphed to Russell, " Mr. Charles Francis Adams, of Massachusetts, is appointed Minister in London. I think it a very good appointment." [2] This news was received in London on April 2, but over six weeks were yet to elapse before Adams reached his post. The appointment of Adams, however, seemed to Lyons a matter of congratulation in his hope that no vicious anti-British policy would be indulged in by Seward. Ten days after his telegram, he wrote at length to Russell, making an excellent statement and analysis in regard to the character of Adams.

> " Mr. Adams is son of John Quincy Adams, the fifth P. of the U.S., and grandson of John Adams, the second P. The grandfather was the first Am. minister in England. The father was one of the Plenipotentiaries who signed in London the Convention of the 3rd July, 1815. Mr. Adams as a member of the H. of R. for one of the districts of Mass., acted with the less violent section of the 'Republican' Party. During the last session of Congress he made a very

[1] Lyons Papers.
[2] F.O., Am., Vol. 761.

remarkable speech on the state of the Union, denying the reasonableness of the complaints of the Southern States, but stating his desire that every concession not inconsistent with honour and principle should be made to them. He is considered to be a man of great independence of character, and has the reputation of being very tenacious of his own opinions. In manner he is quiet and unassuming. He is a man of good fortune. Mrs. Adams comes of a considerable family in Mass., of the name of Brooks. The late wife of Mr. Edward Everett, who, as your L. is aware, has held the offices of Minister in London and Secretary of State, was her sister."[1]

Similar characterizations were being forwarded at almost the same time by Bunch in regard to the Southern Commissioners, now being despatched to London, but they were not so favourable. Mann, wrote Bunch, was the son of a "bankrupt grocer." His personal character was "not good," yet he alone of the three Commissioners appointed had had diplomatic experience. Yancey, it was stated, was an able lawyer, a stirring orator, and a recognized leader of the secession movement, but he was also extremely pro-slavery in his views, had expressed himself in favour of a renewal of the slave trade, and throughout his career had been a "manifest destiny" man. Of Rost, Bunch had no knowledge. In conclusion Bunch described the extreme confidence expressed in the South in "King Cotton," and in rather bitter criticism stated that the Southern Commissioners thought even England, the foe of slavery, would now be compelled to bend the knee and recognize the South in order to get cotton.[2]

The Northern British Consuls on the other hand took an astonishingly pro-Northern view of the whole situation. Archibald, consul at New York, wrote to Russell soon after the fall of Sumter, an exceedingly strong statement of his

[1] F.O., Am., Vol. 762. No. 122. March 30, 1861. Received April 16.
[2] F.O., Am., Vol. 780. No. 37. March 21, 1861. Received April 9.

faith in the power of the North and its fixed and unalterable determination to force the South back into the Union, his confidence in Northern success, and his belief in the justice of the Northern cause. He ventured to suggest the proper policy for England to pursue, viz., to offer immediately her services in mediation but wholly and clearly on the side of the North. He stated that if England did not feel free to offer mediation, she should at least show " such a consistent and effective demonstration of sympathy and aid " for the North as would help in shortening the war.[1] The British Consul at Boston wrote to Russell in much the same vein. So far, indeed, did these men go in expressing their sympathy with the North, that Lyons, on April 27, commented to Russell that these consuls had " taken the Northern War Fever," and that he had mildly reproved Archibald.[2]

With the inauguration of Lincoln on March 4, and the installation of Seward as Secretary of State, it was possible for Lyons to become more active in his efforts to prevent a disruption of British Trade. On March 20 he told Seward in a confidential conversation:

> " . . . If the United States determined to stop by force so important a commerce as that of Great Britain with the cotton-growing States, I could not answer for what might happen.
>
> " . . . It was, however, a matter of the greatest consequence to England to procure cheap cotton. If a considerable rise were to take place in the price of cotton, and British ships were to be at the same time excluded from the Southern Ports, an immense pressure would be put upon Her Majesty's Government to use all the means in their power to open those ports. If Her Majesty's Government felt it to be their duty to do so, they would naturally endeavour to effect their object in a manner as consistent as possible, first with their friendly feelings towards both Sections of this Country, and secondly with

[1] F.O., Am., Vol. 778, No. 26. April 24, 1861.
[2] Russell Papers.

> the recognized principles of International Law. As regards the latter point in particular, it certainly appeared that the most simple, if not the only way, would be to recognize the Southern Confederacy."[1]

This was plain speaking, and Lyons' threat of recognizing the South did not at the moment stir Seward to any retort. But five days later, on March 25, Lyons gave a dinner to Seward and a number of the foreign Ministers, and there Seward's violent talk about seizing any and all ships that tried to trade with the South, even if there was no blockade, made Lyons very anxious. As a host he diverted the conversation lest it become too acrimonious, but he himself told Seward

> ". . . . that it was really a matter so very serious that I was unwilling to discuss it; that his plan seemed to me to amount in fact to a paper blockade of the enormous extent of coast comprised in the seceding States; that the calling it an enforcement of the Revenue Laws appeared to me to increase the gravity of the measure, for it placed Foreign Powers in the dilemma of recognizing the Southern Confederation or of submitting to the interruption of their commerce."[2]

Lyons' advice to Russell was that no rebuff should be given the Southern Commissioners when they arrived in London, but that they be treated well. This, he thought, might open Seward's eyes to his folly. Still Lyons did not yet fully believe that Seward would be so vigorous as his language seemed to imply, and on March 29 he wrote that "prudent counsels" were in the ascendant, that there would be no interference with trade "*at present*," and that a quieter tone was everywhere perceptible in Washington.[3]

From the point of view of the British Minister at

[1] Russell Papers. Lyons to Russell, March 26, 1861. Printed in Newton, *Lord Lyons*, Vol. I., p. 31.

[2] *Ibid.*

[3] Russell Papers.

Washington, the danger spot in relations between the United States and Great Britain lay in this matter of interference with trade to Southern ports. Naturally, and as in duty bound, he sought to preserve that trade. At first, indeed, he seems to have thought that even though a civil war really ensued the trade might continue uninterrupted. Certainly he bore hard and constantly on this one point, seeking to influence not only officials at Washington but the public press. Thus, in a letter to Bunch dated April 12, 1861, at a time when he knew that W. H. Russell, the *Times* correspondent, would shortly appear in Charleston, he instructed Bunch to remember that in talking to Russell he must especially impress him with the idea that any interruption of trade might and probably would result in a British recognition of the South. Lyons wrote, ". . . the *only* chance, if chance there still be of preventing an interruption of the English commerce with the S. is the fear entertained here, that it would lead to our recognizing the S.C." [1] In these words is revealed, however, as in other communications from Lyons, the fact that he was striving to prevent an interruption of trade rather than that he was convinced such interruption ought to result in a British recognition of the South. Indeed, as will be seen, when the blockade was at last declared, Lyons thought it no cause for recognition and was most tolerant of its early ineffectiveness.

While Lyons was thus keeping in close touch with Seward, the relations between England and America at London were exceedingly meagre. All that the American Minister Dallas knew of Russell's intentions is summed up in his despatches to Seward of March 22 and April 9, 1861. [2] On the former date, he gave an account of an interview with Russell in which the latter simply refused to

[1] Lyons Papers.
[2] *U.S. Messages and Documents*, 1861-2, pp. 80-81.

pledge himself against a recognition of the Confederacy; in the latter, presenting a long memorial written by Seward to all of the larger European Governments arguing in friendly spirit the cause of the North, Dallas reported that he drew from Russell merely a general expression of England's kindly feeling towards the United States and her hope that there might still be a peaceful solution. Russell again refused to make any pledge in regard to English policy. In this interview it was tacitly agreed that it would be better for Great Britain to await Adams' arrival before taking any definite action, or so at least Dallas understood Russell—though the latter later denied that any pledge of delay was given. There is no doubt, however, that in Russell's mind, whatever he might say to Dallas, the separation in America was an accomplished fact and the hope of Great Britain was centred upon the idea of a peaceful separation.

Up to and including April 1, indeed, Lyons had been reporting that no definite stand was yet being taken by the American Government. At the same time Russell was continuing his instructions to Lyons to recommend conciliation "but never to obtrude advice unasked." [1] Yet Russell was not wholly undisturbed by the reports of Seward's quarrelsome attitude, for in a private letter of the same date as the preceding, he wrote to Lyons, "I rely upon your wisdom, patience, and prudence, to steer us through the dangers of this crisis. If it can possibly be helped Mr. Seward must not be allowed to get us into a quarrel. I shall see the Southerners when they come, but not officially, and keep them at a proper distance." [2] It is an interesting query, whether this fear thus expressed of Seward's temper was not of distinct benefit to the United States at the moment when the Southern Commissioners

[1] F.O., Am., Vol. 754, No. 79. Russell to Lyons, April 6, 1861.
[2] Lyons Papers. Russell to Lyons, April 6, 1861.

arrived in England. The inference would seem to be clear, that in spite of Lyons' advice to treat them well, the effect upon Russell of Seward's attitude was to treat them coolly. Russell was indeed distinctly worried by Seward's unfriendly attitude.

In the meantime the British press and public, while still uncertain and divided as to the merits of the conflict were now substantially a unit in accepting separation as final. The *Times*, with judicial ponderosity declared: "The new nationality has been brought forth after a very short period of gestation. . . . and the Seceding States have now constituted themselves a nation . . ." [1] At the other end of the scale in newspaper "tone," the *London Press* jeered at the Northern American eagle as having "had his tail pulled out and his wings clipped—yet the meek bird now holds out his claws to be pared, with a resignation that would be degrading in the most henpecked of domestic fowls." [2] Having now veered about to expressions of confidence in the permanency of the Southern Confederacy the *Times* was also compelled to alter its opinion of Southern Statesmen. An editorial gave high praise to the Confederate Congress sitting at Montgomery, stated its personnel to be far superior to that of the Congress at Washington, yet was unable to resist making the customary reference to manners traditionally American:

> "With regard to the Congress itself, we cannot refrain from quoting the *naïve* testimony of a visitor in its favour. 'Gentlemen here [Montgomery] who have spent much time in Washington city declare that they have never witnessed such industry, care, propriety, courtesy, and pleasant Congressional action. *Not one member has appeared in his seat under the influence of liquors or wines*, not a harsh word

[1] The *Times*, February 26, 1861.

[2] *London Press*, March 30, 1861. Cited in Littell's *Living Age*, Vol. 69, p. 379.

has been uttered in debate, and all exhibit the most unflagging energy and determination.' "[1]

The most of the British press quickly followed the lead of the *Times*, forgot its previous dictum that the South was in the control of " ignorant ruffians," and dilated upon the statemanlike directness and sagacity of Southern leaders as contrasted with the stupidity of the North, displayed in its tariff policy.[2] A few journals thought that the North might eventually win in a prolonged struggle but that such a victory would be disastrous to the principles of federalism,[3] and, in any case, that this civil war was one without " a noble cause to sustain either side."[4] By May nearly all the older journals were aligned on the right of the South to secede, and on the fact of a successful secession, though still differing as to the basic causes and essential justice involved. In this same month, however, there emerged a few vigorous champions of the Northern cause and prospects. In April the *Spectator* agreed that the Great Republic was at an end ;[5] in May it urged the North to fight it out with hope, asserting a chance of ultimate victory because of superior resources and the sympathy of all European nations.[6] A small newspaper of limited circulation, the *Morning Star*, organ of John Bright, had from the first championed the Northern cause. Now, as the armed conflict broke in America, it was joined by a more important paper, the *Daily News*, which set itself the task of controverting the *Times*. Moreover the *Daily News* was all the more influential in that it was not uncritical of the North, yet consistently, throughout the war, expressed sympathy for the cause and

[1] The *Times*, March 26, 1861.

[2] *Saturday Review*, May 11, 1861, pp. 465-6.

[3] *Economist*, May 4, 1861.

[4] *Examiner*, January 5 and (as quoted) April 27, 1861. Cited in Littell's *Living Age*, Vol. 68, p. 758 and Vol. 69, p. 570.

[5] *Spectator*, April 27, 1861.

[6] *Ibid.*, May 4, 1861.

principles behind the efforts of the Northern Government. Selling for a low price, twopence-halfpenny, the *Daily News*, like the *Westminster* among the Reviews, appealed to a broader and more popular constituency than the older publications, especially to a constituency not yet vocal, since still unrepresented, in Parliament.[1]

The *Daily News* was fortunate in having, after 1862, the best-informed New York correspondent writing to the London press. This was an Irishman, E. L. Godkin, who, both at home and in America, was the intimate friend of literary men, and himself, later, a great moulder of public opinion.[2] Harriet Martineau further aided the *Daily News* by contributing pro-Northern articles, and was a power in Radical circles.[3] But literary England in general, was slow to express itself with conviction, though Robert Browning, by April, 1861, was firmly determined in his pro-Northern sentiment. In August he was writing in letters of the "good cause."[4] But Browning was a rare exception and it was not until the Civil War had been under way for many months that men of talent in the non-political world were drawn to make comment or to take sides. Their influence at the outset was negligible.[5]

[1] These four publications, the *Spectator*, the *Westminster*, the *Daily News*, and the *Morning Star*, were the principal British pro-Northern organs. In addition *The Liberator* names among the lesser and provincial press the following: *Nonconformist*, *British Standard*, *Dial*, *Birmingham Post*, *Manchester Examiner*, *Newcastle Chronicle*, *Caledonian Mercury* and *Belfast Whig*. Duffus, "English Opinion," p. 40.

[2] Godkin had joined the staff of the *Daily News* in 1853. During the Crimea War he was special war correspondent. He had travelled extensively in America in the late 'fifties and was thoroughly well informed. From 1862 to 1865 his letters to the *Daily News* were of great value in encouraging the British friends of the North. In 1865 Godkin became editor of the New York *Nation*.

[3] W. E. Forster said of her, "It was Harriet Martineau alone who was keeping English opinion about America on the right side through the Press." The *Daily News* Jubilee Edition, p. 46.

[4] James, *William Wetmore Story and His Friends*, Vol. II, p. 92.

[5] Moncure D. Conway's *Autobiography* asserts that two-thirds of the English authors "espoused the Union cause, some of them actively—Professor Newman, Mill, Tom Hughes, Sir Charles Lyell, Huxley, Tyndall, Swinburne, Lord Houghton, Cairns, Fawcett, Frederic Harrison, Leslie

In spite of press utterances, or literary silence, alike indicative of a widespread conviction that Southern independence was assured, there still remained both in those circles where anti-slavery sentiment was strong, and in others more neutral in sympathy, a distaste for the newly-born State as the embodiment of a degrading institution. Lincoln's inaugural address denying an intention to interfere with slavery was a weapon for the friends of the South, but it could not wholly still that issue. Even in the *Times*, through the medium of W. H. Russell's descriptive letters, there appeared caustic criticisms. He wrote in his "Diary," "I declare that to me the more orderly, methodical, and perfect the arrangements for economizing slave labour . . . are, the more hateful and odious does slavery become,"[2] and in his letter of May 8, from Montgomery, having witnessed an auction sale of slaves he stated:

> "I am neither sentimentalist nor Black Republican, nor negro worshipper, but I confess the sight caused a strange thrill through my heart. I tried in vain to make myself familiar with the fact that I could, for the sum of $975, become as absolutely the owner of that mass of blood, bones, sinew, flesh and brains as of the horse which stood by my side. There was no sophistry which could persuade me the man was not a man—he was, indeed, by no means my brother, but assuredly he was a fellow creature."[3]

This was hard printing for the *Times*, in its new advocacy of the South, and Russell's description was made much of by the *Westminster Review* and other publications that soon began to sound again the "issue" of slavery.[4] Yet the

Stephen, Allingham, the Rossettis," Vol. I, p. 406. This is probably true of ultimate, though not of initial, interest and attitude. But for many writers their published works give no clue to their opinions on the Civil War—as for example the works of Dickens, Thackeray, William Morris, or Ruskin. See Duffus, "English Opinion," p. 103.

[2] Russell, *My Diary*, I, p. 398.

[3] The *Times*, May 30, 1861.

[4] *Westminster Review*, Vol. 76, pp. 487-509, October, 1861.

Westminster itself in the same article decried the folly of the Northern attempt at reconquest. So also thought even John Bright at the moment, when expressing himself privately to friends in America.[1]

Slavery, then, still remained an issue before the British public, but of what use was it to upbraid the South, if a new world State were in fact born? And if a State in power, why not give it prompt recognition? The extreme British anti-slavery opponents feared that this was just what the Government was inclined to do, and with promptness. Here and there meetings were hurriedly called to protest against recognition.[2] This fear was unfounded. Neither in London nor at Washington was there any official inclination to hasten recognition. Lyons had held up to Seward the logic of such action, if British trade were illegally interfered with. By April 9 Lyons was aware that the so-called Radical Party in the Cabinet would probably have its way, that conciliation would no longer be attempted, and that a coercive policy toward the South was soon to follow. On that date he wrote to Russell stating that people in Washington seemed so convinced that Europe would *not* interfere to protect its trade that they were willing to venture any act embarrassing to that trade. He himself was still insisting, but with dwindling confidence, that the trade must not be interfered with under any circumstances. And in a second letter of this same date, he repeated to Russell his advice of treating the Southern Commissioners with deference. Any rebuff to them, he asserts again, will but increase the Northern confidence that they may do anything without provoking the resistance of England.[3]

[1] Bright to Sumner, September 6, 1861. Cited in Rhodes, *United States*, Vol III, p. 509.

[2] A meeting held in Edinburgh, May 9, 1861, declared that anti-slavery England ought never to recognize the South. Reported in *Liberator*, May 31, 1861.

[3] F.O., Am., Vol. 762. Nos. 141 and 142.

Like a good diplomat Lyons was merely pushing the argument for all it was worth, hoping to prevent an injury to his country, yet if that injury did come (provided it were sanctioned by the law of nations) he did not see in it an injury sufficient to warrant precipitate action by Great Britain. When indeed the Southern capture of Fort Sumter in Charleston harbour finally brought the actual clash of arms, Lyons expressed himself with regard to other elements in the struggle previously neglected in his correspondence. On April 15 describing to Russell the fall of Sumter, he stated that civil war had at last begun. The North he believed to be very much more powerful than the South, the South more "eager" and united as yet, but, he added, "the taint of slavery will render the cause of the South loathsome to the civilized world." It was true that "commercial intercourse with the cotton States is of vital importance to manufacturing nations . . ." [1] but Lyons was now facing an actual situation rather than a possible one, and as will be seen later, he soon ceased to insist that an interruption of this "commercial intercourse" gave reasonable ground for recognition of the South.

With the fall of Fort Sumter and the European recognition that a civil war was actually under way in America, a large number of new and vexing problems was presented to Russell. His treatment of them furnishes the subject matter of later chapters. For the period previous to April, 1861, British official attitude may be summed up in the statement that the British Minister at Washington hoped against hope that some solution might be found for the preservation of the Union, but that at the same time, looking to future British interests and possibly believing also that his attitude would tend to preserve the Union, he asserted vehemently the impossibility of any Northern interference with British trade to Southern ports. Across

[1] *Ibid.*, No. 146.

the water, Russell also hoped faintly that there might be no separation. Very soon, however, believing that separation inevitable and the disruption of the Union final, he fixed his hope on peaceful rather than warlike secession. Even of this, however, he had little real expectation, but neither he nor anyone else in England, nor even in America, had any idea that the war would be a long and severe one. It is evident that he was already considering the arrival of that day when recognition must be granted to a new, independent and slave-holding State. But this estimate of the future is no proof that the Russian Ambassador's accusation of British governmental pleasure in American disruption was justified.[1] Russell, cautious in refusing to pledge himself to Dallas, was using exactly such caution as a Foreign Secretary was bound to exercise. He would have been a rash man who, in view of the uncertainty and irresolution of Northern statesmen, would have committed Great Britain in March, 1861, to a definite line of policy.

On April 6, Russell was still instructing Lyons to recommend reconciliation. April 8, Dallas communicated to Russell an instruction from Seward dated March 9, arguing on lines of "traditional friendship" against a British recognition of the Confederacy. Russell again refused to pledge his Government, but on April 12 he wrote to Lyons that British Ministers were "in no hurry to recognize the separation as complete and final."[2] In the early morning of that same day the armed conflict in America had begun, and on the day following, April 13, the first Southern victory had been recorded in the capture of Fort Sumter. The important question which the man at the head of the British Foreign Office had now immediately to decide was, what was to be England's attitude, under international

[1] See *ante*, pp. 50-51.

[2] *Parliamentary Papers*, 1862, *Lords*, Vol. XXV. "Correspondence on Civil War in the United States." Nos. 24, 25 and 26.

law, toward the two combatants in America. In deciding this question, neither sentiment nor ideals of morality, nor humanitarianism need play any part ; England's *first* need and duty were to determine and announce for the benefit of her citizens the correct position, under International law, which must be assumed in the presence of certain definite facts.

CHAPTER III

THE DEVELOPMENT OF A POLICY, MAY, 1861

IN June, 1859, a short-lived Conservative Government under the leadership of Lord Derby had been replaced by a "coalition" Liberal Government, at the head of which stood Palmerston, but so constituted that almost equal influence was attributed to the Foreign Secretary, Lord John Russell. Both men had previously held the Premiership, and, as they represented different wings of the Whig-Liberal party, it was prophesied by political wiseacres that personal friction would soon lead to a new disruption. Nor were the possible elements of discord confined to these two. Gladstone, formerly a Peelite Tory, and for a time uncertain whether to return to the Tory fold or to join the Liberals, had yielded to Palmerston's promise of a free hand in financial matters, and had joined the Ministry as Chancellor of the Exchequer. Opposed to him in a certain sense, as the rival claimant for political leadership among the younger group, was Sir George Cornewall Lewis, Home Secretary until July, 1861, thereafter until his death in April, 1863, Secretary for War. Acting in some degree as intermediary and conciliator between these divergent interests stood Lord Granville, President of Council, then a "Conservative-Liberal," especially valuable to the Cabinet for the confidence reposed in him by Queen Victoria and Prince Albert.

In 1861 Palmerston was seventy-seven years old. Long before this he had built his popularity upon a vigorous British "patriotism," assertive of England's honour and jealous for British advantage. Now, however, as head of a Government requiring the most delicate handling to maintain itself, he devoted his energies to details of political management in which he had great skill. His ambition was, primarily, to retain office, and in this purpose he was fortunate because, unknown to his ministerial colleagues, he had received an indirect pledge from Lord Derby, the Opposition leader, that there would be, for a time at least, no determined effort to unseat him so long as his Ministry brought forward no Bill for a further expansion of the franchise. In the unwillingness to make any further adventure toward an expanded democracy Palmerston was wholly at one with Derby. Of like opinion, though less strongly so, was Russell, whose popular nickname, "Finality John," gained by his assertion that the Reform Bill of 1832 was England's last step toward democracy, sufficiently indicates his stand on the franchise question. In fact every member of the Cabinet belonged to the "Conservative-Liberal" group, though with shades of political faith, and none were really Liberals—far less Radicals. The outspoken Radicals in Parliament, like John Bright, and his friend Cobden, who had refused to take office under Palmerston, gave a lukewarm support to the Ministry, but would not pledge themselves to steadfast adherence. They had hopes of Gladstone, believed that he would ultimately come into their group, but meanwhile watched with anxiety his delighted immersion, as indeed Palmerston desired it, in the details of financial management to the exclusion of other questions.

The matter of ministerial and general British attitude toward democracy as affecting British policy during the American Civil War will be considered in a later chapter. In the spring of 1861 it had not become a clear-cut British opinion and did not, so far as historical evidence can determine, affect early governmental policy toward America.

The outstanding feature of the British Government in 1861 is that it was made up of various so-called "Liberal" elements, the representatives of each of which carried on the business of his own department much as he pleased. Palmerston's was, of course, the deciding opinion, whenever he cared to express it, but this he did but rarely. His great concern was to keep his all-star associates running smoothly together and thus to give no occasion for parliamentary criticism and attack. It followed that Russell, eight years the junior of Palmerston, was in foreign affairs more powerful and independent than is customary. Indeed the Government was at times spoken of as the "Palmerston-Russell Ministry." These two were the leaders of the team; next came Gladstone and Cornewall Lewis, rivals of the younger generation, and each eager to lead when their elders should retire from harness. Gladstone's great ability was already recognized, but his personal political faith was not yet clear. Lewis, lacking his rival's magnetic and emotional qualities, cold, scholarly, and accurate in performance, was regarded as a statesman of high promise.[1] Other Cabinet members, as is the custom of coalitions, were more free in opinion and action than in a strict party ministry where one dominating personality imposes his will upon his colleagues.

Lord John Russell, then, in foreign policy, was more than the main voice of the Government; rather, save in times of extreme crisis, governmental foreign policy was Russell's policy. This was even more true as regards American than European affairs, for the former were little understood, and dependence was necessarily placed upon the man whose business it was to be familiar with them.

[1] Sir George Cornewall Lewis was better informed in the early stages of the American conflict than any of his ministerial colleagues. He was an occasional contributor to the reviews and his unsigned article in the *Edinburgh*, April, 1861, on "The Election of President Lincoln and its Consequences," was the first analysis of real merit in any of the reviews.

Indeed there was little actual parliamentary or governmental interest, before midsummer of 1861, in the American question, attention in foreign affairs being directed toward Italian expansion, to the difficulties related to the control of the Ionian islands, and to the developing Danish troubles in Schleswig-Holstein. Neither did the opposition party venture to express a policy as regards America. Lord Derby, able but indolent, occasionally indulged in caustic criticism, but made no attempt to push his attack home. Malmesbury, his former Foreign Secretary, was active and alert in French affairs, but gave no thought to relations across the Atlantic.[1] Disraeli, Tory leader in the Commons, skilfully led a strong minority in attacks on the Government's policy, but never on the American question, though frequently urged to do so by the friends of the South. In short for the first year of the Civil War, 1861, the policy of Great Britain toward America was the policy of Lord John Russell, unhampered by friend or foe.

This being the case, what did Russell know about the American crisis? Briefly, no more than has already been stated as derived from the reports of British officials in the United States, and from the pages of the public press. The salient facts known to Russell were few. Lincoln's Cabinet had been named. Lincoln himself was absolutely an unknown quantity, but it was unbelievable that a man of his origins and history could be more than a mere figurehead—an opinion then held as widely in America as in England. But someone must determine American policy, and by universal consent, this would be Seward.

The new Secretary of State was at the moment better known in England than any other American statesman, with the possible exception of Charles Sumner, whose visits and personal contacts had established a circle of British

[1] In his *Memoirs of an Ex-Minister*, Malmesbury makes but three important references to the Civil War in America.

friendships. Both men were accepted as champions of anti-slavery, Sumner for his vigorous denunciations and his so-called "martyrdom" under the physical violence of the South Carolinan, Brooks; and Seward for his clever political anti-Southern leadership in the United States Senate. But Seward's reputation in this respect was offset by the belief that he was anti-British in his personal sentiments, or at least that he was very ready to arouse for political ends the customary anti-British sentiment of his Irish constituents in the State of New York. In 1860, on the occasion of the visit to the United States of the Prince of Wales, Seward is alleged to have stated to the Duke of Newcastle that in case he became Secretary of State it would then "become my duty to insult England, and I mean to do so"—a threat, whether jocose or not, that aroused much serious and anxious speculation in British governmental circles.[1] Moreover Seward's reputation was that of a wily, clever politician, rather unscrupulous in methods which British politicians professed to disdain—a reputation serving to dim somewhat, as indeed it did in America also, the sincere idealisms and patriotism of the statesman. Altogether, Seward was regarded in Great Britain as a rather dangerous man, yet as the inevitable guiding power in the new Republican administration.

This estimate was shared by many in the United States also, but not by all. The new American Minister to London, Charles Francis Adams, himself a most stiffly upright politician, both regarded Seward as the only possible leader of Republican party policy and rejoiced that this was so, having great confidence in his chief's integrity and wisdom. Adams himself was well suited to his new post. He was known as having early in 1849 fought the battle of anti-slavery as a "Free Soil Whig," and later as a leading Republican member of Congress from Massachusetts.

[1] Adams, *Charles Francis Adams*, p. 165.

Principally, however, he was suited to his post by education, family, and character. He had been taken as a boy to Russia during his father's ministry at St. Petersburg, and later had been educated in England. His father and grandfather, John Quincy Adams and John Adams, both Presidents of the United States, had both, also, been American Ministers at London. Intensely patriotic, but having wide acquaintance through training and study with European affairs, especially those of Britain, and equipped with high intellectual gifts, Adams was still further fitted to his new post by his power of cool judgment and careful expression in critical times. His very coolness, sometimes appearing as coldness and stiff dignity, rendered him an especially fit agent to deal with Russell, a man of very similar characteristics. The two men quickly learned to respect and esteem each other, whatever clash arose in national policies.

But meanwhile Adams, in April, 1861, was not yet arrived in London. The Southern Government organized at Montgomery, Alabama, but soon transferred to Richmond, Virginia, was headed by Jefferson Davis as President and Alexander Stephens as Vice-President. Neither man was well known in England, though both had long been prominent in American politics. The little British information on Davis, that he had served in the United States Senate and as a Cabinet member, seemed to indicate that he was better fitted to executive duties than his rival, Lincoln. But Davis' foreign policy was wholly a matter for speculation, and his Cabinet consisted of men absolutely unknown to British statesmen. In truth it was not a Cabinet of distinction, for it was the misfortune of the South that everywhere, as the Civil War developed, Southern gentlemen sought reputation and glory in the army rather than in political position. Nor did President Davis himself ever fully grasp the importance to the South of a well-considered and energetic foreign policy. At first, indeed, home controversy compelled anxious attention to the exclusion of other matters. Until war cemented Southern patriotism, Davis, himself regarded as an extremist, felt it necessary in denial of an asserted unreasonableness of personal attitude, to appoint to office men known for their earlier moderate opinions on both slavery and secession.[1] "The single exception to this general policy"[2] was the appointment as agents to Europe of Yancey, Rost and Mann, all of them extreme pro-slavery men and eager secessionists. Of these Mann was the only one with any previous diplomatic experience. Yancey's choice was particularly inappropriate, for he at least was known abroad as the extreme fire-eating Southern orator, demanding for ten years past, that Southern action in defence of states rights and Southern "interests," which now, at last, the South was attempting.[3]

Yancey and Rost, starting on their journey on March 16, reached London on April 29.[4] Meanwhile in this same month of April, conditions in America, so long confused and uncertain, were being rapidly clarified. The South, earlier than the North, had come to a determined policy, for while during January and February, at the Montgomery convention, there had been uncertainty as to actively applying the doctrinaire right of secession, by March the party of action had triumphed, and though there was still talk of conferences with the North, and commissioners actually appointed, no real expectation existed of a favourable result. In the North, the determination of policy was more slowly developed. Lincoln was not inaugurated

[1] Dodd, *Jefferson Davis*, pp. 227-8.

[2] *Ibid.*

[3] It was generally whispered in Southern political circles that Davis sent Yancey abroad to get rid of him, fearing his interference at home. If true, this is further evidence of Davis' neglect of foreign policy.

[4] Du Bose, *Yancey*, p. 604.

until March 4, and no positive pronouncement was earlier possible. Even after that date uncertainty still prevailed. European correspondents were reporting men like Sumner as willing to let the South go in peace. The Mayor of New York City was discussing the advisability of a separate secession by that financial centre from Nation and State alike—and of setting up as a "free town." Seward, just appointed Secretary of State, was repudiating in both official and private talk any intention to coerce the South by force of arms.[1] It is no wonder that British statesmen were largely at sea over the American situation.

But on April 13, 1861, the Stars and Stripes floating over Fort Sumter in Charleston harbour was lowered in surrender of a Federal fortress under the armed attack of the newly-born Confederacy. That event drove away as by magic the uncertainty of the North, and removed the last vestiges of Southern doubt. A great wave of militant patriotism swept over both sections.[2] Hurriedly both North and South prepared for war, issuing calls for volunteers and organizing in all accustomed warlike preparations. The news of Sumter reached London or April 27, and that civil war seemed certain was known on April 29. On April 17, Davis, since the South lacked a navy, approved a proclamation offering to issue letters of marque and reprisal. On April 19 Lincoln proclaimed a Northern intention to treat as pirates any privateers acting under such letters, and also gave notice of a blockade of Southern ports, to be instituted later. Thus suddenly, so it seemed to British officials and public after the long delay and uncertainty of months, events in America had precipitated a state of war, though in fact there were still to elapse other months in which both North and South laboured to trans-

[1] Adams, *Charles Francis Adams*, pp. 149-51.

[2] Possibly the best concise statement of the effect on the North is given in Carl Schurz, *Reminiscences*, Vol. II, p. 223. Or see my citation of this in *The Power of Ideals in American History*, ch. I, "Nationality."

form a peaceful society into one capable of waging effective battle.

The result of this sudden change in the American horizon was to alter, almost as quickly, the previous delay in outlining a British policy, though, presumably, the British Government, while waiting the turn of events, had given careful consideration to the steps required of it in just such a situation as had now arisen. Certainly both Lyons and Russell had been deeply anxious for some time, and had visualized a proper British policy. The movement in Great Britain now became rapid. On April 29, Malmesbury, in the Lords, spoke of the news of civil war which had arrived "this morning," and asked if the Government had tried to prevent it, or had set on foot negotiations with other powers to check it. Wodehouse, replying for the Government, stated that the United States as an independent State would have resented any suggestions from Great Britain, and that Lyons had been instructed to be extremely careful about offering advice unless "asked for by the contending parties themselves." Both speakers commented on the "ties of blood" rendering Britain especially anxious in this American quarrel, and regretted the conflict.[1] Malmesbury's query as to the approach to another government, meaning France, was evaded. That some such approach, in accordance with the earlier advice of Lyons,[2] had already been made, is evident from the fact that three days later, on May 1, Dallas learned from Russell of the plan of joint action with France, though what that action would be was not made clear.[3] As Dallas' report was soon the basis of an American complaint shortly to be considered, the paragraph referring to this matter is important:

[1] Hansard, 3rd. Ser., Vol. CLXII, pp. 1207-9

[2] See *ante*, p. 60.

[3] *U.S. Messages and Documents*, 1861-62, pp. 83-4. Dallas to Seward, May 2, 1862.

"The solicitude felt by Lord John Russell as to the effect of certain measures represented as likely to be adopted by the President induced him to request me to call at his private residence yesterday. I did so. He told me that the three representatives of the Southern confederacy were here;[1] that he had not seen them, but was not unwilling to do so, *unofficially*; that there existed an understanding between this government and that of France which would lead both to take the same course as to recognition, whatever that course might be; and he then referred to the rumour of a meditated blockade of Southern ports and their discontinuance as ports of entry—topics on which I had heard nothing. But as I informed him that Mr. Adams had apprised me of his intention to be on his way hither, in the steamship 'Niagara,' which left Boston on the 1st May, and that he would probably arrive in less than two weeks, by the 12th or 15th instant, his lordship acquiesced in the expediency of disregarding mere rumour, and waiting the full knowledge to be brought by my successor. The motion, therefore, of Mr. Gregory may be further postponed, at his lordship's suggestion."

May 3rd, Russell held an unofficial interview with the two Southern commissioners in fact arrived, Yancey and Rost. As reported by them,[2] Russell listened with attention to their representation, but made no informing comment. They argued the constitutional right of secession, depicted the firm determination of the South, were confident of early acquiescence by the North, and especially laid stress on the Southern desire for free trade. Russell's own report to Lyons on this interview and on one held six days later, May 9, is in substantial agreement, but much more is made by him than by the Commissioners of a question put by Russell as to a Southern plan of reviving the African slave-

[1] An error. Mann did not arrive in London until May 15. Du Bose, *Yancey*, p. 604.

[2] Richardson, *Messages and Papers of the Confederacy*, Vol. II, p. 34. This report also shows that Mann was not present at the first interview with Russell.

trade.[1] Yancey and Rost denied this and asserted "that they had prohibited the slave-trade, and did not mean to revive it." Their report to Richmond does not depict this matter as of special significance in the interview; Russell's report to Lyons lays stress upon it. The general result of the interview was that Russell listened, but refused, as to Dallas, to make any pledge on recognition. But the Southern Commissioners came away with a feeling of confidence and were content to wait on British action.[2]

On this same day, May 3, Russell received from the Attorney-General a memorandum in reply to a query as to recognizing the belligerency of the South and as to the right of the South to issue letters of marque and reprisal. The memorandum notes that Southern privateering would be dangerous to British commerce with the North, but sees no help for it. "The best solution," wrote the Attorney-General, "would be for the European nations to determine that the war between the two Confederacies shall be carried on on the principles of 'Justum Bellum,' and shall be conducted according to the rules of the Treaty of Paris. Recognize the Southern States as a Belligerent on this condition only."[3] The next day, referring to this memorandum, Russell wrote Lyons that the law officers "are of opinion that we must consider the Civil War in America as regular war,"[4] but he does *not* comment on the legal advice to press the South to abandon privateering before recognizing her belligerent rights, for this is the only meaning that can be attached to the last sentence quoted

[1] F.O., America, Vol. 755. No. 128, Russell to Lyons, May 11, 1861. This document is marked "Seen by Lord Palmerston and the Queen." The greater and essential part has been printed in *Parliamentary Papers*, 1862, *Lords*, Vol. XXV. "Correspondence on Civil War in United States." No. 33.

[2] Du Bose, *Yancey*, p. 604.

[3] Lyons Papers. The copy of the Memorandum sent to Lyons is undated, but from Russell's letter to Lyons of May 4, in which it was enclosed, it is presumable that the date of May 3 for the Memorandum is correct.

[4] *Ibid.* Russell to Lyons, May 4, 1861.

from the Attorney-General's memorandum. This advice, however, in view of the opinion that there was "no help for it," was presumably but a suggestion as to a possible diplomatic manœuvre with little confidence that it would succeed. The "best solution" was not the probable one, for the South, without a navy, would not readily yield its only naval weapon.

In these few days British policy was rapidly matured and announced. The letter of May 4 to Lyons, stating the Civil War to be a "regular war" was followed on May 6 by a formal instruction giving Lyons advance notice of the determination reached by the Cabinet to recognize the belligerent rights of the South. Russell indulged in many expressions of regret and sympathy, but Lyons was not to conceal that this British action represented the Government's view of the actualities of the American situation. Yet while Lyons was not to conceal this opinion he was not instructed to notify Seward, officially, of the recognition of Southern belligerency.[1] Here was a correct understanding of the difficulty of the diplomatic position at Washington, and a permitted avoidance by Lyons of dangerous ground.[2] Russell was not then aware of the tenacity with which Seward was to cling to a theory, not yet clearly formulated for foreign governments, that the Civil War was a rebellion of peoples rather than a conflict of governments, but he does appear to have understood the delicacy of formal notification to the constituted government at Washington.[3] Moreover his instructions were in line with the British policy of refusing, at present, a recognition of Southern sovereignty.

[1] F.O., Am., Vol. 755. No. 121, Russell to Lyons, May 6, 1861.

[2] It is to be remembered that the United States had given no notice of the existence of a state of war.

[3] In diplomatic usage official notification of neutrality to a belligerent has varied, but Russell's letters show him to have appreciated a peculiar delicacy here.

On the same day, May 6, a copy of the instructions to Lyons was sent to Cowley, British Ambassador at Paris, directing him to request France to join, promptly, in recognizing Southern belligerent rights. Cowley was also instructed that the blockade and privateering required precautions by European governments, and it was suggested that France and England unite in requesting both belligerents to accede to the second and third articles of the Declaration of Paris.[1] These articles refer to the exemption from capture, except contraband, of enemy's goods under a neutral flag, and of neutral goods under an enemy's flag.[2] This day, also, Russell stated in Parliament that England was about to recognize the belligerent rights of the South, and spoke of the measure as a necessary and inevitable one. May 7, Cowley notified Russell that Thouvenel, the French Foreign Minister, was in complete agreement with England's policy,[3] and on May 9, in a more extended communication, Cowley sent word of Thouvenel's suggestion that both powers issue a declaration that they "intended to abstain from all interference," and that M. de Flahault, French Ambassador at London, had

[1] F.O., France, Vol. 1376. No. 553. Draft. Printed in *Parliamentary Papers*, 1862, *Lords*, Vol. XXV. "Correspondence on International Maritime Law." No. 1.

[2] It is interesting that on this same day Lyons was writing from Washington advocating, regretfully, because of his sympathy with the North, a strict British neutrality:

> "The sympathies of an Englishman are naturally inclined towards the North—but I am afraid we should find that anything like a quasi alliance with the men in office here would place us in a position which would soon become untenable. There would be no end to the exactions which they would make upon us, there would be no end to the disregard of our neutral rights, which they would show if they once felt sure of us. If I had the least hope of their being able to reconstruct the Union, or even of their being able to reduce the South to the condition of a tolerably contented or at all events obedient dependency, my feeling against Slavery might lead me to desire to co-operate with them. But I conceive all chance of this to be gone for ever."

Russell Papers. Lyons to Russell, May 6, 1861.

[3] F.O., France, Vol. 1390. No. 677.

been given instructions to act in close harmony with Russell.[1]

The rapidity of movement in formulating policy in the six days from May 1 to May 6, seems to have taken the British public and press somewhat by surprise, for there is a lack of newspaper comment even after Russell's parliamentary announcement of policy on the last-named date. But on May 9 the *Times* set the fashion of general approval in an editorial stating that Great Britain was now coming to see the American conflict in a new light—as a conflict where there were in fact no such ideals involved as had been earlier attributed to it. Southern rights were now more clearly understood, and in any case since war, though greatly to be regretted, was now at hand, it was England's business to keep strictly out of it and to maintain neutrality.[2] This generalization was no doubt satisfactory to the public, but in the Government and in Parliament men who were thinking seriously of specific difficulties realized that the two main problems immediately confronting a British neutral policy were privateering and blockade. The South had declared its *intention* to use privateers. The North had declared its *intention*, first to hang those who engaged in privateering, and second to establish a blockade. Neither declaration had as yet been put into effect.

The first action of the British Government was directed toward privateering. On May 1, Russell sent a note to the Lords Commissioners of the Admiralty calling attention to the Southern plan to issue letters of marque and reprisal and directing that reinforcements be sent to the British fleet in American waters. This was prompt action on unofficial information, for Davis' proclamation bore date of April 17, and Lyons' despatch containing copies of it,

[1] *Ibid.*, No. 684. Printed in part in *Parliamentary Papers*, 1862, *Lords*, Vol. XXV. "Correspondence on International Maritime Law." No. 3.

[2] *Times*, May 9, 1861.

sent on April 22, was not received by Russell until May 10.[1] Ordinary news from the United States required ten days to get into print in London,[2] but official messages might be sent more rapidly by way of telegraph to Halifax, thence by steamer to Liverpool and by telegraph again to London. In case the telegram to Halifax coincided with the departure of a fast vessel the time was occasionally reduced to seven days, but never less. At the best the exact information as to the contents of the Davis and Lincoln proclamations of April 17 and 19 respectively, could have been received only a few days before the order was issued to reinforce the British fleet.

The next day, May 2, Ewart, in the Commons, asked "if Privateers sailing under the flag of an unrecognized Power will be dealt with as Pirates," thus showing the immediate parliamentary concern at the Davis and Lincoln proclamations. Russell stated in reply that a British fleet had been sent to protect British interests and took occasion to indicate British policy by adding, "we have not been involved in any way in that contest by any act or giving any advice in the matter, and, for God's sake, let us if possible keep out of it."[3] May 6, Gregory, a friend of the

[1] *Parliamentary Papers*, 1862, *Lords*, Vol. XXV. "Correspondence on Civil War in the United States." No. 31.

[2] So stated by the *Times*, May 9, 1861.

[3] Hansard, 3rd. Ser., Vol. CLXII, pp. 1378-9. This blunt expression of Great Britain's Foreign Secretary offers an interesting comparison with the words of the American President Wilson, in a parallel statement at the outbreak of the Great War in 1914. Wilson on August 3, 1914, gave a special audience to newspaper correspondents, begging them to maintain an attitude of calm impartiality. On August 4 he issued the first of several neutrality proclamations in which, following the customary language of such documents, the people were notified that neutrality did not restrict the "full and free expression of sympathies in public and in private." But on August 18 in an address to the people of the United States, this legal phraseology, required by traditional usage was negatived by Wilson's appeal that "we must be impartial in thought as well as in action, must put a curb upon our sentiments as well as upon every transaction that might be construed as a preference of one party to the struggle before another." And three weeks later, on September 8, came the proclamation setting aside October 4 "as a day of prayer to Almighty God," informing Him that war existed and asking His intervention. Possibly Russell's more blunt and pithy expression was better suited to the forthrightness of the British public.

Photo: F. Hollyer.

SIR WILLIAM GREGORY, K.C.M.G.

(From Lady Gregory's "Sir William Gregory, K.C.M.G.: An Autobiography," by kind permission)

South, who had already given notice of a motion for the recognition of the Confederacy as an independent State, asked whether the United States had been informed that a blockade of Southern ports would not be recognized unless effective, and whether there would be acquiescence in the belligerent right of the South to issue letters of marque and reprisal.[1] Russell replied that Lincoln had *not* been informed that a blockade must be effective to be respected since the Washington Government did not need to be told of an international rule which it had itself long proclaimed. As to the second point, he now announced what heretofore had not been clearly stated, that Southern privateers could not be regarded by Great Britain as pirates, for if so regarded Britain would herself have to treat them as pirates and would thus be unneutral. This was in fact, in spite of Northern bitter accusations that Britain was exhibiting governmental sympathy with the South by her tolerance of the plan of Southern privateering, an inescapable conclusion. Russell added, however, that the matter of privateering involved some new questions under the Declaration of Paris upon which the Government had not yet decided what stand to take.[2] It was on this same day, in fact, that Russell had instructed Cowley to take up with France the question of the Declaration of Paris,[3]

[1] Hansard, *ibid.*, pp. 1564-7. Gregory, a "Liberal-Conservative," though never a "good party man" was then supporting Palmerston's ministry. He was very popular in Parliament, representing by his prominence in sport and society alike, the "gentleman ruling class" of the House of Commons, and was a valuable influence for the South.

[2] This subject is developed at length in Chapter V on "The Declaration of Paris Negotiation."

[3] See *ante*, p. 88. The chronology of these rapidly succeeding events is interesting :

April 29—Malmesbury states in the Lords that "news was received this day."
May 1—Naval reinforcements sent to American waters.
May 1—Russell's interview with Dallas.
May 2—Russell's plea in Parliament, "For God's sake keep out of it."
May 3—Russell's first interview with Yancey and Rost.
May 3—Attorney-General's memorandum.
May 4—Russell's note to Lyons that this is a "regular war."

Privateering and blockade, declared in America months before there was any possibility of putting them into effect, and months before there were any military operations in the field, forced this rapid European action, especially the action of Great Britain, which, more than any other European nation, feared belligerent interference with her carrying and export trade. How was the British Government to know that Davis would not bend every energy in sending out privateers, and Lincoln to establish a blockade? The respective declarations of Davis and Lincoln were the *first* evidences offered of belligerent status. It was reasonable to assume that here would come the first energetic efforts of the belligerents. Nor was British governmental intelligence sufficiently informed to be aware that Davis, in fact, controlled few ships that could be fitted out as privateers, or that two-thirds of the Northern navy was at the moment widely scattered in foreign seas, making impossible a prompt blockade.

To the British view the immediate danger to its commercial interests lay in this announced maritime war, and it felt the necessity of defining its neutral position with speed. The underlying fact of the fixity of Southern

May 6—Cowley instructed to ask France to recognize Southern belligerency.
May 6—Lyons notified that England will recognize Southern belligerency.
May 6—Russell states in Parliament that privateers can not be treated as pirates.
[Presumably, since parliamentary sittings begin in the late afternoons, the instructions to diplomats were drawn before the statement in Parliament.]
May 9—Russell's second interview with Yancey and Rost.
May 9—Sir George Lewis announces that a Proclamation of Neutrality will be issued soon.
May 13—The Proclamation authorized.
May 13—Adams reaches Liverpool.
May 14—The Proclamation officially published in the *London Gazette*.
May 14—Adams in London "ready for business."

It would appear that Russell's expressions in Parliament on May 2 indicated clearly the purpose of the Government. This was notified to Lyons on May 4, which may be taken as the date when the governmental position had become definitely fixed, even though official instructions were not sent Lyons until the 6th.

determination to maintain secession had in the last few weeks become clearly recognized.

Moreover the latest information sent by British officials in America, some of it received just before the issue of the Proclamation of Neutrality, some just after, was all confirmative of the rapid approach of a great war. A letter from Bunch, at Charleston, was received on May 10, depicting the united Southern will to resist Northern attack, and asserting that the South had no purpose save to conduct a strictly defensive war. Bunch was no longer caustic; he now felt that a new nation was in process of birth.[1] May 4, Monson, writing from Washington, and just returned from a trip through the South, in the course of which he had visited Montgomery, stated "*no reconstruction* of the Union is possible," and added that there was no danger of a servile insurrection, a matter that now somewhat began to disturb the British Government and public.[2] A few days later on, May 12, Lyons expressed his strong sympathy with the North for reasons of anti-slavery, law, and race, but added that he shrank from expressions of sympathy for fear of thus encouraging the Northern Cabinet in its plan of prosecuting civil war since such a war would be frightful in its consequences both to America and to England.[3]

Such reports if received before the issue of the Pro-

[1] F.O., Am., Vol. 780. No. 50. Bunch to Russell, April 19, 1861.

[2] F.O., Am., 789. Monson to Alston, received May 21.

[3] F.O., Am., 763. No. 197. Lyons to Russell, received May 26. The full statement is:

> "To an Englishman, sincerely interested in the welfare of this country, the present state of things is peculiarly painful. Abhorrence of slavery, respect for law, more complete community of race and language, enlist his sympathies on the side of the North. On the other hand, he cannot but reflect that any encouragement to the predominant war feeling in the North cannot but be injurious to both sections of the country. The prosecution of the war can lead only to the exhaustion of the North by an expenditure of life and money on an enterprise in which success and failure would be alike disastrous. It must tend to the utter devastation of the South. It would at all events occasion a suspension of Southern cultivation which would be calamitous even more to England than to the Northern States themselves."

clamation of Neutrality must have strengthened the feeling that prompt action was necessary; if received later, they gave confidence that that action had been wise. May 9, Forster asked in the Commons a series of questions as to the application of the British Foreign Enlistment Act in the American crisis. What would be the status of British citizens serving on Confederate privateers? How would the Government treat citizens who aided in equipping such privateers? Did not the Government intend to take measures to prevent the infringement of law in British ports? Here was pressure by a friend of the North to hasten an official announcement of the policy already notified to Parliament. Sir George Lewis replied stating that the Government was about to issue a general proclamation warning British subjects not to take any part in the war.[1] Similar questions were asked by Derby in the Lords on May 10, and received a similar answer.[2] The few days' delay following Russell's statement of May 6 was due to consideration given by the Law Officers to the exact form required. The Proclamation as issued was dated May 13, and was officially printed in the *London Gazette* on May 14.

In form and in substance the Proclamation of Neutrality did not differ from customary usage.[3] It spoke of the Confederacy as "states styling themselves the Confederate States of America," prohibited to Englishmen enlistment on either side, or efforts to enlist others, or equipment of ships of war, or delivery of commissions to such ships. War vessels being equipped in British ports would be seized and forfeited to the British Government. If a belligerent

[1] Hansard, 3rd. Ser., CLXII, p. 1763.

[2] *Ibid.*, pp. 1830-34. In the general discussion in the Lords there appeared disagreement as to the status of privateering. Granville, Derby, and Brougham, spoke of it as piracy. Earl Hardwicke thought privateering justifiable. The general tone of the debate, though only on this matter of international practice, was favourable to the North.

[3] For example see Hertslet, *Map of Europe by Treaty*, Vol. I, p. 698, for the Proclamation issued in 1813 during the Spanish-American colonial revolutions.

war-ship came into a British port, no change or increase of equipment was to be permitted. If a subject violated the Proclamation he was both punishable in British courts and forfeited any claim to British protection. The Parliamentary discussion on May 16 brought out more clearly and in general unanimity of opinion the policy of the Government in application of the Proclamation; the South was definitely recognized as a belligerent, but recognition of independence was for the future to determine; the right of the South to send out privateers was regretfully recognized; such privateers could not be regarded as pirates and the North would have no right to treat them as such, but if the North in defiance of international opinion did so treat them, Great Britain had at least warned its subjects that they, if engaged in service on a Southern privateer, had no claim to British protection; a blockade of the South to be respected must be effective at least to the point where a vessel attempting to pass through was likely to be captured; the plan of blockading the entire Southern coast, with its three thousand miles of coast line, was on the face of it ridiculous—evidence that Members of Parliament were profoundly ignorant of the physical geography of the Southern seaboard.[1]

The Parliamentary discussion did not reveal any partiality for one side in the American quarrel above the other. It turned wholly on legal questions and their probable application. On May 15 Russell sent to Lyons the official text of the Proclamation, but did not instruct him to communicate it officially to Seward, leaving this rather to Lyons' discretion. This was discretionary in diplomatic usage since in strict fact the Proclamation was addressed to British subjects and need not be communicated officially to the belligerents. In the result the discretion permitted to Lyons had an important bearing, for recognition of

[1] Hansard, 3rd. Ser., CLXII, pp. 2077-2088.

Southern belligerency was opposed to the theory upon which the Northern Government was attempting to proceed. Lyons did not then, or later, make official communication to Seward of the Proclamation.[1] The fact soon appeared that the United States seriously objected to the Proclamation of Neutrality, protesting first, its having been issued at all, and, in the second place, resenting what was considered its "premature" announcement by a friendly nation. This matter developed so serious a criticism by both American Government and public, both during and after the Civil War, that it requires a close examination. Did the British Government exhibit an unfriendly attitude toward the North by a "premature" Proclamation of Neutrality?

On May 13 the new American Minister landed at Liverpool, and on the morning of the fourteenth he was "ready for business" in London,[2] but the interview with Russell arranged for that day by Dallas was prevented by the illness of Russell's brother, the Duke of Bedford.[3] All that was immediately possible was to make official notification of arrival and to secure the customary audience with the Queen. This was promptly arranged, and on May 16 Adams was presented, Palmerston attending in the enforced absence of Russell. Adams' first report to Seward was therefore brief, merely noting that public opinion was "not exactly what we would wish." In this

[1] *Parliamentary Papers*, 1862, *Lords*, Vol. XXV, "Correspondence on Civil War in the United States." No. 35. Russell to Lyons, May 15, 1861. Another reason for Lyons' precaution was that while his French colleague, Mercier, had been instructed to support the British Proclamation, no official French Proclamation was issued until June 10, and Lyons, while he trusted Mercier, felt that this French delay needed some explanation. Mercier told Seward, unofficially, of his instructions and even left a copy of them, but at Seward's request made no official communication. Lyons, later, followed the same procedure. This method of dealing with Seward came to be a not unusual one, though it irritated both the British and French Ministers.

[2] *U.S. Messages and Documents*, 1861-2, p. 85. Adams to Seward, May 17, 1861.

[3] Bedford died that day.

he referred to the utterances of the press, particularly those of the *Times*, which from day to day and with increasing vigour sounded the note of strict neutrality in a "non-idealistic" war. On May 30 the *Times*, asserting that both parties in America were bidding for English support, summed up public opinion as follows:

> "We have been told, in fact, by Northern politicians, that it does not become us to be indifferent, and by Southern leaders that they are half inclined to become British once more. Both sides are bidding for us, and both sides have their partisans over here. On such perilous ground we cannot walk too warily.
>
> "For our own part, we are free to confess that the march of events has induced us to regard the dispute as a more commonplace kind of quarrel than it at first appeared to be. The real motives of the belligerents, as the truth transpires, appear to be exactly such motives as have caused wars in all times and countries. They are essentially selfish motives—that is to say, they are based upon speculations of national power, territorial aggrandizement, political advantage, and commercial gain. Neither side can claim any superiority of principle, or any peculiar purity of patriotism. . . .
>
> "We certainly cannot discover in these arguments anything to remove the case from the common category of national or monarchical quarrels. The representations of the North might be made word for word by any autocrat or conqueror desirous of 'rectifying' his frontier, consolidating his empire, or retaining a disaffected province in subjection. The manifestos of the South might be put forth by any State desirous of terminating an unpleasant connexion or exchanging union for independence. . . .
>
> "It is just such a question as has been left times out of mind in this Old World to the decision of the sword. The sword will be the arbitrator in the New World too; but the event teaches us plainly enough that Republics and Democracies enjoy no exemption from the passions and follies of humanity."

Under these impressions Adams presented himself

on May 18 for his first interview with Russell.[1] He stated that he had come with the idea that there was

> ". . . little to do beyond the duty of preserving the relations actually existing between the two nations from the risk of being unfavourably affected by the unfortunate domestic disturbances prevailing in my own country. It was not without pain that I was compelled to admit that from the day of my arrival I had felt in the proceedings of both houses of Parliament, in the language of Her Majesty's ministers, and in the tone of opinion prevailing in private circles, more of uncertainty about this than I had before thought possible."

Adams then inquired whether the replies given by Russell to Dallas refusing to indicate a policy as to recognition of the South implied a British purpose " to adopt a policy which would have the effect to widen, if not to make irreparable, a breach [between North and South] which we believed yet to be entirely manageable by ourselves."

Russell here replied that " there was no such intention " ; he had simply meant to say to Dallas that the British Government " were not disposed in any way to interfere." To this Adams answered that :

> ". . . it was deserving of grave consideration whether great caution was not to be used in adopting any course that might, even in the most indirect way, have an effect to encourage the hopes of the disaffected in America. . . . It was in this view that I must be permitted to express the great regret I had felt on learning the decision to issue the Queen's proclamation, which at once raised the insurgents to the level of a belligerent State, and still more the language used in regard to it by Her Majesty's ministers in both houses of Parliament before and since. Whatever might be the design, there could be no shadow of doubt that the effect of these events had been to encourage the friends of the disaffected here. The tone of the press and of private opinion indicated it strongly."

[1] *U.S. Messages and Documents*, 1861-2, pp. 90-96. Adams to Seward, May 21, 1861.

Russell's answer was that Adams was placing more stress on recent events than they deserved. The Government had taken the advice of the Law Officers and as a result had concluded that "as a question merely of *fact*, a war existed. . . . Under such circumstances

> it seemed scarcely possible to avoid speaking of this in the technical sense as *justum bellum*, that is, a war of two sides, without in any way implying an opinion of its justice, as well as to withhold an endeavour, so far as possible, to bring the management of it within the rules of modern civilized warfare. This was all that was contemplated by the Queen's proclamation. It was designed to show the purport of existing laws, and to explain to British subjects their liabilities in case they should engage in the war."

To this Adams answered " . . . that under other circumstances

> I should be very ready to give my cheerful assent to this view of his lordship's. But I must be permitted frankly to remark that the action taken seemed, at least to my mind, a little more rapid than was absolutely called for by the occasion. . . . And furthermore, it pronounced the insurgents to be a belligerent State before they had ever shown their capacity to maintain any kind of warfare whatever, except within one of their own harbours, and under every possible advantage. It considered them a marine power before they had ever exhibited a single privateer on the ocean. . . . The rule was very clear, that whenever it became apparent that any organized form of society had advanced so far as to prove its power to defend and protect itself against the assaults of enemies, and at the same time to manifest a capacity to maintain binding relations with foreign nations, then a measure of recognition could not be justly objected to on any side. The case was very different when such an interference should take place, prior to the establishment of the proof required, as to bring about a result which would not probably have happened but for that external agency."

This representation by the American Minister, thus

early made, contains the whole argument advanced against the British Proclamation of Neutrality, though there were many similar representations made at greater length both by Adams later, and by Seward at Washington. They are all well summarized by Bernard as "a rejection . . . of the proposition that the existence of war is a simple matter of fact, to be ascertained as other facts are—and an assertion . . . of the dogma that there can be no war, so far as foreign nations are concerned, and, therefore, no neutrality, so long as there is a sovereignty *de jure*."[1] But in this first representation Adams, in the main, laid stress upon the *haste* with which the Proclamation of Neutrality had been issued, and, by inference, upon the evidence that British sympathies were with the South.

One British journal was, indeed, at this very moment voicing exactly those opinions advanced by Adams. The *Spectator* declared that while the Proclamation, on the face of it, appeared to be one of strict neutrality, it in reality tended "directly to the benefit of the South."[2] A fortnight later this paper asserted, "The quarrel, cover it with cotton as we may, is between freedom and slavery, right and wrong, the dominion of God and the dominion of the Devil, and the duty of England, we submit, is clear." She should, even though forced to declare her neutrality, refuse for all time to recognize the slave-holding Confederacy.[3] But the *Spectator* stood nearly alone in this view. The *Saturday Review* defended in every respect the issue of the Proclamation and added, "In a short time, it will be necessary further to recognize the legitimacy of the Southern Government; but the United States have a right to require that the acknowledgment shall be postponed until the failure of the effort

[1] Bernard, *The Neutrality of Great Britain during the American Civil War*, p. 161. The author cites at length despatches and documents of the period.

[2] *Spectator*, May 18, 1861.

[3] *Spectator*, June 1, 1861.

which they assert or believe that they are about to make has resulted in an experimental proof that subjugation is impossible.[1] A few provincial papers supported the view of the *Spectator*, but they were of minor importance, and generally the press heartily approved the Proclamation.

At the time of Adams' interview with Russell on May 18 he has just received an instruction from Seward written under the impression aroused by Dallas' report of Russell's refusal on April 8 to make any pledge as to British policy on the recognition of Southern independence. Seward was very much disturbed by what Russell had said to Dallas. In this instruction, dated April 27,[2] he wrote:

> "When you shall have read the instructions at large which have been sent to you, you will hardly need to be told that these last remarks of his lordship are by no means satisfactory to this government. Her Britannic Majesty's government is at liberty to choose whether it will retain the friendship of this government by refusing all aid and comfort to its enemies, now in flagrant rebellion against it, as we think the treaties existing between the two countries require, or whether the government of Her Majesty will take the precarious benefits of a different course.
>
> "You will lose no time in making known to Her Britannic Majesty's Government that the President regards the answer of his lordship as possibly indicating a policy that this government would be obliged to deem injurious to its rights and derogating from its dignity."

Having promptly carried out these instructions, as he understood them, Adams soon began to report an improved British attitude, and especially in the Government, stating that this improvement was due, in part, to the vigour now being shown by the Northern Government, in part "to a sense that the preceding action of Her Majesty's ministers has been construed to mean more than they

[1] *Saturday Review*, June 1, 1861.
[2] *U.S. Messages and Documents*, 1861-2, p. 82.

intended by it."[1] But at Washington the American irritation was not so easily allayed. Lyons was reporting Seward and, indeed, the whole North, as very angry with the Proclamation of Neutrality.[2] On June 14, Lyons had a long conversation with Seward in which the latter stubbornly denied that the South could possess any belligerent rights. Lyons left the conference feeling that Seward was trying to divide France and England on this point, and Lyons was himself somewhat anxious because France was so long delaying her own Proclamation.[3] To meet the situation, he and Mercier, the French Minister, went the next day, June 15, on an official visit to Seward with the intention of formally presenting the British Proclamation and Thouvenel's instructions to Mercier to support it.[4] But Seward "said at once that he could not receive from us a communication founded on the assumption that

> the Southern Rebels were to be regarded as Belligerents; that this was a determination to which the Cabinet had come deliberately; that he could not admit that recent events had in any respect altered the relations between Foreign Powers and the Southern States; that he would not discuss the question with us, but that he should give instructions to the United States Ministers in London and Paris who would thus be enabled to state the reasons for the course taken by their Government to Your Lordship and to M. Thouvenel, if you should be desirous to hear them. . . . He should not take Official cognizance of the recognition of the Belligerent Rights of Southern Rebels by Great Britain and France, unless he should be forced to do so by an Official communication addressed to the Government of the United States itself."

[1] *Ibid.*, p. 98. Adams to Seward, June 7, 1861. See also p. 96, Adams to Seward, May 31, 1861.

[2] Russell Papers. Lyons to Russell, June 10, 1861.

[3] *Ibid.* Lyons to Russell, June 14, 1861.

[4] F.O., Am., Vol. 766 No. 282. Lyons to Russell, June 17, 1861. Seward's account, in close agreement with that of Lyons, is in *U.S. Messages and Documents*, 1861-2, p. 106. Seward to Adams, June 19, 1861.

In the result the two Ministers submitted their papers to Seward "for his own use only." They did not regard the moment well chosen "to be punctilious." Lyons reported that Seward's language and demeanour throughout the interview were "calm, friendly, and good humoured," but the fact remained that the United States had not been officially notified of the Proclamation of Neutrality, and that the American Government, sensitive to popular excitement in the matter and committed to the theory of a rebellion of peoples, was thus left free to continue argument in London without any necessity of making formal protest and of taking active steps to support such protest.[1] The official relation was eased by the conciliatory acquiescence of Lyons. The public anger of America, expressed in her newspapers, astonished the British press and, temporarily, made them more careful in comment on American affairs. The *Times* told its readers to keep cool. "It is plain that the utmost care and circumspection must be used by every man or party in England to avoid giving offence to either of the two incensed belligerents."[2] In answer to the Northern outcry at the lack of British sym-

[1] Bancroft in his *Seward* (II, p. 183) prints a portion of an unpublished despatch of Seward to Dayton in Paris, July 1, 1861, as "his clearest and most characteristic explanation of what the attitude of the government must be in regard to the action of the foreign nations that have recognized the belligerency of the 'insurgents.'"

> "Neither Great Britain nor France, separately nor both together, can, by any declaration they can make, impair the sovereignty of the United States over the insurgents, nor confer upon them any public rights whatever. From first to last we have acted, and we shall continue to act, for the whole people of the United States, and to make treaties for disloyal as well as loyal citizens with foreign nations, and shall expect, when the public welfare requires it, foreign nations to respect and observe the treaties.
>
> "We do not admit, and we never shall admit, even the fundamental statement you assume—namely, that Great Britain and France have recognized the insurgents as a belligerent party. True, you say they have so declared. We reply: Yes, but they have not declared so to us. You may rejoin: Their public declaration concludes the fact. We, nevertheless, reply: It must be not their declaration, but the fact, that concludes the fact."

[2] The *Times*, June 3, 1861.

pathy, it declared "Neutrality—strict neutrality—is all that the United States Government can claim."[1]

While the burden of American criticism was thus directed toward the British recognition of Southern belligerency, there were two other matters of great moment to the American view—the attitude of the British Government toward Southern privateers, and the hearing given by Russell to the Confederate envoys. On the former, Seward, on May 21, wrote to Adams: "As to the treatment of privateers in the insurgent service, you will say that this is a question exclusively our own. We treat them as pirates. They are our own citizens, or persons employed by our own citizens, preying on the commerce of our country. If Great Britain shall choose to recognize them as lawful belligerents and give them shelter from our pursuit and punishment, the law of nations affords an adequate and proper remedy."[2] This was threatening language, but was for Adams' own eye, and in the next sentence of his letter Seward stated that avoidance of friction on this point was easy, since in 1856 Great Britain had invited the United States to adhere to the Declaration of Paris everywhere abolishing privateering, and to this the United States was now ready to accede.

What Seward really meant to accomplish by this was not made clear for the question of privateering did not constitute the main point of his belligerent letter of May 21. In fact the proposed treatment of privateers as pirates might have resulted in very serious complications, for though the Proclamation of Neutrality had warned British subjects that they would forfeit any claim to protection if they engaged in the conflict, it is obvious that the hanging as a pirate of a British seaman would have aroused a national outcry almost certain to have forced the Government into

[1] *Ibid.*, June 11, 1861.
[2] *U.S. Messages and Documents*, 1861-2, p. 87.

protest and action against America. Fortunately the cooler judgment of the United States soon led to quiet abandonment of the plan of treating privateers as pirates, while on the other point of giving "shelter" to Confederate privateers Seward himself received from Lyons assurance, even before Adams had made a protest, that no such shelter would be available in British ports.[1]

In this same letter of May 21 Seward, writing of the rumour that the Southern envoys were to be received by Russell "unofficially," instructed Adams that he must use efforts to stop this and that: "You will, in any event, desist from all intercourse whatever, unofficial as well as official, with the British Government, so long as it shall continue intercourse of either kind with the domestic enemies of this country." Here was a positive instruction as to the American Minister's conduct in a given situation, and a very serious instruction, nearly equivalent to "taking leave" after a rupture of diplomatic relations, but the method to be used in avoiding if possible the necessity of the serious step was left to Adams' discretion. Well might Adams' comment, when reporting the outcome, that this was the "most delicate portion of my task."[2] Adams again went over with Russell the suspicion as to British intentions aroused in America by the Queen's Proclamation, but added that he had not been able to convince himself of the existence of an unfriendly design. "But it was not to be disguised that the fact of the continued stay of the pseudo-commissioners in this city, and still more the knowledge that they had been admitted to more or less interviews with his lordship, was calculated to excite uneasiness. Indeed, it had already given great dissatisfaction to my

[1] *Parliamentary Papers*, 1862, *Lords*, Vol. XXV. "Correspondence on Civil War in the United States." No. 56. Lyons to Russell, June 17, 1861, reporting conference with Seward on June 15.

[2] *U.S. Messages and Documents*, 1861-62, p. 104. Adams to Seward, June 14, 1861.

Government. I added, as moderately as I could, that in all frankness any further protraction of this relation could scarcely fail to be viewed by us as hostile in spirit, and to require some corresponding action accordingly." Russell replied that both France and England had long been accustomed to receive such persons unofficially, as in the case of "Poles, Hungarians, Italians, etc.," to hear what they had to say. "But this did not imply recognition in their case any more than in ours. He added that he had seen the gentlemen once some time ago, and once more some time since; he had no expectation of seeing them any more."[1]

For the moment, then, a matter which under Seward's instructions might have brought on a serious crisis was averted by the tact of Adams and the acquiescence of Russell. Yet no pledge had been given; Russell merely stated that he had "no expectation" of further interviews with the Southern commissioners; he was still ready to hear from them in writing. This caused a division of opinion between the commissioners; Yancey argued that Russell's concession to Adams was itself a violation of the neutrality the British Government had announced, and that it should be met by a formal protest. But the other members insisted on a reference to Richmond for instructions.[2] On the same day that Adams reported the result to Seward he wrote privately to his son in Boston:

[1] Bancroft, the biographer of Seward, takes the view that the protests against the Queen's Proclamation, in regard to privateering and against interviews with the Southern commissioners were all unjustifiable. The first, he says, was based on "unsound reasoning" (II, 177). On the second he quotes with approval a letter from Russell to Edward Everett, July 12, 1861, showing the British dilemma: "Unless we meant to treat them as pirates and to hang them we could not deny them belligerent rights" (II, 178). And as to the Southern commissioners he asserts that Seward, later, ceased protest and writes: "Perhaps he remembered that he himself had recently communicated, through three different intermediaries, with the Confederate commissioners to Washington, and would have met them if the President had not forbidden it." Bancroft, *Seward*, II, 179.

[2] Du Bose, *Yancey*, p. 606.

> "My position here thus far has not been difficult or painful. If I had followed the course of some of my colleagues in the diplomatic line, this country might have been on the high road to the confederate camp before now. It did not seem to me to be expedient so to play into the hands of our opponents. Although there has been and is more or less of sympathy with the slave-holders in certain circles, they are not so powerful as to overbear the general sentiment of the people. The ministry has been placed in rather delicate circumstances, when a small loss of power on either extreme would have thrown them out."[1]

In Adams' opinion the Liberals were on the whole more friendly, at least, to the North than were the Conservatives, and he therefore considered it best not to press too harshly upon the Government.

But the concluding sentence of this same letter was significant: "I wait with patience—but as yet I have not gone so far as to engage a house for more than a month at a time. . . ." He might himself be inclined to view more leniently the Proclamation of Neutrality and be able to find excuses for the alleged haste with which it had been issued, but his instructions required strong representations, especially on the latter point. Adams' report to Seward of June 14, just noted, on the interview with Russell of June 12, after treating of privateering and the Southern commissioners, turns in greater length to the alleged pledge of delay given by Russell to Dallas, and to the violation of that pledge in a hasty issue of the Proclamation. He renews attack on the line already taken on May 18.[2] From this time on, throughout and after the war, this criticism was repeatedly made and with increasing bitterness. British friends of the North joined in the American outcry.

[1] *A Cycle of Adams' Letters*, 1861-1865, Vol. I, p. 11. Adams to C. F. Adams, Jnr., June 14, 1861.

[2] See *ante*, p. 98. Russell's report to Lyons of this interview of June 12, lays special emphasis on Adams' complaint of haste. *Parliamentary Papers*, 1862, *Lords*, Vol. XXV, "Correspondence on Civil War in the United States." No. 52. Russell to Lyons, June 21, 1861.

By mere reiteration it became in the popular mind on both sides of the Atlantic an accepted and well-founded evidence of British governmental unfriendliness in May, 1861. At the conclusion of the Civil War, John Bright in Parliament, commenting on the causes of American ill-will, declared that the Government of 1861, knowing that Adams was on his way, should in mere courtesy, have waited his arrival. Then, said Bright, the Proclamation, entirely justifiable in itself, might have been issued without offence and without embittering the United States.[1]

Had in fact a "pledge to wait" been given to Dallas; and was the Proclamation hasty and premature? Russell always denied he had given any such pledge, and the text of Dallas' report of the interview of May 1 would seem to support that denial.[2] On that day Russell for the second time told Dallas that England would not commit herself, as yet, as regards Southern recognition, clearly meaning a recognition of *sovereignty*, not of belligerency, and immediately asked Dallas what the rumours of a blockade meant. Dallas replied that he had no information on this point, and Russell "acquiesced in the expediency of disregarding mere rumour, and waiting the full knowledge to be brought by my successor. The motion, therefore, of Mr. Gregory may be further postponed, at his lordship's suggestion."

The unprejudiced interpretation of this report is merely that Russell refrained from pressing Dallas about a matter—blockade—of which Dallas knew nothing, agreeing that this would be explained by Adams, and especially that he let Dallas understand that Gregory's motion, which was one for *recognizing the independence and sovereignty of the South*, would be postponed. If there was a pledge here it was a pledge not to recognize Southern sovereignty until after Adams' arrival.

[1] Hansard, 3rd. Ser., CLXXVII, pp. 1620-21, March 13, 1865.

[2] See *ante*, p. 85.

But even if there was no promise of delay "there can be no question," writes the son of Adams in a brief biography of his father, "that the proclamation of the 13th was issued with unseemly haste. . . . The purpose was manifest. It was to have the status of the Confederacy as a belligerent an accomplished fact before the arrival of the newly accredited minister. This precipitate action was chiefly significant as indicating an animus; that animus being really based on . . . the belief, already matured into a conviction, that the full recognition of the Confederacy as an independent power was merely a question of time, and probably of a very short time."[1] The author does not, however, support the contemporary American contention that *any* Proclamation was contrary to international custom and that no recognition of belligerent status was permissible to neutrals until the "insurgents" had forced the mother country itself to recognize the division as fully accomplished, even while war still continued. Indeed American practice was flatly contradictory of the argument, as in the very pertinent example of the petty Canadian rebellion of 1837, when President Van Buren had promptly issued a proclamation of neutrality. It is curious that in his several replies to Seward's complaints Russell did not quote a letter from Stevenson, the American Minister to London, addressed to Palmerston, May 22, 1838. Stevenson was demanding disavowal and disapproval of the "Caroline" affair, and incidentally he asserted as an incontrovertible principle "that civil wars are not distinguished from other wars, as to belligerent and neutral rights; that they stand upon the same ground, and are governed by the same principles; that whenever

[1] C. F. Adams, *Charles Francis Adams*, p. 172. In preparing a larger life of his father, never printed, the son later came to a different opinion, crediting Russell with foresight in hastening the Proclamation to avoid possible embarrassment with Adams on his arrival. The quotation from the printed "Life" well summarizes, however, current American opinion.

a portion of a State seek by force of arms to overthrow the Government, and maintain independence, the contest becomes one *de facto* of war."[1] This was as exact, and correct, a statement of the British view as could have been desired.[2]

The American Minister, whatever his official representation, did not then hold, privately, the view of "unfriendly animus." On July 2, 1861, his secretary son wrote: "The English are really on our side; of that I have no doubt whatever. [Later he was less sure of this.] But they thought that as a dissolution seemed inevitable and as we seemed to have made up our minds to it, that their Proclamation was just the thing to keep them straight with both sides, and when it turned out otherwise they did their best to correct their mistake."[3] The modern historical judgment of the best American writers likewise exonerates the British Government of "unfriendly animus,"[4] but is still apt to refer to the "premature" issue of the Proclamation.

This was also John Bright's view. But can Russell and the Government be criticized even as exercising an unwise (not unfriendly) haste? Henry Adams wrote that the British thought the "dissolution seemed inevitable" and "we seemed to have made up our minds to it." Certainly this was a justifiable conclusion from the events in America from Lincoln's election in November, 1860, to his inauguration in March, 1861—and even to a later date, almost in

[1] *U.S. Documents*, Ser. No. 347, Doc. 183, p. 6.

[2] The United States Supreme Court in 1862, decided that Lincoln's blockade proclamation of April 19, 1861, was "itself official and conclusive evidence . . . that a state of war existed." (Moore, Int. Law Digest, I, p. 190.)

[3] *A Cycle of Adams' Letters*, I, p. 16. Henry Adams to C. F. Adams, Jnr.

[4] Rhodes, *History of the United States*, III, p. 420 (*note*) summarizes arguments on this point, but thinks that the Proclamation might have been delayed without harm to British interests. This is perhaps true as a matter of historical fact, but such fact in no way alters the compulsion to quick action felt by the Ministry in the presence of probable *immediate* fact.

fact to the first week in April. During this period the British Ministry preserved a strictly "hands off" policy. Then, suddenly, actual conflict begins and at once each side in America issues declarations, Davis on privateering, Lincoln on blockade and piracy, indicative that *maritime* war, the form of war at once most dangerous to British interests and most likely to draw in British citizens, was the method first to be tried by the contestants. Unless these declarations were mere bluff and bluster England could not dare wait their application. She must at once warn her citizens and make clear her position as a neutral. The Proclamation was no effort "to keep straight with both sides"; it was simply the natural, direct, and prompt notification to British subjects required in the presence of a *de facto* war.

Moreover, merely as a matter of historical speculation, it was fortunate that the Proclamation antedated the arrival of Adams. The theory of the Northern administration under which the Civil War was begun and concluded was that a portion of the people of the United States were striving as "insurgents" to throw off their allegiance, and that there could be no recognition of any Southern *Government* in the conflict. In actual practice in war, the exchange of prisoners and like matters, this theory had soon to be discarded. Yet it was a far-seeing and wise theory nevertheless in looking forward to the purely domestic and constitutional problem of the return to the Union, when conquered, of the sections in rebellion. This, unfortunately, was not clear to foreign nations, and it necessarily complicated relations with them. Yet under that theory Adams had to act. Had he arrived before the Proclamation of Neutrality it is difficult to see how he could have proceeded otherwise than to protest, officially, against any British declaration of neutrality, declaring that his Government did not acknowledge a state of war as existing, and threatening to take his leave. It would have been his duty to *prevent*, if possible, the issue of the Proclamation. Dallas, fortunately, had been left uninformed and uninstructed. Adams, fortunately, arrived too late to prevent and had, therefore, merely to complain. The "premature" issue of the Proclamation averted an inevitable rupture of relations on a clash between the American theory of "no state of war" and the international fact that war existed. Had that rupture occurred, how long would the British Government and people have remained neutral, and what would have been the ultimate fate of the United States?[1]

[1] This was the later view of C. F. Adams, Jnr. He came to regard the delay in his father's journey to England as the most fortunate single incident in American foreign relations during the Civil War.

CHAPTER IV

BRITISH SUSPICION OF SEWARD

THE incidents narrated in the preceding chapter have been considered solely from the point of view of a formal American contention as to correct international practice and the British answer to that contention. In fact, however, there were intimately connected with these formal arguments and instructions of the American Secretary of State a plan of possible militant action against Great Britain and a suspicion, in British Governmental circles, that this plan was being rapidly matured. American historians have come to stigmatize this plan as " Seward's Foreign War Panacea," and it has been examined by them in great detail, so that there is no need here to do more than state its main features. That which is new in the present treatment is the British information in regard to the plan and the resultant British suspicion of Seward's intentions.

The British public, as distinguished from the Government, deriving its knowledge of Seward from newspaper reports of his career and past utterances, might well consider him as traditionally unfriendly to Great Britain. He had, in the 'fifties, vigorously attacked the British interpretation of the Clayton-Bulwer Treaty and characterized Great Britain as " the most grasping and the most rapacious Power in the world " ; he had long prophesied the ultimate annexation of Canada to the United States ; he had not disdained, in political struggles in the State of New York, to whip up, for the sake of votes, Irish antagonism to Great Britain ; and more especially and more recently he had been reported to have expressed to the Duke of Newcastle a belief that civil conflict in America could easily be avoided, or quieted, by fomenting a quarrel with England and engaging in a war against her.[1] Earlier expressions might easily be overlooked as emanating from a politician never over-careful about wounding the sensibilities of foreign nations and peoples, for he had been even more outspoken against the France of Louis Napoleon, but the Newcastle conversation stuck in the British mind as indicative of a probable animus when the politician had become the statesman responsible for foreign policy. Seward might deny, as he did, that he had ever uttered the words alleged,[2] and his friend Thurlow Weed might describe the words as "badinage," in a letter to the London *Times*,[3] but the "Newcastle story" continued to be matter for frequent comment both in the Press and in private circles.

British Ministers, however, would have paid little attention to Seward's speeches intended for home political consumption, or to a careless bit of social talk, had there not been suspicion of other and more serious evidences of unfriendliness. Lyons was an unusually able and well-informed Minister, and from the first he had pictured the leadership of Seward in the new administration at Washington, and had himself been worried by his inability to understand what policy Seward was formulating. But, in fact, he did not see clearly what was going on in the camp of the Republican party now dominant in the North. The essential feature of the situation was that Seward, generally regarded as the man whose wisdom must guide the ill-trained Lincoln, and himself thinking this to be his destined function, early found his authority challenged by other leaders, and his

[1] See *ante*, p. 80.

[2] Barnes, *Life of Thurlow Weed*, II, p. 378. Seward to Weed, December 27, 1861.

[3] *Ibid.*, p. 355. Weed's letter was on the *Trent* affair, but he went out of his way to depict Seward as attempting a bit of humour with Newcastle.

William Henry Seward
(From Lord Newton's "Life of Lord Lyons," by kind permission)

policies not certain of acceptance by the President. It is necessary to review, briefly, the situation at Washington.

Lincoln was inaugurated as President on March 4. He had been elected as a Republican by a political party never before in power. Many of the leading members of this party were drawn from the older parties and had been in administrative positions in either State or National Governments, but there were no party traditions, save the lately created one of opposition to the expansion of slavery to the Territories. All was new, then, to the men now in power in the National Government, and a new and vital issue, that of secession already declared by seven Southern States, had to be met by a definite policy. The important immediate question was as to whether Lincoln had a policy, or, if not, upon whom he would depend to guide him.

In the newly-appointed Cabinet were two men who, in popular estimate, were expected to take the lead—Chase, of Ohio, the Secretary of the Treasury, and Seward, of New York, Secretary of State. Both were experienced in political matters and both stood high in the esteem of the anti-slavery element in the North, but Seward, all things considered, was regarded as the logical leading member of the Cabinet. He had been the favoured candidate for Republican Presidential nomination in 1860, making way for Lincoln only on the theory that the latter as less Radical on anti-slavery, could be more easily elected. Also, he now held that position which by American tradition was regarded as the highest in the Cabinet.

In fact, everyone at Washington regarded it as certain that Seward would determine the policy of the new administration. Seward's own attitude is well summed up in a despatch to his Government, February 18, 1861, by Rudolph Schleiden, Minister from the Republic of Bremen. He described a conversation with Seward in regard to his relations with Lincoln :

"Seward, however, consoled himself with the clever remark, that there is no great difference between an elected president of the United States and an hereditary monarch. The latter is called to the throne through the accident of birth, the former through the chances which make his election possible. The actual direction of public affairs belongs to the leader of the ruling party, here as well as in any hereditary principality.

"The future President is a self-made man and there is therefore as little doubt of his energy as of his proverbial honesty ('honest old Abe'). It is also acknowledged that he does not lack common sense. But his other qualities for the highest office are practically unknown. His election may therefore be readily compared with a lottery. It is possible that the United States has drawn the first prize, on the other hand the gain may only have been a small one. But unfortunately the possibility is not excluded that it may have been merely a blank."

The first paragraph of this quotation reports Seward's opinion; the second is apparently Schleiden's own estimate. Two weeks later Schleiden sent home a further analysis of Lincoln:

"He makes the impression of a natural man of clear and healthy mind, great good-naturedness and best intentions. He seems to be fully conscious of the great responsibility which rests upon him. But at the same time it appears as if he had lost some of his famous firmness and resoluteness through the novelty of the conditions which surround him and the hourly renewed attempts from various sides to gain influence over him. He is therefore at present inclined to concede double weight to the superior political experience of his Secretary of State."[1]

[1] Schleiden, a native of Schleswig, was educated at the University of Berlin, and entered the Danish customs service. In the German revolution of 1848 he was a delegate from Schleswig-Holstein to the Frankfort Parliament. After the failure of that revolution he withdrew to Bremen and in 1853 was sent by that Republic to the United States as Minister. By 1860 he had become one of the best known and socially popular of the Washington diplomatic corps, holding intimate relations with leading Americans both North and South. His reports on events preceding and

This was written on March 4, and the situation was correctly described. Seward led for the moment, but his supremacy was not unchallenged and soon a decision was called for that in its final solution was to completely overthrow his already matured policy towards the seceding States. Buchanan had been pressed by South Carolina to yield possession of federal property in that State and especially to withdraw Federal troops from Fort Sumter in Charleston Harbour. After some vacillation he had refused to do this, but had taken no steps to reinforce and re-supply the weak garrison under the command of Major Anderson. On March 5, Lincoln learned that Sumter would soon have to be yielded unless reinforcements were sent. There followed ten days of delay and indecision ; then on March 15 Lincoln requested from each member of his Cabinet an opinion on what should be done. This brought to an issue the whole question of Seward's policy and leadership.

For Seward's policy, like that of Buchanan, was one of conciliatory delay, taking no steps to bring matters to an issue, and trusting to time and a sobering second thought to bring Southern leaders and people to a less violent attitude. He sincerely believed in the existence of an as yet unvoiced strong Union sentiment in the South, especially in those States which were wavering on secession. He was holding communications, through intermediaries, with certain Confederate "Commissioners" in Washington, and

during the Civil War were examined in the archives of Bremen in 1910 by Dr. Ralph H. Lutz when preparing his doctor's thesis, "Die Beziehungen zwischen Deutschland und den Vereinigten Staaten während des Sezessionskrieges" (Heidelberg, 1911). My facts with regard to Schleiden are drawn in part from this thesis, in part from an article by him, "Rudolph Schleiden and the Visit to Richmond, April 25, 1861," printed in the *Annual Report of the American Historical Association* for 1915, pp. 207-216. Copies of some of Schleiden's despatches are on deposit in the Library of Congress among the papers of Carl Schurz. Through the courtesy of Mr. Frederic Bancroft, who organized the Schurz papers, I have been permitted to take copies of a few Schleiden despatches relating to the visit to Richmond, an incident apparently unknown to history until Dr. Lutz called attention to it.

he had agents in Virginia attempting to influence that State against secession. To all these Southern representatives he now conveyed assurances quite without warrant from Lincoln, that Sumter would be evacuated, acting solely in the belief that his own " policy " would be approved by the President. His argument in reply to Lincoln's call for an opinion was positive against reinforcing Fort Sumter, and it seemed to meet, for the moment, with the approval of the majority of his Cabinet colleagues. Lincoln himself made no pertinent comment, yet did not commit himself.

There the matter rested for a time, for the Confederate Commissioners, regarding Seward's policy of delay as wholly beneficial to the maturing of Southern plans, and Seward " as their cat's-paw,"[1] did not care to press for a decision. Moreover, Seward had given a personal pledge that in case it were, after all, determined to reinforce Sumter, notification of that determination would at once be given to South Carolina. The days went by, and it was not until the last week of March that Lincoln, disillusioned as to the feasibility of Seward's policy of conciliation, reached the conclusion that in his conception of his duty as President of the United States he must defend and retain Federal forts, or attempt to retain them, for the preservation of the Union, and decided to reinforce Fort Sumter. On March 29, the Cabinet assembled at noon and learned Lincoln's determination.

This was a sharp blow to Seward's prestige in the Cabinet; it also threatened his " peaceful " policy. Yet he did not as yet understand fully that either supreme leadership, or control of policy, had been assumed by Lincoln. On April 1 he drafted that astonishing document entitled, " Some Thoughts for the President's Consideration," which at once reveals his alarm and his supreme personal self-confidence. This document begins, " We are at the end of a month's administration, and yet without a policy

[1] This is Bancroft's expression. *Seward*, II, p. 118.

either domestic or foreign." It then advocates as a domestic policy, "*Change The Question Before The Public From One Upon Slavery, Or About Slavery*, for a question upon *Union or Disunion*." Then in a second section, headed "For Foreign Nations," there followed:

> "I would demand explanations from Spain and France, categorically, at once.
> "I would seek explanations from Great Britain and Russia, and send agents into Canada, Mexico and Central America to rouse a vigorous continental spirit of independence on this continent against European intervention.
> "And, if satisfactory explanations are not received from Spain and France,
> "Would convene Congress and declare war against them.
> "But whatever policy we adopt, there must be energetic prosecution of it.
> "For this purpose it must be somebody's business to pursue and direct it incessantly.
> "Either the President must do it himself, and be all the while active in it, or
> "Devolve it on some member of his Cabinet. Once adopted, debates on it must end, and all agree and abide.
> "It is not in my especial province;
> "But I neither seek to evade nor assume responsibility."[1]

Lincoln's reply of the same day, April 1, was characteristically gentle, yet no less positive and definite to any save one obsessed with his own superior wisdom. Lincoln merely noted that Seward's "domestic policy" was exactly his own, except that he did not intend to abandon Fort Sumter. As to the warlike foreign policy Lincoln pointed out that this would be a sharp reversal of that already being prepared in circulars and instructions to Ministers abroad. This was, indeed, the case, for the first instructions, soon despatched, were drawn on lines of recalling to foreign powers their established and long-continued friendly

[1] Lincoln, *Works*, II, 29.

relations with the United States. Finally, Lincoln stated as to the required "guiding hand," "I remark that if this must be done, I must do it. . . . I wish, and suppose I am entitled to have, the advice of all the Cabinet."[1]

This should have been clear indication of Lincoln's will to direct affairs, and even to Seward would have been sufficient had he not, momentarily, been so disturbed by the wreck of his pacific policy toward the South, and as yet so ignorant of the strength of Lincoln's quiet persistence. As it was, he yielded on the immediate issue, the relief of Sumter (though attempting to divert reinforcements to another quarter) but did not as yet wholly yield either his policy of conciliation and delay, nor give up immediately his insane scheme of saving the Union by plunging it into a foreign war. He was, in fact, still giving assurances to the Confederate commissioners, through indirect channels, that he could and would prevent the outbreak of civil war, and in this confidence that his ideas would finally control Lincoln he remained up to the second week in April. But on April 8 the first of the ships despatched to the aid of Sumter left New York, and on that day Governor Pickens of South Carolina was officially notified of the Northern purpose. This threw the burden of striking the first blow upon the South; if Southern threats were now made good, civil war seemed inevitable, and there could be no peaceful decision of the quarrel.

The reinforcements did not arrive in time. Fort Sumter, after a day and a half of dogged fighting, was surrendered to the enemy on April 13—for as an enemy in arms the South now stood. The fall of Sumter changed, as in a moment, the whole attitude of the Northern people. There was now a nearly unanimous cry for the preservation of the Union *by force*. Yet Seward still clung, privately, to his belief that even now the "sober second thought" of the

[1] *Ibid.*, p. 30.

South would offer a way out toward reunion without war. In official utterances and acts he was apparently in complete harmony with the popular will to reconquer the South. Davis' proclamation on marque and privateering, of April 17, was answered by the Lincoln blockade proclamation of April 19. But Virginia had not yet officially seceded, and until this occurred there seemed to Seward at least one last straw of conciliation available. In this situation Schleiden, Minister for Bremen, came to Seward on the morning of April 24 and offered his services as a mediator.[1]

Schleiden's idea was that an armistice be agreed upon with the South until the Northern Congress should meet in July, thus giving a breathing spell and permitting saner second judgment to both sides. He had consulted with his Prussian colleague, who approved, and he found Seward favourable to the plan. Alexander H. Stephens, Vice-President of the Confederacy, was then at Richmond, and to him, as an old friend, Schleiden proposed to go and make the same appeal. Seward at once took Schleiden to see Lincoln. The three men, with Chase (and the Prussian Minister) were the only ones in the secret. Lincoln's first comment was that he was " willing to make an attempt of contributing to the prevention of bloodshed and regretted that Schleiden had not gone to Richmond without consulting him or Seward." Lincoln further stated that " he did not have in mind any aggression against the Southern States, but merely the safety of the Government in the Capitol and the possibility to govern everywhere," a concluding phrase that should have enlightened Schleiden as to Lincoln's determination to preserve the Union. Lincoln said he could neither authorize negotiations nor invite proposals, but that he would gladly consider any such proposals voluntarily made. Schleiden asked for a definite

[1] For references to this whole matter of Schleiden's visit to Richmond see *ante*, p. 116, note 1.

statement as to whether Lincoln would recall the blockade proclamation and sign an armistice if Davis would recall the letters of marque proclamation, but Lincoln refused to commit himself.

This was scant encouragement from the President, but Seward still thought something might result from the venture, and on that evening, April 24, Schleiden started for Richmond, being provided by Seward with a pass through the Union lines. He arrived on the afternoon of the twenty-fifth, but even before reaching the city was convinced that his mission would be a failure. All along his journey, at each little station, he saw excited crowds assembled enthusiastic for secession, bands of militia training, and every indication of preparation for war. Already, on that same day, the Virginia secession ordinance had been published, and the State convention had ratified the provisional constitution of the Southern Confederacy. Schleiden immediately notified Stephens of his presence in Richmond and desire for an interview, and was at once received. The talk lasted three hours. Stephens was frank and positive in asserting the belief that " all attempts to settle peacefully the differences between the two sections were futile." Formal letters were exchanged after this conference, but in these the extent to which Stephens would go was to promise to use his influence in favour of giving consideration to any indication made by the North of a desire " for an amicable adjustment of the questions at issue," and he was positive that there could be no return of the South to the Union.

On the afternoon of April 27 Schleiden was back in Washington. He found that three days had made a great change in the sentiment of the Capitol. " During my short absence," he wrote, " many thousands of volunteers had arrived from the North. There was not only a feeling of security noticeable, but even of combativeness." He found

Seward not at all disposed to pursue the matter, and was not given an opportunity to talk to Lincoln; therefore, he merely submitted copies of the letters that had passed between him and Stephens, adding for himself that the South was arming *because* of Lincoln's proclamation calling for volunteers. Seward replied on April 29, stating his personal regards and that he had no fault to find with Schleiden's efforts, but concluding that Stephens' letters gave no ground for action since the "Union of these States is the supreme as it is the organic law of this country," and must be maintained.

This adventure to Richmond by the Minister of Bremen may be regarded as Seward's last struggle to carry out his long-pursued policy of conciliatory delay. He had not officially sent Schleiden to Richmond, but he had grasped eagerly at the opening and had encouraged and aided Schleiden in his journey. Now, by April 27, hope had vanished, and Seward's "domestic policy," as set forth in his "Thoughts for the President's Consideration" on April 1, was discredited, and inevitably, in some measure, their author also. The dates are important in appreciating Seward's purposes. On April 27, the day of Schleiden's return to Washington, there was sent to Adams that "sharp" despatch, taking issue with British action as foreshadowed by Dallas on April 9, and concluding by instructing Adams to lose no time in warning Russell that such action would be regarded by the United States as "injurious to its rights and derogating from its dignity."[1] It appears, therefore, that Seward, defeated on one line of "policy," eager to regain prestige, and still obsessed with the idea that some means could yet be found to avert

[1] *U.S. Messages and Documents*, 1861-2, p. 82. This, and other despatches have been examined at length in the previous chapter in relation to the American protest on the Queen's Proclamation of Neutrality. In the present chapter they are merely noted again in their bearing on Seward's "foreign war policy."

domestic conflict, was, on April 27, beginning to pick at those threads which, to his excited thought, might yet save the Union through a foreign war. He was now seeking to force the acceptance of the second, and alternative, portion of his "Thoughts for the President."

Seward's theory of the cementing effect of a foreign war was no secret at Washington. As early as January 26 he had unfolded to Schleiden this fantastic plan. "If the Lord would only give the United States an excuse for a war with England, France, or Spain," he said "that would be the best means of re-establishing internal peace."[1] Again, on February 10, he conversed with Schleiden on the same topic, and complained that there was no foreign complication offering an excuse for a break. Lyons knew of this attitude, and by February 4 had sent Russell a warning, to which the latter had replied on February 20 that England could afford to be patient for a time but that too much "blustering demonstration" must not be indulged in. But the new administration, as Lincoln had remarked in his reply to Seward on April 1, had taken quite another line, addressing foreign powers in terms of high regard for established friendly relations. This was the tone of Seward's first instruction to Adams, April 10,[2] in the concluding paragraph of which Seward wrote, "The United States are not indifferent to the circumstances of common descent, language, customs, sentiments, and religion, which recommend a closer sympathy between themselves and Great Britain than either might expect in its intercourse with any other nation." True, on this basis, Seward claimed a special sympathy from Great Britain for the United States, that is to

[1] Quoted by Lutz, *Am. Hist. Assn. Rep.* 1915, p. 210.

[2] *U.S. Messages and Documents*, 1861-2, p. 80. This despatch was read by Seward on April 8 to W. H. Russell, correspondent of the *Times*, who commented that it contained some elements of danger to good relations, but it is difficult to see to what he could have had objection.—Russell, *My Diary*, I, p. 103.

say, the North, but most certainly the tone of this first instruction was one of established friendship.

Yet now, April 27, merely on learning from Dallas that Russell "refuses to pledge himself" on British policy, Seward resorts to threats. What other explanation is possible except that, seeking to save his domestic policy of conciliation and to regain his leadership, he now was adventuring toward the application of his "foreign war panacea" idea. Lyons quickly learned of the changed tone, and that England, especially, was to hear American complaint. On May 2 Lyons wrote to Russell in cypher characterizing Seward as "arrogant and reckless toward Foreign Powers."[1] Evidently Seward was making little concealment of his belligerent attitude, and when the news was received of the speeches in Parliament of the first week in May by which it became clear that Great Britain would declare neutrality and was planning joint action with France, he became much excited. On May 17 he wrote a letter home exhibiting, still, an extraordinary faith in his own wisdom and his own foreign policy.

> "A country so largely relying on my poor efforts to save it had [has] refused me the full measure of its confidence, needful to that end. I am a chief reduced to a subordinate position, and surrounded by a guard, to see that I do not do too much for my country, lest some advantage may revert indirectly to my own fame.
>
> ". . . They have misunderstood things fearfully, in Europe, Great Britain is in danger of sympathizing so much with the South, for the sake of peace and cotton, as to drive us to make war against her, as the ally of the traitors. . . . I am trying to get a bold remonstrance through the Cabinet before it is too late."[2]

The "bold remonstrance" was the famous "Despatch No. 10," of May 21, already commented upon in the pre-

[1] Russell Papers.
[2] Bancroft, *Seward*, II, p. 169.

ceding chapter. But as sent to Adams it varied in very important details from the draft submitted by Seward to Lincoln.[1]

Seward's draft was not merely a "remonstrance"; it was a challenge. Its language implied that the United States desired war, and Seward's plan was to have Adams read the despatch to Russell, give him a copy of it, and then discontinue diplomatic relations so long as Russell held either official or unofficial intercourse with the Southern Commissioners. This last instruction was, indeed, retained in the final form of the despatch, but here, as elsewhere, Lincoln modified the stiff expressions of the original. Most important of all, he directed Adams to consider the whole despatch as for his own guidance, relying on his discretion. The despatch, as amended, began with the statement that the United States "neither means to menace Great Britain nor to wound the sensibilities of that or any other European nation. . . . The paper itself is not to be read or shown to the British Secretary of State, nor any of its positions to be prematurely, unnecessarily, or indiscreetly made known. But its spirit will be your guide."[2] Thus were the teeth skil-

[1] Yet at this very time Seward was suggesting, May 14, to Prussia, Great Britain, France, Russia and Holland a joint naval demonstration with America against Japan because of anti-foreign demonstrations in that country. This has been interpreted as an attempt to tie European powers to the United States in such a way as to hamper any friendly inclination they may have entertained toward the Confederacy (Treat, *Japan and the United States*, 1853-1921, pp. 49-50. Also Dennet, "Seward's Far Eastern Policy," in *Am. Hist. Rev.*, Vol. XXVIII, No. 1. Dennet, however, also regards Seward's overture as in harmony with his determined policy in the Far East.) Like Seward's overture, made a few days before, to Great Britain for a convention to guarantee the independence of San Domingo (F.O., Am., Vol. 763, No. 196, Lyons to Russell, May 12, 1861) the proposal on Japan seems to me to have been an erratic feeling-out of international attitude while in the process of developing a really serious policy—the plunging of America into a foreign war.

[2] *U.S. Messages and Documents*, 1861-2, p. 88. The exact facts of Lincoln's alteration of Despatch No. 10, though soon known in diplomatic circles, were not published until the appearance in 1890 of Nicolay and Hay's *Lincoln*, where the text of a portion of the original draft, with Lincoln's changes were printed (IV, p. 270). Gideon Welles, Secretary of the Navy in Lincoln's Cabinet, published a short book in 1874, *Lincoln and Seward*, in which

fully drawn from the threat of war. Even the positive instructions, later in the despatch, as to the Southern Commissioners, need not have been acted upon by Adams had he not thought it wise to do so. But even with alterations, the American remonstrance was so bold as to alarm Adams. On first perusual he wrote in his diary, June 10, "The Government seems almost ready to declare war with all the powers of Europe, and almost instructs me to withdraw from communication with the Ministers here in a certain contingency. . . . I scarcely know how to understand Mr. Seward. The rest of the Government may be demented for all I know; but he surely is calm and wise. My duty here is in so far as I can do it honestly to prevent the irritation from coming to a downright quarrel. It seems to me like throwing the game into the hands of the enemy."[2]

Adams, a sincere admirer of Seward, was in error as to the source of American belligerent attitude. Fortunately, his judgment of what was wise at the moment coincided with that of Lincoln's—though of this he had no knowledge. In the event Adams' skilful handling of the situation resulted favourably—even to the cessation of intercourse between Russell and the Southern Commissioners. For his part, Lincoln, no more than earlier, was to be hurried into foreign complications, and Seward's "foreign war panacea" was stillborn.

The incident was a vital one in the Northern administration, for Seward at last realized that the President intended to control policy, and though it was yet long before he came to appreciate fully Lincoln's customary calm judgment, he did understand the relation now established between

the story was told, but without dates and so vaguely that no attention was directed to it. Apparently the matter was not brought before the Cabinet and the contents of the despatch were known only to Lincoln, Seward, and the Chairman of the Senate Committee on Foreign Relations, Sumner.

[2] C. F. Adams, "Seward and the Declaration of Paris," p. 21. Reprint from *Mass. Hist. Soc. Proceedings*, XLVI, pp. 23-81.

himself and his chief. Henceforth, he obeyed orders, though free in suggestion and criticism, always welcome to Lincoln. The latter, avowedly ignorant of diplomacy, gladly left details to Seward, and the altered despatch, far from making relations difficult, rendered them simple and easy, by clearing the atmosphere. But it was otherwise with Foreign Ministers at Washington, for even though there was soon a "leak" of gossip informing them of what had taken place in regard to Despatch No. 10, they one and all were fearful of a recovery of influence by Seward and of a resumption of belligerent policy. This was particularly true of Lord Lyons, for rumour had it that it was against England that Seward most directed his enmity. There resulted for British diplomats both at Washington and in London a deep-seated suspicion of Seward, long after he had made a complete face-about in policy. This suspicion influenced relations greatly in the earlier years of the Civil War.

On May 20, the day before Seward's No. 10 was dated, Lyons wrote a long twelve-page despatch to Russell, anxious, and very full of Seward's warlike projects. "The President is, of course, wholly ignorant of foreign countries, and of foreign affairs." "Seward, having lost strength by the failure of his peace policy, is seeking to recover influence by leading a foreign war party; no one in the Cabinet is strong enough to combat him." Britain, Lyons thought, should maintain a stiff attitude, prepare to defend Canada, and make close contacts with France. He was evidently anxious to impress upon Russell that Seward really might mean war, but he declared the chief danger to lie in the fact of American belief that England and France could not be driven into war with the United States, and that they would submit to any insult. Lyons urged some action, or declaration (he did not know what), to correct this false impression.[1]

[1] F.O., Am., Vol. 764, No. 206, Confidential.

Again, on the next day, May 21, the information in his official despatch was repeated in a private letter to Russell, but Lyons here interprets Seward's threats as mere bluster. Yet he is not absolutely sure of this, and in any case insists that the best preventative of war with the United States is to show that England is ready for it.[1]

It was an anxious time for the British Minister in Washington. May 22, he warned Sir Edmund Head, Governor of Canada, urging him to make defensive preparation.[2] The following day he dilated to Russell, privately, on "the difficulty of keeping Mr. Seward within the bounds of decency even in ordinary social intercourse . . ."[3] and in an official communication of this same day he records Washington rumours of a belligerent despatch read by Seward before the Cabinet, of objections by other members, and that Seward's insistence has carried the day.[4] That Seward was, in fact, still smarting over his reverse is shown by a letter, written on this same May 23, to his intimate friend and political adviser, Thurlow Weed, who had evidently cautioned him against precipitate action. Seward wrote, "The European phase is bad. But your apprehension that I may be too decisive alarms me more. Will you consent, or advise us to consent, that Adams and Dayton have audiences and compliments in the Ministers' Audience Chamber, and Toombs' [Confederate Secretary of State] emissaries have access to his bedroom?"[5]

Two interpretations are possible from this: either

[1] Russell Papers. This letter has been printed, in part, in Newton, *Lyons*, I, 41.

[2] Lyons Papers.

[3] *Ibid.*, Lyons to Russell, May 23, 1861.

[4] F.O., Am., Vol. 764, No. 209, Confidential, Lyons to Russell, May 23, 1861. A brief "extract" from this despatch was printed in the British *Parliamentary Papers*, 1862, *Lords*, Vol. XXV. "Correspondence on Civil War in the United States," No. 48. The "extract" in question consists of two short paragraphs only, printed, without any indication of important elisions, in each of the paragraphs,

[5] Bancroft, *Seward*, II, p. 174.

that Seward knowing himself defeated was bitter in retrospect, or that he had not yet yielded his will to that of Lincoln, in spite of the changes made in his Despatch No. 10. The former interpretation seems the more likely, for though Seward continued to write for a time "vigorous" despatches to Adams, they none of them approached the vigour of even the amended despatch. Moreover, the exact facts of the Cabinet of May 21, and the complete reversal of Seward's policy were sufficiently known by May 24 to have reached the ears of Schleiden, who reported them in a letter to Bremen of that date.[1] And on the same day Seward himself told Schleiden that he did "not fear any longer that it would come to a break with England."[2] On May 27 Lyons himself, though still suspicious that an attempt was being made to separate France and England, was able to report a better tone from Seward.[3]

British Ministers in London were not so alarmed as was Lyons, but they were disturbed, nevertheless, and long preserved a suspicion of the American Secretary of State. May 23, Palmerston wrote to Russell in comment on Lyons' despatch of May 2: "These communications are very unpleasant. It is not at all unlikely that either from foolish and uncalculating arrogance and self-sufficiency or from political calculation Mr. Seward may bring on a quarrel with us."[4] He believed that more troops ought

[1] Lutz, "Notes." The source of Schleiden's information is not given in his despatch. He was intimate with many persons closely in touch with events, especially with Sumner, Chairman of the Senate Committee on Foreign Relations, and with Blair, a member of the Cabinet.

[2] *Ibid.*, Schleiden to Republic of Bremen, May 27, 1861.

[3] Bancroft, *Seward*, II, p. 179, sets the date as June 8 when Seward's instructions for England and France show that he had "recovered his balance." This is correct for the change in tone of despatches, but the acceptance of Lincoln's policy must have been immediate. C. F. Adams places the date for Seward's complete change of policy much later, describing his "war mania" as lasting until the Northern defeat of Bull Run, July 21. I think this an error, and evidence that it is such appears later in the present chapter. See Charles Francis Adams, "Seward and the Declaration of Paris," *Mass. Hist. Soc. Proceedings*, XLVI, pp. 23-81.

[4] Russell Papers.

to be sent to Canada, as a precautionary measure, but, he added, "the main Force for Defence must, of course, be local"—a situation necessarily a cause for anxiety by British Ministers. Russell was less perturbed. He had previously expressed appreciation of Adams' conduct, writing to Lyons: "Mr. Adams has made a very favourable impression on my mind as a calm and judicious man,"[1] and he now wrote: "I do not think Mr. Seward's colleagues will encourage him in a game of brag with England. . . . I am sorry Seward turns out so reckless and ruthless. Adams seems a sensible man."[2] But at Washington Lyons was again hot on the trail of warlike rumours. As a result of a series of conversations with Northern politicians, not Cabinet members, he sent a cipher telegram to Russell on June 6, stating: "No new event has occurred but sudden declaration of war by the United States against Great Britain appears to me by no means impossible, especially so long as Canada seems open to invasion."[3] This was followed two days later by a despatch dilating upon the probability of war, and ending with Lyons' opinion of how it should be conducted. England should strike at once with the largest possible naval force and bring the war to an end before the United States could prepare. Otherwise, "the spirit, the energy, and the resources of this people" would make them difficult to overcome. England, on her part, must be prepared to suffer severely from American privateers, and she would be forced to help the South, at least to the extent of keeping Southern ports open. Finally, Lyons concluded, all of this letter and advice were extremely distasteful to him, yet he felt compelled to write it by the seriousness of the situation. Nevertheless, he would exert every effort and use every method to conciliate America.[4]

[1] Lyons Papers, May 21, 1861.
[2] *Ibid.*, Russell to Lyons, May 25, 1861.
[3] F.O., Am., Vol. 765, No. 253.
[4] *Ibid.*, No. 263, Lyons to Russell, June 8, 1861.

In truth, it was not any further belligerent talk by Seward that had so renewed Lyons' anxiety. Rather it was the public and Press reception of the news of the Queen's Proclamation of Neutrality. The Northern people, counting beyond all reasonable expectation upon British sympathy on anti-slavery grounds, had been angrily disappointed, and were at the moment loudly voicing their vexation. Had Seward not already been turned from his foreign war policy he now would have received strong public support in it. But he made no effort to utilize public excitement to his own advantage in the Cabinet. In England, Adams was able to report on June 14 that Russell had no intention of holding further interviews with the Southern Commissioners,[1] but before anyone in Washington could learn of this there was general knowledge of a changed tone from the Secretary of State, and Lyons' fears were considerably allayed. On June 15, occurred that interview between Seward, Lyons, and Mercier, in which Seward had positively refused to receive the Queen's Proclamation, but had throughout evinced the greatest courtesy and goodwill. Lyons so reported the conversation.[2] June 15 may, in fact, be taken as the date when Lyons ceased to be alarmed over an immediate war. Possibly he found it a little difficult to report so sudden a shift from stormy to fair weather. June 21, he wrote that the "lull" was still continuing.[3] June 24, he at last learned and described at length the details of Lincoln's alteration of Despatch No. 10.[4] He

[1] See *ante*, p. 106.

[2] See *ante*, p. 102. Bancroft, *Seward*, II, p. 181, using Seward's description to Adams (*U.S. Messages and Documents*, 1861-2, p. 106) of this interview expands upon the Secretary's skill in thus preventing a joint notification by England and France of their intention to act together. He rightly characterizes Seward's tactics as "diplomatic skill of the best quality." But in Lyons' report the emphasis is placed upon Seward's courtesy in argument, and Lyons felt that the knowledge of British-French joint action had been made sufficiently clear by his taking Mercier with him and by their common though unofficial representation to Seward.

[3] Russell Papers. To Russell.

[4] *Ibid*. To Russell. Lyons' source of information was not revealed,

did not know the exact date but he expressed the opinion that "a month or three weeks ago" war was very near—a misjudgment, since it should be remembered that war seemed advisable to one man only—Seward; and that on this issue he had been definitely cast down from his self-assumed leadership into the ranks of Lincoln's lieutenants.

Lyons was, then, nearly a month behindhand in exact knowledge of American foreign policy toward England, and he was in error in thinking that an American attack on England was either imminent or intended. Nevertheless, he surely was excusable, considering Seward's prestige and Lincoln's lack of it, in reporting as he did. It was long, indeed, before he could escape from suspicion of Seward's purposes, though dropping, abruptly, further comment on the chances of war. A month later, on July 20, he wrote that Seward had himself asked for a confidential and unofficial interview, in order to make clear that there never had been any intention of stirring agitation against England. Personally, Seward took credit for avoiding trouble "by refusing to take official cognizance of the recognition [by England] of the belligerent rights of the South," and he asked Lyons to explain to Russell that previous strong language was intended merely to make foreign Powers understand the intensity of Northern feeling.[1]

Lyons put no faith in all this but was happy to note the change, mistakenly attributing it to England's "stiff tone," and not at all to the veto of the President. Since Lyons himself had gone to the utmost bounds in seeking conciliation (so he had reported), and, in London, Russell also had taken no forward step since the issue of the Queen's Proclamation—indeed, had rather yielded somewhat to Adams' representations—it is not clear in what the "stiff tone" consisted.

Indeed, the cause of Seward's explanation to Lyons

[1] *Ibid.* To Russell.

was the receipt of a despatch from Adams, dated June 28, in which the latter had reported that all was now smooth sailing. He had told Russell that the knowledge in Washington of the result of their previous interviews had brought satisfaction, and Russell, for his part, said that Lyons had "learned, through another member of the diplomatic corps, that no further expression of opinion on the subject in question would be necessary."[1] This referred, presumably, to the question of British intention, for the future, in relation to the Proclamation of Neutrality. Adams wrote: "This led to the most frank and pleasant conversation which I have yet had with his lordship. . . . I added that I believed the popular feeling in the United States would subside the moment that all the later action on this side was known. . . . My own reception has been all that I could desire. I attach value to this, however, only as it indicates the establishment of a policy that will keep us at peace during the continuance of the present convulsion." In reply to Adams' despatch, Seward wrote on July 21, the day after his interview with Lyons, arguing at great length the American view that the British Proclamation of Neutrality in a domestic quarrel was not defensible in international law. There was not now, nor later, any yielding on this point. But, for the present, this was intended for Adams' eye alone, and Seward prefaced his argument by a disclaimer, much as stated to Lyons, of any ill-will to Great Britain:

> "I may add, also, for myself, that however otherwise I may at any time have been understood, it has been an earnest and profound solicitude to avert from foreign war; that alone has prompted the emphatic and sometimes, perhaps, impassioned remonstrances I have hitherto made against any form or measure of recognition of the insurgents by the government of Great Britain. I write in the same spirit now; and I invoke on the part of the British govern-

[1] *U.S. Messages and Documents*, 1861-2, p. 110.

ment, as I propose to exercise on my own, the calmness which all counsellors ought to practise in debates which involve the peace and happiness of mankind."[1]

Diplomatic correspondence couched in the form of platform oratory leads to the suspicion that the writer is thinking, primarily, of the ultimate publication of his despatches. Thus Seward seems to have been laying the ground for a denial that he had ever developed a foolish foreign war policy. History pins him to that folly. But in another respect the interview with Lyons on July 20 and the letter to Adams of the day following overthrow for both Seward and for the United States the accusations sometimes made that it was the Northern disaster at Bull Run, July 21, in the first pitched battle with the South, which made more temperate the Northern tone toward foreign powers.[2] It is true that the despatch to Adams was not actually sent until July 26, but internal evidence shows it to have been written on the 21st before there was any news from the battle-field, and the interview with Lyons on the 20th proves that the military set-back had no influence on Seward's friendly expressions. Moreover, these expressions officially made were but a delayed voicing of a determination of policy arrived at many weeks earlier. The chronology of events and despatches cited in this chapter will have shown that the refusal of Lincoln to follow Seward's leadership, and the consequent lessening of the latter's "high tone," preceded any news whatever from England, lightening the first impressions. The Administration at Washington did not on May 21, even know that England had issued a Proclamation of Neutrality; it knew merely of Russell's statement that one would have to be issued; and the friendly explanations of Russell to Adams were not received in Washington until the month following.

[1] *Ibid.*, p. 118. To Adams.

[2] C. F. Adams, "Seward and the Declaration of Paris." p. 29, and so argued by the author throughout this monograph. I think this an error.

In itself, Seward's "foreign war panacea" policy does not deserve the place in history usually accorded it as a moment of extreme crisis in British-American relations. There was never any danger of war from it, for Lincoln nipped the policy in the bud. The public excitement in America over the Queen's Proclamation was, indeed, intense; but this did not alter the Governmental attitude. In England all that the public knew was this American irritation and clamour. The London press expressed itself a bit more cautiously, for the moment, merely defending the necessity of British neutrality.[1] But if regarded from the effect upon British Ministers the incident was one of great, possibly even vital, importance in the relations of the two countries. Lyons had been gravely anxious to the point of alarm. Russell, less acutely alarmed, was yet seriously disturbed. Both at Washington and in London the suspicion of Seward lasted throughout the earlier years of the war, and to British Ministers it seemed that at any moment he might recover leadership and revert to a dangerous mood. British attitude toward America was affected in two opposite ways; Britain was determined not to be bullied, and Russell himself sometimes went to the point of arrogance in answer to American complaints; this was an unfortunate result. But more fortunate, and *also a result*, was the British Government's determination to step warily in the American conflict and to give no just cause, unless on due consideration of policy, for a rupture of relations with the United States. Seward's folly in May of 1861, from every angle but a short-lived "brain-storm," served America well in the first years of her great crisis.

[1] The *Spectator*, friend of the North, argued, June 15, 1861, that the Queen's Proclamation was the next best thing for the North to a definite British alliance. Southern privateers could not now be obtained from England. And the United States was surely too proud to accept direct British aid.

CHAPTER V

THE DECLARATION OF PARIS NEGOTIATION

If regarded merely from the view-point of strict chronology there accompanied Seward's "foreign war" policy a negotiation with Great Britain which was of importance as the first effort of the American Secretary of State to bring European nations to a definite support of the Northern cause. It was also the first negotiation undertaken by Adams in London, and as a man new to the diplomatic service he attached to it an unusual importance, even, seemingly, to the extent of permitting personal chagrin at the ultimate failure of the negotiation to distort his usually cool and fair judgment. The matter in question was the offer of the United States to accede by a convention to the Declaration of Paris of 1856, establishing certain international rules for the conduct of maritime warfare.

This negotiation has received scant attention in history. It failed to result in a treaty, therefore it has appeared to be negligible. Yet it was at the time of very great importance in affecting the attitude toward each other of Great Britain and the United States, and of the men who spoke for their respective countries. The bald facts of the negotiation appear with exactness in Moore's *Digest of International Law*.[1] but without comment as to motives, and, more briefly, in Bernard's *Neutrality of Great Britain during the American Civil War*,[2] at the conclusion of which the author

[1] VII., pp. 568-583.
[2] Ch. 8.

writes, with sarcasm, " I refrain from any comment on this negotiation."[1] Nicolay and Hay's *Lincoln*, and Rhodes' *United States*, give the matter but passing and inadequate treatment. It was reviewed in some detail in the American argument before the Geneva court of arbitration in the case of the *Alabama*, but was there presented merely as a part of the general American complaint of British neutrality. In fact, but three historical students, so far as the present writer has been able to discover, have examined this negotiation in detail and presented their conclusions as to purposes and motives—so important to an understanding of British intentions at the moment when the flames of civil war were rapidly spreading in America.

These three, each with an established historical reputation, exhibit decided differences in interpretation of diplomatic incidents and documents. The first careful analysis was presented by Henry Adams, son of the American Minister in London during the Civil War, and then acting as his private secretary, in his *Historical Essays*, published in 1891; the second study is by Bancroft, in his *Life of Seward*, 1900; while the third is by Charles Francis Adams (also son of the American Minister), who, in his *Life* of his father, published 1900, gave a chapter to the subject and treated it on lines similar to those laid down by his brother Henry, but who, in 1912, came to the conclusion, through further study, that he had earlier been in error and developed a very different view in a monograph entitled, " Seward and the Declaration of Paris."

If these historiographic details seem unduly minute, partaking as they do of the nature of a foot-note, in a work otherwise general in treatment, the author's answer is that the personality of two of the writers mentioned and their intimate knowledge of the effect of the negotiation upon the mind of the American Minister in London are themselves

[1] *Ibid.*, p. 181.

C. F. Adams

(From a photograph in the United States Embassy, London, by kind permission)

important historical data ; a further answer is the fact that the materials now available from the British Foreign Office archives throw much new light both on the course of the negotiation and on British purposes. It is here planned, therefore, first to review the main facts as previously known ; second, to summarize the arguments and conclusions of the three historians ; third, to re-examine the negotiation in the light of the new material; and, finally, to express an opinion on its conduct and conclusions as an evidence of British policy.

In 1854, during the Crimean War, Great Britain and France, the chief maritime belligerents engaged against Russia, voluntarily agreed to respect neutral commerce under either the neutral's or the enemy's flag. This was a distinct step forward in the practice of maritime warfare, the accepted international rules of which had not been formally altered since the Napoleonic period. The action of Great Britain was due in part, according to a later statement in Parliament by Palmerston, March 18, 1862, to a fear that unless a greater respect were paid than formerly to neutral rights, the Allies would quickly win the ill-will of the United States, then the most powerful maritime neutral, and would run the danger of forcing that country into belligerent alliance with Russia.[1] No doubt there were other reasons, also, for the barbarous rules and practices of maritime warfare in earlier times were by now regarded as semi-civilized by the writers of all nations. Certainly the action of the belligerents in 1854 met with general approval and in the result was written into international law at the Congress of Paris in 1856, where, at the conclusion of the war, the belligerents and some leading neutrals were gathered.

The Declaration of Paris on maritime warfare covered four points :

[1] Henry Adams, *Historical Essays*, p. 275.

"1. Privateering is, and remains, abolished.

"2. The neutral flag covers enemy's goods, with the exception of contraband of war.

"3. Neutral goods, with the exception of contraband of war, are not liable to capture under enemy's flag.

"4. Blockades, in order to be binding, must be effective; that is to say, maintained by a force sufficient really to prevent access to the coast of the enemy."[1]

This agreement was adopted by Austria, France, Great Britain, Prussia, Russia, Sardinia and Turkey, and it was further agreed that a general invitation to accede should be extended to all nations, but with the proviso "that the powers which shall have signed it, or which shall accede thereto, shall not in future enter into any arrangement, concerning the application of the law of neutrals in time of war, which does not rest altogether upon the four principles embodied in the said declaration."[2] In other words it must be accepted in whole, and not in part, and the powers acceding pledging themselves not to enter into any subsequent treaties or engagements on maritime law which did not stipulate observance of all four points. Within a short time nearly all the maritime nations of the world had given official adherence to the Declaration of Paris.

But the United States refused to do so. She had long stood in the advance guard of nations demanding respect for neutral rights. Little by little her avowed principles of international law as regards neutrals, first scoffed at, had crept into acceptance in treaty stipulations. Secretary of State Marcy now declared, in July, 1856, that the United

[1] Text as given in Moore, *Digest*, VII, p. 562.

[2] *Ibid.*, p. 563.

States would accede to the Declaration if a fifth article were added to it protecting all private property at sea, when not contraband. This covered not only cargo, but the vessel as well, and its effect would have been to exclude from belligerent operations non-contraband enemy's goods under the enemy's flag, if goods and ship were privately owned. Maritime warfare on the high seas would have been limited to battles between governmentally operated warships. Unless this rule were adopted also, Secretary Marcy declared that "the United States could not forgo the right to send out privateers, which in the past had proved her most effective maritime weapon in time of war, and which, since she had no large navy, were essential to her fighting power."

"War on private property," said the Americans, "had been abolished on land; why should it not be abolished also on the sea?" The American proposal met with general support among the smaller maritime nations. It was believed that the one great obstacle to the adoption of Marcy's amendment lay in the naval supremacy of Great Britain, and that obstacle proved insurmountable. Thus the United States refused to accede to the Declaration, and there the matter rested until 1861. But on April 17 Jefferson Davis proclaimed for the Southern Confederacy the issue of privateers against Northern commerce. On April 24 Seward instructed representatives abroad, recounting the Marcy proposal and expressing the hope that it still might meet with a favourable reception, but authorizing them to enter into conventions for American adherence to the Declaration of 1856 on the four points alone. This instruction was sent to the Ministers in Great Britain, France, Russia, Prussia, Austria, Belgium, Italy, and Denmark; and on May 10 to the Netherlands.

Having received this instruction, Adams, at the close of his first meeting with Russell on May 18, after having developed at length the American position relative to the issue of the British Proclamation of Neutrality, briefly added that he was directed to offer adherence by means of a convention, to the Declaration of Paris. Russell replied that Great Britain was willing to negotiate, but "seemed to desire to leave the subject in the hands of Lord Lyons, to whom he intimated that he had already transmitted authority. . . ."[1] Adams therefore did not press the matter, waiting further information and instruction from Washington. Nearly two weeks earlier Russell had, in fact, approached the Government of France with a suggestion that the two leading maritime powers should propose to the American belligerents adherence to the second and third articles of the Declaration of Paris. France had agreed and the date of Russell's instruction to Lyons was May 18, the day of the interview with Adams. Confusion now arose in both London and Washington as to the place where the arrangement was to be concluded. The causes of this confusion will be considered later in this chapter; here it is sufficient to note that the negotiation was finally undertaken at London.

On July 18 Russell informed Adams that Great Britain was ready to enter into a convention with the United States, provided a similar convention was signed with France at the same time. This convention, as submitted by Adams, simply recorded an agreement by the two powers to abide by the four points of the Declaration of Paris, using the exact wording of that document.[2] Adams' draft had been communicated to Russell on July 13. There then followed a delay required by the necessity of securing similar action by Dayton, the American Minister at Paris, but on July 29 Adams reported to Russell that this had

[1] *U.S. Messages and Documents*, 1861-2, p. 94. Adams to Seward, May 21, 1861.

[2] Text given in *Parliamentary Papers*, 1862, *Lords*, Vol XXV. "Correspondence respecting International Maritime Law." No. 18.

been done and that he was ready to sign. Two days later, July 31, Russell replied that he, also, was ready, but concluded his letter, "I need scarcely add that on the part of Great Britain the engagement will be prospective, and will not invalidate anything already done."[1] It was not until August 8, however, that Cowley, the British Ambassador to France, reported that Dayton had informed Thouvenel, French Foreign Minister, that he was ready to sign the similar convention with France.[2] With no understanding, apparently, of the causes of further delay, and professing complete ignorance of the meaning of Russell's phrase, just quoted,[3] Adams waited the expected invitation to an official interview for the affixing of signatures. Since it was a condition of the negotiation that this should be done simultaneously in London and Paris, the further delay that now occurred caused him no misgivings.

On August 19 Russell requested Adams to name a convenient day "in the course of this week," and prefaced this request with the statement that he enclosed a copy of a Declaration which he proposed to make in writing, upon signing the convention. "You will observe," he wrote, "that it is intended to prevent any misconception as to the nature of the engagement to be taken by Her Majesty." The proposed Declaration read:

> "In affixing his signature to the Convention of this day between Her Majesty the Queen of Great Britain and Ireland and the United States of America, the Earl Russell declares, by order of Her Majesty, that Her Majesty does not intend thereby to undertake any engagement which shall have any bearing, direct or indirect, on the internal differences now prevailing in the United States."[4]

[1] *Ibid.*, No. 25.

[2] *Ibid.*, No. 26.

[3] *U.S. Messages and Documents*, 1861-2, p. 124. Adams to Seward, Aug. 2, 1861.

[4] *Parliamentary Papers*, 1862, *Lords*, Vol. XXV. "Correspondence respecting International Maritime Law." No. 28.

Under his instructions to negotiate a convention for a pure and simple adherence to the Declaration of Paris, Adams could not now go on to official signature. Nor was he inclined to do so. Sincerely believing, as he stated to Russell in a communication of August 23, that the United States was "acting with the single purpose of aiding to establish a permanent doctrine for all time," and with the object of "ameliorating the horrors of warfare all over the globe," he objected "to accompany the act with a proceeding somewhat novel and anomalous," which on the face of it seemed to imply a suspicion on the part of Great Britain that the United States was "desirous at this time to take a part in the Declaration [of Paris], not from any high purpose or durable policy, but with the view of securing some small temporary object in the unhappy struggle which is going on at home."[1] He also pointed out that Russell's proposed declaration either was or was not a part of the convention. If it was a part then the Senate of the United States must ratify it as well as the convention itself, and he would have gone beyond his instructions in submitting it. If not a part of the convention there could be no advantage in making the Declaration since, unratified by the Senate, it would have no force. Adams therefore declined to proceed further with the matter until he had received new instructions from Washington

To this Russell answered, August 28, with a very explicit exposition of his reasons. Great Britain, he said, had declared her neutrality in the American conflict, thereby recognizing the belligerent rights of the South. It followed that the South "might by the law of nations arm privateers," and that these "must be regarded as the armed vessels of a belligerent." But the United States had refused to recognize the status of belligerency, and could therefore maintain that privateers issued by the Southern

[1] *Ibid.*, No. 31.

States were in fact pirates, and might argue that a European Power signing a convention with the United States, embodying the principles of the Declaration of Paris, "would be bound to treat the privateers of the so-called Confederate States as pirates." Hence Russell pointed out, the two countries, arguing from contradictory premises as to the status of the conflict in America, might become involved in charges of bad faith and of violation of the convention. He had therefore merely intended by his suggested declaration to prevent any misconception by the United States.

> "It is in this spirit that Her Majesty's Government decline to bind themselves, without a clear explanation on their part, to a Convention which, seemingly confined to an adoption of the Declaration of Paris of 1856, might be construed as an engagement to interfere in the unhappy dissensions now prevailing in the United States; an interference which would be contrary to Her Majesty's public declarations, and would be a reversal of the policy which Her Majesty has deliberately sanctioned."[1]

Thus the negotiation closed. Seward in declining to accept the proposed declaration gave varying reasons in his instructions to Adams, in London, and to Dayton, in Paris, for an exactly similar declaration had been insisted upon by France, but he did not argue the question save in generalities. He told Dayton that the supposed possible "intervention" which Great Britain and France seemed to fear they would be called upon to make was exactly the action which the United States desired to forestall, and he notified Adams that he could not consent since the proposed Declaration "would be virtually a new and distinct article incorporated into the projected convention."[2] The first formal negotiation of the United States during the Civil War, and of the new American Minister in London, had come

[1] *Ibid.*, No. 32.
[2] Moore, *Digest*, VII, pp. 578 and 581.

to an inglorious conclusion. Diplomats and Foreign Secretaries were, quite naturally, disturbed, and were even suspicious of each others' motives, but the public, not at the moment informed save on the American offer and the result, paid little attention to these "inner circle" controversies.[1]

What then were the hidden purposes, if such existed, of the negotiating powers. The first answer in historical writing was that offered by Henry Adams,[2] in an essay entitled "The Declaration of Paris, 1861," in the preparation of which the author studied with care all the diplomatic correspondence available in print.[3] His treatment presents Russell as engaged in a policy of deception with the view of obtaining an ultimate advantage to Great Britain in the field of commercial rivalry and maritime supremacy. Following Henry Adams' argument Russell, on May 9, brought to the attention of France a proposal for a joint request on the American belligerents to respect the second and third articles of the Declaration of Paris, and received an acquiescent reply. After some further exchanges of proposed terms of instructions to the British and French Ministers at Washington, Russell, on May 18, sent a despatch to Lyons with instructions for his action. On this same day Russell, in his first interview with Adams, "before these despatches [to Lyons] could have left the Foreign Office," and replying to Adams' proposal to nego-

[1] The point of Russell's Declaration was made very early in the London press. Thus the *Saturday Review*, June 8, 1861, commenting on the report that America was ready to adhere to the Declaration of Paris, stated that this could have no effect on the present war but would be welcomed for its application after this war was over.

[2] In the general American argument before the Geneva Arbitration Court it was stated that the practical effect of British diplomacy in this connection was that "Great Britain was thus to gain the benefit to its neutral commerce of the recognition of the second and third articles, the rebel privateers and cruisers were to be protected and their devastation legalized, while the United States were to be deprived of a dangerous weapon of assault upon Great Britain." Cited in Nicolay and Hay, *Lincoln*, IV, p. 280.

[3] Henry Adams, *Historical Essays*, pp. 237-279.

tiate on the Declaration of Paris as a *whole*—that is to say, on all four articles—intimated that instructions had already gone to Lyons, with directions to assent to any modification of the article on privateering that the United States might desire. Adams understood Russell to prefer that the negotiation (for such Adams thought it was to be) should take place in Washington, and did not press the matter.

This was deliberate deceit; first in a statement of fact since the interview with Adams took place at noon on May 18, at Russell's country house nine miles from London, and in all reasonable supposition the despatch to Lyons would not have been sent until the Foreign Secretary's return to his office; second because Lyons was not instructed to *negotiate* on the Declaration. The interpretation is justified therefore that Russell "evaded the offer of the United States Government." The result of this evasion was delay, but when Seward learned from Lyons that he had no authority to negotiate a convention and Adams received renewed instructions to proceed, the latter "kept his temper, but the affair made a lasting impression on his mind, and shook his faith in the straightforwardness of the British Government." In renewing his overtures at London, Adams made explanations of the previous "misunderstanding" and to these Russell replied with further "inaccuracies" as to what had been said at the first interview.

Thus beginning his survey with an assertion of British deceit and evasion from the very outset, and incidentally remarking that Lyons, at Washington, "made little disguise of his leanings" toward the South, Henry Adams depicts Russell as leading France along a line of policy distinctly unfriendly to the North. Examining each point in the negotiation as already narrated, he summarized it as follows:

"The story has shown that Russell and his colleagues . . . induced the French Government to violate the pledge in the protocol of the Declaration of Paris in order to offer to both belligerents a partial adhesion, which must exclude the United States from a simple adhesion, to the Declaration of Paris, while it placed both belligerents on the same apparent footing. These steps were taken in haste before Adams could obtain an interview. When Adams by an effort unexpected to Russell obtained an interview at Pembroke Lodge at noon of Saturday, May 18, and according to Russell's report of May 21, said that the United States were 'disposed to adhere to the Declaration of Paris,' Russell evaded the offer, saying that he had already sent sufficient instructions to Lyons, although the instructions were not sufficient, nor had they been sent. When this evasion was afterward brought to his notice by Adams, Russell, revising his report to Lyons, made such changes in it as should represent the first proposal as coming from himself, and the evasion to have come from Adams. When at last obliged to read the American offer, Russell declared that he had never heard of it before, although he had himself reported it to Lyons and Lyons had reported it to him. When compelled to take the offer for consideration, Russell, though always professing to welcome adhesion pure and simple, required the co-operation of Dayton. When Adams overcame this last obstacle, Russell interposed a written proviso, which as he knew from Lyons would prevent ratification. When Adams paid no attention to the proviso but insisted on signature of the treaty, Russell at last wrote a declaration in the nature of an insult, which could not be disregarded."[1]

In this presentation of the case to the jury certain minor points are insisted upon to establish a ground for suspicion —as the question of who first made the proposal—that are not essential to Henry Adams' conclusions. This conclusion is that "From the delays interposed by Russell, Adams must conclude that the British Cabinet was trying one device after another to evade the proposition; and finally, from the written declaration of August 19, he could draw no other inference than that Russell had resorted to

[1] *Ibid.*, p. 271.

the only defensive weapon left to him, in order to avoid the avowal of his true motives and policy."[1] The *motive* of this tortuous proceeding, the author believed to have been a deep-laid scheme to revive, *after* the American War was ended, the earlier international practice of Great Britain, in treating as subject to belligerent seizure enemy's goods under the neutral flag. It was the American stand, argues Henry Adams, that in 1854 had compelled Great Britain to renounce this practice. A complete American adherence, now, to the Declaration, would for ever tie Britain's hands, but if there were no such complete adherence and only temporary observation of the second article, after the war had resulted in the disruption of the United States, thus removing the chief supporter of that article, Great Britain would feel free to resume her old-time practice when she engaged in war. If Great Britain made a formal treaty with the United States she would feel bound to respect it; the Declaration of Paris as it stood constituted "a mere agreement, which was binding, as Lord Malmesbury declared, only so long as it was convenient to respect it."[2] Thus the second article of the Declaration of Paris, not the first on privateering, was in the eye of the British Cabinet in the negotiation of 1861. Henry Adams ends his essay: "After the manner in which Russell received the advances of President Lincoln, no American Minister in London could safely act on any other assumption than that the British Government meant, at the first convenient opportunity, to revive the belligerent pretensions dormant since the War of 1812."[3]

This analysis was published in 1891. Still more briefly summarized it depicts an unfriendly, almost hostile attitude

[1] *Ibid.*, p. 273.
[2] *Ibid.*, p. 277.
[3] This same view was maintained, though without stating details, by Henry Adams, as late as 1907. See his "Education of Henry Adams," Private Edition, p. 128.

on the part of Russell and Lyons, deceit and evasion by the former, selfish British policy, and throughout a blind following on by France, yielding to Russell's leadership. The American proposal is regarded merely as a simple and sincere offer to join in supporting an improved international practice in war-times. But when Frederic Bancroft, the biographer of Seward, examined the negotiation he was compelled to ask himself whether this was all, indeed, that the American Secretary of State had in view. Bancroft's analysis may be stated more briefly.[1]

Seward's general instruction, Bancroft notes, bore date of April 24, nearly a month before any foreign Power had recognized Southern belligerent rights; it indicates "a plan by which he hoped to remove all excuse for such action." In despatches to Dayton, Seward asserted a twofold motive: "a sincere desire to co-operate with other progressive nations in the melioration of the rigours of maritime war," and "to remove every cause that any foreign Power could have for the recognition of the insurgents as a belligerent Power."[2] This last result was not so clear to Dayton at Paris, nor was the mechanism of operation ever openly stated by Seward. But he did write, later, that the proposal of accession to the Declaration of Paris was tendered "as the act of this Federal Government, to be obligatory equally upon disloyal as upon loyal citizens." "It did not," writes Bancroft, "require the gift of prophecy to tell what would result in case the offer of accession on the part of the United States should be accepted."[3]

Seward's object was to place the European nations in a position where they, as well as the United States, would be forced to regard Southern privateers as pirates, and treat

[1] Bancroft, *Seward*, II, Ch. 31.
[2] Cited by Bancroft, *Seward*, II, p. 189.
[3] *Ibid*.

them as such. This was a conceivable result of the negotiation before European recognition of Southern belligerency, but even after that recognition and after Dayton had pointed out the impossibility of such a result, Seward pressed for the treaty and instructed Dayton not to raise the question with France. He still had in mind this main object. "If Seward," says Bancroft, "had not intended to use the adherence of the United States to the declaration as a lever to force the other Powers to treat the Confederates as pirates, or at least to cease regarding them as belligerents, he might easily and unofficially have removed all such suspicions."[1] In an interview with Lyons on July 6 Seward urged a quick conclusion of the treaty, arguing that its effect upon the revolted states could be determined afterwards. Naturally Lyons was alarmed and gave warning to Russell. "Probably it was this advice that caused Russell to insist on the explanatory declaration."[2]

It would appear, then, that Seward much underestimated the acuteness of Russell and Thouvenel, and expected them "to walk into a trap." Nor could his claim "that there was no difference between a nation entirely at peace and one in circumstances like those of the United States at this time" be taken seriously. "He was furnishing his opponent with evidences of his lack of candour." This clouded the effect that would have followed "a wise and generous policy toward neutrals, which had doubtless been in Seward's mind from the beginning."[3] In the end he concluded the negotiation gracefully, writing to Adams a pledge of American respect for the second and third articles of the Declaration of Paris—exactly that which Lyons had originally been instructed by Russell to secure.

[1] *Ibid.*, p. 193.
[2] *Ibid.*
[3] *Ibid.*

"We regard Great Britain as a friend. Her Majesty's flag, according to our traditional principles, covers enemy's goods not contraband of war. Goods of Her Majesty's subjects, not contraband of war, are exempt from confiscation, though found under a neutral or disloyal flag. No depredations shall be committed by our naval forces or by those of any of our citizens, so far as we can prevent it, upon the vessels or property of British subjects. Our blockade, being effective, must be respected."[1]

Thus Bancroft regards Seward's proposals of April 24 as in part the result of humanitarian motives and in part as having a concealed purpose of Northern advantage. This last he calls a "trap." And it is to be noted that in Seward's final pledge to Adams the phrase "those of any of our citizens" reserves, for the North, since the negotiation had failed, the right to issue privateers on her own account. But Russell also, says Bancroft, was not "altogether artless and frank." He had in view a British commercial advantage during the war, since if the United States respected the second and third articles of the Declaration of Paris, and "if Confederate privateers should roam the ocean and seize the ships and goods of citizens of the North, all the better for other commercial nations; for it would soon cause the commerce of the United States to be carried on under foreign flags, especially the British and French."[2] Ulterior motive is, therefore, ascribed to both parties in the negotiation, and that of Seward is treated as conceived at the moment when a policy of seeking European friendship was dominant at Washington, but with the hope of securing at least negative European support. Seward's persistence after European recognition of Southern belligerency is

[1] *U.S. Messages and Documents*, 1861-2, p. 143. Seward to Adams, Sept. 7, 1861.

[2] Bancroft, *Seward*, II, p. 196. This speculation is not supported by any reference to documents revealing such a purpose. While it may seem a reasonable speculation it does not appear to be borne out by the new British materials cited later in this chapter.

regarded as a characteristic obstinacy without a clear view of possible resulting dangerous complications.

This view discredits the acumen of the American Secretary of State and it does not completely satisfy the third historian to examine the incident in detail. Nor does he agree on the basis of British policy. Charles Francis Adams, in his "Life" of his father, writing in 1899, followed in the main the view of his brother, Henry Adams. But in 1912 he reviewed the negotiation at great length with different conclusions.[1] His thesis is that the Declaration of Paris negotiation was an essential part of Seward's "foreign war policy," in that in case a treaty was signed with Great Britain and France and then those Powers refused to aid in the suppression of Southern privateering, or at least permitted them access to British and French ports, a good ground of complaint leading to war would be established. *This* was the ultimate ulterior purpose in Seward's mind; the negotiation was but a method of fixing a quarrel on some foreign Power in case the United States should seek, as Seward desired, a cementing of the rift at home by a foreign war.

In the details of the negotiation C. F. Adams agrees with Bancroft, but with this new interpretation. The opening misunderstanding he ascribed, as did Lyons, to the simple fact that Seward "had refused to see the despatch" in which Russell's proposals were made.[2] Seward's instruc-

[1] C. F. Adams, "Seward and The Declaration of Paris" *Mass. Hist. Soc. Proceedings*, XLVI, pp. 23–81.

[2] *Ibid.*, p. 57. The quotation is from a despatch by Lyons of Dec. 6, 1861; but this is inexact language. It is true that Seward had refused to receive officially this despatch, but he had read and considered it in private. Hence he knew *privately* the facts of Russell's proposal and that Lyons had no instructions to negotiate. The incident of this despatch has been treated by me in Chapter IV, where I regard Seward's refusal to receive officially the despatch as primarily a refusal to be notified of Great Britain's proclamation of neutrality. Bancroft treats this incident as primarily a clever refusal by Seward to be approached officially by Lyons and Mercier in a joint representation, thus blocking a plan of joint action. (Bancroft, *Seward*, II, p. 181.) I agree with C. F. Adams that the only effect of this, so far as the negotiation is concerned was that

tions of July 6, after the misunderstanding was made clear to him, pushing the negotiation, were drawn when he was "still riding a very high horse—the No. 10 charger, in fact, he had mounted on the 21st of the previous May,"[1] and this warlike charger he continued to ride until the sobering Northern defeat at Bull Run, July 21, put an end to his folly. If that battle had been a Northern victory he would have gone on with his project. Now, with the end of a period of brain-storm and the emergence of sanity in foreign policy, "Secretary Seward in due time (September 7) pronounced the proposed reservation [by Russell] quite 'inadmissible.' And here the curtain fell on this somewhat prolonged and not altogether creditable diplomatic farce."[2]

Incidentally C. F. Adams examined also British action and intention. Lyons is wholly exonerated. "Of him it may be fairly said that his course throughout seems to furnish no ground for criticism."[3] And Lyons is quoted as having understood, in the end, the real purpose of Seward's policy in seeking embroilment with Europe He wrote to Russell on December 6 upon the American publication of despatches, accompanying the President's annual message: "Little doubt can remain, after reading the papers, that the accession was offered solely with the view to the effect it would have on the privateering operations of the Southern States; and that a refusal on the part of England and France, after having accepted the accession, to treat the Southern privateers as pirates, would have been made a serious grievance, if not a ground of quarrel. . . ."[4] As to

"Seward, by what has always, for some reason not at once apparent, passed for a very astute proceeding, caused a transfer of the whole negotiation from Washington to London and Paris." ("Seward and the Declaration of Paris," p. 50.)

[1] *Ibid.*, p. 51.

[2] *Ibid.*, p. 64.

[3] *Ibid.*, p. 60.

[4] *Ibid.*, p. 58.

Russell, combating Henry Adams' view, it is asserted that it was the great good fortune of the United States that the British Foreign Secretary, having declared a policy of neutrality, was not to be driven from its honest application by irritations, nor seduced into a position where the continuation of that policy would be difficult.

Before entering upon an account of the bearing of the newly available British materials on the negotiation—materials which will in themselves offer sufficient comment on the theories of Henry Adams, and in less degree of Bancroft—it is best to note here the fallacy in C. F. Adams' main thesis. If the analysis given in the preceding chapter of the initiation and duration of Seward's "foreign war policy" is correct, then the Declaration of Paris negotiation had no essential relation whatever to that policy. The instructions to Adams were sent to eight other Ministers. Is it conceivable that Seward desired a war with the whole maritime world? The date, April 24, antedates any deliberate proposal of a foreign war, whatever he may have been brooding, and in fact stamps the offer as part of that friendly policy toward Europe which Lincoln had insisted upon. Seward's frenzy for a foreign war did not come to a head until the news had been received of England's determination to recognize Southern belligerency. This was in the second week of May and on the twenty-first Despatch No. 10 marked the decline, not the beginning, of a belligerent policy, and by the President's orders. By May 24 probably, by the twenty-seventh certainly, Seward had yielded and was rapidly beginning to turn to expressions of friendship.[1] Yet it was only on May 18 that Russell's first instructions to Lyons were sent, and not until late in June that the "misunderstanding" cleared away, instructions were despatched by Seward to push the Declaration of Paris negotiations at London and Paris. The battle of Bull Run

[1] Bancroft says June 8. But see *ante*, p. 130.

had nothing to do with a new policy. Thus chronology forbids the inclusion of this negotiation, either in its inception, progress, or conclusion, as an agency intended to make possible, on just grounds, a foreign war.

A mere chronological examination of documents, both printed and in archives, permits a clearer view of British policy on the Declaration of Paris. Recalling the facts of the American situation known in London it will be remembered that on May 1 the British Government and Parliament became aware that a civil war was inevitable and that the South planned to issue privateers. On that day Russell asked the Admiralty to reinforce the British fleet in West Indian waters that British commerce might be adequately protected. Five days later, May 6, he announced in the Commons that Great Britain must be strictly neutral, and that a policy of close harmony with France was being matured; and on this day he proposed through Cowley, in Paris, that Great Britain and France each ask *both* the contending parties in America to abide by the second and third articles of the Declaration of Paris.[1] If there was ulterior motive here it does not appear in any despatch either then or later, passing between any of the British diplomats concerned—Russell, Cowley, and Lyons. The plain fact was that the United States was not an adherent to the Declaration, that the South had announced privateering, and the North a blockade, and that the only portions of the Declaration in regard to which the belligerents had as yet made no statement were the second and third articles.

[1] *Parliamentary Papers*, 1862, *Lords*, Vol. XXV. "Correspondence respecting International Maritime Law." No. 1. It was with reference to this that Palmerston, on May 5, wrote to Russell: "If any step were thought advisable, perhaps the best mode of our feeling our way would be to communicate confidentially with the South by the men who have come over here from thence, and with the North by Dallas, who is about to return in a few days. Dallas, it is true, is not a political friend of Lincoln, but on the contrary rather leans to the South; but still he might be an organ, if it should be deemed prudent to take any step." (Palmerston MS.)

It was, indeed, an anxious time for the British Government. On May 9 Forster asked in the Commons what would be the Government's attitude toward a British subject serving on a Southern privateer.[1] The next day in the Lords there occurred a debate the general burden of which was that privateering was in fact piracy, but that under the conditions of the American previous stand, it could not be treated as such.[2] Both in the Commons and the Lords speakers were referred to the forthcoming Proclamation of Neutrality, but the uncertainty developed in both debates is very probably reflected in the new despatch now sent to Cowley, on May 11.[3] By that despatch France was asked to send an instruction to Mercier in Washington similar to a draft instruction intended for Lyons, a copy of which was enclosed to Cowley, the object being to secure from the American belligerents adherence to *all* the articles, privateering included, of the Declaration of Paris.[4]

Whatever Russell's purpose in thus altering his original suggestion, it met with a prompt check from France. On May 9 Thouvenel had agreed heartily to the proposal of May 6, adding the practical advice that the best method of approach to the Confederacy would be through the consuls in the South.[5] Now, on May 13, Russell was informed that Thouvenel feared that England and France would get into serious trouble if the North agreed to accede on privateering and the South did not. Cowley reported that he had argued with Thouvenel that privateers were

[1] Hansard, 3rd. Ser., Vol. CLXII, p. 1763.

[2] *Ibid.*, pp. 1830-34.

[3] This instruction never got into the printed Parliamentary papers, nor did any others of the many containing the like suggestion, for they would have revealed a persistence by Russell against French advice—to which he ultimately was forced to yield—a persistence in seeking to bind the belligerents on the first article of the Declaration of Paris, as well as on articles two and three. The points at which Russell returned to this idea are indicated in this chapter.

[4] F.O., France, Vol. 1376. No. 563. Draft.

[5] F. O., France, Vol. 1390. No. 684. Cowley to Russell, May 9, 1861.

pirates and ought to be treated as such, but that Thouvenel refused to do more than instruct Mercier on the second and third articles.[1] For the moment Russell appears to have yielded easily to this French advice. On May 13 he had that interview with the Southern commissioners in which he mentioned a communication about to be made to the South;[2] and on May 15 the London *Times*, presumably reflecting governmental decision, in commenting on the Proclamation of Neutrality, developed at some length the idea that British citizens, if they served on Southern privateers, could claim no protection from Great Britain if the North chose to treat them as pirates. May 16, Cowley reported that Thouvenel had written Mercier in the terms of Russell's draft to Lyons of the eleventh, but omitting the part about privateering,[3] and on this same day Russell sent to Cowley a copy of a *new* draft of instructions to Lyons, seemingly in exact accord with the French idea.[4] On the seventeenth, Cowley reported this as highly satisfactory to Thouvenel.[5] Finally on May 18 the completed instruction was despatched.

It was on this same day, May 18, that Adams had his first interview with Russell. All that had been planned by Great Britain and France had been based on their estimate of the necessity of the situation. They had no knowledge of Seward's instructions of April 24. When therefore Adams, toward the conclusion of his interview, stated his authority to negotiate a convention, he undoubtedly took Russell by surprise. So far as he was concerned a suggestion to the North, the result of an agreement made with France

[1] F. O., France, Vol. 1391. No. 713. Cowley to Russell, May 13, 1861.

[2] Richardson, *Messages and Papers of the Confederacy*, II, p. 40.

[3] F. O., France, Vol. 1391. No. 733.

[4] *Parliamentary Papers*, 1862, *Lords*, Vol. XXV. "Correspondence respecting International Maritime Law." No. 5.

[5] *Ibid.*, No. 6. Note that this and the preceding document are all that appeared in the Parliamentary Papers. Thouvenel's amendment of Russell's plan did not appear.

after some discussion and delay, was in fact completed, and the draft finally drawn *two days before*, on the sixteenth. Even if not actually sent, as Henry Adams thinks, it was a completed agreement. Russell might well speak of it as an instruction already given to Lyons. Moreover there were two points in Adams' conversation of the eighteenth likely to give Russell cause for thought. The first was Adams' protest against the British recognition of a status of belligerency. If the North felt so earnestly about this, had it been wise to instruct Lyons to make an approach to the South? This required consideration. And in the second place did not Adams' offer again open up the prospect of somehow getting from the North at least a formal and permanent renunciation of privateering?

For if an examination is made of Russell's instruction to Lyons of May 18 it appears that he had not, after all, dropped that reference to privateering which Thouvenel had omitted in his own instructions to Mercier. Adams understood Russell to have said that he "had already transmitted authority [to Lyons] to assent to any modification of the only point in issue which the Government of the United States might prefer. On that matter he believed that there would be no difficulty whatever."[1] This clearly referred to privateering. Russell's instructions to Lyons took up the points of the Declaration of Paris in reverse order. That on blockades was now generally accepted by all nations. The principle of the third article had "long been recognized as law, both in Great Britain and in the United States." The second article, "sanctioned by the United States in the earliest period of the history of their independence," had been opposed, formerly, by Great Britain, but having acquiesced in the Declaration of 1856, "she means to adhere to the principle she then adopted."

[1] *U.S. Messages and Documents*, 1861-2, Adams to Seward, May 21, 1861.

Thus briefly stating his confidence that the United States would agree on three of the articles, Russell explained at length his views as to privateering in the American crisis.

> "There remains only to be considered Article I, namely, that relating to privateering, from which the Government of the United States withheld their assent. Under these circumstances it is expedient to consider what is required on this subject by the general law of nations. Now it must be borne in mind that privateers bearing the flag of one or other of the belligerents may be manned by lawless and abandoned men, who may commit, for the sake of plunder, the most destructive and sanguinary outrages. There can be no question, however, but that the commander and crew of a ship bearing a letter of marque must, by the law of nations, carry on their hostilities according to the established laws of war. Her Majesty's Government must, therefore, hold any Government issuing such letters of marque responsible for, and liable to make good, any losses sustained by Her Majesty's subjects in consequence of wrongful proceedings of vessels sailing under such letters of marque.
>
> "In this way, the object of the Declaration of Paris may to a certain extent be attained without the adoption of any new principle.
>
> "You will urge these points upon Mr. Seward."[1]

What did Russell mean by this cautious statement? The facts known to him were that Davis had proclaimed the issue of letters of marque and that Lincoln had countered by proclaiming Southern privateering to be piracy.[2] He did not know that Seward was prepared to renounce privateering, but he must have thought it likely from Lincoln's proclamation, and have regarded this as a good time to strike for an object desired by all the European maritime nations since 1856. Russell could not, while Great Britain was neutral, join the United States in treating Southern privateers as pirates, but he here offered to come as close

[1] *Parliamentary Papers*, 1862, *Lords*, Vol. XXV. "Correspondence respecting International Maritime Law." No. 7.

[2] The text of these proclamations, transmitted by Lyons, had been officially received in London on May 10.

to it as he dared, by asserting that Great Britain would use vigilance in upholding the law of nations. This language might be interpreted as intended for the admonition of the North also, but the *facts* of the then known situation make it applicable to Southern activities alone. Russell had desired to include privateering in the proposals to the United States and to the South, but Thouvenel's criticisms forced him to a half-measure of suggestion to the North, and a full statement of the delicacy of the situation in the less formal letter to Lyons accompanying his official instructions. This was also dated May 18. In it Russell directed Lyons to transmit to the British Consul at Charleston or New Orleans a copy of the official instruction "to be communicated at Montgomery to the President of the so-styled Confederate States," and he further explained his purpose and the British position:

> ". . . You will not err in encouraging the Government to which you are accredited to carry into effect any disposition which they may evince to recognize the Declaration of Paris in regard to privateering. . . .
>
> "You will clearly understand that Her Majesty's Government cannot accept the renunciation of privateering on the part of the Government of the United States if coupled with the condition that they should enforce its renunciation on the Confederate States, either by denying their right to issue letters of marque, or by interfering with the belligerent operations of vessels holding from them such letters of marque, so long as they carry on hostilities according to the recognized principles and under the admitted liabilities of the law of nations."[1]

Certainly this was clear enough and was demanded by the British policy of neutrality. Russell had guarded against the complication feared by Thouvenel, but he still hoped by a half-pledge to the North and a half-threat to the

[1] *Parliamentary Papers*, 1862, *Lords*, Vol. XXV. "Correspondence respecting International Maritime Law." No. 8.

South to secure from both belligerents a renunciation of privateering. In short he was not yet fully convinced of the wisdom of the French limitation. Moreover he believed that Thouvenel might yet be won to his own opinion, for in an unprinted portion of this same private letter to Lyons of May 18 Russell wrote:

> "I have further to state to you, with reference to my despatch of this day that H.M. Govt. were in the first instance inclined to propose to both of the contending parties to adopt the first clause of the Declaration of Paris, by which privateering is renounced. But after communication with the French Govt. it appeared best to limit our propositions in the manner explained in my despatch.
>
> "I understand however from Lord Cowley that, although M. Mercier is not absolutely instructed to advert to the abolition of privateering, yet that some latitude of action is left to him on that point should he deem it advisable to exercise it."[1]

Lyons and Mercier saw more clearly than did Russell what was in Seward's mind. Lyons had been instructed in the despatch just cited to use his own discretion as to joint action with the French Minister so long only as the two countries took the same stand. He was to pursue whatever method seemed most "conciliatory." His first private comment on receiving Russell's instruction was, "Mr. Seward will be furious when he finds that his adherence to the Declaration of Paris will not stop the Southern privateering,"[2] and in an official confidential despatch of the same day, June 4, he gave Russell clear warning of what Seward expected from his overture through Adams.[3] So delicate did the matter appear to Lyons and Mercier that

[1] F. O., Am., Vol. 755. No. 139. "Seen by Ld. P. and the Queen."

[2] Russell Papers. Lyons to Russell, June 4, 1861. (Printed in Newton, *Lyons*, I, 42.)

[3] *Parliamentary Papers*, 1862, *Lords*, Vol. XXV. "Correspondence respecting International Maritime Law." No. 12. Marked "Received," June 17.

they agreed to keep quiet for a time at least about their instructions, hoping to be relieved by the transfer of the whole matter to London and Paris.[1] But in London Russell was at this moment taking up again his favoured purpose. On June 6 he wrote to Grey (temporarily replacing Cowley at Paris) that he understood a communication had been made in Paris, as in London, for an American adherence to the Declaration of Paris; ". . . it may open the way to the abolition of Privateering all over the world. But . . . we ought not to use any menace to the Confederate States with a view of obtaining this desirable object."[2] Evidently, in his opinion, the South would not dare to hold out and no "menace" would be required.[3] Six days later, however, having learned from the French Ambassador that Dayton in Paris had made clear to Thouvenel the expectation of the United States that France would treat Southern privateers as pirates, Russell wrote that England, of course, could not agree to any such conclusion.[4] Nevertheless this did not mean that Russell yet saw any real objection to concluding a convention with the United States. Apparently he could not believe that so obvious an incon-

[1] F. O., Am., Vol. 765. No. 262. Lyons to Russell, June 8, 1861. Also Russell Papers, June 10, 1861. This disinclination to act extended also to the matter of getting in touch with the South, which they also postponed. It appeared that Mercier was instructed to order the French Consul at New Orleans to go in person to President Davis. Both diplomats were very fearful of an "outbreak" from Seward on this planned proposal to the Confederacy.

[2] F. O., France, Vol. 1376. No. 35. Draft. "Seen by Ld. Palmerston and the Queen."

[3] In Washington, so different was the point of view, Lyons and Mercier were now convinced they could not let Seward know of the proposal to be made to the South. They feared he would send them their passports. Mercier in informal talk had explained to Seward his instructions on the Declaration of Paris in so far as the North was concerned. Lyons and Mercier now planned a joint visit and representation to Seward—that which was actually attempted on June 15—but were decided to say nothing about the South, until they learned the effect of this "joint proposal." F. O., Am., Vol. 765. No. 262. Lyons to Russell, June 8, 1861.

[4] *Parliamentary Papers*, 1862, *Lords*, Vol. XXV. "Correspondence respecting International Maritime Law." No. 10. Russell to Grey, June 12, 1861.

sistency with the declared neutrality of Great Britain was expected to be obtained by the American Secretary of State.

Others were more suspicious. Lyons reported on June 13 that Seward had specifically informed Mercier of his belief that a convention signed would bind England and France to aid in suppressing Southern privateering.[1] The effect of this on Lyons and Mercier was to impress upon them the advisability of an *official* notification to Seward, of English and French neutrality—a step not yet taken and which was still postponed, awaiting further instructions.[2] On June 15 the two Ministers finally concluded they could no longer delay and made that joint visit to Seward which resulted in his refusal to receive them as acting together, or to receive officially their instructions, though he read these for his private information. The remainder of June was spent by Lyons in attempting to put matters on a more formal basis, yet not pushing them unduly for fear of arousing Seward's anger. June 17, Lyons told Seward, privately, and alone, that Great Britain *must* have some intercourse with the South if only for the protection of British interests. Seward's reply was that the United States might "shut its eyes" to this, but that if notified of what England and France were doing, the United States would be compelled to make protest. Lyons thereupon urged Seward to distinguish between his official and personal knowledge, but Lyons and Mercier again postponed beginning the negotiation with the Confederacy.[3] Yet while thus reporting this

[1] Stoeckl was writing his Government that the state to which the negotiation had come was full of danger and might lead to a serious quarrel. He thought Russia should keep out of it until results were clearer. On this report Gortchakoff margined "C'est aussi mon avis." (Russian Archives, Stoeckl to F. O., June 12-24, 1861. No. 1359.)

[2] F. O., Am., Vol. 766. No. 278.

[3] *Parliamentary Papers*, 1862, *Lords*, Vol. XXV. "Correspondence respecting International Maritime Law." No. 14. Lyons to Russell, June 17, 1861. "Recd. June 30." It was in this interview that Lyons discovered Seward's misconception as to the position of the proposed negotiation, and made clear to Seward that he had no instructions to sign a convention.

postponement in one letter, Lyons, in another letter of the same date, indicated that the two Ministers thought that they had found a solution of the problem of how to approach, yet not negotiate with, the Confederacy. The idea was Mercier's. Their consuls in the South were to be instructed to go, not to the Southern President, but to the Governor of the State selected, thus avoiding any overture to the Confederate Government.[1] Even with this solution possible they still hesitated, feeling as Lyons wrote " a little pusillanimous," but believing they had prevented an explosion.[2] Moreover Lyons was a bit uneasy because of an important difference, so it seemed to him, in his formal instructions and those of Mercier. The latter had no orders, as had Lyons, to notify Seward, if the agreement on maritime law was made in Washington, that such agreement would not affect the belligerent right of the South to issue privateers.[3] Apparently Mercier had been given no instructions to make this clear—let alone any " latitude " to deal with privateering—although, as a matter of fact, he had already given Seward his personal opinion in accord with Lyons' instructions ; but this was not an official French stand. Lyons was therefore greatly relieved, the " misunderstanding " now cleared away, that new instructions were being sent to Adams to go on with the convention in London. His only subsequent comment of moment was sent to Russell on July 8, when he learned from Seward that Dayton, in Paris, had been directed to raise no further question as to what would or would not be demanded of France in case a convention were signed for an American adherence to the Declaration of Paris. Lyons now repeated his former advice that under no circumstances should a convention be signed without a distinct declaration of no

[1] F. O., Am., Vol. 766. No. 284.
[2] Russell Papers. Lyons to Russell, June 18, 1861.
[3] *Ibid*. Lyons to Russell, June 21, 1861.

British responsibility or duty as regards Southern privateers.[1]

The entire matter was now transferred to London and Paris. Lyons' report of the misunderstanding and that new instructions were being sent to Adams was received on June 30. Russell replied to Lyons on July 5 that Adams had "never made any proposition" on the Declaration of Paris, and that he would now await one.[2] July 11, Adams made his formal offer to sign a convention and communicated a draft of it on the thirteenth. On the day intervening, the twelfth, Russell took a very important step indicative of his sincerity throughout, of his lack of any ulterior motive, and of his anxiety to carry through the negotiation with no resulting irritations or complications with the United States. He recalled his instructions to Lyons about communicating with the Confederacy, stating that in any case he had never intended that Lyons should act without first officially notifying Seward. This recall was now made, he wrote, because to go on might "create fresh irritation without any adequate result," but if in the meantime Lyons had already started negotiations with the South he might "proceed in them to the end."[3]

Having taken this step in the hope that it might avert friction with the United States, Russell, now distinctly eager to secure American adherence to the Declaration in

[1] *Parliamentary Papers*, 1862, *Lords*, Vol. XXV. "Correspondence respecting International Maritime Law." No. 22. Writing privately on the same day Lyons comments on Mercier's "extreme caution" in his relations with Seward. Lyons implied that all this personal, rather than official communication of documents to Seward was Mercier's idea, and that he, Lyons, doubted the wisdom of this course, but had agreed to it because of the desire to act in perfect harmony with France. Russell Papers, Lyons to Russell, July 8, 1861.

[2] Lyons Papers.

[3] F. O., Am., Vol 756. No. 227. On this same day Russell was writing privately to Edward Everett, in Boston, a clear statement of the British position, defending the Proclamation of Neutrality and adding, "It is not our practice to treat five millions of freemen as pirates, and to hang their sailors if they stop our merchantmen. But unless we mean to treat them as pirates and to hang them, we could not deny them belligerent rights." C. F. Adams, "Seward and the Declaration of Paris," pp. 49-50.

full, was ready to conclude the convention at once. The warnings received from many sources did not dismay him. He probably thought that no actual difficulties would ensue, believing that the South would not venture to continue privateering. Even if France were disinclined to make a convention he appears to have been ready for signature by Great Britain alone, for on July 15 he telegraphed Cowley, "I conclude there can be no objection to my signing a Convention with the U.S. Minister giving the adherence of the U.S. to the Declaration of Paris so far as concerns Gt. Britain. Answer immediately by telegraph."[1] Cowley replied on the sixteenth that Thouvenel could not object, but thought it a wrong move.[2] Cowley in a private letter of the same day thought that unless there were "very cogent reasons for signing a Convention at once with Adams," it would be better to wait until France could be brought in, and he expressed again his fear of the danger involved in Adams' proposal.[3] The same objection was promptly made by Palmerston when shown the draft of a reply to Adams. Palmerston suggested the insertion of a statement that while ready to sign a convention Great Britain would do so only at the same time with France.[4] Thus advised Russell telegraphed in the late afternoon of the sixteenth to Cowley that he would "wait for your despatches to-morrow," and that no reply had yet been given Adams,[5] and on the seventeenth he wrote enclosing a draft,

[1] F. O., France, Vol. 1377. No. 176. Draft. Russell to Cowley, July 15, 1861.

[2] F. O., France, Vol. 1394. No. 871.

[3] Russell Papers. Also in a despatch of July 16 Cowley repeated his objections and stated that Dayton had not yet approached France. (F. O., France, Vol. 1394. No. 871.)

[4] F. O., Am., Vol. 755. No. 168. Enclosure. Palmerston's Note to Russell was not sent to Adams but his exact language is used in the last paragraph of the communication to Adams, November 18, as printed in *Parliamentary Papers*, 1862, *Lords*, Vol. XXV. "Correspondence respecting International Maritime Law." No. 19.

[5] F. O., France, Vol. 1378. No. 730. Russell to Cowley, July 17, 1861. Containing draft of telegram sent on 16th at 4.30 p.m.

approved by Palmerston and the Queen, stating that Great Britain had no desire to act alone if Dayton really had instructions identical with those of Adams. He added that if thought desirable Adams and Dayton might be informed verbally, that the proposed Convention would in no way alter the Proclamation of Neutrality.[1]

The remaining steps in the negotiation have already been narrated.[2] Russell informed Adams of the requirement of a similar French convention, Adams secured action by Dayton, and in spite of continued French reluctance and suspicion[3] all was ready in mid-August for the affixing of signatures, when Russell, in execution of his previous promise, and evidently now impressed with the need of an explicit understanding, gave notice of his intended declaration in writing to be attached to the convention.[4] On August 20 both Adams and Dayton refused to sign, the former taking the ground, and with evident sincerity, that the "exception" gave evidence of a British suspicion that was insulting to his country, while Dayton had "hardly concealed" from Thouvenel that this same "exception" was the very object of the Convention.[5] While preparing his rejoinder to Adams' complaint Russell wrote in a note to Palmerston "it all looks as if a trap had been prepared."[6] He, too, at last, was forced to a conclusion long since reached by every other diplomat, save Adams, engaged in this negotiation.

But in reviewing the details of the entire affair it would

[1] *Ibid.* No. 729.

[2] See *ante* pp. 142-45.

[3] F. O., France, Vol. 1394. No. 905. Cowley to Russell, July 26, 1861.

[4] It should be noted that during this period Russell learned that on July 5, Lyons, before receiving the recall of instructions, had finally begun through Consul Bunch at Charleston the overtures to the South. On July 24, Russell approved this action (*Parliamentary Papers*, 1862, *Lords*, Vol. XXV. "Correspondence respecting International Maritime Law." No. 23.)

[5] F. O., France, Vol. 1395. No. 1031. Cowley to Russell, August 20, 1861.

[6] Palmerston MS., Russell to Palmerston, August 26, 1861.

appear that in its initiation by Seward there is no proof that he then thought of any definite "trap." April 24 antedated any knowledge by Seward of British or French policy on neutrality, and he was engaged in attempting to secure a friendly attitude by foreign Powers. One means of doing this was by giving assurances on maritime law in time of war. True he probably foresaw an advantage through expected aid in repressing privateering, but primarily he hoped to persuade the maritime Powers not to recognize Southern belligerency. It was in fact this question of belligerency that determined all his policy throughout the first six months of the American conflict. He was obstinately determined to maintain that no such status existed, and throughout the whole war he returned again and again to pressure on foreign Powers to recall their proclamations of neutrality. Refusing to recognize foreign neutrality as final Seward persisted in this negotiation in the hope that if completed it would place Great Britain and France in a position where they would be forced to reconsider their declared policy. A demand upon them to aid in suppressing privateering might indeed then be used as an argument, but the object was not privateering in itself; that object was the recall of the recognition of Southern belligerency. In the end he simply could not agree to the limiting declaration for it would have constituted an acknowledgment by the United States itself of the existence of a state of war.

In all of this Adams, seemingly, had no share. He acted on the simple and straightforward theory that the United States, pursuing a conciliatory policy, was now offering to adhere to international rules advocated by all the maritime powers. As a result he felt both personally and patriotically aggrieved that suspicion was directed toward the American overtures.[1] For him the failure of the

[1] See C. F Adams, "Seward and the Declaration of Paris," pp. 58 and 74.

negotiation had temporarily, at least, an unfortunate result : " So far as the assumed friendliness of Earl Russell to the United States was concerned, the scales had fallen from his eyes. His faith in the straightforwardness of any portion of the Palmerston-Russell Ministry was gone."[1]

And for Russell also the affair spelled a certain disillusionment, not, it is true, in the good faith of Adams, for whom he still preserved a high regard. Russell felt that his policy of a straightforward British neutrality, his quick acquiescence in the blockade, even before actually effective, his early order closing British ports to prizes of Confederate privateers,[2] were all evidences of at least a friendly attitude toward the North. He may, as did nearly every Englishman at the moment, think the re-union of America impossible, but he had begun with the plan of strict neutrality, and certainly with no thought of offensive action against the North. His first thought in the Declaration of Paris negotiation was to persuade both belligerents to acquiesce in a portion of the rules of that Declaration, but almost at once he saw the larger advantage to the world of a complete adherence by the United States. This became Russell's fixed idea in which he persisted against warnings and obstacles. Because of this he attempted to recall the instruction to approach the South, was ready even, until prohibited by Palmerston, to depart from a policy of close joint action with France, and in the end was forced by that prohibition to make a limiting declaration guarding British neutrality. In it all there is no evidence of any hidden motive nor of any other than a straightforward, even if obstinately blind, procedure. The effect on Russell, at last grudgingly admitting that there had been a " trap,"

[1] Adams, *Life of C. F. Adams*, p. 209.

[2] The Confederate Commissions on August 14, 1861, just before the critical moment in the Declaration of Paris negotiation, had made vigorous protest against this British order, characterizing it as giving a " favour " to the Government at Washington, and thus as lacking in neutrality. Quoted by C. F. Adams, " Seward and the Declaration of Paris," p. 31.

was as unfortunate for good understanding as in the case of Adams. He also was irritated, suspicious, and soon less convinced that a policy of strict neutrality could long be maintained.[1]

[1] A few facts about Southern privateering not directly pertinent to this chapter are yet not without interest. There was no case during the Civil War of a vessel actually going out as a privateer (i.e., a private vessel operating under government letters of marque) from a foreign port. (Adams, "Seward and the Declaration of Paris," p. 38.) No Southern privateer ever entered a British port. (Bernard, *Neutrality of Great Britain*, p. 181). As a result of Seward's general instruction of April 24, a convention was actually signed with Russia in August, but it was not presented by Seward for ratification to the United States Senate. Schleiden in a report to the Senate of Bremen at the time of the *Trent* affair, Nov. 14, 1861, stated that the Russian Ambassador, von Stoeckl, inquired of Seward "whether the U.S. would equip privateers in case war should break out with England and France. Seward replied 'that is a matter of course.' Mr. Stoeckl thereupon remarked that in any case no American privateer would be permitted to cruise in the northern part of the Pacific because Russia, which is the only state that has ports in those regions, would treat them as pirates in accordance with the Convention of August 24. Mr. Seward then exclaimed: 'I never thought of that. I must write to Mr. Clay about it.'" (Schleiden MS.)

CHAPTER VI

BULL RUN; CONSUL BUNCH; COTTON AND MERCIER

THE diplomatic manœuvres and interchanges recounted in the preceding chapter were regarded by Foreign Secretaries and Ministers as important in themselves and as indicative of national policy and purpose. Upon all parties concerned they left a feeling of irritation and suspicion. But the public knew nothing of the details of the inconclusive negotiation and the Press merely gave a hint now and then of its reported progress and ultimate failure. Newspapers continued to report the news from America in unaccustomed detail, but that news, after the attack on Fort Sumter, was for some time lacking in striking incident, since both sides in America were busily engaged in preparing for a struggle in arms for which neither was immediately prepared. April 15, Lincoln called for 75,000 volunteers, and three weeks later for 42,000 additional. The regular army was increased by 23,000 and the navy by 18,000 men. Naval vessels widely scattered over the globe, were instructed to hasten their home-coming. By July 1 Lincoln had an available land force, however badly trained and organized, of over 300,000, though these were widely scattered from the Potomac in the east to the Missouri in the west.

In the South, Davis was equally busy, calling at first for 100,000 volunteers to wage defensive battle in protection of the newly-born Confederacy. The seven states already in secession were soon joined, between May 4 and June 24, by four others, Arkansas, Virginia, North Carolina and

Tennessee in order, but the border states of Maryland, Kentucky, and Missouri, though strongly sympathetic with the rest of the South, were held to the Union by the "border state policy" of Lincoln, the first pronouncement of which asserted that the North had no purpose of attacking slavery where it existed, but merely was determined to preserve the Union. The Northern Congress, meeting in extra session on July 4, heartily approved Lincoln's emergency measures. It authorized an army of 500,000, provided for a loan of $200,000,000, sanctioned the issue of $50,000,000 in Treasury notes and levied new taxes, both direct and by tariffs to meet these expenditures.

In the months preceding the attack on Sumter the fixed determination of the South to secede and the uncertainty of the North had led the British press to believe that the decision rested wholly with the South. Now the North by its preparations was exhibiting an equally fixed determination to preserve the Union, and while the British press was sceptical of the permanence of this determination, it became, for a short time, until editorial policy was crystallized, more cautious in prophecy. The *Economist* on May 4 declared that the responsibility for the "fatal step" rested wholly on Southern leaders because of their passionate desire to extend the shameful institution of which they were so proud, but that the North must inevitably, by mere weight of population and wealth, be the victor, though this could not conceivably result in any real reunion, rather in a conquest requiring permanent military occupation. Southern leaders were mad: "to rouse by gratuitous insult the mettle of a nation three times as numerous and far more than three times as powerful, to force them by aggressive steps into a struggle in which the sympathy of every free and civilized nation will be with the North, seems like the madness of men whose eyes are blinded and hearts hardened by the evil cause they defend."

Two weeks later, the *Economist*, while still maintaining the justice of the Northern cause, though with lessened vigour, appealed to the common sense of the North to refrain from a civil war whose professed object was unattainable. "Everyone knows and admits that the secession is an accomplished, irrevocable, fact. . . . Even if the North were sure of an easy and complete victory—short, of course, of actual subjugation of the South (which no one dreams of) —the war which was to end in such a victory would still be, in the eyes of prudence and worldly wisdom, an objectless and unprofitable folly."[1] But by the middle of June the American irritation at the British Proclamation of Neutrality, loudly and angrily voiced by the Northern press, had caused a British press resentment at this "wilful misrepresentation and misjudgment" of British attitude. "We *do* believe the secession of the Slave States to be a *fait accompli*—a completed and irreversible transaction. We believe it to be impossible now for the North to lure back the South into the Union by any compromise, or to compel them back by any force." "If this is an offence it cannot be helped."[2]

The majority of the London papers, though not all, passed through the same shifts of opinion and expression as the *Economist*; first upbraiding the South, next appealing to the North not to wage a useless war, finally committing themselves to the theory of an accomplished break-up of the Union and berating the North for continuing, through pride alone, a bloody conflict doomed to failure. Meanwhile in midsummer attention was diverted from the ethical causes at issue by the publication in the *Times* of Motley's letter analysing the nature of the American constitution and defending the legal position of the North in its resistance to secession. Motley wrote in protest against the general

[1] *Economist*, May 18, 1861.

[2] *Ibid.*, June 29, 1861.

British press attitude: "There is, perhaps, a readiness in England to prejudge the case; a disposition not to exult in our downfall, but to accept the fact. . . ."[1]

He argued the right and the duty of the North to force the South into subjection. "The right of revolution is indisputable. It is written on the record of our race. British and American history is made up of rebellion and revolution. . . . There can be nothing plainer, then, than the American right of revolution. But, then, it should be called revolution." "It is strange that Englishmen should find difficulty in understanding that the United States Government is a nation among the nations of the earth; a constituted authority, which may be overthrown by violence, as may be the fate of any state, whether kingdom or republic, but which is false to the people if it does not its best to preserve them from the horrors of anarchy, even at the cost of blood."

Motley denied any *right* of *peaceful* secession, and his constitutional argument presented adequately the Northern view. But he was compelled also to refer to slavery and did so in the sense of Lincoln's inaugural, asserting that the North had no purpose of emancipating the slaves. "It was no question at all that slavery within a state was sacred from all interference by the general government, or by the free states, or by individuals in those states; and the Chicago Convention [which nominated Lincoln] strenuously asserted that doctrine." Coming at the moment when the British press and public were seeking ground for a shift from earlier pro-Northern expressions of sympathy to some justification for the South, it may be doubted whether Motley's letter did not do more harm than good to the Northern cause. His denial of a Northern anti-slavery purpose gave excuse for a, professedly, more calm

[1] J. L. Motley, *The Causes of the American Civil War*. Published as a pamphlet. N.Y., 1861.

and judicial examination of the claimed *Southern right* of secession, and his legal argument could be met, and was met, with equally logical, apparently, pro-Southern argument as to the nature of the American constitution. Thus early did the necessity of Lincoln's "border state policy"—a policy which extended even to warnings from Seward to American diplomats abroad not to bring into consideration the future of slavery—give ground for foreign denial that there were any great moral principles at stake in the American conflict.

In the meantime the two sections in America were busily preparing for a test of strength, and for that test the British press, reporting preparations, waited with interest. It came on July 21 in the first battle of Bull Run, when approximately equal forces of raw levies, 30,000 each, met in the first pitched battle of the war, and where the Northern army, after an initial success, ultimately fled in disgraceful rout. Before Bull Run the few British papers early taking strong ground for the North had pictured Lincoln's preparations as so tremendous as inevitably destined to crush, quickly, all Southern resistance. The *Daily News* lauded Lincoln's message to Congress as the speech of a great leader, and asserted that the issue in America was for all free people a question of upholding the eternal principles of liberty, morality and justice. "War for such a cause, though it be civil war, may perhaps without impiety be called 'God's most perfect instrument in working out a pure intent.'"[1] The disaster to the Northern army, its apparent testimony that the North lacked real fighting men, bolstered that British opinion which regarded military measures against the South as folly—an impression reinforced in the next few months by the long pause by the North before undertaking any further great effort in the field. The North was not really ready for determined war,

[1] *Daily News*, July 19, 1861.

indeed, until later in the year. Meanwhile many were the moralizations in the British press upon Bull Run's revelation of Northern military weakness.

Probably the most influential newspaper utterances of the moment were the letters of W. H. Russell to the *Times*. This famous war-correspondent had been sent to America in the spring of 1861 by Delane, editor of the *Times*, his first letter, written on March 29, appearing in the issue of April 16. He travelled through the South, was met everywhere with eager courtesy as became a man of his reputation and one representing the most important organ of British public opinion, returned to the North in late June, and at Washington was given intimate interviews by Seward and other leaders. For a time his utterances were watched for, in both England and America, with the greatest interest and expectancy, as the opinions of an unusually able and thoroughly honest, dispassionate observer. He never concealed his abhorrence of slavery, terming apologists of that institution "the miserable sophists who expose themselves to the contempt of the world by their paltry theiscles on the divine origin and uses of Slavery . . ."[1] and writing "day after day . . . the impression of my mind was strengthened that 'States Rights' meant protection to slavery, extension of slave territory, and free-trade in slave produce with the other world."[2] But at the same time he depicted the energy, ability, and determination of the South in high colours, and was a bit doubtful of similar virtues in the North. The battle of Bull Run itself he did not see, but he rode out from Washington to meet the defeated army, and his description of the routed rabble, jostling and pushing, in frenzy toward the Capitol, so ridiculed Northern fighting spirit as to leave a permanent

[1] Russell, *My Diary, North and South*, p. 159, Boston, 1863. This work is in effect a condensation of Russell's letters to the *Times*, but contains many intimate descriptions not given in the newspaper.

[2] *Ibid.*, p. 315.

sting behind it. At the same time it convinced the British pro-Southern reader that the Northern effort was doomed to failure, even though Russell was himself guarded in opinion as to ultimate result. "'What will England and France think of it?' is the question which is asked over and over again," wrote Russell on July 24,[1] expatiating on American anxiety and chagrin in the face of probable foreign opinion. On August 22 he recorded in his diary the beginnings of the American newspaper storm of personal attack because of his description of the battle in the *Times*—an attack which before long became the alleged cause of his recall by Delane.[2] In fact Russell's letters added nothing in humiliating description to the outpourings of the Northern press, itself greedily quoted by pro-Southern foreign papers. The impression of Northern military incapacity was not confined to Great Britain—it was general throughout Europe, and for the remainder of 1861 there were few who ventured to assert a Northern success in the war.[3]

Official Britain, however, saw no cause for any change in the policy of strict neutrality. Palmerston commented privately, "The truth is, the North are fighting for an Idea chiefly entertained by professional politicians, while the South are fighting for what they consider rightly or wrongly vital interests," thus explaining to his own satisfaction why a Northern army of brave men had *chosen*

[1] The *Times*, August 10, 1861.

[2] Russell, *My Diary*, London, 1863, II, p. 296. This edition varies somewhat from that published at Boston and previously cited. The *New York Times* became Russell's most vicious critic, labelling him "Bull Run Russell," a name which stuck, and beginning its first article on his sins "The terrible epistle has been read with quite as much avidity as an average President's message. We scarcely exaggerate the fact when we say, the first and foremost thought on the minds of a very large portion of our people after the repulse at *Bull's Run* was, what will Russell say?" *Ibid.*, p. 297. As to his recall Russell afterwards asserted that it was really due to a variance of opinion with Delane, the former being really pro-Northern in sympathy and in conviction of ultimate victory. This will be examined later when Russell's position as an independent editor in London becomes important.

[3] For similar German impressions see G. H. Putnam, *Memories of My Youth*, N.Y., 1914, p. 187.

to *run* away,[1] but the Government was careful to refrain from any official utterances likely to irritate the North. The battle served, in some degree, to bring into the open the metropolitan British papers which hitherto professing neutrality and careful not to reveal too openly their leanings, now each took a definite stand and became an advocate of a cause. The Duke of Argyll might write reassuringly to Mrs. Motley to have no fear of British interference,[2] and to Gladstone (evidently controverting the latter's opinion) that slavery was and would continue to be an object in the war,[3] but the press, certainly, was not united either as to future British policy or on basic causes and objects of the war. The *Economist* believed that a second Southern victory like Bull Run, if coming soon, would "so disgust and dishearten the shouters for the Union that the contest will be abandoned on the instant. . . . Some day, with scarcely any notice, we may receive tidings that an armistice has been agreed upon and preliminaries of peace have been signed."[4] John Bright's paper, the *Morning Star*, argued long and feverishly that Englishmen must not lose sight of the fact that slavery was an issue, and made appeal for expressions, badly needed at the moment, of pro-Northern sympathy.[5] To this *John Bull* retorted:

> "Nothing can be clearer than this, that black slavery has nothing whatever to do with this Civil War in America. . . . The people of America have erected a political idol. The Northerners have talked and written and boasted so much about their Republic that they have now become perfectly furious to find that their idol can be overthrown,

[1] Newton, *Lord Lyons*, I, p. 48. In the same view Russell wrote to Lyons, August 16. "The defeat of Manassas or Bull's Run seems to me to show a great want of zeal. For I cannot believe the descendants of the men of 1776 and indeed of 1815 to be totally wanting in courage." (Lyons Papers.)

[2] Motley, *Correspondence*, II, p. 31. August 20, 1861.

[3] Gladstone Papers, August 29, 1861.

[4] *Economist*, Aug. 17, 1861.

[5] *Morning Star*, Sept. 10, 1861.

> and that the false principles upon which the American Republic is built should be exhibited to the world, that their vaunted democracy should be exposed as a mere bubble or a piece of rotten timber, an abominable and worthless tyranny of the sovereign mob."[1]

Here was an early hint of the future of democracy as at issue.[2] *John Bull*, the "country squire's paper," might venture to voice the thought, but more important papers were still cautious in expressing it. W. H. Russell, privately, wrote to Delane: "It is quite obvious, I think, that the North will succeed in reducing the South."[3] But Delane permitted no such positive prophecy to appear in the *Times*. Darwin is good testimony of the all-prevalent British feeling: "I hope to God we English are utterly wrong in doubting whether the North can conquer the South." "How curious it is that you seem to think that you can conquer the South; and I never meet a soul, even those who would most wish it, who think it possible—that is, to conquer and retain it."[4]

In September, after the first interest in Bull Run had waned, there appeared several books and articles on the American question which gave opportunity for renewal of newspaper comment and controversy. A Dr. Lempriere, "of the Inner Temple, law fellow of St. John's College, Oxford," published a work, *The American Crisis Considered*, chiefly declamatory, upholding the right of Southern secession, stating that no one "who has the slightest acquaintance with the political action of history would term the present movement rebellion." With this the *Spectator* begged leave to differ.[5] The *Saturday Review*

[1] *John Bull*, Sept. 14, 1861.

[2] To be discussed fully in Chapter XVIII.

[3] Sept. 13, 1861. Dasent, *Delane*, II, p. 34.

[4] Darwin to Asa Gray, Sept. 17 and Dec. 11, 1861. Cited in *Rhodes*, III, p. 510.

[5] *Spectator*, Sept. 14, 1861.

acknowledged that a prolonged war might force slavery and emancipation to the front, but denied them as vital at present, and offered this view as a defence against the recrimination of Mrs. Harriet Beecher Stowe, who had accused the paper of unfair treatment in a review of her pamphlet exhibiting emancipation as the object of the North. Under the caption, "Mrs. Beecher Stowe's Wounded Feelings," the *Saturday Review* avowed disbelief in the existence of a "Holy War" in America. "The North does not proclaim abolition and never pretended to fight for anti-slavery. The North has not hoisted for its oriflamme the Sacred Symbol of Justice to the Negro; its *cri de guerre* is not unconditional emancipation." "The Governmental course of the British nation . . . is not yet directed by small novelists and their small talk"[1] Thomas Hughes also came in for sarcastic reference in this article, having promptly taken up the cudgels for Mrs. Stowe. He returned to the attack through the columns of the *Spectator*, reasserting slavery as an issue and calling on Englishmen to put themselves in the place of Americans and realize the anger aroused by "deliberate imputations of mean motives," and by the cruel spirit of the utterances. A nation engaged in a life and death struggle should not be treated in a tone of flippant and contemptuous serenity. The British press had chosen "to impute the lowest motives, to cull out and exult over all the meanness, and bragging, and disorder which the contest has brought out, and while we sit on the bank, to make no allowances for those who are struggling in the waves."[2]

Besides the *Spectator*, on the Northern side, stood the *Daily News*, declaring that the South could not hold out, and adding, "The Confederate States may be ten millions,

[1] *Saturday Review*, Sept. 14, 1861.
[2] *Spectator*, Sept. 21, 1861.

but they *are* wrong—notoriously, flagrantly wrong."[1] The *Daily News*, according to its "Jubilee" historians, stood almost alone in steadfast advocacy of the Northern cause.[2] This claim of unique service to the North is not borne out by an examination of newspaper files, but is true if only metropolitan dailies of large circulation are considered. The *Spectator* was a determined and consistent friend of the North. In its issue of September 28 a speech made by Bulwer Lytton was summarized and attacked. The speaker had argued that the dissolution of the Union would be beneficial to all Europe, which had begun to fear the swollen size and strength of the young nation across the Atlantic. He hoped that the final outcome would be not two, but at least four separate nations, and stated his belief that the friendly emulation of these nations would result for Americans in a rapid advance in art and commerce such as had been produced in the old commonwealths of Greece. The *Spectator* answered that such a breaking up of America was much more likely to result in a situation comparable to that in South America, inquired caustically whether Bulwer Lytton had heard that slavery was in question, and asserted that his speech presumably represented the official view of the Tories, and embodied that of the English governing class.[3]

In press utterances during the autumn and early fall of 1861 there is little on British policy toward America. Strict neutrality is approved by all papers and public speakers. But as the months passed without further important military engagements attention began to be directed toward the economic effects on England of the war

[1] *Daily News*, Sept. 17 and Oct. 10, 1861. The statement is in reply to an article in the *Times* of October 9, arguing that even if the South were regarded as in the wrong, they had ten millions, a fact that was conclusive.

[2] *The Daily News Jubilee.* By Justin McCarthy and John R. Robinson, pp. 69-77.

[3] *Spectator*, Sept. 28, 1861.

in America and to the blockade, now beginning to be made effective by the North. The *Saturday Review*, though pro-Southern, declared for neutrality, but distinguished between strict observance of the blockade and a reasonable recognition of the *de facto* government of the Confederacy "as soon as the Southern States had achieved for their independence that amount of security with which Great Britain had been satisfied in former cases."[1] But another article in the same issue contained a warning against forcibly raising the blockade since this must lead to war with the North, and that would commend itself to no thoughtful Englishman. Two weeks later appeared a long review of Spence's *American Union*, a work very influential in confirming British pro-Southern belief in the constitutional right of the South to secede and in the certainty of Southern victory. Spence was "likely to succeed with English readers, because all his views are taken from a thoroughly English standpoint."[2] The week following compliments are showered upon the "young professor" Montague Bernard for his "Two Lectures on the Present American War," in which he distinguished between recognition of belligerency and recognition of sovereignty, asserting that the former was inevitable and logical. The *Saturday Review*, without direct quotation, treated Bernard as an advocate also of the early recognition of Southern independence on the ground that it was a *fait accompli*, and expressed approval.[3]

These few citations, taken with intent from the more sober and reputable journals, summarize the prevailing attitude on one side or the other throughout the months from June to December, 1861. All publications had much

[1] *Saturday Review*, Nov. 2, 1861.

[2] *Ibid.*, Nov. 16. Spence's book rapidly went through many editions, was widely read, and furnished the argument for many a pro-Southern editorial. Spence himself soon became the intimate friend and adviser of Mason, the Confederate envoy to England.

[3] *Ibid.*, Nov. 23, 1861. The inference from Bernard's la guage is perhaps permissible, but not inevitable.

to say of the American struggle and varied in tone from dignified criticism to extreme vituperation, this last usually being the resort of lesser journals, whose leader writers had no skill in "vigorous" writing in a seemingly restrained manner. "Vigorous" leader writing was a characteristic of the British press of the day, and when combined with a supercilious British tone of advice, as from a superior nation, gave great offence to Americans, whether North or South. But the British press was yet united in proclaiming as correct the governmental policy of neutrality, and in any event Motley was right in stating "the Press is not the Government," adding his opinion that "the present English Government has thus far given us no just cause of offence."[1] Meanwhile the Government, just at the moment when the Declaration of Paris negotiation had reached an inglorious conclusion, especially irritating to Earl Russell, was suddenly plunged into a sharp controversy with the United States by an incident growing out of Russell's first instructions to Lyons in regard to that negotiation and which, though of minor importance in itself, aroused an intensity of feeling beyond its merits. This was the recall by Seward of the exequatur of the British consul Bunch, at Charleston, South Carolina.

It will be remembered that in his first instruction to Lyons on the Declaration of Paris Russell had directed that Bunch, at Charleston, be commissioned to seek a Southern official acceptance of the binding force of the second and third articles, but that Lyons and Mercier, fearing Seward's irritation, had hesitated to proceed in the matter. Later Russell had recalled his instructions, but before this recall could reach Lyons the latter had decided to act.[2] On July 5 Lyons gave explicit directions to Bunch not to approach the Confederate Government directly, but to go

[1] Motley, *Correspondence*, II, p. 37. To his mother, Oct. 18, 1861.
[2] See *ante*, Ch. V.

to Governor Pickens of South Carolina and explain the matter to him verbally, adding "you should act with great caution, in order to avoid raising the question of the recognition of the new Confederation by Great Britain." Unfortunately Lyons also wrote, "I am authorized by Lord John Russell to confide the negotiation on this matter to you," thus after all implying that a real *negotiation* with the South was being undertaken. On the same day Mercier sent similar instructions to St. André, the French Acting-Consul at Charleston.[1] Bunch received Lyons' official letter on July 19,[2] together with a private one of July 5, emphasizing that Bunch was to put nothing in writing, and that he and his French colleagues were to keep the names of Lyons and Mercier out of any talk, even, about the matter. Bunch was to talk as if his instructions came directly from Russell. Lyons hoped the South would be wise enough not to indulge in undue publicity, since if "trumpeted" it might elicit "by such conduct some strong disavowal from France and England." Both the official and the private letter must, however, have impressed Bunch with the idea that this was after all a negotiation and that he had been entrusted with it.[3]

Bunch, whose early reports had been far from sympathetic with the Southern cause, had gradually, and quite naturally from his environment, become more friendly to it.[4] He now acted with promptness and with some

[1] *Parliamentary Papers*, 1862, *Lords*, Vol. XXV. "Correspondence respecting International Maritime Law." No. 21 and Inclosure. Belligny was in fact the French agent at Charleston who acted with Bunch.

[2] F. O., Am., Vol. 768. No. 392. Lyons to Russell, Aug. 2, 1861. It is interesting to note that fourteen days were here required to transmit a letter that in ordinary times would have reached its destination in two days. Lyons states that he does not intend to inform Mercier of Russell's attempted recall of instructions.

[3] F. O., Am., Vol. 767. No. 324. Inclosure No. 2. Private. Lyons to Bunch, July 5, 1861. Bunch in reporting to Lyons, also used the word "negotiation."

[4] When Davis proclaimed privateering Bunch had thought this indicated a "low morality" and that Southern privateers would be in reality pirates. F. O., Am., Vol. 763. Inclosure in No. 162. Bunch to Russell, April 18, 1861.

evident exultation at the importance given him personally. In place of Governor Pickens an experienced diplomat, William Henry Trescott, was approached by Bunch and Belligny, who, not St. André, was then the French agent at Charleston.[1] Trescott went directly to President Davis, who at once asked why the British proposal had not been made through the Confederate Commissioners in London, and who somewhat unwillingly yielded to Trescott's urging. On August 13 the Confederate Congress resolved approval of the Declaration of Paris except for the article on privateering.[2] Bunch took great pride in the secrecy observed. "I do not see how any clue is given to the way in which the Resolutions have been procured. . . . We made a positive stipulation that France and England were not to be alluded to in the event of the compliance of the Confederate Govt.,"[3] he wrote Lyons on August 16. But he failed to take account either of the penetrating power of mouth-to-mouth gossip or of the efficacy of Seward's secret agents. On this same day, August 16, Lyons reported the arrest in New York, on the fourteenth, of one Robert Mure, just as he was about to take passage for Liverpool carrying a sealed bag from the Charleston consulate to the British Foreign Office, as well as some two hundred private letters. The letters were examined and among them was one which related Bunch's recent activities and stated that "Mr. B., on oath of secrecy, communicated to me also that the first step of recognition was taken."[4] The sealed bag was sent unopened to be handed by Adams to Russell with an

[1] Bancroft's account, *Seward*, II, pp. 197-203, states that Pickens was absent from Charleston. Bunch's account privately was that he and Belligny thought Pickens "totally unfit to be intrusted with anything in which judgment and discretion are at all necessary." (Lyons Papers. Bunch to Lyons, Aug. 16, 1861.)

[2] Bancroft, *Seward*, II, p. 198.

[3] Lyons Papers. Bunch to Lyons.

[4] *Parliamentary Papers*, 1862, *Lords*, Vol. XXV. "Correspondence on Withdrawal of Bunch's Exequatur." No. 4. Adams to Russell, Sept. 3, 1861.

enquiry whether in fact it contained any papers on the alleged "negotiation" with the South.

Bunch had issued to Mure a paper which the latter regarded as a passport, as did the United States. This also was made matter of complaint by Adams, when on September 3 the affair was presented to Russell. America complained of Bunch on several counts, the three principal ones being (1) that he had apparently conducted a negotiation with the Confederacy, (2) that he had issued a passport, not countersigned by the Secretary of State as required by the United States rules respecting foreign consuls, (3) that he had permitted the person to whom this passport was issued to carry letters from the enemies of the United States to their agents abroad. On these grounds the British Government was requested to remove Bunch from his office. On first learning of Mure's arrest Lyons expressed the firm belief that Bunch's conduct had been perfectly proper and that the sealed bag would be found to contain nothing supporting the suspicion of the American Government.[1] The language used by Lyons was such as to provide an excellent defence in published despatches, and it was later so used. But privately neither Lyons nor Russell were wholly convinced of the correctness of Bunch's actions. Bunch had heard of Mure's arrest on August 18, and at once protested that no passport had been given, but merely a "Certificate to the effect that he [Mure] was a British Merchant residing in Charleston" on his way to England, and that he was carrying official despatches to the Foreign Office.[2] In fact Mure had long since taken out American citizenship papers, and the distinction between passport and certificate seems an evasion. Officially Lyons could report "it is clear that Mr. Robert Mure, in taking charge

[1] *Ibid.* No. 2. Lyons to Russell, Aug. 19, 1861.

[2] Russell Papers. Bunch to Lyons, Aug. 18, 1861. Copy in Lyons to Russell, Aug. 31, 1861.

of the letters which have been seized, abused Mr. Bunch's confidence, for Mr. Bunch had positive instructions from me not to forward himself any letters alluding to military or political events, excepting letters to or from British officials."[1] This made good reading when put in the published Parliamentary Papers. But in reality the sending of private letters by messenger also carrying an official pouch was no novelty. Bunch had explained to Lyons on June 23 that this was his practice on the ground that " there is really no way left for the merchants but through me. If Mr. Seward objects I cannot help it. I must leave it to your Lordship and H.M.'s Government to support me. My own despatch to Lord J. Russell I must send in some way, and so I take the responsibility of aiding British interests by sending the mercantile letters as well."[2] And in Bunch's printed report to Lyons on Mure's arrest, his reply as to the private letters was, " I could not consider him [Mure] as being disqualified from being the bearer of a bag to Earl Russell, by his doing what everyone who left Charleston was doing daily. . . ."[3]

Officially Lyons, on September 2, had reported a conversation with Belligny, the French Consul at Charleston, now in Washington, writing, " I am confirmed in the opinion that the negotiation, which was difficult and delicate, was managed with great tact and good judgment by the two Consuls."[4] But this referred merely to the use of Trescott and its results, not to Bunch's use of Mure. The British Government was, indeed, prepared to defend the action of its agents in securing, *indirectly*, from the South, an

[1] *Parliamentary Papers*, 1862, *Lords*, Vol. XXV. " Correspondence on the Withdrawal of Bunch's Exequatur." No. 7. Lyons to Russell, Aug. 23, 1861.

[2] Lyons Papers. Bunch to Lyons, June 23, 1861.

[3] *Parliamentary Papers*, 1862, *Lords*, Vol. XXV. " Correspondence on the Withdrawal of Bunch's Exequatur." No. 15. Inclosures. Bunch to Lyons, Sept. 30, 1861.

[4] *Ibid.* " Correspondence respecting International Maritime Law." No. 39. Lyons to Russell.

acknowledgment of certain principles of international law. Russell did not believe that Lincoln was "foolhardy enough to quarrel with England and France," though Hammond (Under Secretary of Foreign Affairs) "is persuaded that Seward wishes to pick a quarrel."[1] Enquiry was promptly made of France, through Cowley, as to her stand in the matter of the consuls at Charleston, Russell intimating by an enquiry (later printed in the Parliamentary Papers), as to the initiation of the Declaration of Paris negotiations, that it was Thouvenel who had first suggested the approach to the South through the Consuls.[2] This was an error of memory,[3] and Cowley was perturbed by Thouvenel's reticence in reply to the main question. The latter stated that if a like American demand were made on France "undoubtedly he could not give up an Agent who had done no more than execute the orders entrusted to him."[4] This looked like harmony, but the situation for the two countries was not the same as no demand had been made for the recall of Belligny. Cowley was, in reality, anxious and suspicious, for Thouvenel, in conversation, attributed Seward's anger to Bunch's alleged indiscretions in talk, and made it clear that France would not "stand by" unless Seward should protest to France against the fact of a communication (not a *negotiation*) having been held with the Confederacy.[5] Before the French reply was secured Russell had prepared but not sent an answer to Adams, notifying him that the bag from Bunch, on examination, was found not to contain "correspondence of the enemies

[1] Palmerston MS. Russell to Palmerston, Sept. 6, 1861.

[2] *Parliamentary Papers*, 1862, *Lords*, Vol. XXV. "Correspondence on the Withdrawal of Bunch's Exequatur." No. 6. Russell to Cowley, Sept. 7, 1861.

[3] Russell Papers. Cowley to Russell. Private. Sept. 17, 1861.

[4] *Parliamentary Papers*, 1862, *Lords*, Vol. XXV. "Correspondence on Withdrawal of Bunch's Exequatur." No. 10. Cowley to Russell, Sept. 10, 1861.

[5] F. O., France, Vol. 1396. No. 1112. Cowley to Russell, Sept. 10, 1861. Also Russell Papers. Cowley to Russell. Private. Sept. 10, 1861.

of the Government of the United States" as had been suspected, and transmitting a copy of Bunch's explanation of the reason for forwarding private letters.[1] In another letter to Adams of the same date Russell avowed the Government's responsibility for Bunch's action on the Declaration of Paris, and declined to recall him, adding:

> "But when it is stated in a letter from some person not named, that the first step to the recognition of the Southern States by Great Britain has been taken, the Undersigned begs to decline all responsibility for such a statement.
>
> "Her Majesty's Government have already recognized the belligerent character of the Southern States, and they will continue to recognize them as belligerents. But Her Majesty's Government have not recognized and are not prepared to recognize the so-called Confederate States as a separate and independent State."[2]

Adams received Russell's two notes on September 13,[3] and merely stated that they would be despatched by the next steamer. That Russell was anxious is shown by a careful letter of caution to Lyons instructing him if sent away from Washington "to express in the most dignified and guarded terms that the course taken by the Washington Government must be the result of a misconception on their part, and that you shall retire to Canada in the persuasion that the misunderstanding will soon cease, and the former friendly relations be restored."[4] Meantime Russell was far from satisfied with Bunch, writing Lyons to inform him that the "statements made in regard to his proceedings

[1] *Parliamentary Papers*, 1862, *Lords*, Vol. XXV. "Correspondence on the Withdrawal of Bunch's Exequatur." No. 9. Russell to Adams, Sept. 9, 1861.

[2] *Ibid.* No. 8. Two days later, September 11, Russell wrote to Palmerston that Motley was ignorant of Seward's intentions, and that the Queen wished a modification of the "phrase about not being prepared to recognize," but that he was against any change. Palmerston MS.

[3] *Ibid.* No. 12. Adams to Russell.

[4] Russell to Lyons, Sept. 13, 1861. (Cited in Newton, *Lyons*, I, p. 52.)

require explanation."[1] The failure of Seward to demand Belligny's recall worried Russell. He wrote to Palmerston on September 19, "I cannot believe that the Americans, having made no demand on the French to disavow Belligny, or Baligny, will send away Lyons," and he thought that Seward ought to be satisfied as England had disavowed the offensive part of Bunch's supposed utterances. He was not in favour of sending reinforcements to the American stations: "If they do not quarrel about Bunch, we may rest on our oars for the winter."[2] There was nothing further to do save to wait Seward's action on receipt of the British refusal to recall Bunch. At this moment Lyons at Washington was writing in a hopeful view of "avoiding abstract assertions of principles," but accustoming the North to the *practice* of British recognition of Southern belligerent rights.[3] Lyons believed that Seward would not go further than to withdraw Bunch's exequatur, but he was anxious for the return of Mercier (long absent with Prince Napoleon), since "our position is unluckily not exactly the same with that of France."[4] On October 12 Lyons conferred at length with Seward on the Bunch matter, as usual, privately and unofficially. Seward dwelt on a letter just received from Motley assuring him that Great Britain was not "unfriendly to the United States," and "appeared anxious not to pick a quarrel, yet hardly knowing how to retract from his original position." Lyons told

[1] *Parliamentary Papers*, 1862, *Lords*, Vol. XXV. "Correspondence on the Withdrawal of Bunch's Exequatur." No. 11. Russell to Lyons, Sept. 14, 1861.

[2] Palmerston MS. Russell to Palmerston, Sept. 19, 1861.

[3] Russell Papers. Lyons to Russell. *Private*. Sept. 24, 1861.

[4] *Ibid*. Sept. 27, 1861. The facts about Belligny were, as reported by Lyons and Cowley, that before Bunch's activities became known, the French Consul had been recalled and replaced by another man, St. André. It will have been noted that when Lyons and Mercier sent their instructions to the consuls at Charleston that of Mercier was addressed to St. André. Apparently he had not reached Charleston. Thus there was no opportunity to demand the recall of Belligny. Bancroft (*Seward*, II, p. 203), unaware of this, presumes that Seward "thought it important not to give them (England and France) a common grievance."

Seward that it would be "impossible to carry on the Diplomatic business . . . on the false hypothesis that the United States Government" did not *know* England and France had recognized the belligerent rights of the South, and he urged Russell to get from France an open acknowledgment, such as England has made, that she "negotiated" with the Confederacy. Lyons thought Mercier would try to avoid this, thus seeking to bring pressure on the British Government to adopt his plan of an early recognition of Southern independence. Like Cowley, Lyons was disturbed at the French evasion of direct support in the Bunch affair.[1]

Bunch's formal denial to Lyons of the charges made against him by the United States was confined to three points; he asserted his disbelief that Mure carried any despatches from the *de facto* government at Richmond; he protested that "there was not one single paper in my bag which was not entirely and altogether on Her Majesty's service"; and he explained the alleged "passport" was not intended as such, but was merely "a certificate stating that Mr. Mure was charged by me with despatches," but he acknowledged that in the certificate's description of Mure as a "British merchant" a possible error had been committed, adding, however, that he had supposed anyone would understand, since the words "British subject" had not been used, that Mure was in reality a naturalized citizen of America.[2] This explanation was received by Russell on October 21. Lyons' comment on Bunch's explanation, made without knowledge of what would be Seward's final determination, was that if Bunch had any further excuses to make about the private letters carried by Mure he should drop two weak points in his argument. "I mean the

[1] *Ibid.* Lyons to Russell, Oct. 14, 1861.

[2] *Parliamentary Papers*, 1862, *Lords*, Vol. XXV. "Correspondence on the Withdrawal of Bunch's Exequatur." No. 15. Inclosure. Bunch to Lyons, Sept. 30, 1861.

distinction between B. merchant and B.S., and the distinction between a document requesting that the bearer '*may be permitted to pass freely and receive all proper protection and assistance*' and a passport."[1] Russell, on receipt of Bunch's explanation was also dissatisfied, first because Bunch had violated Lyons' instructions against entrusting despatches to persons carrying private correspondence, and second, because Bunch "gives no distinct denial" to the newspaper stories that he had gossiped about his activities and had stated them to be "a first step toward recognition." These criticisms were directed entirely to Bunch's conduct subsequent to the overture to the South; on the propriety of that act Russell supported Bunch with vigour.[3] October 26, Seward read to Lyons the instruction to Adams on the revocation of Bunch's exequatur. The ground taken for this, reported Lyons, was an evasion of that charge of communicating with the South for which Russell had avowed responsibility, and a turning to the charge that Bunch was personally unacceptable longer to the United States because of his partisanship to the South, as evidenced by various acts and especially as shown by his reported assertion that Great Britain had taken "a first step to recognition." "Never," wrote Lyons, "were serious charges brought upon a slighter foundation." "No one who has read Mr. Bunch's despatches to your Lordship and to me can consider him as in the least degree a partisan of the Southern cause." "When Mr. Seward had finished reading the despatch I remained silent. After a

[1] Lyons Papers. Copy, Private and Confidential, Lyons to Bunch, Oct. 24, 1861. Bunch was informed in this letter that Mure had been set free.

[2] F. O., Am., Vol. 757. No. 381. Russell to Lyons. Draft. Oct. 26, 1861.

[3] The criticisms of Lyons and Russell were not printed in the *Parliamentary Papers*. Bunch did later deny specifically that he had told anyone of his activities. (*Parliamentary Papers*, 1862, *Lords*, Vol. XXV. "Correspondence on the Withdrawal of Bunch's Exequatur." No. 22. Inclosure. Bunch to Lyons. Oct. 31, 1861.)

short pause I took leave of him courteously, and withdrew."[1]

As will have been noted, Lyons had foreseen the American decision against Bunch on purely personal grounds, had been relieved that this would be the issue, and had forewarned Russell. His despatch just cited may be regarded as a suggestion of the proper British refutation of charges, but with acceptance of the American decision. Nevertheless he wrote gloomily on the same day of future relations with the United States.[2] At the same time Russell, also foreseeing Seward's action, was not disturbed. He thought it still "not off the cards that the Southern Confederates may return to the Union. . . . Our conduct must be strictly neutral, and it will be."[3] Upon receipt of Lyons' despatch and letter of October 28 Russell wrote to Palmerston, "I do not attach much importance to this letter of Lyons. It is the business of Seward to feed the mob with sacrifices every day, and we happen to be the most grateful food he can offer."[4] For Russell saw clearly that Great Britain could not object to the removal of Bunch on the purely personal grounds alleged by Seward. There followed in

[1] *Parliamentary Papers*, 1862, *Lords*, Vol. XXV. "Correspondence on the Withdrawal of Bunch's Exequatur." No. 17. Lyons to Russell, Oct. 28, 1861. There are two interesting unindicated elisions in the printed text of this letter. Indicating them in brackets the sentences run: first:—

"It may seem superfluous to make any observations on the charges brought against Mr. Bunch. [For it is plain that a high-handed proceeding being deemed advisable with a view to gratify the American Public, Mr. Bunch has merely been selected as a safer object of attack than the British or French Government.] I can not help saying that never were more serious charges, etc.," and second:—

"When Mr. Seward had finished reading the despatch I remained silent. [I allowed the pain which the contents of it had caused me to be apparent in my countenance, but I said nothing. From my knowledge of Mr. Seward's character, I was sure that at the moment nothing which I could say would make so much impression upon him as my maintaining an absolute silence.] After a short pause, etc." (F. O., America, Vol. 773. No. 607. Lyons to Russell, Oct. 28, 1861).

[2] Russell Papers. Lyons to Russell, Oct. 28, 1861.

[3] Lyons Papers. Russell to Lyons, Nov. 2, 1861.

[4] Palmerston MS. Russell to Palmerston, Nov. 12, 1861. He added, "The dismissal of Bunch seems to me a singular mixture of the bully and coward."

due course the formal notification by Adams on November 21, just six days before he learned of the *Trent* affair, which had occurred on November 8. That alarming incident no doubt coloured the later communications of both parties, for while both Adams and Russell indulged in several lengthy argumentative papers, such as are dear to the hearts of lawyers and diplomats, the only point of possible further dispute was on the claim of Great Britain that future occasions might arise where, in defence of British interests, it would be absolutely necessary to communicate with the Confederacy. Adams acknowledged a British duty to protect its citizens, but reasserted the American right to dismiss any British agent who should act as Bunch had done. On December 9, Russell closed the matter by stating that he did " not perceive that any advantage would be obtained by the continuance of this correspondence."[1] Bunch was expected to leave Charleston as soon as a safe conveyance could be provided for him, but this was not immediately forthcoming. In fact he remained at Charleston until February, 1863, actively engaged, but official papers were signed by his vice-consul. In the excitement over the *Trent*, he seems rapidly to have disappeared from the official as he did from the public horizon.[2]

The Bunch controversy, seemingly of no great importance in so far as the alleged personal grounds of complaint are concerned, had its real significance in the effort of Great

[1] *Parliamentary Papers*, 1862, *Lords*, Vol. XXV. " Correspondence on the Withdrawal of Bunch's Exequatur." No. 26. Russell to Adams, Dec. 9, 1861.

[2] Bonham, *British Consuls in the Confederacy*, p. 45. Columbia University, *Studies in History, Economics and Public Law*, XI-III. No. 3. Bonham shows that Bunch was more pro-Southern than Lyons thought. Lyons had suggested that Bunch be permitted to remain privately at Charleston. (*Parliamentary Papers*, 1862, *Lords*, Vol. XXV. " Correspondence on the Withdrawal of Bunch's Exequatur." No. 29. Lyons to Russell, Dec. 31, 1861.) That Bunch was after all regarded by the United States as a scapegoat may be argued from the " curious circumstance that in 1875, Mr. Bunch, being then British Minister resident at Bogota, acted as arbitrator in a case between the United States and Colombia." (Moore, *Int. Law Digest*, V, p. 22.)

Britain to make contact with the Southern Government—an effort incautiously entered upon, and from which an attempt to withdraw had come too late. The result was British assertion of a right in case of necessity to make such contact, having recognized the South as a belligerent, but a discontinuance of the practice, under the American protest.[1] While this controversy was in progress the attention of the British Government was directed to a proposal urged by Mercier upon Lyons in Washington, which appeared to have the support of the French Government. On September 30, Mercier, so Lyons reported, had received a private letter from Thouvenel expressing great concern over the prospective scarcity of cotton from America, due to the blockade, and asking Mercier's advice. The latter now informed Lyons that his reply had outlined the following steps: first, complete harmony of action between England and France; second, recognition of Southern independence; third, refusal longer to recognize the blockade; fourth, England and France to be alert to seize the "favourable moment," when the North became disheartened, the present moment not being a good one.[2] This policy Mercier thought so "bold" that the North would be deterred from declaring war. The two diplomats held long argument over this suggestion. Lyons acknowledged the general pressure for cotton, but thought there was no need of great alarm as yet and also advanced the idea that in the end Europe would benefit by being forced to develop other sources of

[1] Bancroft, *Seward*, *II*, p. 203, says that if Great Britain ever attempted another negotiation "that British representatives were careful to preserve perfect secrecy." I have found no evidence of any similar communication with the South.

[2] As early as April, 1861, Stoeckl reported Mercier as urging Lyons and Stoeckl to secure from their respective Governments authority to recognize the South whenever they thought "the right time" had come. Lyons did not wish to have this responsibility, arguing that the mere fact of such a decision being left to him would embarrass him in his relations with the North. Stoeckl also opposed Mercier's idea, and added that Russia could well afford to wait until England and France had acted. Russia could then also recognize the South without offending the North. (Russian Archives. Stoeckl to F. O., April 2-14, 1861. No. 863.)

supply, thus being freed from such exclusive dependence on the United States. Mercier answered that France was in dire need and could not wait and he urged that mere recognition of the South would not secure cotton—it was necessary also to break the blockade. In comment to Russell, Lyons agreed that this was true, but thought the fact in itself an argument against accepting Mercier's ideas: "The time is far distant when the intervention of England and France in the quarrel would be welcomed, or, unless under compulsion, tolerated by the American peoples." The South had not yet "gone far enough in establishing its independence to render a recognition of it either proper or desirable for European powers," and he stated with emphasis that recognition would *not* end the war unless there was also an *alliance* with the South.[1]

In the British Cabinet also, at this same time, attention was being directed to the question of cotton, not, primarily, by any push from the British manufacturing interest, but because of queries addressed to it by the French Minister in London. Russell wrote to Palmerston, referring to the inquiry of Flahault, "I agree with you that the cotton question may become serious at the end of the year," but he added that Lindsay had informed him that in any case cotton could not be brought in the winter-time from the interior to the Southern ports.[2] In truth any serious thought given at this time to the question of cotton appears to be the result of the French arguments at London and Washington advocating a vigorous American policy. October 19, Lyons and Mercier renewed debate on exactly the same lines as previously, Mercier this time reading to Lyons an instruction from Thouvenel and his reply. Lyons insisted

[1] Russell Papers. Lyons to Russell, Oct. 4, 1861.

[2] Palmerston MS. Russell to Palmerston, Oct. 8, 1861. On Oct. 7, Lyons wrote to Head, "If we can get through the winter and spring without American cotton, and keep the peace, we shall attain a great object." (Lyons Papers.)

that the North would most certainly declare war on any power that recognized the South and asserted that such a war would cause more suffering many times than all the suffering now caused by the shortage of cotton. Yet Lyons felt compelled to use caution and conciliation in dealing with Mercier, because of the desire to preserve close harmony of attitude.[1] A few days later Lyons' comments seemed wholly justified when Mercier reported to him the tone of a conversation with Seward, after having left with him a copy of Thouvenel's instruction. Seward said plainly that the United States would go to war with any foreign power that tried to interfere and that the only way in which France could get cotton was by a Northern conquest of the South. He acknowledged that the United States might be defeated, but he informed Mercier that France would at least know there had been a war. On his part Mercier told Seward that in his opinion there was but one possible outcome in America—separation—and that he had advised Thouvenel that the true policy of England and France was to recognize the South and "bring about a peaceful separation." Lyons' comment to Russell is that Seward had certainly taken a "high" tone—evident justification of Lyons' previously expressed opinion. Seward had been very eager to learn whether England knew of Thouvenel's instruction, to which Mercier replied "no," and was now anxious that Russell should not reveal to Adams that Lyons had known the contents before delivery to Seward—a caution with which Lyons was very content.[2]

Lyons' first report of Mercier's ideas had been received in London at a rather critical moment. On October 17, just after Adams' complaint about Bunch and Russell's answer, while waiting to see whether Seward would magnify

[1] F. O., America, 772. No. 585. Lyons to Russell, Oct. 21, 1861.
[2] *Ibid.*, Vol. 773. No. 606. Lyons to Russell. Confidential. Oct. 28, 1861.

that incident into a cause of rupture, and four days before Bunch's "unsatisfactory explanation" had been received, Russell wrote to Palmerston:

> "There is much good sense in Mercier's observations. But we must wait. I am persuaded that if we do anything, it must be on a grand scale. It will not do for England and France to break a blockade for the sake of getting cotton. But, in Europe, powers have often said to belligerents, Make up your quarrels. We propose to give terms of pacification which we think fair and equitable. If you accept them, well and good. But, if your adversary accepts them and you refuse them, our mediation is at an end, and you may expect to see us your enemies. France would be quite ready to hold this language with us.
>
> "If such a policy were to be adopted the time for it would be the end of the year, or immediately before the meeting of Parliament."[1]

Apparently Russell under the irritations of the moment was somewhat carried away by Mercier's suggestion. That it was but a briefly held thought has been shown by expressions from him already cited.[2] Nor was he alone in ministerial uncertainty,[3] but Palmerston was not inclined to alter British policy. October 18, he replied to Russell:

> "As to North America, our best and true policy seems to be to go on as we have begun, and to keep quite clear of the conflict between North and South. . . . The only excuse [for intervention] would be the danger to the intervening parties if the conflict went on; but in the American case this can not be pleaded by the Powers of Europe.
>
> "I quite agree with you that the want of cotton would not justify such a proceeding, unless, indeed, the distress

[1] Walpole, *Russell*, II, 344.

[2] See *ante*, p. 194.

[3] "The Americans certainly seem inclined to pick a quarrel with us; but I doubt their going far enough even to oblige us to recognize the Southern States. A step further would enable us to open the Southern ports, but a war would nevertheless be a great calamity." (Maxwell, *Clarendon*, II, 245. Granville to Clarendon. No exact date is given but the context shows it to have been in October, 1861.)

created by that want was far more serious than it is likely to be. The probability is that some cotton will find its way to us from America, and that we shall get a greater supply than usual from other quarters.

"The only thing to do seems to be to lie on our oars and to give no pretext to the Washingtonians to quarrel with us, while, on the other hand, we maintain our rights and those of our fellow countrymen."[1]

In Washington the result of Mercier's conversation with Seward, outlining Thouvenel's suggestions, was a long and carefully prepared despatch to Dayton, in Paris, which the biographer of Seward thinks was one of his "great despatches; perhaps it was his greatest, if we consider his perfect balance and the diplomatic way in which he seemed to ignore what was menacing, while he adroitly let Thouvenel see what the result would be if the implied threats should be carried out."[2] Seward argued with skill the entire matter of cotton, but he was none the less firm in diplomatic defiance of foreign intervention. Since Great Britain had taken no part in the French scheme—a point which Seward was careful to make clear to Dayton—the despatch needs no expanded treatment here. Its significance is that when reported to Lyons by Mercier (for Seward had read it to the latter) the British Minister could pride himself on having already pointed out to both Mercier and Russell that Seward's line was exactly that which he had prophesied. Mercier again was very anxious that his confidences to Lyons should not become known, and Lyons was glad indeed to be wholly free from any share in the discussion.[3]

[1] Ashley, *Palmerston*, II, 218-19. On October 30, Russell wrote to Gladstone expressing himself as worried about cotton but stating that the North was about to try to take New Orleans and thus release cotton. (Gladstone Papers).

[2] Bancroft, *Seward*, II, p. 219. Bancroft cites also a letter from Seward to his wife showing that he appreciated thoroughly the probability of a foreign war if France should press on in the line taken.

[3] F. O., America, Vol. 773. No. 623. Confidential. Lyons to Russell, Nov. 4, 1861.

Two days after thus describing events, Lyons, on November 6, had still another communication, and apparently a last on this topic, with Mercier, in which the two men again went over the whole ground of national policy toward America, and in which their divergent views became very apparent. The arguments were the same, but expressed with more vigour. Mercier seems, indeed, to have attempted to "rush" Lyons into acquiescence in his policy. Lyons finally observed to him that he "had no reason to suppose that Her Majesty's Government considered the time was come for entertaining at all the question of recognizing the South" and asked what good such a step would do anyway. Mercier replied that he did not believe that the North would declare war, and so it would be a step toward settlement. To this Lyons took positive exception.[1] Lyons' report of this conversation was written on November 8, a date which was soon to stand out as that on which occurred an event more immediately threatening to British-American relations than any other during the Civil War.

The battle of Bull Run had left on British minds an impression of Northern incapacity in war—even a doubt of Northern courage and determination. On August 19 the Declaration of Paris negotiation, a favourable result from which was eagerly desired by Russell, had failed, as he well knew when he attached to the convention that explanatory statement limiting its action in point of time. In the end Russell felt that Britain had just escaped a "trap." Two weeks after this Russell learned of the arrest of Mure, and soon of the demand for Bunch's recall, finally and formally made by Adams on November 21. Just six days later, on November 27, London heard of the *Trent* affair of November 8. It is small wonder that Russell

[1] *Ibid.* No. 634. Confidential. Lyons to Russell, Nov. 8, 1861. In truth Lyons felt something of that suspicion of France indicated by Cowley, and for both men these suspicions date from the moment when France seemed lukewarm in support of England in the matter of Bunch.

and his colleagues felt an increasing uncertainty as to the intent of the United States, and also an increasing irritation at having to guard their steps with such care in a situation where they sincerely believed the only possible outcome was the dissolution of the American Union. But up to the moment when the news of the *Trent* affair was received they had pursued a policy, so they believed, of strict and upright neutrality, and were fixed in the determination not to permit minor controversies or economic advantage to divert them from it.

CHAPTER VII

THE "TRENT"

THE *Trent* affair seemed to Great Britain like the climax of American arrogance.[1] The Confederate agents sent to Europe at the outbreak of the Civil War had accomplished little, and after seven months of waiting for a more favourable turn in foreign relations, President Davis determined to replace them by two "Special Commissioners of the Confederate States of America." These were James M. Mason of Virginia, for Great Britain, and John Slidell of Louisiana, for France. Their appointment indicated that the South had at last awakened to the need of a serious foreign policy. It was publicly and widely commented on by the Southern press, thereby arousing an excited apprehension in the North, almost as if the mere sending of two new men with instructions to secure recognition abroad were tantamount to the actual accomplishment of their object.

[1] The *Trent* was the cause of the outpouring of more contemporary articles and pamphlets and has been the subject of more historical writing later, than any other incident of diplomatic relations between the United States and Great Britain during the Civil War—possibly more than all other incidents combined. The account given in this chapter, therefore, is mainly limited to a brief statement of the facts together with such new sidelights as are brought out by hitherto unknown letters of British statesman; to a summary of British public attitude as shown in the press; and to an estimate of the *after effect* of the *Trent* on British policy. It would be of no service to list all of the writings. The incident is thoroughly discussed in all histories, whether British or American and in works devoted to international law. The contemporary American view is well stated, though from a strongly anti-British point of view, in Harris, T. L., *The Trent Affair*, but this monograph is lacking in exact reference for its many citations and can not be accepted as authoritative. The latest review is that of C. F. Adams in the *Proceedings* of the Massachusetts Historical Society for November, 1911, which called out a reply from R. H. Dana, and a rejoinder by Mr. Adams in the *Proceedings* for March, 1912.

Mason and Slidell succeeded in running the blockade at Charleston on the night of October 12, 1861, on the Confederate steamer *Theodora*,[1] and arrived at New Providence, Nassau, on the fourteenth, thence proceeded by the same vessel to Cardenas, Cuba, and from that point journeyed overland to Havana, arriving October 22. In the party there were, besides the two envoys, their secretaries, McFarland and Eustis, and the family of Slidell. On November 7 they sailed for the Danish island of St. Thomas, expecting thence to take a British steamer for Southampton. The vessel on which they left Havana was the British contract mail-packet *Trent*, whose captain had full knowledge of the diplomatic character of his passengers. About noon on November 8 the *Trent* was stopped in the Bahama Channel by the United States sloop of war, *San Jacinto*, Captain Wilkes commanding, by a shot across the bows, and a boarding party took from the *Trent* Mason and Slidell with their secretaries, transferred them to the *San Jacinto*, and proceeded to an American port. Protest was made both by the captain of the *Trent* and by Commander Williams, R.N., admiralty agent in charge of mails on board the ship.[2] The two envoys also declared that they would yield only to personal compulsion, whereupon hands were laid upon shoulders and coat collars, and, accepting this as the application of *force*, they were transferred to the *San Jacinto's* boats. The scene on the *Trent*, as described by all parties, both then and later, partakes of the nature of comic opera, yet was serious enough to the participants. In fact, the envoys, especially Slidell, were exultant in the conviction that the action of Wilkes would inevitably result in the early realization of the object of their

[1] C. F. Adams, *The Trent Affair*. (*Proceedings*, Mass. Hist. Soc., XLV, pp. 41-2.)

[2] *Parliamentary Papers*, 1862, *Lords*, Vol. XXV. "Correspondence respecting the *Trent*." No. 1. Inclosure. Williams to Patey, Nov. 9, 1861.

journey—recognition of the South, at least by Great Britain.[1] Once on board the *San Jacinto* they were treated more like guests on a private yacht, having "seats at the captain's table," than as enemy prisoners on an American war-ship.

Captain Wilkes had acted without orders, and, indeed, even without any recent official information from Washington. He was returning from a cruise off the African coast, and had reached St. Thomas on October 10. A few days later, when off the south coat of Cuba, he had learned of the Confederate appointment of Mason and Slidell, and on the twenty-eighth, in Havana harbour, he heard that the Commissioners were to sail on the *Trent*. At once he conceived the idea of intercepting the *Trent*, exercising the right of search, and seizing the envoys, in spite of the alleged objections of his executive officer, Lieutenant Fairfax. The result was that quite without authority from the United States Navy Department, and solely upon his own responsibility, a challenge was addressed to Britain, the "mistress of the seas," certain to be accepted by that nation as an insult to national prestige and national pride not quietly to be suffered.

The *San Jacinto* reached Fortress Monroe on the evening of November 15. The next day the news was known, but since it was Saturday, few papers contained more than brief and inaccurate accounts and, there being then few Sunday papers, it was not until Monday, the eighteenth, that there broke out a widespread rejoicing and glorification in the Northern press.[2] America, for a few days, passed through a spasm of exultation hard to understand, even by those who felt it, once the first emotion had subsided. This had various causes, but among them is evident a quite

[1] Harris, *The Trent Affair*, pp. 103-109, describes the exact *force* used.

[2] Dana, *The Trent Affair*. (*Proceedings*, Mass. Hist. Soc., XLV, pp. 509-22.)

childish fear of the acuteness and abilities of Mason and Slidell. Both men were indeed persons of distinction in the politics of the previous decades. Mason had always been open in his expressed antipathy to the North, especially to New England, had long been a leader in Virginia, and at the time of the Southern secession, was a United States Senator from that State. Slidell, a Northerner by birth, but early removed to Louisiana, had acquired fortune in business there, and had for nearly twenty years been the political "boss" of one faction of the Democratic Party in New Orleans and in the State. With much previous experience in diplomacy, especially that requiring intrigue and indirect methods (as in the preliminaries of the Mexican War), and having held his seat in the United States Senate until the withdrawal of Louisiana from the Union, he was, of the two men, more feared and more detested, but both were thoroughly obnoxious to the North. Merely on the personal side their capture was cause for wide rejoicing.[1]

Surprise was also an element in the American elation, for until the news of the capture was received no portion of the public had given serious thought to any attempt to stop the envoys. Surprise also played its part when the affair became known in England, though in official circles there had been some warning. It had already been reported in the British press that Mason and Slidell had run the blockade at Charleston, were in Cuba, and were about to set sail for England on the Confederate steamer *Nashville*, but the British Government, considering that the envoys might perhaps sail rather on the West India Mail Steamer for Southampton, became much concerned over a possible American interference with that vessel. On November 9 Hammond sent an urgent enquiry to the Advocate-General stating the situation, calling attention to the presence at

[1] C. F. Adams, *The Trent Affair*. (*Proceedings*, Mass Hist. Soc., XLV, pp. 39-40.)

Photo: Handy, Washington

JAMES M. MASON

Southampton of an American war-vessel, and asking whether this vessel, or any other American man-of-war, "would be entitled to interfere with the mail steamer if fallen in with beyond the territorial limits of the United Kingdom, that is beyond three miles from the British Coast."

> "Whether for instance she might cause the West India Mail Steamer to bring to, might board her, examine her Papers, open the Mail Bags and examine the contents thereof, examine the luggage of passengers, seize and carry away Messrs. Mason and Slidell in person, or seize their Credentials and Instructions and Despatches, or even put a Prize Crew on board the West India Steamer and carry her off to a Port of the United States; in other words what would be the right of the American Cruiser with regard to her passengers and crew and lawful papers and correspondence on board our packet on the assumption that the said packet was liable to capture and confiscation on the ground of carrying enemies' despatches; would the Cruiser be entitled to carry the packet and all and everything in her back to America or would she be obliged to land in this Country or in some near port all the people and all the unseizable goods?"[1]

Hammond further stated that Russell was anxious to have an immediate reply, inasmuch as the mail packet was due to arrive in Southampton on November 12. The opinion of the law officer consulted is best given in Palmerston's own words in a letter to Delane, Editor of the *Times*:

> "94 *Piccadilly*,
> *November* 11, 1861.
>
> "MY DEAR DELANE,
>
> "It may be useful to you to know that the Chancellor, Dr. Lushington, the three Law Officers, Sir G. Grey, the Duke of Somerset, and myself, met at the Treasury to-day to consider what we could properly do about the American cruiser come, no doubt, to search the West Indian packet

[1] F.O., America, Vol. 805. Copy, E. Hammond to Advocate-General, Nov. 9, 1861.

supposed to be bringing hither the two Southern envoys; and, much to my regret, it appeared that, according to the principles of international law laid down in our courts by Lord Stowell, and practised and enforced by us, a belligerent has a right to stop and search any neutral not being a ship of war, and being found on the high seas and being suspected of carrying enemy's despatches; and that consequently this American cruiser might, by our own principles of international law, stop the West Indian packet, search her, and if the Southern men and their despatches and credentials were found on board, either take them out, or seize the packet and carry her back to New York for trial. Such being the opinion of our men learned in the law, we have determined to do no more than to order the *Phaeton* frigate to drop down to Yarmouth Roads and watch the proceedings of the American within our three-mile limit of territorial jurisdiction, and to prevent her from exercising within that limit those rights which we cannot dispute as belonging to her beyond that limit.

"In the meanwhile the American captain, having got very drunk this morning at Southampton with some excellent brandy, and finding it blow heavily at sea, has come to an anchor for the night within Calshot Castle, at the entrance of the Southampton river.

"I mention these things for your private information.

Yours sincerely,

PALMERSTON." [1]

Not completely satisfied with this decision as reported to Delane, and sincerely anxious to avert what he foresaw would be a difficult situation, Palmerston took the unusual step of writing to Adams on the next day, November 12, and asking for an interview. His note took Adams by surprise, but he promptly waited upon Palmerston, and was told of the latter's disturbance at the presence of the American ship *James Adger*, Captain Marchand commanding, in Southampton Harbour, with the alleged purpose of stopping the British West India steamer and intercepting

[1] C. F. Adams, *The Trent Affair*. (*Proceedings*, Mass. Hist. Soc., XLV, p. 54.)

the journey of Mason and Slidell. Palmerston stated that he "did not pretend to judge absolutely of the question whether we had a right to stop a foreign vessel for such a purpose as was indicated," and he urged on Adams the unwisdom of such an act in any case. "Neither did the object to be gained seem commensurate with the risk. For it was surely of no consequence whether one or two more men were added to the two or three who had already been so long here. They would scarcely make a difference in the action of the Government after once having made up its mind."[1]

The interview with Adams, so Palmerston wrote to Delane on the same day, November 12, was reassuring:

> "MY DEAR DELANE,
>
> "I have seen Adams to-day, and he assures me that the American paddle-wheel was sent to intercept the *Nashville* if found in these seas, but not to meddle with any ship under a foreign flag. He said he had seen the commander, and had advised him to go straight home; and he believed the steamer to be now on her way back to the United States. This is a very satisfactory explanation.
>
> Yours sincerely,
>
> PALMERSTON."[2]

In fact, neither Adams' diary nor his report to Seward recorded quite the same statement as that here attributed to him by Palmerston, and this became later, but fortunately after the question of the *Trent* had passed off the stage, a matter of minor dispute. Adams' own statement was that he had told Palmerston the *James Adger* was seeking to intercept the *Nashville* and "had no instruction" to interfere with a British Packet—which is not the same as saying that she already had instructions "not to meddle with any ship

[1] *Ibid.*, pp. 53-4. Adams' Diary MS. Nov. 12, 1861.

[2] *Ibid.*, p. 55.

under a foreign flag."[1] But in any case, it would appear that the British Government had been warned by its legal advisers that if that which actually happened in the case of the *Trent* should occur, English practice, if followed, would compel acquiescence in it.[2] This is not to say that a first legal advice thus given on a problematical case necessarily bound the Government to a fixed line of action, but that the opinion of the Government was one of "no help for it" if the case should actually arise is shown by the instructions to Lyons and by his reaction. On November 16, Hammond wrote to Lyons stating the opinion of the Law Officers that "we could do nothing to save the Packet being interfered with outside our three miles; so Lord Palmerston sent for Adams, who assured him that the American [the *James Adger*] had no instructions to meddle with any ship under English colours . . . that her orders were not to endeavour to take Mason and Slidell out of any ship under

[1] A full year later, after the publication of the American volume of despatches for the year 1862, Russell took up this matter with Adams and as a result of an interview wrote to Lyons, November 28, 1862:

"Lord Palmerston stated to Mr. Adams on the occasion in question that Her Majesty's Government could not permit any interference with any vessel, British or Foreign, within British waters; that with regard to vessels met with at sea, Her Majesty's Government did not mean to dispute the Belligerent right of the United States Ships of War to search them; but that the exercise of that right and the right of detention in certain conditions must in each case be dealt with according to the circumstances of the case, and that it was not necessary for him to discuss such matters then because they were not in point; but that it would not do for the United States Ships of War to harass British Commerce on the High Seas under the pretence of preventing the Confederates from receiving things that are Contraband of War.

"I took an opportunity of mentioning to Mr. Adams, the account which Lord Palmerston had given me of the language which he had thus held, and Mr. Adams agreed in its accuracy.

"Nothing must be said on this subject unless the false statements as to Lord Palmerston's language should be renewed, when you will state the real facts to Mr. Seward." (F. O., Am., Vol. 822. No. 295. *Draft.*)

This résumé by Russell contained still other variations from the original reports of both Palmerston and Adams, but the latter did not think it worth while to call attention to them.

[2] Walpole, *Russell*, II, p. 357, is evidently in error in stating that the law officers, while admitting the right of an American war vessel to carry the British Packet into an American port for adjudication, added, "she would have no right to remove Messrs. Mason and Slidell and carry them off as prisoners, leaving the ship to pursue her voyage." Certainly Palmerston did not so understand the advice given.

foreign colours."[1] On receipt of this letter subsequent to the actual seizure of the envoys, Lyons hardly knew what to expect. He reported Hammond's account to Admiral Milne, writing that the legal opinion was that " Nothing could be done to save the Packet's being interfered with outside of the Marine league from the British Coast " ; but he added, " I am not informed that the Law Officers decided that Mason and Slidell might be taken out of the Packet, but only that we could not prevent the Packet's being interfered with," thus previsioning that shift in British legal opinion which was to come *after* the event. Meanwhile Lyons was so uncertain as to what his instructions would be that he thought he " ought to maintain the greatest reserve here on the matter of the *Trent*."[2]

This British anxiety and the efforts to prevent a dangerous complication occurred after the envoys had been seized but some two weeks before that fact was known in London. " Adams," wrote Russell, " says it was all a false alarm, and wonders at our susceptibility and exaggerated notions."[3] But Russell was not equally convinced with Adams that the North, especially Seward, was so eager

[1] Lyons Papers. Hammond to Lyons. F. O., Private. Nov. 16, 1861. This statement about explicit orders to Captain Marchand " not to endeavour, etc.," is in line with Palmerston's understanding of the conversation with Adams. But that there was carelessness in reporting Adams is evident from Hammond's own language for " no instructions to meddle," which Adams did state, is not the same thing as " instructions not to meddle." Adams had no intent to deceive, but was misunderstood. He was himself very anxious over the presence of the *James Adger* at Southampton, and hurried her Captain away. Adams informed Russell that Palmerston had not understood him correctly. He had told Palmerston, " I had seen the Captain's [Marchand's] instructions, which directed him to intercept the *Nashville* if he could, and in case of inability to do so, to return at once to New York, keeping his eye on such British ships as might be going to the United States with contraband of war. Lord Palmerston's recollections and mine differed mainly in this last particular. Lord Russell then remarked that this statement was exactly that which he had recollected my making to him. Nothing had been said in the instructions about other British ships." (State Dept., Eng., Vol. 78. No. 80. Adams to Seward. Nov. 29, 1861.) Hammond's letter mentions also the excitement of " the Southerners " in England and that they had " sent out Pilot Boats to intercept and warn the Packet. . . ."

[2] Lyons Papers. Lyons to Milne, Dec. 1, 1861.

[3] *Ibid.* Russell to Lyons, Nov. 16, 1861.

for continued British neutrality, and when, on November 27, the news of Captain Wilkes' action was received, Russell and many others in the Cabinet saw in it a continuation of unfriendly Northern policy now culminating in a direct affront. Argyll, the most avowed friend of the North in the Cabinet, was stirred at first to keen resentment, writing "of this wretched piece of American folly. . . . I am all against submitting to any clean breach of International Law, such as I can hardly doubt this has been."[1] The Law Officers now held that "Captain Wilkes had undertaken to pass upon the issue of a violation of neutrality on the spot, instead of sending the *Trent* as a prize into port for judicial adjudication."[2] This was still later further expanded by an opinion that the envoys could not be considered as contraband, and thus subject to capture nor the *Trent* as having violated neutrality, since the destination of the vessel was to a neutral, not to an enemy port.[3] This opinion would have prohibited even the carrying of the *Trent* into an American port for trial by a prize court.

But the British Government did not argue the matter in its demand upon the United States. The case was one for a quick demand of prompt reparation. Russell's instruction to Lyons, sent on November 30, was couched in coldly correct language, showing neither a friendly nor an unfriendly attitude. The seizure of the envoys was asserted to be a breach of international law, which, it was hoped, had occurred without orders, and Lyons was to demand the restoration of the prisoners with an apology. If Seward had not already offered these terms Lyons was to propose them, but as a preliminary step in making clear the British position, he might read the instruction to Seward, leaving

[1] Gladstone Papers. Argyll to Gladstone, Nov. 29, 1861.

[2] C. F. Adams, *The Trent Affair*. (*Proceedings*, Mass. Hist. Soc., XLV, p. 58.)

[3] Moore, *Int. Law Digest*, VII, p. 772. The much argued international law points in the case of the *Trent* are given *in extenso* by Moore.

him a copy of it if desired.[1] In another instruction of the same date Russell authorized a delay of seven days in insisting upon an answer by Seward, if the latter wished it, and gave Lyons liberty to determine whether "the requirements of Her Majesty's Government are substantially complied with."[2] And on December 1, Russell writing privately to Lyons instructed him, while upholding English dignity, to abstain from anything like menace.[3] On November 30, also, the Government hurriedly sent out orders to hold the British Fleet in readiness, began preparations for the sending of troops to Canada, and initiated munitions and supply activities. Evidently there was at first but faint hope that a break in relations, soon to be followed by war, was to be avoided.[4]

It has long been known to history, and was known to Adams almost immediately, that the first draft of the instruction to Lyons was softened in language by the advice of Prince Albert, the material point being the expression of a hope that the action of Captain Wilkes was unauthorized.[5] That instruction had been sent previous to

[1] *Parliamentary Papers,* 1862, *Lords,* Vol. XXV. "Correspondence respecting the *Trent.*" No. 2.

[2] *Ibid.* No. 4.

[3] *Ibid.* No. 29. Inclosure.

[4] Troops were in fact shipped for Canada. This resulted, after the *Trent* affair had blown over, in a circumstance which permitted Seward, with keen delight, to extend a courtesy to Great Britain. Bancroft (II, 245) states that these troops "finding the St. Lawrence river full of ice, had entered Portland harbour. When permission was asked for them to cross Maine, Seward promptly ordered that all facilities should be granted for 'landing and transporting to Canada or elsewhere troops, stores, and munitions of war of every kind without exception or reservation.'" It is true that the American press made much of this, and in tones of derision. The facts, as reported by Lyons, were that the request was merely "a superfluous application from a private firm at Montreal for permission to land some Officers' Baggage at Portland." (Russell Papers, Lyons to Russell, Jan. 20, 1862.) Lyons was much vexed with this "trick" of Seward's. He wrote to the Governor-General of Canada and the Lieutenant-Governors of Nova Scotia and New Brunswick, protesting against an acceptance of Seward's permission, and finally informed Russell that no English troops were marched across the State of Maine. (Russell Papers. Lyons to Russell, Feb. 14, 1862. Also Lyons Papers. Lyons to Monck, Feb. 1, 1862.)

[5] Martin, *Life of the Prince Consort,* V, pp. 418-26.

the receipt of a report from Lyons in which, very fearful of results, he stated that, waiting instructions, he would preserve a strict silence.[1] Equally anxious was Cowley at Paris, who feared the realization of Seward's former "foreign war panacea." "I wish I could divest myself of the idea that the North and South will not shake hands over a war with us."[2] Considering the bitterness of the quarrel in America this was a far-fetched notion. The efforts promptly made by the Confederate agents in London to make use of the *Trent* affair showed how little Cowley understood the American temper. Having remained very quiet since August when Russell had informed them that Great Britain intended remaining strictly neutral,[3] they now, on November 27 and 30, renewed their argument and application for recognition, but received in reply a curt letter declining any official communication with them "in the present state of affairs."[4]

The delay of at least three weeks imposed by methods of transportation before even the first American reaction to

[1] Still another letter from Russell to Lyons on November 30, but not intended for Seward, outlined the points of complaint and argument. (1) The *San Jacinto* did not happen to fall in with the *Trent*, but laid in wait for her. (2) "Unnecessary and dangerous Acts of violence" were used. (3) The *Trent*, when stopped was not "searched" in the "ordinary way," but "certain Passengers" were demanded and taken by force. (4) No charge was made that the *Trent* was violating neutrality, and no authority for his act was offered by Captain Wilkes. (5) No force ought to be used against an "*unresisting* Neutral Ship" except just so much as is necessary to bring her before a prize court. (6) In the present case the British vessel had done nothing, and intended nothing, warranting even an inquiry by a prize court. (7) "It is essential for British Interests, that consistently with the obligations of neutrality, and of observing any *legal* and *effective* blockade, there should be communication between the Dominions of Her Majesty and the Countries forming the Confederate States." These seven points were for Lyons' eye alone. They certainly add no strength to the British position and reflect the uncertainty and confusion of the Cabinet. The fifth and sixth points contain the essence of what, on more mature reflection, was to be the British argument. (F. O., Am., Vol. 758. No. 447. Draft. Russell to Lyons, Nov. 30, 1861).

[2] Russell Papers. Cowley to Russell, Dec. 2, 1861.

[3] *Parliamentary Papers*, 1862, *Lords*, Vol. XXV. "Correspondence on Civil War in the United States." No. 78. Russell to Yancey, Rost and Mann, Aug. 24, 1861.

[4] *Ibid.* No. 124. Russell to Yancey, Rost and Mann, Dec. 7, 1861.

the British demand could be received in London gave time for a lessening of excitement and a more careful self-analysis by British statesmen as to what they really felt and desired. Gladstone wrote : " It is a very sad and heart-sickening business, and I sincerely trust with you that war may be averted."[1] Argyll hurried home from the Continent, being much disturbed by the tone of the British press, and stating that he was against standing on technical grounds of international law. " War with America is such a calamity that we must do all we can to avoid it. It involves not only ourselves, but all our North American colonies."[2] But war seemed to both men scarcely avoidable, an opinion held also by Cornewall Lewis[3] and by Clarendon, the latter standing at the moment in a position midway between the Whig and Tory parties.[4] Yet Russell, with more cause than others to mistrust Seward's policy, as also believing that he had more cause, personally, to resent it, was less pessimistic and was already thinking of at least postponing immediate hostilities in the event of an American refusal to make just recompense. On December 16 he wrote to Palmerston : " I incline more and more to the opinion that if the answer is a reasoning, and not a blunt offensive answer, we should send once more across the Atlantic to ask compliance. . . . I do not think the country would approve an immediate declaration of war. But I think we must abide by our demand of a restoration of the prisoners. . . . Lyons gives a sad account of Canada. Your foresight of last year is amply justified."[5] And on December 20 he wrote, " Adams' language yesterday was entirely in favour of yielding to us, if our tone is not too peremptory. . . . If our demands are refused, we must, of course, call Parliament

[1] Gladstone Papers. Gladstone to Robertson Gladstone, Dec. 7, 1861.
[2] *Ibid.* Argyll to Gladstone, Mentone, Dec. 10, 1861.
[3] Maxwell, *Clarendon*, II, p. 255. Lewis to Clarendon, Dec. 18, 1861.
[4] *Ibid.*, p. 254. Clarendon to Duchess of Manchester, Dec. 17, 1861.
[5] Palmerston MS.

together. The sixth of February will do. In any other case we must decide according to circumstances."[1]

Thus Russell would not have Great Britain go to war with America without the sanction of Parliament, and was seeking reasons for delay. He was reacting, in fact, to a more sobering second thought which was experienced also by nearly everyone, save the eager British "Southerner," in public and in newspaper circles. The first explosion of the Press, on receipt of the news of the *Trent*, had been a terrific one. The British lion, insulted in its chosen field of supremacy, the sea, had pawed the air in frenzy though at first preserving a certain slow dignity of motion. Customary "strong leader-writing" became vigorous, indeed, in editorial treatment of America and in demand for the prompt release of the envoys with suitable apology. The close touch of leading papers with Governmental opinion is well shown, as in the *Times*, by the day-to-day editorials of the first week. On November 28 there was solemn and anxious consideration of a grave crisis with much questioning of international law, which was acknowledged to be doubtful. But even if old British practice seemed to support Captain Wilkes, the present was not to be controlled by a discarded past, and "essential differences" were pointed out. This tone of vexed uncertainty changed to a note of positive assurance and militant patriotism on November 30 when the Government made its demand. The *Times* up to December 2, thought it absolutely certain that Wilkes had acted on authorization, and devoted much space to Seward as the evil genius of American warlike policy toward England. The old "Duke of Newcastle story" was revamped. But on December 2 there reached London the first, very brief, American news of the arrival of the *San Jacinto* at Fortress Monroe, and this contained a positive statement by Wilkes that he had had no orders. The

[1] *Ibid.*, Russell to Palmerston, Dec. 20, 1861.

Times was sceptical, but printed the news as having an important bearing, if true, and, at the same time, printed communications by "Justicia" and others advising a "go slowly" policy.[1] Yet all British papers indulged in sharp reflections on American insults, displayed keen resentment, and demanded a prompt yielding to the Governmental demand.

An intelligent American long resident in London, wrote to Seward on November 29: "There never was within memory such a burst of feeling as has been created by the news of the boarding of [the Trent]. The people are frantic with rage, and were the country polled, I fear 999 men out of a thousand would declare for immediate war. Lord Palmerston cannot resist the impulse if he would." And another American, in Edinburgh, wrote to his uncle in New York: "I have never seen so intense a feeling of indignation exhibited in my life. It pervades all classes, and may make itself heard above the wiser theories of the Cabinet officers."[2] If such were the British temper, it would require skilful handling by even a pacific-minded Government to avoid war. Even without belligerent newspaper utterances the tone of arrogance as in *Punch's* cartoon, "You do what's right, my son, or I'll blow you out of the

[1] Many citations from the *Times* are given in Harris, *The Trent Affair*, to show a violent, not to say scurrilous, anti-Americanism. Unfortunately dates are not cited, and an examination of the files of the paper shows that Harris' references are frequently to communications, not to editorials. Also his citations give but one side of these communications even, for as many argued caution and fair treatment as expressed violence. Harris apparently did not consult the *Times* itself, but used quotations appearing in American papers. Naturally these would print, in the height of American anti-British feeling, the bits exhibiting a peevish and unjust British temper. The British press made exactly similar quotations from the American newspapers.

[2] C. F. Adams, *The Trent Affair* (*Proceedings*, Mass. Hist. Soc. XLV, p. 43, note.) John Bigelow, at Paris, reported that the London Press, especially the Tory, was eager to make trouble, and that there were but two British papers of importance that did not join the hue and cry—these being controlled by friends of Bright, one in London and one in Manchester (Bigelow, *Retrospections of An Active Life*, I, p. 384.) This is not exactly true, but seems to me more nearly so than the picture presented by Rhodes (III, 526) of England as united in a "calm, sorrowful, astonished determination."

water," portended no happy solution. Yet this cartoon at least implied a hope of peaceful outcome, and that this was soon a general hope is shown by the prompt publicity given to a statement from the American General, Winfield Scott, in Paris, denying that he had said the action of Captain Wilkes had been decided upon at Washington before he sailed for Europe, and asserting that no orders were given tc seize the envoys on board any British or foreign vessel.[1] Nevertheless, Adams, for the moment intensely aroused, and suspicious of the whole purpose of British policy, could write to his friend Dana in Boston: "The expression of the past summer might have convinced you that she [Great Britain] was not indifferent to the disruption of the Union. In May she drove in the tip of the wedge, and now you can't imagine that a few spiders' webs of a half a century back will not be strong enough to hold her from driving it home. Little do you understand of this fast-anchored isle."[2]

There can be no doubt that one cause of a more bitter and sharper tone in the British press was the reception of the counter-exultation of the American press on learning of the detention and the exercise of "right of search" on a British ship. The American public equally went "off its head" in its expressions. Writing in 1911, the son of the American Minister to Great Britain, Charles Francis Adams, jun., in 1861, a young law-student in Boston, stated: "I do not remember in the whole course of the half-century's retrospect . . . any occurrence in which the American people were so completely swept off their feet, for the moment losing possession of their senses, as during the weeks which immediately followed the seizure of Mason and Slidell."[3] There were evident two principal causes for

[1] Cowley sent to Russell on December 3, a letter from Percy Doyle recounting an interview with Scott in which these statements were made. (F. O., France, Vol. 1399. No. 1404. Inclosure.)

[2] Dec. 13, 1861. C. F. Adams, *The Trent Affair*. (*Proceedings*, Mass. Hist. Soc., XLV, p. 95.)

[3] *Ibid.*, p. 37.

this elation. The North with much emotion and high courage entering in April, 1861, upon the task of restoring the Union and hoping for quick success, had now passed through a wearisome six months with no evident progress towards its object. Northern failure had developed a deep mortification when, suddenly and unexpectedly, a bold naval captain, on his own initiative, appeared to have struck a real blow at the South. His action seemed to indicate that the fighting forces of the North, if free from the trammels of Washington red tape, could, and would, carry on energetic war. Certainly it was but a slight incident to create such Northern emotion, yet the result was a sudden lifting from despondency to elation.

But almost equally with this cause of joy there operated on American minds the notion that the United States had at last given to Great Britain a dose of her own medicine in a previous era—had exercised upon a British ship that "right of search" which had been so keenly resented by America as to have become almost a *permanent* cause of a sense of injury once received and never to be forgotten. There was no clear thinking about this; the obnoxious right of search in times of peace for vagrant seamen, the belligerent right exercised by Britain while America was a neutral, the practice of a "right of visit" claimed by Britain as necessary in suppression of the African Slave Trade—all were confused by the American public (as they are still in many history textbooks to this day), and the total result of this mixing of ideas was a general American jubilation that the United States had now revenged herself for British offences, in a manner of which Great Britain could not consistently complain. These two main reasons for exultation were shared by all classes, not merely by the uninformed mob of newspaper readers. At a banquet tendered Captain Wilkes in Boston on November 26, Governor Andrews of Massachusetts called Wilkes' action "one of the most illustrious services that had made the war memorable," and added "that there might be nothing left [in the episode] to crown the exultation of the American heart, Commodore Wilkes fired his shot across the bows of the ship that bore the British lion at its head."[1]

All America first applauded the act, then plunged into discussion of its legality as doubts began to arise of its defensibility—and wisdom. It became a sort of temporarily popular "parlour game" to argue the international law of the case and decide that Great Britain could have no cause of complaint.[2] Meanwhile at Washington itself there was evidenced almost equal excitement and approval—but not, fortunately, by the Department responsible for the conduct of foreign relations. Secretary of the Navy Welles congratulated Wilkes on his "great public service," though criticizing him for not having brought the *Trent* into port for adjudication. Congress passed a joint resolution, December 2, thanking Wilkes for his conduct, and the President was requested to give him a gold medal commemorative of his act. Indeed, no evidence of approbation was withheld save the formal approval and avowal of national responsibility by the Secretary of State, Seward. On him, therefore, and on the wisdom of men high in the confidence of the Cabinet, like Sumner, Lyons pinned his faint hope of a peaceful solution. Thoroughly alarmed and

[1] *Ibid.*, p. 49. The *New York Times*, November 19, stated, "We do not believe the American heart ever thrilled with more genuine delight than it did yesterday, at the intelligence of the capture of Messrs. Slidell and Mason. . . . We have not the slightest idea that England will even remonstrate. On the contrary, she will applaud the gallant act of Lieut. Wilkes, so full of spirit and good sense, and such an exact imitation of the policy she has always stoutly defended and invariably pursued . . . as for Commodore Wilkes and his command, let the handsome thing be done, consecrate another *Fourth* of July to him. Load him down with services of plate and swords of the cunningest and costliest art. Let us encourage the happy inspiration that achieved such a victory." Note the "*Fourth* of July."

[2] Lyons Papers. Lousada to Lyons. Boston, Nov. 17, 1861. "Every other man is walking about with a Law Book under his arm and proving the *right* of the Ss. Jacintho to stop H.M.'s mail boat."

despondent, anxious as to the possible fate of Canada,[1] he advised against any public preparations in Canada for defence, on the ground that if the *Trent* affair did blow over it should not appear that we ever thought it an insult which would endanger peace."[2] This was very different from the action and attitude of the Government at home, as yet unknown to Lyons. He wisely waited in silence, advising like caution to others, until the receipt of instructions. Silence, at the moment, was also a friendly service to the United States.

The earliest American reactions, the national rejoicing, became known to the British press some six days after its own spasm of anger, and three days after the Government had despatched its demand for release of the prisoners and begun its hurried military preparations. On December 3 the *Times* contained the first summary of American press outpourings. The first effect in England was astonishment, followed by renewed and more intense evidences of a belligerent disposition. Soon, however, there began to appear a note of caution and more sane judgment of the situation, though with no lessening of the assertion that Britain had suffered an injury that must be redressed. The American frenzy of delight seemingly indicated a deep-seated hostility to Britain that gave pause to British clamour for revenge. On December 4 John Bright made a great speech at Rochdale, arguing a possible British precedent for Wilkes' act, urging caution, lauding American leadership in democracy, and stating his positive conviction that the United States Government was as much astonished as was that of Great Britain by the attack on the *Trent*.[3] To this the *Times* gave a full column of report on December 5

[1] "Mr. Galt, Canadian Minister, is here. He has frightened me by his account of the defencelessness of the Province at this moment." (Russell Papers. Lyons to Russell. Private. Dec. 3, 1861.)

[2] Lyons Papers. Lyons to Monck, Dec. 9, 1861.

[3] Rogers, *Speeches by John Bright*, I, p. 189 *seq.*

and the day following printed five close-type columns of the speech itself. Editorially it attacked Bright's position, belittling the speech for having been made at the one "inconspicuous" place where the orator would be sure of a warm welcome, and asking why Manchester or Liverpool had not been chosen. In fact, however, the *Times* was attempting to controvert "our ancient enemy" Bright as an apostle of democracy rather than to fan the flames of irritation over the *Trent*, and the prominence given to Bright's speech indicates a greater readiness to consider as hopeful an escape from the existing crisis.

After December 3 and up to the ninth, the *Times* was more caustic about America than previously. The impression of its editorials read to-day is that more hopeful of a peaceful solution it was more free to snarl. But with the issue of December 10 there began a series of leaders and communications, though occasionally with a relapse to the former tone, distinctly less irritating to Americans, and indicating a real desire for peace.[1] Other newspapers either followed the *Times*, or were slightly in advance of it in a change to more considerate and peaceful expressions. Adams could write to Seward on December 6 that he saw

[1] Among the communications were several on international law points by "Historicus," answering and belittling American legal argument. W. V. Harcourt, under this pseudonym, frequently contributed very acute and very readable articles to the *Times* on the American civil war. The *Times* was berated by English friends of the North. Cobden wrote Sumner, December 12, "The *Times* and its yelping imitators are still doing their worst." (Morley, *Cobden*, II, 392.) Cobden was himself at one with the *Times* in suspicion of Seward. "I confess I have not much opinion of Seward. He is a kind of American Thiers or Palmerston or Russell—and talks Bunkum. Fortunately, my friend Mr. Charles Sumner, who is Chairman of the Senate Committee on Foreign Relations, and has really a kind of veto on the acts of Seward, is a very peaceable and safe man." (*ibid.*, p. 386, to Lieut.-Col. Fitzmayer, Dec. 3, 1861.) It is interesting that Canadian opinion regarded the *Times* as the great cause of American ill-will toward Britain. A letter to Galt asserted that the "war talk" was all a "farce" (J. H. Pope to Galt, Dec. 26, 1861) and the Toronto *Globe* attacked the *Times* for the creation of bad feeling. The general attitude was that if *British* policy resulted in an American blow at Canada, it was a British, not a Canadian duty, to maintain her defence (Skelton, *Life of Sir Alexander Tilloch Galt*, pp. 340, 348.) Yet the author states that in the beginning Canada went through the same phases of feeling on the *Trent* as did Great Britain.

no change in the universality of the British demand for satisfaction of the "insult and injury thought to be endured," but he recognized in the next few days that a slow shift was taking place in the British temper and regretted the violence of American utterances. December 12, he wrote to his son in America: "It has given us here an indescribably sad feeling to witness the exultation in America over an event which bids fair to be the final calamity in this contest. . . ." Great Britain "is right in principle and only wrong in point of consistency. Our mistake is that we are donning ourselves in her cast-off suit, when our own is better worth wearing."[1] His secretarial son was more vehement: "Angry and hateful as I am of Great Britain, I still can't help laughing and cursing at the same time as I see the accounts of the talk of our people. What a bloody set of fools they are! How in the name of all that's conceivable could you suppose that England would sit quiet under such an insult. *We* should have jumped out of our boots at such a one."[2]

The British Cabinet members were divided in sentiments of hope or pessimism as to the outcome, and were increasingly anxious for an honourable escape from a possible situation in which, if they trusted the observations of Lyons, they might find themselves aiding a slave as against a free State. On November 29, Lyons had written a long account of the changes taking place in Northern feeling as regards slavery. He thought it very probable that the issue of emancipation would soon be forced upon Lincoln, and that the American conflict would then take on a new and more ideal character.[3] This letter, arriving in the midst of uncertainty about the *Trent* solution, was in line with news published in the British papers calling out

[1] *A Cycle of Adams' Letters*, I, pp. 81-2.
[2] *Ibid.*, I, p. 83. Henry Adams to Charles Francis Adams, Jr., Dec. 13, 1861.
[3] Russell Papers. Lyons to Russell. Private. Nov. 29, 1861.

editorials from them largely in disapproval.[1] Certainly Russell was averse to war. If the prisoners were not given up, what, he asked, ought England then to do? Would it be wise to delay hostilities or to begin them at once?

"An early resort to hostilities will enable us at once to raise the blockade of the South, to blockade the North, and to prevent the egress of numerous ships, commissioned as privateers which will be sent against our commerce." But then, there was Canada, at present not defensible. He had been reading Alison on the War of 1812, and found that then the American army of invasion had numbered but 2,500 men. "We may now expect 40 or 50,000."[2] Two days later he wrote to Gladstone that if America would only "let the Commissioners free to go where they pleased," he would be satisfied. He added that in that case, "I should be very glad to make a treaty with the U. S., giving up our pretensions of 1812 and securing immunity to persons not in arms on board neutral vessels or to persons going bona fide from one neutral port to another. This would be a triumph to the U. S. in principle while the particular case would be decided in our favour."[3]

On Saturday, December 14, the Prince Consort died. It was well-known that he had long been a brake upon the wheel of Palmerston's foreign policy and, to the initiated, his last effort in this direction—the modification of the instruction to Lyons on the *Trent*—was no secret. There is no evidence that his death made any change in the British

[1] See the *Times*, Dec. 14, 1861. Here for the first time the *Times* used the expression "the last card" as applied to emancipation.

[2] Palmerston MS. Russell to Palmerston, Dec. 11, 1861.

[3] Gladstone Papers. Russell to Gladstone, Dec. 13, 1861. On the same day Lady Russell wrote Lady Dumfermline: "There can be no doubt that we have done deeds very like that of Captain Wilkes . . . but I wish we had not done them. . . . It is all terrible and awful, and I hope and pray war may be averted—and whatever may have been the first natural burst of indignation in this country, I believe it would be ready to execrate the Ministry if all right and honourable means were not taken to prevent so fearful a calamity." (Dana, *The Trent Affair*. (*Proceedings*, Mass. Hist. Soc., XLV, p. 528.)

position, but it was true, as the American Minister wrote, that "Now they [the British public] are beginning to open their eyes to a sense of his value. They discover that much of their political quietude has been due to the judicious exercise of his influence over the Queen and the Court, and they do not conceal their uneasiness as to the future without him."[1] The nation was plunged into deep mourning, but not to distraction from the American crisis, for on the day when all papers were black with mourning borders, December 16, they printed the news of the approval of Wilkes by the United States Congress, and gave a summary of Lincoln's message of December 2, which, to their astonishment, made no mention of the *Trent* affair. The Congressional approval caused "almost a feeling of consternation among ourselves," but Lincoln's silence, it was argued, might possibly be taken as a good omen, since it might indicate that he had as yet reached no decision.[2] Evidently there was more real alarm caused by the applause given Wilkes by one branch of the government than by the outpourings of the American press. The next day several papers printed Lincoln's message in full and the *Times* gave a long editorial analysis, showing much spleen that he had ignored the issue with Great Britain.[3] On the eighteenth this journal also called attention, in a column and a half editorial, to the report of the American Secretary of War, expressing astonishment, not unmixed with anxiety, at the energy which had resulted in the increase of the army to 700,000 men in less than nine months. The *Times* continued, even increased, its "vigour" of utterance on the *Trent*, but devoted most of its energy to combating the suggestions, now being made very generally,

[1] *A Cycle of Adams' Letters*, I, p. 87. Charles Francis Adams to his son, Dec. 20, 1861.

[2] The *Times*, Dec. 16, 1861.

[3] The *Times* twice printed the full text of the message, on December 16 and 17.

advocating a recourse to arbitration. This would be "weak concession," and less likely to secure redress and peace for the future, than an insistence on the original demands.

Statesmen also were puzzled by Lincoln's silence. Milner Gibson wrote that "even though Lyons should come away, I think the dispute may after all be settled without war."[1] Cornewall Lewis thought the "last mail from America is decidedly threatening, not encouraging."[2] But on December 19, Adams was at last able to give Russell official assurance that Wilkes had acted without authorization. Russell at once informed Lyons of this communication and that he had now told Adams the exact terms of his two instructions to Lyons of November 30. He instructed Lyons to accept in place of an apology an explanation that Wilkes' action was unauthorized—a very important further British modification, but one which did not reach Lyons until after the conclusion of the affair at Washington.[3] Meanwhile a notable change had taken place in American public expressions. It now regarded "the Wilkes affair unfavourably, and would much prefer it had not occurred at all,"[4] a re-action without question almost wholly caused by the knowledge of the British demand and the unanimous

[1] Gladstone Papers. Milner-Gibson to Gladstone, Dec. 18, 1861.

[2] Maxwell, *Clarendon*, II, p. 225. Lewis to Clarendon, Dec. 18, 1861.

[3] *Parliamentary Papers*, 1862, *Lords*, Vol. XXV. "Correspondence respecting the *Trent*." No 14. Russell to Lyons, Dec. 19, 1861. The Government did not make public Adams' confirmation of "no authorization of Wilkes." Possibly it saw no reason for doing so, since this had been established already by Wilkes' own statements. The point was later a matter of complaint by Americans, who regarded it as indicating a peevish and unfriendly attitude. (Willard, *Letter to an English Friend on the Rebellion in the United States*, p. 23. Boston, 1862.) Also by English friends; Cobden thought Palmerston had intentionally prolonged British feeling for political purposes. "Seward's despatch to Adams on the 19th December [*communicated to Russell* on the 19th] . . . virtually settled the matter. To keep alive the wicked passions in this country as Palmerston and his *Post* did, was like the man, and that is the worst that can be said of it." (Morley, *Cobden*, II, p. 389. To Mr. Paulton, Jan., 1862.)

[4] Davis to Adams. New York. Dec. 21, 1861. C. F. Adams, *The Trent Affair*, (*Proceedings*, Mass. Hist. Soc., XLV, p. 107.)

support given it by the British public.[1] On Great Britain the alteration in the American tone produced less effect than might have been expected, and this because of the persistent fear and suspicion of Seward. His voice, it was felt, would in the end be the determining one, and if British belief that he had long sought an occasion for war was correct, this surely was the time when he could be confident of popular support. Thurlow Weed, Seward's most intimate political adviser, was now in London and attempted to disabuse the British public through the columns of the *Times*. His communication was printed, but his assertion that Seward's unfriendly utterances, beginning with the "Newcastle story," were misunderstood, did not convince the *Times*, which answered him at length,[2] and asserted its belief ". . . that upon his ability to involve the United States in a war with England, Mr. Seward has staked his official, and, most probably, also his political existence." The Duke of Newcastle's report of Seward's remarks, wrote George Peabody later, "has strongly influenced the Government in war preparations for several months past."[3] Adams himself, though convinced that Seward's supposed animosity "was a mistake founded on a bad joke of his to the Duke of Newcastle," acknowledged

[1] There has crept into American historical writing of lesser authenticity a story that just at this juncture there appeared, in the harbours of New York and San Francisco, Russian fleets whose commanders let it be understood that they had come under "sealed orders" not to be opened except in a certain grave event and that their presence was, at least, not an unfriendly indication of Russian sentiment in the *Trent* crisis. This is asserted to have bolstered American courage and to give warrant for the argument that America finally yielded to Great Britain from no fear of consequences, but merely on a clearer recognition of the justice of the case. In fact the story is wholly a myth. The Russian fleets appeared two years later in the fall of 1863, not in 1861. Harris, *The Trent Affair*, pp. 208-10, is mainly responsible for this story, quoting the inaccurate memory of Thurlow Weed. (*Autobiography*, II, pp. 346-7.) Reliable historians like Rhodes make no mention of such an incident. The whole story of the Russian fleets with their exact instructions is told by F. A. Golder, "The Russian Fleet and the Civil War," *Am. Hist. Rev.*, July, 1915.

[2] Weed, *Autobiography*, II, pp. 354-61.

[3] *Ibid.*, p. 365. Peabody to Weed, Jan. 17, 1862.

that: "The Duke has, however, succeeded in making everybody in authority here believe it."[1] Surely no "joke" to an Englishman ever so plagued an American statesman; but British Ministers founded their suspicions on far more serious reasons, as previously related.[2]

As time passed without an answer from America, British speculation turned to estimates of the probable conditions of a war. These were not reassuring since even though postulating a British victory, it appeared inevitable that England would not escape without considerable damage from the American navy and from privateers. Americans were "a powerful and adventurous people, strong in maritime resources, and participating in our own national familiarity with the risks and dangers of the deep."[3] Englishmen must not think that a war would be fought only on the shores of America and in Canada. The legal question was re-hashed and intelligent American vexation re-stated in three letters printed in the *Daily News* on December 25, 26 and 27, by W. W. Story, an artist resident in Rome, but known in England as the son of Justice Story, whose fame as a jurist stood high in Great Britain.[4] By the last week of the year Adams felt that the Ministry, at least, was eager to find a way out: "The Government here will not press the thing to an extreme unless they are driven to it by the impetus of the wave they have themselves created."[5] He greatly regretted the death of the Prince Consort who "believed in the policy of conciliating the United States instead of repelling them." On December 27, Adams wrote Seward: "I think the signs are clear of a

[1] *A Cycle of Adams' Letters*, I, p. 91. Charles Francis Adams to his son, Dec. 27, 1861.

[2] See *ante*, Ch. IV.

[3] The *Times*, Dec. 25, 1861.

[4] James, *William Wetmore Story and his Friends*, II, pp. 108-9. The letters were sent to Robert Browning, who secured their publication through Dicey.

[5] C. F. Adams, *The Trent Affair*. Adams to Motley, Dec. 26, 1861. (*Proceedings*, Mass. Hist. Soc., XLV, p. 109).

considerable degree of reaction." He also explained the causes of the nearly unanimous European support of England in this contention: "Unquestionably the view of all other countries is that the opportunity is most fortunate for obtaining new and large modifications of international law which will hereafter materially restrain the proverbial tendency of this country on the ocean."[1]

Adams' estimate was correct. Even the *Morning Post*, generally accepted as Palmerston's organ,[2] and in the *Trent* crisis the most 'vigorous' of all metropolitan journals, commented upon the general public hope of a peaceful solution, but asked on December 30, ". . . can a Government [the American] elected but a few months since by the popular choice, depending exclusively for existence on popular support, afford to disappoint the popular expectation? The answer to this question must, we fear, be in the negative. . . ." The *Post* (thereby Palmerston?) did indeed, as later charged, "prolong the excitement," but not with its earlier animosity to America. The very fact that the *Post* was accepted as Palmerston's organ justified this attitude for it would have been folly for the Government to announce prematurely a result of which there was as yet no definite assurance. Yet *within* the Cabinet there was a more hopeful feeling. Argyll believed Adams' statement to Russell of December 19 was practically conclusive,[3] and Adams himself now thought that the prevalent idea was waning of an American plan to inflict persistent "indignities" on Britain: "at least in this case nothing of the kind had been intended."[4] Everyone wondered at and was vexed with the delay of an answer from America, yet hopefully believed that this indicated

[1] *Ibid.*, p. 110.

[2] Palmerston had very close relations with Delane, of the *Times*, but that paper carefully maintained its independence of any party or faction.

[3] Gladstone Papers. Argyll to Gladstone, Dec. 30, 1861.

[4] State Dept., Eng., Vol. 78. No. 97. Adams to Seward, Jan. 2, 1862.

ultimate yielding. There could be no surety until the event. Russell wrote to Palmerston on January 7, "I still incline to think Lincoln will submit, but not until the clock is 59 minutes past 11. If it is war, I fear we must summon Parliament forthwith."[1]

The last moment for reply was indeed very nearly taken advantage of at Washington, but not to the full seven days permitted for consideration by Russell's November thirtieth instructions to Lyons. These were received on December 18, and on the next day Lyons unofficially acquainted Seward with their nature.[2] The latter expressed gratification with the "friendly and conciliatory manner" of Lyons and asked for two days' time for consideration. On Saturday, December 21, therefore, Lyons again appeared to make a formal presentation of demands but was met with a statement that the press of other business had prevented sufficient consideration and was asked for a further two days' postponement until Monday. Hence December 23 became the day from which the seven days permitted for consideration and reply dated. In the meantime, Mercier, on December 21, had told Seward of the strong support given by France to the British position.

The month that had elapsed since the American outburst on first learning of Wilkes' act had given time for a cooling of patriotic fever and for a saner judgment. Henry Adams in London had written to his brother that if the prisoners were not given up, "this nation means to make war." To this the brother in America replied "this nation doesn't,"[3] an answer that sums up public determination no matter how loud the talk or deep the feeling. Seward understood

[1] Palmerston MS.

[2] Bancroft, *Seward*, II, p. 233. Lyons officially reported that he carried no papers with him (*Parliamentary Papers*, 1862, *Lords*, Vol. XXV. "Correspondence respecting the *Trent*." No. 19. Lyons to Russell, Dec. 19, 1861). Newton (*Lyons*, I, pp. 55-78) shows that Seward was, in fact, permitted to read the instructions on the nineteenth.

[3] *A Cycle of Adams' Letters*, I, p. 86. C. F. Adams, Jr., to Henry Adams, Dec. 19, 1861.

the change and had now received strong warnings from Adams and Weed in London, and from Dayton in Paris,[1] but these were not needed to convince him that America must yield. Apparently, he had recognized from the first that America was in an impossible situation and that the prisoners must be released *if the demand were made.* The comment of those who were "wise after the event" was that true policy would have dictated an immediate release of the prisoners as seized in violation of international law, before any complaint could be received from Great Britain. This leaves out of consideration the political difficulties at home of an administration already seriously weakened by a long-continued failure to "press the war," and it also fails to recognize that in the American Cabinet itself a proposal by Seward to release, made immediately, would in all probability have been negatived. Blair, in the Cabinet, and Sumner in the Senate, were, indeed, in favour of prompt release, but Lincoln seems to have thought the prisoners must be held, even though he feared they might become "white elephants." All that Seward could do at first was to notify Adams that Wilkes had acted without instructions.[2]

[1] Bancroft, *Seward,* II, p. 234. Adams' letter of December 3 was received on December 21; Dayton's of December 3, on the 24th.

[2] Much ink has flowed to prove that Lincoln's was the wise view, seeing from the first the necessity of giving up Mason and Slidell, and that he overrode Seward, e.g., Welles, *Lincoln and Seward,* and Harris, *The Trent Affair.* Rhodes, III, pp. 522-24, and Bancroft, *Seward,* II, pp. 232-37, disprove this. Yet the general contemporary suspicion of Seward's "anti-British policy," even in Washington, is shown by a despatch sent by Schleiden to the Senate of Bremen. On December 23 he wrote that letters from Cobden and Lyndhurst had been seen by Lincoln.

"Both letters have been submitted to the President. He returned them with the remark that 'peace will not be broken if England is not bent on war.' At the same time the President has assured my informant that he would examine the answer of his Secretary of State, word for word, in order that no expression should remain which could create bad blood anew, because the strong language which Mr. Seward had used in some of his former despatches seems to have irritated and insulted England" (Schleiden Papers). No doubt Sumner was Schleiden's informant. At first glance Lincoln's reported language would seem to imply that he was putting pressure on Seward to release the prisoners and Schleiden apparently so interpreted them. But the fact was that at the date when this was written Lincoln had not yet committed himself to accepting Seward's view. He told Seward, "You will go on, of course, preparing your answer,

On Christmas morning the Cabinet met to consider the answer to Great Britain. Sumner attended and read letters from Bright and Cobden, earnestly urging a yielding by America and depicting the strength of British feeling. Bright wrote: "If you are resolved to succeed against the South, *have no war with England;* make every concession that can be made; don't even hesitate to tell the world *that you will even concede what two years ago no Power would have asked of you*, rather than give another nation a pretence for assisting in the breaking up of your country."[1] Without doubt Bright's letters had great influence on Lincoln and on other Cabinet members, greatly aiding Seward, but that his task was difficult is shown by the fact that an entire morning's discussion brought no conclusion. Adjournment was taken until the next day and after another long debate Seward had the fortune to persuade his associates to a hearty unanimity on December 26. The American reply in the form of a communication to Lyons was presented to him by Seward on the 27th, and on that same day Lyons forwarded it to Russell. It did not contain an apology, but Lyons wrote that since the prisoners were to be released and acknowledgment was made that reparation was due to Great Britain, he considered that British demands were "so far substantially complied with" that he should remain at his post until he received further orders.[2]

Seward's reply was immediately printed in the American papers. Lyons reported that it was very well received and that the public was calm and apparently contented with the

which, as I understood it, will state the reasons why they ought to be given up. Now, I have a mind to try my hand at stating the reasons why they ought *not* to be given up. We will compare the points on each side." Lincoln's idea was, in short, to return an answer to Great Britain, proposing arbitration (Bancroft, *Seward*, II, 234).

[1] Mass. Hist. Soc. *Proceedings*, XLV, 155. Bright to Sumner, Dec. 14, 1861. The letters to Sumner on the *Trent* are all printed in this volume of the *Proceedings*. The originals are in the *Sumner Papers* in the library of Harvard University.

[2] *Parliamentary Papers*, 1862, *Lords*, Vol. XXV. "Correspondence respecting the *Trent*." No. 24. Lyons to Russell, Dec. 27, 1861.

outcome.[1] He thought that "thus the preparation for war . . . has prevented war." Seward's argument reviewed at great length all the conditions of the incident, dilated on many points of international law both relevant and irrelevant, narrated the past relations of the two nations on "right of search," and finally took the ground that Mason and Slidell were contraband of war and justly subject to capture, but that Wilkes had erred in not bringing the *Trent*, with her passengers, into port for trial by an American prize court. Therefore the two envoys with their secretaries would be handed over promptly to such persons as Lyons might designate. It was, says Seward's biographer, not a great state paper, was defective in argument, and contained many contradictions,[2] but, he adds, that it was intended primarily for the American public and to meet the situation at home. Another critic sums up Seward's difficulties: he had to persuade a President and a reluctant Cabinet, to support the naval idol of the day, to reconcile a Congress which had passed resolutions highly commending Wilkes, and to pacify a public earlier worked up to fever pitch.[3] Still more important than ill-founded assertions about the nature of contraband of war, a term not reconcilable with the *neutral port* destination of the *Trent*, was the likening of Mason and Slidell to "ambassadors of independent states." For eight months Seward had protested to Europe "that the Confederates were not belligerents, but insurgents," and now "his whole argu-

[1] F. O., Am., Vol. 777. No. 807. Lyons to Russell, Dec. 31, 1861. But he transmitted a few days later, a "shocking prayer" in the Senate on December 30, by the Rev. Dr. Sutherland, which showed a bitter feeling. "O Thou, just Ruler of the world . . . we ask help of Thee for our rulers and our people, that we may patiently, resolutely, and with one heart abide our time; for it is indeed a day of darkness and reproach—a day when the high principle of human equity constrained by the remorseless sweep of physical and armed force, must for the moment, succumb under the plastic forms of soft diplomacy" (Russell Papers. Lyons to Russell, Jan. 3, 1862).

[2] Bancroft, *Seward*, II, 249-53.

[3] C. F. Adams, *The Trent Affair*. (*Proceedings*, Mass. Hist. Soc., XLV, p. 75).

ment rested on the fact that they were belligerents. . . .[1] But this did not later alter a return to his old position nor prevent renewed arguments to induce a recall by European states of their proclamations of neutrality.

On the afternoon of January 8, a telegram from Lyons was received in London, stating that the envoys would be released and the next day came his despatch enclosing a copy of Seward's answer. The envoys themselves did not reach England until January 30, and the delay in their voyage gave time for an almost complete disappearance of public interest in them.[2] January 10, Russell instructed Lyons that Great Britain was well satisfied with the fact and manner of the American answer, and regarded the incident as closed, but that it could not agree with portions of Seward's argument and would answer these later. This was done on January 23, but the reply was mainly a mere formality and is of interest only as revealing a further shift in the opinion of the legal advisers, with emphasis on the question of what constitutes contraband.[3] Possibly the British Government was embarrassed by the fact that while France had strongly supported England at Washington, Thouvenel had told Cowley ". . . that the conduct pursued by Capt. Wilkes, whether the United States claimed to be considered as Belligerents, *or as a Government engaged in putting down a rebellion*, was a violation of all those principles of Maritime international law, which France had

[1] Bancroft, *Seward*, II, 250.

[2] Mason, Slidell, Eustis and McFarland were delivered to the British ship *Rinaldo*, January 1, 1862. *En route* to Halifax the ship encountered a storm that drove her south and finally brought her to St. Thomas, where the passengers embarked on a packet for Southampton.

[3] *Parliamentary Papers*, 1862, *Lords*, Vol. XXV. "Correspondence respecting the *Trent*." Nos. 27 and 35. February 3, Lyons reported that Sumner, in a fireside talk, had revealed that he was in possession of copies of the Law Officers' opinions given on November 12 and 28 respectively. Lyons was astounded and commented that the Law Officers, before giving any more opinions, ought to know this fact (F. O., Am., Vol. 824. No. 76. Lyons to Russell).

ever supported . . ."[1] and had instructed Mercier to so state to Seward. This implied a reflection on former British practice, especially as regards the exercise of a right of search to recover its own citizens and is indicative of the correctness of Adams' judgment that one main reason for European support of Great Britain in the *Trent* crisis, was the general desire to tie her to a limitation of belligerent maritime power.

In notifying Russell of the release of the prisoners, Lyons had stated that he would caution the Commander of the ship conveying them that they were "not to be received with honours or treated otherwise than as distinguished *private* gentlemen."[2] Russell was equally cautious, seeing Mason, shortly after arrival in London, "unofficially at my own house," on February 10, refusing to read his credentials, and after listening to a statement of his instructions, replying that "nothing had hitherto occurred which would justify or induce" Great Britain to depart from a position of neutrality.[3] Russell had already suggested that Thouvenel use the same method with Slidell.[4] This procedure does not necessarily indicate a change in governmental attitude, for it is exactly in line with that pursued toward the Confederate Commissioners before the *Trent*; but the *Trent* controversy might naturally have been expected to have brought about an *easier* relation between Russell and a Southern representative. That it did not do so is evidence of Russell's care not to give offence to Northern susceptibilities. Also, in relief at the outcome of the *Trent*, he was convinced, momentarily at least, that the general British suspicion of Seward was unfounded. "I do not," he wrote to Gladstone, "believe that Seward has any ani-

[1] F. O., France, Vol. 1399. No. 1397. Cowley to Russell, Dec. 3, 1861. The italics are mine.

[2] Newton, *Lyons*, I, 73.

[3] F. O., Am., Vol. 817. No. 57. Draft. Russell to Lyons, Feb. 11, 1861.

[4] F. O., France, Vol. 1419. No. 73. Draft. Russell to Cowley, Jan. 20, 1862.

mosity to this country. It is all buncom" (*sic*).[1] Apparently it was beginning to be realized by British statesmen that Seward's "high tone" which they had interpreted, with some justification earlier, as especially inimical to England, now indicated a foreign policy based upon one object only—the restoration of the Union, and that in pursuit of this object he was but seeking to make clear to European nations that the United States was still powerful enough to resent foreign interference. The final decision in the *Trent* affair, such was the situation in the American Cabinet, rested on Seward alone and that decision was, from the first, for peace.

Nor did Seward later hold any grudge over the outcome. America in general, however, though breathing freely again as the war cloud passed, was bitter. "The feeling against Great Britain is of intense hatred and the conclusion of the whole matter is, that we must give up the traitors, put down the rebellion, increase our navy, perfect the discipline of the 600,000 men in the field, and then fight Great Britain."[2] Lowell, in one of the most emotional of his "Bigelow Papers," wrote, on January 6, 1862:

> "It don't seem hardly right, John,
> When both my hands was full,
> To stump me to a fight, John—
> Your cousin, tu, John Bull!
> Ole Uncle S., sez he, 'I guess
> We know it now,' sez he,
> 'The lion's paw is all the law,
> Accordin' to J.B.,
> Thet's fit for you an' me!'"[3]

[1] Gladstone Papers. Russell to Gladstone, Jan. 26, 1862.

[2] Bigelow, *Retrospections*, I, 424. Bowen to Bigelow, Dec. 27, 1861.

[3] *Poems. Bigelow Papers.* "Jonathan to John." After the release of the envoys there was much correspondence between friends across the water as to the merits of the case. British friends attempted to explain and to soothe, usually to their astonished discomfiture on receiving angry American replies. An excellent illustration of this is in a pamphlet published in Boston in the fall of 1862, entitled, Field and Loring, *Corres-*

It was not the demand itself for the release of Mason and Slidell that in the end so stirred America as the warlike tone of the British press and the preparations of the Government. Even after their surrender America was further incensed by British boasting that America had yielded to a threat of war, as in the *Punch* cartoon of a penitent small boy, Uncle Sam, who "says he is very sorry and that he didn't mean to do it," and so escapes the birching Britannia was about to administer. America had, in all truth, yielded to a threat, but disliked being told so, and regarded the threat itself as evidence of British ill-will.[1] This was long the attitude of the American public.

In England the knowledge of America's decision caused a great national sigh of relief, coupled with a determination to turn the cold shoulder to the released envoys. On January 11, the *Times* recounted the earlier careers of Mason and Slidell, and stated that these two "more than any other men," were responsible for the traditional American "insane prejudice against England," an assertion for which no facts were offered in proof, and one much overestimating the influence of Mason and Slidell on American politics before secession. They were "about the most worthless booty it would be possible to extract from the jaws of the American lion. . . . So we do sincerely hope that our countrymen will not give these fellows anything in the shape of an ovation." Continuing, the *Times* argued:

> "What they and their secretaries are to do here passes our conjecture. They are personally nothing to us. They must not suppose, because we have gone to the very verge of a great war to rescue them, that therefore they are

pondence on the Present Relations between Great Britain and the United States of America. The American, Loring, wrote, "The conviction is nearly if not quite universal that we have foes where we thought we had friends," p. 7.

[1] Dana, *The Trent Affair.* (*Proceedings*, Mass. Hist. Soc., XLV, pp. 508-22).

precious in our eyes. We should have done just as much to rescue two of their own Negroes, and, had that been the object of the rescue, the swarthy Pompey and Cæsar would have had just the same right to triumphal arches and municipal addresses as Messrs. Mason and Slidell. So, please, British public, let's have none of these things. Let the Commissioners come up quietly to town, and have their say with anybody who may have time to listen to them. For our part, we cannot see how anything they have to tell can turn the scale of British duty and deliberation."

This complete reversal, not to say somersault, by the leading British newspaper, was in line with public expressions from all sections save the extreme pro-Southern. Adams was astonished, writing privately: "The first effect of the surrender . . . has been extraordinary. The current which ran against us with such extreme violence six weeks ago now seems to be going with equal fury in our favour."[1] Officially on the same day he explained this to Seward as caused by a late development in the crisis of a full understanding, especially "among the quiet and religious citizens of the middle classes," that if Great Britain did engage in war with the United States she would be forced to become the ally of a "slave-holding oligarchy."[2]

Here, in truth, lay the greatest cause of British anxiety during the period of waiting for an answer and of relief when that answer was received. If England and America became enemies, wrote Argyll, "we necessarily became virtually the *Allies* of the *Scoundrelism* of the South."[3] Robert Browning, attempting to explain to his friend Story the British attitude, declared that early in the war Britain was with the North, expecting "that the pure and simple rights [of anti-slavery] in the case would be declared and vigorously carried out without one let or stop," but

[1] *A Cycle of Adams' Letters*, I, 99. To his son, Jan. 10, 1862.
[2] State Dept., Eng., Vol. 78. No. 99. Adams to Seward, Jan. 10, 1862.
[3] Gladstone Papers. Argyll to Gladstone, Dec. 7, 1861. Also expressed again to Gladstone. *Ibid.*, Jan. 1, 1862.

that Lincoln's denial of emancipation as an object had largely destroyed this sympathy. Browning thought this an excusable though a mistaken judgment since at least: "The *spirit* of all of Mr. Lincoln's acts is altogether against Slavery in the end."[1] He assured Story that the latter was in error "as to men's 'fury' here": "I have not heard one man, woman or child express anything but dismay at the prospect of being obliged to go to war on any grounds with America."[2] And after the affair was over he affirmed: "The purpose of the North is also understood at last; . . . there is no longer the notion that 'Slavery has nothing to do with it.'"[3]

A few extreme pro-Northern enthusiasts held public meetings and passed resolutions commending the "statesmanlike ability and moderation of Seward," and rejoicing that Great Britain had not taken sides with a slave power.[4] In general, however, such sentiments were not *publicly* expressed. That they were keenly felt, nevertheless, is certain. During the height of the crisis, Anthony Trollope, then touring America, even while sharing fully in the intense British indignation against Captain Wilkes, wrote:

> "These people speak our language, use our prayers, read our books, are ruled by our laws, dress themselves in our image, are warm with our blood. They have all our virtues; and their vices are our own too, loudly as we call out against them. They are our sons and our daughters, the source of our greatest pride, and as we grow old they should be the staff of our age. Such a war as we should now wage with the States would be an unloosing of hell upon all that is best upon the world's surface."[5]

[1] James, *William Wetmore Story and His Friends*, II, 105. Browning to Story, Dec. 17, 1861.

[2] *Ibid.*, p. 109. To Story, Dec. 31, 1861.

[3] *Ibid.*, p. 110. To Story, Jan. 21, 1862.

[4] *Liberator*, Feb. 7, 1862. Giving an account of a meeting at Bromley-by-Bow.

[5] Trollope, *North America* (Chapman & Hall, London, 1862), I, p. 446. Trollope left England in August, 1861, and returned in the spring

The expressions of men like Browning and Trollope may not indeed, be regarded as typical of either governmental or general public reactions. Much more exactly and with more authority as representing that thoughtful opinion of which Adams wrote were the conclusions of John Stuart Mill. In an article in *Fraser's Magazine*, February, 1862, making a strong plea for the North, he summarized British feeling about the *Trent*:

> "We had indeed, been wronged. We had suffered an indignity, and something more than an indignity, which, not to have resented, would have been to invite a constant succession of insults and injuries from the same and from every other quarter. We could have acted no otherwise than we have done; yet it is impossible to think, without something like a shudder, from what we have escaped. We, the emancipators of the slave—who have wearied every Court and Government in Europe and America with our protests and remonstrances, until we goaded them into at least ostensibly co-operating with us to prevent the enslaving of the negro . . . *we* should have lent a hand to setting up, in one of the most commanding positions of the world, a powerful republic, devoted not only to slavery, but to pro-slavery propagandism. . . ."

No such protestations of relief over escape from a possible alliance with the South were made officially by the Government, or in a debate upon the *Trent*, February 6, when Parliament reassembled. In the Lords the Earl of Shelburne thought that America should have made a frank and open apology. The Earl of Derby twitted the United States with having yielded to force alone, but said the time "had not yet come" for recognizing the Confederacy. Lord Dufferin expressed great friendship for America and declared that Englishmen ought to make themselves better

of 1862. He toured the North and the West, was a close observer, and his work, published in midsummer 1862, was very serviceable to the North, since he both stated the justice of the Northern cause and prophesied its victory.

informed of the real merits of the Civil War. Earl Granville, speaking for the Government, laid stress upon the difficulties at home of the Washington administration in pacifying public opinion and asserted a personal belief that strict neutrality was England's best policy, "although circumstances may arise which may call for a different course." On the same day in the Commons the debate was of a like general tenor to that in the Lords, but Disraeli differed from his chief (Derby) in that he thought America had been placed in a very difficult position in which she had acted very honourably. Palmerston took much credit for the energetic military preparations, but stated "from that position of strict neutrality, it is not our intention to depart"—an important declaration if taken, as apparently it was not, as fixing a policy. In substance all speakers, whether Whig or Tory, praised the Government's stand, and expressed gratification with the peaceful outcome.[1]

A further debate on the *Trent* was precipitated by Bright on February 17, in connection with the estimates to cover the cost of the military contingents sent to Canada. He asserted that England by generously trusting to American honour, might have won her lasting friendship, and it is worthy of note that for the first time in any speech made by him *in Parliament*, Bright declared that the war was one for the abolition of slavery. Palmerston in reply made no comment on the matter of slavery, but energetically defended the military preparations as a necessary precaution. Bright's speech was probably intended for American consumption with the purpose of easing American ill-will, by showing that even in Parliament there were those who disapproved of that show of force to which America so much objected. He foresaw that this would long be the basis of American bitterness. But Palmerston was undoubtedly

[1] Hansard, 3rd. Ser., CLXV, p. 12 *seq.*, though not consecutive as the speeches were made in the course of the debate on the Address to the Throne.

correct in characterizing Bright's opinion as a "solitary one." And looked at from a distance of time it would seem that a British Government, impressed as it was with a sense of Seward's unfriendliness, which had not prepared for war when making so strong a demand for reparation, would have merited the heaviest condemnation. If Mill was right in stating that the demand for reparation was a necessity, then so also were the military preparations.

Upon the Government the *Trent* acted to bring to a head and make more clear the British relation to the Civil War in America. By November, 1861, the policy of strict neutrality adopted in May, had begun to be weakened for various reasons already recited—weakened not to the point of any Cabinet member's advocacy of change, but in a restlessness at the slow development of a solution in America. Russell was beginning to *think*, at least, of recognition of the Confederacy. This was clear to Lyons who, though against such recognition, had understood the drift, if Schleiden is to be trusted, of Ministerial opinion. Schleiden reported on December 31 that Lyons had expressed to him much pleasure at the peaceful conclusion of the *Trent* affair, and had added, "England will be too generous not to postpone the recognition of the independence of the South as long as possible after this experience."[1] But the *Trent* operated like a thunder-storm to clear the atmosphere. It brought out plainly the practical difficulties and dangers, at least as regards Canada, of a war with America; it resulted in a weakening of the conviction that Seward was unfriendly; it produced from the British public an even greater expression of relief, when the incident was closed, than of anger when it occurred; and it created in a section of that public a fixed belief, shared by at least one member of the Cabinet, that the issue in America was that of slavery, in support of which England could not possibly take a stand.

[1] Schleiden Papers. Schleiden to the Senate of Bremen.

This did not mean that the British Government, nor any large section of the public, believed the North could conquer the South. But it did indicate a renewed vigour for the policy of neutrality and a determination not to get into war with America. Adams wrote to Seward, "I am inclined to believe that the happening of the affair of the *Trent* just when it did, with just the issue that it had, was rather opportune than otherwise."[1] Hotze, the confidential agent of the Confederacy in London, stated, "the *Trent* affair has done us incalculable injury," Russell is now "an avowed enemy of our nationality."[2] Hotze was over-gloomy, but Russell himself declared to Lyons: "At all events I am heart and soul a neutral . . . what a fuss we have had about these two men."[3]

[1] State Dept., Eng., Vol. 78. No. 114. Adams to Seward, Feb. 13, 1862.

[2] Pickett Papers. Hotze to Hunter, March 11, 1862.

[3] Lyons Papers. Russell to Lyons, Feb. 8, 1862.

CHAPTER VIII

THE BLOCKADE

THE six months following the affair of the *Trent* constituted a period of comparative calm in the relations of Great Britain and America, but throughout that period there was steadily coming to the front a Northern belligerent effort increasingly effective, increasingly a cause for disturbance to British trade, and therefore more and more a matter for anxious governmental consideration. This was the blockade of Southern ports and coast line, which Lincoln had declared *in intention* in his proclamation of April 19, 1861.

As early as December, 1860, Lyons had raised the question of the relation of British ships and merchants to the secession port of Charleston, South Carolina, and had received from Judge Black an evasive reply.[1] In March, 1861, Russell had foreseen the possibility of a blockade, writing to Lyons that American precedent would at least require it to be an effective one, while Lyons made great efforts to convince Seward that *any* interference with British trade would be disastrous to the Northern cause in England. He even went so far as to hint at British intervention to preserve trade.[2] But on April 15, Lyons, while believing that no effective blockade was possible, thought that the attempt to institute one was less objectionable than legislation " closing the Southern Ports as Ports of Entry," in reality a mere paper blockade and one which would " justify Great Britain and France in recognizing the Southern

[1] See *ante*, p. 52.
[2] See *ante*, pp. 61 and 65-66.

Confederacy. . . ." Thus he began to weaken in opposition to *any* interference.[1] His earlier expressions to Seward were but arguments, without committing his Government to a line of policy, and were intended to make Seward step cautiously.

Possibly Lyons thought he could frighten the North out of a blockade campaign. But when the Civil War actually began and Lincoln, on April 19, declared he had "deemed it advisable to set on foot a blockade," and that when a "competent force" had been posted "so as to prevent entrance and exit of vessels," warning would be given to any vessel attempting to enter or to leave a blockaded port, with endorsement on her register of such warning, followed by seizure if she again attempted to pass the blockade, Lyons felt that: "If it be carried on, with reasonable consideration for Foreign Flags, and in strict conformity with the Law of Nations, I suppose it must be recognized."[2] The Proclamation named the original seven seceding states, and on April 27 Virginia was added. The blockade was actually begun at certain Virginia ports on April 30, and by the end of May there were a few war-ships off all the more important Southern harbours.[3] This method of putting a blockade into effect by warning at the port rather than by a general notification communicated to European governments and setting a date, involved a hardship on British merchants since they were thereby made uncertain whether goods started for a Southern port would be permitted to enter. In practice vessels on their first departure from a blockaded harbour were warned and permitted to go out, but those seeking to enter were warned and turned back. In *effect*, while the blockade was being established, Lincoln's Proclamation had something of the nature for

[1] Russell Papers. Lyons to Russell, April 15, 1861.
[2] *Ibid.* Lyons to Russell. Private. April 23, 1861.
[3] Bernard, *Neutrality of Great Britain*, pp. 80-1.

the timid British merchant, though not for the bold one, of a paper blockade. This was not clearly understood by Lyons, who thought neutrals must acquiesce, having "exhausted every possible means of opposition," but who consoled himself with the idea that "for some time yet" British trade could be carried on.[1]

Lyons was in fact sceptical, as he told Seward in a long conversation on April 29 of the possibility of blockading a 3,000 mile coast line, but Seward assured him it would be done and effectively.[2] The British press was equally sceptical, and in any case believed that the war would be of short duration, so that there need be no anxiety over next year's supply of cotton.[3] In Parliament Russell took the stand that the blockade, if carried on in accordance with international law and made effective, required British recognition and respect. He also defended Lincoln's "notification at the port" method, stating that it might seem a hardship, but was perfectly legal.[4] Thus there was early and easy acquiescence in the American effort, but when, in June, there was revived a Northern plan to close Southern ports by legislative action, Britain was stirred to quick and vigorous opposition. Lyons learned that a Bill would be introduced in Congress giving the President authority, among other powers, to "proclaim" the ports closed, thus notifying foreign nations not to attempt to use them. He saw in it an unexpected application of the Northern theory that the South was not a belligerent and had no rights as such, and he regarded it as in effect a paper blockade.[5]

The fourth section of the Bill as introduced in Congress did not direct the President to issue a proclamation closing Southern ports—it merely gave him the power to do so.

[1] Russell Papers. Lyons to Russell, April 27, 1861.
[2] Bernard, p. 229.
[3] *Saturday Review*, May 18, 1861.
[4] Hansard, 3rd. Ser., CLXIII, pp. 188-195.
[5] Russell Papers. Lyons to Russell, June 24, 1861.

Almost from the first Lyons thought that Lincoln and Seward were too wise to issue such a proclamation.[1] Nevertheless it was his duty to be on guard and to oppose the plan. For six weeks there was much communication in regard to the " Southern Ports Bill," as all parties called it, from Russell to Lyons, and also with Cowley in France. The British Foreign Office interest in the matter, almost rising to excitement, is somewhat astonishing in view of the small importance evidently attached to the plan at Washington and the reluctance of France to be as vigorous as Great Britain in protest. Vigorous Russell certainly was, using a " high tone " in official remonstrance to America not unlike that taken by Seward on British recognition of Southern belligerency.

Immediately on learning of the introduction of the Bill Russell addressed enquiries to Cowley asking what France intended and urged a stiff protest. Thouvenel had not heard of the Bill and was seemingly indifferent. At first he acquiesced in Russell's protest, then drew back and on three separate occasions promised support only to withdraw such promise. He was disinclined, said Cowley, to join in a " friendly hint " to America because of the touchy sensibilities lately shown by Seward, and feared a direct protest might result in an American declaration of war. In any case why not wait until the President *did* act, and even then the proper method would be a protest rather than " reprisals." " I wish," wrote Cowley, on July 28, " that the French were inclined to be more *bumptious*, as they seemed to be at first. I would at all times rather have the task of calming them, than of urging them on. . . ."[2]

[1] *Ibid.* Lyons to Russell, July 2, 1861.

[2] Russell Papers. Cowley to Russell. The important correspondence on this subject is found in: F. O., France, Vol. 1393. No. 796. Cowley to Russell, July 2, 1861. *Ibid.*, No. 804. Cowley to Russell, July 4, 1861. *Ibid.*, Vol. 1377. No. 704. Russell to Cowley, July 10, 1861. *Ibid.*, Vol. 1394. No. 874. Cowley to Russell, July 17, 1861. *Ibid.*, No. 922. Cowley to Russell, July 28, 1861. *Ibid.*, No. 923. Confidential

Nevertheless Russell on July 19 notified Lyons that England would not observe a "legislative closing" of Southern ports.[1] On July 12 Lyons telegraphed that the Bill had passed both Houses of Congress, and on the sixteenth he wrote privately to Russell that he was much disturbed over its possible consequences since "even Sumner was for it,"[2] as this indicated a real intention to carry it into effect.[3] On August 8, Russell sent formal instructions of protest, a copy of which was to be handed to Seward, but the next day authorized Lyons to exercise discretion as to communicating the despatch.[4]

The original form of this instruction, dated in June and revised in July, concluded with language that might well draw out Thouvenel's objection to a threat of "reprisals." It read that "H.M.G. . . . reserve . . . the right of acting in concert with other Nations in opposition to so violent an attack on the rights of Commercial Countries and so manifest a violation of International Law."[5] This

Cowley to Russell, July 29, 1861. Russell Papers. Cowley to Russell, July 19, 1861. *Ibid.*, Cowley to Russell, July 28, 1861. It is interesting that the promise of France to support England in remonstrance against the "Southern Ports Bill" appears, through Cowley's communications, in the printed Parliamentary Papers. A study of these alone would lead to the judgment that France *had been the first* to raise the question with England and had heartily supported England. The facts were otherwise, though Mercier, without exact instructions from Thouvenel, aided Lyons in argument with Seward (*Parliamentary Papers*, 1862, *Lords*, Vol. XXV. "Correspondence on Civil War in the United States." No. 68. Lyons to Russell, July 20, 1861).

[1] *Parliamentary Papers*, 1862, *Lords*, Vol. XXV. "Correspondence on Civil War in the United States." No. 61.

[2] Russell Papers. Lyons to Russell, July 16, 1861.

[3] Schleiden reported Seward as objecting to the Bill and Sumner as "vainly opposing" it. Sumner had in fact spoken publicly in favour of the measure. Probably he told Schleiden that privately he was against it. Schleiden reported Sumner as active in urging the Cabinet not to issue a Proclamation closing the ports (Schleiden Papers. Schleiden to Senate of Bremen, July 10 and 19, 1861). Mercier later informed Thouvenel that Sumner declared the Bill intended for the Northern public only, to show administration "energy," and that there was never any intention of putting it into effect. F. O., France, 1394. No. 931. Cowley to Russell, Aug. 1, 1861.

[4] *Parliamentary Papers*, 1862, *Lords*, Vol. XXV. "Correspondence on Civil War in the United States." Nos. 70 and 71. Thouvenel did finally consent to support Russell's protest.

[5] F. O., Am., Vol. 755. No. 168.

high tone had been modified possibly by French opposition, possibly by Lyons' early opinion that the Bill would not be made operative. Indeed on July 24 Russell told Lyons that no final instruction of protest would be sent him until the President actually issued a proclamation.[1] Yet in spite of being fairly well assured that there was no danger in the "Southern Ports Bill," Russell did send the instruction of August 8, still distinctly "vigorous" in tone, though with no threat of "reprisals." His reason for doing so is difficult to understand. Certainly he was hardly serious in arguing to Thouvenel that a stiff instruction would strengthen the hands of the "moderate section" of the American Cabinet,[2] or else he strangely misjudged American temperament. Probably a greater reason was his wish to be able to print a Parliamentary Paper indicating the watchful care he was exercising in guarding British interests.

Before Russell's instruction could reach America Seward had voluntarily reassured Lyons as to American intentions. Lyons reported this, privately, on July 20,[3] but on the same day also reported, officially, that two days earlier, that is on the eighteenth, he and Mercier had discussed the 'Southern Ports" Bill and that as a result Mercier had then gone, that same day, to Seward to state that France must regard such a measure as merely a paper blockade.[4] "We were not very sanguine of success," wrote Lyons, but Seward "had listened to him [Mercier] with calmness," and personally seemed disinclined to issue the required Proclamation. This despatch, making it appear that Eng-

[1] F. O., Am., Vol. 756.

[2] F. O., France, Vol. 1395. No. 967. Cowley to Russell, Aug. 8, 1861.

[3] Russell Papers. Lyons to Russell.

[4] *Parliamentary Papers*, 1862, *Lords*, Vol. XXV. "Correspondence on Civil War in the United States." No. 68. Lyons to Russell, July 20, 1861. Enclosed was a copy of the six lines of Thouvenel's "instruction" to Mercier, dated July 4, the very brevity of which shows that this was in fact no instruction at all, but merely a comment by Thouvenel to Mercier.

land and France were in close harmony and that Lyons and Mercier were having a difficult time at Washington was printed, later, in the Parliamentary Papers. It was received by Russell on August 5, and in spite of the reassurances of Lyons' private letter (naturally not for printing) presumably received in the same mail with the official despatch, it furnished the basis of his "strong" instruction of August 8.

At Washington also there were indications of an effort to prepare a good case for the British public and Parliament: July 23, so Lyons wrote privately, Seward had prevented the issue of the "Southern Ports" Proclamation,[1] and on the next day he was shown by Seward, confidentially, an instruction to Adams and other Ministers abroad in which was maintained the right to close the ports by proclamation, but stating the Government's decision not to exercise the right. Lyons believed this was the end of the matter.[2] Yet on August 12, he presented himself formally at the Department of State and stated that he had instructions to declare that "Her Majesty's Government would consider a decree closing the ports of the South actually in possession of the insurgent or Confederate States as null and void, and that they would not submit to measures taken on the high seas in pursuance of such decree." . . . "Mr. Seward thanked me for the consideration I had shown; and begged me to confine myself for the present to the verbal announcement I had just made. He said it would be difficult for me to draw up a written communication which would not have the air of a threat." To this Lyons agreed.[3]

This permitted a warmth-creating impression to Englishmen of the "forthright yet friendly" tone of British

[1] Russell Papers. Lyons to Russell, July 30, 1861.

[2] *Ibid.* Lyons to Russell, August 1, 1861.

[3] *Parliamentary Papers*, 1862, *Lords*, Vol. XXV. "Correspondence on Civil War in the United States." No. 81. Lyons to Russell, Aug. 12, 1861.

diplomats when dealing with Seward. So also did Russell's instruction of August 8, not yet received by Lyons when he took the stage at Washington. Yet there is a possibility that Lyons was in fact merely playing his part as Seward had asked him to play it. On the next day, August 13, he acknowledged the receipt of Russell's communication of July 24, in which it was stated that while Great Britain could not acquiesce in the "Southern Ports" Bill *no final instructions* would be sent until Lincoln issued a Proclamation. Lyons now explained, "As Mr. Seward is undoubtedly at this moment opposed to closing the Ports, I have thought it wiser to be guided by him for the present as to the mode of communicating your decision about the matter."[1] Is it possible that Seward really wished to have a "strong," yet not "too strong" statement from Lyons in order to combat the advocates of the "Ports" Bill? There are many ramifications of diplomatic policy—especially in a popular government. At any rate on August 16 Lyons could assure Russell that there "was no question now of issuing the Proclamation."[2] And on the nineteenth could write officially that a Proclamation based on the Bill had indeed been issued, but without the objectionable fourth section.[3]

The whole affair of the "Southern Ports" Bill occupies more space in the British Parliamentary Papers, and excited more attention from the British Government than it would seem to have merited from the Washington attitude toward it. The Bill had been drawn by the Secretary of the Treasury, and its other sections related to methods of meeting a situation where former customs houses and places for the collection of import duties were now in the hands of the Confederacy. The fourth section alone

[1] Russell Papers. Lyons to Russell. Private. Aug. 13, 1861.

[2] *Ibid.* Russell Papers.

[3] *Parliamentary Papers*, 1862, *Lords*, Vol. XXV. "Correspondence on Civil War in the United States." No. 83.

implied a purpose to declare a paper blockade. The idea of proclaiming closed the Southern ports may have at first received the sanction of Seward as consistent with his denial of the existence of a war; or it may have been a part of his "high tone" foreign policy,[1] but the more reasonable supposition is that the Bill was merely one of many ill-considered measures put forth in the first months of the war by the North in its spasm of energy seeking to use every and any public means to attack the South. But the interest attached to the measure in this work is the British attitude. There can be no doubt that Russell, in presenting papers to Parliament was desirous of making clear two points: first, the close harmony with France—which in fact was not so close as was made to appear; second, the care and vigour of the Foreign Secretary in guarding British interests. Now in fact British trade was destined to be badly hurt by the blockade, but as yet had not been greatly hampered. Nor did Russell yet think an effective blockade feasible. Writing to Lyons a week after his official protest on the "Southern Ports" Bill, he expressed the opinion that a "*regular* blockade" could not possibly prevent trade with the South:

> "If our ships can go in ballast for cotton to the Southern Ports it will be well, but if this cannot be done by agreement there will be surely, in the extent of 3,000 miles, creeks and bays out of which small vessels may come, and run for Jamaica or the Bahamas where the cargoes might be transhipped. But it is not for Downing Street to suggest such plans to Cheapside and Tooley Street."[2]

[1] Lyons thought this possible. Russell Papers. Lyons to Russell. Private. July 20, 1861.

[2] Lyons Papers. Russell to Lyons. Private. Aug. 16, 1861. And again he wrote the next day, "To prevent smuggling over 3,000 miles of coast and 1,500 miles of land frontier seems to me impossible" (*Ibid.*, Aug. 17, 1861). Russell had received some two weeks earlier, a letter from Bunch at Charleston, urging that England make no objection to the blockade in order that the South might be taught the lesson that "King Cotton," was not, after all, powerful enough to compel British recognition and support. He stated that Southerners, angry at the failure to secure

A better knowledge of American geography would have made clear to Russell that if but seven Southern ports were effectively blockaded the remaining 2,550 miles of coast line would be useless for the export of cotton in any considerable amount. His bays and creeks did indeed long provide access to small vessels, but these were not adequate for the transport of a bulky export like cotton.[1] To Russell, however, the blockade appearing negligible in probable effect and also not open to objection by neutrals if regularly established, it seemed that any immediate danger to British trade was averted by the final American action on the "Southern Ports" Bill. It was not until the blockade did begin to be thoroughly effective that either the British public or Government gave it serious consideration.

Not again until late November did Russell return with any interest to the subject of the blockade and then it was again on an American effort which seemed to indicate the ineffectiveness of blockading squadrons and a plan to remedy this by unusual, even "uncivilized," if not illegal, methods. This was the "Stone Boat Fleet" plan of blocking Charleston harbour by sinking vessels across the entrance bar.[2] The plan was reported by Lyons and the news received in England at the most uncertain moment as to the outcome of the *Trent* controversy.[3] British press and

recognition, were loudly proclaiming that they both could and would humble and embarrass Great Britain (F. O., Am., Vol. 781. No. 82. Bunch to Russell, July 8, 1861). Bunch wrote on July 23 that the South planned to hold back its cotton until Great Britain and France raised the blockade (*Ibid.* No. 87). Bunch was now impressed with Southern determination.

[1] The seven ports were Norfolk (Virginia), Wilmington (North Carolina), Charleston (South Carolina), Savannah (Georgia), Mobile (Alabama), New Orleans (Louisiana), and Galveston (Texas).

[2] The first important reference to the blockade after mid-August, 1861, is in an order to Bunch, conveyed through Lyons, not to give advice to British merchants in Charleston as to blockade runners that had gotten into port having any "right" to go out again (F. O., Am., Vol. 757. No. 402. Russell to Lyons, Nov. 8, 1861).

[3] *Parliamentary Papers*, 1862, *Lords*, Vol. XXV. "Correspondence on Civil War in the United States." No. 125. Lyons to Russell, Nov. 25, 1861. Received Dec. 9.

Government at first placed no stress on it, presumably because of the feeling that in view of the existing crisis it was a minor matter. In the same week Lyons, having been asked by Russell for an opinion on the blockade, answered:

> "I am a good deal puzzled as to how I ought to answer your question whether I consider the Blockade effective. It is certainly by no means strict or vigorous along the immense extent of coast to which it is supposed to apply. I suppose the ships which run it successfully both in and out are more numerous than those which are intercepted. On the other hand it is very far from being a mere Paper Blockade. A great many vessels are captured; it is a most serious interruption to Trade; and if it were as ineffective as Mr. Jefferson Davis says in his Message, he would not be so very anxious to get rid of it."[1]

This was a very fair description of the blockade situation. Lyons, unaffected by irritations resulting from the *Trent*, showed the frame of mind of a "determined neutral," as he was fond of describing himself. His answer was the first given to Russell indicating a possibility that the blockade might, after all, become strictly effective and thus exceedingly harmful to British trade. There is no direct *proof* that this influenced Russell to denounce the plan of blocking Southern harbours with stone-laden boats sunk in the channel, but the existence of such a motive seems probable. Moreover his protest was not made until December 20, the *day after* he had learned officially from Adams that Wilkes was unauthorized in searching the *Trent*—a day on which strain and uncertainty regarding American intentions were greatly lessened. Russell then wrote to Lyons that he observed it to be stated, "apparently on good authority," that the declared purpose of the stone boat fleet was "of destroying these harbours for

[1] Russell Papers. Lyons to Russell, Nov. 29, 1861.

ever." He characterized this as implying "utter despair of the restoration of the Union," and as being only "a measure of revenge and irremediable injury against an enemy."

> "But even in this view, as a scheme of embittered and sanguinary war, such a measure is not justifiable. It is a plot against the commerce of nations and the free intercourse of the Southern States of America with the civilized world. It is a project worthy only of times of barbarism."

Lyons was instructed to speak in this sense to Seward, who, it was hoped, would disavow the project.[1]

There was nothing in Lyons' despatches, nor in the American newspaper extracts accompanying them, to warrant such accusation and expostulation. Lyons had merely commented that by some in America the project had been characterized as "odious and barbarous," adding, "The question seems to depend on the extent to which the harbours will be permanently injured."[2] It will be noted that Russell did not refer to information received from Lyons (though it was already in hand), but to "apparently good authority" in justification of his vigorous denunciation. But like vigour, and like characterization of American "barbarism" did not appear in the British press until after the news arrived of the release of Mason and Slidell. Then the storm broke, well summed up in the Punch cartoon entitled "Retrogression. (A Very Sad Picture.) War Dance of the I. O. U. Indian," and showing Uncle Sam in war-feathers and with war-club, in his hand a flag made of the *New York Herald,* dancing in glee on the shores of a deserted harbour across which stretched a row of sunken ships.[3]

[1] *Parliamentary Papers,* 1862, *Lords,* Vol. XXV. "Correspondence on Civil War in the United States." No. 127.

[2] *Ibid.* No. 126. Lyons to Russell, Nov. 29, 1861. Received Dec. 12.

[3] *Punch,* Feb. 1, 1862.

On January 13 the Liverpool Shipowners' Association called the attention of the Foreign Office to the news that Charleston harbour had been closed by stone boats and urged governmental remonstrance.[1] Hammond at once replied quoting the language of Russell's letter of December 20 and stating that further representations would be made.[2] On the sixteenth Russell again instructed Lyons to speak to Seward, but now was much less rasping in language, arguing, rather, the injury in the future to the United States itself in case the harbours were permanently destroyed since ". . . the object of war is peace, and the purposes of peace are mutual good-will and advantageous commercial intercourse."[3] To-day it seems absurd that any save the most ignorant observer should have thought the North contemplated a permanent and revengeful destruction of Southern port facilities. Nor was there any just ground for such an extreme British view of the Northern plan. Yet even Robert Browning was affected by the popular outcry. "For what will you do," he wrote Story, "if Charleston becomes loyal again?"[4] a query expressive of the increasing English concern, even alarm, at the intense bitterness, indicating a long war, of the American belligerents. How absurd, not to say ridiculous, was this British concern at an American "lapse toward barbarism" was soon made evident. On January 11 Lyons, acting on the instructions of December 20, brought up the matter with Seward and was promptly assured that there was no plan whatever "to injure the harbours permanently." Seward stated that there had never been any plan, even, to sink boats in the main entrance channels, but merely the lesser channels, because the Secretary of

[1] *Parliamentary Papers*, 1862, *Lords*, Vol. XXV. "Correspondence on Civil War in the United States." No. 141.

[2] *Ibid.* No. 142. Jan. 15, 1861.

[3] *Ibid.* No. 143.

[4] James, *W. W. Story*, II, p. 111, Jan. 21, 1862.

the Navy had reported that with the blockading fleet he could "stop up the 'large holes,'" but "could not stop up the 'small ones.'" Seward assured Lyons that just as soon as the Union was restored all obstructions would be removed, and he added that the best proof that the entrance to Charleston harbour had not been destroyed was the fact that in spite of blockading vessels and stone boats "a British steamer laden with contraband of war had just succeeded in getting in."[1] Again, on February 10, this time following Russell's instruction of January 16, Lyons approached Seward and was told that he might inform Russell that "all the vessels laden with stone, which had been prepared for obstructing the harbours, had been already sunk, and that it is not likely that any others will be used for that purpose."[2] This was no yielding to Great Britain, nor even an answer to Russell's accusation of barbarity. The fact was that the plan of obstruction of harbours, extending even to placing a complete barrier, had been undertaken by the Navy with little expectation of success, and, on the first appearance of new channels made by the wash of waters, was soon abandoned.[3]

The British outcry, Russell's assumption in protest that America was conducting war with barbarity, and the protest itself, may seem at first glance to have been merely manifestations of a British tendency to meddle, as a "superior nation" in the affairs of other states and to give unasked-for advice. A hectoring of peoples whose civilization was presumably less advanced than that which stamped the

[1] *Parliamentary Papers*, 1862, *Lords*, Vol. XXV. "Correspondence on Civil War in the United States." No. 153. Lyons to Russell, Jan. 14, 1862. Received Jan. 27.

[2] *Ibid.*, *Lords*, Vol. XXV. "Despatch from Lord Lyons respecting the Obstruction of the Southern Harbours." Lyons to Russell, Feb. 11, 1862. Received Feb. 24.

[3] Thompson and Wainwright, *Confidential Correspondence of G. V. Fox, Assistant Secretary of the Navy*, 1861-65, I, p. 79. Du Pont to Fox, Dec. 16, 1861. Hereafter cited as *Fox, Confid. Corresp.* This letter shows clearly also that the Navy had no thought of a *permanent* obstruction.

Englishman was, according to Matthew Arnold, traditional—was a characteristic of British public and Government alike.[1] But this is scarcely a satisfactory explanation in the present case. For in the first place it is to be remarked that the sinking of obstructions in an enemy's harbours in order to render more effective a blockade was no novelty in maritime warfare, as Russell must have well known, and that there was no modern record of such obstructions having permanently destroyed a harbour. A far more reasonable explanation is that which connects the energy of the British Government in opposing a proposed American closing of Southern harbours by Presidential proclamation, with a like energy against the stone boat project. The first method was indeed rightly regarded as a violation of accustomed maritime belligerency, but both methods were primarily objectionable in British eyes because they were very evidently the result of efforts to find a way in which an as yet ineffective blockade could be made more rigorous. On the impossibility of an effective blockade, if conducted on customary lines, the British people and Foreign Secretary had pinned their faith that there would be no serious interruption of trade. This was still the view in January, 1862, though doubts were arising, and the "stone boat" protest must be regarded as another evidence of watchful guardianship of commerce with the South. The very thought that the blockade might become effective, in which case all precedent would demand respect for it, possibly caused Russell to use a tone not customary with him in upbraiding the North for a planned "barbarity."

Within three months the blockade and its effectiveness was to be made the subject of the first serious parliamentary discussion on the Civil War in America. In another three months the Government began to feel a pressure from its associate in "joint attitude," France, to examine again

[1] *Vide* Arnold, *Friendship's Garland.*

with much care its asserted policy of strict neutrality, and this because of the increased effectiveness of the blockade. Meanwhile another "American question" was serving to cool somewhat British eagerness to go hand in hand with France. For nearly forty years since independence from Spain the Mexican Republic had offered a thorny problem to European nations since it was difficult, in the face of the American Monroe Doctrine, to put sufficient pressure upon her for the satisfaction of the just claims of foreign creditors. In 1860 measures were being prepared by France, Great Britain and Spain to act jointly in the matter of Mexican debts. Commenting on these measures, President Buchanan in his annual message to Congress of December 3, 1860, had sounded a note of warning to Europe indicating that American principles would compel the use of force in aid of Mexico if debt-collecting efforts were made the excuse for a plan "to deprive our neighbouring Republic of portions of her territory." But this was at the moment of the break-up of the Union and attracted little attention in the United States. For the same reason, no longer fearing an American block to these plans, the three European Governments, after their invitation to the United States to join them had been refused, signed a convention, October 31, 1861, to force a payment of debts by Mexico. They pledged themselves, however, to seek no accession of territory and not to interfere in the internal affairs of Mexico.

In this pledge Great Britain and Spain were sincere. Napoleon III was not—was indeed pursuing a policy not at first understood even by his Ministers.[1] A joint expedition under the leadership of the Spanish General Prim was despatched, and once in Mexico took possession of customs houses and began to collect duties. It soon became evident

[1] Thouvenel, *Le Secret de l'Empereur*, II, 249. Thouvenel could mistakenly write to Mercier on March 13, 1862. "Nous ne voulons pas cependant imposer une forme de gouvernement aux Mexicains . . ."

to the British and Spanish agents on the spot that France had far other objects than the mere satisfaction of debts. The result was a clash of interests, followed by separate agreements with Mexico and the withdrawal of forces by Great Britain and Spain. This difference of view on Mexican policy had become clear to Cowley, British Ambassador at Paris, by January, 1862, and from that month until the end of March his private letters to Russell referring to American affairs in general are almost wholly concerned with French designs on Mexico. Cowley learned that earlier rumours of Napoleon's purpose to place the Archduke Maximilian of Austria upon the *Throne* of Mexico, far from being unfounded, were but faint indications of a great French "colonial Empire" scheme, and he thought that there was "some ill-will to the United States at the bottom of all this. . . ."[1] He feared that the Mexican question would "give us a deal of trouble yet,"[2] and by March was writing of the "monstrous claims on the Mexican Govt." made by France.[3]

These reactions of Cowley were fully shared by Russell, and he hastened, in March, to withdraw British forces in Mexico, as also did Spain. Great Britain believed that she had been tricked into a false position in Mexico, hastened to escape from it, but in view of the close relation of joint policy with France toward the Civil War in America, undertook no direct opposition though prophesying an evil result. This situation required France to refrain, for a time, from criticism of British policy and action toward the North—to pursue, in brief, a "follow on" policy, rather than one based on its own initiative. On the British side

[1] Russell Papers. Cowley to Russell. Private. Jan. 17, 1862. On this same date Thouvenel, writing to Flahault in London, hoped England would feel that she had a common interest with France in preventing Mexico from falling under the yoke of Americans either "unis ou sécédés." (Thouvenel, *Le Secret de l'Empereur*, II, 226).

[2] *Ibid.*, Jan. 24, 1862.

[3] *Ibid.*, March 6, 1862.

the French Mexican policy created a suspicion of Napoleon's hidden purposes and objects in the Civil War and made the British Government slow to accept French suggestions. The result was that in relation to that war Great Britain set the pace and France had to keep step—a very advantageous situation for the North, as the event was to prove. On the purely Mexican question Lyons early took opportunity to assure Seward that Great Britain was "entirely averse to any interference in the internal affairs of Mexico, and that nothing could be further from their wishes than to impose upon the Mexican Nation any Government not of its own choice.[1]

British dislike of France's Mexican venture served to

[1] F. O., Am., Vol. 825. No. 146. Lyons to Russell, Feb. 28, 1862. The fact that Slidell arrived in France just as Napoleon's plans for Mexico took clearer form has been made the ground for assumptions that he immediately gave assurance of Southern acquiescence and encouraged Napoleon to go forward. I have found no good evidence of this—rather the contrary. The whole plan was clear to Cowley by mid-January before Slidell reached Paris, and Slidell's own correspondence shows no early push on Mexico. The Confederate agents' correspondence, both official and private, will be much used later in this work and here requires explanation. But four historical works of importance deal with it extensively. (1) Richardson, *Messages and Papers of the Confederacy*, 2 vols., 1905, purports to include the despatches of Mason and Slidell to Richmond, but is very unsatisfactory. Important despatches are missing, and elisions sometimes occur without indication. (2) Virginia Mason, *The Public Life and Diplomatic Correspondence of James M. Mason*, 1906, contains most of Mason's despatches, including some not given by Richardson. The author also used the *Mason Papers* (see below). (3) Callahan, *The Diplomatic History of the Southern Confederacy*, 1901, is the most complete and authoritative work on Southern diplomacy yet published. He used the collection known as the "Pickett Papers," for official despatches, supplementing these when gaps occurred by a study of the *Mason Papers*, but his work, narrative in form, permits no extended printing of documents. (4) L. M. Sears, *A Confederate Diplomat at the Court of Napoleon III*. (Am. Hist. Rev. Jan., 1921), is a study drawn from Slidell's private letters in the *Mason Papers*. The Mason Papers exist in eight folios or packages in the Manuscript Division of the Library of Congress, and in addition there is one bound volume of Mason's despatches to Richmond. These contain the private correspondence of Mason and Slidell while in Europe. Slidell's letters are originals. Mason's letters are copies in Slidell's hand-writing, made apparently at Mason's request and sent to him in May, 1865. A complete typed copy of this correspondence was taken by me in 1913, but this has not hitherto been used save in a manuscript Master's degree thesis by Walter M. Case, "James M. Mason, Confederate Diplomat," Stanford University, 1915, and for a few citations by C. F. Adams, *A Crisis in Downing Street* (Mass. Hist. Soc. *Proceedings*, May, 1914). The Mason Papers also contain many letters from Mason's English friends, Spence, Lindsay, Gregory and others.

swell the breeze of amity toward America that had sprung up once the *Trent* was beyond the horizon, and made, temporarily, for smooth sailing in the relations of Great Britain and the North. Lyons wrote on February 7 that the "present notion appears to be to overwhelm us with demonstrations of friendship and confidence."[1] Adams' son in London thought "our work here is past its crisis," and that, "Our victory is won on this side the water,"[2] while the American Minister himself believed that "the prospect of interference with us is growing more and more remote."[3] Russell also was optimistic, writing to Lyons, "Our relations have now got into a very smooth groove. . . . There is no longer any excitement here upon the question of America. I fear Europe is going to supplant the affairs of America as an exciting topic,"[4] meaning, presumably, disturbances arising in Italy. On April 4 Adams described his diplomatic duties as "almost in a state of profound calm."[5]

This quiet in relation to America is evidence that no matter what anxiety was felt by British statesmen over the effects of the blockade there was as yet no inclination seriously to question its legality. That there was, nevertheless, real anxiety is shown by an urgent letter from Westbury to Palmerston upon the blockade, asserting that if cotton brought but four pence at Charleston and thirteen pence at Liverpool there must be some truth in its alleged effectiveness:

> "I am greatly opposed to any violent interference. Do not let us give the Federal States any pretence for saying that they failed thro' our interference. . . . Patience for

[1] Russell Papers. To Russell. Lyons thought France also included in these demonstrations.

[2] *A Cycle of Adams' Letters*, I, 113. Henry Adams to Charles Francis Adams, Jr., Feb. 14, 1862.

[3] *Ibid.*, p. 115. To his son, Feb. 21, 1862.

[4] Lyons Papers. March 1, 1862.

[5] *A Cycle of Adams' Letters*, I, 123. To his son.

KING COTTON BOUND:

Or, The Modern Prometheus.

Reproduced by permission of the Proprietors of "Punch"

a few more weeks is I am satisfied the wiser and the more expedient policy."[1]

This would indicate some Cabinet discussion, at least, on the blockade and on British trade interests. But Westbury's "few more weeks" had no place in Russell's thought, for on February 15 he wrote to Lyons in regard to assertions being made that the blockade was ineffective because certain vessels had eluded it:

> "Her Majesty's Government, however, are of opinion that, assuming that the blockade is duly notified, and also that a number of ships is stationed and remains at the entrance of a port, sufficient really to prevent access to it or to create an evident danger of entering or leaving it, and that these ships do not voluntarily permit ingress or egress, the fact that various ships may have successfully escaped through it (as in the particular instances here referred to) will not of itself prevent the blockade from being an effective one by international law." [2]

From this view Russell never departed in official instructions.[3] England's position as the leading maritime Power made it inevitable that she should promptly approve the Northern blockade effort and be cautious in criticizing its legitimate operation. Both her own history and probable future interests when a belligerent, required such a policy far more important in the eyes of statesmen than any temporary injury to British commerce. English merchants, if determined to trade with the South, must take their own risks, and that Russell believed they would do so is evidenced by his comment to Adams that it was a tradition of the sea that Englishmen "would, if money were to be made by it, send supplies even to hell at the risk of burning their sails."

[1] Palmerston MS. Feb. 9, 1862.

[2] Bernard, p. 245. The author agrees with Russell but adds that Great Britain, in the early stages of the blockade, was indulgent to the North, and rightly so considering the difficulties of instituting it.

[3] He wrote to Mason on February 10, 1863, that he saw "no reason to qualify the language employed in my despatch to Lord Lyons of the 15th of February last." (Bernard, p. 293).

But trade problems with the South soon brought real pressure on the Government. In January, while marking time until Mason should arrive at his post, the Confederate commissioners already in London very nearly took a step that might have prejudiced the new envoy's position. They had now learned through public documents that Russell had informed Adams he "had no intention of seeing them again." Very angry they planned a formal protest to the British Government, but in the end Mann and Rost counselled silence, outvoting Yancey.[1] On his arrival Mason ignored this situation and with cause for, warmly received socially in pro-Southern circles, he felt confident that at least a private reception would soon be given him by Russell. He became, indeed, somewhat of a social lion, and mistaking this personal popularity for evidence of parliamentary, if not governmental, attitude, was confident of quick advantages for the South. On the day after his arrival he wrote unofficially to Hunter, Confederate Secretary of State ". . . although the Ministry may hang back in regard to the blockade and recognition through the Queen's speech, at the opening of Parliament next week the popular voice through the House of Commons will demand both." . . . "I shall be disappointed if the Parliament does not insist on definite action by the Ministry. . . ."[2]

Carefully considering the situation and taking the advice of many English friends, Mason and Slidell agreed that the best line to take was to lay aside for the moment the claim to recognition and to urge European repudiation of the blockade. Slidell, arrived in Paris, wrote Mason that in his coming interview with Thouvenel he should "make only a passing allusion to the question of recognition, intimating that on that point I am not disposed at present

[1] Richardson, *Messages and Papers of the Confederacy*, II, p. 155. Yancey and Mann to Hunter, Jan. 27, 1862.

[2] Mason, *Mason*, pp. 257-8, Jan. 30, 1862.

to press consideration. But I shall insist upon the inefficiency of the blockade, the 'vandalism of the stone fleet,' etc."[1] Mason was urged to take a like course with Russell. Both men were much excited by a document a copy of which had been secured by Mann purporting to be a "confidential memorandum" addressed by England to the Continental Powers, asking whether the time had not come to raise the blockade. No such memorandum existed, but Slidell and Mason believed it genuine.[2] They had great hopes of the opening of Parliament, but when that event took place, February 6, and the only references in debate were to the *Trent* and its fortunate outcome, Mason was puzzled and chagrined. He wrote: "It is thought that silence as to the blockade was intended to leave that question open."[3] This, no doubt, was the consolatory explanation of his friends, but the unofficial interview with Russell, at his home, on February 10, chilled Mason's hopes.

As agreed with Slidell, emphasis in this interview was laid by Mason on the blockade, though recognition was asked. His report to Richmond shows that he proceeded with great caution, omitting portions of his instructions on cotton for fear of arousing antagonism, and venturing only a slight departure by expressing the hope that if Great Britain wished to renew communication with the Confederacy it might be made through him, rather than through the British consuls at the South. Russell's "only reply was, he hoped I might find my residence in London agreeable." He refused to see Mason's credentials, stating this to be "unnecessary, our relations being unofficial." He listened with courtesy, asked a few questions, but "seemed utterly

[1] Mason Papers. Feb. 5, 1862.

[2] Mann sent this "confidential memorandum" to Jefferson Davis, Feb. 1, 1862 (Richardson, II, 160). There is no indication of how he obtained it. It was a fake pure and simple. To his astonishment Slidell soon learned from Thouvenel that France knew nothing of such a memorandum. It was probably sold to Mann by some enterprising "Southern friend" in need of money.

[3] Mason, *Mason*, p. 258. Mason to Hunter, Feb. 7, 1862.

disinclined to enter into conversation at all as to the policy of his Government, and only said, in substance, they must await events." Certainly it was a cool reception, and Mason departed with the conviction that Russell's "personal sympathies were not with us, and his policy inaction."[1] But Mason still counted on parliamentary pressure on the Government, and he was further encouraged in this view by a letter from Spence, at Liverpool, stating that he had just received a request to come to London "from a government quarter, of all the *most important*."[2]

The summons of Spence to London shows that the Government itself feared somewhat a pro-Southern move in Parliament. He reported to Mason that interviews had taken place with Palmerston and with Russell, that he had unfortunately missed one with Gladstone, and, while not citing these men directly, declared the general "London idea" to be that of "postponement"; since it was inevitable that "the North will break down in a few months on the score of money," and that "We have only to wait three months." Evidently Spence believed he was being used as an intermediary and influential adviser in pro-Southern circles to persuade them to a period of quiet.

[1] *Ibid.*, pp. 260-62. Mason's despatch No. 4. Feb. 22, 1862. (This despatch is not given by Richardson.) Slidell was more warmly received by Thouvenel. He followed the same line of argument and apparently made a favourable impression. Cowley reported Thouvenel, after the interview, as expressing himself as "hoping that in two or three months matters would have reached such a crisis in America that both parties would be willing to accept a Mediation. . . ."

(F. O., France., Vol. 1432. No. 132. Confidential. Cowley to Russell, Feb. 10, 1862.)

[2] Mason Papers. Spence to Mason, Feb. 13, 1862. This was that James Spence, author of *The American Union*, a work strongly espousing the Southern cause. This book was not only widely read in England but portions of it were translated into other languages for use on the Continent. Spence was a manufacturer and trader and also operated in the Liverpool Cotton Exchange. He made a strong impression on Mason, was early active in planning and administering Southern cotton loans in England, and was in constant touch with Mason. By Slidell he was much less favourably regarded and the impression created by his frequent letters to Mason is that of a man of second-rate calibre elated by the prominent part he seemed to be playing in what he took to be the birth of a new State.

This, he thought, was unwise since delay would be injurious.[1] Of like opinion were the two Members of Parliament who were, throughout Mason's career in England, to be his closest advisers. These were Gregory and Lindsay, the former possessing somewhat of a following in the "gentleman-ruler" class, the latter the largest shipowner in Great Britain. Their advice also was to press on the blockade question,[2] as a matter of primary British commercial interest, and they believed that France was eager to follow a British lead. This was contrary to Slidell's notion at the moment, but of this Mason was unaware.[3]

The Government did indeed feel compelled to lay before Parliament the papers on the blockade. This was a bulky document of one hundred and twenty-six pages and covered the period from May 3, 1861, to February 17, 1862. In it were the details of the institution of the blockade, reports from British consuls on its effectiveness, lists of vessels captured and of vessels evading it, all together furnishing a very complete view of this, the principal maritime belligerent effort of the North.[4] The Blockade Papers gave opportunity for debate, if desired, and especially so as almost at the end of this document appeared that instruction of February 15 by Russell to Lyons, which clearly stated British acceptance of the blockade as effective. Mason's interview with Russell occurred on the tenth. Five days later, after Spence had been urged vainly to use his influence for "postponement," Russell, so it must appear, gave challenge to pro-Southern sentiment by asserting the effectiveness of the blockade, a challenge almost immediately made known to Parliament by the presentation of papers.

[1] *Ibid.* Spence to Mason, Feb. 20, 1862.

[2] Mason, *Mason.* p. 258.

[3] Slidell in France at first took the tack of urging that Continental interests and British interests in the blockade were "directly antagonistic," basing his argument on England's forward look as a sea power (Slidell to Hunter, Feb. 26, 1862. Richardson, II, p. 186).

[4] *Parliamentary Papers*, 1862, *Lords*, Vol. XXV. "Papers relating to the Blockade."

Unless Southern sympathizers were meekly to acquiesce, without further protest, in governmental policy they must now make some decided effort. This came in the shape of a debate in the Commons, on March 7, of a motion by Gregory urging the Government to declare the blockade ineffective,[1] and of a similar debate on March 10 in the Lords. As is inevitable where many speakers participate in a debate the arguments advanced were repeated and reiterated. In the Commons important speeches for the motion were made by Gregory, Bentinck, Sir James Ferguson, Lord Robert Cecil and Lindsay, while against it appeared Forster and Monckton Milnes. The Solicitor-General, Roundell Palmer, presented the Government view. Gregory opened the debate by seeking to make clear that while himself favourable to recognition of the South the present motion had no essential bearing on that question and was directed wholly to a *fact*—that the blockade was not in reality effective and should not be recognized as such. He presented and analysed statistics to prove the frequency with which vessels passed through the blockade, using the summaries given by Mason to Russell in their interview of February 10, which were now before Parliament in the document on the blockade just presented, and he cited the reports of Bunch at Charleston as further evidence. This was the burden of Gregory's argument,[2] but he glanced in passing at many

[1] Hansard, 3rd. Ser., CLXV, pp. 1158-1230, and pp. 1233-43.

[2] Mason's authenticated statistics, unfortunately for his cause, only came down to Oct. 31, 1861, a fact which might imply that after that date the blockade was rapidly becoming effective and which certainly did indicate that it was at least sufficiently effective to prevent regular and frequent communications between the government at Richmond and its agents abroad. Did Russell have this in mind when he promptly incorporated Mason's figures in the papers presented to Parliament? These figures showed that according to reports from four Southern ports, sixty vessels had entered and cleared between April 29 and October 31, 1861; unauthenticated statistics extending to the date December 31, presented by Mason of vessels arrived at and departing from Cuban ports showed forty-eight vessels, each way engaged in blockade running. Seven of these were listed as "captured." Those reaching Cuba were described as twenty-six British, 14 Confederate, 3 Spanish, 3 American and 2 Mexican, but in none of these statistics were the names of the vessels given, for

other points favourable to the South, commenting on its free trade principles, depicting the "Stone Fleet" as a barbarity, asserting the right of the South to secede, declaring that France regarded British attitude as determined by a selfish policy looking to future wars, and attacking Seward on the ground of American inconsistency, falsely paraphrasing him as stating that "as for all those principles of international law, which we have ever upheld, they are as but dust in the balance compared with the exigencies of the moment."[1] Gregory concluded with the statement that the United States should be treated "with justice and nothing more."

When presenting a cause in Parliament its advocates should agree on a line of argument. The whole theory of this movement on the blockade was that it was wise to minimize the question of recognition, and Gregory had laboured to prove that this was not related to a refusal longer to recognize the blockade. But Bentinck, the second speaker for the motion, promptly undid him for he unhappily

obvious reasons, in the printed paper though apparently included in the list submitted by Mason. These figures did in fact but reveal a situation existing even after 1861. The American blockading fleets had to be created from all sorts of available material and were slow in getting under way. Regular ships of the old Navy could not enforce it being too few in number, and also, at first, directing their efforts to the capture of shore positions which would render a large blockading squadron unnecessary. This proved an abortive effort and it was not until 1862 that the development of a large fleet of blockaders was seriously undertaken. (See *Fox, Confid. Corresp.*, I, pp. 110, 115, 119 and especially 122, which, May 31, 1862, pays tribute to the energy with which the South for "thirteen long months" had defended its important port shore lines.) If Gregory had been able to quote a report by Bunch from Charleston of April 5, 1862, he would have had a strong argument. "The blockade runners are doing a great business. . . . Everything is brought in in abundance. Not a day passes without an arrival or a departure. The Richmond Government sent about a month ago an order to Nassau for Medicines, Quinine, etc. It went from Nassau to New York, was executed there, came back to Nassau, thence here, and was on its way to Richmond in 21 days from the date of the order. Nearly all the trade is under the British flag. The vessels are all changed in Nassau and Havana. Passengers come and go freely and no one seems to think that there is the slightest risk—which, indeed, there is not" (Lyons Papers. Bunch to Lyons, April 5, 1862).

[1] I have nowhere found any such statement by Seward. Gregory's reference is to a note from Seward to Lyons of May 27, 1861, printed in the Blockade Papers. This merely holds that temporary absence of blockading ships does not impair the blockade nor render "necessary a new notice of its existence."

admitted that recognition and blockade questions were so closely interwoven that they could not be considered separately. This was promptly seized upon by Forster, who led in opposition. Forster's main argument, however, was a very able tearing to pieces of Gregory's figures, showing that nearly all the alleged blockade runners were in reality merely small coasting steamers, which, by use of shallow inner channels, could creep along the shore and then make a dash for the West Indies. The effectiveness of the blockade of main ports for ocean-going vessels carrying bulky cargoes was proved, he declared, by the price of raw cotton in England, where it was 100 per cent. greater than in the South, and of salt in Charleston, where the importer could make a profit of 1,000 per cent. To raise the blockade, he argued, would be a direct violation by Britain of her neutrality. The real reason for this motion was not the *ineffectiveness* of the blockade, but the effectiveness, and the real object an English object, not a Southern one. Gregory was taunted for changing a motion to recognize the Confederacy into the present one because he knew the former would fail while the present motion was deceitfully intended to secure the same end. Forster strongly approved the conduct of the Government in preserving strict neutrality, alleging that any other conduct would have meant "a war in which she [England] would have had to fight for slavery against her kinsmen."

Gregory's speech was cautious and attempted to preserve a judicial tone of argument on fact. Forster's reads like that of one who knows his cause already won. Gregory's had no fire in it and was characterized by Henry Adams, an interested auditor, as "listened to as you would listen to a funeral eulogy." . . . "The blockade is now universally acknowledged to be unobjectionable."[1] This estimate is

[1] *A Cycle of Adams' Letters*, I, pp. 119-20. Henry Adams to Charles Francis Adams, Jr., March 15, 1862.

borne out by the speech for the Government by the Solicitor-General, who maintained the effectiveness of the blockade and who answered Gregory's argument that recognition was not in question by stating that to refuse longer to recognize the blockade would result in a situation of "armed neutrality"—that is of "unproclaimed war." He pictured the disgust of Europe if England should enter upon such a war in alliance "with a country . . . which is still one of the last strongholds of slavery"—an admission made in the fervour of debate that was dangerous as tending to tie the Government's hands in the future, but which was, no doubt, merely a personal and carelessly ventured view, not a governmentally authorized one. In general the most interesting feature of this debate is the hearty approval given by friends of the North to the Government's entire line of policy and conduct in relation to America. Their play at the moment, feeling insecure as to the fixity of governmental policy, was to approve heartily the neutrality now existing, and to make no criticisms. Later, when more confident of the permanency of British neutrality, they in turn became critics on the score of failure, in specific cases, in neutral duty.

The Solicitor-General's speech showed that there was no hope for the motion unless it could be made a party question. Of that there was no indication, and the motion was withdrawn. Three days later a similar debate in the Lords was of importance only as offering Russell, since he was now a member of the upper chamber, an opportunity to speak for himself. Lord Campbell had disavowed any intention to attack the blockade since Russell, on February 15, had officially approved it, but criticized the sending to Lyons of the despatch itself. Russell upheld the strict legality and effectiveness of the blockade, stated that if England sided with the South in any way the North would appeal to a slave insurrection—the first reference to an idea which was to play a very important rôle with Russell and others later—and concluded by expressing the opinion that three months would see the end of the struggle on lines of separation, but with some form of union between the two sovereignties.[1] Russell's speech was an unneeded but emphatic negative of the pro-Southern effort.

Clearly Southern sympathizers had committed an error in tactics by pressing for a change of British policy. The rosy hopes of Mason were dashed and the effect of the efforts of his friends was to force the Government to a decided stand when they preferred, as the summons of Spence to conference makes evident, to leave in abeyance for a time any further declaration on the blockade. The refusal of Mason and his Southern friends to wait compelled a governmental decision and the result was Russell's instruction to Lyons of February 15. The effect of the debate on Mason was not to cause distrust of his English advisers, but to convince him that the existing Government was more determined in unfriendliness than he had supposed. Of the blockade he wrote: "... no step will be taken by this Government to interfere with it."[2] He thought the military news from America in part responsible as: "The late reverses at Fort Henry and Fort Donelson have had an unfortunate effect upon the minds of our friends

[1] This "three months" statement returned to plague Russell later, British merchants complaining that upon it they had based plans in the belief that the Government had something definite in view. Spence's reference to this "three months" idea, after his conferences in London, would indicate that Russell was merely indulging in a generalization due to the expected financial collapse of the North. The Russian Ambassador in London gave a different interpretation. He wrote that the Northern victories in the West had caused Great Britain to think the time near when the "border states," now tied to the Union by these victories, would lead in a pacification on lines of separation from the Southern slave states. "It is in this sense, and no other that Russell's 'three months' speech in the Lords is to be taken" (Brunow to F. O., March 3-15, 1862. No 33). Brunow does not so state, but his despatch sounds as if this were the result of a talk with Russell. If so, it would indicate an attempt to interpret Lincoln's "border state policy" in a sense that would appear reasonable in the British view that there could be no real hope at Washington of restoring the Union.

[2] Mason, *Mason*, p. 264. Despatch No. 6. March 11, 1862,

here. . . ."[1] Spence was opposed to any further move in Parliament until some more definite push on the Government from France should occur.[2] Slidell, anxiously watching from Paris the effort in England, had now altered his view of policy and was convinced there was no hope in France until England gave the signal. Referring to his previous idea that the Continent could be put in opposition to Great Britain on the blockade he wrote :

> " I then supposed that the influence of the Emperor was such that any view of the question which he might urge on the British Cabinet would be adopted. I have since had reason to change entirely this opinion. I am now satisfied that in all that concerns us the initiative must be taken by England ; that the Emperor sets such value on her good will that he will make any sacrifice of his own opinions and policy to retain it." [3]

On March 28 he repeated this conviction to Mason.[4] It was a correct judgment. Mason was thereby exalted with the knowledge that his was to be the first place in importance in any and all operations intended to secure European support for the Confederacy, but he could not conceal from himself that the first steps undertaken in that direction had been premature. From this first failure dated his fixed belief, no matter what hopes were sometimes expressed later, that only a change of Government in England would help the Southern cause.

[1] *Ibid.*, p. 266. Fort Henry was taken by Grant on February 6 and Fort Donelson on the 15th. The capture of these two places gave an opening for the advance of the Western army southwards into Tennessee and Mississippi.

[2] Mason Papers. Spence to Mason, March 18, 1862.

[3] Richardson, II, 207. Slidell to Hunter, March 26, 1862.

[4] Mason Papers.

CHAPTER IX

ENTER MR. LINDSAY

THE friendly atmosphere created by the lifting of the threatening *Trent* episode, appears to have made Secretary Seward believe that the moment was opportune for a renewal of pressure on Great Britain and France for the recall of their Proclamations of Neutrality. Seizing upon the victories of Grant at Forts Henry and Donelson, he wrote to Adams on February 28 explaining that as a result the United States, now having access to the interior districts of Alabama, Mississippi and Arkansas, "had determined to permit the restoration of trade upon our inland ways and waters" under certain limitations, and that if this experiment succeeded similar measures would be applied "to the country on the sea-coast, which would be some alleviation of the rigour of the blockade." He added that these "concessions" to foreign nations would "go much further and faster" if those nations would withdraw their "belligerent privileges heretofore so unnecessarily conceded, as we conceive, to the insurgents."[1] This was large talk for a relatively unchanged military situation. Grant had as yet but forced open the door in the West and was still far from having "access to the interior districts" of the states named. Lyons, being shown a copy of this despatch to Adams, commented to Russell that while it might be said the position and the spirit of the Northern armies were greatly improved and notable successes probable, it could not be maintained that hostilities were "so near

[1] *U. S. Messages and Documents*, 1862-63, Pt. I, p. 41.

their conclusion or are carried on upon so small a scale as to disqualify either party for the title of Belligerents."[1] Lyons and Mercier were agreed that this was no time for the withdrawal of belligerent rights to the South, and when the hint was received that the purpose of making such a request was in Seward's mind, the news quite took Thouvenel's breath away.[2] As yet, however, Seward did no more than hint and Adams was quick to advise that the moment had not yet come "when such a proceeding might seem to me likely to be of use."[3]

Just at this time Seward was engaged in forwarding a measure no doubt intended to secure British anti-slavery sympathy for the North, yet also truly indicative of a Northern temper toward the South and its "domestic institution." This was the negotiation of a Slave-Trade treaty with Great Britain, by which America joined, at last, the nations agreeing to unite their efforts in suppression of the African Slave Trade. The treaty was signed by Seward and Lyons at Washington on April 7. On the next day Seward wrote to Adams that had such a treaty been ratified "in 1808, there would now have been no sedition here, and no disagreement between the United States and foreign nations,"[4] a melancholy reflection intended to suggest that the South alone had been responsible for the long delay of American participation in a world humanitarian movement. But the real purpose of the treaty, Lyons thought, was "to save the credit of the President with the Party which elected him if he should make concessions to the South, with a view of reconstructing the Union"[5]—an erroneous view evincing a misconception of

[1] F. O., Am., Vol. 826. Nos. 154 and 155. March 3, 1862.

[2] F. O., France, Vol. 1435. No. 362. Cowley to Russell, March 18, 1862.

[3] *U. S. Messages and Documents*, 1862-63, Pt. I, p. 54. Adams to Seward, March 27, 1862.

[4] *Ibid.*, p. 65.

[5] Russell Papers. Lyons to Russell. Private. April 8, 1862.

the intensity of both Northern and Southern feeling if regarded from our present knowledge, but a view natural enough to the foreign observer at the moment. Lyons, in this letter, correctly stated the rising determination of the North to restore the Union, but underestimated the rapid growth of an equal determination against a restoration with slavery. The real motive for Seward's eagerness to sign the Slave Trade treaty was the thought of its influence on foreign, not domestic, affairs. Lyons, being confident that Russell would approve, had taken "the risk of going a little faster" than his instructions had indicated.[1]

In this same letter Lyons dwelt upon the Northern elation over recent military successes. The campaign in the West had been followed in the East by a great effort under McClellan to advance on Richmond up the peninsula of the James river and using Chesapeake Bay as a means of water transportation and supply. This campaign had been threatened by the appearance of the iron-clad ram *Merrimac* and her attack on the wooden naval vessels operating in support of McClellan, but on March 9 the *Monitor*, a slow-moving floating iron-clad fortress, drove the *Merrimac* from her helpless prey, and removed the Southern threat to McClellan's communications. More than any other one battle of the Civil War the duel between the *Merrimac* and the *Monitor* struck the imagination of the British people, and justly so because of its significance in relation to the power of the British Navy. It "has been the main talk of the town," wrote Adams, "ever since the news came, in Parliament, in the clubs, in the city, among the military and naval people. The impression is that it dates the commencement of a new era in warfare, and that Great Britain must consent to begin over again."[2] The victory of the *Monitor* was relatively unimportant in

[1] *Ibid.*

[2] *A Cycle of Adams' Letters*, I, 123. To his son, April 4, 1862.

British eyes, but a fight between two completely armoured ships, and especially the ease with which the *Merrimac* had vanquished wooden ships on the day previous, were cause of anxious consideration for the future. Russell was more concerned over the immediate lessons of the battle. "Only think," he wrote, "of our position if in case of the Yankees turning upon us they should by means of iron ships renew the triumphs they achieved in 1812-13 by means of superior size and weight of metal."[1]

This, however, was but early and hasty speculation, and while American ingenuity and experiment in naval warfare had, indeed, sounded the death-knell of wooden ships of war, no great change in the character of navies was immediately possible. Moreover British shipbuilders could surely keep pace in iron-clad construction with America or any other nation. The success of the *Monitor* was soon regarded by the British Government as important mainly as indicative of a new energy in the North promising further and more important successes on land. The Government hoped for such Northern success not because of any belief that these would go to the extent of forcing the South into submission, for they were still, and for a long time to come, obsessed with the conviction that Southern independence must ultimately be achieved. The idea was, rather, that the North, having vindicated its fighting ability and realizing that the South, even though losing battle after battle, was stubborn in the will to independence, would reach the conclusion that the game was not worth the price and would consent to separation. Russell wrote in this vein to Lyons, even though he thought that the "morale of the Southern army seems to be ruined for the time."[2] He believed that the end of the war would be hastened by Northern victories, and he therefore rejoiced in them.

[1] Palmerston MS. Russell to Palmerston, March 31, 1862.

[2] Lyons Papers. March 22, 1862.

Of somewhat like opinion up to the end of March, 1862, Lyons, in April, began to doubt his previous analysis of Northern temper and to write warnings that the end was not near. Grant's hard-won victory in the West at Shiloh, April 6-7, the first great pitched battle of the war, called out such a flood of Northern expressions of determination to drive the war to the bitter end as to startle Lyons and cause him, in a remarkably clear letter of survey, to recast his opinions. He wrote:

> "The general opinion is that the Campaign of this Spring will clear up most of the doubts as to the result of the War If the Military successes of the North continue, the determination of the South, will (it is asserted) be at last really put to the test. If notwithstanding great Military reverses, the loss of the Border States, and the occupation of the most important points on the Coast, the Southern men hold out, if they destroy as they threaten to do, their cotton, tobacco and all other property which cannot be removed and then retire into the interior with their families and slaves, the Northern Conquests may prove to be but barren. The climate may be a fatal enemy to the Federal Armies. The Northern people may be unable or unwilling to continue the enormous expenditure. They may prefer Separation to protracting the War indefinitely. I confess, however, that I fear that a protraction of the War during another year or longer, is a not less probable result of the present posture of affairs than either the immediate subjugation of the South or the immediate recognition of its independence." [1]

This itemization of Southern methods of resistance was in line with Confederate threats at a moment when the sky looked black. There was indeed much Southern talk of "retiring" into a hypothetical defensible interior which impressed Englishmen, but had no foundation in geographical fact. Meanwhile British attention was eagerly fixed on the Northern advance, and it was at least generally hoped

[1] F. O., Am., Vol. 827. No. 244. Extract. Lyons to Russell, April 11, 1862.

that the projected attack on New Orleans and McClellan's advance up the peninsula toward Richmond would bring to a more definite status the conflict in America. Extreme Southern sympathizers scouted the possibility of any conclusive Northern success, ignoring, because ignorant, the importance of Grant's western campaign. They "were quite struck aback" by the news of the capture of New Orleans, April 25. "It took them three days to make up their minds to believe it,"[1] but even the capture of this the most important commercial city of the South was not regarded as of great importance in view of the eastern effort toward Richmond.

News of the operations in the peninsula was as slow in reaching England as was McClellan's slow and cautious advance. It was during this advance and previous to the capture of New Orleans that two remarkable adventures toward a solution in America were made, apparently wholly on individual initiative, by a Frenchman in America and an Englishman in France. Mercier at Washington and Lindsay at Paris conceived, quite independently, that the time had come for projects of foreign mediation.

French opinion, like that expressed in England, appears to have been that the Northern successes in the spring of 1862 might result in such a rehabilitation of Northern self-esteem that suggestions of now recognizing the *facts* of the situation and acknowledging the independence of the South would not be unfavourably received. In this sense Thouvenel wrote to Mercier, privately, on March 13, but was careful to state that the word "mediation" ought not to be uttered. His letter dilated, also, on French manufacturing difficulties at home due to the lack of cotton.[2] This was in no way an instruction to Mercier, but the ideas

[1] *A Cycle of Adams' Letters*, I, 143. Adams to his son, May 16, 1862.
[2] Thouvenel, *Le Secret de l'Empereur*, II, p. 247.

expressed were broached by him in a conversation with Seward, only to be met with such positive assertions of intention and ability soon to recover the South as somewhat to stagger the French Minister. He remarked, according to his report to Thouvenel, that he wished it were possible to visit Richmond and assure himself that there also they recognized the truth of Seward's statements, upon which the latter at once offered to further such a trip. Mercier asserted to Thouvenel that he was taken by surprise, having foreseen no such eager acquiescence in a suggestion made *without previous thought*, but that on consideration he returned to Seward and accepted the proposal, outlining the substance of what he intended to say at Richmond. He should there make clear that the anxiety of France was above all directed toward peace as essential to French commercial interests; that France had always regarded the separation of North and South with regret; that the North was evidently determined in its will to restore the Union; and, in repetition, that France wished to aid in any way possible the early cessation of war. Seward, wrote Mercier, told him to add that he, personally, would welcome "the presence in the Senate" of any persons whom the South wished to elect.[1]

Mercier, writes Bancroft, "from the first had been an impatient sympathizer with the Confederacy, and he was quite devoid of the balance and good judgment that characterized Lord Lyons." "Quite unnecessarily, Seward

[1] *Documents Diplomatiques*, 1862, pp. 120-122. Mercier to Thouvenel, April 13, 1862. A translation of this despatch was printed, with some minor inaccuracies, in the New York *Tribune*, Feb. 5, 1863, and of Mercier's report, April 28, on his return from Richmond, on Feb. 9, under the caption "The Yellow Book." It is interesting that the concluding paragraphs of this report of April 28, as printed in the *Tribune*, are not given in the printed volume of *Documents Diplomatiques*, 1862. These refer to difficulties about cotton and to certain pledges given by Seward as to cessation of illegal interferences with French vessels. How the *Tribune* secured these paragraphs, if authentic, is not clear. The whole purpose of the publication was an attack by Horace Greeley, editor, on Seward in an effort to cause his removal from the Cabinet. See Bancroft, *Seward*, II, 371-2.

helped him to make the trip."[1] A circumstance apparently not known to Bancroft was Mercier's consultation with Lyons, before departure, in which were revealed an initiative of the adventure, and a proposed representation to the authorities in Richmond materially different from the report made by Mercier to Thouvenel. These merit expanded treatment as new light on a curious episode and especially as revealing the British policy of the moment, represented in the person of the British Minister in Washington.[2]

On April 10 Mercier came to Lyons, told him that he was about to set out for Richmond and that he had "been for some little time thinking of making this journey." He told of *making the suggestion to Seward*, and that this "rather to his surprise" had been "eagerly" taken up.

> "Monsieur Mercier observed that the object of vital importance to France, and to England also, as he supposed, was to put an end, as soon as possible, to the blockade, and generally to a state of things which caused so grievous an interruption of the trade between Europe and this country. It was, he said, possible that he might hasten the attainment of this object by conferring personally with the Secession leaders. He should frankly tell them that to all appearances their cause was desperate; that their Armies were beaten in all quarters; and that the time had arrived when they ought to come to some arrangement, which would put an end to a state of affairs ruinous to themselves and intolerable to Europe. It was useless to expect any countenance from the European Powers. Those Powers could but act on their avowed principles. They would recognize any people which

[1] Bancroft, *Seward*, II, 298-99. Bancroft's account is based on the *Tribune* translation and on Seward's own comments to Weed and Bigelow. *Ibid.*, 371-72.

[2] Newton. *Lord Lyons*, I, pp. 82-85, gives an account of the initiation of Mercier's trip and prints Lyons' private letter to Russell of April 25, describing the results, but does not bring out sufficiently Lyons' objections and misgivings. Newton thinks that Mercier "whether instructed from home or not . . . after the manner of French diplomatists of the period . . . was probably unable to resist the temptation of trying to effect a striking *coup*. . . ."

established its independence, but they could not encourage the prolongation of a fruitless struggle.

"Monsieur Mercier thought that if the Confederates were very much discouraged by their recent reverses, such language from the Minister of a great European Power might be a knock-down blow ('Coup d'assommoir' was the expression he used) to them. It might induce them to come to terms with the North. At all events it might lead to an Armistice, under which trade might be immediately resumed. He had (he told me) mentioned to Mr. Seward his notion of using this language, and had added that of course as a Minister accredited to the United States, and visiting Richmond with the consent of the United States Government, he could not speak to the Southern men of any other terms for ending the War than a return to the Union.

"Monsieur Mercier proceeded to say that Mr. Seward entirely approved of the language he thus proposed to hold, and had authorized him to say to the Southern leaders, not of course from the United States Government, but from him Mr. Seward, personally, that they had no spirit of vengeance to apprehend, that they would be cordially welcomed back to their Seats in the Senate, and to their due share of political influence. Mr. Seward added that he had not said so much to any other person, but that he would tell Monsieur Mercier that he was willing to risk his own political station and reputation in pursuing a conciliatory course towards the South, that he was ready to make this his policy and to stand or fall by it."

This was certainly sufficiently strong language to have pleased the American Secretary of State, and if actually used at Richmond to have constituted Mercier a valuable Northern agent. It cannot be regarded as at all in harmony with Mercier's previous opinions, nor as expressive of Thouvenel's views. Lyons was careful to refrain from much comment on the matter of Mercier's proposed representations at Richmond. He was more concerned that the trip was to be made at all; was in fact much opposed to it, fearing that it would appear like a break in that unity of French-British attitude which was so desirable. Nor was he without suspicion of a hidden French purpose to secure some special and separate advantages in the way of prospective commercial relations with the South. Mercier told Lyons that he knew he could not ask Lyons to accompany him because of American "extreme susceptibility" to any interference by Great Britain, but he thought of taking Stoeckl, the Russian Minister, and that Stoeckl was "pleased with the idea." Lyons frankly replied that he was glad to be relieved of the necessity of declining to go and was sorry Mercier was determined to proceed since this certainly looked like a break in "joint policy," and he objected positively on the same ground to Stoeckl's going.[1] Mercier yielded the latter point, but argued that by informing Seward of his consultation with Lyons, which he proposed doing, the former objection would be obviated. Finding that Mercier "was bent on going," Lyons thought it best not to object too much and confined his efforts to driving home the idea that no opening should be given for a "separate agreement" with the South.

> "I therefore entered with him into the details of his plans, and made some suggestions as to his language and conduct. I said that one delusion which he might find it desirable to remove from the minds of men in the South, was that it would be possible to inveigle France or any other great European Power into an exclusive Alliance with them. I had reason to believe that some of them imagine that this might be effected by an offer of great commercial privileges to one Power, to the exclusion of others. I hardly supposed that Mr. Jefferson Davis himself, or men of his stamp could entertain so foolish a notion, but still it might be well to eradicate it from any mind in which it had found place." [2]

[1] Stoeckl's report does not agree with Mercier's statement. He wrote that he had been asked to accompany Mercier but had refused and reported a conversation with Seward in which the latter declared the time had not yet come for mediation, that in any case France would not be accepted in that rôle, and that if ever mediation should become acceptable, Russia would be asked to act (Russian Archives, Stoeckl to F. O., April 23-May 5, 1862. No. 927).

[2] F. O., Am., Vol. 828. No. 250. Confidential. Lyons to Russell, April 14, 1862.

Lyons saw Mercier "two or three times" between the tenth and fourteenth and on the twelfth spoke to Seward about the trip, "without saying anything to lead him to suppose that I had any objection to it." This was intended to preserve the impression of close harmony with France, and Lyons wrote, "I consider that the result of my communications with M. Mercier entitles him to say that he makes his journey to Richmond with my acquiescence."[1] Nevertheless he both believed, and declared to Mercier, that the views expressed on Southern weakening of determination were wholly erroneous, and that neither North nor South was ready for any efforts, still less mediation, looking toward peace. He prophesied failure of Mercier's avowed hopes. His prophecy proved well founded. On April 28 Lyons reported Mercier's account to him of the results of the journey. Mercier returned to Washington on April 24, reported at once to Seward the results of his trip, and on the same day called on Lyons. Having conversed with Benjamin, the new Confederate Secretary of State, he was now wholly convinced of the settled determination of the South to maintain its independence, even under extreme reverses. Upon enquiry by Lyons whether the South expected European assistance, Mercier "replied that the Confederate leaders professed to have abandoned all hope of succour from Europe," and that confident in their own power they "desired no aid." Cautiously adverting to his suspicion that Mercier's trip might have had in view French commercial advantage, Lyons asked whether France had received any proposals of benefit in return for recognition. Mercier answered with a simple negative. He then further developed the interview with Benjamin.[2]

[1] *Ibid.*

[2] This suspicion was a natural one but that it was unfounded is indicated by Benjamin's report to Slidell of Mercier's visit, describing the language used in almost exactly the same terms that Lyons reported to Russell. That little importance was attached by Benjamin to Mercier's visit is also indicated by the fact that he did not write to Slidell about it until July. Richardson, II, 260. Benjamin to Slidell, July 19, 1862.

"He said that he had spoken while at Richmond as a friend of the Union, and a friend of all parties, but that the particular language which he had intended to hold was entirely inapplicable to the state of mind in which he found the Confederates one and all. It was idle to tell them that they were worsted on all sides; that the time was come for making terms with the North. What he had said to them about the recognition of their Independence was that the principal inducement to France to recognize it would be a hope that her doing so would have a great moral effect towards hastening peace; that at this moment it would certainly not have any such effect; that it would embroil France with the United States, and that would be all."[1]

Thus none of the strong representations intended to be made by Mercier to convince the South of the uselessness of further resistance had, in fact, been made. In his report to Thouvenel, Mercier stated that he had approached Benjamin with the simple declaration "that the purpose of my journey was merely to assure myself, for myself, of the true condition of things; and that I called to beg him to aid me in attaining it." Since the proposed strong representations were not reported to Thouvenel, either, in the explanation given of the initiation of the trip, the doubt must be entertained that Mercier ever intended to make them. They bear the appearance of arguments to Seward—and in some degree also to Lyons—made to secure acquiescence in his plan. The report to Thouvenel omits also any reference to expressions, as narrated to Lyons, about recognition of the Confederacy, or a "principal inducement" thereto.[2] Mercier now declared to Lyons his own views on recognition:

"He was himself more than ever convinced that the restoration of the old Union was impossible. He believed

[1] F. O., Am., Vol. 828. No. 284. Confidential. Lyons to Russell, April 24, 1862.

[2] *Documents Diplomatiques*, 1862, pp. 122-124.

that, if the Powers of Europe exercised no influence, the War would last for years. He conceived that the Independence of the South must be recognized sooner or later; and in his opinion the Governments of Europe should be on the watch for a favourable opportunity of doing this in such a manner as to end the War. The present opportunity would however, he thought, be particularly unfavourable."

Lyons writes:

"I did not express any opinion as to the policy to be eventually pursued by France or England, but I told Monsieur Mercier that I entirely agreed with him in thinking that there was nothing to do at the present moment but to watch events."

On the day following this interview, Lyons spoke to Seward of Mercier's trip and was given a very different view of the situation at Richmond. Seward said:

"He himself was quite convinced, from Monsieur Mercier's account of what had passed, that the Confederates were about to make a last effort, that their last resources were brought into play; that their last Armies were in the field. If they were now defeated, they would accept the terms which would be offered them. Their talking of retiring into the interior was idle. If the United States were undisputed masters of the Border States and the Sea Coast, there would be no occasion for any more fighting. Those who chose to retire into the interior were welcome to do so, and to stay there till they were tired."

"The truth," wrote Lyons, "as to the state of feeling in the South probably lies somewhere between Mr. Seward's views and those of Monsieur Mercier." Lyons concluded his report of the whole matter:

"The result of Monsieur Mercier's journey has been to bring him back precisely to the point at which he was three months ago. The Federal successes which occurred afterwards had somewhat shaken his conviction in the ultimate success of the South, and consequently his opinions as to the policy to be adopted by France. The sentiments he now expresses are exactly those which he expressed at the beginning of the year." [1]

In other words, Mercier was now again pressing for early recognition of the South at the first favourable moment. On Lyons the effect of the adventure to Richmond was just the reverse of this; and on Russell also its influence was to cause some doubt of Southern success. Appended to Lyons' report stands Russell's initialled comment:

> "It is desirable to know what is the Interior to which the Southern Confederates propose if beaten to retire. If in Arms they will be pursued, if not in Arms their discontent will cause but little embarrassment to their Conquerors. But can the country be held permanently by the U.S. Armies if the Confederates have small bodies in Arms resisting the authority of the U.S. Congress?
>
> Any facts shewing the strength or weakness of the Union feeling in the South will be of great value in forming a judgment on the final issue."

Seward, in conversation with Lyons, had said that to avoid public misconceptions a newspaper statement would be prepared on Mercier's trip. This appeared May 6, in the New York *Times*, the paper more closely Seward's "organ" than any other throughout the war, representing Mercier as having gone to Richmond by order of Napoleon and with Lincoln's approval to urge the Confederates to surrender and to encourage them to expect favourable terms. Lyons commented on this article that the language attributed to Mercier was "not very unlike that which he intended to hold," but that in fact he had not used it. [2] Nor had Napoleon ordered the move. Indeed everyone in London and Paris was much astonished, and many were

[1] F. O., Am., Vol. 828. No. 284. Confidential. Lyons to Russell, April 28, 1862.

[2] F. O., Am., Vol. 829. No. 315. Confidential. Lyons to Russell, May 9, 1862.

the speculations as to the meaning of Mercier's unusual procedure. Russell was puzzled, writing "Que diable allait il faire dans cette galére?"[1] and Cowley, at Paris, could give no light, being assured by Thouvenel on first rumours of Mercier's trip to Richmond that "he had not a notion that this could be true."[2] May 1, Cowley wrote, "The whole thing is inexplicable unless the Emperor is at the bottom of it, which Thouvenel thinks is not the case."[3] The next day Thouvenel, having consulted Napoleon, was assured by the latter that "he could not account for Monsieur Mercier's conduct, and that he greatly regretted it," being especially disturbed by a seeming break in the previous "complete harmony with the British Representative" at Washington.[4] This was reassuring to Russell, yet there is no question that Mercier's conduct long left a certain suspicion in British official circles. On May 2, also, Thouvenel wrote to Flahault in London of the Emperor's displeasure, evidently with the intention that this should be conveyed to Russell.[5]

Naturally the persons most excited were the two Confederate agents in Europe. At first they believed Mercier must have had secret orders from Napoleon, and were delighted; then on denials made to Slidell by Thouvenel they feared Mercier was acting in an unfavourable sense as Seward's agent. Later they returned to the theory of Napoleon's private manipulation, and being confident of his friendship were content to wait events.[6] Slidell had just received assurance from M. Billault, through whom most of his information came, "that the Emperor and all

[1] Lyons Papers. Russell to Lyons, May 10, 1862.

[2] F. O., France, Vol. 1427. No. 544. Cowley to Russell, April 28, 1862.

[3] *Ibid.* Vol. 1438. No. 563. To Russell. Mercier's conduct appeared to Cowley as "want of courtesy" and "tardy confidence" to Lyons. *Ibid.* No. 566. May 1, 1862. To Russell.

[4] *Ibid.* No. 574. Cowley to Russell, May 2, 1862.

[5] Thouvenel, *Le Secret de l'Empereur*, II, p. 299.

[6] Mason Papers. Slidell to Mason, May 3, 14 and 16, 1862. Mason to Slidell, May 5, 14 and 16, 1862.

the Ministers are favourable to our cause, have been so for the last year, and are now quite as warmly so as they have ever been. M. Thouvenel is of course excepted, but then he has no hostility."[1] But a greater source of Southern hope at this juncture was another "diplomatic adventure," though by no accredited diplomat, which antedated Mercier's trip to Richmond and which still agitated not only the Confederate agents, but the British Ministry as well.

This was the appearance of the British Member of Parliament, Lindsay, in the rôle of self-constituted Southern emissary to Napoleon. Lindsay, as one of the principal shipowners in England, had long been an earnest advocate of more free commercial intercourse between nations, supporting in general the principles of Cobden and Bright, and being a warm personal friend of the latter, though disagreeing with him on the American Civil War. He had been in some sense a minor expert consulted by both French and British Governments in the preparation of the commercial treaty of 1860, so that when on April 9 he presented himself to Cowley asking that an audience with the Emperor be procured for him to talk over some needed alterations in the Navigation Laws, the request seemed reasonable, and the interview was arranged for April 11. On the twelfth Lindsay reported to Cowley that the burden of Napoleon's conversation, much to his surprise, was on American affairs.[2]

The Emperor, said Lindsay, expressed the conviction

[1] *Ibid.* Slidell to Mason, May 16, 1862. Billault was a member of the French Ministry, but without portfolio.

[2] Several accounts have been given of this episode. The two known to me treating it at greatest length are (1) Callahan, *Diplomatic History of the Southern Confederacy* and (2) Sears, *A Confederate Diplomat at the Court of Napoleon III*, Am. Hist. Rev., Jan., 1921. Both writers drew their information wholly from Confederate documents, using, especially, the private correspondence of Mason and Slidell, and neither treats the matter from the English view point. I have therefore based my account on the unused letters of British officials, citing other materials only where they offer a side light. The principal new sources are Cowley's private and official letters to Russell.

that re-union between North and South was an impossibility, and declared that he was ready to recognize the South "if Great Britain would set him the example." More than once he had expressed these ideas to England, but "they had not been attended to" and he should not try again. He continued:

> "... that France ought not to interfere in the internal affairs of the United States, but that the United States ought equally to abstain from all interference in the internal concerns of France; and that His Majesty considered that the hindrance placed by the Northern States upon the exportation of cotton from the South was not justifiable, and was tantamount to interference with the legal commerce of France."

He also "denied the efficiency of the blockade so established. He had made observations in this sense to Her Majesty's Government, but they had not been replied to." Then "His Majesty asked what were the opinions of Her Majesty's Govt.; adding that if Her Majesty's Govt. agreed with him as to the inefficiency of the blockade, he was ready to send ships of war to co-operate with others of Her Majesty to keep the Southern ports open." Finally Napoleon requested Lindsay to see Cowley and find out what he thought of these ideas.

Cowley told Lindsay he did not know of any "offer" whatever having been made by France to England, that his (Cowley's) opinion was "that it might be true that the North and the South would never re-unite, but that it was not yet proved; that the efficiency of the blockade was a legal and international question, and that upon the whole it had been considered by Her Majesty's Govt. as efficient, though doubtless many ships had been enabled to run it"; and "that at all events there could not be a more inopportune moment for mooting the question both of the recognition of the South and of the efficiency of the blockade,

The time was gone by when such measures could, if ever, have been taken—for every mail brought news of expeditions from the North acting with success upon the South; and every day added to the efficiency of the blockade"; and "that I did not think therefore that Her Majesty's Govt. would consent to send a squadron to act as the Emperor had indicated, but that I could only give a personal opinion, which might be corrected if I was in error by Mr. Lindsay himself seeing Lord Russell."

On April 13th a second interview took place between Lindsay and Napoleon, of which Lindsay reported that having conveyed to Napoleon Cowley's denial of any offer made to England, as well as a contrary view of the situation, Napoleon:

> "... repeated the statement that two long despatches with his opinion had been written to M. de Flahault, which had not been attended to by Her Majesty's Government, and he expressed a desire that Mr. Lindsay should return to London, lay His Majesty's views before Lord Palmerston and Lord Russell, and bring their answers direct to him as quickly as possible, His Majesty observing that these matters were better arranged by private than official hands. ... Mr. Lindsay said that he had promised the Emperor to be back in Paris on Thursday morning."

In his letter to Russell, Cowley called all this a "nasty intrigue." Cowley had asked Thouvenel for enlightenment, and Thouvenel had denied all knowledge and declared that certainly no such proposals as Lindsay reported the Emperor to have mentioned had ever been sent to England. Cowley wrote:

> "My own conviction is, from Lindsay's conversations with me, which are full of hesitations, and I fear much falsehood hidden under apparent candour, that he has told the Emperor his own views, and that those views are supported by the majority of the people of England, and by the present Opposition in Parliament, who would denounce

the blockade if in power; that he has found a willing listener in the Emperor, who would gladly obtain cotton by any means; and I am much mistaken if Lindsay will not attempt to make political capital of his interviews with the Emperor with the Opposition, and that you may hear of it in Parliament. I lose no time therefore, in writing to you as Lindsay goes over to-night, and will probably endeavour to see you and Lord Palmerston as soon as possible." [1]

The close touch between Lindsay and the Southern agents is shown by his conveyance to Slidell of the good news. Slidell was jubilant, writing to Mason:

"Mr. Lindsay has had a long interview with the Emperor who is prepared to act at once decidedly in our favour; he has always been ready to do so and has twice made representations to England, but has received evasive responses. He has now for the third time given them but in a more decided tone. Mr. Lindsay will give you all the particulars. This is entirely confidential but you can say to Lord Campbell, Mr. Gregory, etc., that I now have positive and *authoritative* evidence that France now waits the assent of England for recognition and other more cogent measures." [2]

Two days later Slidell made a report to Benjamin, which was in substance very similar to that given by Lindsay to Cowley, though more highly coloured as favourable to the South, but he added an important feature which, as has been seen, was suspected by Cowley, but which had not been stated to him. Napoleon had asked Lindsay to see Derby and Disraeli, the leaders of the parliamentary opposition, and inform them of his views—a suggestion which if known to the British Ministry as coming from Napoleon could not fail to arouse resentment. Slidell even believed that, failing British participation, the Emperor might act separately in recognition of the South. [3]

[1] Russell Papers. Cowley to Russell. Private. April 13, 1862.
[2] Mason Papers. April 12, 1862.
[3] Richardson, II, 239. April 14, 1862.

April 15, Cowley, having received, privately, Russell's approval of the language used to Lindsay and believing that Thouvenel was about to write to Flahault on the interviews, felt it "necessary to bring them also on my part officially to your [Russell's] notice."[1] This official report does not differ materially from that in Cowley's private letter of the thirteenth, but omitted, naturally, aspersions on Lindsay and suspicions of the use to which he might put his information.[2] Cowley had held a long conversation with Thouvenel, in which it was developed that the source of the Emperor's views was Rouher, Minister of Commerce, who was very anxious over the future of cotton supply. It appeared that Lindsay in conversation with Thouvenel had affirmed that "*I* [Cowley] *coincided in his views.*" This exasperated Cowley, and he resented Lindsay's "unofficial diplomacy," telling Thouvenel that he "was placed in a false position by Mr. Lindsay's interference. M. Thouvenel exclaimed that his own position was still more false, and that he should make a point of seeing the Emperor, on the following morning, and of ascertaining the extent of His Majesty's participation in the proceeding." This was done, with the result that Napoleon acknowledged that on Lindsay's request he had authorized him to recount to Russell and Palmerston the views expressed, but asserted that "he had not charged him to convey those opinions." Cowley concluded his despatch:

> "Monsieur Thouvenel said that the Emperor did not understand the intricacies of this question—that His Majesty had confounded remarks conveyed in despatches with deliberate proposals—that no doubt the French Government was more preoccupied with the Cotton question than Her Majesty's Government seemed to be, and this he (Thouvenel) had shewn in his communications with M. de

[1] Russell Papers. Cowley to Russell. Private.

[2] F. O., France, Vol. 1437. No. 497. *Confidential.* Cowley to Russell April 15, 1862.

Flahault, but that he knew too well the general opinions prevailing in England to have made proposals. Nor, indeed, did he see what proposals could have been made. He had endeavoured to shew both the Emperor and M. Rouher, that to recognize the independence of the South would not bring Cotton into the markets, while any interference with the blockade would probably have produced a collision. At the same time he could not conceal from me the just anxiety he experienced to reopen the Cotton trade. Might not the Northern States be induced to declare some one port Neutral, at which the trade could be carried on?

I said that the events which were now passing in America demonstrated the prudence of the policy pursued by the two Governments. The recognition of the South would not have prevented the North from continuing its armaments and undertaking the expedition now in progress, and a refusal to acknowledge the blockade as efficient must have been followed by the employment of force, on a question of extreme delicacy."[1]

Formal approval was given Cowley by Russell on April 16. In this Russell stated that he agreed with Thouvenel the cotton situation was alarming, but he added: "The evil is evident—not equally so the remedy." He assured Cowley that "Her Majesty's Government wish to take no step in respect to the Civil War in America except in concert with France and upon full deliberation."[2] Meanwhile Lindsay's diplomatic career had received a severe jolt in London. Confidently addressing to Russell a request for an interview, he received the reply "that I thought the best way for two Govts. to communicate with each other was through their respective Embassies. . . . He [Lindsay] rejoined that he feared you [Cowley] had not stated the reason why the Emperor wished to make the proposal through him rather than the usual channel, and again asked to see me, but I declined to give any other answer, adding that you and the French Ambassr. could make the

[1] *Ibid.*

[2] F. O., France, Vol. 1422. No. 403. Russell to Cowley, April 16, 1862.

most Confidential as well as Official Communications."[1] This rebuff was not regarded as final, though exasperating, by Lindsay, nor by the Confederate agents, all being agreed that Napoleon was about to take an active hand in their favour. Lindsay returned to Paris accompanied by Mason, and on April 18 had still another conversation with Napoleon. He reported Russell's refusal of an interview, and that he had seen Disraeli, but not Derby, who was ill. Disraeli had declared that he believed Russell and Seward to have a "secret understanding" on the blockade, but that if France should make a definite proposal it would probably be supported by a majority in Parliament, and that Russell would be compelled to assent in order to avoid a change of Ministry. In this third interview with Lindsay expressions of vexation with British policy were used by Napoleon (according to Slidell), but he now intimated that he was waiting to learn the result of the Northern effort to capture New Orleans, an event which "he did not anticipate," but which, if it occurred, "might render it inexpedient to act."[2]

Evidently the wedge was losing its force. Mason, returning to London, found that the "pulsations" in Paris had no English repetition. He wrote that Lindsay, failing to reach Russell, had attempted to get at Palmerston, but

[1] *Ibid.* No. 415. Russell to Cowley, April 16, 1862. Whether Napoleon had in fact "charged" Lindsay with a mission must remain in doubt. Cowley believed Lindsay to have prevaricated—or at least so officially reported. He had written a note to Napoleon explaining Russell's refusal to see Lindsay and had received this reply:

"Le 20 Avril, 1862.

Mon cher Lord Cowley:

Je vous remercie de votre billet. J'espère comme vous que bientôt nos manufactures auront du coton. Je n'ai pas de tout été choqué de ce que Lord Russell n'ait pas reçu Mr. Lindsay. Celui-ci m'avait demandé l'autorisation de rapporter au principal secretaire d'Etat notre conversation et j'y avais consenti et voilà tout.

Croyez à mes sentiments d'amitié.

Napoleon."

(Copy. Russell Papers, Cowley to Russell, April 22, 1862).

[2] Richardson, II, 239. Slidell to Benjamin, April 18, 1862. New Orleans was captured on April 25.

with no success. Thereupon Lindsay turning to the Opposition had visited Disraeli a "second time and submitted to him Palmerston's rebuff The strongest expression that fell from Disraeli was—"if it is found that the Emperor and Russell are at issue on the question the session of Parliament would not be as quiet as had been anticipated." This was scant encouragement, for Disraeli's "if" was all important. Yet "on the whole Lindsay is hopeful," wrote Mason in conclusion.[1] Within a fortnight following arrived the news of the capture of New Orleans, an event upon which Seward had postulated the relief of a European scarcity of cotton and to Southern sympathizers a serious blow. May 13, Cowley reported that the Emperor had told him, personally, that "he quite agreed that nothing was to be done for the moment but to watch events."[2] Thouvenel asked Slidell as to the effect of the loss of New Orleans, and received the frank answer, "that it would be most disastrous, as it would give the enemy the control of the Mississippi and its tributaries, [but] that it would not in any way modify the fixed purpose of our people to carry on the war even to an extermination."[3] Mason, a Virginian, and like nearly all from his section, never fully realizing the importance of the Confederate South-West, his eyes fixed on the campaigns about Richmond, was telling the "nervous amongst our friends" that New Orleans would "form a barren acquisition to the enemy, and will on our side serve only as a stimulant."[4]

If the South needed such stimulants she was certainly getting repeated doses in the three months from February to May, 1862. In England, Lindsay might be hopeful of a movement by the Tory opposition, but thought it wiser to postpone for a time further pressure in that direction.

[1] Mason Papers. Mason to Slidell, April 30, 1862.
[2] Russell Papers. Cowley to Russell.
[3] Mason Papers. Slidell to Mason, May 14, 1862.
[4] *Ibid.* Mason to Slidell, May 14, 1862.

May 8, Henry Adams could write to his brother of British public opinion, " there is no doubt that the idea here is as strong as ever that we must ultimately fail,"[1] but on May 16, that " the effect of the news here [of New Orleans] has been greater than anything yet . . . the *Times* came out and gave fairly in that it had been mistaken ; it had believed Southern accounts and was deceived by them. This morning it has an article still more remarkable and intimates for the first time that it sees little more chance for the South. There is, we think, a preparation for withdrawing their belligerent declaration and acknowledging again the authority of the Federal Government over all the national territory to be absolute and undisputed. One more victory will bring us up to this, I am confident."[2]

This was mistaken confidence. Nor did governmental reaction keep pace with Southern depression or Northern elation ; the British Ministry was simply made more determined to preserve strict neutrality and to restrain its French partner in a " wait for events " policy. The " one more victory " so eagerly desired by Henry Adams was not forthcoming, and the attention, now all focused on McClellan's slow-moving campaign, waited in vain for the demonstration of another and more striking evidence of Northern power—the capture of the Confederate Capital, Richmond. McClellan's delays coincided with a bruiting of the news at Washington that foreign Powers were about to offer mediation. This was treated at some length in the semi-official *National Intelligencer* of May 16 in an article which Lyons thought inspired by Seward, stating that mediation would be welcome if offered for the purpose of re-union, but would otherwise be resented, a view which Lyons thought fairly represented the situation.[3]

[1] *A Cycle of Adams' Letters*, I, 139.

[2] *Ibid.*, p. 146.

[3] F. O., Am., Vol. 830. No. 338. Lyons to Russell, May 16, 1862.

There can be little doubt that this Washington rumour was largely the result of the very positive opinion held by Mercier of ultimate Southern success and his somewhat free private communications. He may, indeed, have been talking more freely than usual exactly because of anxiety at Northern success, for McClellan, so far as was then known, was steadily, if slowly, progressing toward a victory. Mercier's most recent instruction from Thouvenel gave him no authority to urge mediation, yet he thought the moment opportune for it and strongly urged this plan on Lyons. The latter's summary of this and his own analysis of the situation were as follows:

> "M. Mercier thinks it quite within the range of possibility that the South may be victorious both in the battle in Virginia and in that in Tennessee. He is at all events quite confident that whether victorious or defeated, they will not give in, and he is certainly disposed to advise his Government to endeavour to put an end to the war by intervening on the first opportunity. He is, however, very much puzzled to devise any mode of intervention, which would have the effect of reviving French trade and obtaining cotton. I should suppose he would think it desirable to go to great lengths to stop the war; because he believes that the South will not give in until the whole country is made desolate and that the North will very soon be led to proclaim immediate emancipation, which would stop the cultivation of cotton for an indefinite time.
>
> I listen and say little when he talks of intervention. It appears to me to be a dangerous subject of conversation. There is a good deal of truth in M. Mercier's anticipations of evil, but I do not see my way to doing any good.
>
> If one is to conjecture what the state of things will be a month or six weeks hence, one may "guess" that McClellan will be at Richmond, having very probably got there without much real fighting. I doubt his getting farther this summer, if so far. . . .
>
> The campaign will not be pushed with any vigour during the summer. It may be begun again in the Autumn. Thus, so far as Trade and Cotton are concerned, we may be next

Autumn, just in the situation we are now. If the South really defeated either or both the Armies opposed to them I think it would disgust the North with the war, rather than excite them to fresh efforts. If the armies suffer much from disease, recruiting will become difficult. The credit of the Government has hitherto been wonderfully kept up, but it would not stand a considerable reverse in the field. It is possible, under such circumstances that a Peace Party might arise ; and perhaps just *possible* that England and France might give weight to such a Party." [1]

In brief, Lyons was all against either intervention or mediation unless a strong reaction toward peace should come in the North, and even then regarded the wisdom of such a policy as only "just *possible*." Nor was Russell inclined to depart from established policy. He wrote to Lyons at nearly the same time :

"The news from York Town, New Orleans, and Corinth seems to portend the conquest of the South. We have now to see therefore, whether a few leaders or the whole population entertain those sentiments of alienation and abhorrence which were so freely expressed to M. Mercier by the Confederate Statesmen at Richmond. I know not how to answer this question. But there are other questions not less important to be solved in the North. Will the Abolitionists succeed in proclaiming freedom to the Slaves of all those who have resisted ? I guess not.

But then the Union will be restored with its old disgrace and its old danger. I confess I do not see any way to any fair solution except separation—but that the North will not hear of—nor in the moment of success would it be of any use to give them unpalatable advice." [2]

Two days preceding this letter, Thouvenel, at last fully informed of Mercier's trip to Richmond, instructed him that France had no intention to depart from her attitude of strict neutrality and that it was more than ever necessary to wait events. [3]

[1] Russell Papers. Lyons to Russell. Private. May 16, 1862.
[2] Lyons Papers. Russell to Lyons. Private. May 17, 1862.
[3] *Documents Diplomatiques*, 1862, p. 124. May 15.

Mercier's renewed efforts to start a movement toward mediation were then wholly personal. Neither France nor Great Britain had as yet taken up this plan, nor were they likely to so long as Northern successes were continued. In London, Mason, suffering a reaction from his former high hopes, summed up the situation in a few words: "This Government passive and ignorant, France alert and mysterious. The Emperor alone knows what is to come out of it, and he keeps his own secret."[1] The Southern play, following the ministerial rebuff to Lindsay, was now to keep quiet and extended even to discouraging public demonstrations against governmental inaction. Spence had prevented such a demonstration by cotton operators in Liverpool. "I have kept them from moving as a matter of judgment. If either of the Southern armies obtain such a victory as I think probable, then a move of this kind may be made with success and power, whilst at the wrong time for it havoc only would have resulted."[2] The wrong time for Southern pressure on Russell was conceived by Seward to be the right time for the North. Immediately following the capture of New Orleans he gave positive instructions to Dayton in Paris and Adams in London to propose the withdrawal of the declaration admitting Southern belligerent rights. Thouvenel replied with some asperity on the folly of Seward's demand, and made a strong representation of the necessity of France to obtain cotton and tobacco.[3] Adams, with evident reluctance, writing, "I had little expectation of success, but I felt it my duty at once to execute the orders," advanced with Russell the now threadbare and customary arguments on the Proclamation of Neutrality, and received the usual refusal to alter

[1] Mason Papers. Mason to Slidell, May 21, 1862.

[2] Mason Papers. Spence to Mason, June 3, 1862.

[3] F. O., France, Vol. 1439. No. 668. Cowley to Russell, May 23, 1862, and *Documents Diplomatiques*, 1862, p. 127. Thouvenel to Mercier, May 21, 1862.

British policy.[1] If Seward was sincere in asking for a retraction of belligerent rights to the South he much mistook European attitude; if he was but making use of Northern victories to return to a high tone of warning to Europe—a tone serviceable in causing foreign governments to step warily—his time was well chosen. Certainly at Washington Lyons did not regard very seriously Seward's renewal of demand on belligerency. Satisfied that there was no immediate reason to require his presence in America, ill and fearing the heat of summer, he had asked on May 9 for permission to take leave of absence for a trip home. On June 6 he received this permission, evidence that Russell also saw no cause for anxiety, and on June 13 he took leave of Lincoln.

> "I had quite an affectionate parting with the President this morning. He told me, as is his wont, a number of stories more or less decorous, but all he said having any bearing on political matters was: 'I suppose my position makes people in England think a great deal more of me than I deserve, pray tell 'em I mean 'em no harm.'"[2]

Fully a month had now elapsed in London since the arrival of news on any striking military event in America. New Orleans was an old story, and while in general it was believed that Richmond must fall before McClellan's army, the persistence of Southern fervid declarations that they would never submit gave renewed courage to their British friends. Lindsay was now of the opinion that it might be wise, after all, to make some effort in Parliament, and since the Washington mediation rumours were becoming current in London also, notice was given of a motion demanding of the Government that, associating itself with France, an offer of mediation be made to the contending

[1] *U. S. Messages and Documents*, 1862, pp. 97-99. Adams to Seward, May 22, 1862.

[2] Newton, *Lord Lyons*, I, 88.

parties in America. Motions on recognition and on the blockade had been tried and had failed. Now the cry was to be "peaceful mediation" to put an end to a terrible war. Friends of the South were not united in this adventure. Spence advised Lindsay to postpone it, but the latter seemed determined to make the effort.[1] Probably he was still smarting under his reverse of April. Possibly also he was aware of a sudden sharp personal clash between Palmerston and Adams that might not be without influence on governmental attitude—perhaps might even indicate a governmental purpose to alter its policy.

This clash was caused by a personal letter written by Palmerston to Adams on the publication in the *Times* of General Butler's famous order in New Orleans authorizing Federal soldiers to treat as "women of the town" those women who publicly insulted Northern troops. The British press indulged in an ecstasy of vicious writing about this order similar to that on the Northern "barbarity" of the Stone Fleet episode. Palmerston's letters to Adams and the replies received need no further notice here, since they did not in fact affect British policy, than to explain that Palmerston wrote in extreme anger, apparently, and with great violence of language, and that Adams replied with equal anger, but in very dignified if irritating terms.[2] In British opinion Butler's order was an incitement to his soldiers to commit atrocities; Americans understood it as merely an authorization to return insult for insult. In fact the order promptly put a stop to attacks on Northern soldiers, whether by act or word, and all disorder ceased. Palmerston was quick to accept the British view, writing to Adams, "it is difficult if not impossible to express adequately the disgust which must be excited in the mind of every honourable man by the general order of General Butler. . . ."

[1] Mason Papers. Spence to Mason, June 11, 1862.

[2] All the letters are given in Adams, *C. F. Adams*, Ch. XIII.

"If the Federal government chooses to be served by men capable of such revolting outrages, they must submit to abide by the deserved opinion which mankind will form of their conduct."[1] This extraordinary letter was written on June 11. Adams was both angry and perturbed, since he thought the letter might indicate an intention to change British policy and that Palmerston was but laying the ground for some "vigorous" utterance in Parliament, after his wont when striking out on a new line. He was further confirmed in this view by an editorial in the *Times* on June 12, hinting at a coming mediation, and by news from France that Persigny was on his way to London to arrange such a step. But however much personally aggrieved, Adams was cool as a diplomat. His first step was to write a brief note to Palmerston enquiring whether he was to consider the letter as addressed to him "officially . . . or purely as a private expression of sentiment between gentlemen."[2]

There is no evidence that Palmerston and Russell were contemplating a change of policy—rather the reverse. But it does appear that Palmerston wished to be able to state in Parliament that he had taken Adams to task for Butler's order, so that he might meet an enquiry already placed on the question paper as to the Ministry's intentions in the matter. This question was due for the sitting of June 13, and on that day Russell wrote to Palmerston that he should call Butler's order "brutal" and that Palmerston might use the term "infamous" if preferred, adding, "I do not see why we should not represent in a friendly way that the usages of war do not sanction such conduct."[3] This was very different from the tone used by Palmerston. His letter was certainly no "friendly way." Again on the same day Russell wrote to Palmerston:

[1] *Ibid.*, pp. 248-9.
[2] *Ibid.*, p. 251.
[3] Palmerston MS.

> "Adams has been here in a dreadful state about the letter you have written him about Butler.
>
> I declined to give him any opinion and asked him to do nothing more till I had seen or written to you.
>
> What you say of Butler is true enough, tho' he denies your interpretation of the order.
>
> But it is not clear that the President approves of the order, and I think if you could add something to the effect that you respect the Government of President Lincoln, and do not wish to impute to them the fault of Butler it might soothe him.
>
> If you could withdraw the letter altogether it would be the best. But this you may not like to do."[1]

It is apparent that Russell did not approve of Palmerston's move against Adams nor of any "vigorous" language in Parliament, and as to the last, he had his way, for the Government, while disapproving Butler's order, was decidedly mild in comment. As to the letter, Adams, the suspicion proving unfounded that an immediate change of policy was intended, returned to the attack as a matter of personal prestige. It was not until June 15 that Palmerston replied to Adams and then in far different language seeking to smooth the Minister's ruffled feathers, yet making no apology and not answering Adams' question. Adams promptly responded with vigour, June 16, again asking his question as to the letter being official or personal, and characterizing Palmerston's previous assertions as "offensive imputations." He also again approached Russell, who stated that he too had written to Palmerston about his letter, but had received no reply, and he acknowledged that Palmerston's proceeding was "altogether irregular."[2] In the end Palmerston was brought, June 19, to write a long and somewhat rambling reply to Adams, in effect still evading the question put him, though acknowledging that

[1] *Ibid.*

[2] Adams, *C. F. Adams*, pp. 252-55.

the "Secretary of State for Foreign Affairs is the regular official organ for communications. . . ." In conclusion he expressed gratification that reports from Lord Lyons showed Butler's authority at New Orleans had been curtailed by Lincoln. The next day Adams answered interpreting Palmerston as withdrawing his "imputations" but stating plainly that he would not again submit "to entertain any similar correspondence."[1]

Adams had been cautious in pushing for an answer until he knew there was to be no change in British policy. Indeed Palmerston's whole move may even have been intended to ease the pressure for a change in that policy. On the very day of Adams' first talk with Russell, friends of the South thought the *Times* editorial indicated "that some movement is to be made at last, and I doubt not we are to thank the Emperor for it."[2] But on this day also Russell was advising Palmerston to state in Parliament that "We have not received at present any proposal from France to offer mediation and no intention at present exists to offer it on our part."[3] This was the exact language used by Palmerston in reply to Hopwood.[4] Mason again saw his hopes dwindling, but was assured by Lindsay that all was not yet lost, and that he would "still hold his motion under consideration."[5] Lindsay, according to his own account, had talked very large in a letter to Russell, but knew privately, and so informed Mason, that the Commons would not vote for his motion if opposed by the Government, and so intended to postpone it.[6] The proposed motion

[1] *Ibid.*, pp. 256-60.

[2] Mason Papers. Mason to Slidell, June 13, 1862.

[3] Palmerston MS.

[4] Hansard, 3rd. Ser., CLXVII, p. 543. June 13, 1862.

[5] Mason Papers. Mason to Slidell, June 14, 1862.

[6] *Ibid.* Lindsay to Mason, June 18, 1862. Lindsay wrote:
"Lord Russell sent to me last night to get the words of my motion. I have sent them to him to-night, and I have embraced the opportunity of opening my mind to his Lordship. I have told him that I have postponed my motion in courtesy to him—that the sympathy of nine-tenths

was now one for recognition instead of mediation, a temporary change of plan due to Palmerston's answer to Hopwood on June 13. But whatever the terms of the motion favourable to the South, it was evident the Government did not wish discussion at the moment, and hesitancy came over pro-Southern friends. Slidell, in despair, declared that for his part he intended, no matter with what prospect of success, to *demand* recognition from France.[1] This alarmed Mason's English advisers, and he wrote at once strongly urging against such a step, for if the demand were presented and refused there would be no recourse but to depart for home.[2] He thought Lindsay's motion dying away for on consultation with "different parties, including Disraeli, Seymour Fitzgerald and Roebuck," it "has been so far reduced and diluted . . . as to make it only expressive of the opinion of the House that the present posture of affairs in America made the question of the recognition of the Confederate States worth the serious consideration of the Government. It was so modified to prevent the Ministry making an issue upon it. . . ." There was "no assurance that it would be sustained . . . even in that form." Lindsay had deter-

of the members of the House was in favour of immediate recognition, and that even if the Government was not prepared to accept my motion, a majority of votes might have been obtained in its favour—that a majority of votes *would* be obtained within the next fortnight, and I expressed the most earnest hope that the Government would move (as the country, and France, are most anxious for them to do so) and thus prevent the necessity of any private member undertaking a duty which belonged to the Executive.

"I further told his Lordship that recognition was a *right* which no one would deny us the form of exercising, that the fear of war if we exercised it was a delusion. That the majority of the leading men in the Northern States would thank us for exercising it, and that even Seward himself might be glad to see it exercised so as to give him an excuse for getting out of the terrible war into which he had dragged his people. I further said, that if the question is settled *without* our recognition of the South, he might *rest certain* that the Northern Armies *would* be marched into Canada. I hope my note may produce the desired results, and thus get the Government to take the matter in hand, for *sub rosa*, I saw that the House was not *yet* prepared to vote, and the question is far too grave to waste time upon it in idle talk, even if talk, without action, did no harm."

[1] *Ibid*. Slidell to Mason, June 17, 1862.

[2] *Ibid* Mason to Slidell, June 19, 1862.

mined to postpone his motion " for a fortnight, so that all expectation from this quarter for the present is dished, and we must wait for 'King Cotton' to turn the screw still further."[1] On June, 20 Lindsay gave this notice of postponement, and no parliamentary comment was made.[2] It was a moment of extreme depression for the Confederate agents in Europe. Slidell, yielding to Mason's pleas, gave up his idea of demanding recognition and wrote :

> " The position of our representatives in Europe is painful and almost humiliating ; it might be tolerated if they could be consoled by the reflection that their presence was in any way advantageous to their cause but I am disposed to believe that we would have done better to withdraw after our first interview with Russell and Thouvenel." [3]

[1] *Ibid.*

[2] Hansard, 3rd. Ser., CLXVII, p. 810.

[3] Mason Papers. Slidell to Mason, June 21, 1862.

PROFESSOR GOLDWIN SMITH
(From a photograph by Elliott & Fry, Ltd.)

CONTENTS

OF

VOLUME TWO

LIST OF ILLUSTRATIONS

PART TWO

GREAT BRITAIN AND THE AMERICAN CIVIL WAR

CHAPTER X

KING COTTON

For two weeks there was no lightening of Southern depression in England. But on June 28 McClellan had been turned back from his advance on Richmond by Lee, the new commander of the Army of Virginia, and the much heralded Peninsular compaign was recognized to have been a disastrous failure. Earlier Northern victories were forgotten and the campaigns in the West, still progressing favourably for the North, were ignored or their significance not understood. Again, to English eyes, the war in America approached a stalemate. The time had come with the near adjournment of Parliament when, if ever, a strong Southern effort must be made, and the time seemed propitious. Moreover by July, 1862, it was hoped that soon, in the cotton districts, the depression steadily increasing since the beginning of the war, would bring an ally to the Southern cause. Before continuing the story of Parliamentary and private efforts by the friends of the South it is here necessary to review the cotton situation—now rapidly becoming a matter of anxious concern to both friend and foe of the North and in less degree to the Ministry itself.

"King Cotton" had long been a boast with the South. "Perhaps no great revolution," says Bancroft, "was ever begun with such convenient and soothing theories as those that were expounded and believed at the time of the organization of the Confederacy. . . . In any case, hostilities could not last long, for France and Great Britain must have what the Confederacy alone could supply, and therefore they could be forced to aid the South, as a condition precedent to relief from the terrible distress that was sure to follow a blockade."[1] This confidence was no new development. For ten years past whenever Southern threats of secession had been indulged in, the writers and politicians of that section had expanded upon cotton as the one great wealth-producing industry of America and as the one product which would compel European acquiescence in American policy, whether of the Union, before 1860, or of the South if she should secede. In the financial depression that swept the Northern States in 1857 *De Bow's Review*, the leading financial journal of the South, declared: "The wealth of the South is permanent and real, that of the North fugitive and fictitious. Events now transpiring expose the fiction, as humbug after humbug explodes."[2] On March 4, 1858, Senator Hammond of South Carolina, asked in a speech, "What would happen if no cotton was furnished for three years? I will not stop to depict what everyone can imagine, but this is certain: England would topple headlong and carry the whole civilized world with her save the South. No, you dare not make war on cotton. No power on earth dares make war upon it. Cotton *is* King."[3] Two years later, writing before the elections of 1860 in which the main question was that of the territorial expansion of slavery, this same Southern statesman expressed himself as believing that "the slave-holding South is now the controlling power of the world. . . . Cotton, rice, tobacco and naval stores command the world; and we have sense enough to know

[1] Bancroft, *Seward*, II, p. 204.
[2] *De Bow's Review*, Dec., 1857. p. 592.
[3] Cited in Adams, *Trans-Atlantic Historical Solidarity*, p. 66.

it, and are sufficiently Teutonic to carry it out successfully."[1]

These quotations indicative of Southern faith in cotton might be amplified and repeated from a hundred sources.

Moreover this faith in the possession of ultimate power went hand in hand with the conviction that the South, more than any other quarter of the world, produced to the benefit of mankind. "In the three million bags of cotton," said a writer in *De Bow's Review*, "the slave-labour annually throws upon the world for the poor and naked, we are doing more to advance civilization . . . than all the canting philanthropists of New England and Old England will do in centuries. Slavery is the backbone of the Northern commercial as it is of the British manufacturing system. . . ."[2] Nor was this idea unfamiliar to Englishmen. Before the Civil War was under way Charles Greville wrote to Clarendon:

> "Any war will be almost sure to interfere with the cotton crops, and this is really what affects us and what we care about. With all our virulent abuse of slavery and slave-owners, and our continual self-laudation on that subject, we are just as anxious for, and as much interested in, the prosperity of the slavery interest in the Southern States as the Carolinan and Georgian planters themselves, and all Lancashire would deplore a successful insurrection of the slaves, if such a thing were possible."[3]

On December 20, 1860, South Carolina led the march in

[1] *Ibid.*, p. 64.

[2] Cited in Smith, *Parties and Slavery*, 68. A remarkable exposition of the "power of cotton" and the righteousness of slavery was published in Augusta, Georgia, in 1860, in the shape of a volume of nine hundred pages, entitled *Cotton is King, and Pro-Slavery Arguments*. This reproduced seven separate works by distinguished Southern writers analysing Slavery from the point of view of political economy, moral and political philosophy, social ethics, political science, ethnology, international law, and the Bible. The purpose of this united publication was to prove the rightfulness, in every aspect, of slavery, the prosperity of America as based on cotton, and the power of the United States as dependent on its control of the cotton supply. The editor was E. N. Elliot, President of Planters' College, Mississippi.

[3] Jan. 26, 1861. Cited in Maxwell, *Clarendon*, II, p. 237.

secession. Fifteen days earlier the British consul at Charleston, Bunch, reported a conversation with Rhett, long a leader of the Southern cause and now a consistent advocate of secession, in which Rhett developed a plan of close commercial alliance with England as the most favoured nation, postulating the dependence of Great Britain on the South for cotton—" upon which supposed axiom, I would remark," wrote Bunch, " all their calculations are based."[1] Such was, indeed, Southern calculation. In January, 1861, *De Bow's Review* contained an article declaring that " the first demonstration of blockade of the Southern ports would be swept away by the English fleets of observation hovering on the Southern coasts, to protect English commerce, and especially the free flow of cotton to English and French factories. . . . A stoppage of the raw material . . . would produce the most disastrous political results—if not a revolution in England. This is the language of English statesmen, manufacturers, and merchants, in Parliament and at cotton associations' debates, and it discloses the truth."[2]

The historical student will find but few such British utterances at the moment, and these few not by men of great weight either in politics or in commerce. The South was labouring under an obsession and prophesied results accordingly. So strong was this obsession that governmental foreign policy neglected all other considerations and the first Commission to Europe had no initial instructions save to demand recognition.[3] The failure of that Com-

[1] *Am. Hist. Rev.*, XVIII, p. 785. Bunch to Russell. No. 51. Confidential. Dec. 5, 1860. As here printed this letter shows two dates, Dec. 5 and Dec. 15, but the original in the Public Record Office is dated Dec. 5.

[2] pp. 94-5. Article by W. H. Chase of Florida.

[3] Rhett, who advocated commercial treaties, learned from Toombs that this was the case. " Rhett hastened to Yancey. Had he been instructed to negotiate commercial treaties with European powers ? Mr. Yancey had received no intimation from any source that authority to negotiate commercial treaties would devolve upon the Commission. ' What then ' exclaimed Rhett, ' can be your instructions ? ' The Presi-

mission, the prompt British acquiescence in the blockade, were harsh blows to Southern confidence but did not for a long time destroy the faith in the power of cotton. In June, 1861, Bunch wrote that there was still a firm belief that "Great Britain will make any sacrifice, even of principle or of honour, to prevent the stoppage of the supply of cotton," and he enclosed a copy of an article in the *Charleston Mercury* of June 4, proclaiming: "The cards are in our hands, and we intend to play them out to *the bankruptcy of every cotton factory in Great Britain and France, or the acknowledgment of our independence.*"[1] As late as March, 1862, Bunch was still writing of this Southern faith in cotton and described the newly-made appointment of Benjamin as Secretary of State as partly due to the fact that he was the leader of the "King Cotton" theory of diplomacy.[2] It was not until the war was well nigh over that British persistence in neutrality, in spite of undoubted hardships caused by the lack of cotton, opened Southern eyes. Pollard, editor of a leading Richmond newspaper, and soon unfriendly to the administration of Jefferson Davis, summed up in *The Lost Cause* his earlier criticisms of Confederate foreign policy:

> "'Cotton,' said the Charleston *Mercury*, 'would bring England to her knees.' The idea was ludicrous enough that England and France would instinctively or readily fling themselves into a convulsion, which their great politicians

dent, Mr. Yancey said, seemed to be impressed with the importance of the cotton crop. A considerable part of the crop of last year was yet on hand and a full crop will soon be planted. The justice of the cause and the cotton, so far as he knew, he regretted to say, would be the basis of diplomacy expected of the Commission" (Du Bose, *Life and Times of Yancey*, 599).

[1] F. O., Am., Vol. 780. No. 69. Bunch to Russell, June 5, 1861. Italics by Bunch. The complete lack of the South in industries other than its staple products is well illustrated by a request from Col. Gorgas, Chief of Ordnance to the Confederacy, to Mason, urging him to secure *three* ironworkers in England and send them over. He wrote, "The reduction of ores with coke seems not to be understood here" (Mason Papers. Gorgas to Mason, Oct. 13, 1861).

[2] F. O., Am., Vol. 843. No. 48. Confidential. Bunch to Russell, March 19, 1862.

> saw was the most tremendous one of modern times. But the puerile argument, which even President Davis did not hesitate to adopt, about the power of 'King Cotton,' amounted to this absurdity: that the great and illustrious power of England would submit to the ineffable humiliation of acknowledging its dependency on the infant Confederacy of the South, and the subserviency of its empire, its political interests and its pride, to a single article of trade that was grown in America!"[1]

But irrespective of the extremes to which Southern confidence in cotton extended the actual hardships of England were in all truth serious enough to cause grave anxiety and to supply an argument to Soutnern sympathizers. The facts of the "Lancashire Cotton Famine" have frequently been treated by historians at much length[2] and need here but a general review. More needed is an examination of some of the erroneous deductions drawn from the facts and especially an examination of the extent to which the question of cotton supply affected or determined British governmental policy toward America.

English cotton manufacturing in 1861 held a position of importance equalled by no other one industry. Estimates based on varying statistics diverge as to exact proportions, but all agree in emphasizing the pre-eminent place of Lancashire in determining the general prosperity of the nation. Surveying the English, not the whole British, situation it is estimated that there were 2,650 factories of which 2,195 were in Lancashire and two adjacent counties. These employed 500,000 operatives and consumed a thousand million pounds of cotton each year.[3] An editorial in the

[1] p. 130.

[2] The two principal British works are: Arnold, *The History of the Cotton Famine*, London, 1864; and Watts, *The Facts of the Cotton Famine*, Manchester, 1866. A remarkable statistical analysis of the world cotton trade was printed in London in 1863, by a Southerner seeking to use his study as an argument for British mediation. George McHenry, *The Cotton Trade*.

[3] Scherer, *Cotton as a World Power*, pp. 263-4.

Times, September 19, 1861, stated that one-fifth of the entire English population was held to be dependent, either directly or indirectly, on the prosperity of the cotton districts,[1] and therefore also dependent on the source of supply, the Confederate South, since statistics, though varying, showed that the raw cotton supplied from America constituted anywhere from 78 to 84 per cent. of the total English importation.[2]

The American crop of 1860 was the largest on record, nearly 4,000,000 bales, and the foreign shipments, without question hurried because of the storm-cloud rising at home, had been practically completed by April, 1861. Of the 3,500,000 bales sent abroad, Liverpool, as usual, received the larger portion.[3] There was, then, no immediate shortage of supply when war came in America, rather an unusual accumulation of raw stocks, even permitting some reshipment to the Northern manufacturing centres of America where the scarcity then brought high prices. In addition, from December, 1860, to at least April, 1861, there had been somewhat of a slump in demand for raw cotton by British manufacturers due to an over-production of goods in the two previous years. There had been a temporary depression in 1856-57 caused by a general financial crisis, but early in 1858 restored confidence and a tremendous demand from the Far East—India especially—set the mills running again on full time, while many new mills were brought into operation. But by May, 1860, the mills had caught up with the heavy demands and the rest of the year saw uncertainty of operations and brought expressions of fear that the

[1] Lack of authentic statistics on indirect interests make this a guess by the *Times*. Other estimates run from one-seventh to one-fourth.

[2] Schmidt, "Wheat and Cotton During the Civil War," p. 408 (in *Iowa Journal of History and Politics*, Vol. 16), 78.8 per cent. (Hereafter cited as Schmidt, *Wheat and Cotton*.) Scherer, *Cotton as a World Power*, p. 264, states 84 per cent. for 1860. Arnold, *Cotton Famine*, pp. 36-39, estimates 83 per cent.

[3] Great Britain ordinarily ran more than twice as many spindles as all the other European nations combined. Schmidt, *Wheat and Cotton*, p. 407, *note*.

"plunge" to produce had been overdone. Manufactured stocks began to accumulate, and money was not easy since 1860 brought also a combination of events—deficient grain harvest at home, withdrawal of gold from England to France for investment in French public works, demand of America for gold in place of goods, due to political uncertainties there—which rapidly raised the discount rate from two and one half per cent. in January, 1860, to six in December. By the end of April, 1861, the Board of Trade Returns indicated that the cotton trade was in a dangerous situation, with large imports of raw cotton and decreased exports of goods.[1] The news of war actually begun in America came as a temporary relief to the English cotton trade and in the prospect of decreased supply prices rose, saving many manufacturers from impending difficulties. A few mills had already begun to work on part-time because of trade depression. The *immediate* effect of Lincoln's blockade proclamation was to check this movement, but by October it had again begun and this time because of the rapid increase in the price of raw cotton as compared with the slower advance of the price of goods.[2]

In substance the principal effect of the War on the English cotton trade for the first seven or eight months was felt, not in the manufacturing districts but in the Liverpool speculative and importing markets of raw cotton. Prices rose steadily to over a shilling a pound in October, 1861. On November 23 there was a near panic caused by rumours of British intervention. These were denounced as false and in five days the price was back above its previous

[1] This Return for April is noteworthy as the first differentiating commerce with the North and the South.

[2] These facts are drawn from Board of Trade Reports, and from the files of the *Economist*, London, and *Hunt's Merchants Magazine*, New York. I am also indebted to a manuscript thesis by T. P. Martin, "The Effects of the Civil War Blockade on the Cotton Trade of the United Kingdom," Stanford University. Mr. Martin in 1921 presented at Harvard University a thesis for the Ph.D degree, entitled "The Influence of Trade (in Cotton and Wheat) on Anglo-American Relations, 1829-1846," but has not yet carried his more matured study to the Civil War period.

figure. Then on November 27 came the news of the *Trent* and the market was thrown into confusion, not because of hopes that cotton would come more freely but in fear that war with America would cause it to do so. The Liverpool speculators breathed freely again only when peace was assured. This speculative British interest was no cause for serious governmental concern and could not affect policy. But the manufacturing trade was, presumably, a more serious anxiety and if cotton became hard, or even impossible to obtain, a serious situation would demand consideration.

In the generally accepted view of a "short war," there was at first no great anticipation of real danger. But beginning with December, 1861, there was almost complete stoppage of supply from America. In the six months to the end of May, 1862, but 11,500 bales were received, less than one per cent. of the amount for the same six months of the previous year.[1] The blockade was making itself felt and not merely in shipments from the South but in prospects of Southern production, for the news came that the negroes were being withdrawn by their masters from the rich sea islands along the coast in fear of their capture by the Northern blockading squadrons.[2] Such a situation seemed bound in the end to result in pressure by the manufacturers for governmental action to secure cotton. That it did not immediately do so is explained by Arnold, whose dictum has been quite generally accepted, as follows:

> "The immediate result of the American war was, at this time, to relieve the English cotton trade, including the dealers in the raw material and the producers and dealers in manufactures, from a serious and impending difficulty.

[1] Adams, *Trans-Atlantic Historical Solidarity*, p. 89.

[2] F. O., Am., Vol. 843. No. 10. Bunch to Russell, Jan. 8, 1862. Bunch also reported that inland fields were being transformed to corn production and that even the cotton on hand was deteriorating because of the lack of bagging, shut off by the blockade.

> They had in hand a stock of goods sufficient for the consumption of two-thirds of a year, therefore a rise in the price of the raw material and the partial closing of their establishments, with a curtailment of their working expenses, was obviously to their advantage. But to make their success complete, this rise in the price of cotton was upon the largest stock ever collected in the country at this season. To the cotton trade there came in these days an unlooked-for accession of wealth, such as even it had never known before. In place of the hard times which had been anticipated, and perhaps deserved, there came a shower of riches." [1]

This was written of the situation in December, 1861. A similar analysis, no doubt on the explanations offered by his English friends, of "the question of cotton supply, which we had supposed would speedily have disturbed the level of their neutral policy" was made by Mason in March, 1862. "Thus," he concluded, "it is that even in Lancashire and other manufacturing districts no open demonstration has been made against the blockade."[2] Manufactures other than cotton were greatly prospering, in particular those of woollen, flax, and iron. And the theory that the cotton lords were not, in reality, hit by the blockade—perhaps profited by it—was bruited even during the war. *Blackwood's Magazine*, October, 1864, held this view, while the *Morning Post* of May 16, 1864, went to the extent of describing the "glut" of goods in 1861, relieved just in the nick of time by the War, preventing a financial crash, "which must sooner or later have caused great suffering in Lancashire."

Arnold's generalization has been taken to prove that the *immediate* effect of the Civil War was to save the cotton industry from great disaster and that there *immediately* resulted large profits to the manufacturers from the increased price of stocks on hand. In fact his description of the

[1] Arnold, *Cotton Famine*, p. 81.
[2] Richardson, II, 198. Mason to Hunter, March 11, 1862.

situation in December, 1861, as his own later pages show, was not applicable, so far as manufacturers' profits are concerned, until the later months of 1862 and the first of 1863. For though prices might be put up, as they were, goods were not sold in any large quantities before the fall of 1862. There were almost no transactions for shipments to America, China, or the Indies.[1] Foreign purchasers as always, and especially when their needs had just been abundantly supplied by the great output of 1858-60, were not keen to place new orders in a rising and uncertain market. The English producers raised their prices, but they held their goods, lacking an effective market. The importance of this in British foreign policy is that at no time, until the accumulated goods were disposed of, was there likely to be any trade eagerness for a British intervention in America. Their only fear, says Arnold, was the sudden opening of Southern ports and a rush of raw cotton,[2] a sneer called out by the alleged great losses incurred and patriotically borne in silence. Certainly in Parliament the members from Lancashire gave no sign of discontent with the Government policy of neutrality for in the various debates on blockade, mediation, and cotton supply but one Member from Lancashire, Hopwood, ever spoke in favour of a departure from neutrality, or referred to the distress in the manufacturing districts as due to any other cause than the shortage in cotton caused by the war.[3]

But it was far otherwise with the operatives of Lancashire. Whatever the causes of short-time operation in the mills or of total cessation of work the situation was such that

[1] Parliamentary Returns, 1861 and 1862. *Monthly Accounts of Trade and Navigation* (in *Parliamentary Papers*, 1862, *Commons*. Vol. LV, and 1863, *Commons*, Vol. LXV).

[2] Arnold, *Cotton Famine*, pp. 174 and 215.

[3] In 1861 there were 26 Members from Lancashire in the Commons, representing 14 boroughs and 2 counties. The suffrage was such that only 1 in every 27 of the population had the vote. For all England the proportion was 1 in 23 (Rhodes, IV, 359). *Parliamentary Papers*, 1867-8, *Lords*, Vol. XXXII, "Report on Boundaries of Boroughs and Counties of England."

from October, 1861, more and more operatives were thrown out of employment. As their little savings disappeared they were put upon public poor relief or upon private charity for subsistence. The governmental statistics do not cover, accurately, the relief offered by private charity, but those of public aid well indicate the loss of wage-earning opportunity. In the so-called "Distressed Districts" of Lancashire and the adjoining counties it appears that poor relief was given to 48,000 persons in normal times, out of a total population of 2,300,000. In the first week of November, 1861, it was 61,207, and for the first week of December, 71,593; thereafter mounting steadily until March, 1862, when a temporary peak of 113,000 was reached. From March until the first week in June there was a slight decrease, but from the second week of June poor relief resumed an upward trend, increasing rapidly until December, 1862, when it reached its highest point of 284,418. In this same first week of December private relief, now thoroughly organized in a great national effort, was extended to 236,000 people, making a grand total at high tide of distress of over 550,000 persons, if private relief was not extended to those receiving public funds. But of this differentiation there is no surety—indeed there are evidences of much duplication of effort in certain districts. In general, however, these statistics do exhibit the great lack of employment in a one-industry district heretofore enjoying unusual prosperity.[1]

[1] The figures are drawn from (1) Farnall's "Reports on Distress in the Manufacturing Districts," 1862. *Parliamentary Papers*, *Commons*, Vol. XLIX, Pt. I, 1863. *Ibid.*, Vol. LII, 1864; and (2) from "Summary of the Number of Paupers in the Distressed Districts," from November, 1861, to December, 1863. *Commons*, Vol. LII. Farnall's reports are less exact than the *Summary* since at times Liverpool is included, at times not, as also six small poor-law unions which do not appear in his reports until 1864. The *Summary* consistently includes Liverpool, and fluctuates violently for that city whenever weather conditions interfered with the ordinary business of the port. It is a striking illustration of the narrow margin of living wages among the dockers of Liverpool that an annotation at the foot of a column of statistics should explain an increase in one week of 21,000 persons thrown on poor relief to the "prevalence of a strong east wind" which prevented vessels from getting up to the docks.

The manufacturing operative population of the district was estimated at between 500,000 and 600,000. At the time of greatest distress some 412,000 of these were receiving either public or private aid, though many were working part-time in the mills or were engaged on public enterprises set on foot to ease the crisis. But there was no starvation and it is absurd to compare the crisis to the Irish famine of the 'forties. This was a *cotton* famine in the shortage of that commodity, but it was not a *human* famine. The country, wrote John Bright, was passing through a terrible crisis, but "our people will be kept alive by the contributions of the country."[1] Nevertheless a rapid change from a condition of adequate wage-earning to one of dependence on charity—a change ultimately felt by the great bulk of those either directly or indirectly dependent upon the cotton industry—might have been expected to arouse popular demonstrations to force governmental action directed to securing cotton that trade might revive. That no such popular effect was made demands careful analysis—to be offered in a later chapter—but here the *fact* is alone important, and the fact was that the operatives sympathized with the North and put no pressure on the Cabinet. Thus at no time during the war was there any attempt from Lancashire, whether of manufacturers or operatives, to force a change of governmental policy.[2]

[1] Trevelyan, *Bright*, p. 309. To Sumner, Dec. 6, 1862.

[2] The historians who see only economic causes have misinterpreted the effects on policy of the "cotton famine." Recently, also, there has been advanced an argument that "wheat defeated cotton"—an idea put forward indeed in England itself during the war by pro-Northern friends who pointed to the great flow of wheat from the North as essential in a short-crop situation in Great Britain. Mr. Schmidt in "The Influence of Wheat and Cotton on Anglo-American Relations during the Civil War," a paper read before the American Historical Association, Dec. 1917, and since published in the *Iowa Journal of History and Politics*, July, 1918, presents with much care all the important statistics for both commodities, but his conclusions seem to me wholly erroneous. He states that "Great Britain's dependence on Northern wheat . . . operated as a contributing influence in keeping the British government officially neutral . . ." (p. 423), a cautious statement soon transformed to the positive one that "this fact did not escape the attention of the English government,"

As the lack of employment developed in Lancashire public discussion and consideration were inevitably aroused. But there was little talk of governmental interference and such as did appear was promptly met with opposition by the leading trade journals. July 13, 1861, the *Economist* viewed the cotton shortage as "a *temporary* and an *immediate* one. . . . We have—on our hypothesis—to provide against the stoppage of our supply for *one* year, and that the very *next* year." Would it *pay*, asked Bright, to break the blockade? "I don't think myself it would be cheap . . . at the cost of a war with the United States."[1] This was also the notion of the London *Shipping Gazette* which, while acknowledging that the mill-owners of England and France were about to be greatly embarrassed, continued: "*But we are not going to add to the difficulty by involving ourselves in a naval war with the Northern States. . . .*"[2] The *Times* commented in substance in several issues in September, 1861, on the "wise policy of working short-

since leading journals referred to it (p. 431). Progressively, it is asserted: "But it was Northern wheat that may well be regarded as the decisive factor, counterbalancing the influence of cotton, in keeping the British government from recognizing the Confederacy" (p. 437). "That the wheat situation must have exerted a profound influence on the government . . ." (p. 438). And finally: "In this contest wheat won, demonstrating its importance as a world power of greater significance than cotton" (p. 439). This interesting thesis has been accepted by William Trimble in "Historical Aspects of the Surplus Food Production of the United States, 1862-1902" (*Am. Hist. Assoc. Reports*, 1918, Vol. 1, p. 224). I think Mr. Schmidt's errors are: (1) a mistake as to the time when recognition of the South was in governmental consideration. He places it in midsummer, 1863, when in fact the danger had passed by January of that year. (2) A mistake in placing cotton and wheat supply on a parity, since the former could not be obtained in quantity from *any* source before 1864, while wheat, though coming from the United States, could have been obtained from interior Russia, as well as from the maritime provinces, in increased supply if Britain had been willing to pay the added price of inland transport. There was a real "famine" of cotton; there would have been none of wheat, merely a higher cost. (This fact, a vital one in determining influence, was brought out by George McHenry in the columns of *The Index*, Sept. 18, 1862.) (3) The fact, in spite of all Mr. Schmidt's suppositions, that while cotton was frequently a subject of governmental concern in *memoranda* and in private notes between members of the Cabinet, I have failed to find one single case of the mention of wheat. This last seems conclusive in negation of Mr. Schmidt's thesis.

[1] Speech at Rochdale, Sept. 1, 1861. Cited in *Hunt's Merchants Magazine*, Vol. 45, pp. 326-7.

[2] *Ibid.*, p. 442.

time as a precaution against the contingencies of the cotton supply, and of the glutted state of distant markets for manufactured goods."[1] October 12, the *Economist* acknowledged that the impatience of some mill-owners was quite understandable as was talk of a European compulsion on America to stop an "objectless and hopeless" quarrel, but then entered upon an elaborate discussion of the principles involved and demonstrated why England ought not to intervene. In November Bright could write: "The notion of getting cotton by interfering with the blockade is abandoned apparently by the simpletons who once entertained it, and it is accepted now as a fixed policy that we are to take no part in your difficulties."[2] Throughout the fall of 1861 the *Economist* was doing its best to quiet apprehensions, urging that due to the "glut" of manufactured goods short-time must have ensued anyway, pointing out that now an advanced price was possible, and arguing that here was a situation likely to result in the development of other sources of supply with an escape from the former dependence on America. In view of the actual conditions of the trade, already recounted, these were appealing arguments to the larger manufacturers, but the small mills, running on short order supplies and with few stocks of goods on hand were less easily convinced. They were, however, without parliamentary influence and hence negligible as affecting public policy. At the opening of the new year, 1862, Bright declared that "with the spinners and manufacturers and merchants, I think generally there is no wish for any *immediate* change."[3]

Bright's letter of November, 1861, was written before news of the *Trent* reached England: that of January, 1862, just after that controversy had been amicably settled. The *Trent* had both diverted attention from cotton and in

[1] e.g., The *Times*, Sept. 19, 1861.
[2] To Sumner, Nov. 20, 1861. Mass Hist. Soc. *Proceedings*, XLVI, p. 97.
[3] *Ibid.* Jan. 11, 1862. Vol. XLV, p. 157.

its immediate result created a general determination to preserve neutrality. It is evident that even without this threat of war there was no real cotton pressure upon the Government. With Northern successes in the spring of 1862 hopes were aroused that the war would soon end or that at least some cotton districts would be captured to the relief of England. Seward held out big promises based on the capture of New Orleans, and these for a time calmed governmental apprehensions, though by midsummer it was clear that the inability to secure the country back of the city, together with the Southern determination to burn their cotton rather than see it fall into the hands of the enemy, would prevent any great supply from the Mississippi valley.[1] This was still not a matter of *immediate* concern, for the Government and the manufacturers both held the opinion that it was not lack of cotton alone that was responsible for the distress and the manufacturers were just beginning to unload their stocks.[2] But in considering and judging the attitude of the British public on this question of cotton it should always be remembered that the great mass of the people sincerely believed that America was responsible for the distress in Lancashire. The error in understanding was more important than the truth.

In judging governmental policy, however, the truth as regards the causes of distress in England is the more important element. The " Cotton Lords " did not choose to reveal it. One must believe that they intentionally dwelt upon the war as the sole responsible cause. In the first important parliamentary debate on cotton, May 9, 1862, not a word

[1] F.O., Am., Vol. 843. No. 85. Bunch to Russell, June 25, 1862. He reported a general burning of cotton estimating the amount so destroyed as nearly one million bales.

[2] Rhodes, III, p. 503, leaves the impression that England was at first unanimous in attributing the cotton disaster to the War. Also, IV, p. 77. I think this an error. It was the general public belief but not that of the well informed. Rhodes, Vol. IV, p. 364, says that it was not until January, 1863, that it was " begun to be understood " that famine was not wholly caused by the War, but partly by glut.

was said of any other element in the situation, and, it is to be noted, not a word advocating a change in British neutral policy.[1] It is to be noted also that this debate occurred when for two months past, the numbers on poor relief in Lancashire were temporarily decreasing,[2] and the general tone of the speakers was that while the distress was serious it was not beyond the power of the local communities to meet it. There was not, then, in May, any reason for grave concern and Russell expressed governmental conviction when he wrote to Gladstone, May 18, "We must, I believe, get thro' the cotton crisis as we can, and promote inland works and railroads in India."[3] Moreover the Southern orders to destroy cotton rather than permit its capture and export by the North disagreeably affected British officials.[4] Up to the end of August, 1862, Russell, while writing much to Lyons on England's necessity for cotton, did not do so in a vein indicative of criticism of Northern policy nor in the sense that British distress demanded special official consideration. Such demands on America as were made up to this time came wholly from France.[5]

It was not then cotton, primarily, which brought a revival in July of the Southern attack on the Government through Parliament.[6] June had seen the collapse of Lindsay's

[1] Hansard, 3d. Ser., CLXVI, pp. 1490-1520. Debate on "The Distress in the Manufacturing Districts." The principal speakers were Egerton, Potter, Villiers and Bright. Another debate on "The Cotton Supply" took place June 19, 1862, with no criticism of America. *Ibid.* CLXVII, pp. 754-93.

[2] See *ante*, p. 12.

[3] Gladstone Papers.

[4] F. O., Am., Vol. 843. No. 73. Bunch to Russell, May 12, 1862. A description of these orders as inclusive of "foreign owned" cotton of which Bunch asserted a great stock had been purchased and stored, waiting export, by British citizens. Molyneaux at Savannah made a similar report. *Ibid.*, Vol. 849. No. 16. To Russell, May 10, 1862.

[5] Bancroft, *Seward*, II, pp. 214-18.

[6] Arnold, *Cotton Famine*, p. 228, quotes a song in the "improvised schoolrooms" of Ashton where operatives were being given a leisure-time education. One verse was:

"Our mules and looms have now ceased work, the Yankees are the cause.
But we will let them fight it out and stand by English laws;
No recognizing shall take place, until the war is o'er;
Our wants are now attended to, we cannot ask for more."

initial move, and Palmerston's answer to Hopwood, June 13, that there was no intention, at present, to offer mediation, appeared final. It was not cotton, but McClellan's defeat, that produced a quick renewal of Lindsay's activities. June 30, Hopwood had withdrawn his motion favouring recognition but in doing so asked whether, "considering the great and increasing distress in the country, the patient manner in which it has hitherto been borne, and the hopelessness of the termination of hostilities, the Government intend to take any steps whatever, either as parties to intervention or otherwise, to endeavour to put an end to the Civil War in America?" This was differently worded, yet contained little variation from his former question of June 13, and this time Palmerston replied briefly that the Government certainly would like to mediate if it saw any hope of success but that at present "both parties would probably reject it. If a different situation should arise the Government would be glad to act."[1] This admission was now seized upon by Lindsay who, on July 11, introduced a motion demanding consideration of "the propriety of offering mediation with the view of terminating hostilities," and insisted upon a debate.

Thus while the first week of June seemed to have quieted rumours of British mediation, the end of the month saw them revived. Adams was keenly aware of the changing temper of opinion and on June 20 presented to Russell a strong representation by Seward who wrote "under the President's instructions" that such recurrent rumours were highly injurious to the North since upon hopes of foreign aid the South has been encouraged and sustained from the first day of secession. Having developed this complaint at some length Seward went on to a brief threat, containing the real meat of the despatch, that if foreign nations did venture to intervene or mediate in favour of the South, the

[1] Hansard, 3rd. Ser., CLXVII, p. 1213.

North would be forced to have recourse to a weapon hitherto not used, namely to aid in a rising of the slaves against their masters. This was clearly a threat of a " servile war " if Great Britain aided the South—a war which would place Britain in a very uncomfortable position in view of her anti-slavery sentiments in the past. It is evidence of Adams' discretion that this despatch, written May 28, was held back from presentation to Russell until revived rumours of mediation made the American Minister anxious.[1] No answer was given by Russell for over a month, a fact in itself indicative of some hesitancy on policy. Soon the indirect diplomacy of Napoleon III was renewed in the hope of British concurrence. July 11, Slidell informed Mason that Persigny in conversation had assured him " that this Government is now more anxious than ever to take prompt and decided action in our favour." Slidell asked if it was impossible to stir Parliament but acknowledged that everything depended on Palmerston : " that august body seems to be as afraid of him as the urchins of a village school of the birch of their pedagogue."[2]

Unquestionably Persigny here gave Slidell a hint of private instructions now being sent by Napoleon to Thouvenel who was on a visit to London. The Emperor telegraphed " Demandez au gouvernement anglais s'il ne croit pas le moment venu de reconnaître le Sud."[3] Palmerston had already answered this question in Parliament and Thouvenel was personally very much opposed to the Emperor's suggestion. There were press rumours that he was in London

[1] *Parliamentary Papers*, 1862, *Lords*, Vol. XXV. " Further Correspondence relating to the Civil War in the United States." No. 1. Recd. June 21, 1862.

[2] Mason Papers.

[3] Thouvenel, *Le Secret de l'Empereur*, II, 352. The exact length of Thouvenel's stay in London is uncertain, but he had arrived by July 10 and was back in Paris by July 21. The text of the telegram is in a letter to Flahault of July 26, in which Thouvenel shows himself very averse to any move which may lead to war with America, " an adventure more serious than that of Mexico " (*Ibid.*, p. 353).

to bring the matter to a head, but his report to Mercier was that interference in America was a very dangerous matter and that he would have been "badly received" by Palmerston and Russell if he had suggested any change in neutral policy.[1]

In spite of this decided opposition by the French Minister of Foreign Affairs it is evident that one ground for renewed Southern hopes was the knowledge of the Emperor's private desires. Lindsay chose his time well for on July 16 the first thorough report on Lancashire was laid before Parliament,[2] revealing an extremity of distress not previously officially authenticated, and during this week the papers were full of an impending disaster to McClellan's army. Lyons, now in London, on his vacation trip, was concerned for the future mainly because of cotton, but did not believe there was much danger of an immediate clash with America.[3] But the great Southern argument of the moment was the Northern military failure, the ability of the South to resist indefinitely and the hopelessness of the war. On the morning of July 18 all London was in excitement over press statements that the latest news from America was not of McClellan's retreat but of the capture of his entire army.

Lindsay's motion was set for debate on this same July 18. Adams thought the story of McClellan's surrender had been set afloat "to carry the House of Commons off

[1] *Ibid.*, p. 349. July 24, 1862. See also résumé in Walpole, *History of Twenty-five Years*, II, 55.

[2] Farnall's First Report. *Parliamentary Papers*, 1862, *Commons*, Vol. XLIX.

[3] Lyons Papers. Lyons to Stuart, July 5, 1862.

"Public opinion will not allow the Government to do more for the North than maintain a strict neutrality, and it may not be easy to do that if there comes any strong provocation from the U.S. . . ."

"However, the real question of the day is cotton. . . ."

"The problem is of how to get over *this next* winter. The prospects of the manufacturing districts are very gloomy."

". . . If you can manage in any way to get a supply of cotton for England before the winter, you will have done a greater service than has been effected by Diplomacy for a century; but nobody expects it."

their feet in its debate to-night."[1] The debate itself may be regarded as a serious attempt to push the Ministry into a position more favourable to the South, and the arguments advanced surveyed the entire ground of the causes of secession and the inevitability of the final separation of North and South. They need but brief summary. Lindsay, refusing to accede to appeals for postponement because "the South was winning anyway," argued that slavery was no element in the conflict, that the Southern cause was just, and that England, because of her own difficulties, should mediate and bring to a conclusion a hopeless war. He claimed the time was opportune since mediation would be welcomed by a great majority in the North, and he quoted from a letter by a labouring man in Lancashire, stating, "We think it high time to give the Southern States the recognition they so richly deserve."

Other pro-Southern speakers emphasized Lancashire distress. Gregory said: "We should remember what is impending over Lancashire—what want, what woe, what humiliation—and that not caused by the decree of God, but by the perversity of man. I leave the statistics of the pauperism that is, and that is to be, to my honourable friends, the representatives of manufacturing England." No statistics were forthcoming from this quarter for not a representative from Lancashire participated in the debate save Hopwood who at the very end upbraided his fellow members from the district for their silence and was interrupted by cries of "Divide, Divide." Lindsay's quoted letter was met by opponents of mediation with the assertion that the operatives were well known to be united against

[1] *A Cycle of Adams' Letters*, I, 166. To his son, July 18, 1862. He noted that the news had come by the *Glasgow* which had sailed for England on July 5, whereas the papers contained also a telegram from McClellan's head-quarters, dated July 7, but "the people here are fully ready to credit anything that is not favourable." Newspaper headings were "Capitulation of McClellan's Army. Flight of McClellan on a steamer." *Ibid.*, 167. Henry Adams to C. F. Adams, Jr., July 19.

any action and that they could be sustained "in luxury" from the public purse for far less a cost than that of a war with America.

But cotton did not play the part expected of it in this debate. Forster in a very able speech cleverly keeping close to a consideration of the effect of mediation on *England*, advanced the idea that such a step would not end the war but would merely intensify it and so prolong English commercial distress. He did state, however, that intervention (as distinct from mediation) would bring on a "servile war" in America, thus giving evidence of his close touch with Adams and his knowledge of Seward's despatch of May 28. In the main the friends of the North were content to be silent and leave it to the Government to answer Lindsay. This was good tactics and they were no doubt encouraged to silence by evidence early given in the debate that there would be no positive result from the motion. Gregory showed that this was a real *attack* on the Government by his bitter criticisms of Russell's "three months" speech.[1]

At the conclusion of Gregory's speech Lindsay and his friends, their immediate purpose accomplished and fearing a vote, wished to adjourn the debate indefinitely. Palmerston objected. He agreed that everyone earnestly wished the war in America to end, but he declared that such debates were a great mistake unless something definite was to follow since they only served to create irritation in America, both North and South. He concluded with a vigorous assertion that if the Ministry were to administer the affairs of the nation it ought to be trusted in foreign affairs and not have its hands tied by parliamentary expressions of opinion at inopportune moments. Finally, the South had

[1] Gregory introduced a ridiculous extract from the *Dubuque Sun*, an Iowa paper, humorously advocating a repudiation of all debts to England, and solemnly held this up as evidence of the lack of financial morality in America. If he knew of this the editor of the small-town American paper must have been tickled at the reverberations of his humour.

not yet securely established its independence and hence could not be recognized. This motion, if carried, would place England on a definite side and thus be fatal to any hope of successful mediation or intervention in the future. Having now made clear the policy of the Government Palmerston did not insist upon a division and the motion was withdrawn.[1]

On the surface Lindsay's effort of July 18 had resulted in ignominious failure. Lyons called it "ill-timed. . . . I do not think we know here sufficiently the extent of the disaster [to McClellan] to be able to come to any conclusion as to what the European Powers should do." But the impression left by the debate that there was a strong parliamentary opinion in favour of mediation made Lyons add: "I suppose Mercier will open full cry on the scent, and be all for mediation. I am still afraid of any attempt of the kind."[2] Very much the same opinion was held by Henry Adams who wrote, "the pinch has again passed by for the moment and we breathe more freely. But I think I wrote to you some time ago that if July found us still in Virginia, we could no longer escape interference. I think now that it is inevitable." A definite stand taken by the North on slavery would bring "the greatest strength in this running battle."[3]

In spite of surface appearances that the debate was "ill-timed" the "pinch" was not in fact passed as the activities of Slidell and Mason and their friends soon indicated. For a fortnight the Cabinet, reacting to the repeated suggestions of Napoleon, the Northern defeats, and the distress in Lancashire, was seriously considering the possibility of taking some step toward mediation. On July 16, two days before the debate in the Commons,

[1] Hansard, 3rd. Ser. CLXVIII, pp. 511-549, for the entire debate.

[2] Lyons Papers. Lyons to Stuart, July 19, 1862.

[3] *A Cycle of Adams' Letters*, I, pp. 168-9. To Charles Francis Adams, Jr., July 19, 1862.

Slidell at last had his first personal contact with Napoleon, and came away from the interview with the conviction that "if England long persists in her inaction he [Napoleon] would be disposed to act without her." This was communicated to Mason on July 20,[1] but Slidell did *not* as yet see fit to reveal to Mason that in the interview with Napoleon he had made a definite push for separate action by France, offering inducements on cotton, a special commercial treaty, and "alliances, defensive, and offensive, for Mexican affairs," this last without any authority from Benjamin, the Confederate Secretary of State. On July 23 Slidell made a similar offer to Thouvenel and left with him a full memorandum of the Southern proposal.[2] He was cautioned that it was undesirable his special offer to France should reach the ears of the British Government—a caution which he transmitted to Mason on July 30, when sending copies of Benjamin's instructions, but still without revealing the full extent of his own overtures to Napoleon.

In all this Slidell was still exhibiting that hankering to

[1] Mason Papers. The larger part of Slidell's letter to Mason is printed in Sears, "A Confederate Diplomat at the Court of Napoleon III," *Am. Hist. Rev.*, Jan., 1921, p. 263. C. F. Adams, "A Crisis in Downing Street," Mass. Hist. Soc. *Proceedings*, May, 1914, p. 379, is in error in dating this letter April 21, an error for which the present writer is responsible, having misread Slidell's difficult hand-writing.

[2] Richardson, II, pp. 268-289. Slidell to Benjamin, July 25, 1862. It is uncertain just when Mason learned the details of Slidell's offer to France. Slidell, in his letter of July 20, wrote: "There is an important part of our conversation that I will give you through Mr. Mann," who, apparently, was to proceed at once to London to enlighten Mason. But the Mason Papers show that Mann did not go to London, and that Mason was left in the dark except in so far as he could guess at what Slidell had done by reading Benjamin's instructions, sent to him by Slidell, on July 30. These did *not* include anything on Mexico, but made clear the plan of a "special commercial advantage" to France. In C. F. Adams, "A Crisis in Downing Street," p. 381, it is stated that Benjamin's instructions were written "at the time of Mercier's visit to Richmond"—with the inference that they were a result of Mercier's conversation at that time. This is an error. Benjamin's instructions were written on April 12, and were sent on April 14, while it was not until April 16 that Mercier reached Richmond. To some it will no doubt seem inconceivable that Benjamin should not have informed Mercier of his plans for France, just formulated. But here, as in Chapter IX, I prefer to accept Mercier's positive assurances to Lyons at their face value. Lyons certainly so accepted them and there is nothing in French documents yet published to cast doubt on Mercier's honour, while the chronology of the Confederate documents supports it.

JOHN SLIDELL

(From Nicolay and Hay's "Life of Abraham Lincoln": The Century Co. New York)

pull off a special diplomatic achievement, characteristic of the man, and in line, also, with a persistent theory that the policy most likely to secure results was that of inducing France to act alone. But he was repeatedly running against advice that France must follow Great Britain, and the burden of his July 20 letter to Mason was an urging that a demand for recognition be now made simultaneously in Paris and London. Thouvenel, not at all enthusiastic over Slidell's proposals, told him that this was at least a prerequisite, and on July 23, Slidell wrote Mason the demand should be made at once.[1] Mason, on the advice of Lindsay, Fitzgerald, and Lord Malmesbury, had already prepared a request for recognition, but had deferred making it after listening to the debate of July 18.[2] Now, on July 24, he addressed Russell referring to their interview of February, 1862, in which he had urged the claims of the Confederacy to recognition and again presented them, asserting that the subsequent failure of Northern campaigns had demonstrated the power of the South to maintain its independence. The South, he wrote, asked neither aid nor intervention; it merely desired recognition and continuation of British neutrality.[3] On the same day Mason also asked for an interview,[4] but received no reply until July 31, when Russell wrote that no definite answer could be sent until "after a Cabinet" and that an interview did not seem necessary.[5]

This answer clearly indicates that the Government was in uncertainty. It is significant that Russell took this moment to reply at last to Seward's protestations of May 28,[6] which had been presented to him by Adams on June 20. He instructed Stuart at Washington that his delay had

[1] Mason Papers.

[2] *Ibid.*, Mason to Slidell, July 18 and 19.

[3] *Parliamentary Papers*, 1863, *Lords*, Vol. XXIX. "Correspondence with Mr. Mason respecting Blockade and Recognition." No. 7.

[4] *Ibid.*, No. 8.

[5] *Ibid.*, No. 9.

[6] See *ante*, p. 18.

been due to a "waiting for military events," but that these had been indecisive. He gave a résumé of all the sins of the North as a belligerent and wrote in a distinctly captious spirit. Yet these sins had not "induced Her Majesty's Government to swerve an inch from an impartial neutrality."[1] Here was no promise of a continuance of neutrality—rather a hint of some coming change. At least one member of the Cabinet was very ready for it. Gladstone wrote privately:

> "It is indeed much to be desired that this bloody and purposeless conflict should cease. From the first it has been plain enough that the whole question was whether the South was earnest and united. That has now for some months been demonstrated; and the fact thus established at once places the question beyond the region even of the most brilliant military successes. . . ."[2]

Gladstone was primarily influenced by the British commercial situation. Lyons, still in England, and a consistent opponent of a change of policy, feared this commercial influence. He wrote to Stuart:

> ". . . I can hardly anticipate any circumstances under which I should think the intervention of England in the quarrel between the North and South advisable. . . .
>
> "But it is very unfortunate that no result whatever is apparent from the nominal re-opening of New Orleans and other ports. And the distress in the manufacturing districts threatens to be so great that a pressure may be put upon the Government which they will find it difficult to resist."[3]

In Parliament sneers were indulged in by Palmerston at the expense of the silent cotton manufacturers of Lancashire, much to the fury of Cobden.[4] Of this period Arnold

[1] *Parliamentary Papers*, 1862, *Lords*, Vol. XXV. "Further Correspondence relating to the Civil War in the United States." No. 2. Russell to Stuart, July 28, 1862.

[2] Gladstone Papers. To Col. Neville, July 26, 1862.

[3] Lyons Papers. July 29, 1862.

[4] Malmesbury, *Memoirs of an Ex-Minister*, II, p. 276. July 31, 1862.

later sarcastically remarked that, "The representatives of Lancashire in the Houses of Parliament did not permit the gaieties of the Exhibition season wholly to divert their attention from the distress which prevailed in the home county."[1]

Being refused an interview, Mason transmitted to Russell on August 1 a long appeal, rather than a demand, for recognition, using exactly those arguments advanced by Lindsay in debate.[2] The answer, evidently given after that "Cabinet" for whose decision Russell had been waiting, was dated August 2. In it Russell, as in his reply to Seward on July 28, called attention to the wholly contradictory statements of North and South on the status of the war, which, in British opinion, had not yet reached a stage positively indicative of the permanence of Southern independence. Great Britain, therefore, still "waited," but the time might come when Southern firmness in resistance would bring recognition.[3] The tone was more friendly than any expressions hitherto used by Russell to Southern representatives. The reply does not reveal the decision actually arrived at by the Ministry. Gladstone wrote to Argyll on August 3 that "yesterday" a Cabinet had been held on the question "to move or not to move, in the matter of the American Civil War. . . ." He had come away before a decision when it became evident the prevailing sentiment would be "nothing shall be done until both parties are desirous of it." Gladstone thought this very foolish; he would have England approach France and Russia, but if they were not ready, wait until they were. "Something, I trust, will be done before the hot weather is over to stop these frightful horrors."[4]

[1] Arnold, *Cotton Famine*, p. 175.

[2] *Parliamentary Papers*, 1863, *Lords*, Vol. XXIX. "Correspondence with Mr. Mason respecting Blockade and Recognition." No. 10.

[3] *Ibid.*, No. 11.

[4] Gladstone Papers. Also Argyll, *Autobiography*, II, p. 191.

All parties had been waiting since the debate of July 18 for the Cabinet decision. It was at once generally known as "no step at present" and wisdom would have decreed quiet acquiescence. Apparently one Southern friend, on his own initiative, felt the need to splutter. On the next day, August 4, Lord Campbell in the Lords moved for the production of Russell's correspondence with Mason, making a very confused speech. "Society and Parliament" were convinced the war ought to end in separation. At one time Campbell argued that reconquest of the South was impossible; at another that England should interfere to prevent such reconquest. Again he urged that the North was in a situation where she could not stop the war without aid from Europe in extricating her. Probably the motion was made merely to draw from Russell an official statement. Production of the papers was refused. Russell stated that the Government still maintained its policy of strict neutrality, that if any action was to be taken it should be by all the maritime powers and that if, in the parliamentary recess, any new policy seemed advisable he would first communicate with those powers. He also declared very positively that as yet no proposal had been received from any foreign power in regard to America, laying stress upon the "perfect accord" between Great Britain and France.[1]

Mason commented on this speech that someone was evidently lying and naturally believed that someone to be Russell. He hoped that France would promptly make this clear.[2] But France gave no sign of lack of "perfect accord." On the contrary Thouvenel even discouraged Slidell from following Mason's example of demanding recognition and the formal communication was withheld, Mason acquiescing.[3] Slidell thought new disturbances in

[1] Hansard, 3rd. Ser., CLXVIII, p. 1177 *seq.*

[2] Mason Papers. Mason to Slidell, Aug. 5, 1862.

[3] F. O., France, Vol. 1443. No. 964. Cowley to Russell, Aug. 8, 1862. Mason Papers. Slidell to Mason, Aug. 20, 1862. Mason to Slidell, Aug. 21.

Italy responsible for this sudden lessening of French interest in the South, but he was gloomy, seeing again the frustration of high hopes. August 24 he wrote Benjamin:

> "You will find by my official correspondence that we are still hard and fast aground here. Nothing will float us off but a strong and continued current of important successes in the field.
>
> I have no hope from England, because I am satisfied that she desires an indefinite prolongation of the war, until the North shall be entirely exhausted and broken down.
>
> Nothing can exceed the selfishness of English statesmen except their wretched hypocrisy. They are continually casting about their disinterested magnaminity and objection of all other considerations than those dictated by a high-toned morality, while their entire policy is marked by egotism and duplicity. I am getting to be heartily tired of Paris." [1]

On August 7 Parliament adjourned, having passed on the last day of the session an Act for the relief of the distress in Lancashire by authorizing an extension of powers to the Poor Law Guardians. Like Slidell and Mason pro-Northern circles in London thought that in August there had come to a disastrous end the Southern push for a change in British policy, and were jubilant. To be sure, Russell had merely declared that the time for action was "not yet" come, but this was regarded as a sop thrown to the South. Neither in informed Southern nor Northern circles outside the Cabinet was there any suspicion, *except by Adams,* that in the six months elapsed since Lindsay had begun his movement the Ministry had been slowly progressing in thoughts of mediation.

In fact the sentiment of the Cabinet as stated by Gladstone had been *favourable* to mediation when "both parties were ready for it" and that such readiness would come soon most Members were convinced. This was a

[1] Richardson, II, p. 315.

convenient and reasonable ground for postponing action but did not imply that if the conviction were unrealized no mediation would be attempted. McClellan, driven out of the Peninsula, had been removed, and August saw the Northern army pressed back from Virginia soil. It was now Washington and not Richmond that seemed in danger of capture. Surely the North must soon realize the futility of further effort, and the reports early in July from Washington dilated upon the rapid emergence of a strong peace party.

But the first panic of dismay once past Stuart sent word of enormous new Northern levies of men and of renewed courage.[1] By mid-August, writing of cotton, he thought the prospect of obtaining any quantity of it "seems hopeless," and at the same time reported the peace party fast losing ground in the face of the great energy of the Administration.[2] As to recognition, Stuart believed: "There is nothing to be done in the presence of these enormous fresh levies, but to wait and see what the next two months will bring forth."[3] The hopes of the British Ministry based on a supposed Northern weariness of the war were being shattered. Argyll, having received from Sumner a letter describing the enthusiasm and determination of the North, wrote to Gladstone:

> "It is evident, whatever may be our opinion of the prospects of 'the North' that they do not yet, at least, feel any approach to such exhaustion as will lead them to admit of mediation. . . ." [4]

To this Gladstone replied:

> "I agree that this is not a state of mind favourable to mediation; and I admit it to be a matter of great difficulty

[1] Russell Papers. Stuart to Russell, July 7, 1862.

[2] *Ibid.* To Russell, Aug. 18, 1862.

[3] *Ibid.* Aug. 26. Stuart's "nothing to be done" refers, not to mediation, but to his idea in June-July that the time was ripe for recognition. He was wholly at variance with Lyons on British policy.

[4] Gladstone Papers. Aug. 26, 1862.

to determine when the first step ought to be taken; but I cannot subscribe to the opinion of those who think that Europe is to stand silent without limit of time and witness these horrors and absurdities, which will soon have consumed more men, and done ten times more mischief than the Crimean War; but with the difference that there the end was uncertain, here it is certain in the opinion of the whole world except one of the parties. I should be puzzled to point out a single case of dismemberment which has been settled by the voluntary concession of the stronger party without any interference or warning from third powers, and as far as principle goes there never was a case in which warning was so proper and becoming, because of the frightful misery which this civil conflict has brought upon other countries, and because of the unanimity with which it is condemned by the civilized world." [1]

The renewal of Northern energy, first reports of which were known to Russell early in August, came as a surprise to the British Ministry. Their progress toward mediation had been slow but steady. Lindsay's initial steps, resented as an effort in indirect diplomacy and not supported by France officially, had received prompt rejection accompanied by no indication of a desire to depart from strict neutrality. With the cessation in late June of the Northern victorious progress in arms and in the face of increasing distress in Lancashire, the second answer to Lindsay was less dogmatic. As given by Palmerston the Government desired to offer mediation, but saw no present hope of doing so successfully. Finally the Government asked for a free hand, making no pledges. Mason might be gloomy, Adams exultant, but when August dawned plans were already on foot for a decided change. The secret was well kept. Four days after the Cabinet decision to wait on events, two days after Russell's refusal to produce the correspondence with Mason, Russell, on the eve of departure for the Continent, was writing to Palmerston:

[1] *Ibid.* Aug. 29, 1862.

> "Mercier's notion that we should make some move in October agrees very well with yours. I shall be back in England before October, and we could then have a Cabinet upon it. Of course the war may flag before that.
>
> "I quite agree with you that a proposal for an armistice should be the first step; but we must be prepared to answer the question on what basis are we to negotiate?" [1]

The next movement to put an end to the war in America was to come, not from Napoleon III, nor from the British friends of the South, but from the British Ministry itself.

[1] Palmerston MS. Aug. 6, 1862.

CHAPTER XI

RUSSELL'S MEDIATION PLAN

THE adjournment of Parliament on August 7 without hint of governmental inclination to act in the American Civil War was accepted by most of the British public as evidence that the Ministry had no intentions in that direction. But keen observers were not so confident. Motley, at Vienna, was keeping close touch with the situation in England through private correspondence. In March, 1862, he thought that "France and England have made their minds up to await the issue of the present campaign"—meaning McClellan's advance on Richmond.[1] With the failure of that campaign he wrote: "Thus far the English Government have resisted his [Napoleon's] importunities. But their resistance will not last long."[2] Meanwhile the recently established pro-Southern weekly, *The Index*, from its first issue, steadily insisted on the wisdom and necessity of British action to end the war.[3] France was declared rapidly to be winning the goodwill of the South at the expense of England; the British aristocracy were appealed to on grounds of close sympathy with a "Southern Aristocracy"; mediation, at first objected to, in view of the more reasonable demand for recognition, was in the end the chief object of *The Index*, after mid-July, when simple recognition seemed impossible of attainment.[4] Especially British

[1] Motley, *Correspondence*, II, 71. To his mother, March 16, 1862.

[2] *Ibid.*, p. 81. Aug. 18, 1862.

[3] *The Index* first appeared on May 1, 1862. Nominally a purely British weekly it was soon recognized as the mouthpiece of the Confederacy.

[4] *The Index*, May 15, 29, June 19 and July 31, 1862.

humiliation because of the timidity of her statesmen, was harped upon and any public manifestation of Southern sympathy was printed in great detail.[1]

The speculations of Motley, the persistent agitation of *The Index* are, however, no indication that either Northern fears or Southern hopes were based on authoritative information as to governmental purpose. The plan now in the minds of Palmerston and Russell and their steps in furthering it have been the subject of much historical study and writing. It is here proposed to review them in the light of all available important materials, both old and new, using a chronological order and with more citation than is customary, in the belief that such citations best tell the story of this, the most critical period in the entire course of British attitude toward the Civil War. Here, and here only, Great Britain voluntarily approached the danger of becoming involved in the American conflict.[2]

Among the few who thought the withdrawal of Lindsay's motion, July 18, and the Prime Minister's comments did *not* indicate safety for the North stood Adams, the American Minister. Of Palmerston's speech he wrote the next day in his diary: "It was cautious and wise, but enough could be gathered from it to show that mischief to us in some shape will only be averted by the favour of Divine Providence or

[1] e.g., the issue of Aug. 14, 1862, contained a long report of a banquet in Sheffield attended by Palmerston and Roebuck. In his speech Roebuck asserted: "A divided America will be a benefit to England." He appealed to Palmerston to consider whether the time had not come to recognize the South. "The North will never be our friends. (Cheers.) Of the South you can make friends. They are Englishmen; they are not the scum and refuse of Europe. (The Mayor of Manchester: 'Don't say that; don't say that.') (Cheers and disapprobation.) I know what I am saying. They are Englishmen, and we must make them our friends."

[2] All American histories treat this incident at much length. The historian who has most thoroughly discussed it is C. F. Adams, with changing interpretation as new facts came to light. See his *Life of C. F. Adams*, Ch. XV; *Studies, Military and Diplomatic*, pp. 400-412; *Trans-Atlantic Historical Solidarity*, pp. 97-106; *A Crisis in Downing Street*, Mass. Hist. Soc. *Proceedings*, May, 1914, pp. 372-424. It will be made clear in a later chapter why Roebuck's motion of midsummer, 1863, was unimportant in considering Ministerial policy.

our own efforts. The anxiety attending my responsibility is only postponed."[1] At this very moment Adams was much disturbed by his failure to secure governmental seizure of a war vessel being built at Liverpool for the South—the famous *Alabama*—which was soon completed and put to sea but ten days later, July 29. Russell's delay in enforcing British neutrality, as Adams saw it, in this matter, reinforcing the latter's fears of a change in policy, had led him to explain his alarm to Seward. On August 16 Adams received an instruction, written August 2, outlining the exact steps to be taken in case the feared change in British policy should occur. As printed in the diplomatic documents later presented to Congress this despatch is merely a very interesting if somewhat discursive essay on the inevitability of European ruminations on the possibility of interference to end the war and argues the unwisdom of such interference, especially for Great Britain's own interests. It does not read as if Seward were alarmed or, indeed, as if he had given serious consideration to the supposed danger.[2] But this conveys a very erroneous impression. An unprinted portion of the despatch very specifically and in a very serious tone, instructs Adams that if approached by the British Government with propositions implying a purpose:

> "To dictate, or to mediate, or to advise, or even to solicit or persuade, you will answer that you are forbidden to debate, to hear, or in any way receive, entertain or transmit, any communication of the kind. . . . If you are asked an opinion what reception the President would give to such a proposition, if made here, you will reply that you are not instructed, but you have no reason for supposing that it would be entertained."

This was to apply either to Great Britain alone or acting in conjunction with other Powers. Further, if the South

[1] Adams, *A Crisis in Downing Street*, p. 388.

[2] *U. S. Messages and Documents*, 1862-3. Pt. I, pp. 165-168.

should be "acknowledged" Adams was immediately to suspend his functions. "You will perceive," wrote Seward, "that we have approached the contemplation of that crisis with the caution which great reluctance has inspired. But I trust that you will also have perceived that the crisis has not appalled us."[1]

This serious and definite determination by the North to resent any intervention by Europe makes evident that Seward and Lincoln were fully committed to forcible resistance of foreign meddling. Briefly, if the need arose, the North would go to war with Europe. Adams at least now knew where he stood and could but await the result. The instruction he held in reserve, nor was it ever officially communicated to Russell. He did, however, state its tenor to Forster who had contacts with the Cabinet through Milner-Gibson and though no proof has been found that the American determination was communicated to the Ministry, the presumption is that this occurred.[2] Such communication could not have taken place before the end of August and possibly was not then made owing to the fact that the Cabinet was scattered in the long vacation and that, apparently, the plan to move *soon* in the American War was as yet unknown save to Palmerston and to Russell.

Russell's letter to Palmerston of August 6, sets the date of their determination.[3] Meanwhile they were depending much upon advices from Washington for the exact moment. Stuart was suggesting, with Mercier, that October should be selected,[4] and continued his urgings even though his immediate chief, Lyons, was writing to him from London strong personal objections to any European intervention whatever and especially any by Great Britain.[5] Lyons

[1] Adams, *A Crisis in Downing Street*, p. 389. First printed in Rhodes, VI, pp. 342-3, in 1899.
[2] *Ibid.*, p. 390.
[3] See *ante*, p. 32.
[4] Russell Papers. Stuart to Russell, July 21, 1862.
[5] Lyons Papers. Lyons to Stuart, July 25, 1862.

explained his objections to Russell as well, but Stuart, having gone to the extent of consulting also with Stoeckl, the Russian Minister at Washington, was now in favour of straight-out recognition of the Confederacy as the better measure. This, thought Stoeckl, was less likely to bring on war with the North than an attempt at mediation.[1] Soon Stuart was able to give notice, a full month in advance of the event, of Lincoln's plan to issue an emancipation proclamation, postponed temporarily on the insistence of Seward,[2] but he attached no importance to this, regarding it as at best a measure of pretence intended to frighten the South and to influence foreign governments.[3] Russell was not impressed with Stuart's shift from mediation to recognition. "I think," he wrote, "we must allow the President to spend his second batch of 600,000 men before we can hope that he and his democracy will listen to reason."[4] But this did not imply that Russell was wavering in the idea that October would be a "ripe time." Soon he was journeying to the Continent in attendance on the Queen and using his leisure to perfect his great plan.[5]

Russell's first positive step was taken on September 13.

[1] Russell Papers. Stuart to Russell, Aug. 8, 1862. Stoeckl's own report hardly agrees with this. He wrote that the newspapers were full of rumours of European mediation but, on consultation with Seward, advised that any offer at present would only make matters worse. It would be best to wait and see what the next spring would bring forth (Russian Archives, Stoeckl to F. O., Aug. 9-21, 1862. No. 1566). Three weeks later Stoeckl was more emphatic; an offer of mediation would accomplish nothing unless backed up by force to open the Southern ports; this had always been Lyons' opinion also; before leaving for England, Lyons had told him "we ought not to venture on mediation unless we are ready to go to war." Mercier, however, was eager for action and believed that if France came forward, supported by the other Powers, especially Rüssia, the United States would be compelled to yield. To this Stoeckl did not agree. He believed Lyons was right (*Ibid.* Sept. 16-28, 1862. No. 1776).

[2] *Ibid.* Aug. 22, 1862. Sumner was Stuart's informant.

[3] *Ibid.* Sept. 26, 1862. When issued on September 22, Stuart found no "humanity" in it. "It is cold, vindictive and entirely political."

[4] Palmerston MS. Russell to Palmerston, Aug. 24, 1862.

[5] The ignorance of other Cabinet members is shown by a letter from Argyll to Gladstone, September 2, 1862, stating as if an accepted conclusion, that there should be no interference and that the war should be allowed to reach its "natural issue" (Gladstone Papers).

On that date he wrote to Cowley in Paris instructing him to sound Thouvenel, *privately*,[1] and the day following he wrote to Palmerston commenting on the news just received of the exploits of Stonewall Jackson in Virginia, " it really looks as if he might end the war. In October the hour will be ripe for the Cabinet."[2] Similar reactions were expressed by Palmerston at the same moment and for the same reasons. Palmerston also wrote on September 14:

> " The Federals . . . got a very complete smashing . . . even Washington or Baltimore may fall into the hands of the Confederates."
>
> " If this should happen, would it not be time for us to consider whether in such a state of things England and France might not address the contending parties and recommend an arrangement upon the basis of separation ? "[3]

Russell replied :

> " . . . I agree with you that the time is come for offering mediation to the United States Government, with a view to the recognition of the independence of the Confederates. I agree further that, in case of failure, we ought ourselves to recognize the Southern States as an independent State. For the purpose of taking so important a step, I think we must have a meeting of the Cabinet. The 23rd or 30th would suit me for the meeting." [4]

The two elder statesmen being in such complete accord the result of the unofficial overture to France was now awaited with interest. This, considering the similar unofficial suggestions previously made by Napoleon, was surprisingly lukewarm. Cowley reported that he had held a long and serious conversation with Thouvenel on the subject of mediation as instructed by Russell on the thirteenth and found a disposition " to wait to see the result

[1] Russell Papers. Cowley to Russell. Sept. 18, 1862, fixes the date of Russell's letter.

[2] Palmerston MS.

[3] Walpole, *Russell*, II, p. 360.

[4] *Ibid.*, p. 361. Sept. 17, 1862.

of the elections" in the North. Mercier apparently had been writing that Southern successes would strengthen the Northern peace party. Thouvenel's idea was that "if the peace party gains the ascendant," Lincoln and Seward, both of whom were too far committed to listen to foreign suggestions, would "probably be set aside." He also emphasized the "serious consequences" England and France might expect if they recognized the South.

> "I said that we might propose an armistice without mediation, and that if the other Powers joined with us in doing so, and let it be seen that a refusal would be followed by the recognition of the Southern States, the certainty of such recognition by all Europe must carry weight with it."
>
> Thouvenel saw some difficulties, especially Russia.
>
> ". . . the French Government had some time back sounded that of Russia as to her joining France and England in an offer of mediation and had been met by an almost scornful refusal. . . ."
>
> "It appears also that there is less public pressure here for the recognition of the South than there is in England."[1]

Thouvenel's lack of enthusiasm might have operated as a check to Russell had he not been aware of two circumstances causing less weight than formerly to be attached to the opinions of the French Secretary for Foreign Affairs. The first was the well-known difference on American policy between Thouvenel and Napoleon III and the well-grounded conviction that the Emperor was at any moment ready to impose his will, if only England would give the signal. The second circumstance was still more important. It was already known through the French press that a sharp conflict had arisen in the Government as to Italian policy and all signs pointed to a reorganization of the Ministry which would exclude Thouvenel. Under these

[1] Russell Papers. Cowley to Russell, Sept. 18, 1862. This is the first reference by Cowley in over three months to mediation—evidence that Russell's instructions took him by surprise.

circumstances Russell could well afford to discount Thouvenel's opinion. The extent to which he was ready to go—much beyond either the offer of mediation, or of armistice evidently in Cowley's mind—is shown by a letter to Gladstone, September 26.

> " I am inclined to think that October 16 may be soon enough for a Cabinet, if I am free to communicate the views which Palmerston and I entertain to France and Russia in the interval between this time and the middle of next month. These views had the offer of mediation to both parties in the first place, and in the case of refusal by the North, to recognition of the South. Mediation on the basis of separation and recognition accompanied by a declaration of neutrality." [1]

The perfected plan, thus outlined, had resulted from a communication to Palmerston of Cowley's report together with a memorandum, proposed to be sent to Cowley, but again *privately*,[2] addressed to France alone. Russell here also stated that he had explained his ideas to the Queen. " She only wishes Austria, Prussia and Russia to be consulted. I said that should be done, but we must consult France first." Also enclosed was a letter from Stuart of September 9, reporting Mercier as just returned from New York and convinced that if advantage were not taken of the present time to do exactly that which was in Russell's mind, Europe would have to wait for the " complete exhaustion " of the North.[3] Russell was now at home again and the next day Palmerston approved the plans as " excellent " ; but he asked whether it would not be well to include Russia in the invitation as a compliment, even though " she might probably decline." As to the other European powers the matter could wait for an " after communication." Yet that Palmerston still wished to go

[1] Gladstone Papers.
[2] Palmerston MS. Russell to Palmerston, Sept. 22, 1862.
[3] Russell Papers.

slowly is shown by a comment on the military situation in America:

> "It is evident that a great conflict is taking place to the north-west of Washington, and its issue must have a great effect on the state of affairs. If the Federals sustain a great defeat, they may be at once ready for mediation, and the iron should be struck while it is hot. If, on the other hand, they should have the best of it, we may wait awhile and see what may follow. . . . "[1]

Thus through Palmerston's caution Russia had been added to France in Russell's proposed memorandum and the communication to Cowley had not been sent off immediately—as the letter to Gladstone of September 26 indicates. But the plan was regarded as so far determined upon that on September 24 Russell requested Lyons not to fix, as yet, upon a date for his departure for America, writing, "M. Mercier is again looking out for an opportunity to offer mediation, and this time he is not so much out in his reckoning."[2] Curiously Mercier had again changed his mind and now thought a proposal of an armistice was the best move, being "particularly anxious that there should be no mention of the word *separation*," but of this Russell had, as yet, no inkling.[3] With full approval of the plan as now outlined, Palmerston wrote to Gladstone, September 24, that he and Russell were in complete agreement that an offer of mediation should be made by the three maritime powers, but that "no actual step would be taken without the sanction of the Cabinet."[4] Two days later Russell explained to Gladstone the exact nature of the proposal,[5] but that there was even now no thoroughly worked out agreement on the sequence of steps necessary is shown by

[1] Walpole, *Russell*, II, p. 362. Sept. 23, 1862.
[2] Lyons Papers.
[3] Lyons Papers. Stuart to Lyons, Sept. 23, 1862.
[4] Morley, *Gladstone*, II, p. 76.
[5] See *ante*, p. 40.

Palmerston's letter to Gladstone of the twenty-fourth, in which is outlined a preliminary proposal of an armistice, cessation of blockade, and negotiation on the basis of separation. [1]

Other members of the Cabinet were likewise informed of the proposed overture to France and Russia and soon it was clear that there would be opposition. Granville had replaced Russell in attendance upon the Queen at Gotha. He now addressed a long and careful argument to Russell opposing the adventure, as he thought it, summing up his opinion in this wise:

> "... I doubt, if the war continues long after our recognition of the South, whether it will be possible for us to avoid drifting into it."
>
> "... I have come to the conclusion that it is premature to depart from the policy which has hitherto been adopted by you and Lord Palmerston, and which, notwithstanding the strong antipathy to the North, the strong sympathy with the South, and the passionate wish to have cotton, has met with such general approval from Parliament, the press, and the public." [2]

But Granville had little hope his views would prevail. A few days later he wrote to Lord Stanley of Alderley:

> "I have written to Johnny my reasons for thinking it decidedly premature. I, however, suspect you will settle to do so! Pam, Johnny, and Gladstone would be in favour of it; and probably Newcastle. I do not know about the others. It appears to me a great mistake." [3]

Opportunely giving added effect to Granville's letter

[1] Adams, *A Crisis in Downing Street*, p. 393, giving the exact text paraphrased by Morley.

[2] Fitzmaurice, *Granville*, I, pp. 442-44, gives the entire letter. Sept. 27, 1862.

[3] *Ibid.*, p. 442. Oct. 1, 1862. Fitzmaurice attributes much influence to Granville in the final decision and presumes that the Queen, also, was opposed to the plan. There is no evidence to show that she otherwise expressed herself than as in the acquiescent suggestion to Russell. As for Granville, his opposition, standing alone, would have counted for little.

there now arrived confused accounts from America of the battles about Washington and of a check to the Southern advance. On September 17 there had been fought the battle of Antietam and two days later Lee, giving up his Maryland campaign, began a retreat through the Shenandoah valley toward the old defensive Southern lines before Richmond. There was no pursuit, for McClellan, again briefly in command, thought his army too shattered for an advance. Palmerston had been counting on a great Southern victory and was now doubtful whether the time had come after all for European overtures to the contestants. October 2 he wrote Russell:

"MY DEAR RUSSELL,

"I return you Granville's letter which contains much deserving of serious consideration. There is no doubt that the offer of Mediation upon the basis of Separation would be accepted by the South. Why should it not be accepted? It would give the South in principle the points for which they are fighting. The refusal, if refusal there was, would come from the North, who would be unwilling to give up the principle for which they have been fighting so long as they had a reasonable expectation that by going on fighting they could carry their point. The condition of things therefore which would be favourable to an offer of mediation would be great success of the South against the North. That state of things seemed ten days ago to be approaching. Its advance has been lately checked, but we do not yet know the real course of recent events, and still less can we foresee what is about to follow. Ten days or a fortnight more may throw a clearer light upon future prospects.

"As regards possible resentment on the part of the Northerns following upon an acknowledgment of the Independence of the South, it is quite true that we should have less to care about that resentment in the spring when communication with Canada was open, and when our naval force could more easily operate upon the American coast, than in winter when we are cut off from Canada and the American coast is not so safe.

"But if the acknowledgment were made at one and the same time by England, France and some other Powers, the Yankees would probably not seek a quarrel with us alone, and would not like one against a European Confederation. Such a quarrel would render certain and permanent that Southern Independence the acknowledgment of which would have caused it.

"The first communication to be made by England and France to the contending parties might be, not an absolute offer of mediation but a friendly suggestion whether the time was not come when it might be well for the two parties to consider whether the war, however long continued, could lead to any other result than separation; and whether it might not therefore be best to avoid the great evils which must necessarily flow from a prolongation of hostilities by at once coming to an agreement to treat upon that principle of separation which must apparently be the inevitable result of the contest, however long it may last.

"The best thing would be that the two parties should settle details by direct negotiation with each other, though perhaps with the rancorous hatred now existing between them this might be difficult. But their quarrels in negotiation would do us no harm if they did not lead to a renewal of war. An armistice, if not accompanied by a cessation of blockades, would be all in favour of the North, especially if New Orleans remained in the hands of the North.

"The whole matter is full of difficulty, and can only be cleared up by some more decided events between the contending armies. . . ."

PALMERSTON."[1]

Very evidently Palmerston was experiencing doubts and was all in favour of cautious delay. American military events more than Granville's arguments influenced him, but almost immediately there appeared a much more vigorous and determined opponent within the Cabinet. Cornewall Lewis was prompt to express objections. October 2, Russell transmitted to Palmerston a letter of disapproval

[1] Russell Papers. A brief extract from this letter is printed in Walpole, *Russell*, II, p. 362.

from Lewis. Russell also, momentarily, was hesitating. He wrote:

> "This American question must be well sifted. I send you a letter of G. Lewis who is against moving . . ."
>
> "My only doubt is whether we and France should stir if Russia holds back. Her separation from our move would ensure the rejection of our proposals. But we shall know more by the 16th. I have desired a cabinet to be summoned for that day, but the summons will not go out till Saturday. So if you wish to stop it, write to Hammond." [1]

From this it would appear that Russia had been approached[2] but that Russell's chief concern was the attitude of France, that his proposed private communication to Cowley had been despatched and that he was waiting an answer which might be expected before the sixteenth. If so his expectations were negatived by that crisis now on in the French Ministry over the Italian question prohibiting consideration of any other matter. On October 15 Thouvenel was dismissed, but his formal retirement from office did not take place until October 24. Several Ministers abroad, among them Flahault, at London, followed him into retirement and foreign affairs were temporarily in confusion.[3] The Emperor was away

[1] Palmerston MS.

[2] Brunow reported Russell's plan October 1, as, summarized, (1) an invitation to France and Russia to join with England in offering good services to the United States looking towards peace. (2) Much importance attached to the adhesion of Russia. (3) Excellent chance of success. (4) Nevertheless a possible refusal by the United States, in which case, (5) recognition by Great Britain of the South if it seemed likely that this could be done without giving the United States a just ground of quarrel. Brunow commented that this would be "eventually" the action of Great Britain, but that meanwhile circumstances might delay it. Especially he was impressed that the Cabinet felt the political necessity of "doing something" before Parliament re-assembled (Russian Archives, Brunow to F. O., London, Oct. 1, 1862 (N. S.). No. 1698. Gortchakoff promptly transmitted this to Stoeckl, together with a letter from Brunow, dated Bristol, Oct. 1, 1862 (N. S.), in which Brunow expressed the opinion that one object of the British Government was to introduce at Washington a topic which would serve to accentuate the differences that were understood to exist in Lincoln's Cabinet. (This seems very far-fetched.) Gortchakoff's comment in sending all this to Stoeckl was that Russia had no intention of changing her policy of extreme friendship to the United States (*Ibid.* F. O. to Stoeckl, Oct. 3, 1862 (O. S.).

[3] Thouvenel, *Le Secret de l'Empereur*, II, pp. 438-9.

from Paris and all that Cowley reported was that the last time he had seen Thouvenel the latter had merely remarked that "as soon as the Emperor came back the two Governments ought to enter into a serious consideration of the whole question. . . ."[1] Cowley himself was more concerned that it was now becoming clear France, in spite of previous protestations, was planning "colonizing" Mexico.[2]

Up to the end of September, therefore, the British Government, while wholly confident that France would agree in any effort whatsoever that England might wish to make, had no recent assurances, either official or private, to this effect. This did not disturb Russell, who took for granted French approval, and soon he cast aside the hesitation caused by the doubts of Granville, the opposition of Lewis, and the caution of Palmerston. Public opinion was certainly turning toward a demand for Ministerial action.[3] Two days of further consideration caused him to return to the attack; October 4 he wrote Palmerston:

> "I think unless some miracle takes place this will be the very time for offering mediation, or as you suggest, proposing to North and South to come to terms.
>
> "Two things however must be made clear:
>
> (i) That we propose separation.
>
> (ii) That we shall take no part in the war unless attacked ourselves."[4]

How Russell proposed to evade a war with an angry North was not made clear, but in this same letter notice was given that he was preparing a memorandum for the Cabinet. Russell was still for a mediation on lines of separation, but his uncertainty, even confusion, of mind became evident

[1] Russell Papers. Cowley to Russell, Sept. 30, 1862.

[2] *Ibid.* Cowley to Russell, Oct. 3, 1862.

[3] Even the *Edinburgh Review* for October, 1862, discussed recognition of the South as possibly near, though on the whole against such action.

[4] Palmerston MS. Walpole makes Palmerston responsible for the original plan and Russell acquiescent and readily agreeing to postpone. This study reverses the rôles.

but another two days later on receipt of a letter from Stuart, written September 23, in which he and Mercier were now all for a suggestion of armistice, with no mention of separation.[1] Russell now thought:

> "If no fresh battles occur, I think the suggestion might be adopted, tho' I am far from thinking with Mercier that the North would accept it. But it would be a fair and defensible course, leaving it open to us to hasten or defer recognition if the proposal is declined. Lord Lyons might carry it over on the 25th." [2]

British policy, as represented by the inclinations of the Foreign Secretary, having started out on a course portending positive and vigorous action, was now evidently in danger of veering far to one side, if not turning completely about. But the day after Russell seemed to be considering such an attenuation of the earlier plan as to be content with a mere suggestion of armistice, a bomb was thrown into the already troubled waters further and violently disturbing them. This was Gladstone's speech at Newcastle, October 7, a good third of which was devoted to the Civil War and in which he asserted that Jefferson Davis had made an army, was making a navy, and had created something still greater—a nation.[3] The chronology of shifts in opinion would, at first glance, indicate that Gladstone made this speech with the intention of forcing Palmerston and Russell to continue in the line earlier adopted, thus hoping to bolster up a cause now losing ground. His declaration, coming from a leading member of of the Cabinet, was certain to be accepted by the public as a foreshadowing of governmental action. If Jefferson Davis

[1] Russell Papers. Also see *ante* p. 41. Stuart to Lyons. The letter to Russell was of exactly the same tenor.

[2] Palmerston MS. Russell to Palmerston, Oct. 6, 1862. Lyons' departure had been altered from October 11 to October 25.

[3] Morley, *Gladstone*, II, p. 79. Morley calls this utterance a great error which was long to embarrass Gladstone, who himself later so characterized it.

had in truth created a nation then early recognition must be given it. But this surmise of intentional pressure is not borne out by any discovered evidence. On the contrary, the truth is, seemingly, that Gladstone, in the north and out of touch, was in complete ignorance that the two weeks elapsed since his letters from Palmerston and Russell had produced any alteration of plan or even any hesitation. Himself long convinced of the wisdom of British intervention in some form Gladstone evidently could not resist the temptation to make the good news known. His declaration, foreshadowing a policy that did not pertain to his own department, and, more especially, that had not yet received Cabinet approval was in itself an offence against the traditions of British Cabinet organization. He had spoken without authorization and " off his own bat."

The speculative market, sensitive barometer of governmental policy, immediately underwent such violent fluctuations as to indicate a general belief that Gladstone's speech meant action in the war. The price of raw cotton dropped so abruptly as to alarm Southern friends and cause them to give assurances that even if the blockade were broken there would be no immediate outpouring of cotton from Southern ports.[1] On the other hand, Bright, staunch friend of the North, *hoped* that Gladstone was merely seeking to overcome a half-hearted reluctance of Palmerston and Russell to move. He was sore at heart over the " vile speech " of " your old acquaintance and friend."[2] The leading newspapers while at first accepting the Newcastle speech as an authoritative statement and generally, though mildly, approving, were quick to feel that there was still uncertainty of policy and became silent

[1] Adams, *A Crisis in Downing Street*, p. 402.

[2] Bright to Sumner, October 10, 1862. Mass. Hist. Soc. *Proceedings*, XLVI, p. 108. Bright was wholly in the dark as to a Ministerial project. Much of this letter is devoted to the emancipation proclamation which did not at first greatly appeal to Bright as a wise measure.

until it should be made clear just what was in the wind.[1] Within the Cabinet it is to be supposed that Gladstone had caused no small stir, both by reason of his unusual procedure and by his sentiments. On Russell, however much disliked was the incursion into his own province, the effect was reinvigoration of a desire to carry through at least some portion of the plan and he determined to go on with the proposal of an armistice. Six days after Gladstone's speech Russell circulated, October 13, a memorandum on America.[2]

This memorandum asserted that the South had shown, conclusively, its power to resist—had maintained a successful defensive; that the notion of a strong pro-Northern element in the South had been shown to be wholly delusive; that the emancipation proclamation, promising a freeing of the slaves in the sections still in rebellion on January 1, 1863, was no humanitarian or idealistic measure (since it left slavery in the loyal or recognized districts) and was but an incitement to servile war—a most "terrible" plan. For these reasons Russell urged that the Great Powers ought seriously to consider whether it was not their duty to propose a "suspension of arms" for the purpose of "weighing calmly the advantages of peace."[3] This was a far cry from mediation and recognition, nor did Russell

[1] The *Times*, October 9 and 10, while surprised that Gladstone and not Palmerston, was the spokesman, accepted the speech as equivalent to a governmental pronouncement. Then the *Times* makes no further comment of moment until November 13. The *Morning Post* (regarded as Palmerston's organ) reported the speech in full on October 9, but did not comment editorially until October 13, and then with much laudation of Gladstone's northern tour but *with no mention whatever* of his utterances on America.

[2] Gladstone wrote to Russell, October 17, explaining that he had intended no "official utterance," and pleaded that Spence, whom he had seen in Liverpool, did not put that construction on his words (Gladstone Papers). Russell replied, October 20. ". . . Still you must allow me to say that I think you went beyond the latitude which all speakers must be allowed when you said that Jeff Davis had made a nation. Negotiations would seem to follow, and for that step I think the Cabinet is not prepared. However we shall soon meet to discuss this very topic" (*Ibid.*).

[3] Palmerston MS. Appended to the Memorandum were the texts of the emancipation proclamation, Seward's circular letter of September 22, and an extract from the *National Intelligencer* of September 26, giving Lincoln's answer to Chicago abolitionists.

indicate either the proposed terms of an armistice or the exact steps to be taken by Europe in bringing it about and making it of value. But the memorandum of October 13 does clearly negative what has been the accepted British political tradition which is to the effect that Palmerston, angered at Gladstone's presumption and now determined against action, had "put up" Cornewall Lewis to reply in a public speech, thereby permitting public information that no Cabinet decision had as yet been reached. Lewis' speech was made at Hereford on October 14. Such were the relations between Palmerston and Russell that it is impossible the former would have so used Lewis without notifying Russell, in which case there would have been no Foreign Office memorandum of the thirteenth.[1] Lewis was, in fact, vigorously maintaining his objections, already made known to Russell, to *any* plan of departure from the hitherto accepted policy of neutrality and his speech at Hereford was the opening gun of active opposition.

Lewis did not in any sense pose as a friend of the North. Rather he treated the whole matter, in his speech at Hereford and later in the Cabinet as one requiring cool judgment and decision on the sole ground of British interests. This was the line best suited to sustain his arguments, but does not prove, as some have thought, that his Cabinet acknowledgment of the impossibility of Northern complete victory, was his private conviction.[2] At Hereford Lewis argued that everyone must acknowledge a great war was in

[1] Morley, *Gladstone*, II, 80, narrates the "tradition." Walpole, *Twenty-five Years*, II, 57, states it as a fact. Also *Education of Henry Adams*, pp. 136, 140. Over forty years later an anonymous writer in the *Daily Telegraph*, Oct. 24, 1908, gave exact details of the "instruction" to Lewis, and of those present. (Cited in Adams, *A Crisis in Downing Street*, pp. 404-5.) C. F. Adams, *Trans-Atlantic Historical Solidarity*, Ch. III, repeats the tradition, but in *A Crisis in Downing Street* he completely refutes his earlier opinion and the entire tradition. The further narrative in this chapter, especially the letters of Clarendon to Lewis, show that Lewis acted solely on his own initiative.

[2] Anonymously, in the *Edinburgh*, for April, 1861, Lewis had written of the Civil War in a pro-Northern sense, and appears never to have accepted fully the theory that it was impossible to reconquer the South.

progress and must admit it " to be undecided. Under such circumstances, the time had not yet arrived when it could be asserted in accordance with the established doctrines of international law that the independence of the Southern States had been established."[1] In effect Lewis gave public notice that no Cabinet decision had yet been reached, a step equally opposed to Cabinet traditions with Gladstone's speech, since equally unauthorized, but excusable in the view that the first offence against tradition had forced a rejoinder.[2] For the public Lewis accomplished his purpose and the press refrained from comment, awaiting results.[3] Meanwhile Palmerston, who must finally determine policy, was remaining in uncertainty and in this situation thought it wise to consult, indirectly, Derby, the leader of the opposition in Parliament. This was done through Clarendon, who wrote to Palmerston on October 16 that Derby was averse to action.

> " He said that he had been constantly urged to *go in for* recognition and mediation, but had always refused on the ground that recognition would merely irritate the North without advancing the cause of the South or procuring a single bale of cotton, and that mediation in the present temper of the Belligerents *must* be rejected even if the mediating Powers themselves knew what to propose as a fair basis of compromise ; for as each party insisted upon having that which the other declared was vitally essential to its existence, it was clear that the war had not yet marked

[1] Cited in Adams, *A Crisis in Downing Street*, p. 407.

[2] Derby, in conversation with Clarendon, had characterized Gladstone's speech as an offence against tradition and best practice. Palmerston agreed, but added that the same objection could be made to Lewis' speech. Maxwell, *Clarendon*, II, 267. Palmerston to Clarendon, Oct. 20, 1862. Clarendon wrote Lewis, Oct. 24, that he did not think this called for any explanation by Lewis to Palmerston, further proof of the falsity of Palmerston's initiative. *Ibid.*, p. 267.

[3] *The Index*, Oct. 16, 1862, warned against acceptance of Gladstone's Newcastle utterances as indicating Government policy, asserted that the bulk of English opinion was with him, but ignorantly interpreted Cabinet hesitation to the " favour of the North and bitter enmity to the South, which has animated the diplomatic career of Lord Russell. . . ." Throughout the war, Russell, to *The Index*, was the evil genius of the Government.

out the stipulations of a treaty of peace. . . . The recognition of the South could be of no benefit to England unless we meant to sweep away the blockade, which would be an act of hostility towards the North." [1]

More than any other member of the Cabinet Lewis was able to guess, fairly accurately, what was in the Premier's mind for Lewis was Clarendon's brother-in-law, and "the most intimate and esteemed of his male friends."[2] They were in constant communication as the Cabinet crisis developed, and Lewis' next step was taken immediately after Palmerston's consultation of Derby through Clarendon. October 17, Lewis circulated a memorandum in reply to that of Russell's of October 13. He agreed with Russell's statement of the facts of the situation in America, but added with sarcasm:

"A dispassionate bystander might be expected to concur in the historical view of Lord Russell, and to desire that the war should be speedily terminated by a pacific agreement between the contending parties. But, unhappily, the decision upon any proposal of the English Government will be made, not by dispassionate bystanders, but by heated and violent partisans; and we have to consider, not how the proposal indicated in the Memorandum ought to be received, or how it would be received by a conclave of philosophers, but how it is likely to be received by the persons to whom it would be addressed."

Lincoln's emancipation proclamation, Lewis admitted, presumably was intended to incite servile war, but that very fact was an argument against, not for, British action, since it revealed an intensity of bitterness prohibitory of any "calm consideration" of issues by the belligerents. And suppose the North did acquiesce in an armistice the only peaceful solution would be an independent slave-holding South for the establishment of which Great Britain

[1] Palmerston MS.
[2] Maxwell, *Clarendon*, II, 279.

would have become intermediary and sponsor. Any policy except that of the continuance of strict neutrality was full of dangers, some evident, some but dimly visible as yet. Statesmanship required great caution; "... looking to the probable consequences," Lewis concluded, "of this philanthropic proposition, we may doubt whether the chances of evil do not preponderate over the chances of good, and whether it is not—

> 'Better to endure the ills we have
> Than fly to others which we know not of.'"[1]

At the exact time when Lewis thus voiced his objections, basing them on the lack of any sentiment toward peace in America, there were received at the Foreign Office and read with interest the reports of a British special agent sent out from Washington on a tour of the Western States. Anderson's reports emphasized three points:

(1) Emancipation was purely a war measure with no thought of ameliorating the condition of the slaves once freed;

(2) Even if the war should stop there was no likelihood of securing cotton for a long time to come;

(3) The Western States, even more then the Eastern, were in favour of vigorous prosecution of the war and the new call for men was being met with enthusiasm.[2]

This was unpromising either for relief to a distressed England or for Northern acceptance of an armistice, yet Russell, commenting on Clarendon's letter to Palmerston, containing Derby's advice, still argued that even if declined a suggestion of armistice could do no harm and might open

[1] Palmerston MS.

[2] *Parliamentary Papers*, 1863. *Commons*, Vol. LXII. "Correspondence relating to the Civil War in the United States of North America." Nos. 33 and 37. Two reports received Oct. 13 and 18, 1862. Anderson's mission was to report on the alleged drafting of British subjects into the Northern Army.

the way for a later move, but he agreed that recognition "would certainly be premature at present."[1] Russell himself now heard from Clarendon and learned that Derby "had been constantly urged to press for recognition and mediation but he had always refused on the ground that the neutral policy hitherto pursued by the Government was the right one and that if we departed from it we should only meet with an insolent rejection of our offer."[2] A long conference with Lyons gave cause for further thought and Russell committed himself to the extent that he acknowledged "we ought not to move *at present* without Russia. . . ."[3] Finally, October 22, Palmerston reached a decision for the immediate present, writing to Russell:

> "Your description of the state of things between the two parties is most comprehensive and just. I am, however, much inclined to agree with Lewis that at present we could take no step nor make any communication of a distinct proposition with any advantage."
>
> . . . . . .
>
> "All that we could possibly do without injury to our position would be to ask the two Parties not whether they would agree to an armistice but whether they might not turn their thoughts towards an arrangement between themselves. But the answer of each might be written by us beforehand. The Northerns would say that the only condition of arrangement would be the restoration of the Union; the South would say their only condition would be an acknowledgment by the North of Southern Independence —we should not be more advanced and should only have pledged each party more strongly to the object for which they are fighting. I am therefore inclined to change the opinion on which I wrote to you when the Confederates seemed to be carrying all before them, and I am very much come back to our original view of the matter, that we must

[1] Palmerston MS. Russell to Palmerston, Oct. 18, 1862.
[2] Russell Papers. Clarendon to Russell, Oct. 19, 1862.
[3] Palmerston MS. Russell to Palmerston, Oct. 20, 1862.

continue merely to be lookers-on till the war shall have taken a more decided turn."[1]

By previous arrangement the date October 23 had been set for a Cabinet to consider the American question but Russell now postponed it, though a few members appeared and held an informal discussion in which Russell still justified his "armistice" policy and was opposed by Lewis and the majority of those present. Palmerston did not attend, no action was possible and technically no Cabinet was held.[2] It soon appeared that Russell, vexed at the turn matters had taken, was reluctant in yielding and did not regard the question as finally settled. Yet on the afternoon of this same day Adams, much disturbed by the rumours attendant upon the speeches of Gladstone and Lewis, sought an explanation from Russell and was informed that the Government was not inclined at present to change its policy but could make no promises for the future.[3] This appeared to Adams to be an assurance against *any* effort by Great Britain and has been interpreted as disingenuous on Russell's part. Certainly Adams' confidence was restored by the interview. But Russell was apparently unconvinced as yet that a suggestion of armistice would necessarily lead to the evil consequences prophesied by Lewis, or would, indeed, require any departure from a policy of strict neutrality. On the one side Russell was being berated by pro-Southerners as weakly continuing an outworn policy and as having "made himself the laughing-stock of Europe and of America;"[4] on the other he was regarded, for the

[1] Russell Papers. It is significant that Palmerston's organ, the *Morning Post*, after a long silence came out on Oct. 21 with a sharp attack on Gladstone for his presumption. Lewis was also reflected upon, but less severely.

[2] Maxwell, *Clarendon*, II, 265.

[3] *U.S. Messages and Documents*, 1862-3, Pt. I, p. 223. Adams to Seward, Oct. 24, 1862. C. F. Adams in *A Crisis in Downing Street*, p. 417, makes Russell state that the Government's intention was "to adhere to the rule of perfect neutrality"—seemingly a more positive assurance, and so understood by the American Minister.

[4] *The Index*, Oct. 23, 1862. "... while our people are starving, our commerce interrupted, our industry paralysed, our Ministry have no plan,

moment, as insisting, through pique, on a line of action highly dangerous to the preservation of peace with the North. October 23 Palmerston wrote his approval of the Cabinet postponement, but declared Lewis' doctrine of "no recognition of Southern independence until the North had admitted it" was unsound.[1] The next day he again wrote: ". . . to talk to the belligerents about peace at present would be as useless as asking the winds during the last week to let the waters remain calm."[2]

This expression by Palmerston on the day after the question apparently had come to a conclusion was the result of the unexpected persistence of Russell and Gladstone. Replying to Palmerston's letter of the twenty-third, Russell wrote: "As no good could come of a Cabinet, I put it off. But tho' I am quite ready to agree to your conclusions for the present, I cannot do so for G. Lewis' reasons. . . ."

> "G. Lewis besides has made a proposition for me which I never thought of making. He says I propose that England and France and perhaps some one Continental power should ask America to suspend the war. I never thought of making such a proposal.
>
> "I think if Russia agreed Prussia would. And if France and England agreed Austria would. Less than the whole five would not do. I thought it right towards the Cabinet to reserve any specific proposition. I am not at all inclined to adopt G. Lewis' invention.
>
> "I have sent off Lyons without instructions, at which he is much pleased."[3]

Russell was shifting ground; first the proposal was to have been made by England and France; then Russia was

no idea, no intention to do anything but fold their hands, talk of strict neutrality, spare the excited feelings of the North, and wait, like Mr. Micawber, for something to turn up."

[1] Russell Papers. To Russell.

[2] *Ibid.* To Russell, Oct. 24, 1862.

[3] Palmerston MS. Russell to Palmerston, Oct. 24, 1862.

necessary; now "less than five powers would not do." But whatever the number required he still desired a proposal of armistice. On October 23, presumably subsequent to the informal meeting of Cabinet members, he drew up a brief memorandum in answer to that of Lewis on October 17, denying that Lewis had correctly interpreted his plan, and declaring that he had always had "in contemplation" a step by the five great powers of Europe. The advisability of trying to secure such joint action, Russell asserted, was all he had had in mind. *If* the Cabinet had approved this advisability, and the powers were acquiescent, *then* (in answer to Lewis' accusation of "no look ahead") he would be ready with definite plans for the negotiation of peace between North and South.[1] Thus by letter to Palmerston and by circulation of a new memorandum Russell gave notice that all was not yet decided. On October 24, Gladstone also circulated a memorandum in reply to Lewis, urging action by England, France and Russia.[2]

Russell's second memorandum was not at first taken seriously by his Cabinet opponents. They believed the issue closed and Russell merely putting out a denial of alleged purposes. Clarendon, though not a member of the Cabinet, was keeping close touch with the situation and on October 24 wrote to Lewis:

> "Thanks for sending me your memorandum on the American question, which I have read with great satisfaction.

[1] Palmerston MS. Marked: "Printed Oct. 24, 1862."

[2] Morley, *Gladstone*, II, 84. Morley was the first to make clear that no final decision was reached on October 23, a date hitherto accepted as the end of the Cabinet crisis. Rhodes, IV, 337-348, gives a résumé of talk and correspondence on mediation, etc., and places October 23 as the date when "the policy of non-intervention was informally agreed upon" (p. 343), Russell's "change of opinion" being also "complete" (p. 342). Curiously the dictum of Rhodes and others depends in some degree on a mistake in copying a date. Slidell had an important interview with Napoleon on October 28 bearing on an armistice, but this was copied as October 22 in Bigelow's *France and the Confederate Navy*, p. 126, and so came to be written into narratives of mediation proposals. Richardson, II, 345, gives the correct date. Rhodes' supposition that Seward's instructions of August 2 became known to Russell and were the determining factor in altering his intentions is evidently erroneous.

Johnny [Russell] always loves to do something when to do nothing is prudent, and I have no doubt that he hoped to get support in his meddling proclivities when he called a Cabinet for yesterday; but its postponement *sine die* is probably due to your memorandum. You have made so clear the idiotic position we should occupy, either in having presented our face gratuitously to the Yankee slap we should receive, or in being asked what practical solution we had to propose after an armistice had been agreed to at our suggestion, that no discussion on the subject would have been possible, and the Foreign Secretary probably thought it would be pleasanter to draw in his horns at Woburn than in Downing Street." [1]

On October 26, having received from Lewis a copy of Russell's newly-circulated paper, Clarendon wrote again:

"The Foreign Secretary's *blatt* exhibits considerable soreness, for which you are specially bound to make allowance, as it was you who procured abortion for him. He had thought to make a great deal of his colt by Meddler out of Vanity, and you have shown his backers that the animal was not fit to start and would not run a yard if he did. He is therefore taken back to the country, where he must have a deal more training before he can appear in public again."

. . . .

"I should say that your speech at Hereford was nearly as effective in checking the alarm and speculation caused by Gladstone's speech, as your memorandum was in smashing the Foreign Secretary's proposed intervention, and that you did so without in the smallest degree committing either the Government or yourself with respect to the future." [2]

In effect Clarendon was advising Lewis to pay no attention to Russell's complaining rejoinder since the object desired had been secured, but there was still one element of strength for Russell and Gladstone which, if obtained, might easily cause a re-opening of the whole question.

[1] Maxwell, *Clarendon*, II, 265.
[2] *Ibid.*, p. 266.

This was the desire of France, still unexpressed in spite of indirect overtures, a silence in part responsible for the expression of an opinion by Palmerston that Napoleon's words could not be depended upon as an indication of what he intended to do.[1] On the day this was written the French ministerial crisis—the real cause of Napoleon's silence—came to an end with the retirement of Thouvenel and the succession of Drouyn de Lhuys. Russell's reply to Palmerston's assertion of the folly of appealing now to the belligerents was that "recognition" was certainly out of the question for the present and that "it should not take place till May or June next year, when circumstances may show pretty clearly whether Gladstone was right."[2] But this yielding to the Premier's decision was quickly withdrawn when, at last, Napoleon and his new Minister could turn their attention to the American question.

On October 27 Cowley reported a conversation with the Emperor in which American affairs were discussed. Napoleon hoped that England, France and Russia would join in an offer of mediation. Cowley replied that he had no instructions and Napoleon then modified his ideas by suggesting a proposal of armistice for six months "in order to give time for the present excitement to calm down. . . ."[3] The next day Cowley reported that Drouyn de Lhuys stated the Emperor to be very anxious to "put an end to the War," but that he was himself doubtful whether it would not be better to "wait a little longer," and in any case if overtures to America were rejected Russia probably would not join Great Britain and France in going on to a recognition of the South.[4] All this was exactly in line with that plan to which

[1] Russell Papers. Palmerston to Russell, Oct. 24, 1862. Palmerston was here writing of Italian and American affairs.

[2] Palmerston MS. Oct. 25, 1862.

[3] Russell Papers. To Russell.

[4] F.O., France, Vol. 1446. Cowley to Russell, Oct. 28, 1862. Cowley, like Lyons, was against action. He approved Drouyn de Lhuys' "hesitation." It appears from the Russian archives that France

Russell had finally come and if officially notified to the British Government would require a renewed consideration by the Cabinet. Presumably Napoleon knew what had been going on in London and he now hastened to give the needed French push. October 28, Slidell was summoned to an audience and told of the Emperor's purpose, acting with England, to bring about an armistice.[1] Three days later, October 31, Cowley wrote that he had now been officially informed by Drouyn de Lhuys, " by the Emperor's orders " that a despatch was about to be sent to the French Ministers in England and Russia instructing them to request joint action by the three powers in suggesting an armistice of six months *including a suspension of the blockade,* thus throwing open Southern ports to European commerce.[2]

Napoleon's proposal evidently took Palmerston by surprise and was not regarded with favour. He wrote to Russell:

> " As to the French scheme of proposals to the United States, we had better keep that question till the Cabinet meets, which would be either on Monday 11th, or Wednesday 12th, as would be most convenient to you and our colleagues.

approached Russia. On October 31, D'Oubril, at Paris, was instructed that while Russia had always been anxious to forward peace in America, she stood in peculiarly friendly relations with the United States, and was against any appearance of pressure. It would have the contrary effect from that hoped for. If England and France should offer mediation Russia, " being too far away," would not join, but might give her moral support. (Russian Archives, F.O. to D'Oubril, Oct. 27, 1862 (O.S.). No. 320.) On the same date Stoeckl was informed of the French overtures, and was instructed not to take a stand with France and Great Britain, but to limit his efforts to approval of any *agreement* by the North and South to end the war. Yet Stoeckl was given liberty of action if (as Gortchakoff did not believe) the time had assuredly come when both North and South were ready for peace, and it needed but the influence of some friendly hand to soothe raging passions and to lead the contending parties themselves to begin direct negotiations (*Ibid.*, F.O. to Stoeckl, Oct. 27, 1862 (O.S.).

[1] Mason Papers. Slidell to Mason, Oct. 29, 1862. Slidell's full report to Benjamin is in Richardson, II, 345.

[2] F.O., France, Vol. 1446, No. 1236. Cowley thought neither party would consent unless it saw some military advantage. (Russell Papers. Cowley to Russell, Oct. 31, 1862.) Morley, *Gladstone*, II, 84-5, speaks of the French offer as " renewed proposals of mediation." There was no renewal for this was the *first* proposal, and it was not one of mediation though that was an implied result.

But is it likely that the Federals would consent to an armistice to be accompanied by a cessation of Blockades, and which would give the Confederates means of getting all the supplies they may want ?"

. . . . . .

"Then comes the difficulty about slavery and the giving up of runaway slaves, about which we could hardly frame a proposal which the Southerns would agree to, and people of England would approve of. The French Government are more free from the shackles of principle and of right and wrong on these matters, as on all others than we are. At all events it would be wiser to wait till the elections in North America are over before any proposal is made. As the Emperor is so anxious to put a stop to bloodshed he might try his hand as a beginning by putting down the stream of ruffians which rolls out from that never-failing fountain at Rome."[1]

But Russell was more optimistic, or at least in favour of some sort of proposal to America. He replied to Palmerston :

"My notion is that as there is little chance of our good offices being accepted in America we should make them such as would be creditable to us in Europe. I should propose to answer the French proposal therefore by saying,

"That in offering our good offices we ought to require both parties to consent to examine, first, whether there are any terms upon which North and South would consent to restore the Union ; and secondly, failing any such terms, whether there are any terms upon which both would consent to separate.

"We should also say that if the Union is to be restored it would be essential in our view, that after what has taken place all the slaves should be emancipated, compensation being granted by Congress at the rate at which Great Britain emancipated her slaves in 1833.

"If separation takes place we must be silent on the trend of slavery, as we are with regard to Spain and Brazil.

[1] Russell Papers, Nov. 2, 1862. Monday, November 1862, was the 10th not the 11th as Palmerston wrote.

"This is a rough sketch, but I will expand it for the Cabinet.

"It will be an honourable proposal to make, but the North and probably the South will refuse it." [1]

Here were several ideas quite impossible of acceptance by North and South in their then frame of mind and Russell himself believed them certain to be refused by the North in any case. But he was eager to present the question for Cabinet discussion hoping for a reversal of the previous decision. Whether from pique or from conviction of the wisdom of a change in British policy, he proposed to press for acceptance of the French plan, with modifications. The news of Napoleon's offer and of Russell's attitude, with some uncertainty as to that of Palmerston, again brought Lewis into action and on November 7 he circulated another memorandum, this time a very long one of some fifteen thousand words. This was in the main an historical résumé of past British policy in relation to revolted peoples, stating the international law of such cases, and pointing out that Great Britain had never recognized a revolted people so long as a *bona fide* struggle was still going on. Peace was no doubt greatly to be desired. "If England could, by legitimate means, and without unduly sacrificing or imperilling her own interests, accelerate this consummation, she would, in my opinion, earn the just gratitude of the civilized world." But the question, as he had previously asserted, was full of grave dangers. The very suggestion of a concert of Powers was itself one to be avoided. "A conference of the five great Powers is an imposing force, but it is a dangerous body to set in motion. A single intervening Power may possibly contrive to satisfy both the adverse parties; but five intervening Powers have first to satisfy one another." Who could tell what divergence might arise on the question

[1] Palmerston MS. Nov. 3, 1862.

of slavery, or on boundaries, or how far England might find her ideals or her vital interests compromised?[1]

Here was vigorous resistance to Russell, especially effective for its appeal to past British policy, and to correct practice in international law. On the same day that Lewis' memorandum was circulated, there appeared a communication in the *Times* by "Historicus," on "The International Doctrine of Recognition," outlining in briefer form exactly those international law arguments presented by Lewis, and advocating a continuation of the policy of strict neutrality. "Historicus" was William Vernon Harcourt, husband of Lewis' stepdaughter who was also the niece of Clarendon. Evidently the family guns were all trained on Russell.[2] "Historicus" drove home the fact that premature action by a neutral was a "hostile act" and ought to be resented by the "Sovereign State" as a "breach of neutrality and friendship."[3]

Thus on receipt of the news of Napoleon's proposal the Cabinet crisis was renewed and even more sharply than on October 23. The French offer was not actually presented until November 10.[4] On the next two days the answer to be made received long discussion in the Cabinet. Lewis described this to Clarendon, prefacing his account by stating that Russell had heard by telegram from Napier at St. Petersburg to the effect that Russia would not join but would support English-French proposals through her Minister at Washington, "provided it would not cause irritation."[5]

[1] Gladstone Papers. The memorandum here preserved has the additional interest of frequent marginal comments by Gladstone.

[2] The letters of "Historicus" early attracted, in the case of the *Trent*, favourable attention and respect. As early as 1863 they were put out in book form to satisfy a public demand: *Letters by Historicus on some questions of International Law*, London, 1863.

[3] The *Times*, Nov. 7, 1862. The letter was dated Nov. 4.

[4] *Parliamentary Papers*, 1863, Lords, Vol. XXIX. "Despatch respecting the Civil War in North America." Russell to Cowley, Nov. 13, 1862.

[5] For substance of the Russian answer to France see *ante*, p. 59, *note* 4. D'Oubril reported Drouyn de Lhuys as unconvinced that the time

"Having made this statement, Lord John proceeded to explain his views on the question. These were, briefly, that the recent successes of the Democrats afforded a most favourable opportunity of intervention, because we should strengthen their hands, and that if we refused the invitation of France, Russia would reconsider her decision, act directly with France, and thus accomplish her favourite purpose of separating France and England. He therefore advised that the proposal of France should be accepted. Palmerston followed Lord John, and supported him, but did not say a great deal. His principal argument was the necessity for showing sympathy with Lancashire, and of not throwing away any chance of mitigating it [*sic*].

"The proposal was now thrown before the Cabinet, who proceeded to pick it to pieces. Everybody present threw a stone at it of greater or less size, except Gladstone, who supported it, and the Chancellor [Westbury] and Cardwell, who expressed no opinion. The principal objection was that the proposed armistice of six months by sea and land, involving a suspension of the commercial blockade, was so grossly unequal—so decidedly in favour of the South, that there was no chance of the North agreeing to it. After a time, Palmerston saw that the general feeling of the Cabinet was against being a party to the representation, and he capitulated. I do not think his support was very sincere: it certainly was not hearty . . . I ought to add that, after the Cabinet had come to a decision and the outline of a draft had been discussed, the Chancellor uttered a few oracular sentences on the danger of refusing the French invitation, and gave a strong support to Lord John. His support came rather late . . . I proposed that we should *tater le terrain* at Washington and ascertain whether there was any chance of the proposal being accepted. Lord John refused this. He admitted there was no chance of an affirmative answer from Washington. I think his principal motive was a fear of displeasing France, and that Palmerston's principal motive was a wish to seem to support him. There is a useful

was inopportune but as stating he had not expected Russia to join. The French Minister of Foreign Affairs was irritated at an article on his overtures that had appeared in the *Journal de Petersbourg*, and thought himself unfairly treated by the Russian Government. (Russian Archives. D'Oubril to F. O., Nov. 15, 1862 (N.S.), Nos. 1908 and 1912.)

article in to-day's *Times* throwing cold water on the invitation. I take for granted that Delane was informed of the result of the Cabinet." [1]

Gladstone, writing to his wife, gave a similar though more brief account:

"Nov. 11. We have had our Cabinet to-day and meet again to-morrow. I am afraid we shall do little or nothing in the business of America. But I will send you definite intelligence. Both Lords Palmerston and Russell are *right*. Nov. 12. The United States affair has ended and not well. Lord Russell rather turned tail. He gave way without resolutely fighting out his battle. However, though we decline for the moment, the answer is put upon grounds and in terms which leave the matter very open for the future. Nov. 13. I think the French will make our answer about America public; at least it is very possible. But I hope they may not take it as a positive refusal, or at any rate that they may themselves act in the matter. It will be clear that we concur with them, that the war should cease. Palmerston gave to Russell's proposal a feeble and half-hearted support."[2]

The reply to France was in fact immediately made public both in France and in England. It was complimentary to the Emperor's "benevolent views and humane intentions," agreed that "if the steps proposed were to be taken, the concurrence of Russia would be extremely desirable" but remarked that as yet Great Britain had not been informed that Russia wished to co-operate, and concluded that since there was no ground to hope the North was ready for the proposal it seemed best to postpone any overture until there was a "greater prospect than now exists of its being accepted

[1] Maxwell, *Clarendon*, II, 268. The letter, as printed, is dated Nov. 11, and speaks of the Cabinet of "yesterday." This appears to be an error. Gladstone's account is of a two-days' discussion on Nov. 11 and 12, with the decision reached and draft of reply to France outlined on the latter date. The article in the *Times*, referred to by Lewis, appeared on Nov. 13.

[2] Morley, *Gladstone*, II, 85.

by the two contending parties."[1] The argument of Russell in the Cabinet had been for acceptance without Russia though earlier he had stipulated her assistance as essential. This was due to the knowledge already at hand through a telegram from Napier at St. Petersburg, November 8, that Russia would refuse.[2] But in the answer to France it is the attitude of Russia that becomes an important reason for British refusal as, indeed, it was the basis for harmonious decision within the British Cabinet. This is not to say that had Russia acceded England also would have done so, for the weight of Cabinet opinion, adroitly encouraged by Palmerston, was against Russell and the result reached was that which the Premier wished. More important in his view than any other matter was the preservation of a united Ministry and at the conclusion of the American debate even Gladstone could write: "As to the state of matters generally in the Cabinet, I have never seen it smoother."[3]

Public opinion in England in the main heartily supported the Cabinet decision. Hammond described it as "almost universal in this country against interference,"[4] an estimate justified if the more important journals are taken into

[1] *Parliamentary Papers*, 1863, *Lords*, Vol. XXIX. "Despatch respecting the Civil War in North America." Russell to Cowley, Nov. 13, 1862.

[2] F. O., Russia, Vol. 609, No. 407. Napier to Russell. The same day Napier wrote giving an account of an interview between the French Minister and Prince Gortchakoff in which the latter stated Russia would take no chances of offending the North. *Ibid.*, No. 408.

[3] Morley, *Gladstone*, II, 85. To his wife, Nov. 13, 1862. Even after the answer to France there was some agitation in the Ministry due to the receipt from Stuart of a letter dated Oct. 31, in which it was urged that this was the most opportune moment for mediation because of Democratic successes in the elections. He enclosed also an account of a "horrible military reprisal" by the Federals in Missouri alleging that *ten* Southerners had been executed because of *one* Northerner seized by Southern guerillas. (Russell Papers.) The Russell Papers contain a series of signed or initialled notes in comment, all dated Nov. 14. "W." (Westbury?) refers to the "horrible atrocities," and urges that, if Russia will join, the French offer should be accepted. Gladstone wrote, "I had supposed the question to be closed." "C. W." (Charles Wood), "This is horrible; but does not change my opinion of the course to be pursued." "C. P. V." (C. P. Villiers) wrote against accepting the French proposal, and commented that Stuart had always been a strong partisan of the South.

[4] Lyons Papers. Hammond to Lyons, Nov. 15, 1862.

account but not true of all. The *Times* of November 13 declared:

> "We are convinced that the present is not the moment for these strong measures. There is now great reason to hope that by means of their own internal action the Americans may themselves settle their own affairs even sooner than Europe could settle them for them. We have waited so long that it would be unpardonable in us to lose the merit of our self-denial at such a moment as this. . . . We quite agree with Mr. Cobden that it would be cheaper to keep all Lancashire on turtle and venison than to plunge into a desperate war with the Northern States of America, even with all Europe at our back. In a good cause, and as a necessity forced upon us in defence of our honour, or of our rightful interests, we are as ready to fight as we ever were; but we do not see our duty or our interest in going blindfold into an adventure such as this. We very much doubt, moreover, whether, if Virginia belonged to France as Canada belongs to England, the Emperor of the French would be so active in beating up for recruits in this American mediation league."

This was followed up two days later by an assertion that no English statesman had at any time contemplated an offer of mediation made in such a way as to lead to actual conflict with the United States.[1] On the other hand the *Herald*, always intense in its pro-Southern utterances, and strongly anti-Palmerston in politics, professed itself unable to credit the rumoured Cabinet decision. "Until we are positively informed that our Ministers are guilty of the great crime attributed to them," the *Herald* declared, "we must hope against hope that they are innocent." If guilty they were responsible for the misery of Lancashire (depicted in lurid colours):

> "A clear, a sacred, an all-important duty was imposed upon them; to perform that duty would have been the pride and delight of almost any other Englishmen; and they,

[1] The *Times*, Nov. 15, 1862.

> with the task before them and the power to perform it in their hands—can it be that they have shrunk back in craven cowardice, deserted their ally, betrayed their country, dishonoured their own names to all eternity, that they might do the bidding of John Bright, and sustain for a while the infamous tyranny of a Butler, a Seward, and a Lincoln ?" [1]

In the non-political *Army and Navy Gazette* the returned editor, W. H. Russell, but lately the *Times* correspondent in America, jeered at the American uproar that might now be expected against France instead of England: "Let the Emperor beware. The scarred veteran of the New York Scarrons of Plum Gut has set his sinister or dexter eye upon him, and threatens him with the loss of his throne," but the British public must expect no lasting change of Northern attitude toward England and must be ready for a war if the North were victorious.[2] *Blackwood's* for November, 1862, strongly censured the Government for its failure to act. The *Edinburgh* for January, 1863, as strongly supported the Ministry and expanded on the fixed determination of Great Britain to keep out of the war. *The Index* naturally frothed in angry disappointment, continuing its attacks, as if in hopes of a reversal of Ministerial decision, even into the next year. "Has it come to this? Is England, or the English Cabinet, afraid of the Northern States? Lord Russell might contrive so to choose his excuses as not to insult at once both his country and her ally."[3] An editorial from the *Richmond* (Virginia) *Whig* was quoted with approval characterizing Russell and Palmerston as "two old painted mummies," who secretly were rejoiced at the war in America as "threatening the complete annihilation" of both sides,

[1] The *Herald*, Nov. 14, 1862. This paper was listed by Hotze of *The Index*, as on his "pay roll." Someone evidently was trying to earn his salary.

[2] Nov. 15, 1862. It is difficult to reconcile Russell's editorials either with his later protestations of early conviction that the North would win or with the belief expressed by Americans that he was *constantly* pro-Northern in sentiment, e.g., Henry Adams, in *A Cycle of Adams' Letters*, I, 141.

[3] *The Index*, Nov. 20, 1862, p. 56.

and expressing the conviction that if the old Union were restored both North and South would eagerly turn on Great Britain.[1] The explanation, said *The Index*, of British supineness was simply the pusillanimous fear of war—and of a war that would not take place in spite of the bluster of Lincoln's "hangers-on."[2] Even as late as May of the year following, this explanation was still harped upon and Russell "a statesman" who belonged "rather to the past than to the present" was primarily responsible for British inaction. "The nominal conduct of Foreign Affairs is in the hands of a diplomatic Malaprop, who has never shown vigour, activity, or determination, except where the display of these qualities was singularly unneeded, or even worse than useless."[3]

The Index never wavered from its assumption that in the Cabinet Russell was the chief enemy of the South. Slidell, better informed, wrote: "Who would have believed that Earl Russell would have been the only member of the Cabinet besides Gladstone in favour of accepting the Emperor's proposition?"[4] He had information that Napoleon had been led to expect his proposal would be accepted and was much irritated—so much so that France would now probably act alone.[5] Gladstone's attitude was a sorrow to many of his friends. Bright believed he was at last weaned from desires for mediation and sympathetic with the answer to France,[6] but Goldwin Smith in correspondence with Gladstone on American affairs knew that the wild idea now in the statesman's mind was of offering

[1] *Ibid.*, Jan. 15, 1863, p. 191.
[2] *Ibid.*, Jan. 22, 1863, p. 201.
[3] *Ibid*,, May 28, 1863, p. 72.
[4] Mason Papers. To Mason, Nov. 28, 1862.
[5] Pickett Papers. Slidell to Benjamin, Nov. 29, 1862. This despatch is not in Richardson, *Messages and Papers of the Confederacy*, and illustrates the gaps in that publication.
[6] Rhodes, IV, 347. Bright to Sumner, Dec. 6, 1862.

Canada to the North if she would let the South go[1]—a plan unknown, fortunately for Gladstone's reputation for good judgment, save to his correspondent.

In general, as the weeks passed, the satisfaction grew both with the public and in the Government that England had made no adventure of new policy towards America. This satisfaction was strongly reinforced when the first reports were received from Lyons on his arrival in America. Reaching New York on November 8 he found that even the "Conservatives" were much opposed to an offer of mediation at present and thought it would only do harm until there was a change of Government in Washington—an event still remote. Lyons himself believed mediation useless unless intended to be followed by recognition of the South and that such recognition was likewise of no value without a raising of the blockade for which he thought the British Cabinet not prepared.[2] Lyons flatly contradicted Stuart's reports, his cool judgment of conditions nowhere more clearly manifested than at this juncture in comparison with his subordinate's excited and eager pro-Southern arguments. Again on November 28 Lyons wrote that he could not find a single Northern paper that did not repudiate

[1] Goldwin Smith told of this plan in 1904, in a speech at a banquet in Ottawa. He had destroyed Gladstone's letter outlining it. *The Ottawa Sun*, Nov. 16, 1904.

[2] Almost immediately after Lyons' return to Washington, Stoeckl learned from him, and from Mercier, also, that England and France planned to offer mediation and that if this were refused the South would be recognized. Stoeckl commented to the Foreign Office: "What good will this do?" It would not procure cotton unless the ports were forced open and a clear rupture made with the North. He thought England understood this, and still hesitated. Stoeckl went on to urge that if all European Powers joined England and France they would be merely tails to the kite and that Russia would be one of the tails. This would weaken the Russian position in Europe as well as forfeit her special relationship with the United States. He was against any *joint* European action. (Russian Archives, Stoeckl to F. O., Nov. 5-17, 1862, No. 2002.) Gortchakoff wrote on the margin of this despatch: "Je trouve son opinion très sage." If Stoeckl understood Lyons correctly then the latter had left England still believing that his arguments with Russell had been of no effect. When the news reached Washington of England's refusal of the French offer, Stoeckl reported Lyons as much surprised (*Ibid.*, to F. O., Nov. 19-Dec. 1, 1862, No. 2170).

foreign intervention.[1] In the South, when it was learned that France had offered to act and England had refused, there was an outburst of bitter anti-British feeling.[2]

The Northern press, as Lyons had reported, was unanimous in rejection of European offers of aid, however friendly, in settling the war. It expressed no gratitude to England, devoting its energy rather to animadversions on Napoleon III who was held to be personally responsible. Since there had been no European offer made there was no cause for governmental action. Seward had given Adams specific instructions in case the emergency arose but there had been no reason to present these or to act upon them and the crisis once past Seward believed all danger of European meddling was over and permanently. He wrote to Bigelow: "We are no longer to be disturbed by Secession intrigues in Europe. They have had their day. We propose to forget them."[3] This was a wise and statesmanlike attitude and was shared by Adams in London. Whatever either man knew or guessed of the prelude to the answer to France, November 13, they were careful to accept that answer as fulfilment of Russell's declaration to Adams, October 23, that Great Britain intended no change of policy.[4]

[1] *Parliamentary Papers*, 1832, *Commons*, Vol. LXXII, "Correspondence relating to the Civil War in the United States of North America." Nos. 47 and 50. Received Nov. 30 and Dec. 11. Mercier, who had been Stuart's informant about political conditions in New York, felt that he had been deceived by the Democrats. F. O., Am., Vol. 784, No. 38. Confidential, Lyons to Russell, Jan. 13, 1863.

[2] F. O., Am., Vol. 840, No. 518. Moore (Richmond) to Lyons, Dec. 4, 1862. Also F. O., Am., Vol. 844, No. 135. Bunch (Charleston) to Russell, Dec. 13, 1862. Bunch wrote of the "Constitutional hatred and jealousy of England, which are as strongly developed here as at the North. Indeed, our known antipathy to Slavery adds another element to Southern dislike."

[3] Bigelow, *Retrospections*, I, 579, Dec. 2, 1862. Bigelow was Consul-General at Paris, and was the most active of the Northern confidential agents abroad. A journalist himself, he had close contacts with the foreign press. It is interesting that he reported the Continental press as largely dependent for its American news and judgments upon the British press which specialized in that field, so that Continental tone was but a reflection of the British tone. *Ibid.*, p. 443. Bigelow to Seward, Jan. 7, 1862.

[4] Lyons placed a high estimate on Adams' abilities. He wrote: "Mr. Adams shows more calmness and good sense than any of the American Ministers abroad." (Russell Papers. To Russell, Dec. 12, 1862.)

So far removed was Seward's attitude toward England from that ascribed to him in 1861, so calm was his treatment of questions now up for immediate consideration, so friendly was he personally toward Lyons, that the British Minister became greatly alarmed when, shortly after his return to Washington, there developed a Cabinet controversy threatening the retirement of the Secretary of State. This was a quarrel brought on by the personal sensibilities of Chase, Secretary of the Treasury, and directed at Seward's conduct of foreign affairs. It was quieted by the tact and authority of Lincoln, who, when Seward handed in his resignation, secured from Chase a similar offer of resignation, refused both and in the result read to Chase that lesson of Presidential control which Seward had learned in May, 1861. Lyons wrote of this controversy "I shall be sorry if it ends in the removal of Mr. Seward. We are much more likely to have a man less disposed to keep the peace than a man more disposed to do so. I should hardly have said this two years ago."[1] After the event of Seward's retention of office Russell wrote: "I see Seward stays in. I am very glad of it."[2] This is a remarkable reversal of former opinion. A better understanding of Seward had come, somewhat slowly, to British diplomats, but since his action in the *Trent* affair former suspicion had steadily waned; his "high tone" being regarded as for home consumption, until now there was both belief in Seward's basic friendliness and respect for his abilities.

Thus Russell's ambitious mediation projects having finally dwindled to a polite refusal of the French offer to join in a mere suggestion of armistice left no open sores in the British relations with America. The projects were unknown; the refusal seemed final to Seward and was indeed destined to prove so. But of this there was no clear

[1] Russell Papers. Lyons to Russell, Dec. 22, 1862.
[2] Lyons Papers. Russell to Lyons, Jan. 3, 1863.

conception in the British Cabinet. Hardly anyone yet believed that reconquest of the South was even a remote possibility and this foretold that the day must some time come when European recognition would have to be given the Confederacy. It is this unanimity of opinion on the ultimate result of the war in America that should always be kept in mind in judging the attitude of British Government and people in the fall of 1862. Their sympathies were of minor concern at the moment, nor were they much in evidence during the Cabinet crisis. All argument was based upon the expediency and wisdom of the present proposal. Could European nations *now* act in such a way as to bring to an early end a war whose result in separation was inevitable? It was the hope that such action promised good results which led Russell to enter upon his policy even though personally his sympathies were unquestionably with the North. It was, in the end, the conviction that *now* was not a favourable time which determined Palmerston, though sympathetic with the South, to withdraw his support when Russell, through pique, insisted on going on. Moreover both statesmen were determined not to become involved in the war and as the possible consequences of even the "most friendly" offers were brought out in discussion it became clear that Great Britain's true policy was to await a return of sanity in the contestants.[1]

For America Russell's mediation plan constitutes the most dangerous crisis in the war for the restoration of the Union. Had that plan been adopted, no matter how friendly in intent, there is little question that Lewis' forebodings

[1] December 1, Brunow related an interview in which Russell expressed his "satisfaction" that England and Russia were in agreement that the moment was not opportune for a joint offer to the United States. Russell also stated that it was unfortunate France had pressed her proposal without a preliminary confidential sounding and understanding between the Powers; the British Government saw no reason for changing its attitude. (Russian Archives. Brunow to F. O., Dec. 1, 1862 (N.S.), No. 1998.) There is no evidence in the despatch that Brunow knew of Russell's preliminary "soundings" of France.

would have been realized and war would have ensued between England and the North. But also whatever its results in other respects the independence of the South would have been established. Slavery, hated of Great Britain, would have received a new lease of life—and by British action. In the Cabinet argument all parties agreed that Lincoln's emancipation proclamation was but an incitement to servile war and it played no part in the final decision. Soon that proclamation was to erect a positive barrier of public opinion against any future efforts to secure British intervention. Never again was there serious governmental consideration of meddling in the American Civil War.[1]

[1] Various writers have treated Roebuck's motion in 1863 as the "crisis" of intervention. In Chapter XIV the error of this will be shown.

CHAPTER XII

THE EMANCIPATION PROCLAMATION

THE finality of the British Cabinet decision in November, 1862, relative to proposals of mediation or intervention was not accepted at the moment though time was to prove its permanence. The British press was full of suggestions that the first trial might more gracefully come from France since that country was presumed to be on more friendly terms with the United States.[1] Others, notably Slidell at Paris, held the same view, and on January 8, 1863, Slidell addressed a memorandum to Napoleon III, asking separate recognition of the South. The next day, Napoleon dictated an instruction to Mercier offering friendly mediation in courteous terms but with no hint of an armistice or of an intended recognition of the South.[2] Meanwhile, Mercier had again approached Lyons alleging that he had been urged by Greeley, editor of the *New York Tribune*, to make an isolated French offer, but that he felt this would be contrary to the close harmony hitherto maintained in French-British relations. But Mercier added that if Lyons was disinclined to a proposal of mediation, he intended to advise his Government to give him authority to act alone.[3] Lyons made no comment to Mercier but wrote to Russell, "I certainly desire that the Settlement of the

[1] *Punch*, Nov. 22, 1862, has a cartoon picturing Palmerston as presenting this view to Napoleon III.

[2] Rhodes, IV, p. 348.

[3] F. O., Am., Vol. 875. No. 80. Confidential. Lyons to Russell, Jan. 27, 1863. This date would have permitted Mercier to be already in receipt of Napoleon's instructions, though he gave no hint of it in the interview with Lyons.

Contest should be made without the intervention of England."

A week later the Russian Minister, Stoeckl, also came to Lyons desiring to discover what would be England's attitude if Russia should act alone, or perhaps with France, leaving England out of a proposal to the North.[1] This was based on the supposition that the North, weary of war, might ask the good offices of Russia. Lyons replied that he did not think that contingency near and otherwise evaded Stoeckl's questions; but he was somewhat suspicious, concluding his report, "I cannot quite forget that Monsieur Mercier and Monsieur de Stoeckl had agreed to go to Richmond together last Spring."[2] The day after this despatch was written Mercier presented, February 3, the isolated French offer and on February 6 received Seward's reply couched in argumentative, yet polite language, but positively declining the proposal.[3] Evidently Lyons was a bit disquieted by the incident; but in London, Napoleon's overture to America was officially stated to be unobjectionable, as indeed was required by the implications of the reply of November 13, to France. Russell, on February 14, answered Lyons' communications in a letter marked "Seen by Lord Palmerston and the Queen":

"Her Majesty's Government have no wish to interfere at present in any way in the Civil War. If France were to offer good offices or mediation, Her Majesty's Government would feel no jealousy or repugnance to such a course on the part of France alone."[4]

[1] Mercier had in fact approached Stoeckl on a joint offer of mediation without England. Evidently Stoeckl had asked instructions and those received made clear that Russia did not wish to be compelled to face such a question. She did not wish to offend France, and an offer without England had no chance of acceptance (Russian Archives, F. O. to Stoeckl, Feb. 16, 1863 (O.S.)).

[2] F. O. Am., Vol. 876. No. 108. Confidential. Lyons to Russell, Feb. 2, 1863.

[3] Rhodes, IV, p. 348.

[4] F. O., Am., Vol. 868, No. 86.

The writing of this despatch antedated the knowledge that France had already acted at Washington, and does not necessarily indicate any governmental feeling of a break in previous close relations with France on the American question. Yet this was indubitably the case and became increasingly evident as time passed. Russell's despatch to Lyons of February 14 appears rather to be evidence of the effect of the debates in Parliament when its sessions were resumed on February 5, for in both Lords and Commons there was given a hearty and nearly unanimous support of the Government's decision to make no overture for a cessation of the conflict in America. Derby clearly outlined the two possible conditions of mediation; first, when efforts by the North to subdue the South had practically ceased; and second, if humane interests required action by neutral states, in which case the intervening parties must be fully prepared to use force. Neither condition had arrived and strict neutrality was the wise course. Disraeli also approved strict neutrality but caustically referred to Gladstone's Newcastle speech and sharply attacked the Cabinet's uncertain and changeable policy—merely a party speech. Russell upheld the Government's decision but went out of his way to assert that the entire subjugation of the South would be a calamity to the United States itself, since it would require an unending use of force to hold the South in submission.[1] Later, when news of the French offer at Washington had been received, the Government was attacked in the Lords by an undaunted friend of the South, Lord Campbell, on the ground of a British divergence from close relations with France. Russell, in a brief reply, reasserted old arguments that the time had "not yet" come, but now declared that events seemed to show the possibility of a complete Northern victory and added with emphasis that recognition of the South

[1] Hansard, 3rd. Ser., CLXIX, pp. 5-53, and 69-152.

could justly be regarded by the North as an "unfriendly act."[1]

Thus Parliament and Cabinet were united against meddling in America, basing this attitude on neutral duty and national interests, and with barely a reference to the new policy of the North toward slavery, declared in the emancipation proclamations of September 22, 1862, and January 1, 1863, Had these great documents then no favourable influence on British opinion and action? Was the Northern determination to root out the institution of slavery, now clearly announced, of no effect in winning the favour of a people and Government long committed to a world policy against that institution? It is here necessary to review early British opinion, the facts preceding the first emancipation proclamation, and to examine its purpose in the mind of Lincoln.

Before the opening of actual military operations, while there was still hope of some peaceful solution, British opinion had been with the North on the alleged ground of sympathy with a free as against a slave-owning society. But war once begun the disturbance to British trade interests and Lincoln's repeated declarations that the North had no intention of destroying slavery combined to offer an excuse and a reason for an almost complete shift of British opinion. The abolitionists of the North and the extreme anti-slavery friends in England, relatively few in number in both countries, still sounded the note of "slavery the cause of the war," but got little hearing. Nevertheless it was seen by thoughtful minds that slavery was certain to have a distinct bearing on the position of Great Britain when the war was concluded. In May, 1861, Palmerston declared that it would be a happy day when "we could succeed in putting an end to this unnatural war between the two sections of our North American cousins," but

[1] *Ibid.*, pp. 1714-41. March 23, 1863.

added that the difficulty for England was that "*We* could not well mix ourselves up with the acknowledgment of slavery. . . ."[1]

Great Britain's long-asserted abhorrence of slavery caused, indeed, a perplexity in governmental attitude. But this looked to the final outcome of an independent South—an outcome long taken for granted. Debate on the existing moralities of the war very soon largely disappeared from British discussion and in its place there cropped out, here and there, expressions indicative of anxiety as to whether the war could long continue without a "servile insurrection," with all its attendant horrors.

On July 6, 1861, the *Economist*, reviewing the progress of the war preparations to date, asserted that it was universally agreed no restoration of the Union was possible and answered British fears by declaring it was impossible to believe that even the American madness could contemplate a servile insurrection. The friendly *Spectator* also discussed the matter and repeatedly. It was a mistaken idea, said this journal, that there could be no enfranchisement without a slave rising, but should this occur, "the right of the slave to regain his freedom, even if the effort involve slaughter, is as clear as any other application of the right of self-defence."[2] Yet English abolitionists should not urge the slave to act for himself, since "as war goes on and all compromise fails the American mind will harden under the white heat and determine that the *cause* of all conflict must cease." That slavery, in spite of any declaration by Lincoln or Northern denial of a purpose to attack it—denials which disgusted Harriet Martineau—was in real fact the basic cause of the war, seemed to her as clear as anything in reason.[3] She had no patience with English

[1] Ashley, *Palmerston*, II, 208-9. To Ellice, May 5, 1861.
[2] July 13, 1861.
[3] Harriet Martineau, *Autobiography*, p. 508. To Mrs. Chapman, Aug. 8, 1861.

anti-slavery people who believed Northern protestations, and she did not express concern over the horrors of a possible servile insurrection. Nevertheless this spectre was constantly appearing. Again the *Spectator* sought to allay such fears ; but yet again also proclaimed that even such a contingency was less fearful than the consolidation of the slave-power in the South.[1]

Thus a servile insurrection was early and frequently an argument which pro-Northern friends were compelled to meet. In truth the bulk of the British press was constant in holding up this bogie to its readers, even going to the point of weakening its argument of the impossibility of a Northern conquest of the South by appealing to history to show that England in her two wars with America had had a comparatively easy time in the South, thus postulating the real danger of some " negro Garibaldi calling his countrymen to arms."[2] Nor was this fear merely a pretended one. It affected all classes and partisans of both sides. Even official England shared in it ; January 20, 1862, Lyons wrote, " The question is rapidly tending towards the issue either of peace and a recognition of the separation, or a Proclamation of Emancipation and the raising of a servile insurrection."[3] At nearly the same time Russell, returning to Gladstone a letter from Sumner to Cobden, expressed his sorrow " that the President intends a war of emancipation, meaning thereby, I fear, a war of greater desolation than has been since the revival of letters."[4] John Stuart Mill, with that clear logic which appealed to the more intelligent reader, in an able examination of the underlying causes and probable results of the American conflict, excused the Northern leaders for early denial of a purpose to attack slavery, but expressed complete confidence that even these

[1] Sept. 21, 1861.
[2] *Saturday Review*, Nov. 17, 1860.
[3] Russell Papers. To Russell.
[4] Gladstone Papers. Russell to Gladstone, Jan. 26, 1862.

leaders by now understood the "almost certain results of success in the present conflict" (the extinction of slavery) and prophesied that "if the writers who so severely criticize the present moderation of the Free-soilers are desirous to see the war become an abolition war, it is probable that if the war lasts long enough they will be gratified."[1] John Bright, reaching a wider public, in speech after speech, expressed faith that the people of the North were "marching on, as I believe, to its [slavery's] entire abolition."[2]

Pro-Southern Englishmen pictured the horrors of an "abolition war," and believed the picture true; strict neutrals, like Lyons, feared the same development; friends of the North pushed aside the thought of a "negro terror," yet even while hoping and declaring that the war would destroy slavery, could not escape from apprehensions of an event that appeared inevitable. Everywhere, to the British mind, it seemed that emancipation was necessarily a provocative to servile insurrection, and this belief largely affected the reception of the emancipation proclamation—a fact almost wholly lost sight of in historical writing.

Nor did the steps taken in America leading up to emancipation weaken this belief—rather they appeared to justify it. The great advocate of abolition as a weapon in the war and for its own sake was Charles Sumner, Chairman of the Senate Committee on Foreign Relations. He early took the ground that a proclamation everywhere emancipating the slaves would give to the Northern cause a moral support hitherto denied it in Europe and would at the same time strike a blow at Southern resistance. This idea was presented in a public speech at Worcester, Massachusetts, in October, 1861, but even Sumner's free-soil friends thought him mistaken and his expressions "unfortunate." By December, however, he found at

[1] Article in *Fraser's Magazine*, Feb. 1862, "The Contest in America."
[2] Hansard, 3rd Ser., CXLV, p. 387, Feb. 17, 1862.

Washington a change in governmental temper and from that date Sumner was constant, through frequent private conversations with Lincoln, in pressing for action. These ideas and his personal activities for their realization were well known to English friends, as in his letters to Cobden and Bright, and to the English public in general through Sumner's speeches, for Sumner had long been a well-known figure in the British press.[1]

Lincoln, never an "Abolitionist," in spite of his famous utterance in the 'fifties that the United States could not indefinitely continue to exist "half-slave and half-free," had, in 1861, disapproved and recalled the orders of some of the military leaders, like Fremont, who without authority had sought to extend emancipation to slaves within the lines of their command. But as early as anyone he had foreseen the gradual emergence of emancipation as a war problem, at first dangerous to that wise "border state policy" which had prevented the more northern of the slave states from seceding. His first duty was to restore the Union and to that he gave all his energy, yet that emancipation, when the time was ripe, was also in Lincoln's mind is evident from the gradual approach through legislation and administrative act. In February, 1862, a Bill was under discussion in Congress, called the "Confiscation Bill," which, among other clauses, provided that all slaves of persons engaged in rebellion against the United States, who should by escape, or capture, come into the possession of the military forces of the United States, should be for ever free; but that this provision should not be operative until the expiration of sixty days, thus giving slave-owners opportunity to cease their rebellion and retain their slaves.[2] This measure did not at first have Lincoln's approval for he feared its effect on the loyalists of the border states. Nevertheless he

[1] Pierce, *Sumner*, IV, pp. 41-48, and 63-69.

[2] Raymond, *Life, Public Services and State Papers of Abraham Lincoln*, p. 243.

realized the growing strength of anti-slavery sentiment in the war and fully sympathized with it where actual realization did not conflict with the one great object of his administration. Hence in March, 1862, he heartily concurred in a measure passed rapidly to Presidential approval, April 16, freeing the slaves in the District of Columbia, a territory where there was no question of the constitutional power of the national Government.

From February, 1862, until the issue of the first emancipation proclamation in September, there was, in truth, a genuine conflict between Congress and President as to methods and extent of emancipation. Congress was in a mood to punish the South ; Lincoln, looking steadily toward re-union, yet realizing the rising strength of anti-slavery in the North, advocated a gradual, voluntary, and compensated emancipation. Neither party spoke the word "servile insurrection," yet both realized its possibility, and Seward, in foreign affairs, was quick to see and use it as a threat. A brief summary of measures will indicate the contest. March 6, Lincoln sent a message to Congress recommending that a joint resolution be passed pledging the pecuniary aid of the national Government to any state voluntarily emancipating its slaves, his avowed purpose being to secure early action by the loyal border states in the hope that this might influence the Southern states.[1] Neither the House of Representatives nor the Senate were really favourable to this resolution and the border states bitterly opposed it in debate, but it passed by substantial majorities in both branches and was approved by Lincoln on April 10. In effect the extreme radical element in Congress had yielded, momentarily, to the President's insistence on an olive-branch offering of compensated emancipation. Both as regards the border states and looking to the restoration of the Union, Lincoln was determined to

[1] *Ibid.*, pp. 229-32.

give this line of policy a trial. The prevailing sentiment of Congress, however, preferred the punitive Confiscation Bill.

At this juncture General Hunter, in command of the "Department of the South," which theoretically included also the States of South Carolina, Georgia and Florida, issued an order declaring the slaves in these states free. This was May 9, 1862. Lincoln immediately countermanded Hunter's order, stating that such action "under my responsibility, I reserve to myself."[1] He renewed, in this same proclamation, earnest appeals to the border states, to embrace the opportunity offered by the Congressional resolution of April 10. In truth, border state attitude was the test of the feasibility of Lincoln's hoped-for voluntary emancipation, but these states were unwilling to accept the plan. Meanwhile pressure was being exerted for action on the Confiscation Bill; it was pushed through Congress and presented to Lincoln for his signature or veto. He signed it on July 12, *but did not notify that fact to Congress until July* 17. On this same day of signature, July 12, Lincoln sent to Congress a proposal of an Act to give pecuniary aid in voluntary state emancipation and held a conference with the congressional representatives of the border states seeking their definite approval of his policy. A minority agreed but the majority were emphatically against him. The Confiscation Bill would not affect the border states; they were not in rebellion. And they did not desire to free the slaves even if compensated.[2]

Thus Lincoln, by the stubbornness of the border states, was forced toward the Congressional point of view as expressed in the Confiscation Bill. On the day following his failure to win the border state representatives he told Seward and Welles who were driving with him, that he had

[1] *Ibid.*, p. 233, May 19, 1862.

[2] A Bill was in fact introduced July 16, 1862, on the lines of Lincoln's "pecuniary aid" proposal of July 12, but no action was taken on it.

come to the conclusion that the time was near for the issue of a proclamation of emancipation as a military measure fully within the competence of the President. This was on July 13.[1] Seward offered a few objections but apparently neither Cabinet official did more than listen to Lincoln's argument of military necessity. Congress adjourned on July 17. On July 22, the President read to the Cabinet a draft of an emancipation proclamation the text of the first paragraph of which referred to the Confiscation Act and declared that this would be rigorously executed unless rebellious subjects returned to their allegiance. But the remainder of the draft reasserted the ideal of a gradual and compensated emancipation and concluded with the warning that for states still in rebellion on January 1, 1863, a general emancipation of slaves would be proclaimed.[2] All of the Cabinet approved except Blair who expressed fears of the effect on the approaching November elections, and Seward who, while professing sympathy with the indicated purpose, argued that the time was badly chosen in view of recent military disasters and the approach of Lee's army toward Washington. The measure, Seward said, might "be viewed as the last measure of an exhausted government, a cry for help; the government stretching forth its hands to Ethiopia, instead of Ethiopia stretching forth her hands to the government. It will be considered our last *shriek* on the retreat." He therefore urged postponement until after a Northern victory. This appealed to Lincoln and he "put the draft of the proclamation aside, waiting for victory."[3]

Victory came in September, with McClellan's defeat of Lee at Antietam, and the retreat of the Southern army toward Richmond. Five days later, September 22, Lincoln

[1] Welles, *Diary,* I, pp. 70-71.
[2] Abraham Lincoln, *Complete Works,* II, p. 213.
[3] Rhodes, IV, pp. 71-2.

issued the proclamation, expanded and altered in text from the draft of July 22, but in substance the same.[1] The loyal border states were not to be affected, but the proclamation renewed the promise of steps to be taken to persuade them to voluntary action. On January 1, 1863, a second proclamation, referring to that of September 22, was issued by Lincoln "by virtue of the power in me vested as commander-in-chief of the army and navy of the United States in time of actual armed rebellion against the authority and Government of the United States. . . ." The states affected were designated by name and all persons held as slaves within them "are, and henceforward shall be, free. . . ." "I hereby enjoin upon the people so declared to be free to abstain from all violence, unless in necessary self-defence. . . ." "And upon this act, sincerely believed to be an act of justice, warranted by the Constitution upon military necessity, I invoke the considerate judgment of mankind, and the gracious favour of Almighty God."[2]

Such were the steps, from December, 1861, when the radical Sumner began his pressure for action, to September, 1862, when Lincoln's pledge of emancipation was made. Did these steps indicate, as British opinion unquestionably held, an intention to rouse a servile insurrection? Was the Confiscation Bill passed with that purpose in view and had Lincoln decided to carry it into effect? The failure of the slaves to rise is, indeed, the great marvel of the Civil War and was so regarded not in England only, but in America also. It was the expectation of the North and the constant fear of the South. But was this, in truth, the *purpose* of the emancipation proclamation?

[1] As issued September 22, the first paragraph refers to his plan of securing legislation to aid compensated voluntary emancipation, the next sets the date January 1, 1863, for completed emancipation of slaves in states still in rebellion and the remaining paragraphs concern the carrying out of the confiscation law. Lincoln, *Complete Works*, II, pp. 237-8.

[2] Raymond, *State Papers of Lincoln*, 260-61.

This purpose has been somewhat summarily treated by American historians, largely because of lack of specific evidence as to motives at the time of issue. Two words "military necessity" are made to cover nearly the entire argument for emancipation in September, 1862, but in just what manner the military prowess of the North was to be increased was not at first indicated. In 1864, Lincoln declared that after the failure of successive efforts to persuade the border states to accept compensated emancipation he had believed there had arrived the "indispensable necessity for military emancipation and arming the blacks."[1] Repeatedly in later defence of the proclamation he urged the benefits that had come from his act and asserted that commanders in the field "believe the emancipation policy and the use of coloured troops constitute the heaviest blow yet dealt to the rebellion."[2] He added: "negroes, like other people, act upon motives. Why should they do anything for us, if we will do nothing for them? If they stake their lives for us, they must be prompted by the strongest motive, even the promise of freedom."

There is no note here of stirring a servile insurrection; nor did Lincoln ever acknowledge that such a purpose had been in his mind, though the thought of such possible result must have been present—was, indeed, present to most minds even without a proclamation of emancipation. Lincoln's alleged purpose was simply to draw away slaves, wherever possible, from their rebellious masters, thus reducing the economic powers of resistance of the South, and then to make these ex-slaves directly useful in winning the war. But after the war, even here and there during it, a theory was advanced that an impelling motive with the President had been the hope of influencing favourably

[1] Rhodes, IV, p. 214.

[2] *Ibid.*, p. 410. In letter, August 26, 1863, addressed to a Springfield mass meeting of "unconditional Union men."

foreign governments and peoples by stamping the Northern cause with a high moral purpose. In popular opinion, Lincoln came to be regarded as a far-visioned statesman in anticipating that which ultimately came to pass. This has important bearing on the relations of the United States and Great Britain.

There is no doubt that nearly every Northern American had believed in 1860, that anti-slavery England would sympathize strongly with the North. The event did not prove this to be the case, nor could the North justly complain in the face of administration denials of an anti-slavery purpose. The English Government therefore was widely upheld by British opinion in regarding the struggle from the point of view of British interests. Yet any Northern step antagonistic to the institution of slavery compelled British governmental consideration. As early as December, 1860, before the war began, Bunch, at Charleston, had reported a conversation with Rhett, in which the latter frankly declared that the South would expect to revive the African Slave Trade.[1] This was limited in the constitution later adopted by the Confederacy which in substance left the matter to the individual states—a condition that Southern agents in England found it hard to explain.[2] As already noted, the ardent friends of the North continued to insist, even after Lincoln's denial, that slavery was the real cause of the American rupture.[3] By September, 1861, John Bright was writing to his friend Sumner that, all indications to the contrary, England would warmly support the North

[1] American Hist. Rev., XVIII, pp. 784-7. Bunch to Russell, Dec. 5, 1860.

[2] Southern Commissioners abroad early reported that recognition of independence and commercial treaties could not be secured unless the South would agree to " mutual right of search " treaties for the suppression of the African Slave Trade. Davis' answer was that the Confederate constitution gave him no authority to negotiate such a treaty; indeed, denied him that authority since the constitution itself prohibited the importation of negroes from Africa. For Benjamin's instructions see Bigelow, *Retrospections*, I, pp. 591-96.

[3] *Spectator*, May 4, 1861.

if only it could be shown that emancipation was an object.[1] Again and again he urged, it is interesting to note, just those ideals of gradual and compensated emancipation which were so strongly held by Lincoln. In this same month the *Spectator* thought it was " idle to strive to ignore the very centre and spring of all disunion," and advised a " prudent audacity in striking at the cause rather than at the effect."[2] Three weeks later the *Spectator*, reviewing general British press comments, summed them up as follows :

> " If you make it a war of emancipation we shall think you madmen, and tell you so, though the ignorant instincts of Englishmen will support you. And if you follow our counsel in holding a tight rein on the Abolitionists, we shall applaud your worldly wisdom so far ; but shall deem it our duty to set forth continually that you have forfeited all claim to the *popular* sympathy of England."

This, said the *Spectator*, had been stated in the most objectionable style by the *Times* in particular, which, editorially, had alleged that " the North has now lost the chance of establishing a high moral superiority by a declaration against slavery." To all this the *Spectator* declared that the North must adopt the bold course and make clear that restoration of the Union was not intended with the old canker at its roots.[3]

Official England held a different view. Russell believed that the separation of North and South would conduce to the extinction of slavery since the South, left to itself and fronted by a great and prosperous free North, with a population united in ideals, would be forced, ultimately, to abandon its " special system." He professed that he could not understand Mrs. Stowe's support of the war

[1] Sept. 6, 1861. In Mass. Hist. Soc. *Proceedings*, Vol. XLVI, p. 95.
[2] Sept. 14, 1861.
[3] October 5, 1861.

and thought she and Sumner "animated by a spirit of vengeance."[1] If the South did yield and the Union were restored *with* slavery, Russell thought that "Slavery would prevail all over the New World. For that reason I wish for separation."[2] These views were repeated frequently by Russell. He long had a fixed idea on the moral value of separation, but was careful to state, "I give you these views merely as speculations," and it is worthy of note that after midsummer of 1862 he rarely indulged in them. Against such speculations, whether by Russell or by others, Mill protested in his famous article in *Fraser's*, February, 1862.[3]

On one aspect of slavery the North was free to act and early did so. Seward proposed to Lyons a treaty giving mutual right of search off the African Coast and on the coasts of Cuba for the suppression of the African Slave Trade. Such a treaty had long been urged by Great Britain but persistently refused by the United States. It could not well be declined now by the British Government and was signed by Seward, April 8, 1862,[4] but if he expected any change in British attitude as a result he was disappointed. The renewal by the South of that trade might be a barrier to British goodwill, but the action of the North was viewed as but a weak attempt to secure British sympathy, and to mark the limits of Northern anti-slavery efforts. Indeed, the Government was not eager for the treaty on other grounds, since the Admiralty had never "felt any interest in the suppression of the slave trade . . . whatever they have done . . . they have done grudgingly and imperfectly."[5]

This was written at the exact period when Palmerston

[1] Lyons Papers. To Lyons, Oct. 26, 1861.

[2] *Ibid.* To Lyons, Nov. 2, 1861. The same ideas are officially expressed by Russell to Lyons, March 7, 1861, and May 1, 1862. (F. O., Am., Vol. 818, No. 104, Draft; and *Ibid.*, Vol. 819, No. 197, Draft.).

[3] See *ante*, p. 81.

[4] *U.S. Messages and Documents*, 1862-3, Pt. I, p. 65.

[5] Ashley, *Palmerston*, II, p. 227. Palmerston to Russell, Aug. 13, 1862.

and Russell were initiating those steps which were to result in the Cabinet crisis on mediation in October-November, 1862. Certainly the Slave Trade treaty with America had not influenced governmental attitude. At this juncture there was founded, November, 1862, the London Emancipation Society, with the avowed object of stirring anti-slavery Englishmen in protest against "favouring the South." But George Thompson, its organizer, had been engaged in the preliminary work of organization for some months and the Society is therefore to be regarded as an expression of that small group who were persistent and determined in assertion of slavery as the cause and object of the Civil War, before the issue of Lincoln's proclamation.[1] Thus for England as a whole and for official England the declarations of these few voices were regarded as expressive of a wish rather than as consistent with the facts. The moral uplift of an anti-slavery object was denied to the North.

This being so did Lincoln seek to correct the foreign view by the emancipation proclamation? There is some, but scant ground for so believing. It is true that this aspect had at various times, though rarely, been presented to the President. Carl Schurz, American Minister at Madrid, wrote to Seward as early as September 14, 1861, strongly urging the declaration of an anti-slavery purpose in the war and asserting that public opinion in Europe would then be such in favour of the North that no government would "dare to place itself, by declaration or act, upon the side of a universally condemned institution."[2] There is no evidence that Seward showed this despatch to Lincoln, but in January, 1862, Schurz returned to America and in

[1] Garrison, *Garrison*, IV, p. 66. Many distinguished names were on the roster of the Society—Mill, Bright, Cobden, Lord Houghton, Samuel Lucas, Forster, Goldwin Smith, Justin McCarthy, Thomas Hughes, Cairns, Herbert Spencer, Francis Newman, the Rev. Newman Hall, and others. Frederick W. Chesson was secretary, and very active in the work.

[2] Schurz, *Speeches and Correspondence*, I, 190.

conversation with the President urged the "moral issue" to prevent foreign intervention. The President replied: "You may be right. Probably you are. I have been thinking so myself. I cannot imagine that any European power would dare to recognize and aid the Southern Confederacy if it became clear that the Confederacy stands for slavery and the Union for freedom."[1] No doubt others urged upon him the same view. Indeed, one sincere foreign friend, Count Gasparin, who had early written in favour of the North,[2] and whose opinions were widely read, produced a second work in the spring of 1862, in which the main theme was "slavery the issue." The author believed emancipation inevitable and urged an instant proclamation of Northern *intention* to free the slaves.[3] Presumably, Lincoln was familiar with this work. Meanwhile Sumner pressed the same idea though adding the prevalent abolition arguments which did not, necessarily, involve thought of foreign effect. On the general question of emancipation Lincoln listened, even telling Sumner that he "was ahead of himself only a month or six weeks."[4]

Yet after the enactment of the "confiscation bill" in July, 1862, when strong abolitionist pressure was brought on the President to issue a general proclamation of emancipation, he reasserted in the famous reply to Greeley, August 22, 1862, his one single purpose to restore the Union "with or without slavery."

> "If there be those who would not save the Union unless they could at the same time save slavery, I do not agree with them.
>
> "If there be those who would not save the Union unless

[1] Schurz, *Reminiscences*, II, 309.

[2] Gasparin, *The Uprising of a Great People*, 1861.

[3] Gasparin, *America before Europe*, Pt. V, Ch. III. The preface is dated March 4, 1862, and the work went through three American editions in 1862.

[4] Pierce, *Sumner*, IV, p. 63. No exact date, but Spring of 1862.

they could at the same time destroy slavery, I do not agree with them.

"*My paramount object is to save the Union, and not either to save or to destroy slavery.*"[1]

Here seemed to be specific denial of raising a moral issue; yet unknown to the public at the moment there had already been drafted and discussed in Cabinet the emancipation proclamation. Greeley had presented abolitionist demands essential to cement the North. A month later, September 13, a delegation of Chicago clergymen came to Washington, had an audience with Lincoln, presented similar arguments, but also laid stress on the necessity of securing the sympathy of Europe. This was but nine days before the first proclamation was issued, but Lincoln replied much as to Greeley, though he stated, "I will also concede that Emancipation would help us in Europe, and convince them that we are incited by something more than ambition."[2] Immediately after the event, September 24, making a short speech to a serenading party, Lincoln said, "I can only trust in God I have made no mistake. . . . It is now for the country and the world to pass judgment and, maybe, take action upon it."[3] Over a year later, December 8, 1863, in his annual message to Congress, he noted a "much improved" tone in foreign countries as resulting from the emancipation proclamation, but dwelt mainly on the beneficial effects at home.[4]

Evidently there is slight ground for believing Lincoln to have been convinced that foreign relations would be improved by the proclamation. On the contrary, if he

[1] Raymond, *State Papers of Lincoln*, p. 253.

[2] *Ibid.*, p. 256.

[3] Rhodes, IV, p. 162.

[4] Lincoln's *Complete Works*, II, p. 454. But the *after-comment* by Lincoln as to purpose was nearly always in line with an unfinished draft of a letter to Charles D. Robinson, Aug. 17, 1864, when the specific object was said to be "inducing the coloured people to come bodily over from the rebel side to ours." *Ibid.*, p. 564.

trusted Seward's judgment he may have *feared* the effect on Europe, for such was Seward's prophecy. Here may have lain the true meaning of Lincoln's speech of September 24—that it was now for "the world to pass judgment and, maybe, take action upon it." After all foreign policy, though its main lines were subject to the President's control, was in the hands of Seward and throughout this entire period of six months since the introduction of the Confiscation Bill up to Lincoln's presentation of his draft proclamation to the Cabinet in July, Seward had been using the threat of a servile insurrection as a deterrent upon French-British talk of intervention. At times Seward connected servile insurrection with emancipation—at times not.

Seward had begun his career as Secretary of State with an appeal to Europe on lines of old friendship and had implied, though he could not state explicitly, the "noble" cause of the North. He had been met with what he considered a "cold" and premature as well as unjustifiable declaration of neutrality. From the first day of the conflict Lyons and Mercier had been constant in representing the hardships inflicted by the American war upon the economic interests of their respective countries. Both men bore down upon the interruption of the cotton trade and Seward kept repeating that Northern victories would soon release the raw cotton. He expected and promised much from the capture of New Orleans, but the results were disappointing. As time went on Seward became convinced that material interests alone would determine the attitude and action of Great Britain and France. But the stored supplies were on hand in the South, locked in by the blockade and would be available when the war was over *provided* the war did not take on an uncivilized and sanguinary character through a rising of the slaves. If that occurred cotton would be burned and destroyed and cotton supply to Europe would be not merely a matter of temporary interruption, but one of long-continued dearth with no certainty of early resumption. Fearing the growth in England, especially, of an intention to intervene, Seward threatened a Northern appeal to the slaves, thinking of the threat not so much in terms of an uncivilized and horrible war as in terms of the material interests of Great Britain. In brief, considering foreign attitude and action in its relation to Northern advantage—to the winning of the war—he would use emancipation as a threat of servile insurrection, but did not desire emancipation itself for fear it would cause that very intervention which it was his object to prevent.

His instructions are wholly in line with this policy. In February, 1862, the Confiscation Bill had been introduced in Congress. In April, Mercier's trip to Richmond[1] had caused much speculation and started many rumours in London of plans of mediation.[2] On May 28, Seward wrote to Adams at great length and especially emphasized two points: first that while diplomats abroad had hitherto been interdicted from discussing slavery as an issue in the war, they were now authorized to state that the war was, in part at least, intended for the suppression of slavery, and secondly, that the North if interfered with by foreign nations would be forced to have recourse to a servile war. Such a war, Seward argued, would be "completely destructive of all European interests. . . ."[3] A copy of this instruction Adams gave to Russell on June 20. Eight days later Adams told Cobden in reply to a query about mediation that it would result in a servile war.[4] Evidently Adams perfectly understood Seward's policy.

[1] See *ante*, Ch. IX.

[2] *U.S. Messages and Documents*, 1862-3, Pt. I, p. 83. Adams to Seward, May 8, 1862.

[3] *Ibid.*, pp. 101-105.

[4] *Ibid.*, p. 122. Adams to Seward, July 3, 1862. In his despatch Adams states the conversation to have occurred "last Saturday," and with an "unofficial person," who was sounding him on mediation. This was Cobden.

On July 13, Lincoln told Seward and Welles of the planned emancipation proclamation and that this was his first mention of it to anyone. Seward commented favourably but wished to consider the proposal in all its bearings before committing himself.[1] The day following he transmitted to agents abroad a copy of the Bill that day introduced into Congress embodying Lincoln's plan for gradual and compensated emancipation. This was prompt transmittal—and was unusual. Seward sent the Bill without material comment,[2] but it is apparent that this method and measure of emancipation would much better fit in with his theory of the slavery question in relation to foreign powers, than would an outright proclamation of emancipation.

Meanwhile American anxiety as to a possible alteration in British neutral policy was increasing. July 11, Adams reported that he had learned "from a credible source" that the British Cabinet might soon "take new ground."[3] This despatch if it reached Seward previous to the Cabinet of July 22, presumably added strength to his conviction of the inadvisability of now issuing the proclamation. In that Cabinet, Seward in fact went much beyond the customary historical statement that he advised postponement of the proclamation until the occurrence of a Northern victory; he argued, according to Secretary of War Stanton's notes of the meeting, "That foreign nations will intervene to prevent the abolition of slavery for the sake of cotton. . . . We break up our relations with foreign nations and the production of cotton for sixty years."[4] These views did not prevail; Lincoln merely postponed action. Ten days later Seward sent that long instruction to Adams covering the whole ground of feared European intervention, which,

[1] Welles, *Diary*, I, p. 70.
[2] *U.S. Messages and Documents*, 1862-3, Pt. I, p. 135.
[3] *Ibid.*, p. 133. To Seward. His informant was Baring.
[4] Bancroft, *Seward*, II, p. 333.

fortunately, Adams was never called upon to carry out.[1] In it there was renewed the threat of a servile war if Europe attempted to aid the South, and again it is the materialistic view that is emphasized. Seward was clinging to his theory of correct policy.

Nor was he mistaken in his view of first reactions in governmental circles abroad—at least in England. On July 21, the day before Lincoln's proposal of emancipation in the Cabinet, Stuart in reviewing military prospects wrote: "Amongst the means relied upon for weakening the South is included a servile war."[2] To this Russell replied: ". . . I have to observe that the prospect of a servile war will only make other nations more desirous to see an end of this desolating and destructive conflict."[3] This was but brief reiteration of a more exact statement by Russell made in comment on Seward's first hint of servile war in his despatch to Adams of May 28, a copy of which had been given to Russell on June 20. On July 28, Russell reviewing Seward's arguments, commented on the fast increasing bitterness of the American conflict, disturbing and unsettling to European Governments, and wrote:

> "The approach of a servile war, so much insisted upon by Mr. Seward in his despatch, only forewarns us that another element of destruction may be added to the slaughter, loss of property, and waste of industry, which already afflict a country so lately prosperous and tranquil." [4]

In this same despatch unfavourable comment was made also on the Confiscation Bill with its punitive emancipation clauses. Stuart presented a copy of the despatch to Seward

[1] See *ante*, p. 35.

[2] *Parliamentary Papers*, 1863, *Lords*, Vol. XXIX. "Correspondence relating to the Civil War in the United States of North America." No. 8. To Russell.

[3] *Ibid.*, No. 10. Russell to Stuart, Aug. 7, 1862.

[4] *Ibid.*, 1863, *Lords*, Vol. XXV. "Further correspondence relating to the Civil War in the United States of North America." No. 2. To Stuart.

on August 16.[1] On August 22, Stuart learned of Lincoln's plan and reported it as purely a manœuvre to affect home politics and to frighten foreign governments.[2] Where did Stuart get the news if not from Seward, since he also reported the latter's success in postponing the proclamation?

In brief both Seward and Russell were regarding emancipation in the light of an incitement to servile insurrection, and both believed such an event would add to the argument for foreign intervention. The *threat* Seward had regarded as useful; the *event* would be highly dangerous to the North. Not so, however, did emancipation appear in prospect to American diplomats abroad. Adams was a faithful servant in attempting to carry out the ideas and plans of his chief, but as early as February, 1862, he had urged a Northern declaration in regard to slavery in order to meet in England Southern private representations that, independence won, the South would enter upon a plan of gradual emancipation to be applied "to all persons born after some specific date."[3] Motley, at Vienna, frequently after February, 1862, in private letters to his friends in America, urged some forward step on slavery,[4] but no such advice in despatches found its way into the selected correspondence annually sent to print by Seward. Far more important was the determination taken by Adams, less than a month after he had presented to Russell the "servile war" threat policy of Seward, to give advice to his chief that the chances of foreign intervention would be best met by the distinct avowal of an anti-slavery object in the

[1] *Ibid.*, 1863, *Lords*, Vol. XXIX. "Correspondence relating to the Civil War in the United States of North America," No. 20. Stuart to Russell, Aug. 16, 1862.

[2] See *ante*, p. 37.

[3] State Department, Eng., Vol. 78, No. 119. Adams to Seward, Feb. 21, 1862. This supplemented a similar representation made on Jan. 17, 1862. (*U.S. Messages and Documents*, 1862–3, Pt. I, p. 16.)

[4] e.g., Motley, *Correspondence*, II, pp. 64-5. To O. W. Holmes, Feb. 26, 1862.

war and that the North should be prepared to meet an European offer of mediation by declaring that if made to extinguish slavery such mediation would be welcome. This Adams thought would probably put an end to the mediation itself, but it would also greatly strengthen the Northern position abroad.[1]

This was no prevision of an emancipation proclamation; but it was assertion of the value of a higher "moral issue." Meanwhile, on July 24, Seward still fearful of the effects abroad of emancipation, wrote to Motley, asking whether he was "sure" that European powers would not be encouraged in interference, because of material interests, by a Northern attempt to free the slaves.[2] Motley's answer began, "A thousand times No," and Adams repeated his plea for a moral issue.[3] September 25, Adams met Seward's "material interests" argument by declaring that for Great Britain the chief difficulty in the cotton situation was not scarcity, but uncertainty, and that if English manufacturers could but know what to expect there would be little "cotton pressure" on the Government.[4] Thus leading diplomats abroad did not agree with Seward, but the later advices of Adams were not yet received when the day, September 22, arrived on which Lincoln issued the proclamation. On that day in sending the text to Adams the comment of Seward was brief. The proclamation, he said, put into effect a policy the approach of which he had "heretofore indicated to our representatives abroad," and he laid emphasis on the idea that the main purpose of the proclamation was to convince the South that its true interests were in the preservation of the Union—which is to say that the hoped-for result was the return of the South

[1] *U.S. Messages and Documents*, 1862-3, Pt. I, p. 140. Adams to Seward, July 17, 1862.

[2] Bancroft, *Seward*, II, p. 336.

[3] *U.S. Messages and Documents*, 1862-3, Pt. I, p. 191. Adams to Seward, Sept. 12, 1862.

[4] *Ibid.*, p. 199.

with its slaves.[1] Certainly this was far from a truthful representation, but its purpose is evident. Seward's first thought was that having held up the threat of servile insurrection he must now remove that bogie. Four days later his judgment was improved, for he began, and thereafter maintained with vigour, the "high moral purpose" argument as evinced in the emancipation proclamation. "The interests of humanity," he wrote to Adams, "have now become identified with the cause of our country. . . ."[2]

That the material interests of Great Britain were still in Seward's thought is shown by the celerity with which under Lincoln's orders he grasped at an unexpected opening in relation to liberated slaves. Stuart wrote in mid-September that Mr. Walker, secretary of the colony of British Guiana, was coming from Demerara to Washington to secure additional labour for the British colony by offering to carry away ex-slaves.[3] This scheme was no secret and five days after the issue of the proclamation Seward proposed to Stuart a convention by which the British Government would be permitted to transport to the West Indies, or to any of its colonies, the negroes about to be emancipated. On September 30, Adams was instructed to take up the matter at London.[4] Russell was at first disinclined to consider such a convention and discussion dragged until the spring of 1864, when it was again proposed, this time by Russell, but now declined by Seward. In its immediate

[1] *Ibid.*, p. 195.

[2] *Ibid.*, p. 202. Seward to Adams, Sept. 26, 1862. Lyons, on his return to Washington, wrote that he found Seward's influence much lessened, and that he had fallen in public estimation by his "signing the Abolition Proclamation, which was imposed upon him, in opposition to all his own views, by the Radical Party in the Cabinet." (Russell Papers. Lyons to Russell, Nov. 14, 1862.)

[3] Russell Papers. Stuart to Russell, Sept. 19, 1862.

[4] *U.S. Messages and Documents*, 1862-3, Pt. I, p. 202. The instruction went into great detail as to conditions and means. A similar instruction was sent to Paris, The Hague, and Copenhagen.

influence in the fall of 1862, Seward's offer had no effect on the attitude of the British Government.[1]

To Englishmen and Americans alike it has been in later years a matter for astonishment that the emancipation proclamation did not at once convince Great Britain of the high purposes of the North. But if it be remembered that in the North itself the proclamation was greeted, save by a small abolitionist faction, with doubt extending even to bitter opposition and that British governmental and public opinion had long dreaded a servile insurrection—even of late taking its cue from Seward's own prophecies—the cool reception given by the Government, the vehement and vituperative explosions of the press do not seem so surprising. "This Emancipation Proclamation," wrote Stuart on September 23, "seems a brutum fulmen."[2] One of the President's motives, he thought, was to affect public opinion in England. "But there is no pretext of humanity about the Proclamation. . . . It is merely a Confiscation Act, or perhaps worse, for it offers direct encouragement to servile insurrections."[3] Received in England during the Cabinet struggle over mediation the proclamation appears not to have affected that controversy, though Russell sought to use it as an argument for British action. In his memorandum, circulated October 13, Russell strove to show that the purpose and result would be servile war. He dwelt both on the horrors of such a war, and on its destruction of industry:

> "What will be the practical effect of declaring emancipation, not as an act of justice and beneficence, dispensed by

[1] There was much talk and correspondence on this project from Sept., 1862, to March, 1864. Stuart was suspicious of some "trap." Russell at one time thought the United States was secretly planning to colonize ex-slaves in Central America. Some of the Colonies were in favour of the plan. (Russell Papers. Stuart to Russell, Sept. 29, 1862. F.O., Am., Vol. 878, No. 177. Lyons to Russell, Feb. 24, 1863.)

[2] Lyons Papers. To Lyons.

[3] Russell Papers. Stuart to Russell, Sept. 26, 1862.

the Supreme Power of the State, but as an act of punishment and retaliation inflicted by a belligerent upon a hostile community, it is not difficult to foresee. Wherever the arms of the United States penetrate, a premium will be given to acts of plunder, of incendiarism, and of revenge. The military and naval authorities of the United States will be bound by their orders to maintain and protect the perpetrators of such acts. Wherever the invasion of the Southern States is crowned by victory, society will be disorganized, industry suspended, large and small proprietors of land alike reduced to beggary."[1]

The London newspaper press was very nearly a unit in treating the proclamation with derision and contempt and no other one situation in the Civil War came in for such vigorous denunciation. Citations setting forth such comment have frequently been gathered together illustrative of the extent of press condemnation and of its unity in vicious editorials.[2] There is no need to repeat many of them here, but a few will indicate their tone. The *Times* greeted the news with an assertion that this was a final desperate play by Lincoln, as hope of victory waned. It was his "last card,"[3] a phrase that caught the fancy of lesser papers and was repeated by them. October 21, appeared the "strongest" of the *Times* editorials:

"... We have here the history of the beginning of the end, but who can tell how the pages will be written which are yet to be filled before the inevitable separation is accomplished? Are scenes like those which we a short time since described from Dahomey yet to interpose, and is the reign of the last PRESIDENT to go out amid horrible massacres of

[1] Gladstone Papers. British agents still residing in the South believed the proclamation would have little practical effect, but added that if actually carried out the cultivation of cotton "would be as completely arrested as if an edict were pronounced against its future growth," and pictured the unfortunate results for the world at large. (F. O., Am., Vol. 846, No. 34. Cridland to Russell, Oct. 29, 1862.)

[2] See Rhodes, IV, 344, *notes*.

[3] October 6, 1862. The *Times* had used the "last card" phrase as early as Dec. 14, 1861, in speculations on the effect of Sumner's agitation for emancipation.

ABE LINCOLN'S LAST CARD; OR, ROUGE-ET-NOIR.

Reproduced by permission of the Proprietors of "Punch"

white women and children, to be followed by the extermination of the black race in the South? Is LINCOLN yet a name not known to us as it will be known to posterity, and is it ultimately to be classed among that catalogue of monsters, the wholesale assassins and butchers of their kind?

"... We will attempt at present to predict nothing as to what the consequence of Mr. Lincoln's new policy may be, except that it certainly will not have the effect of restoring the Union. It will not deprive Mr. Lincoln of the distinctive affix which he will share with many, for the most part foolish and incompetent, Kings and Emperors, Caliphs and Doges, that of being LINCOLN—'the Last.'"

The *Times* led the way; other papers followed on. The *Liverpool Post* thought a slave rising inevitable,[1] as did also nearly every paper acknowledging anti-Northern sentiments, or professedly neutral, while even pro-Northern journals at first feared the same results.[2] Another striking phrase, "Brutum Fulmen," ran through many editorials. The *Edinburgh Review* talked of Lincoln's "cry of despair,"[3] which was little different from Seward's feared "last shriek." *Blackwood's* thought the proclamation "monstrous, reckless, devilish." It "justifies the South in raising the black flag, and proclaiming a war without quarter."[4] But there is no need to expand the citation of the well-nigh universal British press pouring out of the wrath of heaven upon Lincoln, and his emancipation proclamation.[5]

Even though there can be no doubt that the bulk of

[1] Oct. 6, 1862.

[2] e.g., *Dublin Nation*, Oct. 11, 1862. *Manchester Guardian*, Oct. 7. *London Morning Advertiser*, Oct. 9. *North British Review*, Oct., 1862. *London Press*, Oct. 11. *London Globe*, Oct. 6. *London Examiner*, Oct. 11, editorial: "The Black Flag," and Oct. 18: "The Instigation to Servile War." *Bell's Weekly Messenger*, Oct. 11.

[3] October, 1862.

[4] November, 1862.

[5] It is worthy of note that the French offer of joint mediation made to Britain in October specified the danger of servile war resulting from the proclamation as a reason for European action. (France, *Documents Diplomatiques*, 1862, p. 142.)

England at first expected servile war to follow the proclamation it is apparent that here and there a part of this British wrath was due to a fear that, in spite of denials of such influence, the proclamation was intended to arouse public opinion against projects of intervention and *might so arouse it.* The New York correspondent of the *Times* wrote that it was "promulgated evidently as a sop to keep England and France quiet,"[1] and on October 9, an editorial asserted that Lincoln had "a very important object. There is a presentiment in the North that recognition cannot be delayed, and this proclamation is aimed, not at the negro or the South, but at Europe." *Bell's Weekly Messenger* believed that it was now "the imperative duty of England and France to do what they can in order to prevent the possible occurrence of a crime which, if carried out, would surpass in atrocity any similar horror the world has ever seen."[2] "Historicus," on the other hand, asked: "What is that solution of the negro question to which an English Government is prepared to affix the seal of English approbation?"[3] Mason, the Confederate Agent in London, wrote home that it was generally believed the proclamation was issued "as the means of warding off recognition. . . . It was seen through at once and condemned accordingly."[4]

This interpretation of Northern purpose in no sense negatives the dictum that the proclamation exercised little influence on immediate British governmental policy, but does offer some ground for the belief that strong pro-Southern sympathizers at once saw the need of combating an argument dangerous to the carrying out of projects of mediation. Yet the new "moral purpose" of Lincoln did not immediately appeal even to his friends. The *Spectator* deplored the lack of a clean-cut declaration in

[1] The *Times*, Oct. 7, 1862.
[2] Oct. 18, 1862.
[3] Communication in the *Times*, Nov. 7, 1862.
[4] Richardson, II, 360. Mason to Benjamin, Nov. 6, 1862.

favour of the principle of human freedom: "The principle asserted is not that a human being cannot justly own another, but that he cannot own him unless he is loyal to the United States." . . . "There is no morality whatever in such a decree, and if approved at all it must be upon its merits as a political measure."[1] Two weeks later, reporting a public speech at Liverpool by ex-governor Morehead of Kentucky, in which Lincoln was accused of treachery to the border states, the *Spectator*, while taking issue with the speaker's statements, commented that it was not to be understood as fully defending a system of government which chose its executive "from the ranks of half-educated mechanics."[2]

Similarly in America the emancipation proclamation, though loudly applauded by the abolitionists, was received with misgivings. Lincoln was disappointed at the public reaction and became very despondent, though this was due, in part, to the failure of McClellan to follow up the victory of Antietam. The elections of October and November went heavily against the administration and largely on the alleged ground of the President's surrender to the radicals.[3] The army as a whole was not favourably stirred by the proclamation; it was considered at best as but a useless bit of "waste paper."[4] In England, John Bright, the most ardent public advocate of the Northern cause, was slow to applaud heartily; not until December did he give distinct approval, and even then in but half-hearted fashion, though he thought public interest was much aroused and that attention was now fixed on January 1, the date set by Lincoln for actual enforcement of emancipation.[5] In a speech at Birmingham, December 18, Bright had little to

[1] *Spectator*, Oct. 11, 1862.
[2] *Ibid.*, Oct. 25, 1862.
[3] Rhodes, IV, 162-64.
[4] Perry, *Henry Lee Higginson*, p. 175.
[5] Rhodes, IV, p. 349, *note*. Bright to Sumner, Dec. 6, 1862.

say of emancipation; rather he continued to use previous arguments against the South for admitting, as Vice-President Stephens had declared, that slavery was the very "corner-stone" of Southern institutions and society.[1] A few public meetings at points where favour to the North had been shown were tried in October and November with some success but with no great show of enthusiasm. It was not until late December that the wind of public opinion, finding that no faintest slave-rising had been created by the proclamation began to veer in favour of the emancipation edict.[2] By the end of the year it appeared that the Press, in holding up horrified hands and prophesying a servile war had "overshot the mark."[3]

Soon the changing wind became a gale of public favour for the cause of emancipation, nor was this lessened—rather increased—by Jefferson Davis' proclamation of December 23, 1862, in which he declared that Lincoln had approved "of the effort to excite a servile insurrection," and that therefore it was now ordered "all negro slaves captured in arms be at once delivered over to the executive authorities of the respective States to which they belong, to be dealt with according to the laws of said State." This by state laws meant death to the slave fighting for his freedom, even as a regular soldier in the Northern armies, and gave a good handle for accusations of Southern ferocity.[4]

Official opinion was not readily altered, Lyons writing in December that the promised January proclamation might still mean servile war. He hoped that neither Lincoln's proclamation nor Davis' threat of retaliation would be

[1] Rogers, *Speeches by John Bright*, I, pp. 216 ff.

[2] *Liberator*, Nov. 28, 1862, reports a meeting at Leigh, Oct. 27, expressing sympathy with the North. At Sheffield, Dec. 31, 1862, an amended resolution calling for recognition of the South was voted down and the original pro-Northern resolutions passed. There were speakers on both sides. *Liberator*, Jan. 23, 1863.

[3] Motley, *Correspondence*, II, p. 113. J. S. Mill to Motley, Jan. 26, 1863.

[4] Richardson, I, p. 273. Davis' order applied also to all Northern white officers commanding negro troops. It proved an idle threat.

carried into effect.[1] Russell regarded the January 1 proclamation as "a measure of war of a very questionable kind."[2]

But the British anti-slavery public, now recovered from its fears of an "abolition war" was of another temper. Beginning with the last week of December, 1862, and increasing in volume in each succeeding month, there took place meeting after meeting at which strong resolutions were passed enthusiastically endorsing the issue of the emancipation proclamation and pledging sympathy to the cause of the North. The *Liberator* from week to week, listed and commented on these public meetings, noting fifty-six held between December 30, 1862, and March 20, 1863. The American Minister reported even more, many of which sent to him engraved resolutions or presented them in person through selected delegations. The resolutions were much of the type of that adopted at Sheffield, January 10:

> "*Resolved:* that this meeting being convinced that slavery is the cause of the tremendous struggle now going on in the American States, and that the object of the leaders of the rebellion is the perpetuation of the unchristian and inhuman system of chattel slavery, earnestly prays that the rebellion may be crushed, and its wicked object defeated, and that the Federal Government may be strengthened to pursue its emancipation policy till not a slave be left on the American soil." [3]

[1] Russell Papers. Lyons to Russell, Dec. 30, 1862. And again, Jan. 2, 1863. "If it do not succeed in raising a servile insurrection, it will be a very unsuccessful political move for its authors." Stoeckl in conference with Seward, expressed regret that the emancipation proclamation had been issued, since it set up a further barrier to the reconciliation of North and South—always the hope of Russia. Seward replied that in executing the proclamation, there would be, no doubt, many modifications. Stoeckl answered that then the proclamation must be regarded as but a futile menace. (Russian Archives. Stoeckl to F. O., Nov. 19–Dec. 1, 1862, No. 2171.)

[2] Rhodes, IV, p. 357.

[3] *U.S. Diplomatic Correspondence*, 1863, Pt. I, p. 55. Adams to Seward, Jan. 16, 1863, transmitting this and other resolutions presented to him. Adams by March 20 had reported meetings which sent resolutions to him, from Sheffield, Chesterfield, Derbyshire, Crophills, Salford, Cobham,

Adams quoted the *Times* as referring to these meetings as made up of "nobodies." Adams commented:

> "They do not indeed belong to the high and noble class, but they are just those nobodies who formerly forced their most exalted countrymen to denounce the prosecution of the Slave Trade by the commercial adventurers at Liverpool and Bristol, and who at a later period overcame all their resistance to the complete emancipation of the negro slaves in the British dependencies. If they become once fully aroused to a sense of the importance of this struggle as a purely moral question, I feel safe in saying there will be an end of all effective sympathy in Great Britain with the rebellion."[1]

Adams had no doubt "that these manifestations are the genuine expression of the feelings of the religious dissenting and of the working classes," and was confident the Government would be much influenced by them.[2] The newspapers, though still editorially unfavourable to the emancipation proclamation, accepted and printed communications with increasing frequency in which were expressed the same ideas as in the public meetings. This was even more noticeable in the provincial press. Samuel A. Goddard, a merchant of Birmingham, was a prolific letter writer to the *Birmingham Post*, consistently upholding the Northern cause and he now reiterated the phrase, "Mr. Lincoln's cause is just and holy."[3] In answer to Southern sneers at the failure of the proclamation to touch slavery in the border states, Goddard made clear the fact that

Ersham, Weybridge, Bradford, Stroud, Bristol, Glasgow, Liverpool, South London, Bath, Leeds, Bromley, Middleton, Edinburgh, Birmingham, Aberdare, Oldham, Merthyr Tydfil, Paisley, Carlisle, Bury, Manchester, Pendleton, Bolton, Newcastle-on-Tyne, Huddersfield, Ashford, Ashton-under-Lyne, Mossley, Southampton, Newark, and York. See also Rhodes, IV, 348-58, for résumé of meetings and opinions expressed.

[1] State Department, Eng., Vol. 81, No. 300. Adams to Seward, Jan. 22, 1863.

[2] *U.S. Diplomatic Correspondence*, 1863, Pt. I, p. 100. Adams to Seward, Feb. 5, 1863.

[3] Goddard, *Letters on the American Rebellion*, p. 287. Goddard contributed seventy letters before 1863.

Lincoln had no constitutional "right" to apply his edict to states not in rebellion.[1] On the public platform no one equalled the old anti-slavery orator, George Thompson, in the number of meetings attended and addresses made. In less than a month he had spoken twenty-one times and often in places where opposition was in evidence. Everywhere Thompson found an aroused and encouraged anti-slavery feeling, now strongly for the North.[2]

Eight years earlier five hundred thousand English women had united in an address to America on behalf of the slaves. Harriet Beecher Stowe now replied to this and asked the renewed sympathy of her English sisters. A largely signed "round robin" letter assured her that English women were still the foes of slavery and were indignantly united against suggestions of British recognition of the South.[3] Working class Britain was making its voice heard in support of the North. To those of Manchester, Lincoln, on January 19, 1863, addressed a special letter of thanks for their earnest support while undergoing personal hardships resulting from the disruption of industry caused by the war. "I cannot" he wrote, "but regard your decisive utterances upon the question [of human slavery] as an instance of sublime Christian heroism which has not been surpassed in any age or in any country."[4] Nonconformist England now came vigorously to the support of the North. Spurgeon, in London, made his great congregation pray with him: "God bless and strengthen

[1] *Ibid.*, p. 307. Letter to *Daily Gazette*, May 2, 1863.

[2] *The Liberator*, Feb. 27, 1863. At Bristol the opposition element introduced a resolution expressing abhorrence of slavery and the hope that the war in America might end in total emancipation, but adding that "at the same time [this meeting] cannot but regard the policy of President Lincoln in relation to slavery, as partial, insincere, inhuman, revengeful and altogether opposed to those high and noble principles of State policy which alone should guide the counsels of a great people." The resolution was voted down, and one passed applauding Lincoln. The proposer of the resolution was also compelled to apologize for slurring remarks on Thompson.

[3] *Atlantic Monthly*, XI, p. 525.

[4] Lincoln, *Complete Works*, II, p. 302.

the North; give victory to their arms."[1] Further and more general expression of Nonconformist church sympathy came as a result of a letter received February 12, 1863, from a number of French pastors and laymen, urging all the Evangelical churches to unite in an address to Lincoln. The London and Manchester Emancipation Societies combined in drawing up a document for signature by pastors and this was presented for adoption at a meeting in Manchester on June 3, 1863. In final form it was "An Address to Ministers and Pastors of All Christian Denominations throughout the States of America." There was a "noisy opposition" but the address was carried by a large majority and two representatives, Massie and Roylance, were selected to bear the message in person to the brethren across the ocean.[2] Discussion arose over the Biblical sanction of slavery. In the *Times* appeared an editorial pleading this sanction and arguing the *duty* of slaves to refuse liberty.[3] Goldwin Smith, Regius Professor of Modern History at Oxford, replied in a pamphlet, "Does the Bible sanction American Slavery?"[4] His position and his skill in presentation made him a valuable ally to the North.

Thus British anti-slavery circles, previously on the defensive, became aroused and enthusiastic when Lincoln's January 1, 1863, proclamation made good his pledge of the previous September: other elements of opinion, and in all classes, were strengthened in like measure, and everywhere the first expression of fear of a servile insurrection largely disappeared. In truth, pro-Northern England went to such

[1] Trevelyan, *John Bright*, p. 306. Also Rhodes, IV, p. 351.

[2] Massie, *America: the Origin of Her Present Conflict*, London, 1864. This action and the tour of the two delegates in America did much to soothe wounded feelings which had been excited by a correspondence in 1862-3 between English, French and American branches of similar church organizations. See *New Englander*, April, 1863, p. 288.

[3] Jan. 6, 1863.

[4] Published Oxford and London, 1863.

lengths in its support of emancipation as to astound and alarm the *Saturday Review*, which called these demonstrations a "carnival of cant."[1] More neutral minds were perplexed over the practical difficulties and might well agree with Schleiden who wrote in January, 1863, quoting Machiavelli: "What is more difficult, to make free men slaves, or slaves free?"[2] But by the end of January the popular approval of emancipation was in full swing. On the evening of the twenty-ninth there took place in London at Exeter Hall, a great mass meeting unprecedented in attendance and enthusiasm. The meeting had been advertised for seven o'clock, but long before the hour arrived the hall was jammed and the corridors filled. A second meeting was promptly organized for the lower hall, but even so the people seeking admission crowded Exeter Street and seriously impeded traffic in the Strand. Outdoor meetings listened to reports of what was going on in the Hall and cheered the speakers. The main address was made by the Rev. Newman Hall, of Surrey Chapel. A few Southern sympathizers who attempted to heckle the speakers were quickly shouted down.[3]

The "carnival of cant," as the *Saturday Review* termed it, was truly a popular demonstration, stirred by anti-slavery leaders, but supported by the working and non-enfranchised classes. Its first effect was to restore courage and confidence to Northern supporters in the upper classes. Bright had welcomed emancipation, yet with some mis-

[1] Rhodes, IV, p. 355.

[2] Lutz, *Notes*. Schleiden's despatch, No. 1, 1863. German opinion on the Civil War was divided; Liberal Germany sympathized strongly with the North; while the aristocratic and the landowning class stood for the South. The historian Karl Friedrich Neumann wrote a three-volume history of the United States wholly lacking in historical impartiality and strongly condemnatory of the South. (Geschichte der Vereinigten Staaten, Berlin, 1863-66.) This work had much influence on German public opinion. (Lutz, *Notes*.)

[3] *Liberator*, Feb. 20, 1863. Letter of J. P. Jewett to W. L. Garrison, Jan. 30, 1863. "The few oligarchs in England who may still sympathize with slavery and the Southern rebels, will be rendered absolutely powerless by these grand and powerful uprisings of THE PEOPLE."

givings. He now joined in the movement and in a speech at Rochdale, February 3, on "Slavery and Secession," gave full approval of Lincoln's efforts.

In 1862, shortly after the appearance of Spence's *American Union*, which had been greeted with great interest in England and had influenced largely upper-class attitude in favour of the South, Cairnes had published his pamphlet, "Slave Power." This was a reasoned analysis of the basis of slavery and a direct challenge to the thesis of Spence.[1] England's "unnatural infatuation" for a slave power, Cairnes prophesied, would be short-lived. His pamphlet began to be read with more conviction by that class which until now had been coldly neutral and which wished a more reassured faith in the Northern cause than that stirred by the emotional reception given the emancipation proclamation. Yet at bottom it was emancipation that brought this reasoning public to seek in such works as that of Cairnes a logical basis for a change of heart. Even in official circles, utterances previously made in private correspondence, or in governmental conversations only, were now ventured in public by friends of the North. On April 1, 1863, at a banquet given to Palmerston in Edinburgh, the Duke of Argyll ventured to answer a reference made by Palmerston in a speech of the evening previous in which had been depicted the horrors of Civil War, by asking if Scotland were historically in a position to object to civil wars having high moral purpose. "I, for one," Argyll said, "have not learned to be ashamed of that ancient combination of the Bible and the sword. Let it be enough for us to pray and hope that the contest, whenever it may be brought to an end, shall bring with it that great blessing to the white race which shall consist in the final freedom of the black."[2]

[1] Duffus, *English Opinion*, p. 51.
[2] Argyll, *Autobiography*, II, pp. 196-7.

The public meetings in England raised high the hope in America that governmental England would show some evidence of a more friendly attitude. Lincoln himself drafted a resolution embodying the ideas he thought it would be wise for the public meetings to adopt. It read:

> "Whereas, while *heretofore* States, and Nations, have tolerated slavery, *recently*, for the first time in the world, an attempt has been made to construct a new Nation, upon the basis of, and with the primary, and fundamental object to maintain, enlarge, and perpetuate human slavery, therefore,
>
> *Resolved:* that no such embryo State should ever be recognized by, or admitted into, the family of Christian and civilized nations; and that all Christian and civilized men everywhere should, by all lawful means, resist to the utmost, such recognition or admission." [1]

This American hope much disturbed Lyons. On his return to Washington, in November, 1862, he had regarded the emancipation proclamation as a political manœuvre purely and an unsuccessful one. The administration he thought was losing ground and the people tired of the war. This was the burden of his private letters to Russell up to March, 1863, but does not appear in his official despatches in which there was nothing to give offence to Northern statesmen. But in March, Lyons began to doubt the correctness of these judgments. He notes a renewed Northern enthusiasm leading to the conferring of extreme powers—the so-called "dictatorship measures"—upon Lincoln. Wise as Lyons ordinarily was he was bound by the social and educational traditions of his class, and had at first not the slightest conception of the force or effect of emancipation upon the public in middle-class England. He feared an American reaction against England when it was under-

[1] Trevelyan, *John Bright*. Facsimile, opp. p. 303. Copy sent by Sumner to Bright, April, 1863.

stood that popular meetings would have no influence on the British Government.

> "Mr. Seward and the whole Party calculate immensely on the effects of the anti-slavery meetings in England, and seem to fancy that public feeling in England is coming so completely round to the North that the Government will be obliged to favour the North in all ways, even if it be disinclined to do so. This notion is unlucky, as it makes those who hold it, unreasonable and presumptuous in dealing with us." [1]

. . . . .

Lincoln's plan of emancipation and his first proclamation had little relation to American foreign policy. Seward's attitude toward emancipation was that the *threat* of it and of a possible servile war might be useful in deterring foreign nations, especially Great Britain, from intervening. But he objected to the carrying of emancipation into effect because he feared it would *induce* intervention. Servile war, in part by Seward's own efforts, in part because of earlier British newspaper speculations, was strongly associated with emancipation, in the English view. Hence the Government received the September, 1862, proclamation with disfavour, the press with contempt, and the public with apprehension—even the friends of the North. But no servile war ensued. In January, 1863, Lincoln kept his promise of wide emancipation and the North stood committed to a high moral object. A great wave of relief and exultation

[1] Russell Papers. Lyons to Russell, March 10, 1863. Lyons was slow to favour the emancipation proclamation. The first favourable mention I have found was on July 26, 1864. (Russell Papers. To Russell.) In this view his diplomatic colleagues coincided. Stoeckl, in December, 1863, wrote that slavery was dead in the Central and Border States, and that even in the South its form must be altered if it survived. (Russian Archives, Stoeckl to F. O., Nov. 22–Dec. 4, 1863, No. 3358.) But immediately after the second proclamation of January, 1863, Stoeckl could see no possible good in such measures. If they had been made of universal application it would have been a "great triumph for the principle of individual liberty," but as issued they could only mean "the hope of stirring a servile war in the South." (*Ibid.*, Dec. 24, 1863-Jan. 5, 1864, No. 70.)

swept over anti-slavery England, but did not so quickly extend to governmental circles. It was largely that England which was as yet without direct influence on Parliament which so exulted and now upheld the North. Could this England of the people affect governmental policy and influence its action toward America? Lyons correctly interpreted the North and Seward as now more inclined to press the British Government on points previously glossed over, and in the same month in which Lyons wrote this opinion there was coming to a head a controversy over Britain's duty as a neutral, which both during the war and afterwards long seemed to Americans a serious and distinctly unfriendly breach of British neutrality. This was the building in British ports of Confederate naval vessels of war.

CHAPTER XIII

THE LAIRD RAMS

THE building in British ports of Confederate war vessels like the *Alabama* and the subsequent controversy and arbitration in relation thereto have been exhaustively studied and discussed from every aspect of legal responsibility, diplomatic relations, and principles of international law. There is no need and no purpose here to review in detail these matters. The purpose is, rather, to consider the development and effect at the time of their occurrence of the principal incidents related to Southern ship-building in British yards. The *intention* of the British Government is of greater importance in this study than the correctness of its action.

Yet it must first be understood that the whole question of a belligerent's right to procure ships of war or to build them in the ports of neutral nations was, in 1860, still lacking definite application in international law. There were general principles already established that the neutral must not do, nor permit its subjects to do, anything directly in aid of belligerents. The British Foreign Enlistment Act, notification of which had been given in May, 1861, forbade subjects to "be concerned in the equipping, furnishing, fitting out, or arming, of any ship or vessel, with intent or in order that such ship or vessel shall be employed in the service . . ." of a belligerent, and provided for punishment of individuals and forfeiture of vessels if this prohibition were disobeyed. But the Act also declared that such punishment, or seizure, would follow on due proof of the offence. Here was the weak point of the Act, for in effect if secrecy were maintained by offenders the proof was available only after the offence had been committed and one of the belligerents injured by the violation of the law. Over twenty years earlier the American Government, seeking to prevent its subjects from committing unneutral acts in connection with the Canadian rebellion of 1837, had realized the weakness of its neutrality laws as they then stood, and by a new law of March 10, 1838, hastily passed and therefore limited to two years' duration, in the expectation of a more perfect law, but intended as a clearer exposition of neutral duty, had given federal officials power to act and seize *on suspicion*, leaving the proof of guilt or innocence to be determined later. But the British interpretation of her own neutrality laws was that proof was required in advance of seizure—an interpretation wholly in line with the basic principle that a man was innocent until proved guilty, but fatal to that preservation of strict neutrality which Great Britain had so promptly asserted at the beginning of the Civil War.[1]

The South wholly lacking a navy or the means to create one, early conceived the idea of using neutral ports for

[1] In other respects, also, this question of belligerent ship-building and equipping in neutral ports was, in practice, vaguely defined. As late as 1843 in the then existing Texan war of independence against Mexico, the British Foreign Secretary, Aberdeen, had been all at sea. Mexico made a contract for two ships of war with the English firm of Lizardi & Company. The crews were to be recruited in England, the ships were to be commanded by British naval officers on leave, and the guns were to be purchased from firms customarily supplying the British Navy. Aberdeen advised the Admiralty to give the necessary authority to purchase guns. When Texas protested he at first seemed to think strict neutrality was secured if the same privileges were offered that country. Later he prohibited naval officers to go in command. One Mexican vessel, the *Guadaloupe*, left England with full equipment as originally planned; the other, the *Montezuma*, was forced to strip her equipment. But both vessels sailed under British naval officers for these were permitted to resign their commissions. They were later reinstated. In all this there was in part a temporary British policy to aid Mexico, but it is also clear that British governmental opinion was much in confusion as to neutral duty in the case of such ships. See my book, *British Interests and Activities in Texas*, Ch. IV.

the construction of war vessels. Advice secured from able British lawyers was to the effect that if care were taken to observe the strict letter of the Foreign Enlistment Act, by avoiding warlike equipment, a ship, even though her construction were such as to indicate that she was destined to become a ship of war, might be built by private parties in British yards. The three main points requiring careful observance by the South were concealment of government ownership and destination, no war equipment and no enlistment of crew in British waters.

The principal agent selected by the South to operate on these lines was Captain J. D. Bullock, who asserts in his book descriptive of his work that he never violated British neutrality law and that prevailing legal opinion in England supported him in this view.[1] In March, 1862, the steamer *Oreto* cleared from Liverpool with a declared destination of "Palermo, the Mediterranean, and Jamaica." She was not heard of until three months later when she was reported to be at Nassau completing her equipment as a Southern war vessel. In June, Adams notified Russell "that a new and still more powerful war-steamer was nearly ready for departure from the port of Liverpool on the same errand."[2] He protested that such ships violated the neutrality of Great Britain and demanded their stoppage and seizure. From June 23 to July 28, when this second ship, "No. 290" (later christened the *Alabama*) left Liverpool, Adams and the United States consul at Liverpool, Dudley, were busy in securing evidence and in renewing protests to the Government. To each protest Russell replied in but a few lines that the matter had been referred to the proper departments, and it was not until July 26, when there was received from Adams an opinion by an eminent Queen's

[1] Bullock, *Secret Service under the Confederacy*.

[2] Bernard, *Neutrality of Great Britain during the American Civil War*, pp. 338-9.

Counsel, Collier, that the affidavits submitted were conclusive against the "290," that Russell appears to have been seriously concerned. On July 28, the law officers of the Crown were asked for an immediate opinion, and on the thirty-first telegrams were sent to Liverpool and to other ports to stop and further examine the vessel. But the "290" was well away and outside of British waters.[1]

The *Alabama*, having received guns and munitions by a ship, the *Bahama*, sent out from England to that end, and having enlisted in the Confederate Navy most of the British crews of the two vessels, now entered upon a career of destruction of Northern commerce. She was not a privateer, as she was commonly called at the time, but a Government vessel of war specially intended to capture and destroy merchant ships. In short her true character, in terms of modern naval usage, was that of a "commerce destroyer." Under an able commander, Captain Semmes, she traversed all oceans, captured merchant ships and after taking coal and stores from them, sank or burnt the captures; for two years she evaded battle with Northern war vessels and spread so wide a fear that an almost wholesale transfer of the flag from American to British or other foreign register took place, in the mercantile marine. The career of the *Alabama* was followed with increasing anger and chagrin by the North; this, said the public, was a British ship, manned by a British crew, using British guns and ammunition, whose escape from Liverpool had been winked at by the British Government. What further evidence was necessary of bad faith in a professed strict neutrality?

Nor were American officials far behind the public in suspicion and anger. At the last moment it had appeared

[1] *Parliamentary Papers*, 1863, *Commons*, LXXII. "Correspondence respecting the 'Alabama.'" Also *ibid.*, "Correspondence between Commissioner of Customs and Custom House Authorities at Liverpool relating to the 'Alabama.'" The last-minute delay was due to the illness of a Crown adviser.

as if the Government were inclined to stop the "290." Was the hurried departure of the vessel due to a warning received from official sources? On November 21, Adams reported that Russell complained in an interview of remarks made privately by Bright, to the effect that warning had come from Russell himself, and "seemed to me a little as if he suspected that Mr. Bright had heard this from me."[1] Adams disavowed, and sincerely, any such imputation, but at the same time expressed to Russell his conviction that there must have been from some source a "leak" of the Government's intention.[2] The question of advance warning to Bullock, or to the Lairds who built the *Alabama*, was not one which was likely to be officially put forward in any case; the real issue was whether an offence to British neutrality law had been committed, whether it would be acknowledged as such, and still more important, whether repetitions of the offence would be permitted. The *Alabama*, even though she might, as the American assistant-secretary of the Navy wrote, be "giving us a sick turn,"[3] could not by herself greatly affect the issue of the war; but many *Alabamas* would be a serious matter. The belated governmental order to stop the vessel was no assurance for the future since in reply to Adams' protests after her escape, and to a prospective claim for damages, Russell replied that in fact the orders to stop had been given merely for the purpose of further investigation, and that

[1] State Department, Eng., Vol. 81, No. 264. Adams to Seward, Nov. 21, 1862.

[2] Selborne, in his *Memorials: Family and Personal*, II, p. 430, declared that in frequent official communication with all members of the Cabinet at the time, "I never heard a word fall from any one of them expressive of anything but regret that the orders for the detention of the *Alabama* were sent too late." Of quite different opinion is Brooks Adams, in his "The Seizure of the Laird Rams" (*Proceedings*, Mass. Hist. Soc., Vol. XLV, pp. 243-333). In 1865 his father, the American Minister, made a diary entry that he had been shown what purported to be a copy of a note from one V. Buckley to Caleb Huse, Southern agent in England, warning him of danger to his "protegé." "This Victor Buckley is a young clerk in the Foreign Office." (*Ibid.*, p. 260, *note.*)

[3] Fox, *Confidential Correspondence*, I, p. 165. Fox to Dupont, Nov. 7, 1862.

in strict law there had been no neglect of governmental duty.[1] If this were so similar precautions and secrecy would prohibit official interference in the issue from British ports of a whole fleet of Southern war-vessels. Russell might himself feel that a real offence to the North had taken place. He might write, "I confess the proceedings of that vessel [the *Alabama*] are enough to *rile* a more temperate nation, and I owe a grudge to the Liverpool people on that account,"[2] but this was of no value to the North if the governmental decision was against interference without complete and absolute proof.

It was therefore the concern of the North to find some means of bringing home to the British Ministry the enormity of the offence in American eyes and the serious danger to good relations if such offences were to be continued. An immediate downright threat of war would have been impolitic and would have stirred British pride to the point of resentment. Yet American pride was aroused also and it was required of Seward that he gain the Northern object and yet make no such threat as would involve the two nations in war—a result that would have marked the success of Southern secession. That Seward was able to find the way in which to do this is evidence of that fertility of imagination and gift in expedient which marked his whole career in the diplomacy of the Civil War.[3]

In that same month when Adams was beginning his protests on the "290," June, 1862, there had already been drawn the plans, and the contracts made with the Laird

[1] It is interesting that the opinion of many Continental writers on international law was immediately expressed in favour of the American and against the British contention. This was especially true of German opinion. (Lutz, *Notes*.)

[2] Lyons Papers. To Lyons, Dec. 20, 1862.

[3] I am aware that Seward's use of the "Privateering Bill," now to be recounted is largely a new interpretation of the play of diplomacy in regard to the question of Southern ship-building in England. Its significance became evident only when British correspondence was available; but that correspondence and a careful comparison of dates permits, and, as I think, requires a revised statement of the incident of the Laird Rams.

Brothers at Liverpool, for the building of two vessels far more dangerous than the *Alabama* to the Northern cause. These were the so-called Laird Rams. They were to be two hundred and thirty feet long, have a beam of forty feet, be armoured with four and one-half inch iron plate and be provided with a "piercer" at the prow, about seven feet long and of great strength. This "piercer" caused the ships to be spoken of as rams, and when the vessels were fully equipped it was expected the "piercer" would be three feet under the surface of the water. This was the distinguishing feature of the two ships; it was unusual construction, nearly impossible of use in an ordinary battle at sea, but highly dangerous to wooden ships maintaining a close blockade at some Southern port. While there was much newspaper comment in England that the vessels were "new *Alabamas*," and in America that they were "floating fortresses," suitable for attack upon defenceless Northern cities, their primary purpose was to break up the blockading squadrons.[1]

Shortly before the escape of the *Alabama* and at a time when there was but little hope the British Government would seize her and shortly after the news was received in Washington that still other vessels were planned for building in the Lairds' yards, a Bill was introduced in Congress authorizing the President to issue letters of marque and privateering. This was in July, 1862, and on the twelfth, Seward wrote to Adams of the proposed measure specifying that the purpose was to permit privateers to seek for and capture or destroy the *Alabama* or other vessels of a like type. He characterized this as a plan "to organize the

[1] Bullock dreamed also of ascending rivers and laying Northern cities under contribution. According to a statement made in 1898 by Captain Page, assigned to command the rams, no instructions as to their use had been given him by the Confederate Government, but his plans were solely to break the blockade with no thought of attacking Northern cities. (Rhodes, IV. 385, *note*.)

militia of the seas by issuing letters of marque and reprisal."[1] Neither here nor at any time did Seward or Adams allege in diplomatic correspondence any other purpose than the pursuit of *Alabamas*, nor is it presumable that in July, 1862, the construction plans of the Rams were sufficiently well known to the North to warrant a conclusion that the later purpose of the proposed privateering fleet was *at first* quite other than the alleged purpose. Probably the Bill introduced in July, 1862, was but a hasty reaction to the sailing of the *Oreto* (or *Florida*) and to the failure of early protests in the case of the *Alabama*. Moreover there had been an earlier newspaper agitation for an increase of naval power by the creation of a "militia of the seas," though with no clear conception of definite objects to be attained. This agitation was now renewed and reinforced and many public speeches made by a General Hiram Wallbridge, who had long advocated an organization of the mercantile marine as an asset in times of war.[2] But though introduced in the summer of 1862, the "privateering bill" was not seriously taken up until February, 1863.

In the Senate discussion of the Bill at the time of introduction, Senator Grimes, its sponsor, declared that the object was to encourage privateers to pursue British ships when, as was expected, they should "turn Confederate." Sumner objected that the true business of privateers was to destroy enemy commerce and that the South had no such *bona fide* commerce. Grimes agreed that this was his opinion also, but explained that the administration wanted

[1] *U.S. Diplomatic Correspondence*, 1862, p. 134.

[2] Wallbridge, *Addresses and Resolutions*. Pamphlet. New York, n.d. He began his agitation in 1856, and now received much popular applause. His pamphlet quotes in support many newspapers from June, 1862, to September, 1863. Wallbridge apparently thought himself better qualified than Welles to be Secretary of the Navy. Welles regarded his agitation as instigated by Seward to get Welles out of the Cabinet. Welles professes that the "Privateering Bill" slipped through Congress unknown to him and "surreptitiously" (Diary, I, 245-50), a statement difficult to accept in view of the Senate debates upon it.

the measure passed so that it might have in its hands a power to be used if the need arose. The general opinion of the Senate was opposed and the matter was permitted to lapse, but without definite action, so that it could at any time be called up again.[1] Six months later the progress of construction and the purpose of the rams at Liverpool were common knowledge. On January 7, 1863, the privateering bill again came before the Senate, was referred to the committee on naval affairs, reported out, and on February 17 was passed and sent to the House of Representatives, where on March 2 it was given a third reading and passed without debate.[2] In the Senate, Grimes now clearly stated that the Bill was needed because the Confederates "are now building in England a fleet of vessels designed to break our blockade of their coast," and that the privateers were to "assist in maintaining blockades." There was no thorough debate but a few perfunctory objections were raised to placing so great a power in the hands of the President, while Sumner alone appears as a consistent opponent arguing that the issue of privateers would be dangerous to the North since it might lead to an unwarranted interference with neutral commerce. No speaker outlined the exact method by which privateers were to be used in "maintaining blockades"; the bill was passed as an "administration measure."

Coincidently, but as yet unknown in Washington, the chagrin of Russell at the escape of the *Alabama* had somewhat lost its edge. At first he had been impressed with the necessity of amending the Foreign Enlistment Act so as to prevent similar offences and had gained the approval of the law officers of the Crown. Russell had even offered to take up with America an agreement by which both

[1] Cong. Globe, 37th Congress, 2nd Session, Pt. IV, pp. 3271, 3325 and 3336.

[2] *Ibid.*, 3rd Session, Pt. I, pp. 220, 393, and Part II, pp. 960, 1028, 1489.

countries were to amend their neutrality laws at the same moment. This was in December, 1862, but now on February 14, 1863, he wrote to Lyons that the project of amendment had been abandoned as the Cabinet saw no way of improving the law.[1] While this letter to Lyons was on its way to America, a letter from Seward was *en route*, explaining to Adams the meaning of the privateering bill.

> "The Senate has prepared a Bill which confers upon the President of the United States the power to grant letters of marque and reprisal in any war in which the country may at any time be engaged, and it is expected that the Bill will become a law. Lord Lyons suggests that the transaction may possibly be misapprehended abroad, if it come upon foreign powers suddenly and without any explanations. You will be at liberty to say that, as the Bill stands, the executive Government will be set at liberty to put the law in force in its discretion, and that thus far the proper policy in regard to the exercise of that discretion has not engaged the President's attention. I have had little hesitation in saying to Lord Lyons that if no extreme circumstances occur, there will be entire frankness on the part of the Government in communicating to him upon the subject, so far as to avoid any surprise on the part of friendly nations, whose commerce or navigation it might be feared would be incidentally and indirectly affected, if it shall be found expedient to put the Act in force against the insurgents of the United States."[2]

Certainly this was vague explanation, yet though the main object might be asserted "to put the act in force against the insurgents," the hint was given that the commerce of friendly neutrals might be "incidentally and indirectly affected." And so both Lyons and Seward understood the matter, for on February 24, Lyons reported a long conversation with Seward in which after pointing out the probable "bad effect" on Europe, Lyons received the

[1] Brooks Adams, "The Seizure of the Laird Rams." (Mass. Hist. Soc. *Proceedings*, Vol. XLV, pp. 265-6.)

[2] *U.S. Diplomatic Correspondence*, 1863, Pt. I, p. 116, Feb. 19, 1863.

reply that some remedy must be found for the fact that " the law did not appear to enable the British Government to prevent " the issue of Confederate " privateers."[1] On March 8, Seward followed this up by sending to Lyons an autograph letter:

> " I am receiving daily such representations from our seaports concerning the depredations on our commerce committed by the vessels built and practically fitted out in England, that I do most sincerely apprehend a new element is entering into the unhappy condition of affairs, which, with all the best dispositions of your Government and my own, cannot long be controlled to the preservation of peace.
>
> " If you think well of it, I should like that you should confidentially inform Earl Russell that the departure of more armed vessels under insurgent-rebel command from English ports is a thing to be deprecated above all things."

On March 9th, Lyons had a long talk with Seward about this, and it appears that Lincoln had seen the letter and approved it. Seward stated that the New York Chamber of Commerce had protested about the *Alabama*, declaring:

> " That no American merchant vessels would get freights—that even war with England was preferable to this—that in that case the maritime enterprise of the country would at least find a profitable employment in cruising against British trade."

Seward went on to show the necessity of letters of marque, and Lyons protested vigorously and implied that war must result.

> " Mr. Seward said that he was well aware of the inconvenience not to say the danger of issuing Letters of Marque: that he should be glad to delay doing so, or to escape the necessity altogether; but that really unless some intelligence came from England to allay the public exasperation, the measure would be unavoidable." [2]

[1] F. O., Am., Vol. 878, No. 180. Lyons to Russell.
[2] *Ibid.*, Vol. 879, No. 227. Lyons to Russell, March 10, 1863.

Lyons was much alarmed, writing that the feeling in the North must not be underestimated and pointing out that the newspapers were dwelling on the notion that under British interpretation of her duty as a neutral Mexico, if she had money, could build ships in British ports to cruise in destruction of French commerce, adding that "one might almost suppose" some rich American would give the funds to Mexico for the purpose and so seek to involve England in trouble with France.[1] Lyons had also been told by Seward in their conversation of March 9, that on that day an instruction had been sent to Adams to present to Russell the delicacy of the situation and to ask for some assurance that no further Southern vessels of war should escape from British ports. This instruction presented the situation in more diplomatic language but in no uncertain tone, yet still confined explanation of the privateering bill as required to prevent the "destruction of our national navigating interest, unless that calamity can be prevented by . . . the enforcement of the neutrality law of Great Britain. . . ."[2]

Lyons' reports reached Russell before Seward's instruction was read to him. Russell had already commented to Adams that American privateers would find no Confederate merchant ships and that if they interfered with neutral commerce the United States Government would be put in an awkward position. To this Adams replied that the privateers would seek and capture, if possible, vessels like the *Alabama*, but Russell asked Lyons to find out "whether in any case they [privateers] will be authorized to interfere with neutral commerce, and if in any case in what case, and to what extent."[3] Three days later, on March 26,

[1] *Ibid.*, No. 235. Lyons to Russell, March 13, 1863. Privately Lyons also emphasized American anger. (Russell Papers. To Russell, March 24, 1863.)

[2] *U.S. Diplomatic Correspondence*, 1863, Pt. I, p. 141. Seward to Adams, March 9, 1863.

[3] F. O., Am., Vol. 869, No. 147. Russell to Lyons, March 24, 1863.

Adams presented his instructions and these Russell regarded as " not unfriendly in tone," but in the long conversation that ensued the old result was reached that Adams declared Great Britain negligent in performance of neutral duty, while Russell professed eagerness to stop Southern ship-building if full evidence was "forthcoming." Adams concluded that " he had worked to the best of his power for peace, but it had become a most difficult task." Upon this Russell commented to Lyons, " Mr. Adams fully deserves the character of having always laboured for peace between our two Nations. Nor I trust will his efforts, and those of the two Governments fail of success."[1]

In these last days of March matters were in fact rapidly drawing to a head both in America and England. At Washington, from March seventh to the thirty-first, the question of issuing letters of marque and reprisal had been prominently before the Cabinet and even Welles who had opposed them was affected by unfavourable reports received from Adams as to the intentions of Great Britain. The final decision was to wait later news from England.[2] This was Seward's idea as he had not as yet received reports of the British reaction to his communications through Lyons and Adams. March 27 was the critical day of decision in London, as it was also the day upon which public and parliamentary opinion was most vigorously debated in regard to Great Britain's neutral duty. Preceding this other factors of influence were coming to the front. In the first days of March, Slidell, at Paris, had received semi-official assurances that if the South wished to build ships in French yards " we should be permitted to arm and equip them and proceed to sea."[3] This suggestion was permitted to percolate in England with the intention, no

[1] *Ibid.*, Vol. 869, No. 155. Russell to Lyons, March 27, 1863.
[2] Welles, *Diary*, I, pp. 245-50.
[3] Bigelow, *Retrospections*, I, 634, Slidell to Benjamin, March 4, 1863.

doubt, of strengthening Bullock's position there. In the winter of 1862-3, orders had been sent to the Russian Baltic fleet to cruise in western waters and there was first a suspicion in America, later a conviction, that the purpose of this cruise was distinctly friendly to the North—that the orders might even extend to actual naval aid in case war should arise with England and France. In March, 1863, this was but vague rumour, by midsummer it was a confident hope, by September-October, when Russian fleets had entered the harbours of New York and San Francisco, the rumour had become a conviction and the silence of Russian naval officers when banqueted and toasted was regarded as discreet confirmation. There was no truth in the rumour, but already in March curious surmises were being made even in England, as to Russian intentions, though there is no evidence that the Government was at all concerned. The truth was that the Russian fleet had been ordered to sea as a precaution against easy destruction in Baltic waters, in case the difficulties developing in relation to Poland should lead to war with France and England.[1]

In England, among the people rather than in governmental England, a feeling was beginning to manifest itself that the Ministry had been lax in regard to the *Alabama*, and as news of her successes was received this feeling was given voice. Liverpool, at first almost wholly on the side of the Lairds and of Southern ship-building, became doubtful

[1] For example of American contemporary belief and later "historical tradition," see Balch, *The Alabama Arbitration*, pp. 24-38. Also for a curious story that a large part of the price paid for Alaska was in reality a repayment of expenses incurred by Russia in sending her fleet to America, see *Letters of Franklin K. Lane*, p. 260. The facts as stated above are given by F. A. Golder, *The Russian Fleet and the Civil War* (*Am. Hist. Rev.*, July, 1915, pp. 801 *seq.*). The plan was to have the fleet attack enemy commerce. The idea of aid to the North was "born on American soil," and Russian officers naturally did nothing to contradict its spread. In one case, however, a Russian commander was ready to help the North. Rear-Admiral Papov with six vessels in the harbour of San Francisco was appealed to by excited citizens on rumours of the approach of the *Alabama* and gave orders to protect the city. He acted without instructions and was later reproved for the order by his superiors at home.

by the very ease with which the *Alabama* destroyed Northern ships. Liverpool merchants looked ahead and saw that their interests might, after all, be directly opposed to those of the ship-builders. Meetings were held and the matter discussed. In February, 1863, such a meeting at Plaistow, attended by the gentry of the neighbourhood, but chiefly by working men, especially by dock labourers and by men from the ship-building yards at Blackwall, resolved that "the Chairman be requested to write to the Prime Minister of our Queen, earnestly entreating him to put in force, with utmost vigilance, the law of England against such ships as the *Alabama*."[1] Such expressions were not as yet wide-spread, nor did the leading papers, up to April, indulge in much discussion, but British *doubt* was developing.[2]

Unquestionably, Russell himself was experiencing a renewed doubt as to Britain's neutral duty. On March 23, he made a speech in Parliament which Adams reported as "the most satisfactory of all the speeches he has made

[1] *The Liberator*, March 6, 1863.

[2] American opinion knew little of this change. An interesting, if somewhat irrational and irregular plan to thwart Southern ship-building operations, had been taken up by the United States Navy Department. This was to buy the Rams outright by the offer of such a price as, it was thought, would be so tempting to the Lairds as to make refusal unlikely. Two men, Forbes and Aspinwall, were sent to England with funds and much embarrassed Adams to whom they discreetly refrained from stating details, but yet permitted him to guess their object. The plan of buying ran wholly counter to Adams' diplomatic protests on England's duty in international law and the agents themselves soon saw the folly of it. Fox, Assistant Secretary of the Navy, wrote to Dupont, March 26, 1863: "The Confederate ironclads in England, I think, will be taken care of." (Correspondence, I, 196.) Thurlow Weed wrote to Bigelow, April 16, of the purpose of the visit of Forbes and Aspinwall. (Bigelow, *Retrospections*, I, 632.) Forbes reported as early as April 18 virtually against going on with the plan. "We must keep cool here, and prepare the way; we have put new fire into Mr. Dudley by furnishing *fuel*, and he is hard at it getting evidence. . . . My opinion *to-day* is that we can and shall stop by legal process and by the British Government the sailing of ironclads and other war-ships." (Forbes MS. To Fox.) That this was wholly a Navy Department plan and was disliked by State Department representatives is shown by Dudley's complaints (Forbes MS.). The whole incident has been adequately discussed by C. F. Adams, though without reference to the preceding citations, in his *Studies Military and Diplomatic*, Ch. IX. "An Historical Residuum," in effect a refutation of an article by Chittenden written in 1890, in which bad memory and misunderstanding played sad havoc with historical truth.

since I have been at this post."[1] On March 26, came the presentation by Adams of Seward's instruction of which Russell wrote to Lyons as made in no unfriendly tone and as a result of which Adams wrote: "The conclusion which I draw . . . is, that the Government is really better disposed to exertion, and feels itself better sustained for action by the popular sentiment than ever before."[2] Russell told Adams that he had received a note from Palmerston "expressing his approbation of every word" of his speech three days before. In a portion of the despatch to Seward, not printed in the Diplomatic Correspondence, Adams advised against the issue of privateers, writing, "In the present favourable state of popular mind, it scarcely seems advisable to run the risk of changing the current in Great Britain by the presentation of a new issue which might rally all national pride against us as was done in the *Trent* case."[3] That Russell was indeed thinking of definite action is foreshadowed by the advice he gave to Palmerston on March 27, as to the latter's language in the debate scheduled for that day on the Foreign Enlistment Act. Russell wrote, referring to the interview with Adams:

> "The only thing which Adams could think of when I asked him what he had to propose in reference to the *Alabama* was that the Government should declare their disapproval of the fitting out of such ships of war to prey on American commerce.
>
> "Now, as the fitting out and escape of the *Alabama* and *Oreto* was clearly an evasion of our law, I think you can have no difficulty in declaring this evening that the Government disapprove of all such attempts to elude our law with a view to assist one of the belligerents." [4]

[1] *U.S. Diplomatic Correspondence*, 1863, Pt. I, p. 157. To Seward, March 24, 1863.

[2] *Ibid.*, p. 160. To Seward, March 27, 1863.

[3] State Department, Eng., Vol. 82, No. 356. Adams to Seward, March 27, 1863.

[4] Palmerston MS. Russell to Palmerston, March 27, 1863.

But the tone of parliamentary debate did not bear out the hopeful view of the American Minister. It was, as Bright wrote to Sumner, " badly managed and told against us,"[1] and Bright himself participated in this " bad management." For over a year he had been advocating the cause of the North in public speeches and everywhere pointing out to unenfranchised England that the victory of the North was essential to democracy in all Europe. Always an orator of power he used freely vigorous language and nowhere more so than in a great public meeting of the Trades Unions of London in St. James' Hall, on March 26, the evening before the parliamentary debate. The purpose of this meeting was to bring public pressure on the Government in favour of the North, and the pith of Bright's speech was to contrast the democratic instincts of working men with the aristocratic inclinations of the Government.[2] Reviewing " aristocratic " attitude toward the Civil War, Bright said :

> " Privilege thinks it has a great interest in this contest, and every morning, with blatant voice, it comes into your streets and curses the American Republic. Privilege has beheld an afflicting spectacle for many years past. It has beheld thirty millions of men, happy and prosperous, without emperor, without king, without the surroundings of a court, without nobles, except such as are made by eminence in intellect and virtue, without State bishops and State priests.
>
> " ' Sole venders of the lore which works salvation,' without great armies and great navies, without great debt and without great taxes.
>
> . . . . . .
>
> " You wish the freedom of your country. You wish it for yourselves. . . . Do not then give the hand of fellowship to the worst foes of freedom that the world has ever seen. . . . You will not do this. I have faith in you. Impartial history

[1] Rhodes, IV, p. 369, *notes*, April 4, 1863. Bright was made very anxious as to Government intentions by this debate.

[2] This topic will be treated at length in Chapter XVIII. It is here cited merely in relation to its effect on the Government at the moment.

will tell that, when your statesmen were hostile or coldly neutral, when many of your rich men were corrupt, when your press—which ought to have instructed and defended—was mainly written to betray, the fate of a Continent and of its vast population being in peril, you clung to freedom with an unfailing trust that God in his infinite mercy will yet make it the heritage of all His children." [1]

The public meeting of March 26 was the most notable one in support of the North held throughout the whole course of the war, and it was also the most notable one as indicating the rising tide of popular demand for more democratic institutions. That it irritated the Government and gave a handle to Southern sympathizers in the parliamentary debate of March 27 is unquestioned. In addition, if that debate was intended to secure from the Government an intimation of future policy against Southern ship-building it was conducted on wrong lines for *immediate* effect—though friends of the North may have thought the method used was wise for *future* effect. This method was vigorous attack. Forster, leading in the debate,[2] called on Ministers to explain the "flagrant" violation of the Foreign Enlistment Act, and to offer some pledge for the future; he asserted that the Government should have been active on its own initiative in seeking evidence instead of waiting to be urged to enforce the law, and he even hinted at a certain degree of complicity in the escape of the *Alabama*. The Solicitor-General answered in a legal defence of the Government, complained of the offence of America in arousing its citizens against Great Britain upon unjustifiable grounds, but did not make so vigorous a reply as might, perhaps, have been expected. Still he stood firmly on the ground that the Government could not act without evidence to convict—in itself a statement that might well preclude

[1] Trevelyan, *John Bright*, 307-8.
[2] Hansard, 3rd Series, CLXX, 33-71, for entire debate.

interference with the Rams. Bright accused the Government of a "cold and unfriendly neutrality," and referred at length to the public meeting of the previous evening:

> "If you had last night looked in the faces of three thousand of the most intelligent of the artisan classes in London, as I did, and heard their cheers, and seen their sympathy for that country for which you appear to care so little, you would imagine that the more forbearing, the more generous, and the more just the conduct of the Government to the United States, the more it would recommend itself to the magnanimous feelings of the people of this country."

This assumption of direct opposition between Parliament and the people was not likely to win or to convince men, whether pro-Southern or not, who were opponents of the speaker's long-avowed advocacy of more democratic institutions in England. It is no wonder then that Laird, who had been castigated in the speeches of the evening, rising in defence of the conduct of his firm, should seek applause by declaring, "I would rather be handed down to posterity as the builder of a dozen *Alabamas* than as a man who applies himself deliberately to set class against class, and to cry up the institutions of another country which, when they come to be tested, are of no value whatever, and which reduce the very name of liberty to an utter absurdity." This utterance was greeted with great cheering—shouted not so much in approval of the *Alabama* as in approval of the speaker's defiance of Bright.

In short, the friends of the North, if they sought some immediate pledge by the Government, had gone the wrong way about to secure it. Vigour in attack was no way to secure a favourable response from Palmerston. Always a fighting politician in public it was inevitable that he should now fight back. Far from making the statement recommended to him by Russell, he concluded the debate by reasserting the correctness of governmental procedure in

William Edward Forster (1851)

the case of the *Alabama*, and himself with vigour accused Forster and Bright of speaking in such a way as to increase rather than allay American irritation. Yet a careful reading of the speeches of both the Solicitor-General and of Palmerston, shows that while vindicating the Government's conduct in the past, they were avoiding *any* pledge of whatever nature, for the future.

Adams was clearly disappointed and thought that the result of the debate was "rather to undo in the popular mind the effect of Lord Russell's speech than to confirm it."[1] He and his English advisers were very uneasy, not knowing whether to trust to Russell's intimations of more active governmental efforts, or to accept the conclusion that his advice had been rejected by Palmerston.[2] Possibly if less anxious and alarmed they would have read more clearly between the lines of parliamentary utterances and have understood that their failure to hurry the Government into public announcement of a new policy was no proof that old policy would be continued. Disappointed at the result in Parliament, they forgot that the real pressure on Government was coming from an American declaration of an intention to issue privateers unless something were done to satisfy that country. Certainly Russell was unmoved by the debate for on April 3 he wrote to Palmerston:

> "The conduct of the gentlemen who have contracted for the ironclads at Birkenhead is so very suspicious that I have thought it necessary to direct that they should be detained. The Attorney-General has been consulted and concurs in the measure, as one of policy, though not of strict law.
>
> "We shall thus test the law, and if we have to pay damages we have satisfied the opinion which prevails here

[1] *U.S. Diplomatic Correspondence*, 1863, Pt. I, p. 164. Adams to Seward, March 28, 1863.

[2] Rhodes, IV, 369-72.

as well as in America that this kind of neutral hostility should not be allowed to go on without some attempt to stop it." [1]

Two days later, on April 5, the *Alexandra*, a vessel being equipped to join the *Alabama* as a commerce destroyer, was seized on the ground that she was about to violate the Enlistment Act and a new policy, at least to make a test case in law, was thereby made public. In fact, on March 30, but three days after the debate of March 27, the case of the *Alexandra* had been taken up by Russell, referred to the law officers on March 31, and approved by them for seizure on April 4. [2] Public meetings were quickly organized in support of the Government's action, as that in Manchester on April 6, when six thousand people applauded the seizure of the *Alexandra*, demanded vigorous prosecution of the Lairds and others, and urged governmental activity to prevent any further ship-building for the South. [3]

On April 7, Russell wrote to Lyons:

> "The orders given to watch, and stop when evidence can be procured, vessels apparently intended for the Confederate service will, it is to be hoped, allay the strong feelings which have been raised in Northern America by the escape from justice of the *Oreto* and *Alabama*." [4]

It thus appears that orders had been issued to stop, on *evidence* to be sure, but on evidence of the vessels being "*apparently* intended" for the South. This was far from being the same thing as the previous assertion that conclusive evidence was required. What, then, was the basic consideration in Russell's mind leading to such a

[1] Palmerston MS.

[2] Bernard, p. 353. The case was heard in June, and the seizure held unwarranted. Appealed by the Government this decision was upheld by the Court of Exchequer in November. It was again appealed, and the Government defeated in the House of Lords in April, 1864.

[3] *Manchester Examiner and Times*, April 7, 1863. Goldwin Smith was one of the principal speakers. Letters were read from Bright, Forster, R. A. Taylor, and others.

[4] F. O., Am., Vol. 869, No. 183.

face-about on declared policy? Chagrin at the very evident failure of existing neutrality law to operate, recognition that there was just cause for the rising ill-will of the North, no doubt influenced him, but more powerful than these elements was the anxiety as to the real purpose and intent in application of the American "privateering" Bill. How did Russell, and Lyons, interpret that Bill and what complications did they foresee and fear?

As previously stated in this chapter, the privateering Bill had been introduced as an "administration measure" and for that reason passed without serious debate. In the Cabinet it was opposed by Welles, Secretary of the Navy, until he was overborne by the feeling that "something must be done" because vessels were building in England intended to destroy the blockade, The Rams under construction were clearly understood to have that purpose. If privateers were to offset the action of the Rams there must be some definite plan for their use. Seward and Adams repeatedly complained of British inaction yet in the same breath asserted that the privateers were intended to chase and destroy *Alabamas*--a plan so foolish, so it seemed to British diplomats, as to be impossible of acceptance as the full purpose of Seward. How, in short, *could* privateers make good an injury to blockade about to be done by the Rams? If added to the blockading squadrons on station off the Southern ports they would but become so much more fodder for the dreaded Rams. If sent to sea in pursuit of *Alabamas* the chances were that they would be the vanquished rather than the victors in battle. There was no Southern mercantile marine for them to attack and privateering against "enemy's commerce" was thus out of the question since there was no such commerce.

There remained but one reasonable supposition as to the intended use of privateers. If the Rams compelled the relaxation of the close blockade the only recourse of the

North would be to establish a "cruising squadron" blockade remote from the shores of the enemy. If conducted by government war-ships such a blockade was not in contravention to British interpretation of international law.[1] But the Northern navy, conducting a cruising squadron blockade was far too small to interfere seriously with neutral vessels bringing supplies to the Confederacy or carrying cotton from Southern ports. A "flood of privateers," scouring the ocean from pole to pole might, conceivably, still render effective that closing in of the South which was so important a weapon in the Northern war programme.

This was Russell's interpretation of the American plan and he saw in it a very great danger to British commerce and an inevitable ultimate clash leading to war. Such, no doubt, it was Seward's desire should be Russell's reaction, though never specifically explaining the exact purpose of the privateers. Moreover, nine-tenths of the actual blockade-running still going on was by British ships, and this being so it was to be presumed that "privateers" searching for possible blockade runners would commit all sorts of indignities and interferences with British merchant ships whether on a blockade-running trip or engaged in ordinary trade between non-belligerent ports.

Immediately on learning from Lyons details of the privateering bill, Russell had instructed the British Minister at Washington to raise objections though not formally making official protest, and had asked for explanation of the exact nature of the proposed activities of such vessels. Also he had prepared instructions to be issued by the

[1] "Historicus," in articles in the *Times*, was at this very moment, from December, 1862, on, discussing international law problems, and in one such article specifically defended the belligerent right to conduct a cruising squadron blockade. See *Historicus on International Law*, pp. 99-118. He stated the established principle to be that search and seizure could be used "not only" for "vessels actually intercepted in the attempt to enter the blockaded port, but those also which shall be elsewhere met with and shall be found to have been destined to such port, with knowledge of the fact and notice of the blockade." (*Ibid.*, p. 108.)

Admiralty to British naval commanders as to their duty of preventing unwarranted interference with legitimate British commerce by privateers.[1] The alteration of governmental policy as indicated in the arrest of the *Alexandra*, it might be hoped, would at least cause a suspension of the American plan, but assurances were strongly desired Presumably Russell knew that Adams as a result of their conversations, had recommended such suspension, but at Washington, Lyons, as yet uninformed of the *Alexandra* action, was still much alarmed. On April 13 he reported that Seward had read to him a despatch to Adams, relative to the ships building in England, indicating that this was "a last effort to avert the evils which the present state of things had made imminent."[2] Lyons had argued with Seward the inadvisabilty of sending such a despatch, since it was now known that Russell had "spoken in a satisfactory manner" about Confederate vessels, but Seward was insistent. Lyons believed there was real cause for anxiety, writing:

> "A good deal of allowance must be made for the evident design of the Government and indeed of the people to intimidate England, but still there can be little doubt that the exasperation has reached such a point as to constitute a serious danger. It is fully shared by many important members of the Cabinet—nor are the men in high office exempt from the overweening idea of the naval power of the United States, which reconciles the people to the notion of a war with England. Mr. Seward for a certain time fanned the flame in order to recover his lost popularity. He is now, I believe, seriously anxious to avoid going farther. But if strong measures against England were taken up as a Party cry by the Republicans, Mr. Seward would oppose very feeble resistance to them. If no military success be obtained within a short time, it may become a Party necessity to resort to some means of producing an excitement

[1] F. O., Am., Vol. 869, No. 158. Russell to Lyons, March 28, 1863.

[2] F. O., Am., Vol. 881, No. 309. To Russell.

in the country sufficient to enable the Government to enforce the Conscription Act, and to exercise the extra-legal powers conferred by the late Congress. To produce such an excitement the more ardent of the party would not hesitate to go, to the verge of a war with England. Nay there are not a few who already declare that if the South must be lost, the best mode to conceal the discomfiture of the party and of the nation, would be to go to war with England and attribute the loss of the South to English interference." [1]

On the same day Lyons wrote, privately:

"I would rather the quarrel came, if come it must, upon some better ground for us than this question of the ships fitted out for the Confederates. The great point to be gained in my opinion, would be to prevent the ships sailing, without leading the people here to think that they had gained their point by threats." [2]

So great was Lyons' alarm that the next day, April 14, he cipher-telegraphed Monck in Canada that trouble was brewing,[3] but soon his fears were somewhat allayed. On the seventeenth he could report that Seward's "strong" despatch to Adams was not intended for communication to Russell,[4] and on the twenty-fourth when presenting, under instructions, Russell's protest against the privateering plan he was pleased, if not surprised, to find that the "latest advices" from England and the news of the seizure of the *Alexandra*, had caused Seward to become very conciliatory. Lyons was assured that the plan "was for the present at rest."[5] Apparently Seward now felt more security than did Lyons as to future British action for three days later the British Minister wrote to Vice-Admiral Milne that an American issue of letters of marque would surely come if

[1] *Ibid.*, No. 310. To Russell, April 13, 1863.

[2] Russell Papers. To Russell, April 13, 1863.

[3] F. O., Am., Vol. 882, No. 324. Copy enclosed in Lyons to Russell, April 17, 1863.

[4] Russell Papers. To Russell.

[5] F. O., Am., Vol. 882, No. 341. Lyons to Russell, April 24, 1863.

England did not stop Southern ship-building, and he wrote in such a way as to indicate his own opinion that effective steps *must* be taken to prevent their escape.[1]

The whole tone and matter of Lyons' despatches to Russell show that he regarded the crisis of relations in regard to Southern ship-building in British yards as occurring in March-April, 1863. Seward became unusually friendly, even embarrassingly so, for in August he virtually forced Lyons to go on tour with him through the State of New York, thus making public demonstration of the good relations of the two Governments. This sweet harmony and mutual confidence is wholly contrary to the usual historical treatment of the Laird Rams incident, which neglects the threat of the privateering bill, regards American protests as steadily increasing in vigour, and concludes with the "threat of war" note by Adams to Russell just previous to the seizure of the Rams, in September. Previously, however, American historians have been able to use only American sources and have been at a loss to understand the privateering plan, since Seward never went beyond a vague generalization of its object in official utterances. It is the British reaction to that plan which reveals the real "threat" made and the actual crisis of the incident.

It follows therefore that the later story of the Rams requires less extended treatment than is customarily given to it. The correct understanding of this later story is the recognition that Great Britain had in April given, a pledge and performed an act which satisfied Seward and Adams that the Rams would not be permitted to escape. It was their duty nevertheless to be on guard against a British relaxation

[1] Lyons Papers, April 27, 1863. Lyons wrote: "The stories in the newspapers about an ultimatum having been sent to England are untrue. But it is true that it had been determined (or very nearly determined) to issue letters of marque, if the answers to the despatches sent were not satisfactory. It is very easy to see that if U.S. privateers were allowed to capture British merchant vessels on charges of breach of blockade or carrying contraband of war, the vexations would have soon become intolerable to our commerce, and a quarrel must have ensued."

of the promise made, and the delay, up to the very last moment, in seizing the Rams, caused American anxiety and ultimately created a doubt of the sincerity of British actions.

Public opinion in England was steadily increasing against Southern ship-building. On June 9, a memorial was sent to the Foreign Office by a group of ship-owners in Liverpool, suggesting an alteration in the Foreign Enlistment Act if this were needed to prevent the issue of Southern ships, and pointing out that the "present policy" of the Government would entail a serious danger to British commerce in the future if, when England herself became a belligerent, neutral ports could be used by the enemy to build commerce destroyers.[1] The memorial concluded that in any case it was a disgrace that British law should be so publicly infringed. To this, Hammond, under-secretary, gave the old answer that the law was adequate "provided proof can be obtained of any act done with the intent to violate it."[2] Evidently ship-owners, as distinguished from ship-builders, were now acutely alarmed. Meanwhile attention was fixed on the trial of the *Alexandra*, and on June 22, a decision was rendered against the Government, but was promptly appealed.

This decision made both Northern and Southern agents anxious and the latter took steps further to becloud the status of the Rams. Rumours were spread that the vessels were in fact intended for France, and when this was disproved that they were being built for the Viceroy of Egypt. This also proved to be untrue. Finally it was declared that the real owners were certain French merchants whose purpose in contracting for such clearly warlike vessels was left in mystery, but with the intimation that Egypt was to be

[1] *Parliamentary Papers*, 1863, *Commons*, LXXII. "Memorial from Shipowners of Liverpool on Foreign Enlistment Act."

[2] *Ibid.*

the ultimate purchaser. Captain Bullock had indeed made such a contract of sale to French merchants but with the proviso of resale to him, after delivery. On his part, Russell was seeking *proof* fully adequate to seizure, but this was difficult to obtain and such as was submitted was regarded by the law officers as inadequate. They reported that there was "no evidence capable of being presented to a court of justice." He informed Adams of this legal opinion at the moment when the latter, knowing the Rams to be nearing completion, and fearing that Russell was weakening in his earlier determination, began that series of diplomatic protests which very nearly approached a threat of war.

At Washington also anxiety was again aroused by the court's decision in the *Alexandra* case, and shortly after the great Northern victories at Vicksburg and Gettysburg, Seward wrote a despatch to Adams, July 11, which has been interpreted as a definite threat of war. In substance Seward wrote that he still felt confident the Government of Great Britain would find a way to nullify the *Alexandra* decision, but renewed, in case this did not prove true, his assertion of Northern intention to issue letters of marque, adding a phrase about the right to "pursue" Southern vessels even into neutral ports.[1] But there are two considerations in respect to this despatch that largely negative the belligerent intent attributed to it: Seward did not read or communicate it to Lyons, as was his wont when anything serious was in mind; and he did not instruct Adams to communicate it to Russell. The latter never heard of it until the publication, in 1864, of the United States diplomatic correspondence.[2]

[1] *U.S. Diplomatic Correspondence*, 1863, Pt. I, pp. 308-10.

[2] The despatch taken in its entirety save for a few vigorous sentences quite typical of Seward's phrase-making, is not at all warlike. Bancroft, II, 385 *seq.*, makes Seward increasingly anxious from March to September, and concludes with a truly warlike despatch to Adams, September 5. This last was the result of Adams' misgivings reported in mid-August, and it is not until these were received (in my interpretation) that Seward

In London, on July 11, Adams began to present to Russell evidence secured by Consul Dudley at Liverpool, relative to the Rams and to urge their immediate seizure. Adams here but performed his duty and was in fact acting in accordance with Russell's own request.[1] On July 16 he reported to Seward that the Roebuck motion for recognition of the South[2] had died ingloriously, but expressed a renewal of anxiety because of the slowness of the government; if the Rams were to escape, Adams wrote to Russell, on July 11, Britain would herself become a participant in the war.[3] Further affidavits were sent to Russell on August 14, and on September 3, having heard from Russell that the Government was legally advised "they cannot interfere in any way with these vessels," Adams sent still more affidavits and expressed his regret that his previous notes had not sufficiently emphasized the grave nature of the crisis pending between the United States and Great Britain. To this Russell replied that the matter was "under serious and anxious consideration," to which, on September 5, in a long communication, Adams wrote that if the Rams escaped: "It would be superfluous in me to point out to your Lordship that this is war."

The phrase was carefully chosen to permit a denial of a threat of war on the explanation that Great Britain would herself be participating in the war. There is no question that at the moment Adams thought Russell's "change of policy" of April was now thrown overboard, but the fact was that on September 1, Russell had already

really began to fear the "pledge" made in April would not be carried out. Adams himself, in 1864, read to Russell a communication from Seward denying that his July 11 despatch was intended as a threat or as in any sense unfriendly to Great Britain. (F. O., Am., Vol. 939, No. 159. Russell to Lyons, April 3, 1864.)

[1] *Parliamentary Papers*, 1864, *Commons*, LXII. "Correspondence respecting iron-clad vessels building at Birkenhead."

[2] See next chapter.

[3] State Department, Eng., Vol. 83, No. 452, and No. 453 with enclosure. Adams to Seward, July 16, 1863.

given directions to take steps for the detention of the Rams and that on September 3, positive instructions were given to that effect,[1] though not carried out until some days later. There had been no alteration in the " new policy " of April; the whole point of the delay was governmental anxiety to secure evidence sufficient to convict and thus to avoid attack for acting in contradiction to those principles which had been declared to be the compelling principles of non-interference in the case of the *Alabama*. But so perfect were the arrangements of Captain Bullock that complete evidence was not procurable and Russell was forced, finally, to act without it.[2]

It would appear from a letter written by Russell to Palmerston, on September 3, the day on which he gave the order to stop, that no Cabinet approval for this step had yet formally been given, since Russell notified Palmerston of his purpose and asked the latter, if he disapproved, to call a Cabinet at once.[3] The *plan* to stop the Rams must have long been understood for Palmerston called no Cabinet. Moreover it is to be presumed that he was preparing the public for the seizure, for on this same September 3, the *Times*, in a long editorial, argued that the law as it stood (or was interpreted), was not in harmony with true neutrality, and pointed out future dangers to British commerce, as had the Liverpool ship-owners. Delane of the *Times* was at this period especially close to Palmerston, and it is at least inferential that the editorial was an advance notice of governmental intention to apply a policy known in intimate circles to have been for some time matured. Four days

[1] Rhodes, IV, 381.

[2] Many of these details were unknown at the time so that on the face of the documents then available, and for long afterwards, there appeared ground for believing that Adams' final protests of September 3 and 5 had forced Russell to yield. Dudley, as late as 1893, thought that " at the crisis " in September, Palmerston, in the absence of Russell, had given the orders to stop the rams. (In *Penn. Magazine of History*, Vol. 17, pp. 34-54. " Diplomatic Relations with England during the Late War.")

[3] Rhodes, IV, p. 382.

later, while governmental action was still unknown to the public another editorial advocated seizure of the Rams.[1] Russell had acted under the fear that one of the Rams might slip away as had the *Alabama* ; he had sent orders to stop and investigate, but he delayed final seizure in the hope that better evidence might yet be secured, conducting a rapid exchange of letters with Lairds (the builders), seeking to get admissions from them. It was only on September 9 that Lairds was officially ordered not to send the vessels on a " trial trip," and it was not until September 16 that public announcement was made of the Government's action.[2]

Russell has been regarded as careless and thoughtless in that it was not until September 8 he relieved Adams' mind by assuring him the Rams would be seized, even though three days before, on September 5, this information had been sent to Washington. The explanation is Russell's eager search for evidence to *convict*, and his correspondence with Lairds which did not come to a head until the eighth, when the builders refused to give information. To the builders Russell was writing as if a governmental decision had not yet been reached. He could take no chance of a " leak " through the American Minister. Once informed, Adams was well satisfied though his immediate reaction was to criticize, not Russell, but the general " timidity and vacillation " of the law officers of the Crown.[3] Two days later, having learned from Russell himself just what was taking place, Adams described the " firm stand " taken by the Foreign Secretary, noted the general approval by the

[1] The *Times*, Sept. 7, 1863.

[2] *Ibid*. Editorial, Sept. 16, 1863. The Governmental correspondence with Lairds was demanded by a motion in Parliament, Feb. 23, 1864, but the Government was supported in refusing it. A printed copy of this correspondence, issued privately, was placed in Adams' hands by persons unnamed and sent to Seward on March 29, 1864. Seward thereupon had this printed in the *Diplomatic Correspondence*, 1864-5, Pt. I, No. 633.

[3] State Department, Eng., Vol. 84, No. 492. Adams to Seward, Sept. 8, 1863.

public press and expressed the opinion that there was now a better prospect of being able to preserve friendly relations with England than at any time since his arrival in London.[1] Across the water British officials were delighted with the seizure of the Rams. Monck in Canada expressed his approval.[2] Lyons reported a "great improvement" in the feeling toward England and that Seward especially was highly pleased with Russell's expressions, conveyed privately, of esteem for Seward together with the hope that he would remain in office.[3]

The actual governmental seizure of the Rams did not occur until mid-October, though they had been placed under official surveillance on September 9. Both sides were jockeying for position in the expected legal battle when the case should be taken up by the courts.[4] At first Russell even thought of making official protest to Mason in London and a draft of such protest was prepared, approved by the Law Officers and subsequently revised by Palmerston,

[1] *U.S. Diplomatic Correspondence*, 1863, Pt. I, p. 370. To Seward, Sept. 10, 1863. Adams, looking at the whole matter of the Rams and the alleged "threat of war" of Sept. 5, from the point of view of his own anxiety at the time, was naturally inclined to magnify the effects of his own efforts and to regard the *crisis* as occurring in September. His notes to Russell and his diary records were early the main basis of historical treatment. Rhodes, IV, 381-84, has disproved the accusation of Russell's yielding to a threat. Brooks Adams (Mass. Hist. Soc. *Proceedings*, Vol. XLV, p. 293, *seq.*) ignores Rhodes, harks back to the old argument and amplifies it with much new and interesting citation, but not to conviction. My interpretation is that the real crisis of Governmental decision to act came in April, and that events in September were but final applications of that decision.

[2] Russell Papers. Monck to Stuart, Sept. 26, 1863. Copy in Stuart to Russell, Oct. 6, 1863.

[3] *Ibid.* Lyons to Russell, Oct. 16, 1863.

[4] Hammond wrote to Lyons, Oct. 17: "You will learn by the papers that we have at last seized the Iron Clads. Whether we shall be able to bring home to them legally that they were Confederate property is another matter. I think we can, but at all events no moral doubt can be entertained of the fact, and, therefore, we are under no anxiety whether as to the public or Parliamentary view of our proceeding. They would have played the devil with the American ships, for they are most formidable ships. I suppose the Yankees will sleep more comfortably in consequence." (Lyons Papers.) The Foreign Office thought that it had thwarted plans to seize violently the vessels and get them to sea. (F. O., Am., Vol. 930. Inglefield to Grey, Oct. 25, and Romaine to Hammond, Oct. 26, 1863.).

but finally was not sent.[1] Possibly it was thought that such a communication to Mason approached too nearly a recognition of him in his desired official capacity, for in December the protest ultimately directed to be made through Consul-General Crawford at Havana, instructed him to go to Richmond and after stating very plainly that he was in no way recognizing the Confederacy to present the following:

> " It appears from various correspondence the authenticity of which cannot be doubted, that the Confederate Government having no good ports free from the blockade of the Federals have conceived the design of using the ports of the United Kingdom for the purpose of constructing ships of war to be equipped and armed to serve as cruisers against the commerce of the United States of America, a State with which Her Majesty is at peace. . . ."
>
> " These acts are inconsistent with the respect and comity which ought to be shewn by a belligerent towards a Neutral Power.
>
> "Her Majesty has declared her Neutrality and means strictly to observe it.
>
> "You will therefore call upon Mr. Benjamin to induce his Government to forbear from all acts tending to affect injuriously Her Majesty's position." [2]

To carry out this instruction there was required permission for Crawford to pass through the blockade but Seward refused this when Lyons made the request.[3]

Not everyone in Britain, however, approved the Government's course in seizing the Rams. Legal opinion especially was very generally against the act. Adams now pressed either for an alteration of the British law or for a convention

[1] F. O., Am., Vol. 929. Marked " September, 1863." The draft summarized the activities of Confederate ship-building and threatened Southern agents in England with " the penalities of the law. . . ."

[2] F. O., Am., Vol. 932, No. 1. F. O. to Consul-General Crawford, Dec. 16, 1863. The South, on October 7, 1863, had already " expelled " the British consuls. Crawford was to protest against this also. (*Ibid.*, No. 4.)

[3] Bonham. *British Consuls in the South*, p. 254. (Columbia Univ. Studies, Vol. 43.)

with America establishing mutual similar interpretation of neutral duty. Russell replied that "until the trials of the *Alexandra* and the steam rams had taken place, we could hardly be said to know what our law was, and therefore not tell whether it required alteration. I said, however, that he might assure Mr. Seward that the wish and intention of Government were to make our neutrality an honest and bona-fide one."[1] But save from extreme and avowed Southern sympathizers criticism of the Government was directed less to the stoppage of the Rams than to attacks of a political character, attempting to depict the weakness of the Foreign Minister and his humiliation of Great Britain in having "yielded to American threats." Thus, February 11, 1864, after the reassembling of Parliament, a party attack was made on Russell and the Government by Derby in the House of Lords. Derby approved the stopping of the Rams but sought to prove that the Government had dishonoured England by failing to act of its own volition until threatened by America. He cited Seward's despatch of July 11 with much unction, that despatch now having appeared in the printed American diplomatic correspondence with no indication that it was not an instruction at once communicated to Russell. The attack fell flat for Russell simply replied that Adams had never presented such an instruction. This forced Derby to seek other ground and on February 15 he returned to the matter, now seeking to show by the dates of various documents that "at the last moment" Adams made a threat of war and Russell had yielded. Again Russell's reply was brief and to the effect that orders to stop the Rams had been given before the communications from Adams were received. Finally, on February 23, a motion in the Commons called for all correspondence with Adams and with Lairds. The

[1] Lyons Papers. Russell to Lyons, Dec. 5, 1863. Bullock, *Secret Service*, declares the British Government to have been neutral but with strong leaning toward the North.

Government consented to the first but refused that with Lairds and was supported by a vote of 187 to 153.[1]

Beginning with an incautious personal and petty criticism of Russell the Tories had been driven to an attempt to pass what was virtually a vote of censure on the Ministry yet they were as loud as was the Government in praise of Adams and in approval of the seizure of the Rams. Naturally their cause was weakened, and the Ministry, referring to expressions made and intentions indicated as far back as March, 1863, thus hinting without directly so stating that the real decision had then been made, was easily the victor in the vote.[1] Derby had committed an error as a party leader and the fault rankled for again in April, 1864, he attempted to draw Russell into still further discussion on dates of documents. Russell's reply ignored that point altogether.[2] It did not suit his purpose to declare, flatly, the fact that in April assurances had been given both to Adams and through Lyons to Seward, that measures would be taken to prevent the departure of Southern vessels from British ports. To have made this disclosure would have required an explanation *why* such assurance had been given and this would have revealed the effect on both Russell and Lyons of the Northern plan to create a *cruising squadron blockade by privateers*. *There* was the real threat. The later delays and seeming uncertainties of British action made Adams anxious but there is no evidence that Russell ever changed his purpose. He sought stronger evidence before acting and he hoped for stronger support

[1] Hansard, 3rd Ser., CLXXIII, pp. 430-41, 544-50, 955-1021. The Tory point of view is argued at length by Brooks Adams, *The Seizure of the Laird Rams*, pp. 312-324.

[2] Hansard, 3rd. Ser., CLXXIV, pp. 1862-1913. *The Index*, naturally vicious in comment on the question of the Rams, summed up its approval of Derby's contentions: "Europe and America alike will inevitably believe that it was the threat of Mr. Adams, and nothing else, which induced the Foreign Secretary to retract his letter of the 1st September, and they will draw the necessary conclusion that the way to extort concessions from England is by bluster and menace." (Feb. 18, 1864, p. 106.)

from legal advisers, but he kept an eye on the Rams and when they had reached the stage where there was danger of escape, he seized them even though the desired evidence was still lacking.[1] Seward's "privateering bill" plan possibly entered upon in a moment of desperation and with no clear statement from him of its exact application had, as the anxiety of British diplomats became pronounced, been used with skill to permit, if not to state, the interpretation they placed upon it, and the result had been the cessation of that inadequate neutrality of which America complained.

[1] Lairds brought suit for damages, but the case never reached a decision, for the vessels were purchased by the Government. This has been regarded as acknowledgment by the Government that it had no case. In my view the failure to push the case to a conclusion was due to the desire not to commit Great Britain on legal questions, in view of the claim for damages certain to be set up by the United States on account of the depredations of the *Alabama*.

CHAPTER XIV

ROEBUCK'S MOTION

In the mid-period during which the British Government was seeking to fulfil its promise of an altered policy as regards ship-building and while the public was unaware that such a promise had been given, certain extreme friends of the South thought the time had come for renewed pressure upon the Government, looking toward recognition of the Confederacy. The *Alexandra* had been seized in April, but the first trial, though appealed, had gone against the Government in June, and there was no knowledge that the Ministry was determined in its stand. From January to the end of March, 1863, the public demonstrations in approval of the emancipation proclamation had somewhat checked expressions of Southern sympathy, but by the month of June old friends had recovered their courage and a new champion of the South came forward in the person of Roebuck.

Meanwhile the activities of Southern agents and Southern friends had not ceased even if they had, for a time, adopted a less vigorous tone. For four months after the British refusal of Napoleon's overtures on mediation, in November, 1862, the friends of the South were against "acting now," but this did not imply that they thought the cause lost or in any sense hopeless. Publicists either neutral in attitude or even professedly sympathetic with the North could see no outcome of the Civil War save separation of North and South. Thus the historian Freeman in the preface to the first volume of his uncompleted *History of Federal Government*, published in 1863, carefully explained that his book did not have its origin in the struggle in America, and argued that the breaking up of the Union in no way proved any inherent weakness in a federal system, but took it for granted that American reunion was impossible. The novelist, Anthony Trollope, after a long tour of the North, beginning in September, 1861, published late in 1862 a two-volume work, *North America*, descriptive of a nation engaged in the business of war and wholly sympathetic with the Northern cause. Yet he, also, could see no hope of forcing the South back into the Union. "The North and South are virtually separated, and the day will come in which the West also will secede."[1]

Such interpretations of conditions in America were not unusual; they were, rather, generally accepted. The Cabinet decision in November, 1862, was not regarded as final, though events were to prove it to be so for never again was there so near an approach to British intervention. Mason's friend, Spence, early began to think that true Southern policy was now to make an appeal to the Tories against the Government. In January, 1863, he was planning a new move:

> "I have written to urge Mr. Gregory to be here in time for a thorough organization so as to push the matter this time to a vote. I think the Conservatives may be got to move as a body and if so the result of a vote seems to me very certain I have seen Mr. Horsfall and Mr. Laird here and will put myself in communication with Mr. Disraeli as the time approaches for action for this seems to me now our best card." [2]

That some such effort was being thought of is evidenced by the attitude of the *Index* which all through the months from November, 1862, to the middle of January, 1863, had

[1] Trollope, *North America*, I, p. 124.
[2] Mason Papers. Spence to Mason, Jan. 3, 1863. Liverpool.

continued to harp on the subject of mediation as if still believing that something yet might be done by the existing Ministry, but which then apparently gave up hope of the Palmerstonian administration:

> "But what the Government means is evident enough. It does not mean to intervene or to interfere. It will not mediate, if it can help it; it will not recognize the Confederate States, unless there should occur some of those 'circumstances over which they have no control,' which leave weak men and weak ministers no choice. They will not, if they are not forced to it, quarrel with Mr. Seward, or with Mr. Bright. They will let Lancashire starve; they will let British merchantmen be plundered off Nassau and burnt off Cuba; they will submit to a blockade of Bermuda or of Liverpool; but they will do nothing which may tend to bring a supply of cotton from the South, or to cut off the supply of eggs and bacon from the North." [1]

But this plan of 'turning to the Tories' received scant encouragement and was of no immediate promise, as soon appeared by the debate in Parliament on reassembling, February 5, 1863. Derby gave explicit approval of the

[1] The *Index*, Jan. 29, 1863, p. 217. The active agent in control of the *Index* was Henry Hotze, who, in addition to managing this journal, used secret service funds of the Confederacy to secure the support of writers in the London press. He was in close touch with all the Southern agents sent to Europe at various times, but appears never to have been fully trusted by either Mason or Slidell. In 1912-13 I made notes from various materials originating with Hotze, these being then in the possession of Mr. Charles Francis Adams. These materials were (1) a letter and cash book marked "C.S.A. Commercial Agency, London"; (2) a copy despatch book, January 6, 1862, to December 31, 1864; (3) a copy letter-book of drafts of "private" letters, May 28, 1864, to June 16, 1865. All these materials were secured by Mr. Adams from Professor J. F. Jameson, who had received them from Henry Vignaud. Since Mr. Adams' death in 1915 no trace of these Hotze materials has been found. My references, then, to "Hotze Papers," must rest on my notes, and transcripts of many letters, taken in 1912-13. Describing his activities to Benjamin, Hotze stated that in addition to maintaining the *Index*, he furnished news items and *editorials* to various London papers, had seven paid writers on these papers, and was a pretty constant distributor of "boxes of cigars imported from Havana . . . American whiskey and other articles." He added: "It is, of course, out of the question to give vouchers." (Hotze Papers MS. Letter Book. Hotze to Benjamin, No. 19, March 14, 1863.) In Hotze's cash book one of his regular payees was Percy Gregg who afterwards wrote a history of the Confederacy. Hotze complained that he could get no "paid writer" on the *Times*.

Government's refusal to listen to Napoleon.[1] By February, Russell, having recovered from the smart of defeat within the Cabinet, declared himself weary of the perpetual talk about mediation and wrote to Lyons, ". . . till both parties are heartily tired and sick of the business, I see no use in talking of good offices. When that time comes Mercier will probably have a hint; let him have all the honour and glory of being the first."[2] For the time being Spence's idea was laid aside, Gregory writing in response to an inquiry from Mason:

> "The House of Commons is opposed to taking any step at present, feeling rightly or wrongly that to do so would be useless to the South, and possibly embroil us with the North. Any motion on the subject will be received with disfavour, consequently the way in which it will be treated will only make the North more elated, and will irritate the South against us. If I saw the slightest chance of a motion being received with any favour I would not let it go into other hands, but I find the most influential men of all Parties opposed to it." [3]

Of like opinion was Slidell who, writing of the situation in France, reported that he had been informed by his "friend at the Foreign Office" that "It is believed that every possible thing has been done here in your behalf—we must now await the action of England, and it is through that you must aim all your efforts in that direction."[4]

With the failure, at least temporary, of Southern efforts to move the British Government or to stir Parliament, energies were now directed toward using financial methods of winning support for the Southern cause. The "Confederate Cotton Loan" was undertaken with the double

[1] See *ante*, Ch. XI.

[2] Lyons Papers, Feb. 14, 1863.

[3] Mason Papers, March 18, 1863.

[4] Pickett Papers. Slidell to Benjamin, No. 34, May 3, 1863. This despatch is omitted by Richardson.

object of providing funds for Southern agents in Europe and of creating an interested support of the South, which might, it was hoped, ultimately influence the British Government.

By 1863 it had become exceedingly difficult, owing to the blockade, for the Government at Richmond to transmit funds to its agents abroad. Bullock, especially, required large amounts in furtherance of his ship-building contracts and was embarrassed by the lack of business methods and the delays of the Government at home. The incompetence of the Confederacy in finance was a weakness that characterized all of its many operations whether at home or abroad[1] and was made evident in England by the confusion in its efforts to establish credits there. At first the Confederate Government supplied its agents abroad with drafts upon the house of Fraser, Trenholm & Company, of Liverpool, a branch of the firm long established at Charleston, South Carolina, purchasing its bills of exchange with its own "home made" money. But as Confederate currency rapidly depreciated this method of transmitting funds became increasingly difficult and costly. The next step was to send to Spence, nominated by Mason as financial adviser in England, Confederate money bonds for sale on the British market, with authority to dispose of them as low as fifty cents on the dollar, but these found no takers.[2] By September, 1862, Bullock's funds for ship-building were exhausted and some new method of supply was required. Temporary relief was found in adopting a suggestion from Lindsay whereby cotton was made the basis for an advance of £60,000, a form of cotton bond being devised which fixed the price of cotton at eightpence the pound. These bonds were not put on the market but were privately

[1] Schwab, *The Confederate States of America* gives the best analysis and history of Southern financing.

[2] It is possible that a few were disposed of to contractors in payment for materials.

placed by Lindsay & Company with a few buyers for the entire sum, the transaction remaining secret.[1]

In the meantime this same recourse to cotton had occurred to the authorities at Richmond and a plan formulated by which cotton should be purchased by the Government, stored, and certificates issued to be sold abroad, the purchaser being assured of "all facilities of shipment." Spence was to be the authorized agent for the sale of these "cotton certificates," but before any reached him various special agents of the Confederacy had arrived in England by December, 1862, with such certificates in their possession and had disposed of some of them, calling them "cotton warrants." The difficulties which might arise from separate action in the market were at once perceived and following a conference with Mason all cotton obligations were turned to Fraser, Trenholm & Company. Spence now had in his hands the "money bonds" but no further attempt was made to dispose of these since the "cotton warrants" were considered a better means of raising funds.

It is no doubt true that since all of these efforts involved a governmental guarantee the various "certificates" or "warrants" partook of the nature of a government bond. Yet up to this point the Richmond authorities, after the first failure to sell "money bonds" abroad were not keen to attempt anything that could be stamped as a foreign "government loan." Their idea was rather that a certain part of the produce of the South was being set aside as the property of those who in England should extend credit to the South. The sole purpose of these earlier operations was to provide funds for Southern agents. By July, 1862, Bullock had exhausted his earlier credit of a million dollars. The £60,000 loan secured through Lindsay then tided over an emergency demand and this had been followed by a development on similar lines of the "cotton certificates"

[1] Mason Papers. Mason to Slidell, Sept. 27, 1862.

and "warrants" which by December, 1862, had secured, through Spence's agency, an additional million dollars or thereabouts. Mason was strongly recommending further expansion of this method and had the utmost confidence in Spence. Now, however, there was broached to the authorities in Richmond a proposal for the definite floating in Europe of a specified "cotton loan."

This proposal came through Slidell at Paris and was made by the well-established firm of Erlanger & Company. First approached by this company in September, 1862, Slidell consulted Mason but found the latter strongly committed to his own plans with Spence.[1] But Slidell persisted and Mason gave way.[2] Representatives of Erlanger proceeded to Richmond and proposed a loan of twenty-five million dollars; they were surprised to find the Confederate Government disinclined to the idea of a foreign loan, and the final agreement, cut to fifteen millions, was largely made because of the argument advanced that as a result powerful influences would thus be brought to the support of the South.[3] The contract was signed at Richmond, January 28, 1863, and legalized by a secret act of Congress on the day following.[4] But there was no Southern enthusiasm for the project. Benjamin wrote to Mason that the Confederacy disclaimed the "desire or intention on our part to effect a loan in Europe . . . . during the war we want only such very moderate sums as are required abroad for the purchase of warlike supplies and for vessels, and even that is not required because of our want of funds,

[1] *Ibid.* Slidell to Mason, Oct. 2, 1862.

[2] Slidell's daughter was engaged to be married to Erlanger's son.

[3] Slidell himself wrote: "I should not have gone so far in recommending these propositions . . . had I not the best reason to believe that even in anticipation of its acceptance the very strongest influence will be enlisted in our favour." (Richardson, II, p. 340. To Benjamin, Oct. 28, 1862.)

[4] Schwab, *The Confederate States of America*, pp. 30-31. Schwab is in error in stating that Erlanger himself went to Richmond, since it appears from Slidell's letters that he was in constant contact with Erlanger in Paris during the time the "agents" were in Richmond.

but because of the difficulties of remittance"; as for the Erlanger contract the Confederacy "would have declined it altogether but for the political considerations indicated by Mr. Slidell. . . ."[1]

From Mason's view-point the prime need was to secure money; from Slidell's (at least so asserted) it was to place a loan with the purpose of establishing strong friends. It had been agreed to suspend the operations of Spence until the result of Erlanger's offer was learned, but pressure brought by Caleb Huse, purchasing agent of the Confederacy, caused a further sale of "cotton warrants."[2] Spence, fearing he was about to be shelved, became vexed and made protest to Mason, while Slidell regarded Spence[3] as a weak and meddlesome agent.[4] But on February 14, 1863, Erlanger's agents returned to Paris and uncertainty was at an end. Spence went to Paris, saw Erlanger, and agreed to co-operate in floating the loan.[5] Then followed a remarkable bond market operation, interesting, not so much as regards the financial returns to the South, for these were negligible, as in relation to the declared object of Slidell and the Richmond Government—namely, the "strong influences" that would accompany the successful flotation of a loan.

Delay in beginning operations was caused by the failure to receive promptly the authenticated copy of the Act of Congress authorizing the loan, which did not arrive until March 18. By this contract Erlanger & Company, sole managers of the loan, had guaranteed flotation of the entire $15,000,000 at not less than 77, the profit of the Company to be five per cent., plus the difference between 77 and the

[1] Richardson, II, 399-401, Jan. 15, 1863.

[2] *Ibid*, p. 420. Mason to Benjamin, Feb. 5, 1863.

[3] Mason Papers, Jan. 23, 1863.

[4] *Ibid.* Slidell to Mason, Feb. 15, 1863.

[5] *Ibid.* Slidell to Mason, Feb. 23, 1863, and Mason to Slidell, Feb. 24, 1863.

actual price received, but the first $300,000 taken was to be placed at once at the disposal of the Government. The bonds were put on the market March 19, in London, Liverpool, Paris, Amsterdam and Frankfurt, but practically all operations were confined to England. The bid for the loan was entitled "*Seven per Cent. Cotton Loan of the Confederate States of America for* 3 *Millions Sterling at* 90 *per Cent.*" The bonds were to bear interest at seven per cent. and were to be exchangeable for cotton at the option of the holder at the price of sixpence "for each pound of cotton, at any time not later than six months after the ratification of a treaty of peace between the present belligerents." There were provisions for the gradual redemption of the bonds in gold for those who did not desire cotton. Subscribers were to pay 5 per cent. on application, 10 per cent. on allotment, 10 per cent. on each of the days, the first of May, June and July, 1863, and 15 per cent. on the first of August, September and October.

Since the price of cotton in England was then 21 pence per pound it was thought here was a sufficiently wide margin to offer at least a good chance of enormous profits to the buyer of the bonds. True "the loan was looked upon as a wild cotton speculation,"[1] but odds were so large as to induce a heavy gamblers' plunge, for it seemed hardly conceivable that cotton could for some years go below sevenpence per pound, and even that figure would have meant profit, *if* the Confederacy were established. Moreover, even though the loan was not given official recognition by the London stock exchange, the financial columns of the *Times* and the *Economist* favoured it and the subscriptions were so prompt and so heavy that in two days the loan was reported as over-subscribed three times in London alone.[2] With the closing of the subscription the bonds went up to 95½.

[1] Schwab, p. 33.

[2] *Ibid.*, p. 33. In France permission to advertise the loan was at first refused, but this was changed by the intervention of the Emperor.

Slidell wrote : " It is a financial recognition of our independence, emanating from a class proverbially cautious, and little given to be influenced by sentiment or sympathy."[1] On Friday, March 27, the allotment took place and three days later Mason wrote, " I think I may congratulate you, therefore, on the triumphant success of our infant credit—it shows, *malgré* all detraction and calumny, that cotton is king at last."[2]

" Alas for the King ! Two days later his throne began to tremble and it took all the King's horses and all the King's men to keep him in state."[3] On April 1, the flurry of speculation had begun to falter and the loan was below par ; on the second it dropped to 3½ discount, and by the third the promoters and the Southern diplomats were very anxious. They agreed that someone must be " bearing " the bonds and suspected Adams of supplying Northern funds for that purpose.[4] Spence wrote from Liverpool in great alarm and coincidently Erlanger & Company urged that Mason should authorize the use of the receipts already secured to hold up the price of the bonds. Mason was very reluctant to do this,[5] but finally yielded when informed of the result of an interview between Spence, Erlanger, and the latter's chief London agent, Schroeder. Spence had proposed a withdrawal of a part of the loan from the market as likely to have a stabilizing effect, and opposed the Erlanger plan of using the funds already in hand. But

[1] Richardson, II, p. 457. To Benjamin, March 21, 1863.

[2] Mason's *Mason*, p. 401. To Benjamin, March 30, 1863.

[3] MS. Thesis, by Walter M. Case, for M.A. degree at Stanford University : *James M. Mason—Confederate Diplomat* (1915). I am much indebted to Mr. Case's Chapter V : " Mason and Confederate Finance."

[4] No evidence has been found to support this. Is not the real reason for the change to be found in British Governmental intentions known or suspected ? March 27 was the day of the Parliamentary debate seemingly antagonistic to the North : while March 31, on the other hand, the *Alexandra* case was referred to the Law Officers, and April 4 they recommend her seizure, which was done on April 5. It is to be presumed that rumours of this seeming face-about by the Government had not failed to reach the bond market.

[5] Mason Papers. Mason to Slidell, April 3, 1863.

Schroeder coolly informed him that if the Confederate representative refused to authorize the use of these funds to sustain the market, then Erlanger would regard his Company as having " completed their contract . . . which was simply to issue the Loan." " Having issued it, they did not and do not guarantee that the public would pay up their instalments. If the public abandon the loan, the 15 per cent sacrificed is, in point of fact, not the property of the Government at all, but the profits of Messrs. Erlanger & Co., actually in their hands, and they cannot be expected to take a worse position. At any rate they will not do so, and unless the compact can be made on the basis we name, matters must take their course."[1]

In the face of this ultimatum, Spence advised yielding as he " could not hesitate . . . seeing that nothing could be so disastrous politically, as well as financially, as the public break-down of the Loan."[2] Mason gave the required authorization and this was later approved from Richmond. For a time the " bulling " of the loan was successful, but again and again required the use of funds received from actual sales of bonds and in the end the loan netted very little to the Confederacy. Some $6,000,000 was squandered in supporting the market and from the entire operation it is estimated that less than $7,000,000 was realized by the Confederacy, although, as stated by the *Economist*, over $12,000,000 of the bonds were outstanding and largely in the hands of British investors at the end of the war.[3]

[1] *Ibid.* Spence to Mason, May 9, 1863. This letter was written a month after the event at Mason's request for an exact statement of what had occurred.

[2] *Ibid.*

[3] Schwab, pp. 39-44. Schwab believes that Erlanger & Company " are certainly open to the grave suspicion of having themselves been large holders of the bonds in question, especially in view of the presumably large amount of lapsed subscriptions, and of having quietly unloaded them on the unsuspecting Confederate agents when the market showed signs of collapsing " (p. 35). Schwab did not have access to Spence's report which gives further ground for this suspicion.

The loan soon became, not as had been hoped and prophesied by Slidell, a source of valuable public support, but rather a mere barometer of Southern fortunes.[1] From first to last the Confederate Cotton Loan bore to subscribers the aspect of a speculative venture and lacked the regard attached to sound investment. This fact in itself denied to the loan any such favourable influence, or "financial recognition of the Confederacy," as Mason and Slidell, in the first flush of success, attributed to it. The rapid fluctuations in price further discredited it and tended to emphasize the uncertainty of Southern victory. Thus "confidence in the South" was, if anything, lessened instead of increased by this turning from political to financial methods of bringing pressure upon the Government.[2]

Southern political and parliamentary pressure had indeed been reserved from January to June, 1863. Public attention was distracted from the war in America by the Polish question, which for a time, particularly during the months of March and April, 1863, disturbed the good relations existing between England and France since the Emperor seemed bent on going beyond British "meddling," even to pursuing a policy that easily might lead to war with Russia. Europe diverted interest from America, and Napoleon himself was for the moment more concerned over the Polish question than with American affairs, even though the Mexican venture was still a worry to him. It was no time for a British parliamentary "push" and when a question was raised on the cotton famine in

[1] A newspaper item that Northern ships had run by Vicksburg sent it down; Lee's advance into Pennsylvania caused a recovery; his retreat from Gettysburg brought it so low as thirty per cent. discount.

[2] After the war was over Bigelow secured possession of and published an alleged list of important subscribers to the loan in which appeared the name of Gladstone. He repeated this accusation—a serious one if true, since Gladstone was a Cabinet member—in his *Retrospections* (I, p. 620), and the story has found place in many writings (e.g., G. P. Putnam, *Memoirs*, p. 213). Gladstone's emphatic denial, calling the story a "mischievous forgery," appears in Morley, *Gladstone*, II, p. 83.

Lancashire little attention was given it, though ordinarily it would have been seized upon as an opportunity for a pro-Southern demonstration. This was a bitter attack by one Ferrand in the Commons, on April 27, directed against the cotton manufacturers as lukewarm over employees' sufferings. Potter, a leading cotton manufacturer, replied to the attack. Potter and his brother were already prominent as strong partisans of the North, yet no effort was made to use the debate to the advantage of the South.[1]

In late May both necessity and fortuitous circumstance seemed to make advisable another Southern effort in Parliament. The cotton loan, though fairly strong again because of Confederate governmental aid, was in fact a failure in its expected result of public support for the South; something must be done to offset that failure. In Polish affairs France had drawn back; presumably Napoleon was again eager for some active effort. Best of all, the military situation in America was thought to indicate Southern success; Grant's western campaign had come to a halt with the stubborn resistance of the great Mississippi stronghold at Vicksburg, while in Virginia, Lee, on May 2-3, had overwhelmingly defeated Hooker at Chancellorsville and was preparing, at last, a definite offensive campaign into Northern territory. Lee's advance north did not begin until June 10, but his plan was early known in a select circle in England and much was expected of it. The time seemed ripe, therefore, and the result was notification by Roebuck of a motion for the recognition of the Confederacy—a first step the real purpose of which was to attempt that 'turning to the Tories' which had been advocated by Spence in January, but postponed on the advice of Gregory.[2] *The Index* clearly indicated where lay the wind: "No one," it declared "now asks what will be the policy of Great

[1] Hansard, 3rd Ser., CLXX, pp. 776-838.
[2] See *ante*, p. 155.

Britain towards America; but everybody anxiously waits on what the Emperor of the French will do."

> "... England to-day pays one of the inevitable penalties of free government and of material prosperity, that of having at times at the head of national affairs statesmen who belong rather to the past than to the present, and whose skill and merit are rather the business tact and knowledge of details, acquired by long experience, than the quick and prescient comprehension of the requirements of sudden emergencies....
>
> "The nominal conduct of Foreign Affairs is in the hands of a diplomatic Malaprop, who has never shown vigour, activity, or determination, except where the display of these qualities was singularly unneeded, or even worse than useless. ... From Great Britain, then, under her actual Government, the Cabinet at Washington has nothing to fear, and the Confederate States nothing to expect."[1]

Of main interest to the public was the military situation. The *Times* minimized the western campaigns, regarding them as required for political effect to hold the north-western states loyal to the Union, and while indulging in no prophecies as to the fate of Vicksburg, expressing the opinion that, if forced to surrender it, the South could easily establish "a new Vicksburg" at some other point.[2] Naturally *The Index* was pleased with and supported this view.[3] Such ignorance of the geographic importance of Vicksburg may seem like wilful misleading of the public; but professed British military experts were equally ignorant. Captain Chesney, Professor of Military History at Sandhurst College, published in 1863, an analysis of American campaigns, centring all attention on the battles in Maryland and Virginia and reaching the conclusion that the South could resist, indefinitely, any Northern attack.[4] He dis-

[1] The *Index*, May 28, 1863, pp. 72-3.

[2] The *Times*, June 1, 1863.

[3] The *Index*, June 4, 1863.

[4] Chesney, *Military View of Recent Campaigns in Maryland and Virginia*, London, 1863.

missed the western campaigns as of no real significance. W. H. Russell, now editor of the *Army and Navy Gazette*, better understood Grant's objectives on the Mississippi but believed Northern reconquest of the South to the point of restoration of the Union to be impossible. If, however, newspaper comments on the success of Southern armies were to be regarded as favourable to Roebuck's motion for recognition, W. H. Russell was against it.

> "If we could perceive the smallest prospect of awaking the North to the truth, or of saving the South from the loss and trials of the contest by recognition, we would vote for it to-morrow. But next to the delusion of the North that it can breathe the breath of life into the corpse of the murdered Union again, is the delusion of some people in England who imagine that by recognition we would give life to the South, divide the nations on each side of the black and white line for ever, and bring this war to the end. There is probably not one of these clamourers for recognition who could define the limits of the State to be recognized. . . . And, over and above all, recognition, unless it meant 'war,' would be an aggravation of the horrors of the contest; it would not aid the South one whit, and it would add immensely to the unity and the fury of the North."[1]

The British Foreign Secretary was at first little concerned at Roebuck's motion, writing to Lyons, "You will see that Roebuck has given notice of a motion to recognize the South. But I think it certain that neither Lord Derby nor Cobden will support it, and I should think no great number of the Liberal party. Offshoots from all parties will compose the minority."[2] Russell was correct in this view but not so did it appear to Southern agents who now became active at the request of Roebuck and Lindsay in securing from the Emperor renewed expressions of willingness to act, and promptly, if England would but give the word. There was no real hope that Russell would change his policy, but

[1] *Army and Navy Gazette*, June 6, 1863.
[2] Lyons Papers, May 30, 1863.

there seemed at least a chance of replacing the Whig Ministry with a Tory one. The date for the discussion of the motion had been set for June 30. On June 13, Lindsay, writing to Slidell, enclosed a letter from Roebuck asking for an interview with Napoleon,[1] and on June 16, Mason wrote that if Slidell saw the Emperor it was of the greatest importance that he, Mason, should be at once informed of the results and how far he might communicate them to "our friends in the House."[2] Slidell saw the Emperor on June 18, talked of the possibility of "forcing the English Cabinet to act or to give way to a new ministry," asked that an interview be given Lindsay and Roebuck, and hinted that Lord Malmesbury, a warm friend of the Emperor, would probably be the Foreign Secretary in a Tory cabinet. Napoleon made no comment indicating any purpose to aid in upsetting the Palmerston Government; but consented to the requested interview and declared he would go to the length of officially informing the British Ministry that France was very ready to discuss the advisability of recognizing the South.[3]

This was good news. June 22, Slidell received a note from Mocquard stating that Baron Gros, the French Ambassador at London, had been instructed to sound Russell. Meanwhile, Roebuck and Lindsay had hurried to Paris, June 20, saw Napoleon and on the twenty-fifth, Slidell reported that they were authorized to state in the House of Commons that France was "not only willing but

[1] Callahan, *Diplomatic History of the Southern Confederacy*, p. 184. Callahan's Chapter VIII, "The Crisis in England" is misnamed, for Roebuck's motion and the whole plan of "bringing in the Tories" never had a chance of succeeding, as, indeed, Callahan himself notes. His detailed examination of the incident has unfortunately misled some historians who have derived from his work the idea that the critical period of British policy towards America was Midsummer, 1863, whereas it occurred, in fact, in October–November, 1862 (e.g., Schmidt, "Wheat and Cotton during the Civil War," pp. 413 *seq*. Schmidt's thesis is largely dependent on placing the critical period in 1863).

[2] Mason Papers. To Slidell.

[3] Callahan, pp. 184-5.

anxious to recognize the Confederate States with the co-operation of England."[1] Slidell added, however, that Napoleon had not promised Roebuck and Lindsay to make a formal proposal to Great Britain. This rested on the assurances received by Slidell from Mocquard, and when Mason, who had let the assurance be known to his friends, wrote that Russell, replying to Clanricarde, on June 26, had denied any official communication from France, and asked for authority from Slidell to back up his statements by being permitted to give Roebuck a copy of the supposed instruction,[2] he received a reply indicating confusion somewhere:

> "I called yesterday on my friend at the Affaires Etrangeres on the subject of your note of Saturday: he has just left me. M. D. de Lh. will not give a copy of his instructions to Baron Gros—but this is the substance of it. On the 19th he directed Baron Gros to take occasion to say to leading Members of Parliament that the Emperor's opinions on the subject of American affairs were unchanged. That he was disposed with the co-operation of England immediately to recognize the Confederate States; this was in the form of a draft letter, not a despatch. On the 22nd, he officially instructed the Baron to sound *Palmerston* on the subject and to inform him of the Emperor's views and wishes. This was done in consequence of a note from the Emperor, to the Minister, in which he said, 'Je me demande, s'il ne serait bien d'avertir Lord Palmerston, que je suis décidé à reconnaitre le Sud.' This is by far the most significant thing that the Emperor has said, either to me or to the others. It renders me comparatively indifferent what England may do or omit doing. At all events, let Mr. Roebuck press his motion and make his statement of the Emperor's declaration. Lord Palmerston will not dare to dispute it and the responsibility of the continuance of the war will rest entirely upon him. M. Drouyn de Lhuys has not heard from Baron Gros the result of his interview with

[1] *Ibid.*, p. 186. To Benjamin.

[2] Mason Papers. Mason to Slidell, June 27, 1863. Mason wrote: "The question of veracity is raised."

Palmerston. I see that the latter has been unwell and it is probable that the former had not been able to see him. There can be no impropriety in Mr. Roebuck's seeing Baron Gros, who will doubtless give him information which he will use to advantage. I write in great haste; will you do me the favour to let Lord Campbell know the substance of this note, omitting that portion of it which relates to the Emperor's inclination to act alone. Pray excuse me to Lord Campbell for not writing to him, time not permitting me to do so."[1]

This did not satisfy Mason; he telegraphed on the twenty-ninth, "Can I put in hands of Roebuck copy of Mocquard's note brought by Corcoran."[2] To which Slidell replied by letter:

"For fear the telegraph may commit some blunder I write to say that M. Mocquard's note, being confidential, cannot be *used in any way*. I showed it to Messrs. Roebuck and Lindsay when they were here and have no objection that they should again see it confidentially."[3]

On June 29, Roebuck went to Baron Gros and received the information that no formal communication had been made to Russell. The next day in an effort in some way to secure an admission of what Mason and his friends believed to be the truth, Lord Campbell asked Russell in the House of Lords if he had received either a document or a verbal communication outlining Napoleon's desires. Russell replied that Baron Gros had told him "an hour ago" that he had not even received any instruction to deliver such a communication.[4] This was in the hours preceding the debate, now finally to occur in the Commons. Evidently there had been an error in the understanding of Napoleon by Slidell, Roebuck and Lindsay, or else there was a question of veracity between Russell, Baron Gros and Napoleon.

[1] *Ibid.* Slidell to Mason, June 29, 1863.
[2] *Ibid.* To Slidell.
[3] *Ibid.* To Mason. "Monday eve." (June 29, 1863.)
[4] Callahan, 186; and Hansard, 3rd Ser., CLXXI, p. 1719.

Roebuck's motion was couched in the form of a reqnest to the Queen to enter into negotiations with foreign powers for co-operation in recognition of the Confederacy. Roebuck argued that the South had in fact established its independence and that this was greatly to England's advantage since it put an end to the "threatening great power" in the West. He repeated old arguments based on suffering in Lancashire—a point his opponents brushed aside as no longer of dangerous concern—attacked British anti-slavery sentiment as mere hypocrisy and minimized the dangers of a war with the North, prophesying an easy victory for Great Britain. Then, warmed to the real attack on the Government Roebuck related at length his interview with Napoleon, claiming to have been commissioned by the Emperor to urge England to action and asserting that since Baron Gros had been instructed to apply again to the British Cabinet it must be evident that the Ministry was concealing something from Parliament. Almost immediately, however, he added that Napoleon had told him no formal French application could be renewed to Great Britain since Russell had revealed to Seward, through Lyons, the contents of a former application.

Thus following the usual pro-Southern arguments, now somewhat perfunctorily given, the bolt against the Government had been shot with all of Roebuck's accustomed "vigour" of utterance.[1] Here was direct attack; that it was a futile one early became evident in the debate. Lord Robert Montagu, while professing himself a friend of the South, was sarcastic at the expense of Roebuck's entrance into the field of diplomacy, enlarged upon the real dangers of becoming involved in the war, and moved an amendment in favour of continued British neutrality. Palmerston was absent, being ill, but Gladstone, for the

[1] Punch's favourite cartoon of Roebuck was of a terrier labelled 'Tear 'em," worrying and snarling at his enemies.

Government, while carefully avoiding expressions of sympathy for either North or South, yet going out of his way to pass a moral judgment on the disaster to political liberty if the North should wholly crush the South, was positive in assertion that it would be unwise to adopt either Roebuck's motion or Montagu's amendment. Great Britain should not *commit* herself to any line of policy, especially as military events were "now occurring" which might greatly alter the whole situation, though "the main result of the contest was not doubtful." Here spoke that element of the Ministry still convinced of ultimate Southern success.

If Gladstone's had been the only reply to Roebuck he and his friends might well have thought they were about to secure a ministerial change of front. But it soon appeared that Gladstone spoke more for himself than for the Government. Roebuck had made a direct accusation and in meeting this, Layard, for the Foreign Office, entered a positive and emphatical denial, in which he was supported by Sir George Grey, Home Secretary, who added sharp criticism of Roebuck for permitting himself to be made the channel of a French complaint against England. It early became evident to the friends of the South that an error in tactics had been committed and in two directions; first, in the assertion that a new French offer had been made when it was impossible to present proof of it; and second, in bringing forward what amounted to an attempt to unseat the Ministry without previously committing the Tories to a support of the motion. Apparently Disraeli was simply letting Roebuck "feel out" the House. The only member of the Tory party strongly supporting him was Lord Robert Cecil, in a speech so clearly a mere party one that it served to increase the strength of ministerial resistance. Friends of the North quickly appreciated the situation and in strong speeches supported the neutrality policy of the Government. Forster laid stress upon the danger of war and the strength of British emancipation sentiment as did Bright in what was, read to-day, the most powerful of all his parliamentary utterances on the American war. In particular Bright voiced a general disbelief in the accuracy of Roebuck's report of his interview with Napoleon, called upon his "friend" Lindsay for his version[1] of the affair, and concluded by recalling former speeches by Roebuck in which the latter had been fond of talking about the "perjured lips" of Napoleon. Bright dilated upon the egotism and insolence of Roebuck in trying to represent the Emperor of France on the floor of the House of Commons. The Emperor, he asserted, was in great danger of being too much represented in Parliament.[2]

The result of this first day's debate on June 30 was disconcerting to Southern friends. It had been adjourned without a vote, for which they were duly thankful. Especially disconcerting was Slidell's refusal to permit the citation of Mocquard's note in proof of Roebuck's assertions. Mason wrote:

> "I have your note of 29th ult. You will see in the papers of to-day the debate in the House last night, at which I was present, and will have seen what in the H. L. Lord Russell said in reply to Lord Campbell. Thus the French affair remains in a 'muss,' unless the Emperor will show his hand *on paper*, we shall never know what he really means, or derive any benefit from his private and individual revelations. As things now stand before the public, there can be but one opinion, i.e., that he holds one language in private com-

[1] Bright and Lindsay had, in fact, long been warm friends. They disagreed on the Civil War, but this did not destroy their friendship.

[2] Hansard, 3rd. Ser., CLXXI, pp. 1771-1842, for debate of June 30. Roebuck's egotism was later related by Lamar, then in London on his way to Russia as representative of the South. A few days before the debate Lamar met Roebuck at Lindsay's house and asked Roebuck whether he expected Bright to take part in the debate. "No, sir," said Roebuck sententiously, "Bright and I have met before. It was the old story—the story of the swordfish and the whale! No, sir! Mr. Bright will not cross swords with me again." Lamar attended the debate and saw Roebuck given by Bright the "most deliberate and tremendous pounding I ever witnessed." (*Education of Henry Adams*, pp. 161-2.)

munications, though 'with liberty to divulge,' and another to his ambassador here. The debate is adjourned to-morrow night, when Lindsay will give in his explanation. It would be uncivil to say that I have no confidence in the Emperor, but certainly what has come from him so far can invite only distrust." [1]

As in Parliament, so in the public press, immediate recognition of the Confederacy received little support. The *Times*, while sympathetic with the purpose was against Roebuck's motion, considering it of no value unless backed up by force; to this the *Times* was decidedly opposed.[2] Of like opinion was the *Economist*, declaring that premature recognition was a justifiable ground for a declaration of war by the North.[3] July 2, Roebuck asked when the debate was to be renewed and was told that must wait on Palmerston's recovery and return to the House. Bright pressed for an immediate decision. Layard reaffirmed very positively that no communication had been received from France and disclosed that Napoleon's alleged complaint of a British revelation to Seward of French overtures was a myth, since the document in question had been printed in the *Moniteur*, thus attracting Seward's attention.[4] Thus Roebuck was further discredited. July 4, Spence wrote strongly urging the withdrawal of the motion:

"I have a letter from an eminent member of the House and great friend of the South urging the danger of carrying Mr. Roebuck's motion to a vote. It is plain it will be defeated by a great majority and the effect of this will encourage the North and distress our friends. It will also strengthen the minority of the Cabinet in favour of the North. . . .

"The fact is the ground of the motion, which was action on the part of France, has failed us—and taken shape which tells injuriously instead of being the great support. . . .

[1] Mason Papers. To Slidell, July 1, 1863.
[2] July 1, 1863.
[3] July 4, 1863.
[4] Hansard, 3rd. Ser., CLXXII, pp. 67-73.

"If a positive engagement were made by Mr. Disraeli to support the motion it would alter the question entirely. In the absence of this I fear the vote would be humiliating and would convey an impression wholly delusive, for the members are 10 to 1 in favour of the South and yet on this point the vote might be 5 to 1 against Southern interests."[1]

On July 6, Palmerston was back in the House and Roebuck secured an agreement for a resumption of the debate on "Monday next."[2] Meantime many powerful organs of the French press had taken up the matter and were full of sharp criticism of Napoleon's supposed policy and actions as stated by Roebuck. The effect in England was to create a feeling that Napoleon might have difficulty in carrying out a pro-Southern policy.[3] Palmerston, wishing to avoid further discussion on Napoleon's share in providing fuel for the debate, wrote in a very conciliatory and pleasant way to Roebuck, on July 9:

"Perhaps you will allow me thus privately to urge upon you, and through you upon Mr. Lindsay, the expediency of dropping altogether, whether your debate goes on or not, all further mention or discussion of what passed between you and Mr. Lindsay on the one hand, and the Emperor of the French on the other. In truth the whole proceeding on this subject the other day seems to me to have been very irregular. The British Parliament receives messages and communications from their own sovereign, but not from the sovereigns of other countries. . . ."

[1] Mason Papers. To Mason, July 4, 1863. In fact Disraeli, throughout the Civil War, favoured strict neutrality, not agreeing with many of his Tory colleagues. He at times expressed himself privately as believing the Union would not be restored but was wise enough to refrain from such comment publicly. (Monypenny, *Disraeli*, IV, p. 328.)

[2] Hansard, 3rd. Ser., CLXXII, p. 252.

[3] *The Index* felt it necessary to combat this, and on July 9 published a "letter from Paris" stating such criticisms to be negligible as emanating wholly from minority and opposition papers. "All the sympathies of the French Government have, from the outset, been with the South, and this, quite independently of other reasons, dictated the line which the opposition press has consistently followed; the Orleanist *Debats*, Republican *Siècle*, The Palais Royal *Opinion*, all join in the halloo against the South."

"No good can come of touching again upon this matter, nor from fixing upon the Emperor a mistake which amid the multiplicity of things he has to think of he may be excused for making. I am very anxious that neither you nor Mr. Lindsay should mention those matters any more, as any discussion about them must tend to impair the good relations between the French and English Governments. Might I ask you to show this note to Mr. Lindsay, your fellow traveller."[1]

The next day, in the Commons, Sir James Ferguson appealed to Roebuck to withdraw his motion altogether as inexpedient, because of the uncertainty of events in America and as sure to be defeated if pressed to a vote. Palmerston approved this suggestion and urged that if the debate be continued speakers should refrain from all further mention of the personal questions that had been raised, since these were not proper matters for discussion in the House and were embarrassing to the French Emperor. But Palmerston's skill in management was unavailing in this case and the "muss" (as Mason called it) was continued when Lindsay entered upon a long account of the interview with Napoleon, renewed the accusations of Russell's "revelations" to Seward and advised Roebuck not to withdraw his motion but to postpone it "until Monday." The *Scotia*, he said was due and any moment news from America might change the governmental policy. Again the fat was in the fire. Palmerston sharply disavowed that news would change policy. Kinglake thought Roebuck's actions should be thoroughly investigated. Forster eagerly pressed for continuation of the debate. There was a general criticism of Roebuck's "diplomacy," and of Lindsay's also. Northern friends were jubilant and those of the South embarrassed and uncertain. Gregory believed that the motion should be withdrawn "in the interest of the South," but Lord Robert Cecil renewed Lindsay's ad-

[1] Palmerston MS. July 9, 1863.

vice to wait "until Monday" and this was finally done.[1]

All England was in fact eagerly waiting for news from America. Lee's advance was known to have passed by Washington, but no reports were yet at hand of the battle which must determine this first great offensive campaign by the South. July 9, the *Times* predicted, editorially, that Lee was about to capture Washington and that this event would be met by a great cry of joy and relief in the North, now weary of the war and eager to escape from the despotism of Lincoln's administration.[2] Nevertheless the *Times*, while still confident of Lee's victorious advance and of the welcome likely to be accorded him in the North, came out strongly on July 13 in an appeal to Roebuck to withdraw his motion, arguing that even if he were successful Great Britain ought to make no hurried change of policy.[3] On this day, the thirteenth, Roebuck moved the discharge

[1] Hansard, 3rd Ser., CLXXII, 554 *seq.*, July 10, 1863.

[2] In the same issue appeared a letter from the New York correspondent of the *Times*, containing a similar prediction but in much stronger terms. For the last half of the war the *Times* was badly served by this correspondent who invariably reported the situation from an extreme anti-Northern point of view. This was Charles Mackay who served the *Times* in New York from March, 1862, to December, 1865. (Mackay, *Forty Years' Recollections*, II, p. 412.) Possibly he had strict instructions. During this same week Lyons, writing privately to Russell, minimized the "scare" about Lee's advance. He reported that Mercier had ordered up a war-ship to take him away if Washington should fall. Lyons cannily decided such a step for himself inadvisable, since it would irritate Seward and in case the unexpected happened he could no doubt get passage on Mercier's ship. When news came of the Southern defeat at Gettysburg and of Grant's capture of Vicksburg, Lyons thought the complete collapse of the Confederacy an imminent possibility. Leslie Stephen is a witness to the close relations of Seward and Lyons at this time. He visited Washington about a month after Gettysburg and met Seward, being received with much cordiality as a *verbal* champion in England of the North. (He had as yet published no signed articles on the war.) In this conversation he was amused that Seward spoke of the friendly services of "Monkton Mill," as a publicist on political economy. (Maitland, *Leslie Stephen*, p. 120.)

[3] In this issue a letter from the New York correspondent, dated July 1, declared that all of the North except New England, would welcome Lee's triumph: "... he and Mr. Jefferson Davis might ride in triumph up Broadway, amid the acclamations of a more enthusiastic multitude than ever assembled on the Continent of America." The New York city which soon after indulged in the "draft riots" might give some ground for such writing, but it was far fetched, nevertheless—and New York was not the North.

of his motion in a speech so mild as to leave the impression that "Tear 'em" had his tail between his legs but, Lindsay, his feelings evidently injured by the aspersions cast upon his own "amateur diplomacy," spoke at much length of the interview with Napoleon and tried to show that on a previous occasion he had been, in fact, "employed" by the Government. Palmerston was pithy and sarcastic in reply. Lindsay, he said, had "employed" himself. He hoped that this would be the "last time when any member of this House shall think it his duty to communicate to the British House of Commons that which may have passed between himself and the Sovereign of a foreign country."[1]

The entire debate on Roebuck's motion was a serious blow to the cause of the South in Parliament. Undertaken on a complete misunderstanding of the position of Tory leaders, begun with a vehemence that led its mover into tactical error, it rapidly dwindled to a mere question of personal veracity and concluded in sharp reproof from the Government. No doubt the very success (so it seemed at the moment) of Southern arms, upon which Roebuck counted to support his motion was, in actual effect, a deterrent, since many Southern sympathizers thought Great Britain might now keep hands off since the South was "winning anyway." There is no evidence that Russell thought this, or that he was moved by any consideration save the fixed determination to remain neutral—even to the extent of reversing a previous decision as to the powers of the Government in relation to Southern ship-building.

Roebuck withdrew his motion, not because of any imminent Southern victory, but because he knew that if pressed to a vote it would be overwhelmingly defeated.

[1] Hansard, 3rd Ser., CLXXII, 661 *seq*. Ever afterwards Roebuck was insistent in expressions of dislike and fear of America. At a banquet to him in Sheffield in 1869 he delivered his "political testament": "Beware of Trades Unions; beware of Ireland; beware of America." (Leader, *Autobiography and Letters of Roebuck*, p. 330.)

The debate was the last one of importance on the topics of mediation or recognition.[1] News of Lee's check at Gettysburg reached London on July 16, but was described by the *Times* two days later as virtually a Southern victory since the Northern army had been compelled to act wholly on the defensive. In the same issue it was stated of Vicksburg, "it is difficult to see what possible hope there can be of reducing the city."[2] But on July 20, full news of the events of July 4, when Vicksburg fell and Lee began his retreat from Gettysburg, was received and its significance acknowledged, though efforts were made to prove that these events simply showed that neither side could conquer the other.[3] In contradiction of previous assertions that "another Vicksburg" might easily be set up to oppose Northern advance in the west there was now acknowledgment that the capture of this one remaining barrier on the Mississippi was a great disaster to the South. *The Index*, forgetful that it was supposedly a British publication, declared: "The saddest news which has reached *us* since the fall of New Orleans is the account of the surrender of Vicksburg. The *very day* on which the capitulation took place renders the blow heavier."[4]

[1] May 31, 1864, Lindsay proposed to introduce another recognition motion, but on July 25 complained he had had no chance to make it, and asked Palmerston if the Government was not going to act. The reply was a brief negative.

[2] The *Times*, July 18, 1863.

[3] The power of the *Times* in influencing public opinion through its news columns was very great. At the time it stood far in the lead in its foreign correspondence and the information printed necessarily was that absorbed by the great majority of the British public. Writing on January 23, 1863, of the mis-information spread about America by the *Times*, Goldwin Smith asserted: "I think I never felt so much as in this matter the enormous power which the *Times* has, not from the quality of its writing, which of late has been rather poor, but from its exclusive command of publicity and its exclusive access to a vast number of minds. The *ignorance* in which it has been able to keep a great part of the public is astounding." (To E. S. Beesly. Haultain, *Correspondence of Goldwin Smith*, p. 11.)

[4] *The Index*, July 23, 1863, p. 200. The italics are mine. The implication is that a day customarily celebrated as one of rejoicing has now become one for gloom. No *Englishman* would be likely to regard July 4 as a day of rejoicing.

"The fall of Vicksburg," wrote Spence, "has made me ill all the week, never yet being able to drive it off my mind."[1] Adams reported that the news had caused a panic among the holders of the Cotton Loan bonds and that the press and upper classes were exceedingly glad they had refused support of Roebuck's motion.[2]

If July, 1863, may in any way be regarded as the "crisis" of Southern effort in England, it is only as a despairing one doomed to failure from the outset, and receiving a further severe set-back by the ill-fortune of Lee's campaign into Pennsylvania. The real crisis of governmental attitude had long since passed. Naturally this was not acknowledged by the staunch friends of the South any more than at Richmond it was acknowledged (or understood) that Gettysburg marked the crisis of the Confederacy. But that the end of Southern hope for British intervention had come at Richmond, was made clear by the action of Benjamin, the Confederate Secretary of State. On August 4, he recalled Mason, writing that the recent debates in Parliament showed the Government determined not to receive him:

> "Under these circumstances, your continued residence in London is neither conducive to the interests nor consistent with the dignity of this Government, and the President therefore requests that you consider your mission at an end, and that you withdraw, with your secretary, from London."[3]

A private letter accompanying the instruction authorized Mason to remain if there were any "marked change" in governmental attitude, but since the decision of the Ministry to seize the Laird Rams had been made public at nearly the same moment when this instruction was received, September

[1] Mason Papers. To Mason, July 25, 1863.

[2] *U.S. Diplomatic Correspondence*, 1863, Pt. I, p. 329. Adams to Seward, July 30, 1863.

[3] Mason, *Mason*, p. 449.

15, Mason could hardly fail to retire promptly. Indeed, the very fact of that seizure gave opportunity for a dramatic exit though there was no connection between Benjamin's instruction and the stopping of Confederate ship-building in England. The real connection was with the failure of the Gettysburg campaign and the humiliating collapse of Roebuck's motion. Even the *Times* was now expanding upon the "serious reverses" of the South and making it clearly understood that England "has not had and will not have the slightest inclination to intervention or mediation, or to take any position except that of strict neutrality."[1]

Mason at once notified Slidell of his receipt of the recall instruction and secured the latter's approval of the communication he proposed making to Russell.[2] A general consultation of Southern agents took place and Mason would have been vexed had he known how small was the regard for his abilities as a diplomat.[3] *The Index* hastened to join in a note already struck at Richmond of warm welcome to France in her conquest of Mexico, reprinting on September 17, an editorial from the *Richmond Enquirer* in which it was declared, "France is the only Power in the world that has manifested any friendly feeling towards the Confederacy in its terrible struggle for independence." Evidently all hope was now centred upon Napoleon, a conclusion without doubt distasteful to Mason and one which he was loth to accept as final.

[1] Sept. 4, 1863. The *Times* was now printing American correspondence sharply in contrast to that which preceded Gettysburg when the exhaustion and financial difficulties of the North were dilated upon. Now, letters from Chicago, dated August 30, declared that, to the writer's astonishment, the West gave every evidence that the war had fostered rather than checked, prosperity. (Sept. 15, 1863.).

[2] Mason Papers. Mason to Slidell, Sept. 14 and 15, 1863. Slidell to Mason, Sept. 16, 1863.

[3] McRea wrote to Hotze, September 17, 1863, that in his opinion Slidell and Hotze were the only Southern agents of value diplomatically in Europe (Hotze Correspondence). He thought all others would soon be recalled. Slidell, himself, even in his letter to Mason, had the questionable taste of drawing a rosy picture of his own and his family's intimate social intercourse with the Emperor and the Empress.

On September 21, Mason notified Russell of his withdrawal very nearly in the words of Benjamin's instruction. The news was at once made public, calling out from the *Times* a hectoring editorial on the folly of the South in demanding recognition before it had won it.[1] In general, however, the press took a tone apparently intended to "let Mason down easily," acknowledging that his act indicated a universal understanding that Great Britain would not alter her policy of strict neutrality, but expressing admiration for the courage and confidence of the South.[2] September 25, Russell replied to Mason with courtesy but also with seeming finality:

> "I have on other occasions explained to you the reasons which have induced Her Majesty's Government to decline the overtures you allude to, and the motives which have hitherto prevented the British Court from recognizing you as the accredited Minister of an established State.
>
> "These reasons are still in force, and it is not necessary to repeat them.
>
> "I regret that circumstances have prevented my cultivating your personal acquaintance, which, in a different state of affairs, I should have done with much pleasure and satisfaction."[3]

Thus Mason took his exit. Brief entrances upon the stage in England were still to be his, but the chief rôle there was now assigned to others and the principal scenes transferred to France. That Mason did not fully concur in this as final, easily as it was accepted by Slidell, is evident from his later correspondence with Lindsay and Spence. He regarded the question of British recognition of the South as mainly an English political question, pinning his hopes on a Tory overthrow of Palmerston's Ministry. This he

[1] Sept. 23, 1863.

[2] e.g., *Manchester Guardian*, Sept. 23, 1863, quoted in *The Index*, Sept. 24, p. 343.

[3] Mason's *Mason*, p. 456.

believed to depend on the life of the Prime Minister and his anxious inquiries as to the health of Palmerston were frequent. Nothing in his instructions indicated a desired course of action and Mason after consulting Slidell and, naturally, securing his acquiescence, determined to remain in Europe waiting events.

If the South was indignant at British inaction the North was correspondingly pleased and after the seizure of the Laird Rams was officially very friendly—at least so Lyons reported.[1] In this same private letter, however, Lyons ventured a strong protest against a notion which now seems to have occurred to Russell of joint action by England, France and Spain to withdraw belligerent rights *to the North,* unless the United States formally "concede to their enemy the status of a Belligerent for all *international* purposes." Why or how this idea came to be taken up by Russell is uncertain. Possibly it was the result of irritation created by the persistence of Seward in denying that the war was other than an effort to crush rebellious subjects—a theory clearly against the fact yet consistently maintained by the American Secretary of State throughout the entire war and constantly causing difficulties in relations with neutral countries. At any rate Lyons was quick to see the danger. He wrote:

> "Such a declaration might produce a furious outburst of wrath from Government and public here. It cannot, however, be denied that the reasoning on which the Declaration would be founded would be incontrovertible, and that in the end firmness answers better with the Americans than coaxing. But then England, France and Spain must be really firm, and not allow their Declaration to be a *brutum fulmen.* If on its being met, as it very probably would be, by a decided refusal on the part of the United States, they did not proceed to break up the Blockade, or at all events to resist by force the exercise of the right of visit on the high seas, the United

[1] Russell Papers. To Russell, Oct. 26, 1863.

> States Government and people would become more difficult to deal with than ever. I find, however, that I am going beyond my own province, and I will therefore add only an excuse for doing so." [1]

Lyons followed this up a week later by a long description of America's readiness for a foreign war, a situation very different from that of 1861. America, he said, had steadily been preparing for such a contingency not with any desire for it but that she might not be caught napping.[2] This was written as if merely an interesting general speculation and was accompanied by the assurance, "I don't think the Government here at all desires to pick a quarrel with us or with any European Power—but the better prepared it is, the less manageable it will be."[3] Nevertheless, Lyons' concern over Russell's motion of withdrawing belligerent rights to the North was great, and his representations presumably had effect, for no more was heard of the matter. Russell relieved Lyons' mind by writing, November 21:

> "I hope you continue to go on quietly with Seward. I think this is better than any violent demonstrations of friendship which might turn sour like beer if there should be a thunder-storm.
>
> "But I am more and more persuaded that amongst the

[1] *Ibid.* Lyons wrote after receiving a copy of a despatch sent by Russell to Grey, in France, dated October 10, 1863.

[2] F. O., Am., 896. No. 788. Confidential. Lyons to Russell, Nov. 3, 1863. "It seems, in fact, to be certain that at the commencement of a war with Great Britain, the relative positions of the United States and its adversary would be very nearly the reverse of what they would have been if a war had broken out three or even two years ago. Of the two Powers, the United States would now be the better prepared for the struggle—the coasts of the United States would present few points open to attack—while the means of assailing suddenly our own ports in the neighbourhood of this country, and especially Bermuda and the Bahamas, would be in immediate readiness. Three years ago Great Britain might at the commencement of a war have thrown a larger number of trained troops into the British Provinces on the continent than could have been immediately sent by the United States to invade those provinces. It seems no exaggeration to say that the United States could now without difficulty send an Army exceeding in number, by five to one, any force which Great Britain would be likely to place there."

[3] *Ibid.* Private. Lyons to Russell, Nov. 3, 1863.

> Powers with whose Ministers I pass my time there is none with whom our relations ought to be so frank and cordial as the United States." [1]

If relations with the North were now to be so "frank and cordial," there was, indeed, little remaining hope possible to English friends of the South. Bright wrote to Sumner: "Neutrality is agreed upon by all, and I hope a more fair and friendly neutrality than we have seen during the past two years."[2] George Thompson, at Exeter Hall, lauding Henry Ward Beecher for his speech there, commented on the many crowded open public meetings in favour of the North as compared with the two pro-Southern ones in London, slimly and privately attended.[3] Jefferson Davis, in addressing the Confederate Congress, December 7, was bitter upon the "unfair and deceptive conduct" of England.[4] Adams, by mid-December, 1863, was sure that previous British confidence in the ultimate success of the South was rapidly declining.[5]

Such utterances, if well founded, might well have portended the cessation of further Southern effort in England. That a renewal of activity soon occurred was due largely to a sudden shift in the military situation in America and to the realization that the heretofore largely negative support given to the Southern cause must be replaced by organized and persistent effort. Grant's victorious progress in the West had been checked by the disaster to Rosencrans at Chicamauga, September 18, and Grant's army forced to

[1] Lyons Papers. To Lyons.

[2] Rhodes, IV, p. 393. Nov. 20, 1863.

[3] *The Liberator*, Nov. 27, 1863. I have not dwelt upon Beecher's tour of England and Scotland in 1863, because its influence in "winning England" seems to me absurdly over-estimated. He was a gifted public orator and knew how to "handle" his audiences, but the majority in each audience was friendly to him, and there was no such "crisis of opinion" in 1863 as has frequently been stated in order to exalt Beecher's services.

[4] Dodd, *Jefferson Davis*, p. 319. The words are Dodd's.

[5] State Department, Eng., Vol. 84, No. 557. Adams to Seward, Dec. 17, 1863.

retrace its steps to recover Chattanooga. It was not until November 24 that the South was compelled to release its grip upon that city. Meanwhile in the East, Lee, fallen back to his old lines before Richmond, presented a still impregnable front to Northern advance. No sudden collapse, such as had been expected, followed the Southern defeats at Vicksburg and Gettysburg. Again the contest presented the appearance of a drawn battle. Small wonder then that McHenry, confident in his statistics, should now declare that at last cotton was to become in truth King,[1] and count much upon the effect of the arguments advanced in his recently published book.[2] Small wonder that Southern friends should hurry the organization of the "Southern Independence Association." Seeking a specific point of attack and again hoping for Tory support they first fixed their attention on the new trial of the *Alexandra*, on appeal from the decision by the Chief Baron of the Court of Exchequer. On December 4, Lindsay wrote to Mason that he had daily been "journeying to town" with the "old Chief Baron" and was confident the Government would again be defeated—in which case it would be very open to attack for the seizure of the Rams also. Nevertheless he was emphatic in his caution to Mason not to place too high a hope on any change in Government policy or on any expectation that the Tories would replace Palmerston.[3]

[1] Hotze Correspondence. McHenry to Hotze, Dec. 1, 1863.

[2] McHenry, *The Cotton Trade*, London, 1863. The preface in the form of a long letter to W. H. Gregory is dated August 31, 1863. For a comprehensive note on McHenry see C. F. Adams in Mass. Hist. Soc. *Proceedings*, March, 1914, Vol. XLVII, 279 *seq*.

[3] Mason Papers.

CHAPTER XV

THE SOUTHERN INDEPENDENCE ASSOCIATION

NORTHERN friends in England were early active in organizing public meetings and after the second emancipation proclamation of January 1, 1863, these became both numerous and notable. Southern friends, confident in the ultimate success of the Confederacy and equally confident that they had with them the great bulk of upper-class opinion in England, at first thought it unnecessary to be active in public expressions aside from such as were made through the newspapers. Up to November, 1862, *The Index* records no Southern public meeting. But by the summer of 1863, the indefatigable Spence had come to the conclusion that something must be done to offset the efforts of Bright and others, especially in the manufacturing districts where a strong Northern sympathy had been created. On June 16, he wrote to Mason that on his initiative a Southern Club had been organized in Manchester and that others were now forming in Oldham, Blackburn and Stockport. In Manchester the Club members had " smashed up the last Abolitionist meeting in the Free Trade Hall ":

> " These parties are not the rich spinners but young men of energy with a taste for agitation but little money. It appears to my judgment that it would be wise not to stint money in aiding this effort to expose cant and diffuse the truth. Manchester is naturally the centre of such a move and you will see there are here the germs of important work —but they need to be tended and fostered. I have supplied

a good deal of money individually but I see room for the use of £30 or £40 a month or more." [1]

The appeal for funds (though Spence wrote that he would advance the required amounts on the chance of reimbursement from the Confederate secret service fund) is interesting in comparison with the contributions willingly made by Bright's friends. "Young men of energy with a taste for agitation but little money" reveals a source of support somewhat dubious in persistent zeal and requiring more than a heavy list of patrons' names to keep up a public interest. Nevertheless, Spence succeeded, for a short time, in arousing a show of energy. November 24, 1863, Mason wrote to Mann that measures were "in progress and in course of execution" to hold public meetings, memorialize Parliament, and form an association for the promotion of Southern independence "under the auspices of such men as the Marquis of Lothian, Lord Robert Cecil, M.P., Lord Wharncliffe, Lord Eustace Cecil, Messrs. Haliburton, Lindsay, Peacocke, Van Stittart, M.P., Beresford Hope, Robert Bourke, and others. . . ."[2] A fortnight later, Spence reported his efforts and postulated that in them, leading to European intervention, lay the principal, if not the only hope, of Southern independence—a view never *publicly* acknowledged by any devoted friend of the South:

"The news is gloomy—very, and I really do not see how the war is to be worked out to success without the action of Europe. That is stopped by our Government but there is a power that will move the latter, if it can only be stirred up, and that, of course, is public opinion. I had a most agreeable and successful visit to Glasgow upon a requisition signed by the citizens. The enemy placarded the walls and brought all their forces to the meeting, in which out of 4,000 I think they were fully 1,000 strong, but we beat them completely, carrying a resolution which embraced a memorial

[1] Mason Papers.
[2] *Ibid.*

to Lord Palmerston. We have now carried six public meetings, Sheffield, Oldham, Stockport, Preston, Ashton, Glasgow. We have three to come off now ready, Burnley, Bury, Macclesfield, and others in preparation. My plan is to work up through the secondary towns to the chief ones and take the latter, Liverpool, Manchester, London, etc., as we come upon the assembling of Parliament. . . . By dint of perseverance I think we shall succeed. The problem is simply to convert latent into active sympathy. There is ample power on our side to move the Cabinet—divided as it is, if we can only arouse that power. At any rate the object is worth the effort." [1]

In the month of November, *The Index* began to report these meetings. In nearly all, Northern partisans were present, attempted to heckle the speakers, and usually presented amendments to the address which were voted down. Spence was given great credit for his energy, being called " indefatigable ":

> " The commencement of the session will see Parliament flooded with petitions from every town and from every mill throughout the North. A loud protest will arise against the *faineant* policy which declines to interfere while men of English blood are uselessly murdering each other by thousands, and while England's most important manufacture is thereby ruined. . . . It remains to be seen whether the voice of the North will have any effect upon the policy of the Government." [2]

By " the North " was meant the manufacturing districts and an explanation was made of the difficulty of similar efforts in London because it was really a " congeries of cities," with no such solidarity of interests as characterized " the North." [3] Without London, however, the movement

[1] *Ibid.* Spence to Mason, Dec. 7, 1863.

[2] *The Index*, Dec. 10, 1863, p. 518.

[3] The success of pro-Northern meetings in London was ignored. Lord Bryce once wrote to C. F. Adams, " My recollection is that while many public meetings were held all over Great Britain by those who favoured the cause which promised the extinction of Slavery, no open (i.e., non-ticket)

lacked driving force and it was determined to create there an association which should become the main-spring of further activities. Spence, Beresford Hope, and Lord Eustace Cecil were made a committee to draft a plan and preliminary address. Funds were now forthcoming from the big blockade-running firms ·

> "Some time ago I saw friend Collie, who had made a terrific sum of money, and told him he must come out for the cause in proportion thereto. To this he responded like a brick, I was near saying, but I mean Briton—by offering at once to devote a percentage of cotton out of each steamer that runs the blockade, to the good of the cause. He has given me at once £500 on account of this—which I got to-day in a cheque and have sent on to Lord Eustace Cecil, our treasurer. Thus, you see, we are fairly afloat there." [1]

Yet Spence was fighting against fear that all this agitation was too late:

> "Nevertheless it is not to be disguised that the evil tidings make uphill work of it—very. Public opinion has quite veered round to the belief that the South will be exhausted. The *Times* correspondent's letters do great harm—more especially Gallenga's—who replaced Chas. Mackay at New York. I have, however, taken a berth for Mackay by Saturday's boat, so he will soon be out again and he is dead for our side." [2]

Again Spence asserted the one great hope to be in European intervention:

> "I am now clear in my own mind that unless we get

meeting ever expressed itself on behalf of the South, much as its splendid courage was admired." (Letter, Dec. 1, 1913, in Mass. Hist. Soc. *Proceedings*, Vol. XLVII, p. 55.) No doubt many of these pro-Southern meetings were by ticket, but that many were not is clear from the reports in *The Index.*

[1] Mason Papers. Spence to Mason, Dec. 17, 1863.

[2] *Ibid.* The *weight* of the *Times* is here evident even though Goldwin Smith's statement, made in a speech at Providence, R.I., in 1864, be true that the London *Daily Telegraph*, a paper not committed to either side in America, had three times the circulation of the *Times.* (*The Liberator*, Sept. 30, 1864.) Smith's speech was made on the occasion of receiving the degree of LL.D. from Brown University.

Europe to move—or some improbable convulsion occur in the North—the end will be a sad one. It seems to me therefore, impossible that too strenuous an effort can be made to move our Government and I cannot understand the Southerners who say: 'Oh, what can you make of it?' I have known a man brought back to life two hours after he seemed stone-dead—the efforts at first seemed hopeless, but in case of life or death what effort should be spared?"[1]

The Manchester Southern Club was the most active of those organized by Spence and was the centre for operations in the manufacturing districts. On December 15, a great gathering (as described by *The Index*) took place there with delegates from many of the near-by towns.[2] Forster referred to this and other meetings as "spasmodic and convulsive efforts being made by Southern Clubs to cause England to interfere in American affairs,"[3] but the enthusiasm at Manchester was unquestioned and plans were on foot to bombard with petitions the Queen, Palmerston, Russell and others in authority, but more especially the members of Parliament as a body. These petitions were "in process of being signed in every town and almost in every cotton-mill throughout the district."[4] It was high time for London, if it was desired that she should lead and *control*

[1] *Ibid.* That Mason did contribute Confederate funds to Spence's meetings comes out in later correspondence, but the amount is uncertain.

[2] *The Index*, Dec. 17, 1863, p. 532. "The attendance of representatives was numerous, and the greatest interest was manifested throughout the proceedings. Manchester was represented by Mr. W. R. Callender (Vice-Chairman of the Central Committee), and by Messrs. Pooley, J. H. Clarke, T. Briggs, Rev. Geo. Huntington, Rev. W. Whitelegge, Messrs. Armstrong, Stutter, Neild, Crowther, Stenhouse, Parker, Hough, W. Potter, Bromley, etc. Mr. Mortimer Collins, the Secretary of the Association, was also present. The districts were severally represented by the following gentlemen: Stockport—Messrs. Constantine and Leigh; Rochdale—Mr. Thos. Staley; Bradford—Mr. J. Leach; Hyde—Messrs. Wild and Fletcher; Glossop—Mr. C. Schofield; Oldham—Messrs. Whittaker, Steeple, and Councillor Harrop; Delf and Saddleworth—Mr. Lees, J.P.; Macclesfield—Messrs. Cheetham and Bridge; Heywood—Mr. Fairbrother; Middleton—Mr. Woolstencroft; Alderley (Chorley)—Mr. J. Beesley, etc., etc."

[3] So reported by *The Index*, Jan. 14, 1864, p. 20, in comment on speeches being made by Forster and Massie throughout Lancashire.

[4] *The Index*, Jan. 14, 1864, p. 22.

these activities, to perfect her own Club. "Next week," wrote Lindsay, on January 8, 1864, it would be formally launched under the name of "The Southern Independence Association,"[1] and would be in working order before the reassembling of Parliament.

The organization of meetings by Spence and the formation of the Southern Independence Association were attempts to do for the South what Bright and others had done earlier and so successfully for the North. Tardily the realization had come that public opinion, even though but slightly represented in Parliament, was yet a powerful weapon with which to influence the Government. Unenfranchised England now received from Southern friends a degree of attention hitherto withheld from it by those gentry who had been confident that the goodwill of the bulk of their own class was sufficient support to the Southern cause. Early in the war one little Southern society had indeed been organized, but on so diffident a basis as almost to escape notice. This was the *London Confederate States Aid Association* which came to the attention of Adams and his friends in December, 1862, through the attendance at an early meeting of one, W. A. Jackson ("Jefferson Davis' ex-coachman"), who reported the proceedings to George Thompson. The meeting was held at 3 Devonshire Street, Portland Place, was attended by some fifty persons and was addressed by Dr. Lempriere. A Mr. Beals, evidently an unwelcome guest, interrupted the speaker, was forcibly ejected by a policeman and got revenge by arranging a demonstration against Mason (who was present), confronting him, on leaving the house, with a placard showing a negro in chains.[2] There was no "public effort" contemplated in such a meeting, although funds were to be

[1] Mason Papers. To Mason.

[2] *The Liberator*, Dec. 26, 1862, giving an extract from the London *Morning Star* of Dec. 4, and a letter from George Thompson.

solicited to aid the South. Adams reported the Association as a sort of Club planning to hold regular Wednesday evening meetings of its members, the dues being a shilling a week and the rules providing for loss of membership for non-attendance.[1]

Nothing more is heard of this Association after December, 1862. Possibly its puerilities killed it and in any case it was not intended to appeal to the public.[2] But the launching of the Southern Independence Association betokened the new policy of constructive effort in London to match and guide that already started in the provinces. A long and carefully worded constitution and address depicted the heroic struggles of the Confederates and the "general sympathy" of England for their cause; dwelt upon the "governmental tyranny, corruption in high places, ruthlessness in war, untruthfulness of speech, and causeless animosity toward Great Britain" of the North; and declared that the interests of America and of the world would be best served by the independence of the South. The effect of a full year's penetration in England of Lincoln's emancipation proclamation is shown in the necessity felt by the framers of this constitution to meet that issue. This required delicate handling and was destined to cause some heart-burnings. The concluding section of the constitution read:

> "The Association will also devote itself to the cultivation of kindly feelings between the people of Great Britain and of the Confederate States; and it will, in particular, steadily but kindly represent to the Southern States, that recognition by Europe must necessarily lead to a revision of the system

[1] *U.S. Diplomatic Correspondence*, 1863, Pt. I, p. 18. Adams to Seward, Dec. 18, 1862, enclosing a pamphlet issued by the Association.

[2] Its appeal for funds was addressed in part to women. "Fairest and best of earth! for the sake of violated innocence, insulted virtue, and the honour of your sex, come in woman's majesty and omnipotence and give strength to a cause that has for its object the highest human aims—the amelioration and exaltation of humanity."

of servile labour, unhappily bequeathed to them by England, in accordance with the spirit of the age, so as to combine the gradual extinction of slavery with the preservation of property, the maintenance of the civil polity, and the true civilization of the negro race." [1]

The Association was unquestionably armed with distinguished guns of heavy calibre in its Committee and officers, and its membership fee (one guinea annually) was large enough to attract the élite, but it remained to be seen whether all this equipment would be sent into action. As yet the vigour of the movement was centred at Manchester and even there a curious situation soon arose. Spence in various speeches, was declaring that the "Petition to Parliament" movement was spreading rapidly. 30,000 at Ashton, he said, had agreed to memoralize the Government. But on January 30, 1864, Mason Jones, a pro-Northern speaker in the Free Trade Hall at Manchester, asked why Southern public meetings had come to a halt.

[1] *The Index*, Jan. 14, 1864, p. 23. The committee of organization was as follows :—

The Most Noble the Marquis of Lothian,
The Most Noble the Marquis of Bath,
The Lord Robert Cecil, M.P.,
The Lord Eustace Cecil,
The Right Honourable Lord Wharncliffe.
The Right Honourable Lord Campbell,
The Hon. C. Fitzwilliam, M.P.,
The Honourable Robt. Bourke,
Edward Akroyd, Esq., Halifax,
Colonel Greville, M.P.,
W. H. Gregory, Esq., M.P.,
T. C. Haliburton, Esq., M.P.,
A. J. B. Beresford Hope, Esq.,
W. S. Lindsay, Esq., M.P.,
G. M. W. Peacocke, Esq., M.P.,
Wm. Scholefield, Esq., M.P.,
James Spence, Esq., Liverpool,
William Vansittart, Esq., M.P.

Chairman : A. J. B. Beresford Hope, Esq.
Treasurer : The Lord Eustace Cecil.

"The Southerners," he declared, "had taken the Free Trade Hall in the outset with that intention and they were obliged to pay the rent of the room, though they did not use it. They knew that their resolutions would be outvoted and that amendments would pass against them."[1] There must have been truth in the taunt for while *The Index* in nearly every issue throughout the middle of 1864 reports great activity there, it does not give any account of a public meeting. The reports were of many applications for membership "from all quarters, from persons of rank and gentlemen of standing in their respective counties."[2]

Just here lay the weakness of the Southern Independence Association programme. It *did* appeal to "persons of rank and gentlemen of standing," but by the very fact of the flocking to it of these classes it precluded appeal to Radical and working-class England—already largely committed to the cause of the North. Goldwin Smith, in his "Letter to a Whig Member of the Southern Independence Association," made the point very clear.[3] In this pamphlet, probably the strongest presentation of the Northern side and the most severe castigation of Southern sympathizers that appeared throughout the whole war, Smith appealed to old Whig ideas of political liberty, attacked the aristocracy and the Church of England, and attempted to make the

[1] *The Liberator*, Feb. 26, 1864.

[2] *The Index*, March 17, 1864, p. 174. An amusing reply from an "historian" inclined to dodge is printed as of importance. One would like to know his identity, and what his "judicial situation" was. "An eminent Conservative historian writes as follows: 'I hesitate to become a member of your Association from a doubt whether I should take that open step to which my inclinations strongly prompt me, or adhere to the neutrality in public life to which, as holding a high and responsible judicial situation in this country, I have hitherto invariably confined myself. And after mature consideration I am of opinion that it will be more decorous to abide in this instance by my former rule. I am the more inclined to follow this course from the reflection that by not appearing in public as an advocate of the Southern States, I shall be able to serve their cause more effectually in my literary character. And the printing of a new edition of my "History" (which is now going on) will afford me several opportunities of doing so, of which I shall not fail gladly to avail myself.'"

[3] Printed, London, 1864.

Radicals of England feel that the Northern cause was their cause. Printing the constitution and address of the Association, with the list of signers, he characterized the movement as fostered by "men of title and family," with "a good sprinkling of clergymen," and as having for its object the plunging of Great Britain into war with the North.[1]

It is significant, in view of Mason Jones' taunt to the Southern Independence Association at Manchester, that *The Index*, from the end of March to August, 1864, was unable to report a single Southern public meeting. The London Association, having completed its top-heavy organization, was content with that act and showed no life. The first move by the Association was planned to be made in connection with the *Alexandra* case when, as was expected, the Exchequer Court should render a decision against the Government's right to detain her. On January 8, 1864, Lindsay wrote to Mason that he had arranged for the public launching of the Association "next week," that he had again seen the Chief Baron who assured him the Court would decide "that the Government is entirely wrong":

> "I told him that if the judgment was clear, and if the Government persisted in proceeding further, that our Association (which he was pleased to learn had been formed) would take up the matter in Parliament and out of it, for if we had no right to seize these ships, it was most unjust that we should detain them by raising legal quibbles for the

[1] At the time a recently-printed work by a clergyman had much vogue: "The South As It Is, or Twenty-one Years' Experience in the Southern States of America." By Rev. T. D. Ozanne. London, 1863. Ozanne wrote: "Southern society has most of the virtues of an aristocracy, increased in zest by the democratic form of government, and the freedom of discussion on all topics fostered by it. It is picturesque, patriarchal, genial. It makes a landed gentry, it founds families, it favours leisure and field sports; it develops a special class of thoughtful, responsible, guiding, and protecting minds; it tends to elevation of sentiment and refinement of manners" (p. 61). Especially he insisted the South was intensely religious and he finally dismissed slavery with the phrase: "The Gospel of the Son of God has higher objects to attain than the mere removal of one social evil" (p. 175).

purpose of keeping them here till the time arrived when the South might not require them. I think public opinion will go with us on this point, for John Bull—with all his failings—loves fair play." [1]

It is apparent from the language used by Lindsay that he was thinking of the Laird Rams and other ships fully as much as of the *Alexandra*,[2] and hoped much from an attack on the Government's policy in detaining Southern vessels. Earl Russell was to be made to bear the brunt of this attack on the reassembling of Parliament. In an *Index* editorial, Adams was pictured as having driven Russell into a corner by "threats which would not have been endured for an hour by a Pitt or a Canning"; the Foreign Secretary as invariably yielding to the "acknowledged mastery of the Yankee Minister":

> "Mr. Adams' pretensions are extravagant, his logic is blundering, his threats laughable; but he has hit his mark. We can trace his influence in the detention of the *Alexandra* and the protracted judicial proceedings which have arisen out of it; in the sudden raid upon the rams at Birkenhead; in the announced intention of the Government to alter the Foreign Enlistment Act of this country in accordance with the views of the United States Cabinet. When one knows the calibre of Mr. Adams one feels inclined to marvel at his success. The astonishment ceases when one reflects that the British Secretary for Foreign Affairs is Earl Russell."[3]

But when, on February 23, the debate on the Laird Rams occurred,[4] the Tory leaders, upon whom Lindsay and others depended to drive home the meaning of the *Alexandra* decision, carefully avoided urging the Govern-

[1] Mason Papers.

[2] The *Alexandra*,, as a result of the Court's decision, was again appealed, but on an adverse decision was released, proceeded to Nassau, where she was again libelled in the Vice-Admiralty Court of the Bahamas, and again released. She remained at Nassau until the close of the war, thus rendering no service to the South. (Bernard, pp. 354-5.)

[3] Feb. 4, 1864, p. 73.

[4] See Ch. XIII.

ment to change its policy and contented themselves with an effort, very much in line with that initiated by *The Index*, to belittle Russell as yielding to a threat. Adams was even applauded by the Tories for his discretion and his anxiety to keep the two countries out of war. The Southern Independence Association remained quiescent. Very evidently someone, presumably Derby or Disraeli, had put a quietus on the plan to make an issue of the stoppage of Southern ship-building. Russell's reply to his accusers was but a curt denial without going into details, in itself testimony that he had no fear of a party attack on the *policy* of stopping the ships. He was disgusted with the result of the *Alexandra* trial and in conversation with Adams reflected upon "the uncertainty and caprice incident everywhere to the administration of justice."[1]

As between Russell and Seward the waters formerly troubled by the stiff manner and tone of the one statesman and the flamboyance of the other were now unusually calm. Russell was less officious and less eager to protest on minor matters and Seward was less belligerent in language. Seward now radiated supreme confidence in the ultimate victory of the North. He had heard rumours of a movement to be made in Parliament for interposition to bring the war to an end by a reunion of North and South on a basis of Abolition and of a Northern assumption of the Confederate debts. Commenting on this to Lyons he merely remarked that the Northern answer could be put briefly as: (1) determination to crush rebellion by force of arms and resentment of any "interposition"; (2) the slaves were already free and would not be made the subject of any bargain; (3) "As to the Confederate debt the United States, Mr. Seward said, would never pay a dollar of it."[2] That there was public animosity to Great Britain, Lyons

[1] State Department, Eng. Adams to Seward, April 7, 1864.
[2] F. O., Am., Vol. 944, No. 81. Lyons to Russell, Feb. 1, 1864.

did not deny and reported a movement in Congress for ending the reciprocity treaty with Canada but, on Seward's advice, paid no attention to this, acknowledging that Seward was very wise in political manipulation and depending on his opposition to the measure.[1] Some alarm was indeed caused through a recurrence by Seward to an idea dating back to the very beginning of the war of establishing ships off the Southern ports which should collect duties on imports. He told Lyons that he had sent a special agent to Adams to explain the proposal with a view to requesting the approval of Great Britain. Lyons urged that no such request be made as it was sure to be refused, interpreting the plan as intended to secure a British withdrawal of belligerent rights to the South, to be followed by a bold Northern defiance to France if she objected.[2] Adams did discuss the project with Russell but easily agreed to postpone consideration of it and in this Seward quietly acquiesced.[3] Apparently this was less a matured plan than a "feeler," put out to sound British attitude and to learn, if possible, whether the tie previously binding England and France in their joint policy toward America was still strong. Certainly at this same time Seward was making it plain to Lyons that while opposed to current Congressional expressions of antagonism to Napoleon's Mexican policy, he was himself in favour, once the Civil War was ended, of helping the republican Juarez drive the French from Mexico.[4]

For nearly three years Russell, like nearly all Englishmen, had held a firm belief that the South could not be conquered and that ultimately the North must accept the bitter pill of Southern independence. Now he began to doubt, yet still held to the theory that even if conquered the South would never yield peaceful obedience to the Federal Govern-

[1] Russell Papers. Lyons to Russell, Feb. 9, 1864.
[2] F. O., Am., Vol. 944, No. 98. Lyons to Russell, Feb. 12, 1864.
[3] *Ibid.*, Vol. 946, No. 201. Lyons to Russell, March 22, 1864.
[4] *Ibid.*, Vol. 945, No. 121. Lyons to Russell, Feb. 23, 1864.

ment. As a reasoning and reasonable statesman he wished that the North could be made to see this.

> "... It is a pity," he wrote to Lyons, "the Federals think it worth their while to go on with the war. The obedience they are ever likely to obtain from the South will not be quiet or lasting, and they must spend much money and blood to get it. If they can obtain the right bank of the Mississippi, and New Orleans, they might as well leave to the Confederates Charleston and Savannah."[1]

This was but private speculation with no intention of urging it upon the United States. Yet it indicated a change in the view held as to the warlike *power* of the North. Similarly the *Quarterly Review*, long confident of Southern success and still prophesying it, was acknowledging that "the unholy [Northern] dream of universal empire" must first have passed.[2] Throughout these spring months of 1864, Lyons continued to dwell upon the now thoroughly developed readiness of the United States for a foreign war and urged the sending of a military expert to report on American preparations.[3] He was disturbed by the arrogance manifested by various members of Lincoln's Cabinet, especially by Welles, Secretary of the Navy, with whom Seward, so Lyons wrote, often had difficulty in demonstrating the unfortunate diplomatic bearing of the acts of naval officers. Seward was as anxious as was Lyons to avoid irritating incidents, "but he is not as much listened to as he ought to be by his colleagues in the War and Navy Departments."[4]

[1] Lyons Papers, April 23, 1864.

[2] April, 1864.

[3] Russell Papers. Lyons to Russell, April 19, 1864, and F. O., Am., Vol. 948, No. 284. Lyons to Russell, April 25, 1864. A Captain Goodenough was sent to America and fully confirmed Lyons' reports.

[4] Russell Papers. Lyons to Russell, May 9, 1864. The tone of the *New York Herald* might well have given cause for anxiety. "In six months at the furthest, this unhappy rebellion will be brought to a close. We shall then have an account to settle with the Governments that have either outraged us by a recognition of what they call 'the belligerent rights'

Such an act by a naval officer, defiant of British authority and disregardful of her law, occurred in connection with a matter already attracting the attention of the British public and causing some anxiety to Russell—the alleged securing in Ireland of enlistments for the Northern forces. The war in America had taken from the ranks of industry in the North great numbers of men and at the same time had created an increased demand for labour. But the war had also abruptly checked, in large part, that emigration from Europe which, since the middle 'forties, had been counted upon as a regular source of labour supply, easily absorbed in the steady growth of productive enterprise. A few Northern emissaries of the Government early sent abroad to revive immigration were soon reinforced by private labour agents and by the efforts of steamship companies.[1] This resulted in a rapid resumption of

of the rebels, or by the active sympathy and aid which they have afforded them. Let France and England beware how they swell up this catalogue of wrongs. By the time specified we shall have unemployed a veteran army of close upon a million of the finest troops in the world, with whom we shall be in a position not only to drive the French out of Mexico and to annex Canada, but, by the aid of our powerful navy, even to return the compliment of intervention in European affairs." (Quoted by *The Index*, July 23, 1863, p. 203.)

[1] Bigelow, *Retrospections*, I, p. 563, states that great efforts were made by the Government to stimulate immigration both to secure a labour supply and to fill up the armies. Throughout and even since the war the charge has been made by the South that the foreign element, after 1862, preponderated in Northern armies. There is no way of determining the exact facts in regard to this for no statistics were kept. A Memorandum prepared by the U.S. War Department, dated July 15, 1898, states that of the men examined for physical fitness by the several boards of enrolment, subsequent to September 1, 1864 (at which time, if ever, the foreign element should have shown preponderance), the figures of nativity stood: United States, 341,569; Germany, 54,944; Ireland, 50,537; British-America, 21,645; England, 16,196; and various other countries no one of which reached the 3,500 mark. These statistics really mean little as regards war-time immigration since they do not show *when* the foreign-born came to America; further, from the very first days of the war there had been a large element of American citizens of German and Irish birth in the Northern armies. Moreover, the British statistics of emigration, examined in relation to the figures given above, negative the Southern accusation. In 1861, but 38,000 subjects of Great Britain emigrated to the United States; in 1862, 48,000; while in 1863 the number suddenly swelled to 130,000, and this figure was repeated in 1864. In each year almost exactly two-thirds were from Ireland. Now of the 94,000 from Ireland in 1863, considering the number of Irish-American citizens already in the army, it is evident that the bulk must have gone into labour supply.

emigration in 1863, and in several cases groups of Irishmen signed contracts of such a nature (with non-governmental agents) that on arrival in America they were virtually black-jacked into the army. The agents thereby secured large profits from the sums offered under the bounty system of some of the Eastern states for each recruit. Lyons soon found himself called upon to protest, on appeal from a few of these hoodwinked British citizens, and Seward did the best he could to secure redress, though the process was usually a long one owing to red-tape and also to the resistance of army officers.

As soon as the scheme of "bounty profiteers" was discovered prompt steps were taken to defeat it by the American Secretary of State. But the few cases occurring, combined with the acknowledged and encouraged agents of *bona fide* labour emigration from Ireland, gave ground for accusations in Parliament that Ireland was being used against the law as a place of enlistments. Russell had early taken up the matter with Adams, investigation had followed, and on it appearing that no authorized Northern agent was engaged in recruiting in Ireland the subject had been dropped.[1] There could be and was no objection to encourage labour emigration, and this was generally recognized as the basis of the sudden increase of the numbers going to America.[2] But diplomatic and public quiescence was disturbed when the United States war vessel *Kearsarge*, while in port at Queenstown, November, 1863, took on board fifteen Irishmen and sailed away with them. Russell at once received indirectly from Mason (who was now in France), charges that these men had been enlisted and in the presence of the American consul at Queenstown; he was prompt in investigation but before this was well under

[1] *Parliamentary Papers*, 1863, *Commons*, LXXII. "Correspondence with Mr. Adams respecting enlistment of British subjects."

[2] The *Times*, Nov. 21, 1863. Also March 31, 1864.

way the *Kearsarge* sailed into Queenstown again and landed the men. She had gone to a French port and no doubt Adams was quick to give orders for her return. Adams was soon able to disprove the accusation against the consul but it still remained a question whether the commander of the vessel was guilty of a bold defiance of British neutrality. On March 31, 1864, the Irishmen, on trial at Cork, pleaded guilty to violation of the Foreign Enlistment Act, but the question of the commander's responsibility was permitted to drop on Adams' promise, April 11, of further investigation.[1]

The *Kearsarge* case occurred as Parliament was drawing to a close in 1863, and at a time when Southern efforts were at low ebb. It was not, therefore, until some months later when a gentleman with a shady past, named Patrick Phinney, succeeded in evading British laws and in carrying off to America a group of Irishmen who found themselves, unwillingly, forced into the Northern army, that the two cases were made the subject of a Southern and Tory attack on Russell. The accusations were sharply made that Russell was not sufficiently active in defending British law and British honour,[2] but these were rather individual accusations than concerted and do not indicate any idea of making an issue with the Government.[3] Whenever opportunity arose some inquiry up to July, 1864, would be made intended to bring out the alleged timidity of Russell's policy towards the North—a method then also being employed on many other matters with the evident intention

[1] *Parliamentary Papers*, 1864, *Commons*, LXII. "Correspondence respecting the Enlistment of British seamen at Queenstown." Also "Further Correspondence," etc.

[2] For facts and much correspondence on the Phinney case see *Parliamentary Papers*, 1864, *Commons*, LXII. "Correspondence respecting the Enlistment of British subjects in the United States Army." Also "Further Correspondence," etc.

[3] Hansard, 3rd Ser., CLXXIV, p. 628, and CLXXV, p. 353, and CLXXVI, p. 2161. In the last of these debates, July 28, 1864, papers were asked for on "Emigration to America," and readily granted by the Government.

of weakening the Ministry for the great Tory attack now being organized on the question of Danish policy.

In truth from the beginning of 1864, America had been pushed to one side in public and parliamentary interest by the threatening Danish question which had long been brewing but which did not come into sharp prominence until March. A year earlier it had become known that Frederick VII of Denmark, in anticipation of a change which, under the operations of the Salic law, would come at his death in the constitutional relations of Denmark to Schleswig-Holstein, was preparing by a new "constitutional act" to secure for his successor the retention of these districts. The law was enacted on November 13, 1863, and Frederick VII died two days later. His successor, Christian IX, promptly declared his intention to hold the duchies in spite of their supposed desire to separate from Denmark and to have their own Prince in the German Confederation. The Federal Diet of the Confederation had early protested the purpose of Denmark and Russell had at first upheld the German arguments but had given no pledges of support to anyone.[1] But Palmerston on various occasions had gone out of his way to express in Parliament his favour for the Danish cause and had used incautious language even to the point of virtually threatening British aid against German ambitions.[2] A distinct crisis was thus gradually created, coming to a head when Prussia, under Bismarck's guiding hand, dragging Austria in with her, thrust the Federal Diet of the Confederation to one side, and assumed command of the movement to wrest Schleswig-Holstein from Denmark.

This occurred in February, 1864, and by this time Palmerston's utterances, made against the wish of the

[1] Walpole, *History of Twenty-five Years*, Vol. I, Ch. VI.

[2] In the Cabinet, Palmerston (and to some extent Russell) was opposed by Granville and Clarendon (the latter of whom just at this time entered the Cabinet) and by the strong pro-German influence of the Queen. (Fitzmaurice, *Granville*, I, Ch. XVI.)

majority of his Cabinet colleagues (though this was not known), had so far aroused the British public as to have created a feeling, widely voiced, that Great Britain could not sit idly by while Prussia and Austria worked their will on Denmark. There was excellent ground for a party attack to unseat the Ministry on the score of a humiliating "Danish policy," at one time threatening vigorous British action, then resorting to weak and unsuccessful diplomatic manœuvres. For three months the Government laboured to bring about through a European council some solution that should both save something for Denmark and save its own prestige. Repeatedly Palmerston, in the many parliamentary debates on Denmark, broke loose from his Cabinet colleagues and indulged in threats which could not fail to give an excellent handle to opponents when once it became clear that the Ministry had no intention of coming in arms to the defence of the Danish King.

From February to June, 1864, this issue was to the fore. In its earlier stages it did not appear to Southern sympathizers to have any essential bearing on the American question, though they were soon to believe that in it lay a great hope. Having set the Southern Independence Association on its feet in London and hoping much from its planned activities, Lindsay, in March, was momentarily excited over rumours of some new move by Napoleon. Being undeceived[1] he gave a ready ear to other rumours, received privately through Delane of the *Times*, that an important Southern victory would soon be forthcoming.[2] Donoughmore, the herald of this glad news also wrote:

> "Our political prospects here are still very uncertain. The Conference on the Danish question will either make or

[1] Mason Papers. Slidell to Mason, March 13, 1864.

[2] This came through a letter from Donoughmore to Mason, April 4, 1864, stating that it was private information received by Delane from Mackay, the *Times* New York correspondent. The expected Southern victory was to come "in about fourteen days." (Mason Papers.)

mar the Government. If they can patch up a peace they will remain in office. If they fail, out they go." [1]

Here was early expressed the real hope of one faction of extreme Southern friends in the Danish question. But Lindsay had not yet made clear where he stood on a possible use of a European situation to affect the cause of the South. Now, as always, he was the principal confidant and friend of Mason in England, but he was on ordinary political questions not in sympathy with Tory principles or measures. He was soon disgusted with the apathy of the London Independence Association and threatened to resign membership if this organization, started with much trumpeting of intended activity, did not come out boldly in a public demand for the recognition of the South. [2] He had already let it be known that another motion would be made in Parliament for mediation and recognition and was indignant that the Association did not at once declare its adherence. Evidently there were internal difficulties. Lindsay wrote Mason that he retained membership only to prevent a break up of the Association and had at last succeeded in securing a meeting of the Executive Committee when his proposed parliamentary resolution would be considered. The Manchester Association was much more alert and ready to support him. "The question is quite ripe *for fresh agitation* and from experience I find that that agitation *must* be started by a debate in Parliament. No notice is taken of lectures or speeches in the provinces." [3]

Before any move was made in Parliament letters to the newspapers began anew to urge that the Ministry should be pressed to offer mediation in America. They met with little favourable response. The *Times*, at the very end of Lindsay's effort, explained its indifference,

[1] *Ibid.*
[2] Mason Papers. Lindsay to Beresford Hope, April 8, 1864.
[3] *Ibid.* Lindsay to Mason, May 10, 1864.

and recited the situation of October-November, 1862, stating that the question had then been decided once for all. It declared that Great Britain had "no moral right to interfere" and added that to attempt to do so would result in filling "the North with the same spirit of patriotism and defiance as animated the invaded Confederates."[1] Thus support to Lindsay was lacking in a hoped-for quarter, but his conferences with Association members had brought a plan of modified action the essential feature of which was that the parliamentary motion must not be made a *party* one and that the only hope of the South lay in the existing Government. This was decidedly Lindsay's own view though it was clearly understood that the opportuneness of the motion lay in ministerial desire for and need of support in its Danish policy. Lindsay expected to find Palmerston more complaisant than formerly as regards American policy and was not disappointed. He wrote to Mason on May 27:

> "I received in due course your note of the 23rd. In a matter of so much importance I shall make no move in the House in regard to American affairs without grave consideration. I am therefore privately consulting the friends of the South. On this subject we had a meeting of our lifeless association on Monday last and on the same subject we are to have another meeting next Monday; but differences of opinion exist there as well as elsewhere, as to the advisability of moving at present. Some say 'move'—others, 'postpone'—but the news by the *Scotia* to-morrow will regulate to a considerable extent our course of action. One thing is now clear to me that the motion must *not* be a party one, and that the main point will be to get the Government to go with *whoever* brings forward the motion, for as you are aware I would rather see the motion in other hands than mine, as my views on the American question are so well known. As no competent member however seems disposed to move or rather to incur the responsibility,

[1] July 18, 1864.

I sent to inquire if it would be agreeable to Lord Palmerston to see me on American affairs and on the subject of a motion to be brought forward in the House. He sent word that he would be very glad to see me, and I had, therefore, a long meeting with him alone last night, the result of which was that if I brought forward a motion somewhat as follows, on the third of June, he would likely be prepared *to accept it,* though he asked if I would see him again after the *Scotia* arrived. The motion we talked about was to this *effect*—'That the House of Commons deeply regretting the great loss of life and the sufferings of the people of the United States and the Confederate States of North America by the continuance of the war which has been so long waged between them, trust that Her Majesty's Government will avail itself of the earliest opportunity of mediating in conjunction with the other powers of Europe to bring about a cessation of hostilities.'"

Lindsay had suggested to Palmerston that it was desirable for Mason to return to England and have a conference with the Premier. To this Palmerston gave a ready consent but, of course, no invitation. Lindsay strongly urged Mason to come over:

"*I think much good will follow your meeting Lord Palmerston. It will lead to other meetings;* and besides in other matters I think if you came here, you might *at present* prove of much service to the South." [1]

Meanwhile the difference within the Southern Independence Association permitted the coming forward of a minor London organization called *The Society for Promoting the Cessation of Hostilities in America.* A letter was addressed by it to Members of Parliament urging that the time had come for action:

"215 *Regent Street,*
London, W.
May 28th, 1864.

"SIR,

"The Society which has the honour to present to you

[1] Mason Papers.

the accompanying pamphlet, begs to state that there now exists in Great Britain and Ireland a strong desire to see steps taken by the Government of this country in concert with other Powers, to bring about peace on a durable basis between the belligerents in North America.

"I am directed by the Committee to express a hope that you will, before the Session closes, support a motion in Parliament to this effect; and should you desire to see evidence of the feeling of a large portion of the country in this matter, I shall be most happy to lay it before you." [1]

Whether Lindsay, vexed with the delays of the Association, had stirred the Society to action, is not clear, but the date of this letter, following on the day after the interview with Palmerston, is suggestive. The pressure put on Mason to come to London was not at first successful. Mason had become fixed in the opinion, arrived at in the previous fall, that there was no favour to be expected from Palmerston or Russell and that the only hope rested in their overthrow. Against this idea Lindsay had now taken definite ground. Moreover, Mason had been instructed to shake the dust of England from off his shoes with no official authority to return. Carefully explaining this last point to Lindsay he declined to hold an interview with Palmerston, except on the latter's invitation, or at least suggestion:

"Had the suggestion you make of an interview and conversation with Lord Palmerston originated with his Lordship I might not have felt myself prohibited by my instructions from at once acceding to it, but as it has the form only of his assent to a proposition from you I must with all respect decline it.

"Although no longer accredited by my Government as Special Commissioner to Great Britain, I am yet in Europe with full powers, and therefore, had Lord Palmerston expressed a desire to see me as his own act (of course unofficially, and even without any reason assigned for the

[1] Sample letter in Mason Papers.

interview) I should have had great pleasure in complying with his request." [1]

The explanation of disinclination to come was lengthy, but the last paragraph indicated an itching to be active in London again. Lindsay renewed his urgings and was not only hopeful but elated over the seeming success of his overtures to the Government. He had again seen Palmerston and had now pushed his proposal beyond the timid suggestion of overtures when the opportune moment should arrive to a definite suggestion of recognition of the Confederacy:

> "I reasoned on the *moral* effect of recognition, considering that the restoration of the Union, which was utterly hopeless, was the object which the North had in view, etc., etc. This reasoning appeared to produce a considerable effect, for he appears now to be very open to conviction. He again said that in his opinion the subjugation of the South could not be effected by the North, and he added that he thought the people of the North were becoming more and more alive to the fact every day."

Lindsay's next step was to be the securing of an interview with Russell and if he was found to be equally acquiescent all would be plain sailing:

> "Now, if by strong reasoning in a quiet way, and by stern facts we can get Lord R. to my views, I think I may say that all difficulty so far as our Cabinet is concerned, *is at an end*. I hope to be able to see Lord Russell alone to-morrow. He used to pay some little attention to any opinions I ventured to express to him, and I am *not* without hope. I may add that I was as frank with Lord Palmerston as he has been pleased to be with me, and I told him at parting to-day, that my present intention was not to proceed with the Motion at least for 10 days or a fortnight, unless he was prepared to support me. He highly commended this course, and seemed much gratified with what I said. The fact is, *sub rosa*, it is clear to me that *no* motion will be carried unless

[1] Mason Papers. Mason to Lindsay, May 29, 1864.

> it is supported by the Government for it is clear that Lord Derby is resolved to leave the responsibility with the Executive, and therefore, *in the present state of matters*, it would seriously injure the cause of the South to bring forward any motion which would not be carried."

Lindsay then urges Mason to come at once to London.

> "Now apart altogether from you seeing Lord Palmerston, I must earnestly entreat you to come here. Unless you are much wanted in Paris, your visit here, as a private gentleman, can do no harm, and *may, at the present moment, be of great service to your country*." [1]

Palmerston's willingness to listen to suggestions of what would have amounted to a complete face-about of British policy on America, his "gratification" that Lindsay intended to postpone the parliamentary motion, his friendly courtesy to a man whom he had but recently rebuked for a meddlesome "amateur diplomacy," can be interpreted in no other light than an evidence of a desire to prevent Southern friends from joining in the attack, daily becoming more dangerous, on the Government's Danish policy. How much of this Lindsay understood is not clear; on the face of his letters to Mason he would seem to have been hoodwinked, but the more reasonable supposition is, perhaps, that much was hoped from the governmental necessity of not alienating supporters. The Danish situation was to be used, but without an open threat. In addition the tone of the public press, for some time gloomy over Southern prospects, was now restored to the point of confidence and in this the *Times* was again leading.[2] The Society for Promoting the Cessation of Hostilities in America quickly issued another circular letter inviting Members of Parliament to join in a deputation to call on Palmerston to urge action

[1] *Ibid.* Lindsay to Mason, May 30, 1864.

[2] Editorials of May 28 and 30, 1864, painted a dark picture for Northern armies.

on the lines of Lindsay's first overture. Such a deputation would represent " more than 5,000 members and the feeling of probably more than twenty millions of people." It should not be a deputation " of parties " but representative of all groups in Parliament :

> " The Society has reason to believe that the Premier is disposed to look favourably upon the attempt here contemplated and that the weight of an influential deputation would strengthen his hands." [1]

This proposal from the Society was now lagging behind Lindsay's later objective—namely, direct recognition. That this was felt to be unfortunate is shown by a letter from Tremlett, Honorary Secretary of the Society, to Mason. He wrote that the *Southern Independence Association*, finally stirred by Lindsay's insistence, had agreed to join the Society in a representation to Palmerston but had favoured some specific statement on recognition. Palmerston had sent word that he favoured the Society's resolution but not that of the Association, and as a result the joint letter of the two organizations would be on the mild lines of Lindsay's original motion:

> " Although this quite expresses the object of our Society, still I do not think the ' Independence Association ' ought to have ' ratted ' from its principles. It ought not to have consented to ignore the question which it was instituted to bring before Parliament—that of the Independence of the Confederacy—and more than that, the ambiguous ending of the resolution to be submitted is not such as I think ought to be allowed. You know the resolution and therefore I need only quote the obnoxious words ' That Her Majesty's Government will avail itself of the earliest opportunity of mediating, etc.'
>
> " This is just leaving the Government where they have been all along. They have always professed to take ' the

[1] Mason Papers. Sample letter, June 1, 1864. Signed by F. W. Tremlett, Hon. Sec.

earliest opportunity' but of which they are to be the judges!"[1]

Evidently there was confusion in the ranks and disagreement among the leaders of Southern friends. Adams, always cool in judgment of where lay the wind, wrote to Seward on this same day that Lindsay was delaying his motion until the receipt of favourable news upon which to spring it. Even such news, Adams believed, would not alter British policy unless it should depict the "complete defeat and dispersion" of Northern forces.[2] The day following the *Times* reported Grant to be meeting fearful reverses in Virginia and professed to regard Sherman's easy advance toward Atlanta as but a trap set for the Northern army in the West.[3] But in reality the gage of battle for Southern advantage in England was fixed upon a European, not an American, field. Mason understood this perfectly. He had yielded to Lindsay's insistence and had come to London. There he listened to Lindsay's account of the interview (now held) with Russell, and June 8 reported it to Slidell:

> "Of his intercourse with Lord Russell he reports in substance that his Lordship was unusually gracious and seemed well disposed to go into conversation. Lord Russell agreed that the war on the part of the United States was hopeless and that neither could union be restored nor the South brought under the yoke. . . . In regard to Lindsay's motion Lord Russell said, that he could not *accept* it, but if brought up for discussion his side would *speak* favourably of it. That is to say they would commend it if they could not vote for it."

This referred to Lindsay's original motion of using the "earliest opportunity of mediation," and the pleasant

[1] *Ibid.* Tremlett to Mason, June 2, 1864.

[2] State Department, Eng., Vol. 86, No. 705. Adams to Seward, June 2, 1864.

[3] June 3, 1864.

reception given by Russell scarcely justified any great hope of decided benefit for the South. It must now have been fairly apparent to Lindsay, as it certainly was to Mason, that all this complaisance by Palmerston and Russell was but political manipulation to retain or to secure support in the coming contest with the Tories. The two old statesmen, wise in parliamentary management, were angling for every doubtful vote. Discussing with Lindsay the prospects for governmental action Mason now ventured to suggest that perhaps the best chances of success lay with the Tories, and found him unexpectedly in agreement:

> "I told Lindsay (but for his ear only) that Mr. Hunter, editor of the *Herald*, had written to Hotze about his connection with Disraeli, and he said at once, that if the latter took it up in earnest, it could not be in better hands and would carry at the expense of the Ministry and that he would most cheerfully and eagerly yield him the *pas*. Disraeli's accession, as you remember, was contingent upon our success in Virginia—and agreeing entirely with Lindsay that the movement could not be in better hands and as there were but 10 days before his motion could again come, I thought the better policy would be for the present that he should be silent and to await events." [1]

Slidell was less sceptical than was Mason but agreed that it might best advantage the South to be rid of Russell:

> "If Russell can be trusted, which to me is very doubtful, Lindsay s motion must succeed. Query, how would its being brought forward by Disraeli affect Russell's action—if he can be beaten on a fair issue it would be better for us perhaps than if it appeared to be carried with his qualified assent." [2]

But Mason understood that Southern expectation of a

[1] Mason Papers. Mason to Slidell, June 8, 1864. Mason wrote to Benjamin that Disraeli had said "to one of his friends and followers" that he would be prepared to bring forward some such motion as that prepared by Lindsay. (Mason's *Mason*, p. 500. To Benjamin, June 9, 1864.) Evidently the friend was Hunter.

[2] Mason Papers. Slidell to Mason, June 9, 1864.

change in British policy toward America must rest (and even then but doubtfully) on a change of Government. By June 29 his personal belief was that the Tory attack on the Danish question would be defeated and that this would "of course postpone Lindsay's projected motion."[1] On June 25, the Danish Conference had ended and the Prussian war with Denmark was renewed. There was a general feeling of shame over Palmerston's bluster followed by a meek British inaction. The debate came on a vote of censure, July 8, in the course of which Derby characterized governmental policy as one of "meddle and muddle." The censure was carried in the Lords by nine votes, but was defeated in the Commons by a ministerial majority of eighteen. It was the sharpest political crisis of Palmerston's Ministry during the Civil War. Every supporting vote was needed.[2]

Not only had Lindsay's motion been postponed but the interview with Palmerston for which Mason had come to London had also been deferred in view of the parliamentary crisis. When finally held on July 14, it resolved itself into a proud and emphatic assertion by Mason that the South could not be conquered, that the North was nearly ready to acknowledge it and that the certainty of Lincoln's defeat in the coming Presidential election was proof of this. Palmerston appears to have said little.

> "At the conclusion I said to him in reply to his remark, that he was gratified in making my acquaintance, that I felt obliged by his invitation to the interview, but that the obligation would be increased if I could take with me any expectation that the Government of Her Majesty was prepared to unite with France, in some act expressive of their sense that the war should come to an end. He said, that perhaps, as I was of opinion that the crisis was at hand,

[1] *Ibid.* Mason to Slidell, June 29, 1864.
[2] Walpole, *History of Twenty-five Years*, Vol. I, Ch. VI.

it might be better to wait until it had arrived. I told him that my opinion was that the crisis had passed, at least so far as that the war of invasion would end with the campaign." [1]

Reporting the interview to Slidell in much the same language, Mason wrote:

"My own impressions derived from the whole interview are, that [while] P. is as well satisfied as I am, that the separation of the States is final and the independence of the South an accomplished fact, the Ministry fears to move under the menaces of the North." [2]

Slidell's comment was bitter:

"I am very much obliged for your account of your interview with Lord Palmerston. It resulted very much as I had anticipated excepting that his Lordship appears to have said even less than I had supposed he would. However, the time has now arrived when it is comparatively of very little importance what Queen or Emperor may say or think about us. A plague, I say, on both your Houses." [3]

Slidell's opinion from this time on was, indeed, that the South had nothing to expect from Europe until the North itself should acknowledge the independence of the Confederacy. July 21, *The Index* expressed much the same view and was equally bitter. It quoted an item in the *Morning Herald* of July 16, to the effect that Mason had secured an interview with Palmerston and that "the meeting was satisfactory to all parties":

"The withdrawal of Mr. Lindsay's motion was, it is said, the result of that interview, the Premier having given a sort of implied promise to support it at a more opportune moment; that is to say, when Grant and Sherman have

[1] Mason's *Mason*, p. 507. Mason to Benjamin, July 14, 1864.
[2] Mason Papers, July 16, 1864.
[3] *Ibid.* To Mason, July 17, 1864.

been defeated, and the Confederacy stand in no need of recognition."

In the same issue *The Index* described a deputation of clergymen, noblemen, Members of Parliament "and other distinguished and influential gentlemen" who had waited upon Palmerston to urge mediation toward a cessation of hostilities in America. Thus at last the joint project of the Southern Independence Association and of the Society for Promoting the Cessation of Hostilities in America had been put in execution *after* the political storm had passed and not before—when the deputation might have had some influence. But the fact was that no deputation, unless a purely party one, could have been collected before the conclusion of the Danish crisis. When finally assembled it "had no party complexion," and the smiling readiness with which it received Palmerston's jocular reply indicating that Britain's safest policy was to keep strictly to neutrality is evidence that even the deputation itself though harassed by Lindsay and others into making this demonstration, was quite content to let well enough alone. Not so *The Index* which sneered at the childishness of Palmerston:

> "... He proved incontestably to his visitors that, though he has been charged with forgetting the vigour of his prime, he can in old age remember the lessons of his childhood, by telling them that
>
> They who in quarrels interpose
> Will often wipe a bloody nose (laughter)—
>
> a quotation which, in the mouth of the Prime Minister of the British Empire, and on such an occasion, must be admitted as not altogether unworthy of Abraham Lincoln himself." [1]

Spence took consolation in the fact that Mason had at last come into personal contact with Palmerston, "even

[1] *The Index*, July 21, 1864, p. 457.

now at his great age a charming contrast to that piece of small human pipe-clay, Lord Russell."[1] But the whole incident of Lindsay's excited efforts, Mason's journey to London and interview with Palmerston, and the deputation, left a bad taste in the mouth of the more determined friends of the South—of those who were Confederates rather than Englishmen. They felt that they had been deceived and toyed with by the Government. Mason's return to London was formally approved at Richmond but Benjamin wrote that the argument for recognition advanced to Palmerston had laid too much stress on the break-down of the North. All that was wanted was recognition which was due the South from the mere facts of the existing situation, and recognition, if accorded, would have at once ended the war without intervention in any form.[2] Similarly *The Index* stated that mediation was an English notion, not a Southern one. The South merely desired justice, that is, recognition.[3] This was a bold front yet one not unwarranted by the military situation in midsummer of 1864, as reported in the press. Sherman's western campaign toward Atlanta had but just started and little was known of the strength of his army or of the powers of Southern resistance. This campaign was therefore regarded as of minor importance. It was on Grant's advance toward Richmond that British attention was fixed; Lee's stiff resistance, the great losses of the North in battle after battle and finally the settling down by Grant to besiege the Southern lines at Petersburg, in late June, 1864, seemed to indicate that once again an offensive in Virginia to " end the war " was doomed to that failure which had marked the similar efforts of each of the three preceding years.

Southern efforts in England to alter British neutrality

[1] Mason Papers. Spence to Mason, July 18, 1864.
[2] Richardson, II, pp. 672-74. Benjamin to Mason, Sept. 20, 1864.
[3] July 21, 1864.

practically ended with Lindsay's proposed but undebated motion of June, 1864, but British confidence in Southern ability to defend herself indefinitely, a confidence somewhat shattered at the beginning of 1864—had renewed its strength by July. For the next six months this was to be the note harped upon in society, by organizations, and in the friendly press.

CHAPTER XVI

BRITISH CONFIDENCE IN THE SOUTH

AFTER three years of great Northern efforts to subdue the South and of Southern campaigns aimed, first, merely toward resistance, but later involving offensive battles, the Civil War, to European eyes, had reached a stalemate where neither side could conquer the other. To the European neutral the situation was much as in the Great War it appeared to the American neutral in December, 1916, at the end of two years of fighting. In both wars the neutral had expected and had prophesied a short conflict. In both, this had proved to be false prophecy and with each additional month of the Civil War there was witnessed an increase of the forces employed and a psychological change in the people whereby war seemed to have become a normal state of society. The American Civil War, as regards continuity, numbers of men steadily engaged, resources employed, and persistence of the combatants, was the "Great War," to date, of all modern conflicts. Not only British, but nearly all foreign observers were of the opinion by midsummer of 1864, after an apparent check to Grant in his campaign toward Richmond, that all America had become engaged in a struggle from which there was scant hope of emergence by a decisive military victory. There was little knowledge of the steady decline of the resources of the South even though Jefferson Davis in a message to the Confederate Congress in February, 1864, had spoken bitterly of Southern disorganization.[1] Yet this belief in stalemate

[1] Dodd, *Jefferson Davis*, p. 232.

in essence still postulated an ultimate Southern victory, for the function of the Confederacy was, after all, to *resist* until its independence was recognized. Ardent friends of the North in England both felt and expressed confidence in the outcome, but the general attitude of neutral England leaned rather to faith in the powers of indefinite Southern resistance, so loudly voiced by Southern champions.

There was now one element in the situation, however, that hampered these Southern champions. The North was at last fully identified with the cause of emancipation; the South with the perpetuation of slavery. By 1864, it was felt to be impossible to remain silent on this subject and even in the original constitution and address of the Southern Independence Association a clause was adopted expressing a hope for the gradual extinction of slavery.[1] This brought Mason some heartburnings and he wrote to Spence in protest, the latter's reply being that he also agreed that the South ought not to be offered gratuitous advice on what was purely "an internal question," but that the topic was full of difficulties and the clause would have to stand, at least in some modified form. At Southern public meetings, also, there arose a tendency to insert in resolutions similar expressions. "In Manchester," Spence wrote, "Mr. Lees, J.P., and the strongest man on the board, brought forward a motion for an address on this subject. I went up to Manchester purposely to quash it and I did so effectually."[2]

Northern friends were quick to strike at this weakness in Southern armour; they repeatedly used a phrase, "The Foul Blot," and by mere iteration gave such currency to it that even in Southern meetings it was repeated. *The Index*, as early as February, 1864, felt compelled to meet the phrase and in an editorial, headed "The Foul Blot,"

[1] See *ante*, p. 192.

[2] Mason Papers. Spence to Mason, Jan. 22, 1864.

argued the error of Southern friends. As long as they could use the word "blot" in characterization of Southern slavery, *The Index* felt that there could be no effective British push for Southern independence and it asserted that slavery, in the sense in which England understood it, did not exist in the Confederacy.

"... It is truly horrible to reduce human beings to the condition of cattle, to breed them, to sell them, and otherwise dispose of them, as cattle. But is it defending such practices to say that the South does none of these things, but that on the contrary, both in theory and in practice, she treats the negro as a fellow-creature, with a soul to be saved, with feelings to be respected, though in the social order in a subordinate place, and of an intellectual organization which requires guardianship with mutual duties and obligations? This system is called slavery, because it developed itself out of an older and very different one of that name, but for this the South is not to blame.

. . . . . .

"But of this the friends of the South may be assured, that so long as they make no determined effort to relieve the Southern character from this false drapery, they will never gain for it that respect, that confidence in the rectitude of Southern motives, that active sympathy, which can alone evoke effective assistance. . . . The best assurance you can give that the destinies of the negro race are safe in Southern hands is, not that the South will repent and reform, but that she has consistently and conscientiously been the friend and benefactor of that race.

. . . . . .

"It is, therefore, always with pain that we hear such expressions as 'the foul blot,' and similar ones, fall from the lips of earnest promoters of Confederate Independence. As a concession they are useless; as a confession they are untrue. . . . Thus the Southerner may retort as we have seen that an Englishman would retort for his country. He might say the South is proud, and of nothing more proud than this—not that she has slaves, but that she has treated them as slaves never were treated before, that she has used power as no nation ever used it under similar circumstances, and that she has solved mercifully and humanely a most difficult problem which has elsewhere defied solution save in blood. Or he might use the unspoken reflection of an honest Southerner at hearing much said of 'the foul blot': 'It was indeed a dark and damnable blot that England left us with, and it required all the efforts of Southern Christianity to pale it as it now is.'" [1]

In 1862 and to the fall of 1863, *The Index* had declared that slavery was not an issue in the war; now its defence of the "domestic institution" of the South, repeatedly made in varying forms, was evidence of the great effect in England of Lincoln's emancipation edicts. *The Index* could not keep away from the subject. In March, quotations were given from the *Reader*, with adverse comments, upon a report of a controversy aroused in scientific circles by a paper read before the Anthropological Society of London. James Hunt was the author and the paper, entitled "The Negro's Place in Nature," aroused the contempt of Huxley who criticized it at the meeting as unscientific and placed upon it the "stigma of public condemnation." The result was a fine controversy among the scientists which could only serve to emphasize the belief that slavery was indeed an issue in the American War and that the South was on the defensive. Winding up a newspaper duel with Hunt who emerged rather badly mauled, Huxley asserted "the North is justified in any expenditure of blood or treasure which shall eradicate a system hopelessly inconsistent with the moral elevation, the political freedom, or the economical progress of the American people. . . ."[2]

Embarrassment caused by the "Foul Blot" issue, the impossibility to many sincere Southern friends of accepting the view-point of *The Index*, acted as a check upon the holding of public meetings and prevented the carrying out of that

[1] *The Index*, Feb. 18, 1864, p. 105.

[2] *The Index*, March 24, 1864, p. 189, quoting the *Reader* for March 19.

intensive public campaign launched by Spence and intended to be fostered by the Southern Independence Association. By the end of June, 1864, there was almost a complete cessation of Southern meetings, not thereafter renewed, except spasmodically for a brief period in the fall just before the Presidential election in America.[1] Northern meetings were continuous throughout the whole period of the war but were less frequent in 1864 than in 1863. They were almost entirely of two types—those held by anti-slavery societies and religious bodies and those organized for, or by, working men. An analysis of those recorded in the files of *The Liberator*, and in the reports sent by Adams to Seward permits the following classification:[2]

Year.	Number.	Character.	
		Anti-Slavery and Religious	Working-men.
1860	3	3	–
1861	7	7	–
1862	16	11	5
1863	82	26	56
1864	21	10	11
1865	5	4	1

Many persons took part in these meetings as presiding

[1] The first Southern meeting in England I have found record of was one reported in the *Spectator*, Nov. 16, 1861, to honour Yancey on his arrival. It was held by the *Fishmongers of London*. Yancey was warmly received and appealed to his hosts on the ground that the South was the best buyer of English goods.

[2] The 134 meetings here listed represent by no means all held, for Goldwin Smith estimated at least 500 after the beginning of 1862., (*The Civil War in America*, London, 1866.) The list may be regarded as an analysis of the more important, attracting the attention of *The Liberator* and of Adams.

officers or as speakers and movers of resolutions; among them those appearing with frequency were George Thompson, Rev. Dr. Cheever, Rev. Newman Hall, John Bright, Professor Newman, Mr. Bagley, M.P., Rev. Francis Bishop, P. A. Taylor, M.P., William Evans, Thomas Bayley Potter, F. W. Chesson and Mason Jones. While held in all parts of England and Scotland the great majority of meetings were held in London and in the manufacturing districts with Manchester as a centre. From the first the old anti-slavery orator of the 'thirties, George Thompson, had been the most active speaker and was credited by all with having given new life to the moribund emancipation sentiment of Great Britain.[1] Thompson asserted that by the end of 1863 there was a "vigilant, active and energetic" anti-slavery society in almost every great town or city.[2] Among the working-men, John Bright was without question the most popular advocate of the Northern cause, but there were many others, not named in the preceding list, constantly active and effective.[3] Forster, in the judgment of many, was the most influential friend of the North in Parliament, but Bright, also an influence in Parliament, rendered his chief service in moulding the opinion of Lancashire and

[1] At a banquet given to Thompson in 1863 he was declared by Bright to have been the "real liberator of the slaves in the English colonies," and by P. A. Taylor as, by his courage "when social obloquy and personal danger had to be incurred for the truth's sake," having rendered great services "to the cause of Abolition in America."

[2] *The Liberator*, Jan. 15, 1864. Letter to James Buffum, of Lynn, Dec. 10, 1863.

[3] Goldwin Smith's pamphlet: "The Civil War in America: An Address read at the last meeting of the Manchester Union and Emancipation Society" (held on January 26, 1866), pays especial tribute to Thomas Bayley Potter, M.P., stating "you boldly allied yourself with the working-men in forming this association." Smith gives a five-page list of other leading members, among whom, in addition to some Northern friends already named, are to be noted Thomas Hughes, Duncan McLaren, John Stuart Mill. There are eleven noted "Professors," among them Cairnes, Thorold Rogers, and Fawcett. The publicity committee of this society during three years had issued and circulated "upwards of four hundred thousand books, pamphlets, and tracts." Here, as previously, the activities of Americans in England are not included. Thus George Francis Train, correspondent of the *New York Herald*, made twenty-three speeches between January, 1861, and March, 1862. ("Union Speeches in England.")

became to American eyes their great English champion, a view attested by the extraordinary act of President Lincoln in pardoning, on the appeal of Bright, and in his honour, a young Englishman named Alfred Rubery, who had become involved in a plot to send out from the port of San Francisco, a Confederate "privateer" to prey on Northern commerce.[1]

This record of the activities of Northern friends and organizations, the relative subsidence of their efforts in the latter part of 1864, thus indicating their confidence in Northern victory, the practical cessation of public Southern meetings, are nevertheless no proof that the bulk of English opinion had greatly wavered in its faith in Southern powers of resistance. The Government, it is true, was better informed and was exceedingly anxious to tread gently in relations with the North, the more so as there was now being voiced by the public in America a sentiment of extreme friendship for Russia as the "true friend" in opposition to the "unfriendly neutrality" of Great Britain and France.[2] It was a period of many minor irritations, arising out of the blockade, inflicted by America on British interests, but to these Russell paid little attention except to enter formal protests. He wrote to Lyons:

> "I do not want to pick a quarrel out of our many just causes of complaint. But it will be as well that Lincoln and Seward should see that we are long patient, and do

[1] For text of Lincoln's pardon see Trevelyan, *Bright*, p. 296. Lincoln gave the pardon "especially as a public mark of the esteem held by the United States of America for the high character and steady friendship of the said John Bright. . . ." The names of leading friends of the South have been given in Chapter XV.

[2] This was a commonplace of American writing at the time and long after. A Rev. C. B. Boynton published a book devoted to the thesis that England and France had united in a "policy" of repressing the development of America and Russia (*English and French Neutrality and the Anglo-French Alliance in their relations to the United States and Russia*, Cincinnati, C. F. Vest & Co., 1864). Boynton wrote: "You have not come to the bottom of the conduct of Great Britain, until you have touched that delicate and real foundation cause—we are too large and strong a nation" (Preface, p. 3). The work has no historical importance except that it was thought worth publication in 1864.

nothing to distract their attention from the arduous task they have so wantonly undertaken."[1]

Lyons was equally desirous of avoiding frictions. In August he thought that the current of political opinion was running against the re-election of Lincoln, noting that the Northern papers were full of expressions favouring an armistice, but pointed out that neither the "peace party" nor the advocates of an armistice ever talked of any solution of the war save on the basis of re-union. Hence Lyons strongly advised that "the quieter England and France were just at this moment the better."[2] Even the suggested armistice was not thought of, he stated, as extending to a relaxation of the blockade. Of military probabilities, Lyons professed himself to be no judge, but throughout all his letters there now ran, as for some time previously, a note of warning as to the great power and high determination of the North.

But if the British Government was now quietly operating upon the theory of an ultimate Northern victory, or at least with the view that the only hope for the South lay in a Northern weariness of war, the leading British newspapers were still indulging in expressions of confidence in the South while at the same time putting much faith in the expected defeat of Lincoln at the polls. As always at this period, save for the few newspapers avowedly friendly to the North and one important daily professing strict neutrality—the *Telegraph*—the bulk of the metropolitan press took its cue, as well as much of its war news, from the columns of the *Times*. This journal, while early assuming a position of belief in Southern success, had yet given both sides in the war fair accuracy in its reports—those of the New York correspondent, Mackay, always excepted. But from June, 1864, a change came over the *Times*; it was either itself

[1] Lyons Papers. July 16, 1864. Copy.
[2] Russell Papers. Lyons to Russell, Aug. 23, 1864.

deceived or was wilfully deceiving its readers, for steadily every event for the rest of the year was coloured to create an impression of the unlimited powers of Southern resistance. Read to-day in the light of modern knowledge of the military situation throughout the war, the *Times* gave accurate reports for the earlier years but became almost hysterical; not to say absurd, for the last year of the conflict. Early in June, 1864, Grant was depicted as meeting reverses in Virginia and as definitely checked, while Sherman in the West was being drawn into a trap in his march toward Atlanta.[1] The same ideas were repeated throughout July. Meanwhile there had begun to be printed a series of letters from a Southern correspondent at Richmond who wrote in contempt of Grant's army.

> "I am at a loss to convey to you the contemptuous tone in which the tried and war-worn soldiers of General Lee talk of the huddled rabble of black, white, and copper-coloured victims (there are Indians serving under the Stars and Stripes) who are at times goaded up to the Southern lines. . . . The truth is that for the first time in modern warfare we are contemplating an army which is at once republican and undisciplined."[2]

At the moment when such effusions could find a place in London's leading paper the facts of the situation were that the South was unable to prevent almost daily desertions and was wholly unable to spare soldiers to recover and punish the deserters. But on this the *Times* was either ignorant or wilfully silent. It was indeed a general British sentiment during the summer of 1864, that the North was losing its power and determination in the war,[3] even though it was unquestioned that the earlier "enthusiasm for the slave-

[1] June 3, 1864.

[2] The *Times*, August 4, 1864. Letters dated June 27 and July 5, 1864.

[3] *A Cycle of Adams' Letters*, II, p. 126. Henry Adams to his brother, May 13, 1864. "The current is dead against us, and the atmosphere so uncongenial that the idea of the possibility of our success is not admitted."

holders" had passed away.[1] One element in the influence of the *Times* was its *seeming* impartiality accompanied by a pretentious assertion of superior information and wisdom that at times irritated its contemporaries, but was recognized as making this journal the most powerful agent in England. Angry at a *Times* editorial in February, 1863, in which Mason had been berated for a speech made at the Lord Mayor's banquet, *The Index* declared:

> "Our contemporary is all things to all men. It not only shouts with the largest crowd, according to the Pickwickian philosophy, but with a skill and daring that command admiration, it shouts simultaneously with opposite and contending crowds. It is everybody's *Times*."[2]

Yet *The Index* knew, and frequently so stated, that the *Times* was at bottom pro-Southern. John Bright's medium, the *Morning Star*, said: "There was something bordering on the sublime in the tremendous audacity of the war news supplied by the *Times*. Of course, its prophecies were in a similar style. None of your doubtful oracles there; none of your double-meaning vaticinations, like that which took poor Pyrrhus in."[3] In short, the *Times* became for the last year of the war the Bible of their faith to Southern sympathizers, and was frequent in its preachments.[4]

There was one journal in London which claimed to have equal if not greater knowledge and authority in military matters. This was the weekly *Army and Navy Gazette*, and its editor, W. H. Russell, in 1861 war correspondent in America of the *Times*, but recalled shortly after his famous letter on the battle of Bull Run, consistently maintained after the war had ended that he had always asserted

[1] *Ibid.*, p. 136. Henry Adams to his brother, June 3, 1864.

[2] *The Index*, Feb. 19, 1863, p. 265.

[3] This was written immediately after the battles of Vicksburg and Gettysburg, but the tone complained of was much more marked in 1864.

[4] The *Times* average of editorials on the Civil War ran two in every three days until May, 1864, and thereafter one in every three days.

the ultimate victory of the North and was, indeed, so pro-Northern in sentiment that this was the real cause of his recall.[1] He even claimed to have believed in Northern victory to the extent of re-union. These protestations after the event are not borne out by the columns of the *Gazette*, for that journal was not far behind the *Times* in its delineation of incidents unfavourable to the North and in its all-wise prophecies of Northern disaster. The *Gazette* had no wide circulation except among those in the service, but its *dicta*, owing to the established reputation of Russell and to the specialist nature of the paper, were naturally quite readily accepted and repeated in the ordinary press. Based on a correct appreciation of man power and resources the *Gazette* did from time to time proclaim its faith in Northern victory,[2] but always in such terms as to render possible a hedge on expressed opinion and always with the assertion that victory would not result in reunion. Russell's most definite prophecy was made on July 30, 1864:

> "The Southern Confederacy, like Denmark, is left to fight by itself, without even a conference or an armistice to

[1] Russell wrote to John Bigelow, March 8, 1865: "You know, perhaps, that, as I from the first maintained the North must win, I was tabooed from dealing with American questions in the *Times* even after my return to England, but *en revanche* I have had my say in the *Army and Navy Gazette*, which I have bought, every week, and if one could be weak and wicked enough to seek for a morbid gratification amid such ruins and blood, I might be proud of the persistence with which I maintained my opinions against adverse and unanimous sentiment" (Bigelow, *Retrospections*, Vol. II, p. 361). Also on June 5, 1865, Russell wrote in his diary: ". . . had the *Times* followed my advice, how different our position would be—not only that of the leading journal, but of England. If ever I did State service, it was in my letters from America." (Atkins, *Life of W. H. Russell*, Vol. II, p. 115.) See also Bigelow, *Retrospections*, I, pp. 344-45. Russell was editor of the *Gazette* on its first appearance as a weekly, January 6, 1860, but left it to go to America. On his return he settled down to his editorial task in November, 1862, and thereafter, throughout the war, the *Gazette* may be regarded as reflecting his views. His entire letters from America to the *Times* constitute a most valuable picture of the months preceding the outbreak of war, but the contempt poured on the Northern army for its defeat at Bull Run made Russell much disliked in the North. This dislike was bitterly displayed in a pamphlet by Andrew D. White ("A Letter to William Howard Russell, LL.D., on passages in his 'Diary North and South'"), published in London in 1863.

[2] June 25, 1864.

aid it ; and it will be strange indeed if the heroism, endurance, and resources of its soldiers and citizens be not eventually dominated by the perseverance and superior means of the Northern States. Let us repeat our profession of faith in the matter. We hold that the Union perished long ago, and that its component parts can never again be welded into a Confederacy of self-governing States, with a common executive, army, fleet, and central government. Not only that. The principle of Union itself among the non-seceding States is so shocked and shattered by the war which has arisen, that the fissures in it are likely to widen and spread, and to form eventually great gulfs separating the Northern Union itself into smaller bodies. But ere the North be convinced of the futility of its efforts to substitute the action of force for that of free will, we think it will reduce the Southern States to the direst misery. . . ." [1]

Such occasional "professions of faith," accompanied by sneers at the "Confederate partisanship" of the *Times*[2] served to differentiate the *Gazette* from other journals, but when it came to description and estimate of specific campaigns there was little to choose between them and consequently little variance in the effect upon the public. Thus a fortnight before his "profession of faith," Russell could comment editorially on Sherman's campaign toward Atlanta :

"The next great Federal army on which the hopes of the North have so long been fixed promises to become a source of fearful anxiety. Sherman, if not retreating, is certainly not advancing ; and, if the Confederates can interfere seriously with his communications, he must fall back as soon as he has eaten up all the supplies of the district. . . . All the enormous advantages possessed by the Federals have been nullified by want of skill, by the interference of Washington civilians, and by the absence of an animating homogeneous spirit on the part of their soldiery." [3]

[1] The *Army and Navy Gazette*, July 30, 1864.
[2] *Ibid.*, June 25, 1864.
[3] *Ibid.*, July 16, 1864. Similar articles and editorials might be quoted from many of the more important papers, but the *Times* and the *Gazette*

Hand in hand with war news adverse to the North went comments on the Presidential election campaign in America, with prophecies of Lincoln's defeat. This was indeed but a reflection of the American press but the citations made in

will suffice as furnishing the keynote. I have not examined in detail the files of the metropolitan press beyond determining their general attitude on the Civil War and for occasional special references. Such examination has been sufficient, however, to warrant the conclusion that the *weight* of the *Times* in influencing opinion was very great. Collating statistics given in:

(1) Grant's *The Newspaper Press;* (2) in a speech in Parliament by Edward Banes in 1864 (Hansard, 3rd Ser., CLXXV, p. 295); and (3) in *Parliamentary Papers*, 1861, *Commons*, Vol. XXXIV, "Return of the Registered Newspapers in the United Kingdom .... from 30 June, 1860, to 30 June, 1861," the following facts of circulation are derived:

(A) *Daily Papers*:

(1) *The Telegraph* (evening), 150,000 (neutral).

(2) *The Standard* (morning and evening), 130,000 (Southern). Under the same management was also *The Herald* (morning), but with small circulation (Southern).

(3) The *Times* (morning), 70,000 (Southern). Grant says: "The prestige of the *Times* was remarkable The same articles appearing in other papers would not produce the same effect as in the *Times*." Of Delane, the editor, Grant declared "His name is just as well-known . . . throughout the civilized world as that of any of our European kings. . . . The *Times* may, indeed, be called the Monarch of the Press." (Grant, II, p. 53.)

(4) *The Morning Advertiser* (circulation uncertain, probably 50,000, but very largely taken in the trades, in public-houses, and in the Clubs (neutral).

(5) *The Daily News* (morning), 6,000 (Northern).

(6) *The Morning Star*, 5,500 (but with evening edition 10,000) (Northern). Grant says that contrary to general belief, John Bright was never a shareholder but at times raised money to meet deficits. *The Star* was regarded as an *anti-British paper* and was very unpopular.

(7) *The Morning Post*, 4,500 (Southern). It was regarded as Palmerston's organ.

(8) *The Morning Chronicle*. Very small circulation in the 'sixties (neutral).

(B) *Weekly Papers*.—No approximate circulation figures are available, but these papers are placed by Grant in supposed order of subscribers.

(1) *Reynolds' Weekly*. Circulation upwards of 350,000. A penny paper, extreme Liberal in politics, and very popular in the manufacturing districts (Northern).

(2) *John Bull* (Southern). "The country squire's paper."

(3) *The Spectator* (Northern).

(4) *The Saturday Review* (Southern).

(5) *The Economist* (Neutral).

(6) *The Press and St. James' Chronicle*. Small circulation (Southern).

In addition to British newspapers listed above as Northern in sentiment *The Liberator* names for Great Britain as a whole *Westminster Review, Nonconformist, British Standard, Birmingham Post, Manchester Examiner, Newcastle Chronicle, Caledonian Mercury, Belfast Whig*, and some few others of lesser importance. (*Liberator*, June 30, 1863.) The attitude of the *Manchester Guardian* seemed to *The Liberator* to be like that of the *Times*.

British papers emphasized especially Northern weariness of Lincoln's despotism and inefficiency. Thus, first printed in *The Index*, an extract from a New York paper, *The New Nation*, got frequent quotation:

> "We have been imposed upon long enough. The ruin which you have been unable to accomplish in four years, would certainly be fully consummated were you to remain in power four years longer. Your military governors and their provost-marshals override the laws, and the *echo of the armed heel rings forth as clearly now in America as in France or Austria. You have encroached upon our liberty without securing victory, and we must have both.*" [1]

It was clearly understood that Northern military efforts would have an important bearing on the election. The *Times* while expressing admiration for Sherman's boldness in the Atlanta campaign was confident of his defeat:

> ". . . it is difficult to see how General Sherman can escape a still more disastrous fate than that which threatened his predecessor. He has advanced nearly one hundred and fifty miles from his base of operations, over a mountainous country; and he has no option but to retreat by the same line as he advanced. This is the first instance of a Federal general having ventured far from water communications. That Sherman has hitherto done so with success is a proof of both courage and ability, but he will need both these qualities in a far greater degree if he is forced to retreat." [2]

And W. H. Russell, in the *Gazette*, included Grant in the approaching disaster:

> "The world has never seen anything in war so slow and fatuous as Grant's recent movements, except it be those of Sherman. Each is wriggling about like a snake in the presence of an ichneumon. They both work round and round, now on one flank and then on the other, and on each move meet the unwinking eye of the enemy, ready for his spring and bite.

[1] *The Index*, April 14, 1864, p. 231.
[2] August 8, 1864.

> In sheer despair Grant and Sherman must do something at last. As to shelling! Will they learn from history? Then they will know that they cannot shell an army provided with as powerful artillery as their own out of a position. . . . The Northerners have, indeed, lost the day solely owing to the want of average ability in their leaders in the field." [1]

On the very day when Russell thus wrote in the *Gazette* the city of Atlanta had been taken by Sherman. When the news reached England the *Times* having declared this impossible, now asserted that it was unimportant, believed that Sherman could not remain in possession and, two days later, turned with vehemence to an analysis of the political struggle as of more vital influence. The Democrats, it was insisted, would place peace "paramount to union" and were sure to win.[2] Russell, in the *Gazette*, coolly ignoring its prophecy of three weeks earlier, now spoke as if he had always foreseen the fall of Atlanta:

> "General Sherman has fully justified his reputation as an able and daring soldier; and the final operations by which he won Atlanta are not the least remarkable of the series which carried him from Chattanooga . . . into the heart of Georgia." [3]

But neither of these political-military "expert" journals would acknowledge any benefit accruing to Lincoln from Sherman's success. Not so, however, Lyons, who kept his chief much better informed than he would have been if credulous of the British press. Lyons, who for some time had been increasingly in bad health, had sought escape from the summer heat of Washington in a visit to Montreal. He now wrote correctly interpreting a great change in Northern attitude and a renewed determination to persevere in the war until reunion was secured. Lincoln, he thought, was likely to be re-elected:

[1] Sept. 3, 1864.
[2] Sept. 20 and 22, 1864.
[3] Sept. 24, 1864.

"The reaction produced by the fall of Atlanta may be taken as an indication of what the real feelings of the people in the Northern States are. The vast majority of them ardently desire to reconquer the lost territory. It is only at moments when they despair of doing this that they listen to plans for recovering the territory by negotiation. The time has not come yet when any proposal to relinquish the territory can be publicly made."[1]

The *Times*, slowly convinced that Atlanta would have influence in the election, and as always clever above its contemporaries in the delicate process of face-about to save its prestige, arrived in October at the point where it could join in prediction of Lincoln's re-election. It did so by throwing the blame on the Democratic platform adopted at the party convention in Chicago, which, so it represented, had cast away an excellent chance of success by declaring for union first and peace afterwards. Since the convention had met in August this was late analysis ; and as a matter of fact the convention platform had called for a "cessation of bloodshed" and the calling of a convention to restore peace—in substance, for an armistice. But the *Times*[2] now assumed temporarily a highly moral and disinterested pose and washed its hands of further responsibility ; Lincoln was likely to be re-elected :

For ourselves we have no particular reason to wish it otherwise. We have no very serious matter of complaint that we are aware of against the present Government of America. Allowance being made for the difficulties of their position, they are conducting the war with a fair regard to the rights of neutral nations. The war has swept American commerce from the sea, and placed it, in great measure, in our hands ; we have supplied the loss of the cotton which was suddenly withdrawn from us ; the returns of our revenue and our trade are thoroughly satisfactory, and we

[1] Russell Papers. Lyons to Russell, Sept. 16, 1864.

[2] General McClellan, the nominee of the convention, modified this in his letter of acceptance.

have received an equivalent for the markets closed to us in America in the vast impulse that has been given towards the development of the prosperity of India. We see a great nation, which has not been in times past sparing of its menaces and predictions of our ruin, apparently resolved to execute, without pause and without remorse, the most dreadful judgments of Heaven upon itself. We see the frantic patient tearing the bandages from his wounds and thrusting aside the hand that would assuage his miseries, and every day that the war goes on we see less and less probability that the great fabric of the Union will ever be reconstructed in its original form, and more and more likelihood that the process of disintegration will extend far beyond the present division between North and South. . . . Were we really animated by the spirit of hostility which is always assumed to prevail among us towards America, we should view the terrible spectacle with exultation and delight, we should rejoice that the American people, untaught by past misfortunes, have resolved to continue the war to the end, and hail the probable continuance of the power of Mr. Lincoln as the event most calculated to pledge the nation to a steady continuance in its suicidal policy. But we are persuaded that the people of this country view the prospect of another four years of war in America with very different feelings. They are not able to divest themselves of sympathy for a people of their own blood and language thus wilfully rushing down the path that leadeth to destruction.[1]

Sherman's capture of Atlanta did indeed make certain that Lincoln would again be chosen President, but the *Times* was more slow to acknowledge its military importance, first hinting and then positively asserting that Sherman had fallen into a trap from which he would have difficulty in escaping.[2] The *Gazette* called this "blind partisanship,"[3] but itself indulged in gloomy prognostications as to the character and results of the Presidential election, regarding it as certain that election day would see the use of "force,

[1] Oct. 10, 1864.
[2] Nov. 10, 1864.
[3] Nov. 12, 1864.

fraud and every mechanism known to the most unscrupulous political agitation." "We confess," it continued, "we are only so far affected by the struggle inasmuch as it dishonours the Anglo-Saxon name, and diminishes its reputation for justice and honour throughout the world."[1] Again official England was striking a note far different from that of the press.[2] Adams paid little attention to newspaper

[1] *Ibid.*

[2] According to *The Index*, the French press was more divided than was the London press in portrayal of military events in America. The *Siècle* and the *Opinion Nationale* pictured Sherman as about to capture Atlanta. Readers of the *Constitutionel*, *Patrie*, *Moniteur*, and *La France* "know quite well that Sherman has neither occupied the centre, the circumference, nor, indeed, any part of the defences of Atlanta; and that he was completely defeated by General Hood on July 22." (*Index*, Aug. 18, 1864, p. 522.) The Paris correspondent wrote, October 19, after the news was received of Sheridan's campaign in the Shenandoah Valley:

"The *Siècle* is triumphant. According to this humanitarian journal, whose sole policy consists in the expression of a double hatred, part of which it bestows on the priests, and part on the slave-dealers, the American contest has assumed its last phase, the Confederates are running in breathless haste to demand pardon, and true patriotism is at last to meet with its reward. This great and noble result will be due to the Northern generals, *who have carried military glory to so high a pitch without at the same time compromising American Democracy!*

"Your readers will doubtless consider that the writer of the above lines undertakes to speak on a subject of which he knows nothing; but what will they say of a writer who, in the same journal, thus expresses himself relative to the issues of the coming election?

'Lincoln being elected, the following will be the results: The South will lose courage and abandon the contest; the lands reduced to barrenness by servile labour will be again rendered productive by the labour of the freeman; the Confederates, *who know only how to fight, and who are supported by the sweat of others*, will purify and regenerate themselves by the exercise of their own brains and of their own hands. . . .'

"These strange remarks conclude with words of encouragement to the robust-shouldered, iron-fronted, firm-lipped Lincoln, and prayers for the welfare of the American brethren.

"You will not easily credit it, but this article—a very masterpiece of delirium and absurdity—bears the signature of one of the most eminent writers of the day, M. Henri Martin, the celebrated historian of France. (*Index*, Oct. 20, 1864, p. 667.)

A week later *The Index* was vicious in comment upon the "men and money" pouring out of *Germany* in aid of the North. German financiers, under the guise of aiding emigration, were engaged in the prosperous business of "selling white-skinned Germans to cut Southern throats for the benefit, as they say, of the poor blacks." (Oct. 27, 1864, p. 685.) This bitter tone was indulged in even by the Confederate Secretary of State. Benjamin wrote to Slidell, September 20, 1864, that France was wilfully deceiving the South by professions of friendship. The President, he stated, "could not escape the painful conviction that the Emperor of the French, knowing that the utmost efforts of this people are engrossed in the defence of their homes against an atrocious warfare waged by greatly superior numbers, has thought the occasion opportune for promoting his own purposes, at no greater cost than a violation of his faith and duty toward us." (Richardson, II, p. 577.)

utterances, but kept his chief informed of opinions expressed by those responsible for, and active in determining, governmental policy. The autumn "season for speeches" by Members of Parliament, he reported, was progressing with a very evident unanimity of expressions, whether from friend or foe, that it was inexpedient to meddle in American affairs. As the Presidential election in America came nearer, attention was diverted from military events. Anti-slavery societies began to hold meetings urging their friends in America to vote for Lincoln.[1] Writing from Washington, Lyons, as always anxious to forestall frictions on immaterial matters, wrote to Russell, "We must be prepared for demonstrations of a '*spirited foreign policy*' by Mr. Seward, during the next fortnight, for electioneering purposes."[2] Possibly his illness made him unduly nervous, for four days later he was relieved to be asked by Seward to "postpone as much as possible all business with him until after the election."[3] By November 1, Lyons was so ill that he asked for immediate leave, and in replying, "You will come away at once," Russell added that he was entirely convinced the United States wished to make no serious difficulties with Great Britain.

> ". . . I do not think the U.S. Government have any ill-intentions towards us, or any fixed purpose of availing themselves of a tide of success to add a war with us to their existing difficulties. Therefore whatever their bluster and buncome may be at times, I think they will subside when the popular clamour is over."[4]

[1] e.g., Meeting of Glasgow Union and Emancipation Society, Oct. 11, 1864. (*The Liberator*, Nov. 4, 1864.)

[2] Russell Papers, Oct. 24, 1864.

[3] *Ibid.* Lyons to Russell, Oct. 28, 1864.

[4] Lyons Papers. Russell to Lyons, Nov. 19, 1864. Lyons reached London December 27, and never returned to his post in America. Lyons' services to the friendly relations of the United States and Great Britain were of the greatest. He upheld British dignity yet never gave offence to that of America; he guarded British interests but with a wise and generous recognition of the difficulties of the Northern Government. No doubt he was at heart so unneutral as to hope for Northern success, even

In early November, Lincoln was triumphantly re-elected receiving 212 electoral votes to 21 cast for McClellan. No disturbances such as the *Gazette* had gloomily foretold attended the event, and the tremendous majority gained by the President somewhat stunned the press. Having prophesied disorders, the *Gazette* now patted America on the back for her behaviour, but took occasion to renew old "professions of faith" against reunion:

> "Abraham Lincoln II reigns in succession to Abraham Lincoln I, the first Republican monarch of the Federal States, and so far as we are concerned we are very glad of it, because the measure of the man is taken and known. . . . It is most creditable to the law-abiding habits of the people that the elections . . . passed off as they have done. . . . Mr. Lincoln has four long years of strife before him; and as he seems little inclined to change his advisers, his course of action, or his generals, we do not believe that the termination of his second period of government will find him President of the United States."[1]

The *Times* was disinclined, for once, to moralize, and was cautious in comment:

> "Ever since he found himself firmly established in his office, and the first effervescence of national feeling had begun to subside, we have had no great reason to complain of the conduct of Mr. Lincoln towards England. His tone has been less exacting, his language has been less offensive and, due allowance being made for the immense difficulties of his situation, we could have parted with Mr. Lincoln, had such been the pleasure of the American people, without any vestige of ill-will or ill-feeling. He has done as regards this country what the necessities of his situation demanded from him, and he has done no more."[2]

though at first sharing in the view that there was small possibility of reunion, but this very hope—unquestionably known to Seward and to Lincoln—frequently eased dangerous moments in the relations with Great Britain, and was in the end a decided asset to the Government at home.

[1] Nov. 26, 1864.

[2] Nov. 22, 1864.

This was to tread gently ; but more exactly and more boldly the real reaction of the press was indicated by *Punch's* cartoon of a phœnix, bearing the grim and forceful face of Lincoln, rising from the ashes where lay the embers of all that of old time had gone to make up the *liberties* of America.[1]

During the months immediately preceding Lincoln's re-election English friends of the South had largely remained inactive. Constantly twitted that at the chief stronghold of the *Southern Independence Association*, Manchester, they did not dare to hold a meeting in the great Free Trade Hall,[2] they tried ticket meetings in smaller halls, but even there met with opposition from those who attended. At three other places, Oldham, Ashton, and Stockport, efforts to break the Northern hold on the manufacturing districts met with little success,[3] and even, as reported in the *Index*, were attended mainly by " magistrates, clergy, leading local gentry, manufacturers, tradesmen, and cotton operatives," the last named being also, evidently, the last considered, and presumably the least represented.[4] The Rev. Mr. Massie conducted " follow up " Northern meetings wherever the Southern friends ventured an appearance.[5] At one town only, Oldham, described by *The Index* as " the most ' Southern ' town in Lancashire," was a meeting held at all comparable with the great demonstrations easily staged by pro-Northern friends. Set for October 31, great efforts were made to picture this meeting as an outburst of indignation from the unemployed. Summoned by

[1] The gradual change in *Punch's* representation of a silly-faced Lincoln to one which bore the stamp of despotic ferocity is an interesting index of British opinion during the war. By 1864 those who watched his career had come to respect Lincoln's ability and power though as yet wholly unappreciative of his still greater qualities.

[2] *The Liberator*, Sept. 23, 1864. Letter from T. H. Barker to Garrison, August 27, 1864.

[3] *Ibid.*, Nov. 4, 1864.

[4] *The Index*, Sept. 29, 1864, p. 618, describing the meeting at Ashton.

[5] *The Liberator*, Nov. 4, 1864.

handbills headed "*The Crisis! The Crisis! The Crisis!*" there gathered, according to *The Index* correspondent, a meeting "of between 5,000 and 6,000 wretched paupers, many of whom were women with children in their arms, who, starved apparently in body and spirit as in raiment, had met together to exchange miseries, and ask one another what was to be done." Desperate speeches were made, the people "almost threatening violence," but finally adopting a resolution now become so hackneyed as to seem ridiculous after a description intended to portray the misery and the revolutionary character of the meeting:

> "That in consequence of the widespread distress that now prevails in the cotton districts by the continuance of the war in America, this meeting is desirous that Her Majesty's Government should use their influence, together with France and other European powers, to bring both belligerents together in order to put a stop to the vast destruction of life and property that is now going on in that unhappy country."[1]

No doubt this spectacular meeting was organized for effect, but in truth it must have overshot the mark, for by October, 1864, the distress in Lancashire was largely alleviated and the public knew it, while elsewhere in the cotton districts the mass of operative feeling was with the North. Even in Ireland petitions were being circulated for signature among the working men, appealing to Irishmen in America to stand by the administration of Lincoln and to enlist in the Northern armies on the ground of emancipation.[2] Here, indeed, was the insuperable barrier, in the fall of 1864, to public support of the South. Deny as he might the presence of the "foul blot" in Southern society, Hotze, of *The Index*, could not counteract that phrase. When the Confederate Congress at Richmond began, in

[1] *The Index*, Nov. 3, 1864, p. 699.
[2] *The Liberator*, Nov. 4, 1864.

the autumn of 1864, seriously to discuss a plan of transforming slaves into soldiers, putting guns in their hands, and thus replenishing the waning man-power of Southern armies, Hotze was hard put to it to explain to his English readers that this was in fact no evidence of lowered strength, but rather a noble determination on the part of the South to permit the negro to win his freedom by bearing arms in defence of his country.[1]

This was far-fetched for a journal that had long insisted upon the absolute incapacity of the black race. Proximity of dates, however, permits another interpretation of Hotze's editorial of November 10, and indeed of the project of arming the slaves, though this, early in the spring of 1865, was actually provided for by law. On November 11, Slidell, Mason and Mann addressed to the Powers of Europe a communication accompanying a Confederate "Manifesto," of which the blockade had long delayed transmissal. This "Manifesto" set forth the objects of the Southern States and flatly demanded recognition:

> "'All they ask is immunity from interference with their internal peace and prosperity and to be left in the undisturbed enjoyment of their inalienable rights of life, liberty and the pursuit of happiness which their common ancestry declared to be the equal heritage of all parties to the Social compact.'"[2]

Russell replied, November 25:

> "Great Britain has since 1783, remained, with the exception of a short period, connected by friendly relations with both the Northern and the Southern States. Since the commencement of the Civil War which broke out in 1861, Her Majesty's Government have continued to entertain sentiments of friendship equally for the North and for the

[1] *The Index*, Nov. 10, 1864, p. 713.

[2] F. O., Am., Vol. 975. Slidell, Mason and Mann to Russell, Nov. 11, 1864, Paris. Replies were received from England, France, Sweden and the Papal States. (Mason Papers, Mason to Slidell, Jan. 4, 1865).

South; of the causes of the rupture Her Majesty's Government have never presumed to judge; they deplored the commencement of this sanguinary struggle, and anxiously look forward to the period of its termination. In the meantime they are convinced that they best consult the interests of peace, and respect the rights of all parties by observing a strict and impartial Neutrality. Such a Neutrality Her Majesty has faithfully maintained and will continue to maintain."[1]

If *The Index* did indeed hope for results from the "Manifesto," and had sought to bolster the appeal by dilating on a Southern plan to "let the slaves win their freedom," the answer of Russell was disappointing. Yet at the moment, in spite of the effect of Lincoln's re-election, the current of alleged expert military opinion was again swinging in favour of the South. The *Times* scored Russell's answer, portraying him as attempting to pose as "Our Mutual Friend":

"The difficulty, of course, was to be polite to the representatives of the Confederate States without appearing rude to the United States; and, on the other hand, to acknowledge the authority of the United States without affronting the dignity of the Confederates. Between these two pitfalls Lord Russell oscillates in his letter, and now puts his foot a little bit in the hole on one side, and then, in recovering himself gets a little way into the hole on the other side. In this way he sways to and fro for a minute or two, but rights himself at last, and declares he has hitherto stood upright between the two pitfalls, and he will continue to do so. . . . Lord Russell seems to be in danger of forgetting that *neuter* does not mean *both*, but *neither*, and that if, therefore, he would maintain even in words a strict neutrality it is necessary to avoid any demonstrations of friendship to either belligerent."[2]

This was harsh criticism, evincing a *Times* partisanship

[1] F. O., Am., Vol. 975. Draft. Russell to the "Commissioners of the so-called Confederate States," Nov. 25, 1864.

[2] Dec. 1, 1864.

justifying the allegations of the *Gazette*, but wholly in line with the opinion to which the *Times* was now desperately clinging that Grant had failed and that Sherman, adventuring on his spectacular " march to the sea " from Atlanta, was courting annihilation. Yet even Northern friends were appalled at Sherman's boldness and discouraged by Grant's slowness. The son of the American Minister could write, " Grant moves like the iron wall in Poe's story. You expect something tremendous, and it's only a step after all."[1]

The *Times* was at least consistent in prophecies until the event falsified them ; the *Gazette* less so. Some six weeks after having acclaimed Sherman's generalship in the capture of Atlanta,[2] the *Gazette's* summary of the military situation was that :

> " . . . if the winter sees Grant still before Petersburg, and Sherman unable to hold what he has gained in Georgia, the South may be nearer its dawning day of independence than could have been expected a few weeks ago, even though Wilmington be captured and Charleston be ground away piecemeal under a distant cannonade. The position of the Democrats would urge them to desperate measures, and the wedge of discord will be driven into the ill-compacted body which now represents the Federal States of North America."[3]

But on December 17, W. H. Russell again changed his view and foretold with accuracy Sherman's movements toward Savannah. Not so the *Times*, privately very anxious as to what Sherman's campaign portended, while publicly belittling it. December 2, it was noted that Sherman had not been heard from for weeks, having left Atlanta with 50,000 men. December 5, his objective was stated to be Savannah, and while the difficulties to be encountered were

[1] *A Cycle of Adams' Letters*, II, p. 207. Henry Adams to his brother, Oct. 21, 1864.

[2] See *ante*, p. 233.

[3] Nov. 12, 1864.

enumerated, no prophecy was indulged in. But on December 22, Sherman's move was called a "desperate" one, forced by his inability to retreat *northward* from Atlanta:

> "If we turn to military affairs, we are informed that the great feature of the year is Sherman's expedition into Georgia. We are not yet able to say whether Sherman will succeed in escaping the fate of Burgoyne; but we know that his apparent rashness is excused by the fact that Sherman was unable to return on the way by which he came; so that the most remarkable feature of the war, according to the President, is the wild and desperate effort of an out-manœuvred General to extricate himself from a position which, whatever effect it may have had on the election, should never, on mere military grounds, have been occupied at all."[1]

This was followed up four days later by a long and careful review of Sherman's whole western campaign, concluding with the dictum that his sole object now was to escape to some undefended point on the coast where he could be rescued by the Northern navy. The war had taken a definite turn in favour of the South; it was impossible to conceive that Sherman would venture to attack Savannah:

> "For the escape or safety of Sherman and his army it is essential he should reach Beaufort, or some neighbouring point on the sea-coast as rapidly as possible. Delay would be equivalent to ruin, and he will do nothing to create it."[2]

Rarely, if ever, did the *Times*, in its now eager and avowed championship so definitely commit itself in an effort to preserve British confidence in the Southern cause.[3] Even friends of the North were made doubtful

[1] Dec. 22, 1864.

[2] Dec. 26, 1864. But this was in reality a mere "keeping up courage" editorial. See Ch. XVIII, p. 300.

[3] That this was very effective championship is shown by Henry Adams' letter to his brother, Dec. 16, 1864. (*A Cycle of Adams' Letters*, II, p. 232.)

by the positiveness of prediction indulged in by that journal whose opinions were supposed to be based on superior information. Their recourse was to a renewal of "deputations" calling on the American Minister to express steady allegiance to the Northern cause,[1] and their relief was great when the news was received that Savannah had fallen, December 20, without a struggle. The *Times* recorded the event, December 29, but with no comment save that Southern prospects were less rosy than had been supposed. Then ensued a long silence, for this time there was no possibility of that editorial wiggling about the circle from excuses for misinterpretation to a complacent resumption of authoritative utterance.

For the editor, Delane, and for wise Southern sympathizers the fall of Savannah was a much harder blow than the mere loss of prestige to the *Times*.[2] Courage failed and confidence in the South waned—momentarily almost vanished. Nearly two weeks passed before the *Times* ventured to lift again the banner of hope, and even then but half-heartedly.

> "The capture of the city completes the history of Sherman's march, and stamps it as one of the ablest, certainly one of the most singular military achievements of the war.
>
> ". . . The advantage gained for the Federal cause by the possession of Savannah is yet to be shown. To Sherman and his army 'the change of base' is indisputably a change for the better. Assuming that his position at Atlanta was as

"Popular opinion here declares louder than ever that Sherman is lost. People are quite angry at his presumption in attempting such a wild project. The interest felt in his march is enormous, however, and if he arrives as successfully as I expect, at the sea, you may rely upon it that the moral effect of his demonstration on Europe will be greater than that of any other event of the war."

[1] State Department, Eng, Adams to Seward, Dec. 16, 1864. Adams expressed to Seward doubts as to the propriety of his receiving such deputations and making replies to them. *The Index* (Dec. 22, 1864, p. 808) was "indignant" that Adams should presume to "hector and threaten" England through his replies. But Adams continued to receive deputations.

[2] Delane's position on the Civil War and the reasons for the importance of Savannah to him, personally, are described in Ch. XVIII.

desperate as shortness of supplies and an interrupted line of retreat could make it, the command of a point near the sea-coast and free communication with the fleet is obviously an improvement. At the least the army secures full means of subsistence, and a point from which further operations may be commenced. On the other hand, the blow, as far as the Confederate Government is concerned, is mitigated by the fact that Savannah has been little used as a seaport since the capture of Fort Pulaski by the Federals at an early stage of the war.

"... But the fall of the city is a patent fact, and it would be absurd to deny that it has produced an impression unfavourable to the *prestige* of the Confederacy."[1]

Far more emphatic of ultimate Northern victory was the picture presented, though in sarcasm, by the *Times* New York correspondent, printed in this same issue:

"No disappointments, however fast they may follow on the heels of each other, can becloud the bright sunshine of conceit and self-worship that glows in the heart of the Yankee. His country is the first in the world, and he is the first man in it. Knock him down, and he will get up again, and brush the dirt from his knees, not a bit the worse for the fall. If he do not win this time, he is bound to win the next. His motto is 'Never say die.' His manifest destiny is to go on—prospering and to prosper—conquering and to conquer."

[1] Jan. 9, 1865.

CHAPTER XVII

THE END OF THE WAR

"I think you need not trouble yourself about England. At this moment opinion seems to have undergone a complete change, and our people and indeed our Government is more moderately disposed than I have ever before known it to be. I hear from a member of the Government that it is believed that the feeling between our Cabinet and the Washington Government has been steadily improving."[1]

THUS wrote Bright to Sumner in the last week of January, 1865. Three weeks later he again wrote in reassurance against American rumours that Europe was still planning some form of intervention to save the South: "*All parties and classes* here are resolved on a strict neutrality. . . ."[2] This was a correct estimate. In spite of a temporary pause in the operations of Northern armies and of renewed assertions from the South that she "would never submit," British opinion was now very nearly unanimous that the end was near. This verdict was soon justified by events. In January, 1865, Wilmington, North Carolina, was at last captured by a combined sea and land attack. Grant, though since midsummer, 1864, held in check by Lee before Petersburg, was yet known to be constantly increasing the strength of his army, while his ability to strike when the time came was made evident by the freedom with which his cavalry scoured the country about the Confederate

[1] Bright to Sumner, Jan. 26, 1865 (Mass. Hist. Soc. *Proceedings*, XLVI, p. 132).

[2] To Sumner, Feb. 17, 1865 (*Ibid*. p. 133).

capital, Richmond—in one raid even completely encircling that city. Steadily Lee's army lost strength by the attrition of the siege, by illness and, what was worse, by desertion since no forces could be spared from the fighting front to recover and punish the deserters. Grant waited for the approach of spring, when, with the advance northwards of the army at Savannah, the pincers could be applied to Lee, to end, it was hoped, in writing *finis* to the war.

From December 20, 1864, to February 1, 1865, Sherman remained in Savannah, renewing by sea the strength of his army. On the latter date he moved north along the coast, meeting at first no resistance and easily overrunning the country. Columbia, capital of South Carolina, was burned. Charleston was evacuated, and it was not until March, in North Carolina, that any real opposition to the northward progress was encountered. Here on the sixteenth and the nineteenth, Johnston, in command of the weak Southern forces in North Carolina, made a desperate effort to stop Sherman, but without avail, and on March 23, Sherman was at Goldsboro, one hundred and sixty miles south of Richmond, prepared to cut off the retreat of Lee when Grant should at last take up an energetic offensive.

In the last week of March, Grant began cutting off supplies to Richmond, thus forcing Lee, if he wished still to protect the Southern capital, to come out of his lines at Petersburg and present an unfortified front. The result was the evacuation of Petersburg and the abandonment of Richmond, Jefferson Davis and his Government fleeing from the city on the night of April 2 Attempting to retreat southwards with the plan of joining Johnston's army, Lee, on April 9, found his forces surrounded at Appomattox and surrendered. Nine days later, on April 18, Johnston surrendered to Sherman at Durham, North Carolina. It was the end of the war and of the Confederacy.

The rapidity with which Southern resistance in arms

THE AMERICAN GLADIATORS—HABET!

crumbled in 1865 when once Sherman and Grant were under way no doubt startled foreign observers, but in British opinion, at least, the end had been foreseen from the moment Sherman reached the sea at Savannah. The desperate courage of the South was admired, but regarded as futile. Equally desperate and futile was the last diplomatic effort of the Confederate agents in Europe, taking the form of an offer to abolish slavery in return for recognition. The plan originated with Benjamin, Southern Secretary of State, was hesitatingly approved by Davis,[1] and was committed to Mason for negotiation with Great Britain. Mason, after his withdrawal from London, had been given duplicate powers in blank for any point to which emergencies might send him, thus becoming a sort of Confederate Commissioner at Large to Europe. Less than any other representative abroad inclined to admit that slavery was other than a beneficent and humane institution, it was felt advisable at Richmond not only to instruct Mason by written despatch, but by personal messenger also of the urgency of presenting the offer of abolition promptly and with full assurance of carrying it into effect. The instruction was therefore entrusted to Duncan F. Kenner, of Louisiana, and he arrived in Paris early in March, 1865, overcame Mason's unwillingness to carry such an offer to England, and accompanied the latter to London.

The time was certainly not propitious, for on the day Mason reached London there came the news of the burning of Columbia and the evacuation of Charleston. Mason hesitated to approach Palmerston, but was pressed by Kenner who urged action on the theory that Great Britain did not wish to see a reconstruction of the Union.[2] Slidell, in Paris, on receiving Mason's doubts, advised waiting until the Emperor had been consulted, was granted an interview

[1] Dodd, *Jefferson Davis*, p. 343

[2] Mason Papers. Mason to Slidell, March 4, 1865.

and reported Napoleon III as ready as ever to act if England would act also, but as advising delay until more favourable news was received from America.[1] But Mason's instructions did not permit delay; he must either carry them out or resign—and Kenner was at his elbow pressing for action. On March 13, therefore, Mason wrote to Palmerston asking for a private interview and was promptly granted one for the day following.

Both personal disinclination to the proposal of abolition and judgment that nothing would come of it made Mason cautious in expressing himself to Palmerston. Mason felt that he was stultifying his country in condemning slavery. Hence in roundabout language, "with such form of allusion to the *concession* we held in reserve, as would make him necessarily comprehend it,"[2] and turning again and again to a supposed "latent, undisclosed obstacle"[3] to British recognition, Mason yet made clear the object of his visit. The word slavery was not mentioned by him, but Palmerston promptly denied that slavery in the South had ever been, or was now, a barrier to recognition; British objections to recognition were those which had long since been stated, and there was nothing "underlying" them. On March 26, Mason called on the Earl of Donoughmore, a Tory friend of the South with whom he had long been in close touch, and asked whether he thought Palmerston's Government could be induced by a Southern abolition of slavery to recognize the Confederacy. The reply was "that the time had gone by now. . . ." This time the words "slavery" and "abolition" were spoken boldly,[4] and Donoughmore was positive that if, in the midsummer of 1863, when Lee was invading Pennsylvania, the South had made its present overture, nothing could have prevented British recognition.

[1] *Ibid.* Slidell to Mason, March 5 and 6, 1865.
[2] *Ibid.* Mason to Slidell, March 15, 1865.
[3] Mason to Benjamin, March 31, 1865. (Richardson, II, pp. 709-17.)
[4] *Ibid.* p. 717.

The opinion clashed with Mason's own conviction, but in any case no more was to be hoped, now, from his overture. Only a favourable turn in the war could help the South.

There was no public knowledge in London of this "last card" Southern effort in diplomacy, though there were newspaper rumours that some such move was on foot, but with a primary motive of restoring Southern fighting power by putting the negroes in arms. British public attention was fixed rather upon a possible last-moment reconciliation of North and South and a restored Union which should forget its domestic troubles in a foreign war. Momentarily somewhat of a panic overcame London society and gloomy were the forebodings that Great Britain would be the chosen enemy of America. Like rumours were afloat at Washington also. The Russian Minister, Stoeckl, reported to his Government that he had learned from "a sure source" of representations made to Jefferson Davis by Blair, a prominent Unionist and politician of the border state of Maryland, looking to reconstruction and to the sending by Lincoln of armies into Canada and Mexico. Stoeckl believed such a war would be popular, but commented that "Lincoln might change his mind[1] to-morrow." In London the *Army and Navy Gazette* declared that Davis could not consent to reunion and that Lincoln could not offer any other terms of peace, but that a truce might be patched up on the basis of a common aggression against supposed foreign enemies.[2] Adams pictured all British society as

[1] Russian Archives. Stoeckl to F. O., Jan. 24, 1865. No. 187. It is nteresting that just at this time Gortchakoff should have sent to Stoeckl the copy of a memorandum by one, C. Catacazy, employé of the Foreign Office and long-time resident in the United States, in which was outlined a plan of a Russian offer of mediation. The memorandum specified that such an offer should be based on the idea that the time had come for a complete restoration of the Union and argued that both North and South regarded Russia as a special friend; it was Russia's interest to see the Union restored as a balance to Great Britain. Gortchakoff's comment was favourable, but he left it wholly to Stoeckl's judgment and discretion to act upon the plan. (Russian Archives. F. O. to Stoeckl, Feb. 6, 1865.)

[2] Feb. 4, 1865.

now convinced that the end of the war was near, and bitter against the previous tone and policy of such leaders of public opinion as the *Times*, adding that it was being "whispered about that if the feud is reconciled and the Union restored, and a great army left on our hands, the next manifestation will be one of hostility to this country."[1]

The basis of all this rumour was Blair's attempt to play the mediator. He so far succeeded that on January 31, 1865, Lincoln instructed Seward to go to Fortress Monroe to meet "commissioners" appointed by Davis. But Lincoln made positive in his instructions three points:

(1) Complete restoration of the Union.
(2) No receding on emancipation.
(3) No cessation of hostilities "short of an end of the war, and the disbanding of all forces hostile to the Government."

A few days later the President decided that his own presence was desirable and joined his Secretary of State in the "Hampton Roads Conference" of February 3. It quickly appeared that the Confederates did indeed hope to draw the North into a foreign war for a "traditional American object," using the argument that *after* such a war restoration of the Union would be easily accomplished. The enemy proposed was not Great Britain but France, and the place of operations Mexico. There was much discussion of this plan between Seward and Stephens, the leading Southern Commissioner, but Lincoln merely listened, and when pressed for comment stuck fast to his decision that no agreement whatever would be entered into until the South had laid down its arms. The Southerners urged that there was precedent for an agreement in advance of cessation of hostilities in the negotiations between Charles I and the Roundheads. Lincoln's reply was pithy: "I do not profess to be posted in history. On all such matters I turn

[1] *A Cycle of Adams' Letters*, II, 254. To his son, Feb. 10, 1865.

you over to Seward. All I distinctly recollect about the case of Charles I is that he lost his head in the end."[1]

When news of the holding of this conference reached England there occurred a panic on the Stock Exchange due to the uncertainty created by the prospect of an immediate end of the American War. "The consternation," wrote Adams, "was extraordinary."[2] What did the United States intend to do? "The impression is now very general that peace and restoration at home are synonymous with war with this country." There existed an "extraordinary uneasiness and indefinite apprehension as to the future." So reported Adams to Seward; and he advised that it might be well for the United States "to consider the question how far its policy may be adapted to quiet this disturbance"; due allowance should be made for the mortification of those leaders who had been so confident of Southern victory and for expressions that might now fall from their lips; it was possible that reassurances given by the United States might aid in the coming elections in retaining the Government in power—evidently, in Adams' opinion, a result to be desired.[3]

Adams' advice as to the forthcoming elections was but repetition of that given earlier and with more emphasis.[4] Apparently Seward was then in no mood to act on it, for his reply was distinctly belligerent in tone, recapitulating British and Canadian offences in permitting the enemy to use their shores, and asserting that the measures now proposed of abrogating the reciprocity treaty of 1854 with Canada and the agreement of 1817 prohibiting armaments on the Great Lakes, were but defensive measures required to protect American soil.[5] These matters Adams had been

[1] Bancroft, *Seward*, II, pp. 410-14.

[2] *A Cycle of Adams' Letters*, II, 256. To his son, Feb. 17, 1865.

[3] *U.S. Messages and Documents*, 1865-66, Pt. I, p. 182. Adams to Seward, Feb. 23, 1865.

[4] *Ibid.* p. 112. Adams to Seward, Feb. 2, 1865.

[5] *Ibid.* p. 180. Seward to Adams, Feb. 21, 1865.

instructed to take up with Russell, but with discretion as to time and he had ventured to postpone them as inopportune. Professing entire agreement with the justice of Seward's complaints he nevertheless wrote that to press them "at this moment would be only playing into the hands of the mischief-makers, and disarming our own friends."[1] The day before this was written home Seward, at Washington, on March 8, recalled his instruction as to the agreement of 1817, stating that Russell might be informed the United States had no intention of increasing its armaments on the Great Lakes.[2]

Thus there were incidents offering ground for a British excitement over a prospective war with America, even though no such intention was seriously entertained by the North. The British Government did not share this fear, but Delane, of the *Times*, kept it alive in the public mind, and indeed was sincere in efforts to arouse his readers to the danger. "I do not know what grounds Delane has for it," wrote W. H. Russell to his American friend Bigelow, "but he is quite sure Uncle Samuel is about to finish off the dreadful Civil War with another war with us scarcely less horrible."[3] Governmental circles, however, belittled the agitation. Burnley, temporarily representing England at Washington, was assured by Seward, and so reported, that all these rumours of a foreign war were of Southern origin, had in fact been actually elaborated at the Hampton Roads Conference, but were perfectly understood by the North as but part of the Southern game, and that the Southern offer had been flatly refused.[4] In a parliamentary debate in the Commons on March 13, arising out of governmental estimates for military expenditures in Canada, opportunity was given for a discussion of relations with

[1] *Ibid.* p. 199. Adams to Seward, March 9, 1865.
[2] *Ibid.* p. 197. Seward to Adams, March 8, 1865.
[3] March 8, 1865. (Bigelow, *Retrospections*, II, p. 361.)
[4] Russell Papers. Burnley to Russell, Feb. 23 and March 13, 1865.

America. A few Members gave voice to the fear of war, but the general tone of the debate was one of confidence in the continuance of peaceful relations. Bright, in a vigorous and witty speech, threw right and left criticisms of Parliament, the Press, and individuals, not sparing members of the Government, but expressed the utmost confidence in the pacific policy of Lincoln. As one known to be in close touch with America his words carried weight.[1] Palmerston gave assurances that the present relations between the two Governments were perfectly friendly and satisfactory. The effect of the debate, reported Adams, was to quiet the panic,[2] yet at the same time England was now awake to and somewhat alarmed by, America's " prodigious development of physical power during the war." To quiet this, Adams recommended " prudence and moderation in tone."[3]

Thus the actual cessation of hostilities in America and the possible effect of this event on foreign relations had been for some time anticipated and estimated in Great Britain.[4] The news of Lee's surrender, therefore, caused no great surprise since the *Times* and other papers had been preparing the public for it.[5] Newspaper comment on the event followed closely that of the *Times*, rendering honour to

[1] " The speech of Mr. Bright is universally admitted to have been one of the most brilliant specimens of his peculiar style of oratory. In its reminiscences, equally unwelcome to both sides of the House, it was yet received after the fashion of an unpleasant medicine, which has the aid of a strong and savoury medium to overwhelm the nauseous taste." (*U.S. Messages and Documents*, 1865-66, Pt. I, p. 246. Adams to Seward, March 16, 1865.)

[2] *Ibid.*

[3] *Ibid.* p. 262. Adams to Seward, March 24, 1865. Adams wrote of his own situation that it " seems at last to be getting easy and comfortable, so far as freedom from anxiety is concerned." (*A Cycle of Adams' Letters*, II, p. 258. To his son, March 24, 1865.)

[4] Bruce, who succeeded Lyons at Washington, reached New York on April 7. His first letter to Russell from Washington, dated April 14, stated that America was certainly preparing to oust Maximilian in Mexico, and that even the Southern prisoners were eager to join the United States troops in an expedition for this purpose. (Russell Papers.)

[5] *U.S. Messages and Documents*, 1865-66, Part II, p. 323. Adams to Seward, April 20, 1865.

the militant qualities of the South and to Lee, but writing *finis* to the war:

> "Such is the end of the great army which, organized by the extraordinary genius of one man, aided by several other commanders of eminent ability, has done such wonders in this war. Not even the Grand Army of Napoleon himself could count a series of more brilliant victories than the force which, raised chiefly from the high-spirited population of Virginia, has defeated so many invasions of the State, and crushed the hopes of so many Northern generals. Chief and soldiers have now failed for the first and last time. They were victorious until victory was no longer to be achieved by human valour, and then they fell with honour."[1]

The people of the North, also, were complimented for their slowly developed but ultimate ability in war, and especially for "a patience, a fortitude, and an energy which entitle them to rank among the very first of military nations."[2] No one remained to uphold the Southern banner in Europe save the Confederate agents, and, privately, even they were hopeless. Mason, it is true, asserted, as if bolstering his own courage, that "this morning's" news did not mean an overwhelming disaster; it could not be wholly true; even if true it must mean peace on the basis of separation; finally, "5th. *I know* that no terms of peace would be accepted that did not embrace independence." But at the conclusion of this letter he acknowledged:

> "I confess that all this speculation rests on, what I assume, that Lee surrendered only in expectation of a peace derived from his interview with Grant—and that no terms of peace would be entertained that did not rest on *independence*." [3]

But Slidell saw more clearly. He replied:

> "I cannot share your hopefulness. We have seen the

[1] April 24, 1865.
[2] *Ibid.*
[3] Mason Papers. Mason to Slidell, April 23, 1865.

beginning of the end. I, for my part, am prepared for the worst. With Lee's surrender there will soon be an end to our regular organized armies and I can see no possible good to result from a protracted guerilla warfare. We are crushed and must submit to the yoke. Our children must bide their time for vengeance, but you and I will never revisit our homes under our glorious flag. For myself I shall never put my foot on a soil from which flaunts the hated Stars and Stripes. . . . I am sick, sick at heart."[1]

The news of Lee's surrender arrived at the same moment with that of a serious injury to Seward in a runaway accident, and in its editorial on the end of the war the *Times* took occasion to pay a tribute to the statesman whom it had been accustomed to berate.

"There seems to be on the part of President Lincoln a desire to conciliate vanquished fellow-citizens. Under the guidance of Mr. Seward, who has creditably distinguished himself in the Cabinet by his moderate counsels, and whose life will, we trust, be spared at this crisis to the Union, he may by gentle measures restore tranquillity, and perhaps, before his term of office expires, calm in some degree the animosities which have been raised by these years of war."[2]

Nor was this insincere, for Seward had, first in the estimate of British statesmen, more slowly in the press and with the public, come to be regarded in an aspect far different from that with which he was generally viewed in 1861. There was real anxiety at the reports of Seward's accident, but when, in less than a week, there was received also the news of the assassination of Lincoln and of the brutal attack on Seward, all England united in expressions of sympathy and horror. "Few events of the present century," wrote Adams, "have created such general consternation and indignation."[3]

[1] *Ibid.* Slidell to Mason, April 26, 1865.
[2] April 24, 1865.
[3] *U.S. Messages and Documents*, 1865-66, Pt. I, p. 331. Adams to Seward, April 28, 1865.

In Ford's Theatre on the evening of April 14, Lincoln was shot by Booth, a fanatical Southerner, who had gained entrance to the box where the President was sitting. Lincoln died early the next morning. On the same evening, at about ten o'clock, an unknown man was admitted to Seward's house on the plea that he had a message from the physician, passed upstairs, but was stopped by Seward's son at the door of the sick room. Beating the son into semi-unconsciousness with a revolver which had missed fire, the stranger burst open the door, attacked the Secretary as he lay in bed with a bowie-knife, slashing at his throat, until Seward rolled off the bed to the floor. Seward's throat was "cut on both sides, his right cheek nearly severed from his face"; his life was saved, probably, because of an iron frame worn to support the jaw fractured in the runaway accident nine days before.[1] The assailant fought his way out of the house and escaped. For some days Seward's life was despaired of, whether from his injuries or from shock.

These tragic occurrences were the outcome of a revengeful spirit in the hearts of a few extreme Southerners, and in no sense represented the feeling of the South. It was inevitable, however, that abroad so horrible a crime should react both to the detriment of the Confederacy and to the advantage of the North. Sympathy with the North took the form of a sudden exaltation of the personality of Lincoln, bringing out characterizations of the man far different from those which had been his earlier in the war. The presence of a "rural attorney" in the Presidential office had seemed like the irony of fate in the great crisis of 1861. Even so acute an observer as Lyons could then write, "Mr. Lincoln has not hitherto given proof of his possessing any natural talents to compensate for his ignorance of everything but Illinois village politics. He seems to be well meaning

[1] Bancroft, *Seward*, II, p. 417.

and conscientious, in the measure of his understanding, but not much more."[1] But Lyons was no more blind than his contemporaries, for nearly all characterizations, whether American or foreign, were of like nature.

But the slow progress of the years of war had brought a different estimate of Lincoln—a curious blending of admiration for the growth of his personal authority and for his steadiness of purpose, with criticism of his alleged despotism. Now, with his death, following so closely the collapse of the Confederacy, there poured out from British press and public a great stream of laudation for Lincoln almost amounting to a national recantation. In this process of "whitening Abraham's tomb," as a few dyed-in-the-wool Southern sympathizers called it, *Punch* led the way in a poem by Tom Taylor:

"*You* lay a wreath on murdered Lincoln's bier,
You, who with mocking pencil wont to trace,
Broad for the self-complacent British sneer,
His length of shambling limb, his furrowed face."

. . . . . .

"Yes, he had lived to shame me from my sneer,
To lame my pencil and confute my pen—
To make me own this hind of princes peer,
This rail-splitter a true-born king of men."[2]

Less emotional than most papers, but with a truer estimate of Lincoln, stood the *Times*. Severely reprobating the act of Booth and prophesying a disastrous effect in the treatment of the conquered South, it proceeded:

"Starting from a humble position to one of the greatest eminence, and adopted by the Republican party as a makeshift, simply because Mr. Seward and their other prominent

[1] Russell Papers. Lyons to Russell, April 9, 1861.
[2] May 6, 1865.

leaders were obnoxious to different sections of the party, it was natural that his career should be watched with jealous suspicion. The office cast upon him was great, its duties most onerous, and the obscurity of his past career afforded no guarantee of his ability to discharge them. His shortcomings moreover were on the surface. The education of a man whose early years had been spent in earning bread by manual labour had necessarily been defective, and faults of manner and errors of taste repelled the observer at the outset. In spite of these drawbacks, Mr. Lincoln slowly won for himself the respect and confidence of all. His perfect honesty speedily became apparent, and, what is, perhaps, more to his credit, amid the many unstudied speeches which he was called upon from time to time to deliver, imbued though they were with the rough humour of his early associates, he was in none of them betrayed into any intemperance of language towards his opponents or towards neutrals. His utterances were apparently careless, but his tongue was always under command. The quality of Mr. Lincoln's administration which served, however, more than any other to enlist the sympathy of bystanders was its conservative progress. He felt his way gradually to his conclusions, and those who will compare the different stages of his career one with another will find that his mind was growing throughout the course of it."

. . . . . .

"The gradual change of his language and of his policy was most remarkable. Englishmen learnt to respect a man who showed the best characteristics of their race in his respect for what is good in the past, acting in unison with a recognition of what was made necessary by the events of passing history."[1]

This was first reaction. Two days later, commenting on the far warmer expressions of horror and sympathy emanating from all England, there appeared another and longer editorial:

"If anything could mitigate the distress of the American people in their present affliction, it might surely be the

[1] April 27, 1865.

sympathy which is expressed by the people of this country. We are not using the language of hyperbole in describing the manifestation of feeling as unexampled. Nothing like it has been witnessed in our generation. . . . But President Lincoln was only the chief of a foreign State, and of a State with which we were not unfrequently in diplomatic or political collision. He might have been regarded as not much more to us than the head of any friendly Government, and yet his end has already stirred the feelings of the public to their uttermost depths."

. . . . . .

" . . . a space of twenty-four hours has sufficed not only to fill the country with grief and indignation, but to evoke almost unprecedented expressions of feeling from constituted bodies. It was but on Wednesday that the intelligence of the murder reached us, and on Thursday the Houses of Lords and Commons, the Corporation of the City of London, and the people of our chief manufacturing towns in public meeting assembled had recorded their sentiments or expressed their views. In the House of Lords the absence of precedent for such a manifestation was actually made the subject of remark.

"That much of this extraordinary feeling is due to the tragical character of the event and the horror with which the crime is regarded is doubtless true, nor need we dissemble the the fact that the loss which the Americans have sustained is also thought our own loss in so far as one valuable guarantee for the amity of the two nations may have been thus removed. But, upon the whole, it is neither the possible embarrassment of international relations nor the infamous wickedness of the act itself which has determined public feeling. The preponderating sentiment is sincere and genuine sympathy—sorrow for the chief of a great people struck down by an assassin, and sympathy for that people in the trouble which at a crisis of their destinies such a catastrophe must bring. Abraham Lincoln was as little of a tyrant as any man who ever lived. He could have been a tyrant had he pleased, but he never uttered so much as an ill-natured speech. . . . In all America there was, perhaps, not one man who less deserved to be the victim of this revolution than he who has just fallen."[1]

[1] April 29, 1865.

The Ministry did not wait for public pressure. Immediately on receipt of the news, motions were made, April 27, in both Lords and Commons for an address to the Queen, to be debated "Monday next," expressing "sorrow and indignation" at the assassination of Lincoln.[1] April 28, Russell instructed Bruce to express at Washington that "the Government, the Parliament, and the Nation are affected by a unanimous feeling of abhorrence of the criminals guilty of these cowardly and atrocious crimes, and sympathy for the Government and People of the United States. . . ."[2] Russell wrote here of both Lincoln and Seward. The Queen wrote a personal letter of sympathy to Mrs. Lincoln. Already Bruce had written from Washington that Lincoln "was the only friend of the South in his party,"[3] and he was extremely anxious that Seward's recovery might be hastened, fearing the possibility of Sumner's assumption of the Secretaryship of State. "We miss terribly the comparative moderation of Lincoln and Seward."[4]

The American Minister naturally became the centre toward which the public outpouring of sympathy was directed. "The excitement in this country has been deep and wide, spreading through all classes of society. My table is piled high with cards, letters and resolutions. . . ."[5] Indeed all the old sources of "addresses" to Adams on emancipation and many organizations having no professed interest in that subject now sent to him resolutions—the emancipation societies, of horror, indignation, and even accusation against the South; the others of sympathy,

[1] Hansard, 3d. Ser., CLXXVIII, pp. 1073 and 1081.

[2] *Parliamentary Papers*, 1865, *Commons*, Vol. LVII. "Correspondence respecting the Assassination of the late President of the United States."

[3] Russell Papers. Bruce to Russell, April 18, 1865.

[4] *Ibid.* April 24, 1865.

[5] *A Cycle of Adams' Letters*, II, 267. Charles Francis Adams to his son, April 28, 1865.

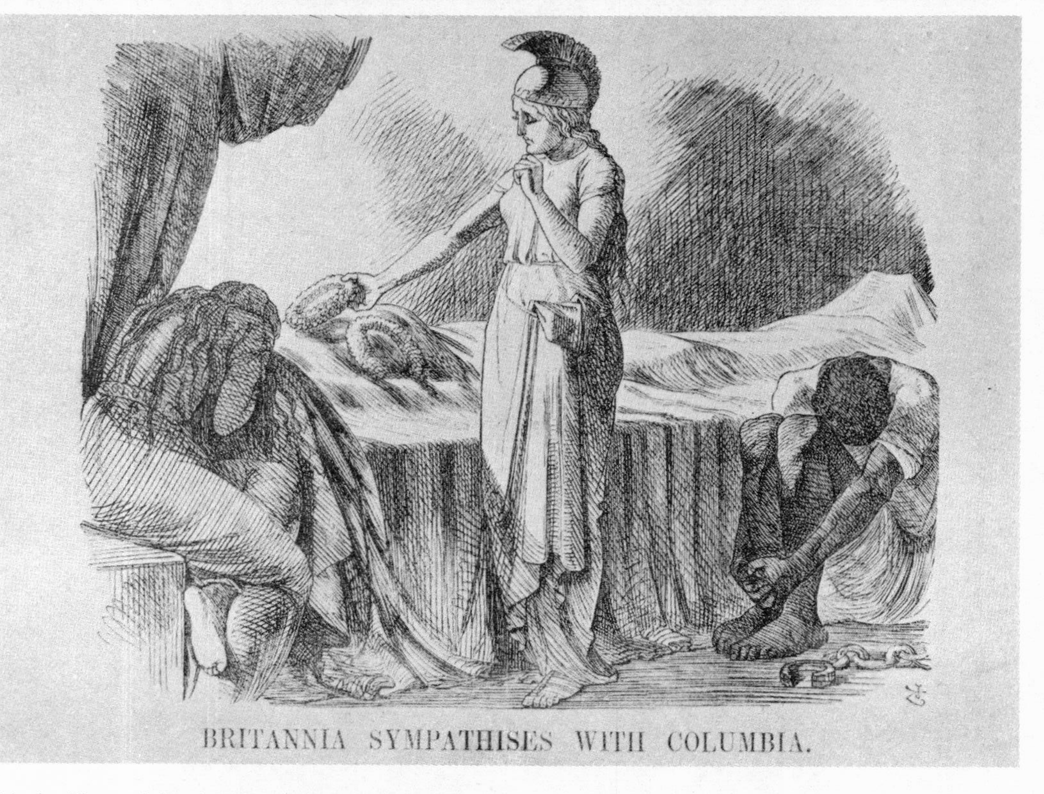

BRITANNIA SYMPATHISES WITH COLUMBIA.

Reproduced by permission of the Proprietors of "Punch"

more moderate in tone, yet all evincing an appreciation of the great qualities of Lincoln and of the justice of the cause of the North, now victorious. Within two weeks Adams reported over four hundred such addresses from Emancipation Societies, Chambers of Commerce, Trades Unions, municipalities, boroughs, churches, indeed from every known type of British organizations.[1]

On May 1 the motion for the address to the Crown came up for debate. In the Lords, Russell emphasized the kindly and forgiving qualities of Lincoln as just those needed in America, and now lost by his death. Derby, for the Opposition, expressed the horror of the world at Booth's act, joined in expressions of sympathy to the United States, but repeated the old phrase about the "North fighting for empire, the South for independence," and hinted that the unusual step now being taken by Parliament had in it a "political object," meaning that the motion had been introduced in the hope of easing American irritation with Great Britain.[2] It was not a tactful speech, but Derby's lieutenant in the Commons, Disraeli, saved his party from criticism by what was distinctly the most thoughtful and best-prepared utterance of the day. Palmerston was ill. The Government speech was made by Grey, who incautiously began by asserting that the majority of the people of Great Britain had always been on the side of the North and was met by cries of "No, no" and "Hear, hear." Disraeli concluded the debate. He said:

> "There are rare instances when the sympathy of a nation approaches those tenderer feelings that generally speaking, are supposed to be peculiar to the individual, and to form the happy privilege of private life; and this is one. Under all circumstances we should have bewailed the catastrophe at Washington; under all circumstances we should have

[1] *U.S. Messages and Documents*, 1865-66, Pt. I, pp. 344, 361. Adams to Hunter, May 4 and May 11, 1865.

[2] Hansard, 3rd. Ser., CLXXVIII, p. 1219.

shuddered at the means by which it was accomplished. But in the character of the victim, and even in the accessories of his last moments there is something so homely and so innocent that it takes as it were the subject out of all the pomp of history and the ceremonial of diplomacy; it touches the heart of nations, and appeals to the domestic sentiment of mankind.

"Sir, whatever the various and varying opinions in this House, and in the country generally on the policy of the late President of the United States, on this, I think, all must agree, that in one of the severest trials which ever tested the moral qualities of man, he fulfilled his duty with simplicity and strength. Nor is it possible for the people of England, at such a moment, to forget that he sprang from the same fatherland, and spoke the same mother tongue.

"When such crimes are perpetrated the public mind is apt to fall into gloom and perplexity; for it is ignorant alike of the causes and the consequences of such deeds. But it is one of our duties to reassure the country under unreasoning panic or despondency. Assassination has never changed the history of the world. . . .

"In expressing our unaffected and profound sympathy with the citizens of the United States at the untimely end of their elected Chief, let us not, therefore, sanction any feeling of depression, but rather let us express a fervent hope that from out the awful trials of the last four years, of which not the least is this violent demise, the various populations of North America may issue elevated and chastened; rich in that accumulated wisdom, and strong in that disciplined energy which a young nation can only acquire in a protracted and perilous struggle. Then they will be enabled not merely to renew their career of power and prosperity, but they will renew it to contribute to the general happiness of mankind. It is with these feelings, Sir, that I second the Address to the Crown."[1]

Lincoln's assassination served to bring out not only British popular sympathy, but also the certitude that the war was over and the North victorious. But officially the Government had not yet recognized this. Even as early as January, 1865, Seward had returned to the old proposal

[1] *Ibid.* pp. 1242-46.

that the nations of Europe should withdraw their recognition of Southern belligerent rights,[1] and in March he had asked Stoeckl, the Russian Minister, whether Russia would not lead in the suggestion of this measure to England and France.[2] Meanwhile Sherman's army was rapidly advancing northward and reports were arriving of its pillagings and burnings. March 20, Gregory asked in the Commons whether the Government was taking any steps to prevent the destruction of British property and received from Layard an evasive reply. Merely a "confident hope" had been expressed to the United States that "every facility will be given" to British subjects to prove ownership of property.[3] Evidently the Government was not eager to raise irritating questions at a moment when all eyes were strained to observe the concluding events of the war.

Then came the news of Lee's surrender and of the assassination of Lincoln, with the attack on Seward, already incapacitated from active duties. Seward's illness delayed American pressure on England—a fortunate circumstance in the relations with Great Britain in that it gave time for a clearer appreciation of the rapidity and completeness of the collapse of the South. May 15, Lord Houghton asked whether the Government did not intend, in view of recent events in America, "to withdraw the admission of belligerent rights conceded to the so-called Confederate States." Russell promptly objected to the form of the question: England had not "conceded" any rights to the South—she had merely issued a proclamation of neutrality after Lincoln had declared the existence of a war by proclaiming a blockade. England had had no other recourse, unless she chose to refuse recognition of the blockade, and this would have drawn her into the war. As to a withdrawal

[1] Russell Papers. Burnley to Russell, Jan. 16, 1865.

[2] Russian Archives. Stoeckl to F. O., March 1-13, 1865. No. 523. Stoeckl was opposed to this.

[3] Hansard, 3rd. Ser., CLXXVII, p. 1922.

of the neutrality proclamation this must wait upon official announcement from the United States that the war was at an end. Texas was still in arms and Galveston still blockaded, and for this section the United States would no doubt continue to exercise on neutral vessels a belligerent right of search. It followed that if Great Britain did prematurely withdraw her proclamation of neutrality and the United States searched a British vessel, it would be the exercise of a right of search in time of peace—an act against which Great Britain would be bound to make vigorous protest. Hence England must wait on American action proclaiming the end of the war. Russell concluded by expressing gratification at the prospect of peace.[1]

But matters were not to take this orderly and logical course. Seward, though still extremely weak and confined to his home, was eager to resume the duties of office, and on May 9 a Cabinet was held at his house. A week later Bruce wrote to Russell in some anxiety that America was about to *demand* the withdrawal by Great Britain of belligerent rights to the South, that if Great Britain would but act before such a demand was made it would serve to continue the existing good feeling in America created by the sympathy over Lincoln's death, and especially, that there was a decided danger to good relations in the fact that Confederate cruisers were still at large. He urged that orders should be sent to stop their presence in British colonial ports securing coal and supplies.[2] Three days later Bruce repeated his warning.[3] This was, apparently, a complication unforeseen at the Foreign Office. In any case Russell at once made a complete face-about from the policy he had outlined in reply to Lord Houghton. On May 30 he instructed Cowley in Paris to notify France

[1] *Ibid.* CLXXIX, p. 286.
[2] F. O., Am., Vol. 1018. No. 297. Bruce to Russell, May 16, 1865.
[3] *Ibid.* No. 303. Bruce to Russell, May 19, 1865.

that England thought the time had arrived for recognition that the war was ended and laid special stress upon the question of Confederate cruisers still at sea and their proper treatment in British ports.[1] Thus having given to France notice of his intention, but without waiting for concurrent action, Russell, on June 2, issued instructions to the Admiralty that the war was ended and stated the lines upon which the Confederate cruisers were to be treated.[2] Here was prompt, even hurried, action though the only additional event of war in America which Russell could at the moment cite to warrant his change of policy was the capture of Jefferson Davis. On the same day Russell wrote to Bruce stating what had been done and recognizing the "re-establishment of peace within the whole territory of which the United States, before the commencement of the civil war, were in undisturbed possession."[3]

This sudden shift by the Government did not escape Derby's caustic criticism. June 12, he referred in Parliament to Houghton's previous inquiry and Russell's answer, asking why the Government had not stuck to its earlier position and calling attention to the fact that the United States, while now proclaiming certain ports open to trade, yet specified others as still closed and threatened with punishment as pirates, any vessel attempting to enter them. Derby desired information as to what the Government had done about this remarkable American proclamation. Russell, "who was very imperfectly heard," answered that undoubtedly it was embarrassing that no "regular communication" had been received from America giving notice of the end of the war, but that the two Confederate

[1] *Parliamentary Papers*, 1865, *Commons*, Vol. LVII. "Further Correspondence respecting the Cessation of Civil War in North America." No. 10.

[2] *Ibid.* "Correspondence respecting the Cessation of Civil War in North America."

[3] *Ibid.* "Further Correspondence respecting the Cessation of Civil War in North America." No. 9.

cruisers still at sea and the entrance of one of them to various Australian ports had compelled some British action. He had consulted Adams, who had no instructions but felt confident the United States would soon formally declare the end of the war. The "piracy proclamation" was certainly a strange proceeding. Derby pushed for an answer as to whether the Government intended to let it go by unnoticed. Russell replied that a despatch from Bruce showed that "notice" had been taken of it. Derby asked whether the papers would be presented to Parliament; Russell "was understood to reply in the affirmative."[1] Derby's inquiry was plainly merely a hectoring of Russell for his quick shift from the position taken a month earlier. But the very indifference of Russell to this attack, his carelessness and evasion in reply, indicate confidence that Parliament was as eager as the Government to satisfy the North and to avoid friction. The only actual "notice" taken by Bruce at Washington of the "piracy proclamation" was in fact, to report it to Russell, commenting that it was "unintelligible" and probably a mere attempt to frighten foreign ship-owners.[2] Russell instructed Bruce not to ask for an explanation since Galveston had been captured subsequent to the date of the proclamation and there was presumably no port left where it could be applied.[3]

In truth the actual events of the closing days of the war had outrun diplomatic action by America. Scattered Southern forces still in the field surrendered with an unexpected rapidity, while at Washington all was temporarily in confusion upon the death of Lincoln and the illness of Seward. Bruce's advice had been wise and the prompt action of Russell fortunate. Seward at once accepted

[1] Hansard, 3rd. Ser., CLXXX, pp. 1-6.

[2] *Parliamentary Papers*, 1865, *Commons*, Vol. LVII. "Correspondence respecting President's Proclamation of 22nd May, 1865. Bruce to Russell, May 26, 1865.

[3] *Ibid.* June 16, 1865.

Russell's notification of June 2 as ending British neutrality. While again insisting upon the essential injustice of the original concession of belligerent rights to the South, and objecting to some details in the instructions to the Admiralty, he yet admitted that normal relations were again established and acknowledged that the United States could no longer exercise a right of search.[1] July 4, Russell presented this paper to Parliament, reading that portion in which Seward expressed his pleasure that the United States could now enter again upon normal relations with Great Britain.[2] Two days later Russell wrote to Bruce that he had not expected Seward to acknowledge the rightfulness of England's neutrality position, pointed out that his Admiralty instructions were misunderstood and were less objectionable than appeared and concluded by the expression of a hope for the "establishment of a lasting and intimate friendship between the two nations."[3]

. . . . .

Great Britain, wrote the Russian Minister in Washington in January, 1860, was about to experience one of those "strokes of fortune" which occurred but rarely in the history of nations, in the approaching dissolution of the American Union. She alone, of all the nations of the world, would benefit by it in the expansion of her power, hitherto blocked by the might of the United States. Broken into two or more hostile pieces America would be at the mercy of England, to become her plaything. "The Cabinet of London is watching attentively the internal dissensions of the Union and awaits the result with an impatience which it has difficulty in disguising." Great Britain would soon,

[1] *Ibid.* "Further Correspondence respecting the Cessation of Civil War in North America." No. 9. Seward to Bruce, June 19, 1865.

[2] Hansard, 3rd. Ser., CLXXX, p. 1143.

[3] *Parliamentary Papers*, 1865, *Commons*, Vol. LVII. "Further Correspondence respecting the Cessation of Civil War in North America." No. 10.

in return for cotton, give recognition to the South and, if required, armed support. For this same cotton she would oppose emancipation of the slaves. The break-up of the Union was no less than a disaster for all nations save England, since hitherto the "struggle" between England and the United States "has been the best guarantee against the ambitious projects and political egotism of the Anglo-Saxon race."[1]

This prophecy, made over a year in advance of events, was repeated frequently as the crisis in America approached and during the first two years of the war. Stoeckl was not solitary in such opinion. The French Minister of Foreign Affairs held it also—and the French Emperor puzzled himself in vain to discover why Great Britain, in furtherance of her own interests, did not eagerly accept his overtures for a vigorous joint action in support of the South.[2]

The preceding chapters of this work will have shown how unfounded was such prophecy. Stoeckl was behind the times, knowing nothing, apparently, of that positive change in British policy in the late 'fifties which resulted in a determination to cease opposition to the expansion of American power. Such opposition was then acknowledged to have been an error and in its place there sprang into being a conviction that the might of America would tend toward the greatness of England itself.[3] In the months preceding the outbreak of the Civil War all British governmental effort was directed toward keeping clear of the quarrel and toward conciliation of the two sections. No doubt there were those in Great Britain who rejoiced at the

[1] Russian Archives, Stoeckl to F. O., Dec. 23, 1859/Jan. 4, 1860. No. 146.

[2] *Ibid.* Stoeckl to F. O., Jan. 17-29, 1861. No. 267. He reports that he has seen a confidential letter from Thouvenel to Mercier outlining exactly his own ideas as to England being the sole gainer by the dissolution of the Union.

[3] For an analysis of this change see *The Cambridge History of British Foreign Policy*, Vol II, p. 277, which also quotes a remarkable speech by Disraeli.

rupture between North and South, but they were not in office and had no control of British policy.

The war once begun, the Government, anxious to keep clear of it, was prompt in proclaiming neutrality and hastened this step for fear of maritime complications with that one of the belligerents, the North, which alone possessed a naval force. But the British Ministry, like that of every other European state, believed that a revolution for independence when undertaken by a people so numerous and powerful as that of the South, must ultimately succeed. Hence as the war dragged on, the Ministry, pressed from various angles at home, ventured, with much uncertainty, upon a movement looking toward mediation. Its desire was first of all for the restoration of world peace, nor can any other motive be discovered in Russell's manœuvres. This attempt, fortunately for America and, it may be believed, for the world, was blocked by cool heads within the Ministry itself. There was quick and, as it proved, permanent readjustment of policy to the earlier decision not to meddle in the American crisis.

This very failure to meddle was cause of great complaint by both North and South, each expectant, from divergent reasons, of British sympathy and aid. The very anger of the North at British "cold neutrality" is evidence of how little America, feeling the ties of race and sentiment, could have understood the mistaken view-point of diplomats like Stoeckl, who dwelt in realms of "reasons of state," unaffected by popular emotions. Aside from race, which could be claimed also by the South, the one great argument of the North in appeal to England lay in the cry of anti-slavery. But the leaders of the North denied its pertinence. Itself unsympathetic with the emotions of emancipation societies at home, the British Government settled down by the end of 1862 to a fixed policy of strict neutrality.

In all this the Government but pursued that line which

is the business of Governments—the preservation of the prosperity and power of the state. With the unexpected prolongation of the war and the British recognition of the Northern " will to conquer " there came, as is evident from a scrutiny of Russell's diplomatic tone and acts, a growing belief that the North might after all succeed in its purpose, at least of subjugating the South. This would mean the possibility of continuing that policy of friendship for a united America which had been determined upon in the 'fifties. Here was no special sympathy, but merely a cool calculation of benefits to Great Britain, but there can be no question that the general attitude of the Government by midsummer of 1863 was distinctly favourable to a restored Union. A " friendly neutrality " began to replace a " cold neutrality."

But it is the business of Governments not merely to guard national interests and prosperity ; they also must guard their own authority and seek to remain in political power. Here emancipation, never greatly stirring the leaders, whether Whig or Tory, exercised an increasing pressure by the force of public approval. It made impossible any attempt to overthrow the Ministry on the score of non-interference in America, or of favouritism toward the North. It gave to an enthusiastic and vociferous section of the British public just ground for strong support of Lincoln and his cause, and in some degree it affected governmental attitude.

There was, however, another question, much more vital than emancipation in its relation to British home politics, that ran like a constant thread through the whole pattern of British public attitude toward America. It had always been so since the days of the American revolution and now was accentuated by the American war. This was the question of the future of democracy. Was its fate bound up with the result of that war ? And if so where lay British interest? Always present in the minds of thoughtful Englishmen, appearing again and again through each changing phase of the war, this question was so much a constant that to have attempted discussion of it while other topics were being treated, would have resulted in repetition and confusion. It is therefore made the subject of a separate and concluding chapter.

CHAPTER XVIII

THE KEY-NOTE OF BRITISH ATTITUDE

On May 8, 1865, the news was received in London of Johnston's surrender to Sherman. On that same day there occurred in the Commons the first serious debate in thirty-three years on a proposed expansion of the electoral franchise. It was a dramatic coincidence and no mere fortuitous one in the minds of thoughtful Englishmen who had seen in the Civil War a struggle as fateful in British domestic policy as in that of America herself. Throughout all British political agitation from the time of the American revolution in 1776, there had run the thread of the American "example" as argument to some for imitation, to others for warning. Nearly every British traveller in America, publishing his impressions, felt compelled to report on American governmental and political institutions, and did so from his preconceived notions of what was desirable in his own country.[1] In the ten years immediately preceding the Civil War most travellers were laudatory of American democracy, and one, the best in acute analysis up to the time of Lord Bryce's great work, had much influence on that class in England which was discontented with existing political institutions at home. This was Mackay's *Western World* which, first published in 1849, had gone through four editions in 1850 and in succeeding years was frequently reprinted.[2] Republicanism, Mackay asserted, was no

[1] See my article, "The Point of View of the British Traveller in America," *Pol. Sci. Quarterly*, June, 1914.

[2] Alexander Mackay, *The Western World; or Travels in the United States in 1846-47.*

longer an experiment ; its success and permanence were evident in the mighty power of the United States ; Canada would soon follow the American example ; the "injustice" of British aristocrats to the United States was intentional, seeking to discredit democracy :

> ". . . Englishmen are too prone to mingle severity with their judgments whenever the Republic is concerned. It is the interest of aristocracy to exhibit republicanism, where-ever it is found, in the worst possible light, and the mass of the people have too long, by pandering to their prejudice, aided them in their object. They recognize America as the stronghold of republicanism. If they can bring it into dis-repute here, they know that they inflict upon it the deadliest blow in Europe."[1]

On the opposing side were other writers. Tremenheere argued the inapplicability of American institutions to Great Britain.[2] The theoretical bases of those institutions were in some respects admirable but in actual practice they had resulted in the rule of the mob and had debased the nation in the estimation of the world ; bribery in elections, the low order of men in politics and in Congress, were proofs of the evils of democracy ; those in England who clamoured for a "numerical" rather than a class representation should take warning from the American experiment. Occasionally, though rarely, there appeared the impressions of some British traveller who had no political axe to grind,[3] but from 1850 to 1860, as in every previous decade, British writing on America was coloured by the author's attitude on

[1] *Ibid.* Fourth Edition, London, 1850, Vol. III, p. 24.

[2] Hugh Seymour Tremenheere, *The Constitution of the United States compared with Our Own,* London, 1854.

[3] e.g., William Kelly, *Across the Rocky Mountains from New York to California,* London, 1852. He made one acute observation on American democracy. "The division of parties is just the reverse in America to what it is in England. In England the stronghold of democracy is in the large towns, and aristocracy has its strongest supporters in the country. In America the ultra-democrat and leveller is the western farmer, and the aristocratic tendency is most visible amongst the manufacturers and merchants of the eastern cities." (p. 181.)

political institutions at home. The "example" of America was constantly on the horizon in British politics.

In 1860, the Liberal movement in England was at its lowest ebb since the high tide of 1832. Palmerston was generally believed to have made a private agreement with Derby that both Whig and Tory parties would oppose any movement toward an expansion of the franchise.[1] Lord John Russell, in his youth an eager supporter of the Reform Bill of 1832, had now gained the name of "Finality John" by his assertion that that Reform was final in British institutions. Political reaction was in full swing much to the discontent of Radicals like Bright and Cobden and their supporters. When the storm broke in America the personal characteristics of the two leaders North and South, Lincoln and Davis, took on, to many British eyes, an altogether extreme importance as if representative of the political philosophies of the two sections. Lincoln's "crudity" was democratic; Davis' "culture" was aristocratic—nor is it to be denied that Davis had "aristocratic" views on government.[2] But that this issue had any vital bearing on the quarrel between the American sections was never generally voiced in England. Rather, British comment was directed to the lesson, taught to the world by the American crisis, of the failure of democratic institutions in *national power.* Bright had long preached to the unenfranchised of England the prosperity and might of America and these had long been denied by the aristocratic faction to be a result of democratic institutions. At first the denial was now repeated, the *Saturday Review,* February 23, 1861, protesting that there was no essential connection between the "shipwreck" of American institutions and the movement in England for an expanded franchise. Even, the article

[1] Monypenny, *Disraeli,* IV, pp. 293-4, states a Tory offer to support Palmerston on these lines.

[2] Dodd, *Jefferson Davis,* p. 217.

continued, if an attempt were made to show such a connection it would convince nobody since "Mr. Bright has succeeded in persuading a great number of influential persons that the admission of working-men into the constituencies is chiefly, if not solely, desirable on the ground that it has succeeded admirably in America and has proved a sovereign panacea against the war, taxation and confusion which are the curses of old Governments in Europe." Yet that the denial was not sincere is shown by the further assertion that "the shallow demagogues of Birmingham and other kindred platforms must bear the blame of the inference, drawn nearly universally at the present moment, that, if the United States become involved in hopeless difficulties, it would be madness to lower the qualification for the suffrage in England."

This pretended disclaimer of any essential relation between the American struggle and British institutions was not long persisted in. A month later the *Saturday Review* was strong in contemptuous criticism of the "promiscuous democracy" of the North.[1] Less political journals followed suit. The *Economist* thought the people of England would now be convinced of the folly of aping America and that those who had advocated universal suffrage would be filled with "mingled alarm, gratitude and shame."[2] Soon W. H. Russell could write, while still at Washington ". . . the world will only see in it all, the failure of republican institutions in time of pressure as demonstrated by all history—that history which America vainly thought she was going to set right and re-establish on new grounds and principles."[3] "The English worshippers of American institutions," said the *Saturday Review*, "are in danger of losing their last pretext for preferring

[1] March, 30, 1861.
[2] March 16, 1861.
[3] To John Bigelow, April 14, 1861. (Bigelow, *Retrospections*, I, p. 347.)

the Republic to the obsolete and tyrannical Monarchy of England. . . . It now appears that the peaceable completion of the secession has become impossible, and it will be necessary to discover some new ground of superiority by which Mr. Buchanan or Mr. Lincoln may be advantageously contrasted with Queen Victoria."[1]

These expressions antedated the news of the actual opening of the war and may be regarded as jeers at Bright and his followers rather than as attempts to read a lesson to the public. No such expressions are to be found in the letters of leading officials though minor ones occasionally indulged in them.[2] As late as June, 1861, Adams declared that while some in England welcomed American disunion as a warning to their countrymen it was evident that but a small number as yet saw the cause of the North as identical with the world progress of free institutions.[3] Evidently he was disappointed that the followers of Bright were not exhibiting more courage and demanding public support of the North as fighting their battle at home. They were indeed strangely silent, depressed no doubt by American events, and discouraged. It required time also to arouse intensity of feeling on the American question and to see clearly the issues involved. Aristocratic Britain was first to declare a definite lesson to be learned, thereby bringing out the fighting qualities of British democracy. Throughout 1861, the comment was relatively mild. In July, *Blackwood's* declared :

> " It is precisely because we do not share the admiration of America for her own institutions and political tendencies that we do not now see in the impending change an event

[1] April 27, 1861.

[2] Bunch wrote to Russell, May 15, 1861, that the war in America was the " natural result of the much vaunted system of government of the United States " ; it had " crumbled to pieces," and this result had long been evident to the public mind of Europe. (F. O., Am., Vol. 780, No. 58.)

[3] State Department, Eng., Vol. 77, No. 9. Adams to Seward, June 21, 1861.

> altogether to be deplored. In those institutions and tendencies we saw what our own might be if the most dangerous elements of our Constitution should become dominant. We saw democracy rampant, with no restriction upon its caprices. We saw a policy which received its impulses always from below . . . nor need we affect particularly to lament the exhibition of the weak point of a Constitution . . . the disruption of which leaves entirely untouched the laws and usages which America owes to England, and which have contributed so powerfully to her prosperity. . . ."
>
> "With a rival Government on the frontier . . . with great principles to be not vapoured about but put to the proof we should probably see the natural aristocracy rise from the dead level of the Republic, raising the national character with its own elevation."[1]

In the same month the *Quarterly*, always more calm, logical and convincing than *Blackwood's*, published "Democracy on its Trial."[2] "The example of America kept alive, as it had created, the party of progress"; now "it has sunk from the decrep tude of premature old age." If England, after such an example, permits herself to be led into democracy she "will have perished by that wilful infatuation which no warning can dispel."

Adams had complained that few British friends of progress identified the cause of the North with their own, but this was true of Americans also. The *Atlantic Monthly* for July 1861, discussed British attitude wholly in terms of cotton supply. But soon there appeared in the British press so many preachments on the "lesson" of America that the aristocratic effort to gain an advantage at home became apparent to all.[3] The *Economist* moralized on the "untried"

[1] I have made an effort to identify writers in *Blackwood's*, but am informed by the editors that it is impossible to do this for the period before 1870, old correspondence having been destroyed.

[2] July, 1861.

[3] The *Atlantic Monthly* for November, 1861, takes up the question, denying that democracy is in any sense "on trial" in America, so far as the permanence of American institutions is concerned. It still does not see clearly the real nature of the controversy in England.

character of American institutions and statesmen, the latter usually as ignorant as the "masses" whom they represented and if more intellectual still more worthy of contempt because of their "voluntary moral degradation" to the level of their constituents.[1] "The upper and ruling class" wrote Bright to Sumner, were observing with satisfaction, "that democracy may get into trouble, and war, and debt, and taxes, as aristocracy has done for this country."[2] Thus Bright could not deny the blow to democracy; nor could the *Spectator*, upbraiding its countrymen for lack of sympathy with the North: "New England will be justified in saying that Old England's anti-slavery sympathies are mere hollow sentimental pretences, since she can rest satisfied to stuff her ears with cotton against the cries of the slaves, and to compensate her gentle regret over the new impulse given to slavery by her lively gratification over the paralyzing shock suffered by Democracy."[3] This was no taking up of cudgels for the North and "Progress" such as Adams had hoped for. Vigour rested with the opposing side and increased when hopes of a short war vanished. The *Saturday Review* asserted:

> "In that reconstruction of political philosophy which the American calamities are likely to inaugurate, the value of the popular element will be reduced to its due proportions. . . . The true guarantee of freedom will be looked for more in the equilibrium of classes than in the equality of individuals. . . . We may hope, at last, that the delusive confusion between freedom and democracy is finally banished from the minds of Englishmen."[4]

"The real secret," wrote Motley, "of the exultation which manifests itself in the *Times* and other organs over our troubles and disasters, is their hatred, not to America,

[1] Aug. 17, 1861.
[2] Sept. 6, 1861. (Mass. Hist. Soc. *Proceedings*, XLVI, p. 94.)
[3] Sept. 7, 1861.
[4] Sept. 14, 1861.

so much as to democracy in England."[1] It was scarcely a secret in the columns of the journals already quoted. But no similar interpretation had as yet appeared in the *Times* and Motley's implication was justified for it and other leading daily newspapers. The Reviews and Weeklies were for the moment leading the attack—possibly one reason for the slowness in reply of Bright and his followers. Not all Reviews joined in the usual analysis. The *Edinburgh* at first saw in slavery the sole cause of the American dispute,[2] then attributed it to the inevitable failure in power of a federal system of government, not mentioning democracy as in question.[3] *Blackwood's* repeatedly pushed home its argument:

> "Independent of motives of humanity, we are glad that the end of the Union seems more likely to be ridiculous than terrible. . . . But for our own benefit and the instruction of the world we wish to see the faults, so specious and so fatal, of their political system exposed, in the most effective way. . . . And the venerable Lincoln, the respectable Seward, the raving editors, the gibbering mob, and the swift-footed warriors of Bull's Run, are no malicious tricks of fortune played off on an unwary nation, but are all of them the legitimate offspring of the great Republic. . . . dandled and nursed—one might say coddled—by Fortune, the spoiled child Democracy, after playing strange pranks before high heaven, and figuring in odd and unexpected disguises, dies as sheerly from lack of vitality as the oldest of worn-out despotisms. . . . In the hope that this contest may end in the extinction of mob rule, we become reconciled to the much slighter amount of suffering that war inflicts on America."[4]

Equally outspoken were a few public men who early espoused the cause of the South. Beresford Hope, before a "distinguished audience" used language insulting to the

[1] Motley, *Correspondence*, II, p. 35. To his mother, Sept. 22, 1861.
[2] April, 1861.
[3] Oct., 1861.
[4] Oct., 1861. Article, "Democracy teaching by Example."

North, fawning upon the South and picturing the latter as wholly admirable for its aristocratic tendencies. For this he was sharply taken to task by the *Spectator*.[1] More sedately the Earl of Shrewsbury proclaimed, "I see in America the trial of Democracy and its failure. I believe that the dissolution of the Union is inevitable, and that men now before me will live to see an aristocracy established in America."[2] In all countries and at all times there are men over-eager in early prophecy on current events, but in such utterances as these there is manifest not merely the customary desire to stand in the limelight of assured knowledge and wisdom, but also the happy conviction that events in America were working to the undoing of the Radicals of Great Britain. If they would not be supine the Radicals must strike back. On December 4, at Rochdale where, as the *Times* asserted, he was sure of an audience sympathetic on purely personal grounds, Bright renewed his profession of faith in the American Republic and sang his accustomed praises of its great accomplishments.[3] The battle, for England, on American democracy, was joined; the challenge issued by aristocratic England, accepted.

But apart from extreme factions at either end of the scale there stood a group holding a middle ground opinion, not yet sure of the historical significance of the American collapse. To this group belonged Gladstone, as yet uncertain of his political philosophy, and regretful, though vainly, it would appear, of the blow to democracy. He wrote his thought to Brougham, no doubt hoping to influence the view-point of the *Edinburgh*.

> "This has without doubt been a deplorable year for poor 'Democracy' and never has the old woman been at a heavier discount since 1793. I see no discredit to the founders of the

[1] Nov. 23, 1861.
[2] Cited by Harris, *The Trent Affair*, p. 28.
[3] Robertson, *Speeches of John Bright*, I, pp. 177 *seq.*

American constitution in the main fact of the rupture. On the contrary it was a great achievement to strike off by the will and wit of man a constitution for two millions of men scattered along a seaboard, which has lasted until they have become more than thirty millions and have covered a whole continent. But the freaks, pranks, and follies, not to say worse, with which the rupture has been met in the Northern States, down to Mr. Chase's financial (not exposition but) exposure have really given as I have said the old lady in question such a heavy blow and great discouragement that I hope you will in the first vigour of your action be a little merciful and human lest you murder her outright."[1]

On this middle group of Englishmen and their moral conceptions the American Minister, Adams, at first pinned his faith, not believing in 1861 that the issues of democracy or of trade advantage would lead Great Britain from just rules of conduct. Even in the crisis of the *Trent* affair he was firm in this opinion:

"Much as the commercial and manufacturing interests may be disposed to view the tariff as the source of all our evils, and much as the aristocratic classes may endeavour to make democracy responsible for them, the inexorable logic of events is contradicting each and every assertion based on these notions, and proving that the American struggle is, after all, the ever-recurring one in human affairs between right and wrong, between labour and capital, between liberty and absolutism. When such an issue comes to be presented to the people of Great Britain, stripped of all the disguises which have been thrown over it, it is not difficult to predict at least which side it will *not* consent to take.[2]

April, 1861, saw the beginning of the aristocratic challenge on American democracy and December its acceptance by Bright. Throughout 1862 he practically deserted his seat in Parliament and devoted himself to

[1] Gladstone Papers, Dec. 27, 1861.

[2] State Dept., Eng., Vol. 78, No. 95. Adams to Seward, Dec. 27, 1861. As printed in *U.S. Messages and Documents*, 1862-63, Pt. I, p. 14. Adams' emphasis on the word "*not*" is unindicated, by the failure to use italics.

stirring up labour and radical sentiment in favour of the North. In January, 1862, a mass meeting at New Hall, Edgware Road, denounced the daily press and was thought of sufficient moment to be reported by Adams. A motion was carried:

> "That in the opinion of this meeting, considering the ill-disguised efforts of the *Times* and other misleading journals to misrepresent public opinion here on all American questions . . . to decry democratic institutions under the trials to which the Republic is exposed, it is the duty of the working-men especially as unrepresented in the National Senate to express their sympathy with the United States in their gigantic struggle for the preservation of the Union. . . ."[1]

The daily press was, in fact, now joining more openly in the controversy. The *Morning Post*, stating with conviction its belief that there could be no re-union in America, added:

> " . . . if the Government of the United States should succeed in reannexing them [the Southern States] to its still extensive dominions, Democracy will have achieved its grandest triumph since the world began. It will have demonstrated to the ample satisfaction of its present and future proselytes that it is even more puissant in war than in peace; that it can navigate not only the smooth seas of unendangered prosperity, but can ride safely through the fiercest tempests that would engulf every other craft laden with human destinies; that it can descend to the darkest depths of adversity, and rise from them all the stronger for the descent. . . . And who can doubt that Democracy will be more arrogant, more aggressive, more levelling and vulgarizing, if that be possible, than it ever had been before." [2]

By midsummer, 1862, Adams was more convinced than in 1861 that the political controversy in England had an important bearing on the attitude toward America. Even the alleged neutrality of *Fraser's Magazine* seemed turning

[1] *Ibid.* No. 110. Enclosure. Adams to Seward, Jan. 31, 1862.
[2] Feb. 22, 1862.

to one-sided presentation of the "lesson" of America. Mill's defence of the North, appearing in the February number, was soon followed in July by the first of a series of articles, "Universal Suffrage in the United States and Its Consequences," depicting the war as the result of mob rule and predicting a military despotism as its inevitable consequence. The Liberals were losing strength, wrote Adams:

> "That the American difficulties have materially contri buted to this result cannot be doubted. The fact that many of the leading Liberals are the declared friends of the United States is a decided disadvantage in the contest now going on. The predominating passion here is the desire for the ultimate subdivision of America into many separate States which will neutralize each other. This is most visible among the conservative class of the Aristocracy who dread the growth of liberal opinions and who habitually regard America as the nursery of them."[1]

From all this controversy Government leaders kept carefully aloof at least in public expression of opinion. Privately, Russell commented to Palmerston, "I have been reading a book on Jefferson by De Witt, which is both interesting and instructive. It shows how the Great Republic of Washington degenerated into the Democracy of Jefferson. They are now reaping the fruit."[2] Was it mere coincidence or was there significance in an editorial in Palmerston's alleged "organ," the *Morning Post*:

> "That any Englishman has looked forward with pleasure to the calamities of America is notoriously and demonstrably

[1] State Dept., Eng., Vol. 80, No. 206. Adams to Seward, Aug. 8, 1862. Of this period in 1862, Rhodes (IV, 78) writes that "the most significant and touching feature of the situation "was that the cotton operative population was frankly on the side of the North." Lutz, *Die Beziehungen zwischen Deutschland und den Vereinigten Staaten während des Sezessionskrieges*, pp. 49-53, makes an interesting analysis of the German press, showing it also determined in its attitude by factional political idealisms in Germany.

[2] Palmerston MS., Aug. 24, 1862.

false. But we have no hesitation in admitting that many thoughtful Englishmen who have watched, in the policy of the United States during the last twenty years, the foreshadowing of a democratic tyranny compared with which the most corrupt despotisms of the Old World appear realms of idyllic happiness and peace, have gratefully recognized the finger of Providence in the strife by which they have been so frightfully rent asunder. . . ."[1]

In October the heavy artillery of the Conservatives was again brought into action and this time with more explicit diagnosis than heretofore. "For a great number of years," said the *Quarterly*, "a certain party among us, great admirers of America . . . have chosen to fight their English battles upon American soil." Now the American Government "has disgracefully and ignominiously failed" at all points. It is evident that "political equality is not merely a folly, it is a chimera."[2] At last, in November, the *Times* openly took the position which its accusers declared to have been the basis of its editorial utterances almost from the beginning of the Civil War.

"These are the consequences of a cheap and simple form of government, having a rural attorney for Sovereign and a city attorney for Prime Minister. We have already said that if such a terrible exposure of incapacity had happened in England we should at the earliest moment possible have sent the incapables about their business, and put ourselves in the hands of better men. . . ."

"This Republic has been so often proposed to us as a model for imitation that we should be unpardonable not to mark how it works now, when for the first time it has some work to do. We believe that if the English system of Parliamentary action had existed in America, the war could not have occurred, but we are quite sure that such Ministers would have long since been changed."[3]

[1] Aug. 30, 1862.
[2] October, 1862. "The Confederate Struggle and Recognition."
[3] Nov. 4, 1862.

In addition to a Conservative ringing the changes upon the failure of democracy, the open friends of the South dilated also upon the "gentlemanly" characteristics of Southern leaders and society. This was the frequent burden of articles in *The Index* in the early weeks of its publication. To this was soon added a picture of Northern democracy as composed of and controlled by the "immigrant element" which was the source of "the enormous increase of population in the last thirty years" from revolutionary areas in Europe. "Germans, Hungarians, Irish carried with them more than their strong arms, they imported also their theories of equality. . . . The revolutionary party which represents them is at this moment master in the States of the North, where it is indulging in all its customary licence."[1] This fact, complained *The Index*, was not sufficiently brought out in the English press. Very different was the picture painted by Anthony Trollope after a tour of the Western states:

> ". . . this man has his romance, his high poetic feeling, and above all his manly dignity. Visit him, and you will find him without coat or waistcoat, unshorn, in ragged blue trousers and old flannel shirt, too often bearing on his lantern jaws the signs of ague and sickness; but he will stand upright before you and speak to you with all the ease of a lettered gentleman in his own library. All the odious incivility of the republican servant has been banished. He is his own master, standing on his own threshold, and finds no need to assert his equality by rudeness. He is delighted to see you, and bids you sit down on his battered bench, without dreaming of any such apology as an English cotter offers to a Lady Bountiful when she calls. He has worked out his independence, and shows it in every easy movement of his body. He tells you of it unconsciously in every tone of his voice. You will always find in his cabin some newspaper, some book, some token of advance in education. When he questions you about the old country he astonishes you by the extent of his knowledge.

[1] *The Index*, Nov. 20, 1862, p. 63. (Communication.)

I defy you not to feel that he is superior to the race from whence he has sprung in England or in Ireland."

. . . . . .

"It is always the same story. With us there is no level of society. Men stand on a long staircase, but the crowd congregates near the bottom, and the lower steps are very broad. In America men stand upon a common platform, but the platform is raised above the ground, though it does not approach in height the top of our staircase. If we take the average altitude in the two countries, we shall find that the American heads are the more elevated of the two."[1]

A comparison of dates shows that the unanimity of conservative and aristocratic expression on the failure of American democracy and its lesson to England was most marked and most open at the moment when the Government was seriously considering an offer of mediation in the war. Meanwhile the emancipation proclamation of September, 1862, had appeared. It did not immediately affect governmental attitude, save adversely to the North, and it gave a handle for pro-Southern outcry on the score of a "servile war." Indeed, the radicals were at first depressed by it; but when months passed with no appearance of a servile war and when the second emancipation proclamation of January, 1863, further certified the moral purpose of the North, a great element of strength was added to the English advocates of democracy. The numerous "addresses" to Lincoln exhibited both a revived moral enthusiasm for the cause of anti-slavery and were frequently combined with a laudation of American political institutions. The great mass-meeting at Exeter Hall, January 29, 1863, was described by the correspondent of an American paper as largely deriving its strength from the universal dissatisfaction

[1] Anthony Trollope, *North America*, London, 1862, Vol. I, p. 198. The work appeared in London in 1862, and was in its third edition by the end of the year. It was also published in New York in 1862 and in Philadelphia in 1863.

of the lower orders of the English people with their existing conditions under the Crown:

> "The descendants of the Roundhead commoners, chafing under the limitations of the franchise, burdensome taxation, the contempt with which they are regarded by the lords of the soil, the grievous effects of the laws of entail and primogeniture, whereby they are kept poor and rendered liable to starvation and pauperism—these have looked to America as the model democracy which proves the poor man's capacity for self-government." The meeting was called for seven o'clock but at half after five the hall was filled, and at six crowded. A second hall was filled and outdoor meetings of two thousand people organized in Exeter Street. "All working-class England was up in arms, not so much against slavery as against British oligarchy."[1]

The correspondent further reported rumours that this meeting had caused anxious consideration to the managers of the *Times*, and the decision to step more warily. No doubt this was exaggeration of the political character and effect of the meeting, but certain it is that the political element was present joining hands with anti-slavery enthusiasm. Also it is noteworthy that the last confident and vigorous expression of the "failure" of democracy, from sources professedly neutral, appeared immediately after the St. James' Hall meeting, but was necessarily written before that meeting took place. *Blackwood's*, in its issue of February, 1863, declared, as before: "Every sensible man in this country now acknowledges . . . that we have already gone as far toward democracy as is safe to go. . . . This is the great moral benefit which we have derived from the events in America." John Blackwood was an intimate friend of Delane, editor of the *Times*, holding similar views on political questions; but the *Times* was suddenly grown cautious in reading English

[1] *The Liberator*, March 13, 1863, quoting a report in the *New York Sunday Mercury*.

political lessons from America. In truth, attack now rested with the Radicals and Bright's oratory was in great demand.[1] He now advanced from the defensive position of laudation of the North to the offensive one of attacking the Southern aristocracy, not merely because it wished to perpetuate African slavery, but because it desired to make all the working-classes as subservient to it as was the negro.[2] It was now Radical purpose to keep the battle raging and they were succeeding. Bigelow believed that the United States might well recognize its opportunity in this controversy and give aid to its friends:

> "After all, this struggle of ours both at home and abroad is but a struggle between the principle of popular government and government by a privileged class. The people therefore all the world over are in a species of solidarity which it is our duty and interest to cultivate to the utmost."[3]

But Adams gave contrary advice. Wholly sympathetic with the democratic movement in England as now, somewhat to his surprise, developed, he yet feared that the extremes to which Bright and others were going in support of the North might create unfortunate reactions in the Government. Especially he was anxious that the United States should not offer opportunity for accusation of interference in a British political quarrel. It is noteworthy that while many addresses to Lincoln were forwarded by him and many were printed in the annual publication of diplomatic correspondence, those that thus appeared dealt almost exclusively with

[1] Lord Salisbury is quoted in Vince, *John Bright*, p. 204, as stating that Bright "was the greatest master of English oratory that this generation—I may say several generations—has seen. I have met men who have heard Pitt and Fox, and in whose judgment their eloquence at its best was inferior to the finest efforts of John Bright. At a time when much speaking has depressed, has almost exterminated, eloquence, he maintained that robust, powerful and vigorous style in which he gave fitting expression to the burning and noble thoughts he desired to utter."

[2] Speech at Rochdale, Feb. 3, 1863. (Robertson, *Speeches of John Bright*, I, pp. 234 *seq.*)

[3] Bigelow to Seward, Feb. 6, 1863. (Bigelow, *Retrospections*, I, p. 600.)

emancipation. Yet Adams was also forwarding addresses and speeches harping on American democracy. A meeting at Edinburgh, February 19, found place, in its emancipation aspect in the United States documents,[1] but the burden of that meeting, democracy, did not. It was there proclaimed that the British press misrepresented conditions in America, "because the future of free political institutions, as sketched in the American Declaration of Independence and in the State Constitutions of the Northern States, would be a standing argument against the expansion of the franchise and the enjoyment of just political rights among us, as well as a convenient argument in favour of the continued domination of our aristocratic parties."[2] The tide of democratic feeling was rising rapidly in England. On March 26, Adams wrote to Seward of a recent debate in Parliament that that body was much more judicious in expressions on America than it had been before 1862. "It will not escape your observation that the question is now felt to be taking a shape which was scarcely anticipated by the managers [of the *Times*] when they first undertook to guide the British mind to the overthrow of free institutions in America."[3]

On the evening of the day on which this was written there occurred the greatest, most outspoken, and most denunciatory to the aristocracy, of the meetings held to support the cause of the North. This was the spectacular gathering of the Trades Unions of London at St. James' Hall, on March 26, usually regarded as the culminating effort in Bright's tour of England for the cause of democracy, but whose origin is somewhat shrouded in mystery. Socialist tradition claims that Karl Marx conceived the idea

[1] *U.S. Messages and Documents*, 1863, Pt. I, p. 123.

[2] State Dept., Eng., Adams to Seward. No. 334. Feb. 26, 1863. enclosing report of the Edinburgh meeting as printed in *The Weekly Herald, Mercury and News*, Feb. 21, 1863.

[3] *U.S. Messages and Documents*, 1863, Pt. I, p. 157.

of the meeting and was responsible for its organization.[1] The press generally reported it as a "Bright Meeting." Adams wrote to Seward of the pressure put on him by Professor Beesly, of the University of London, to send a representative from the American Ministry, Beesly expanding upon the importance and high standing of the Trades Unions. To this Adams demurred but finally sent his son to sit in the audience and report the proceedings.

Whatever its origin there can be no doubt that this was the most important of all pro-Northern meetings held in England during the Civil War, nor that its keynote was "America fighting the battle of democracy." Save for some distinguished speakers those in attendance consisted almost wholly of three thousand picked representatives of the Trades Unions of London. Adams transmitted to Seward his son's report of the meeting, its character, composition, names of speakers and their emphatic expressions of friendship for the North,[2] but it is again noteworthy that Henry Adams' clear analysis of the real significance of the meeting was not printed in the published diplomatic correspondence. Giving due praise to the speeches of Bright and Beesly, and commenting on press assertions that "the extraordinary numbers there were only brought together by their curiosity to hear Mr. Bright," Henry Adams continued: "That this was not the case

[1] Spargo, *Karl Marx*, pp. 224-5. Spargo claims that Marx bent every effort to stir working men to a sense of class interest in the cause of the North and even went so far as to secure the presence of Bright at the meeting, as the most stirring orator of the day, though personally he regarded Bright "with an almost unspeakable loathing." On reading this statement I wrote to Mr. Spargo asking for evidence and received the reply that he believed the tradition unquestionably well founded, though "almost the only testimony available consists of a reference or two in one of his [Marx's] letters and the ample corroborative testimony of such friends as Lessner, Jung and others." This is scant historical proof; but some years later in a personal talk with Henry Adams, who was in 1863 his father's private secretary, and who attended and reported the meeting, the information was given that Henry Adams himself had then understood and always since believed Marx's to have been the guiding hand in organizing the meeting.

[2] *U.S. Messages and Documents*, 1863, Pt. I, p. 162. (Adams to Seward, March 27, 1863.)

must have been evident to every person present. In fact, it was only after he closed that the real business of the evening began." Then followed speeches and the introduction of resolutions by "Mr. Howell, a bricklayer . . . Mr. Odgers, a shoemaker . . . Mr. Mantz, a compositor. . . Mr. Cremer, a joiner, who was bitter against Lord Palmerston . . . Mr. Conolly, a mason . . ." and other labouring men, all asserting "that the success of free institutions in America was a political question of deep consequence in England and that they would not tolerate any interference unfavourable to the North." No one, the report emphasized, "could doubt what was intended."

> "The meeting was a demonstration of democratic strength and no concealment of this fact was made. If it did not have a direct political bearing on internal politics in England it needed little of doing so. There was not even a profession of faith in the government of England as at present constituted. Every hostile allusion to the Aristocracy, the Church, the opinions of the 'privileged classes,' was received with warm cheers. Every allusion to the republican institutions of America, the right of suffrage, the right of self-taxation, the 'sunlight' of republican influence, was caught up by the audience with vehement applause. It may therefore be considered as fairly and authoritatively announced that the class of skilled workmen in London—that is the leaders of the pure popular movement in England—have announced by an act almost without precedent in their history, the principle that they make common cause with the Americans who are struggling for the restoration of the Union and that all their power and influence shall be used on behalf of the North."[1]

Bright's words of most scarifying indictment of "Privilege," and his appeal to workers to join hands with their fellows in America have been given in a previous

[1] State Dept., Eng., Vol. 82, No. 358. Adams to Seward, March 27, 1863, enclosing report by Henry Adams. There was also enclosed the printed report, giving speeches at length, as printed by *The Bee Hive*, the organ of the London Trades Unions.

chapter.[1] Evidently that appeal, though enthusiastically received for its oratorical brilliance, was unneeded. His was but an eloquent expression of that which was in the minds of his audience. Upon the American Minister the effect was to cause him to renew warnings against showing too keen an appreciation of the support of political radicalism in England. The meeting, he wrote, had at once stirred anxiety in Parliament and verged:

> ". . . much too closely upon the minatory in the domestic politics of this Kingdom to make it easy to recognize or sympathize with by Foreign Governments. . . . Hence it seems to me of the greatest consequence that the treatment of all present questions between the two nations should be regulated by a provident forecast of what may follow it [the political struggle in England] hereafter. I am not sure that some parties here would not now be willing even to take the risk of a war in order the more effectually to turn the scale against us, and thus, as they think, to crush the rising spirit of their own population. That this is only a feeling at present and has not yet risen to the dignity of a policy may be true enough; but that does not the less impose upon the Government at home a duty so to shape its actions as, if possible, to defeat all such calculations and dissipate such hopes. . . . We owe this duty not less to the great body of those who in this kingdom are friends to us and our institutions, than to ourselves." [2]

Thus Adams advised his Government to tread lightly in respect to democratic agitation in England. Over a month later he received a deputation headed by Bright, come to present to him the resolutions passed at the Trades Unions' meeting. The deputation expressed fears that a rupture was imminent in the relations of Great Britain and America, and that this would have a disastrous influence on the aspirations of working-class Europe. Adams replied in general terms of appreciation for the sympathies expressed

[1] See *ante*, p. 132.

[2] State Dept., Eng., Vol. 82, No. 360. Adams to Seward, April 2, 1863.

JOHN BRIGHT

(From a photograph taken of him in the attitude in which he usually spoke)
(From Trevelyan's "Life of John Bright")

by the meeting but carefully avoided specific comment on its democratic purpose. "He was too prudent," said the *Times* in reporting the deputation, "to appraise the importance of the particular demonstration to which his notice was invited . . ." and his reply was given favourable comment.[1] This reply, wrote Adams, "appears to have had a sedative effect."[2] Meanwhile, Bright continued his preachment to the English people though modifying his tone of fierce accusation against "privilege," and confining himself to declaring the interest of the unenfranchised in the American conflict. In a speech before the Union and Emancipation Society of London, on June 16, he asserted for the "twenty millions of people in this country" as yet without representation in Parliament, "I say that these have an interest, almost as great and direct as though they were living in Massachusetts or New York, in the tremendous struggle for freedom which is now shaking the whole North American Continent."[3] Like utterances were repeated at further public meetings and so insistent were they as to require reply by the conservative faction, even if, as was supposed, the effect of the Trades' Union attitude had been to give a halt to the vehemence of those who had been sounding the "lesson" of American failure in democracy. Bright became the centre of attack. The *Times* led.

> "His is a political fanaticism. He used to idolize the Constitution of the United States as the one great dominant Democracy of the world. He believes in it still, and, if it must go, he is ready to idolize its memory. For this he gives up all his most cherished notions and all his less absorbing principles. . . ."
>
> "Yet Mr. Bright is consistent. He has one master passion

[1] May 5, 1863.

[2] *U.S. Diplomatic Correspondence*, 1863, Pt. I, p. 243. Adams to Seward, May 7, 1863.

[3] Robertson, *Speeches of John Bright*, I, p. 264. In a letter to Bigelow, March 16, 1863, Bright estimated that there were seven millions of men of twenty-one years of age and upward in the United Kingdom, of whom slightly over one million had the vote. (Bigelow, *Retrospections*, I, p. 610.)

> and his breast, capacious as it is, can hold no more. That master passion is the love of that great dominant Democracy. He worshipped it while rising to its culminating point, and he is obliged to turn right round to worship it while setting. He did not himself know, until tested by this great trial, how entirely his opinions as to war and peace, and slavery and freedom, and lust of conquest and hatred of oppression, were all the mere accidents which hung loosely upon him, and were capable of being detached at once in the interest of the ruling passion of his soul for that great dominant Democracy. Nor need we wonder; for if that great Democracy has been a failure, then men will say that the life of Mr. John Bright up to this time has been but a foolish dream." [1]

Evidently Bright's speeches were causing anxiety and bitterness; but an "if" had crept into the estimate of the future of American democracy, caused less by the progress of the war than by the rising excitement of democratic England. The *Times* editorial just quoted appeared when the faith was generally professed that Lee was about to end the war through the invasion of Pennsylvania. In the reaction created by the arrival of the news of Gettysburg and Vicksburg, Adams still again warned his Government against either a belligerent or interfering attitude toward Great Britain, but stated plainly that Northern victory was of supreme importance in Europe itself. "We have a mission to fulfill. It is to show, by our example to the people of England in particular, and to all nations in general, the value of republican institutions." There was still a general belief in the incompetency of those institutions. "The greatest triumph of all would be to prove these calculations vain. In comparison with this, what would be the gain to be derived from any collision with the powers of Europe?" [2]

[1] July 2, 1863. The editorial was written in connection with Roebuck's motion for mediation and is otherwise interesting for an attempt to characterize each of the speakers in the Commons.

[2] *U.S. Diplomatic Correspondence*, 1863, Part I, p. 319. To Seward, July 23, 1863.

It is strange that with so clearly-expressed a division of English opinion on American democracy few in America itself appreciated the significance of the British controversy. J. M. Forbes, who had been on a special mission to England, wrote to Lincoln, on his return:[1]

> "Our friends abroad see it! John Bright and his glorious band of English Republicans see that we are fighting for Democracy or (to get rid of the technical name) for liberal institutions; the Democrats and the liberals of the old world are as much and as heartily with us as any supporters we have on this side.
>
> Our enemies too see it in the same light; the Aristocrats and the Despots of the old world see that our quarrel is that of the People against an Aristocracy."[2]

But there are few similar expressions and these few nearly always came from men who had been abroad and had thus come into direct contact with British political movements. Meanwhile, Lee's retreat from Pennsylvania had produced a like retreat in the opinions on the failure of democracy earlier confidently held by the professedly neutral press. In September, having arrived at the point by the usual process of gradually facing about, the *Times* was bold enough to deny that England had any personal feeling or concern about democracy in America or that this had anything to do with English attitude on the war.[3] Thenceforth neither the *Times* nor any of the leading papers saw fit to revive with vigour the cry of "democracy's failure," no matter how persistent in proclaiming ultimate victory for the South. Aristocratic exultation had given place to alarm and it seemed wiser, if possible, to quiet the issue.[4] Not so the

[1] See *ante*, p. 130, *note* 2.

[2] MS. letter, Sept. 8, 1863, in possession of C. F. Adams, Jr.

[3] Sept. 24, 1863.

[4] Even the friendly Russian Minister in Washington was at this time writing of the "rule of the mob" in America and trusting that the war, "the result of democracy," would serve as a warning to Europe. (Russian Archives, Stoeckl to F. O., Nov. 29-Dec. 11, 1864, No. 1900.)

Radicals, who made every effort to keep the issue alive in the minds of the British public, and whose leaders with less violence but increased firmness debated the question in every public meeting favourable to the North.[1] Many Conservatives, Adams reported, were now anxiously sitting on the fence yet finding the posture a difficult one because of their irritation at Bright's taunts.[2] Bright's star was rising. "The very moment the war comes to an end," wrote Adams, "and a restoration of the Union follows, it will be the signal for a reaction that will make Mr. Bright perhaps the most formidable public man in England."[3]

The continuation of the controversy was not, however, wholly one-sided. In the silence of the daily press it seemed incumbent upon the more eager and professed friends of the South to take up the cudgels. Hence, in part, came the organization of the Southern Independence Association and the attempt to hold public meetings favourable to the South, in the early months of 1864. Much talk had been spent on the "British issue" involved in the war; there was now to be vigorous work to secure it.[4] *The Index* plunged into vigorous denunciation of "The Manchester School, which, for convenience and truth, we had better for the future call the American School." Even the Government was attacked for its complacence under the "American danger" and for retaining as a member Milner-Gibson, who, in a recent speech, had shown that he shared Bright's views on democracy:

> "That gentleman [Bright] could not be asked to enter the Cabinet in person. The country abhorred him; Parliament despised him; his inveterate habits of slander and vitupera-

[1] State Dept., Eng., Vol. 84, Nos. 557 and 559. Adams to Seward, Dec. 17, 1863. Adams repeated his advice to "keep out of it."

[2] *Ibid.* Vol. 85, No. 587. Adams to Seward, Jan. 29, 1864. Adams here expressed the opinion that it was partly the aristocratic antipathy to Bright that had *produced* the ill-will to the United States.

[3] *Ibid.*

[4] See Ch. XV.

tion, his vulgarity, and his incurable want of veracity, had made him so hateful to the educated classes that it would have required no common courage to give him office; his insolent sneers at royalty would have made his appointment little less than a personal insult to the Queen; and his bad temper would have made him an intolerable colleague in the Council. But Mr. Bright had another self; a faithful shadow, which had no ideas, no soul, no other existence but what it borrowed from him, while its previous life and education had accustomed it to the society of statesmen and of gentlemen."[1]

Such expressions gained nothing for the Conservative cause; they were too evidently the result of alarm at the progress of Radical and pro-Northern sentiment. Goldwin Smith in a "Letter" to the Southern Independence Association, analysed with clarity the situation. Answering criticisms of the passionate mob spirit of Northern press and people, he accused the *Times* of having

"... pandered to the hatred of America among the upper classes of this country during the present war. Some of us at least had been taught by what we have lately seen not to shrink from an extension of the suffrage, if the only bad consequence of that measure of justice would be a change in government from the passions of the privileged class to the passions of the people. ... History will not mistake the meaning of the loud cry of triumph which burst from the hearts of all who openly or secretly hated liberty and progress, at the fall, as they fondly supposed, of the Great Republic." British working men "are for the most part as well aware that the cause of those who are fighting for the right of labour is theirs, as any nobleman in your Association can be that the other cause in his."[2]

The question of democracy as a political philosophy and as an institution for Great Britain was, by 1864, rapidly coming to the front in politics. This was very largely a result of the American Civil War. Roebuck, after the failure of his

[1] *The Index*, Jan. 28, 1864, p. 58.

[2] Goldwin Smith, *A Letter to a Whig Member of the Southern Independence Association*, London, 1864, pp. 14, 68, and 71.

effort for mediation in 1863, was obsessed with a fear of the tendency in England. "I have great faith in my countrymen," he wrote, "but the experience of America frightens me. I am not ashamed to use the word *frightened*. During my whole life I have looked to that country as about to solve the great problem of self-government, and now, in my old age, the hopes of my youth and manhood are destroyed, and I am left to reconstruct my political philosophy, and doubt and hesitation beset me on every point."[1] More philosophically Matthew Arnold, in 1864, characterized the rule of aristocracy as inevitably passing, but bent his thought to the discovery of some middle ground or method—some "influence [which] may help us to prevent the English people from becoming, with the growth of democracy, *Americanized*."[2] "There is no longer any sort of disguise maintained," wrote Adams, "as to the wishes of the privileged classes. Very little genuine sympathy is entertained for the rebels. The true motive is apparent enough. It is the fear of the spread of democratic feeling at home in the event of our success."[3]

The year 1864 had witnessed a rapid retreat by wiser Conservative elements in proclaming the "lesson" of American democracy—a retreat caused by alarm at the vigour with which Radicals had taken up the challenge. Conservative hopes were still fixed upon Southern success and Conservative confidence loudly voiced. Even the pride of the *Times* in the accuracy of its news and in its military forecasts was subordinated to the purpose of keeping up the courage of the faction it represented.[4] Small wonder, then, that Delane, on receiving the news of Sherman's arrival before Savannah, should be made physically ill and write to Dasent: "The American news is a heavy blow

[1] Leader, *Roebuck*, p. 299. To William Ibbitt, April 26, 1864.
[2] Arnold, *Mixed Essays*, p. 17. (N. Y., Macmillan, 1883.)
[3] State Dept., Eng., Vol. 86, No. 709. Adams to Seward, June 9, 1864.
[4] See *ante*, Ch. XVI.

to us as well as to the South." The next day he added: "I am still sore vexed about Sherman, but Chenery did his best to attenuate the mischief."[1] "Attenuation" of Northern progress in arms was, indeed, attempted, but the facts of the military situation were too strong for continued concealment. From January, 1865, only the most stubborn of Southern friends could remain blind to the approaching Northern victory. Lord Acton, a hero-worshipper of the great Confederate military leader, "broke his heart over the surrender of Lee," but was moved also by keen insight as to the political meaning of that surrender.[2]

So assured were all parties in England that the great Civil War in America was closing in Northern victory that the final event was discounted in advance and the lines were rapidly being formed for an English political struggle on the great issue heralded as involved in the American conflict. Again, on the introduction of a motion in Parliament for expansion of the franchise the ultra-Conservatives attempted to read a "lesson" from America. The *Quarterly* for April, 1865, asserted that even yet "the mass of educated men in England retain the sympathy for the South which they have nourished ever since the conflict assumed a decided shape." America was plainly headed in the direction of a military despotism. Her example should warn England from a move in the same direction. "The classes which govern this country are in a minority," and should beware of majority rule. But events discredited the prophecy of a military despotism. The assassination of Lincoln gave opportunity not merely for a general outpouring of expressions of sympathy but also to the Radicals a chance to exalt Lincoln's leadership in democracy.[3]

[1] Dasent, *Delane*, II, pp. 135-6. Delane to Dasent, Dec. 25 and 26, 1864. The *Times* on December 26 pictured Sherman as having *escaped* to the sea, but on the 29th acknowledged his achievements.

[2] *Lord Acton's Letters to Mary Gladstone*, p. 183.

[3] These were not confined to Great Britain. The American Legation in Berlin received addresses of sympathy from many organizations, especially

In July Great Britain was holding elections for a new Parliament. Not a single member who had supported the cause of the North failed of re-election, several additional Northern "friends" were chosen, and some outspoken members for the South were defeated. Adams thought this a matter deserving special notice in America, and prophesied a new era approaching in England:

> "As it is, I cannot resist the belief that this period marks an era in the political movement of Great Britain. Pure old-fashioned conservatism has so far lost its hold on the confidence of the country that it will not appear in that guise any more. Unless some new and foreign element should interpose, I look for decided progress in enlarging the popular features of the constitution, and diminishing the influence of the aristocracy. . . . It is impossible not to perceive traces of the influence of our institutions upon all these changes. . . . The progress of the liberal cause, not in England alone, but all over the world, is, in a measure, in our hands."[1]

The "Liberal progress" was more rapid, even, than Adams anticipated. Palmerston, ill for some months past, died on October 18, 1865. Russell succeeded him as head of the Ministry, and almost immediately declared himself in favour of Parliamentary reform even though a majority in both Houses was still opposed to such a measure. Russell's desertion of his earlier attitude of "finality" on franchise expansion correctly represented the acceptance, though unwillingly, by both political parties of the necessity of reform. The battle, long waged, but reaching its decisive moment during the American Civil War, had finally gone

labour unions. One such, drawn by W. Liebknecht, A. Vogt, and C. Schilling read in part: "Members of the working-class, we need not affirm to you the sincerity of these our sympathies; for with pride we can point to the fact, that, while the aristocracy of the Old World took openly the part of the southern slaveholder, and while the middle class was divided in its opinions, the working-men in all countries of Europe have unanimously and firmly stood on the side of the Union." (*U.S. Diplomatic Correspondence*, 1865, Pt. IV, p. 500.)

[1] *U.S. Messages and Documents*, 1865, Pt. I, p. 417. Adams to Hunter, July 13, 1865.

against Conservatism when Lee surrendered at Appomatox. Russell's Reform Bill of 1866 was defeated by Tory opposition in combination with a small Whig faction which refused to desert the "principle" of aristocratic government—the "government by the wise," but the Tories who came into power under Derby were forced by the popular demand voiced even to the point of rioting, themselves to present a Reform Bill. Disraeli's measure, introduced with a number of "fancy franchises," which, in effect, sought to counteract the giving of the vote to British working-men, was quickly subjected to such caustic criticism that all the planned advantages to Conservatism were soon thrown overboard, and a Bill presented so Radical as to permit a transfer of political power to the working classes.[1] The Reform Bill of 1867 changed Great Britain from a government by aristocracy to one by democracy. A new nation came into being. The friends of the North had triumphed.

Thus in addition to the play of diplomatic incidents, the incidental frictions, the effect on trade relations, the applications of British neutrality, and the general policy of the Government, there existed for Great Britain a great issue in the outcome of the Civil War—the issue of the adoption of democratic institutions. It affected at every turn British public attitude, creating an intensity and bitterness of tone, on both sides, unexampled in the expressions of a neutral people. In America this was little understood, and American writers both during the war and long afterwards, gave little attention to it.[2] Immediately upon the conclusion of the war, Goldwin Smith, whose words during the conflict were bitter toward the aristocracy, declared that

[1] Disraeli was less disturbed by this than were other Tory leaders. He had long before, in his historical novels, advocated an aristocratic leadership of democracy, as against the middle class. Derby called the Bill "a leap in the dark," but assented to it.

[2] Pierce, *Sumner*, IV, pp. 151-153, summarizes the factors determining British attitude and places first the fear of the privileged classes of the example of America, but his treatment really minimizes this element.

"the territorial aristocracy of this country and the clergy of the Established Church" would have been excusable "if they could only have said frankly that they desired the downfall of institutions opposed to their own, instead of talking about their sympathy for the weak, and their respect for national independence, and their anxiety for the triumph of Free Trade."[1] This was stated before the democratic hope in England had been realized. Three years later the same staunch friend of the North, now removed to America and occupying a chair of history at Cornell University, wrote of the British aristocracy in excuse of their attitude: "I fought these men hard; I believed, and believe now, that their defeat was essential to the progress of civilization. But I daresay we should have done pretty much as they did, if we had been born members of a privileged order, instead of being brought up under the blessed influence of equality and justice."[2]

Such judgment and such excuses will appear to the historian as well-founded. But to Americans who conceived the Civil War as one fought first of all for the preservation of the nation, the issue of democracy in England seemed of little moment and little to excuse either the "cold neutrality" of the Government or the tone of the press. To Americans Great Britain appeared friendly to the dissolution of the Union and the destruction of a rival power. Nationality was the issue for the North; that democracy was an issue in America was denied, nor could it, in the intensity of the conflict, be conceived as the vital question determining British attitude. The Reform Bill of 1867 brought a new British nation into existence, the nation decrying American institutions was dead and a "sister democracy" holding

[1] Goldwin Smith, "The Civil War in America: An Address read at the last meeting of the Manchester Union and Emancipation Society." (Jan. 26, 1866.) London, 1866. pp. 71-75.

[2] Goldwin Smith, *America and England in their present relations*, London, 1869, p. 30.

out hands to the United States had replaced it, but to this the men who had won the war for the North long remained blind. Not during the generation when Americans, immersed in a life and death struggle for national existence, felt that "he who is not for me is against me," could the generally correct neutrality of the British Government and the whole-hearted support of Radical England be accepted at their true value to the North. For nearly half a century after the American Civil War the natural sentiments of friendship, based upon ties of blood and a common heritage of literature and history and law, were distorted by bitter and exaggerated memories.

INDEX